KEEPERS OF A MOVEMENT

OTHER SCHIFFER BOOKS BY THE AUTHOR:
Brooklyn on My Mind, ISBN: 978-0-7643-5652-0

Library of Congress Control Number: 2018937433

Edited by Ian Robertson
Designed by Molly Shields
Cover design by Molly Shields

Type set in Mr Eaves San OT/Mrs Eaves XL Serif Nar OT

ISBN: 978-0-7643-7125-7
ePub: 978-1-5073-0682-6
Printed in China

10 9 8 7 6 5 4 3 2 1

Published by Schiffer Publishing, Ltd.
4880 Lower Valley Road
Atglen, PA 19310
Phone: (610) 593-1777; Fax: (610) 593-2002
Email: info@schifferbooks.com
Web: www.schifferbooks.com

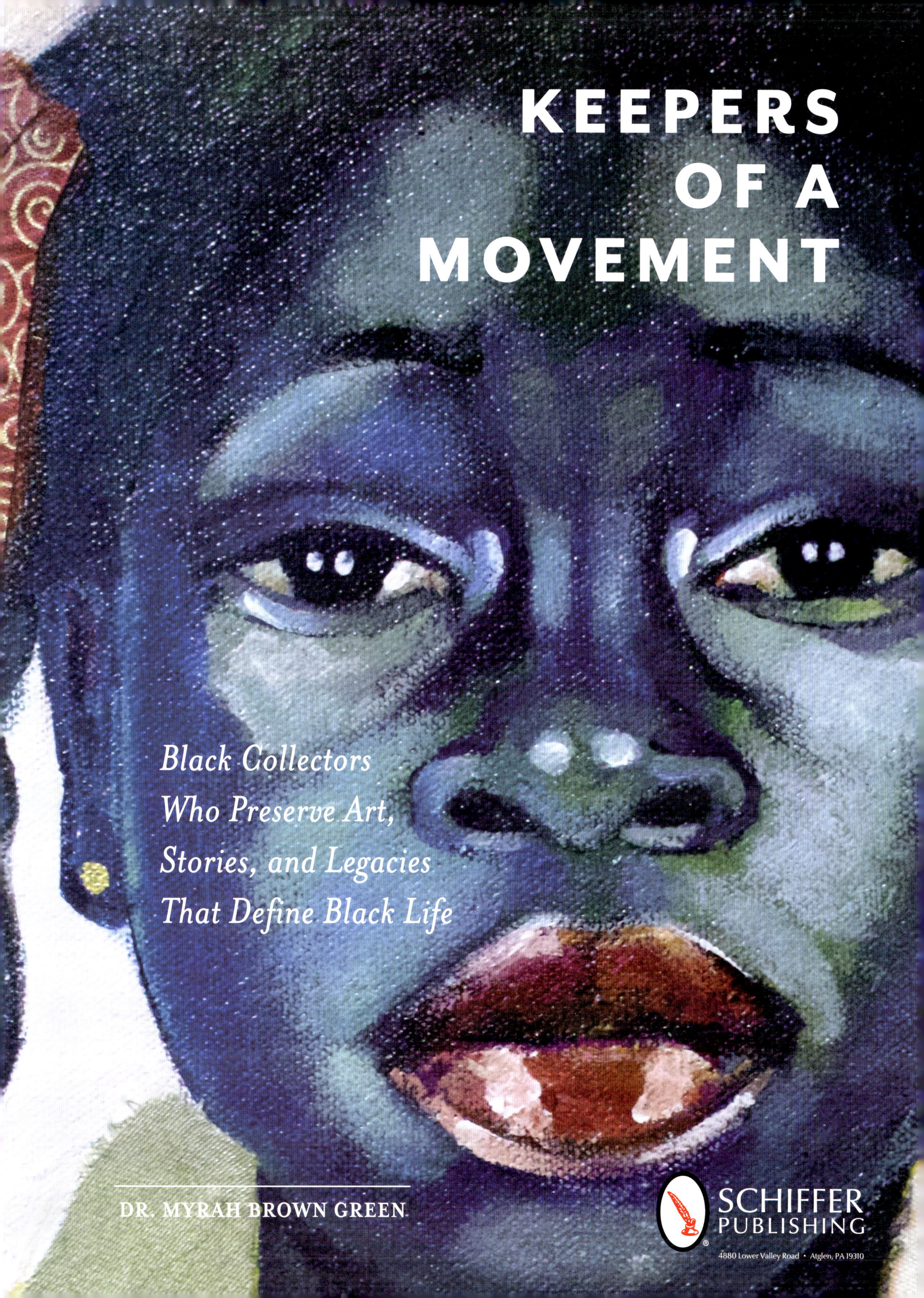

KEEPERS OF A MOVEMENT

Black Collectors Who Preserve Art, Stories, and Legacies That Define Black Life

DR. MYRAH BROWN GREEN

SCHIFFER PUBLISHING
4880 Lower Valley Road • Atglen, PA 19310

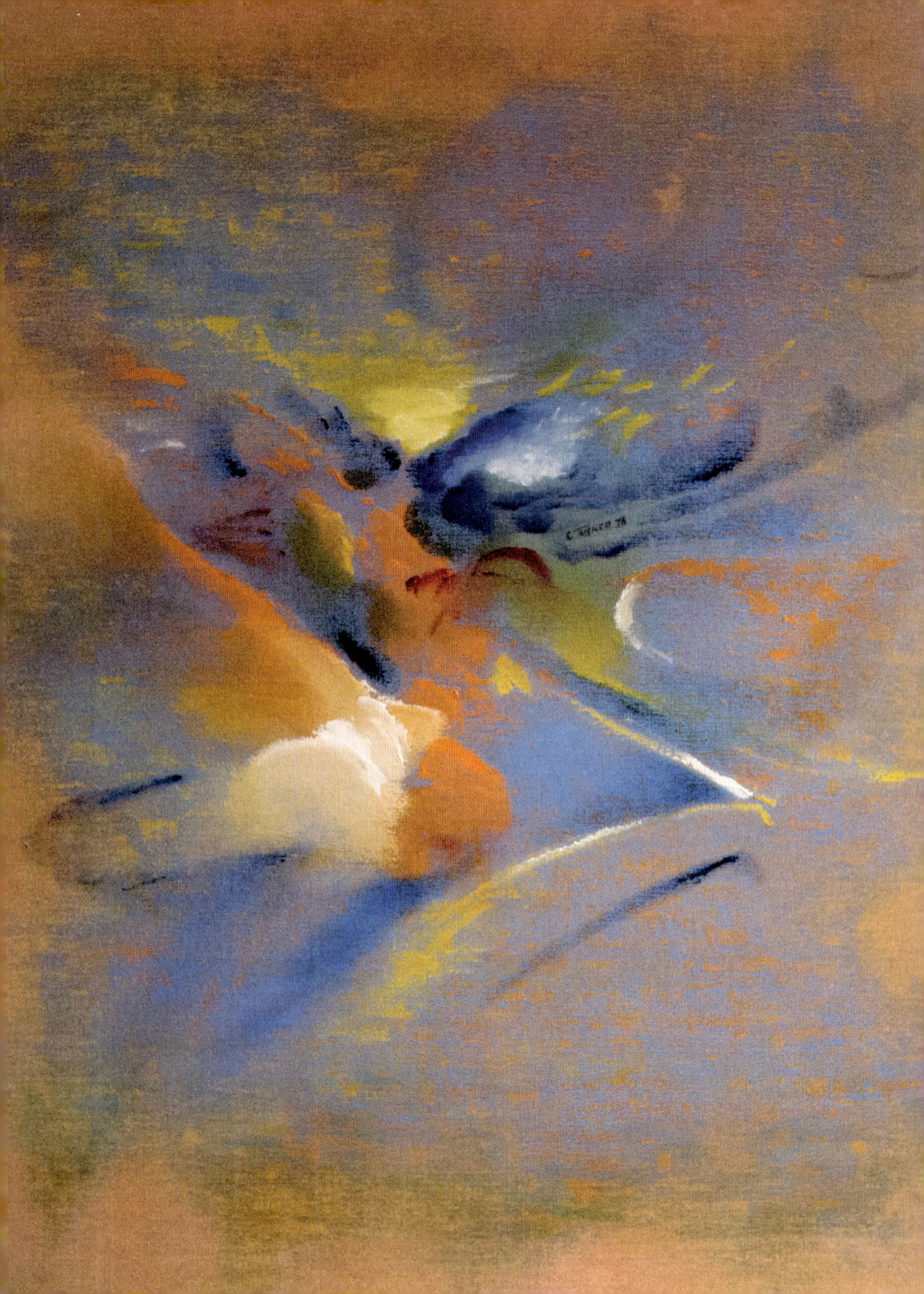

CONTENTS

FOREWORD

In April 2018, I had the pleasure of meeting Dr. Myrah Brown Green at the unveiling of the Fairmount Heights Art Wall at Fairmount Heights Switching Station in Newark, New Jersey. Dr. Myrah played a pivotal role in representing and assisting several New York–based artists involved in the project. Our connection was immediate, rooted in shared values, experiences, and a mutual passion for the arts. Both of us hail from New England—Dr. Myrah from Cambridge, Massachusetts, and myself from Hartford, Connecticut—and we are both married to community activists who share our deep commitment to serving and uplifting our people. Like Dr. Myrah, I am an arts practitioner, often working in nontraditional ways—sometimes as an administrator, other times behind the scenes—but always in service to the arts. For more than two decades, I have been immersed in this work, while Dr. Myrah's contributions extend significantly further. It is a shared calling, a testament to the profound role art plays in our lives as a source of solace, joy, and inspiration.

Art moves and inspires, offering clarity in a complex world. It connects us to culture, people, places, and time. Immersing oneself in art is a meditative act, opening doors to self-discovery and new perspectives. Collecting art deepens this connection, requiring focus, openness, and a willingness to embrace a spectrum of emotions—wonder, discomfort, curiosity, or joy. Whether motivated by aesthetic appeal, cultural significance, historical documentation, or investment potential, collecting art is a profound act of engagement.

In *Keepers of a Movement: Black Collectors Who Preserve Art, Stories, and Legacies That Define Black Life*, Dr. Myrah underscores the vital importance of Black people actively collecting and documenting their history and culture. Through collecting we preserve our stories, establish provenance, and celebrate our identities. Documenting and publicizing these collections not only affirms our place in history but also inspires creativity and fosters generational wealth. This work educates and empowers, reminding us of the connections to those who came before us and lighting the way for those who will come after.

Dr. Myrah's career is deeply rooted in exploring the creative practices of the African diaspora. Her work as an archivist, curator, and chronicler of art history is invaluable. She is the author of celebrated works that include *Brooklyn on My Mind: Black Artists from the WPA to the Present* and *Pieced Symbols: Quilt Blocks from the Global Village*. An accomplished professional quilt maker, Dr. Green also teaches quilting and textiles while dabbling in photography and printmaking. In addition to her creative pursuits, she serves as an educator at Medgar Evers College, nurturing the next generation of cultural stewards.

I invite you to immerse yourself in this extraordinary survey of diverse collections representing just a glimpse of the countless Black collectors worldwide. These collections are more than assemblages of art—they are meditative spaces that inspire reflection, joy, and a deeper understanding of our collective journey. Welcome to *Keepers of a Movement: Black Collectors Who Preserve Art, Stories, and Legacies That Define Black Life*.

KEIA D. CARTER SIMMONS
Independent Cultural Facilitator Associate Director, Temple Contemporary Art Gallery, Tyler School of Art and Architecture

ACKNOWLEDGMENTS

To celebrate his first one hundred days of school, my six-year-old grandson wanted to write one hundred words that he knew how to spell and read himself. When I scanned the list, THANK and YOU stood out on the page. In that moment I was reminded that learning to feel and express gratitude is an essential part of life. To me, those two words are just as powerful as the phrase I love you . . . and so I thank the Infinite One, who reminds me every day that this work of archiving will benefit generations to come.

My ancestors taught me how to stand on their shoulders, and whew, I have a strong and powerful foundation—my mother, Dorothy; my grandmothers, Dora and Amy; Mama Lura; and Aunt Louise. Richard, my love, you support me every step of the way. There is no idea I bring to you that you don't make me believe is the best one ever. Daddy, after all these decades, you still tell me I'm smart—LOL! My four phenomenal children, Adero-Zaire, Assantwa-Nzinga, Amenawon, and Talu, thank you for enjoying and sharing what I do. Your support means the world to me. Cyrie and Summer-Zaire, watching you both grow, I see so much of my artistic self in you—my grands, my artists, my Keepers of Nana's gifts. My siblings Ina, Sonya, and Hodges Jr. keep me grounded. My nieces Varonica, Shani, and Isabella, I love that you are a part of this legacy too.

I am so grateful to have such an extended arsenal of art sisters. Thank you Jennifer Stewart-Hutchinson, Shelly Innis, Valerie Pilgrim Bell-Bey, Corrine Jennings, and Dr. Carolyn L. Mazloomi. Each of you has taken the lead in counseling me as I gathered the information needed for this document. I was privileged to have an up-close-and personal view of your extensive collections, and you know how I feel about Black women collectors being hidden figures. My goal has always been to let the world know how knowledgeable you all are about Black art, the great taste each of you has as collectors, and the invaluable support you give artists through your nurturing spirits. In my last book, *Brooklyn on My Mind: Black Artists from the WPA to the Present*, I wrote that I looked forward to writing about you one day. That wish has now been manifested. The world will see you as a collector in the following pages.

Thank you Sannii Crespina-Flores, Zarinah Shabazz, Keia Simmons, Vanessa Greene, and Pamela Elaine (my SG coach)—you all became my hype sisters. Each of you gave me the gentle nudge I needed whenever I thought I was journeying down the wrong road. And Donna Actie, who through it all took on the responsibilities of editor and tech specialist, I am deeply grateful for your commitment to this project.

Finally, I am thankful to all of the collectors. You graciously allowed me to collaborate with you in choosing these magnificent works of art. Each artist's work represents a moment in world history—moments of the past, moments of the present, and moments yet to come.

Thanks to all who chose to make this book a part of your collection. I am so proud and grateful to share this platform with all of you!

INTRODUCTION

When I was ten years old, my class took a school trip to a museum in Massachusetts, the state where I grew up. My mother had given me some money to purchase a treat in the gift shop, and as I browsed the shelves my eyes landed on a small, rectangular object that I felt an irresistible urge to have. I had no idea what it was, but something about it spoke to me.

Curious, my teacher asked if I knew what I had chosen. When I said no, she explained that it was a mezuzah—a sacred artifact in Jewish culture. She told me it contained a prayer inside and was traditionally mounted on the doorframe of a home, touched by the people living there as they came and went. Then she asked if I still wanted it. I nodded firmly.

Somehow I convinced my parents to hang it in our doorway. It isn't there anymore, but I'll never forget that moment: my first act of collecting something that felt like art to me, and the way my parents supported my curiosity and growing passion.

For centuries, Black artists across the African Diaspora have been architects of cultural innovation, resilience, and transformation. Their art, music, literature, and activism have profoundly shaped the world. I've been fortunate to meet many of these creators over the years. But behind these celebrated figures stands another equally vital force: the Black collector.

These keepers of history and culture play a crucial role in preserving the artifacts, stories, and legacies that define Black life. They safeguard what might otherwise be lost—rare books, heirlooms, works of art, and ephemera that bear witness to the depth and complexity of our experiences.

Keepers of a Movement: Black Collectors Who Preserve Art, Stories, and Legacies That Define Black Life honors these individuals whose passion and dedication ensure that the narratives of the past remain alive for future generations. Their collections illuminate the threads of heritage and identity that connect us, providing a richer, more nuanced understanding of history. I have curated the works in a way that shows a specific area of each collector's collection, so that the world may get a taste of the depth and breadth of how broadly the Black collector collects. You will also have the opportunity to hear directly from the collector as to why they have connected with the works they have featured in their section.

This celebration goes beyond objects to focus on the lives, communities, and movements they represent. Through the stories of Black collectors, we explore the power of preservation and ownership—the commitment to ensuring that Black voices are heard, remembered, and celebrated.

Together we honor these keepers of a movement. They are the custodians of our collective memory, ensuring that the legacy of a people endures.

DR. MYRAH BROWN GREEN
Author, Art Historian, Independent Curator, Artist Doula, and Master Quiltmaker

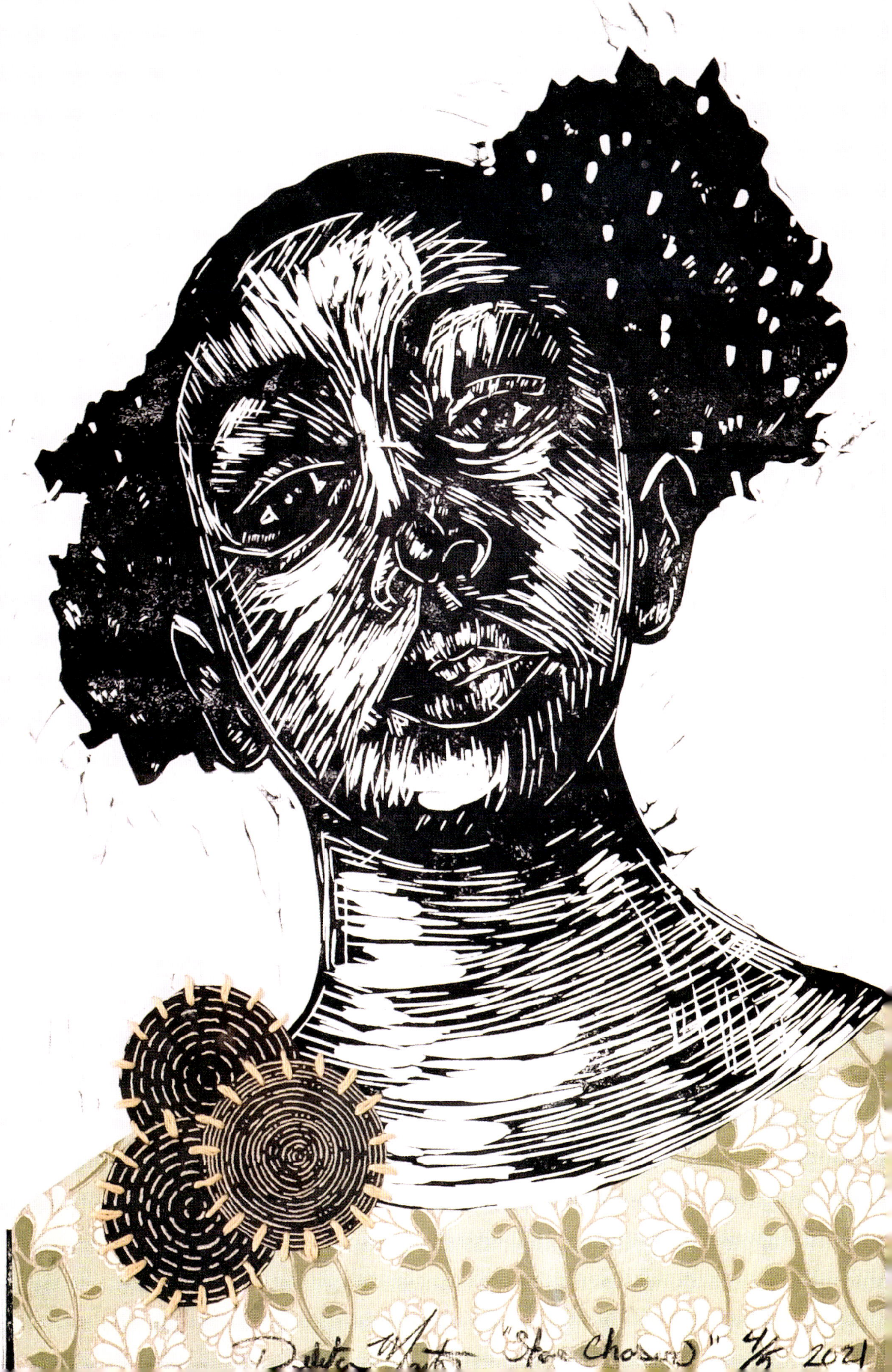
2021

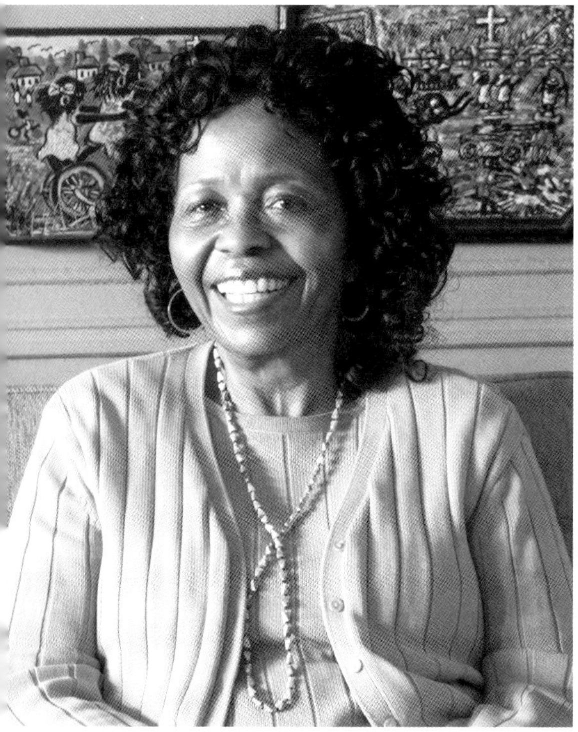

Photo: Myrah Brown Green

DR. CYNTHIA D. BARNES
OUTSIDER ART

DR. MYRAH: What was the first piece of art that you collected and when?

DR. CYNTHIA D. BARNES: The first piece of art I ever collected was *Market Place* by Jamaican artist Lester Gunther, purchased around 1979 from the Essie Green Gallery in Brooklyn, New York. It was a vibrant introduction into the world of art collecting, a path that has brought me endless inspiration and joy ever since.

DR. MYRAH: Why are you a Keeper of Outsider Art?

DR. CYNTHIA D. BARNES: My journey as a keeper of outsider art is rooted in the stories shared with me by Thurlow Tibbs, who opened my eyes to the richness of early-twentieth-century outsider art. During my biannual visits to his gallery in Washington, DC, Thurlow would share tales of extraordinary self-taught artists—artists like William Traylor, F. L. "Doc" Spellmon, and Clementine Hunter, whose lives were often marked by economic hardship, but whose creativity and resilience shone brilliantly through their work. They transformed found objects into profound expressions of life and culture, capturing the essence of the African American experience in the South.

In the mid-1990s, Joan Smith, Jennifer Stewart, and I began making an annual pilgrimage to the Outsider Art Fair in New York City. Among the diverse crowd, we were often the only African Americans, but we felt a kinship with the art we encountered there. These works held a raw, unpolished beauty that spoke to us deeply. Through these visits, we connected with gallery owners dedicated to outsider art, but none was more influential than Jimmy Hedges of the Rising Fawn Gallery in Lookout Mountain, Georgia. Jimmy introduced us to remarkable artists like Mose Tolliver, Jimmy Lee Sudduth, and Purvis Young. He encouraged us to delve deeper, to study, and to preserve these precious works, and even brought us handpicked pieces to choose from.

I am a keeper of outsider art because I believe in honoring the legacy of these untrained artists, whose creativity knows no bounds and whose works echo with stories of resilience, community, and spirit. I feel a responsibility to carry forward their legacy, to ensure that future generations appreciate and understand the strength, ingenuity, and beauty of these works. It is a privilege to be part of this lineage, a guardian of art that transcends formal boundaries and speaks to the heart.

Pervis Young, *Untitled* (Pregnant Woman), 2000. Acrylic on wood, 46" × 23". *Photo: Myrah Brown Green*

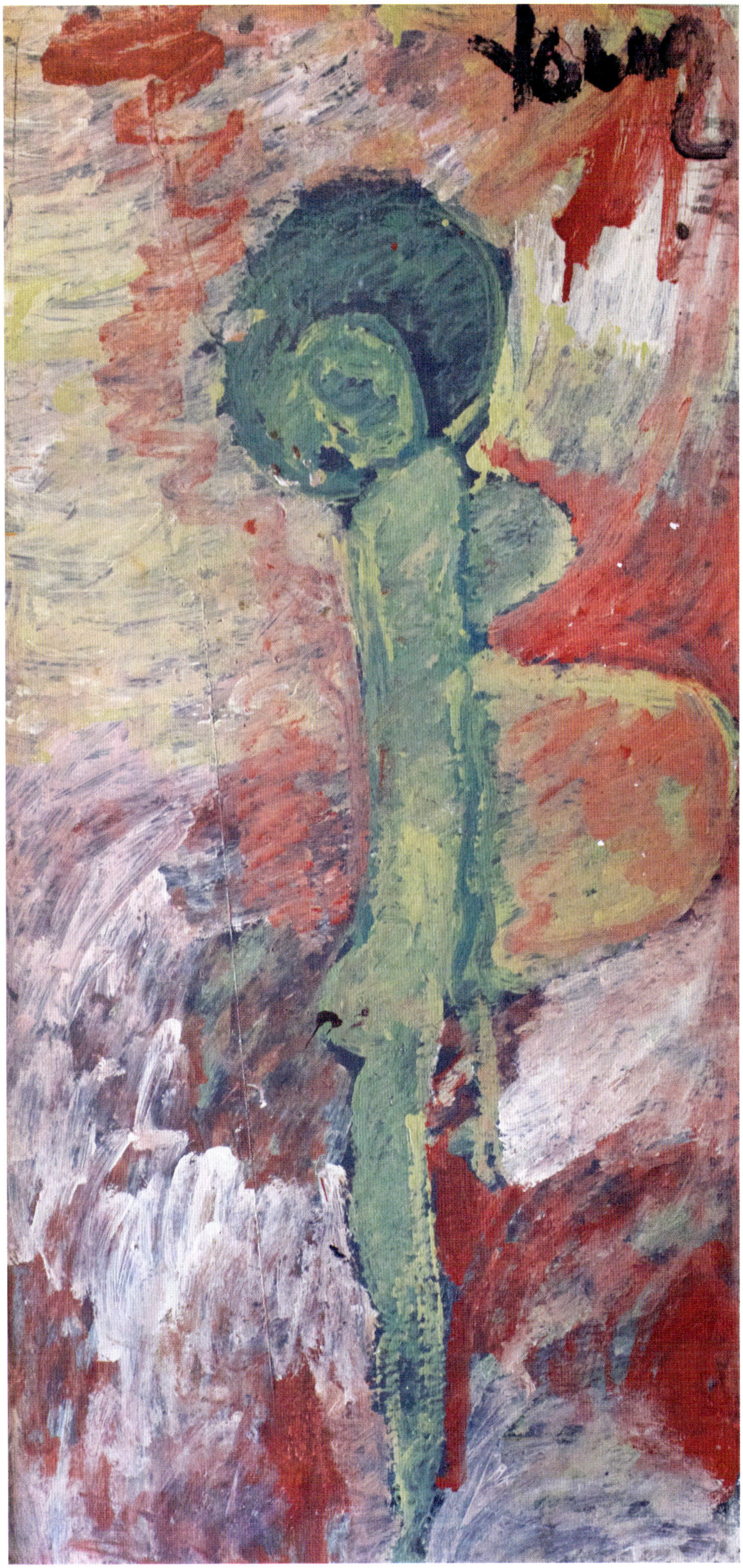
Young

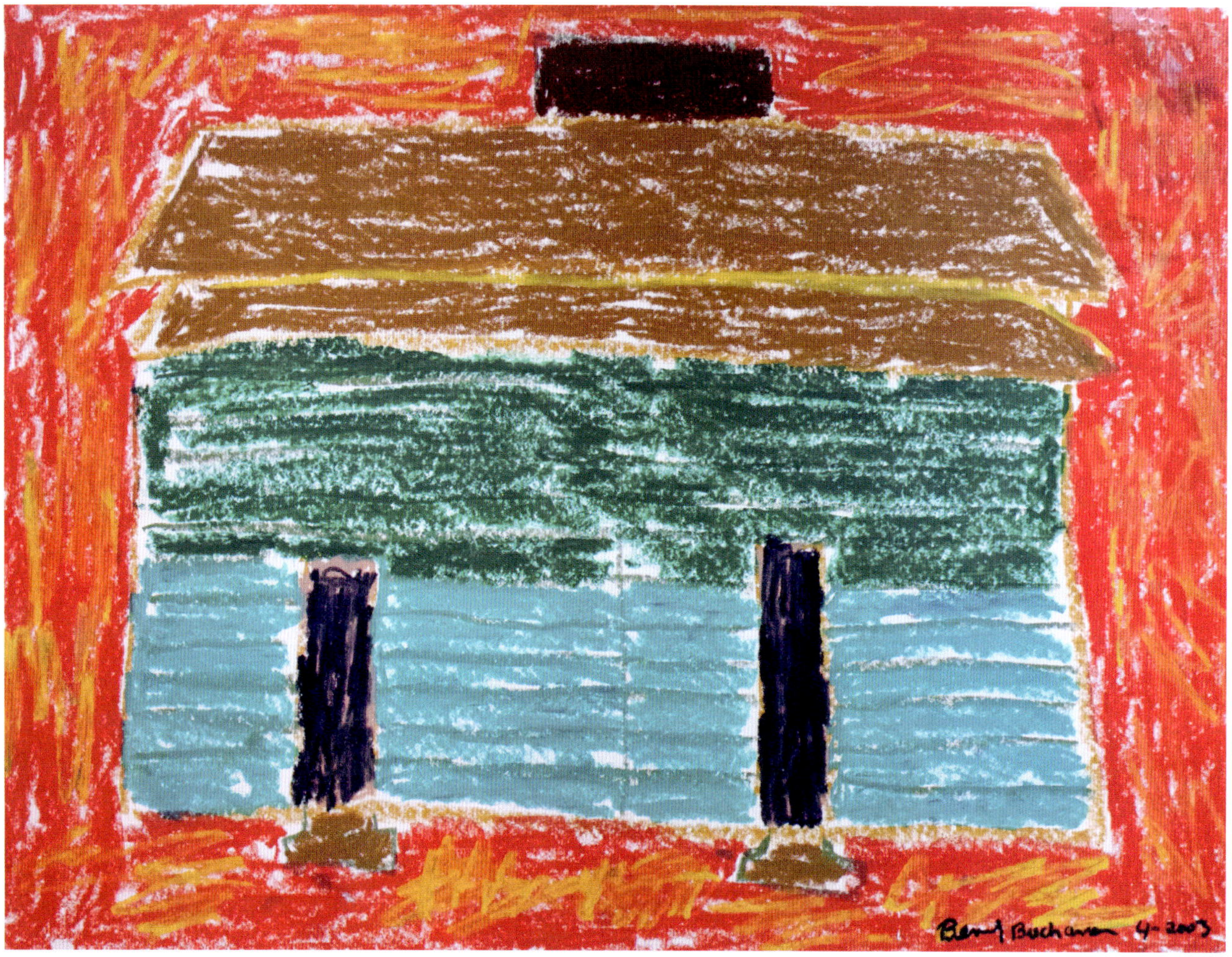

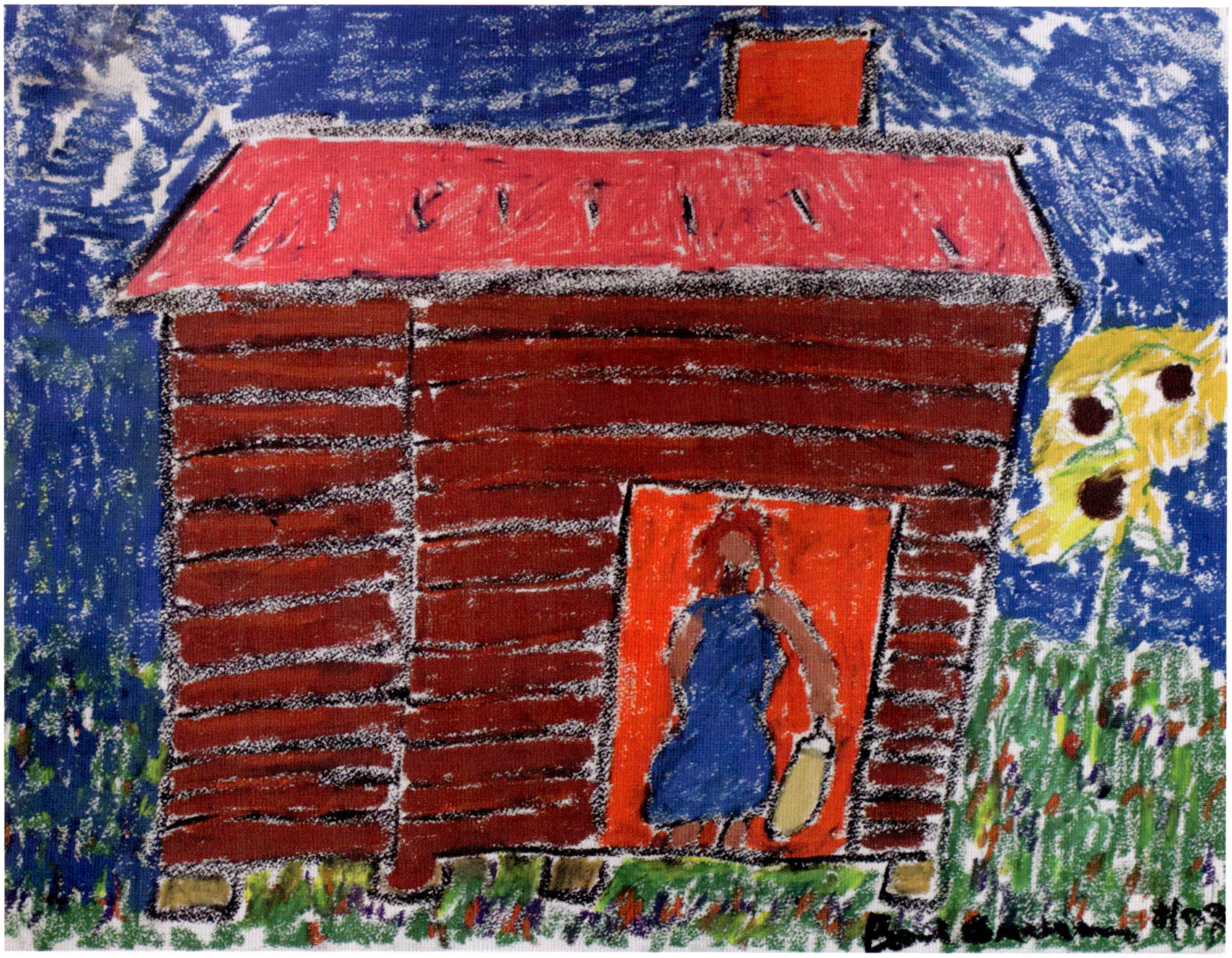

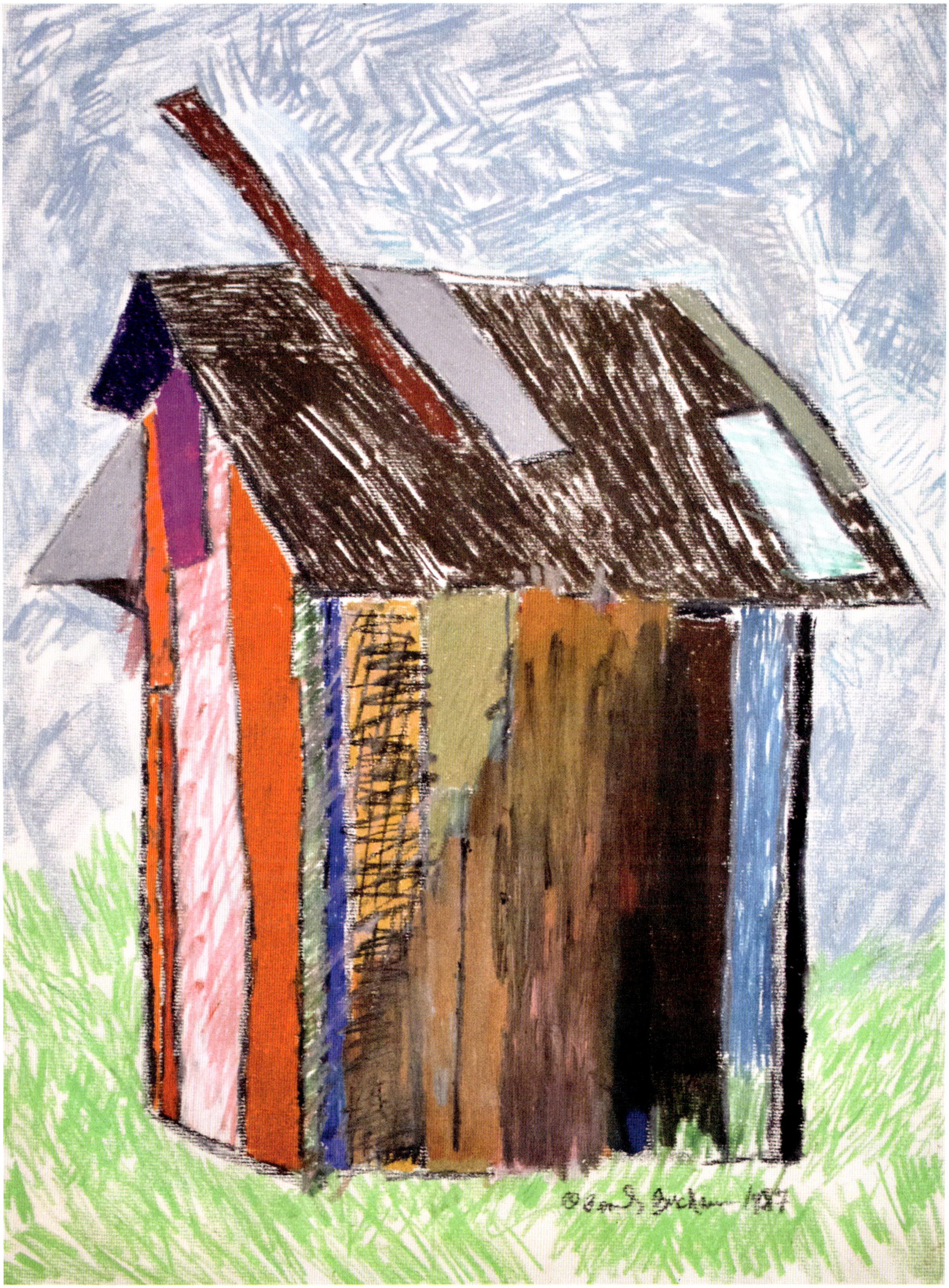

Beverly Buchanan, *Green Saddle Bag*, 2003.
Pastel on paper, 22" × 30". *Photo: Myrah Brown Green*

Beverly Buchanan, *Watering Flowers*, 2003.
Pastel on paper, 22" × 30". *Photo: Myrah Brown Green*

Above: Beverly Buchanan, *Untitled*, 1987.
Pastel on paper, 24" × 18". *Photo: Myrah Brown Green*

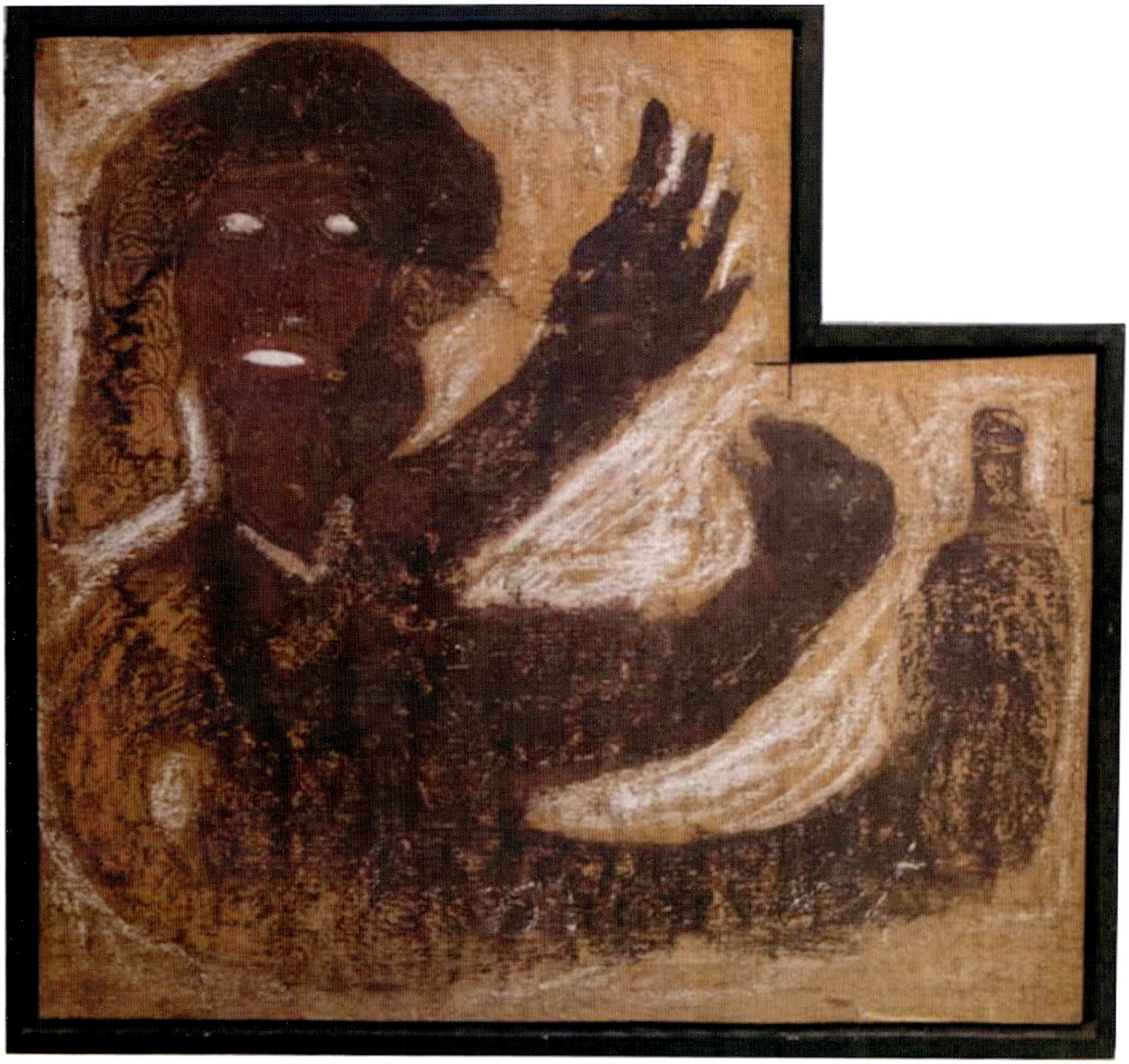

Above: Jimmy Lee Sudduth, *Untitled*, 1969. Mud and paint on wood panel, 32" × 36". *Photo: Myrah Brown Green*

Mose Toliver, *Untitled*, 1960. House paint and marker on wood, 23" × 15". *Photo: Myrah Brown Green*

Mose Toliver, *Untitled*, 1980. House paint and marker on wood, 23" × 23". *Photo: Myrah Brown Green*

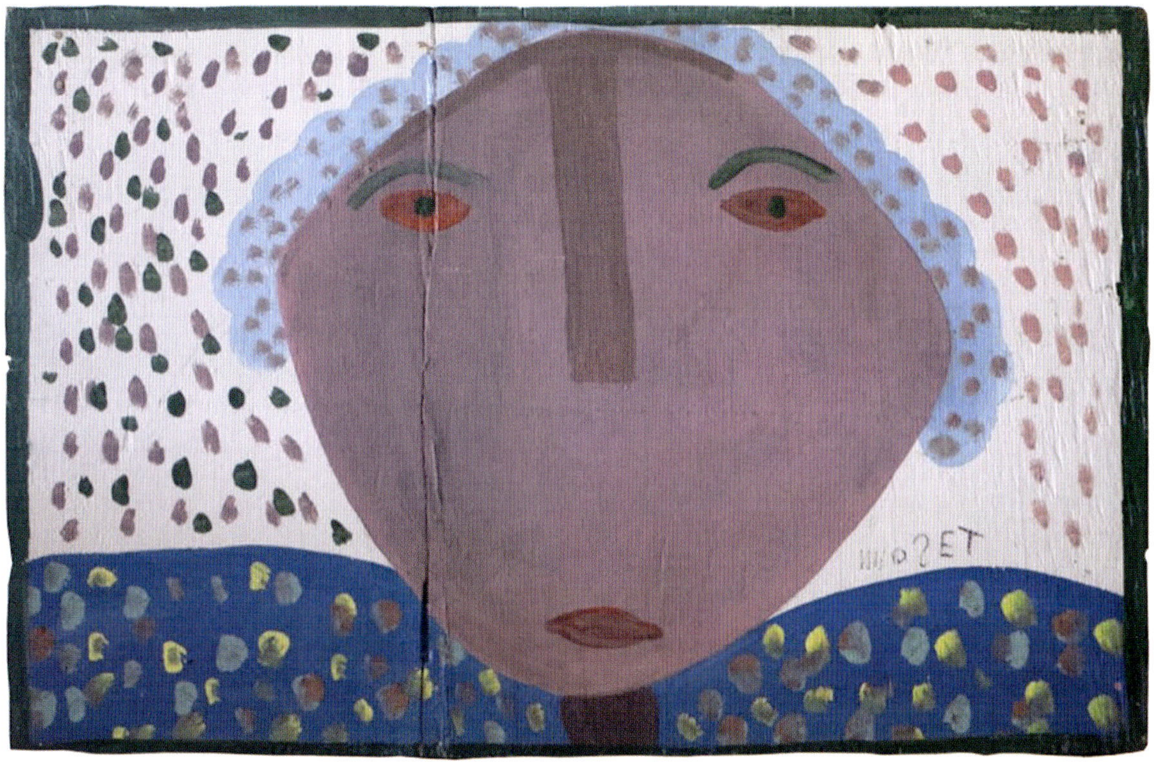
MoSET

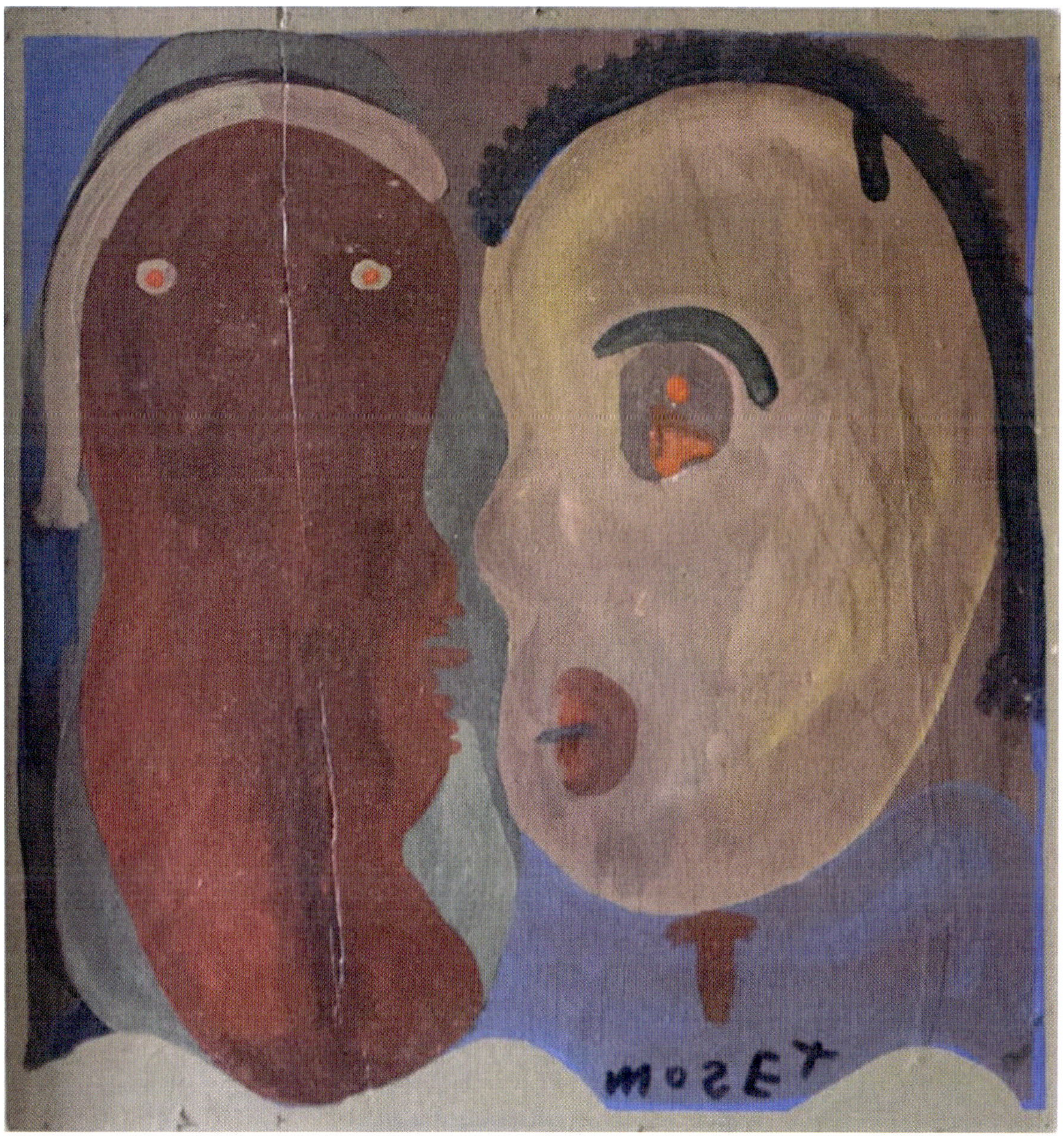
MoSE

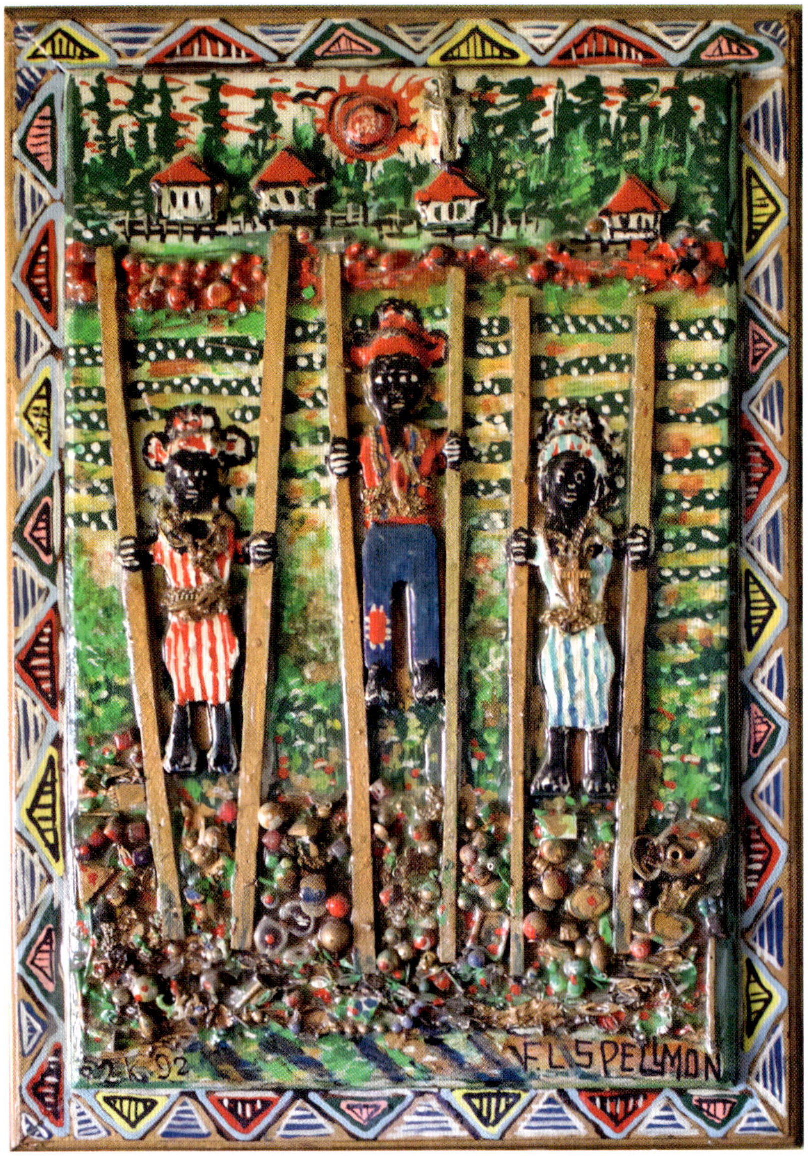

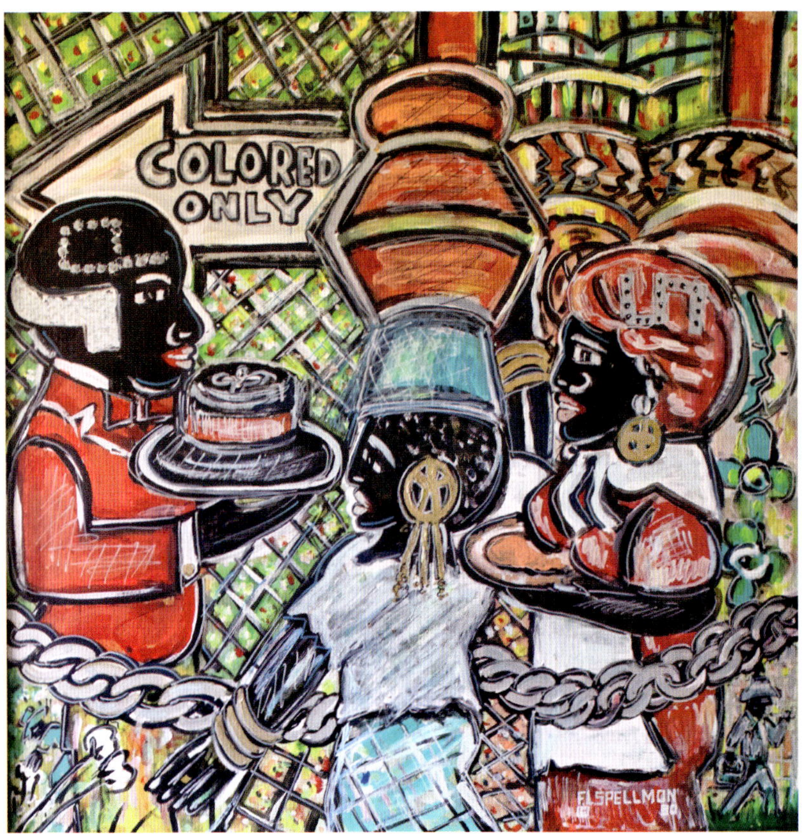

F. L. (DOC) Spellmon, *Children on Stilts*, 1992. Mixed media, found objects, 15.5" × 21.5". *Photo: Myrah Brown Green*

F. L. (DOC) Spellmon, *Colored Only #2*, 1980–1988. Mixed media, 37" × 37". *Photo: Myrah Brown Green*

Opposite: Mr. Imagination, *Untitled*, 1990. Paint and mixed media, 10" × 4.5". *Photo: Myrah Brown Green*

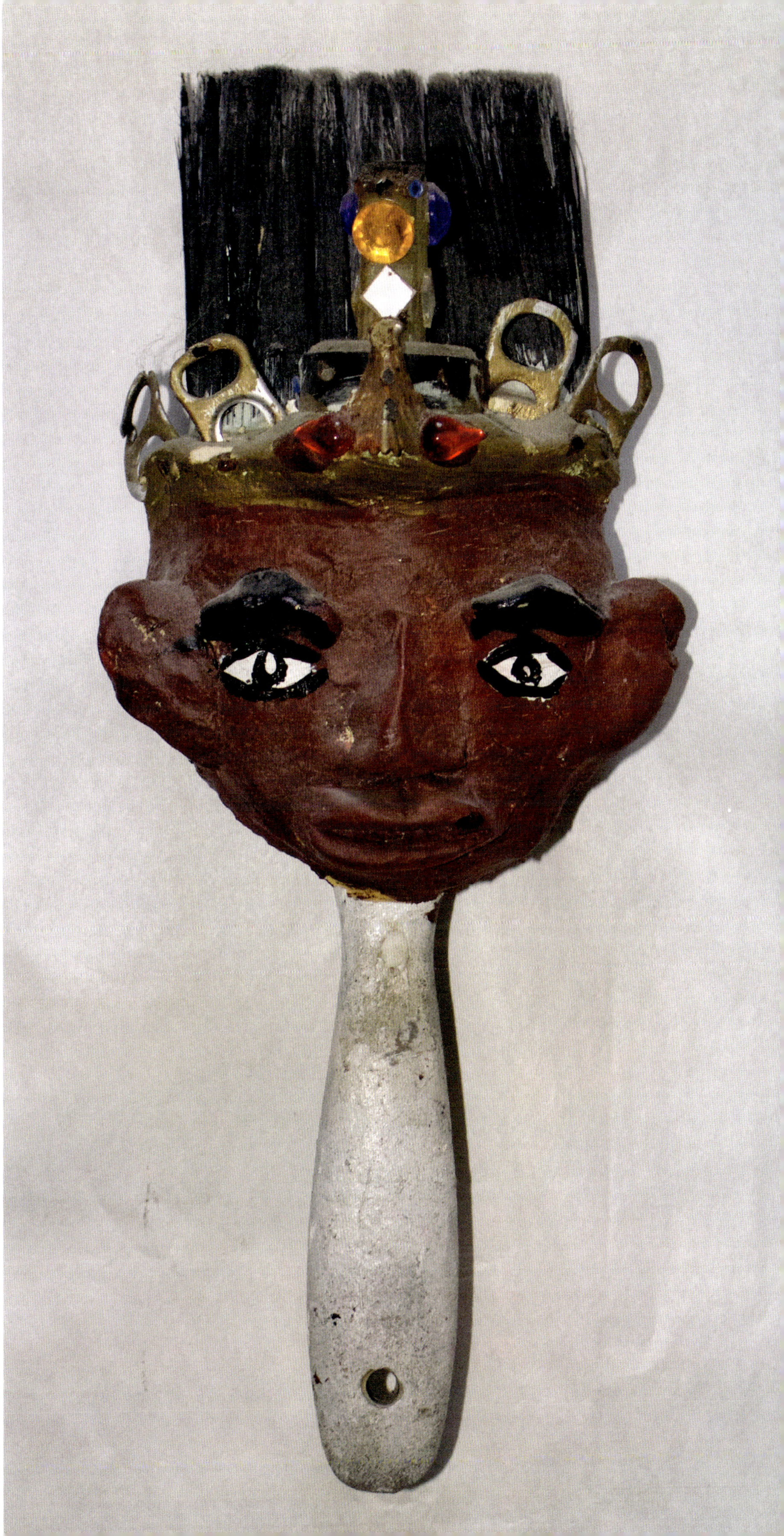

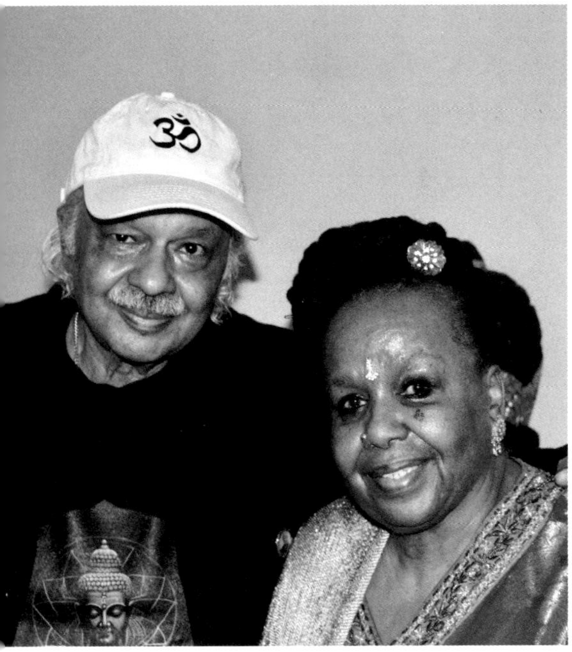

Photo: Myrah Brown Green

THE BARTLEY COLLECTION

BLACK BUDDHAS

DR. MYRAH: What was the first piece of art that you collected and when?

AJUBA AND HASSANI BARTLEY: One of the first things that we collected was *Black Woman with a Hoe and Rake* in 1980. It was a beautiful piece of artwork. We don't know the artist, but we know that a person named Wilson did it. We got it at a street fair in the village. It depicted Post-Reconstruction. It made me think of my grandmother, because she worked in the fields.

DR. MYRAH: Why are you a Keeper of Black Buddhas?

AJUBA AND HASSANI BARTLEY: We feel akin to them. I've seen the African presence in Asia, especially while traveling through India and encountering the Black Buddhas. What we've collected over the years, we identify with. It's just like saying, "We are everywhere."

We were fascinated. There was an attraction, something we hadn't seen before. We had seen brass Buddhas. We had seen pictures of Buddhas. But at that time, none of them reflected Black skin. That's when we began to investigate. The more we saw them, the more we knew we wanted one in our home.

Then it became something more. Almost like an obsession. We started collecting them in all sizes. That's what made it exciting.

And then you look at the hair. It's a Black hairstyle. Cornrows. Knots. It's not spoken about much. We have seen Buddhas with wavy hair, which are more common in India. But the ones we were drawn to, the ones we saw most often, had coils or African knots.

In the caves in China, there are so many Black Buddhas. But no one talks about them. In Cambodia they are present in the temples as well. In Southern China, the Mogao Caves hold many of them. That's where you can find these depictions carved into history.

We were fascinated. Some of them even had the third eye in the center of their forehead. A star. Shining outward. Looking right at you.

What an experience.

Artist unknown, *Meditating Buddha* (Thailand), 1997. Marble. *Photo: Myrah Brown Green*

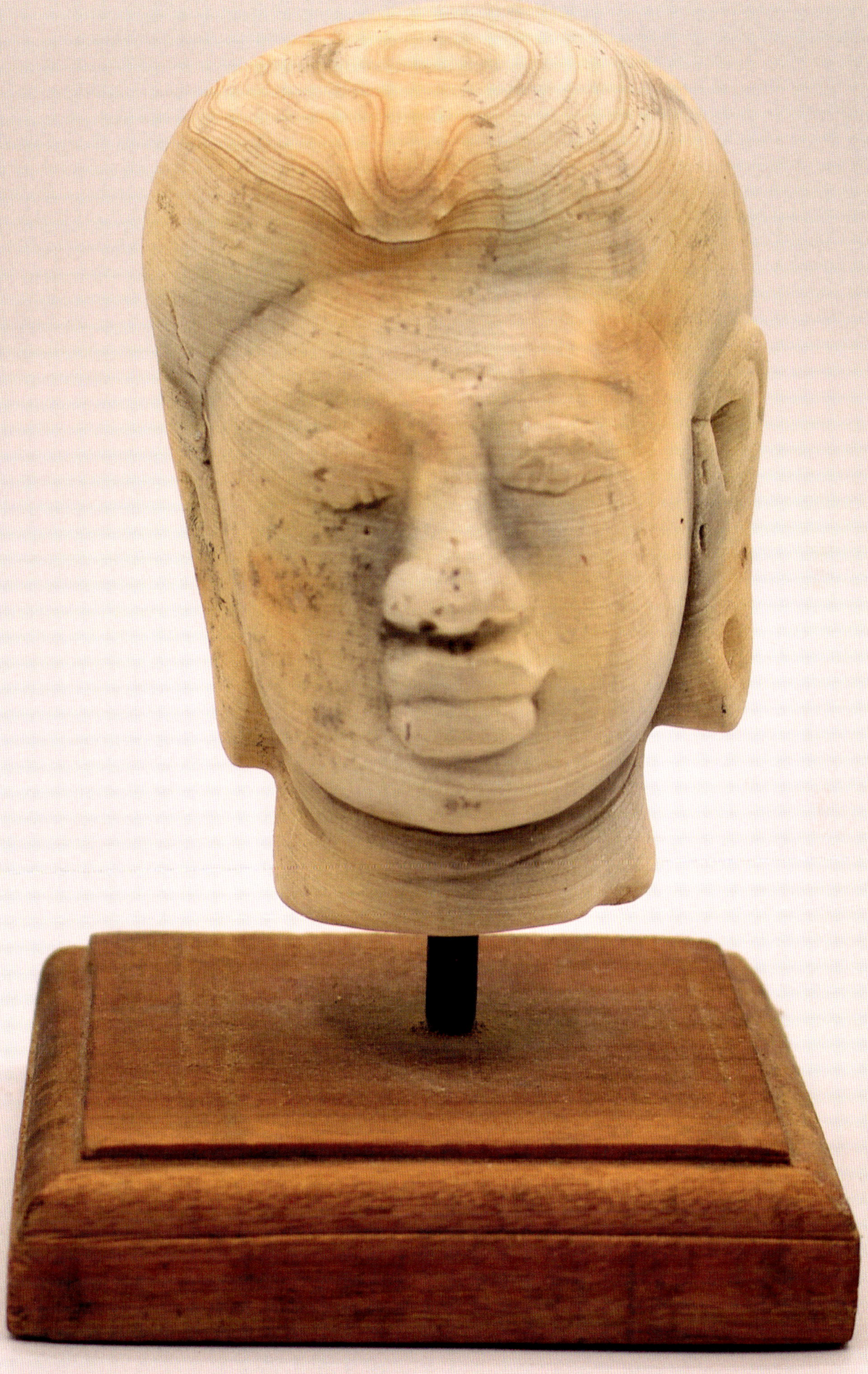

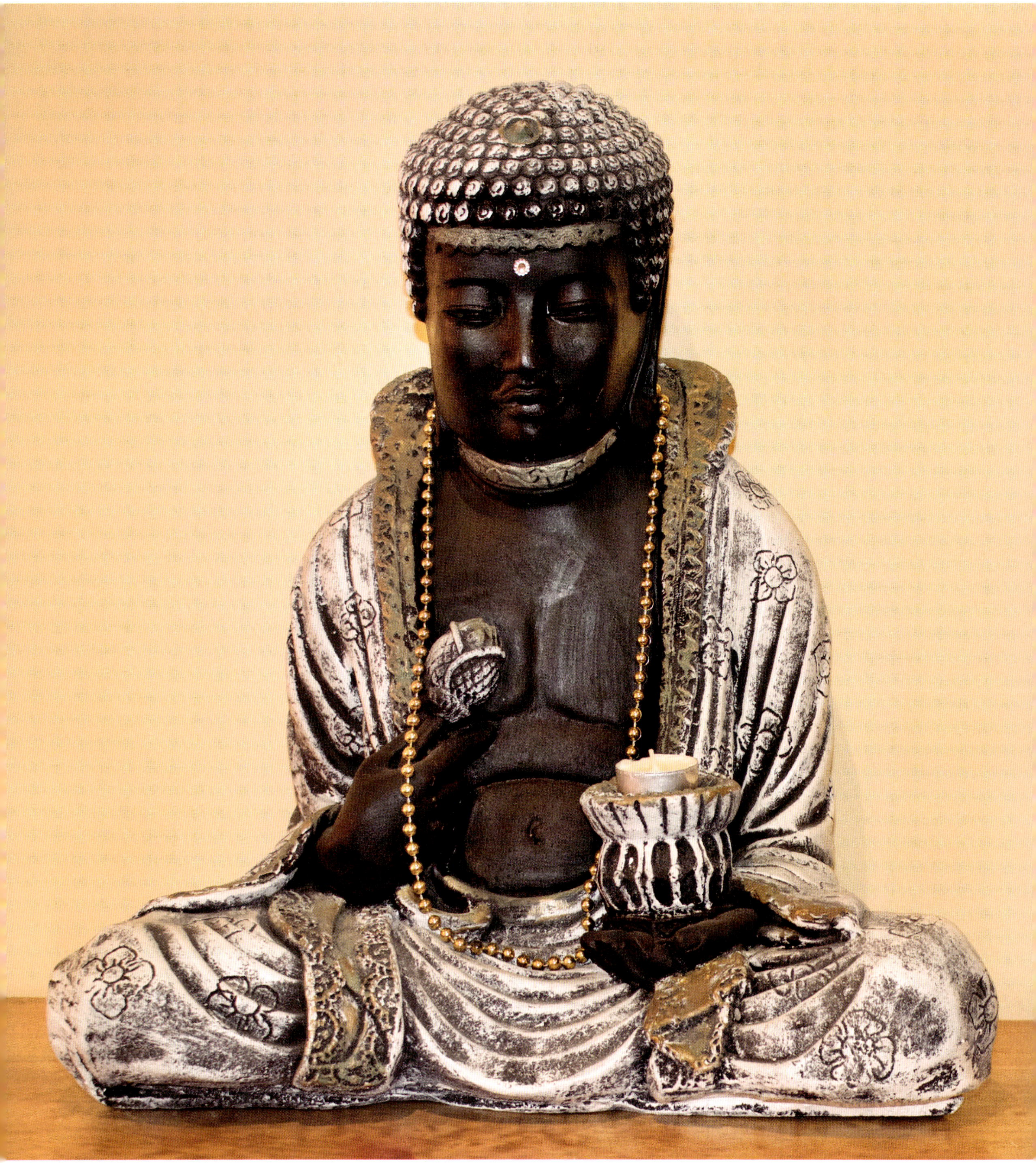

Artist unknown, *Healing Buddha* (Thailand), 1980. Resin.
Photo: Myrah Brown Green

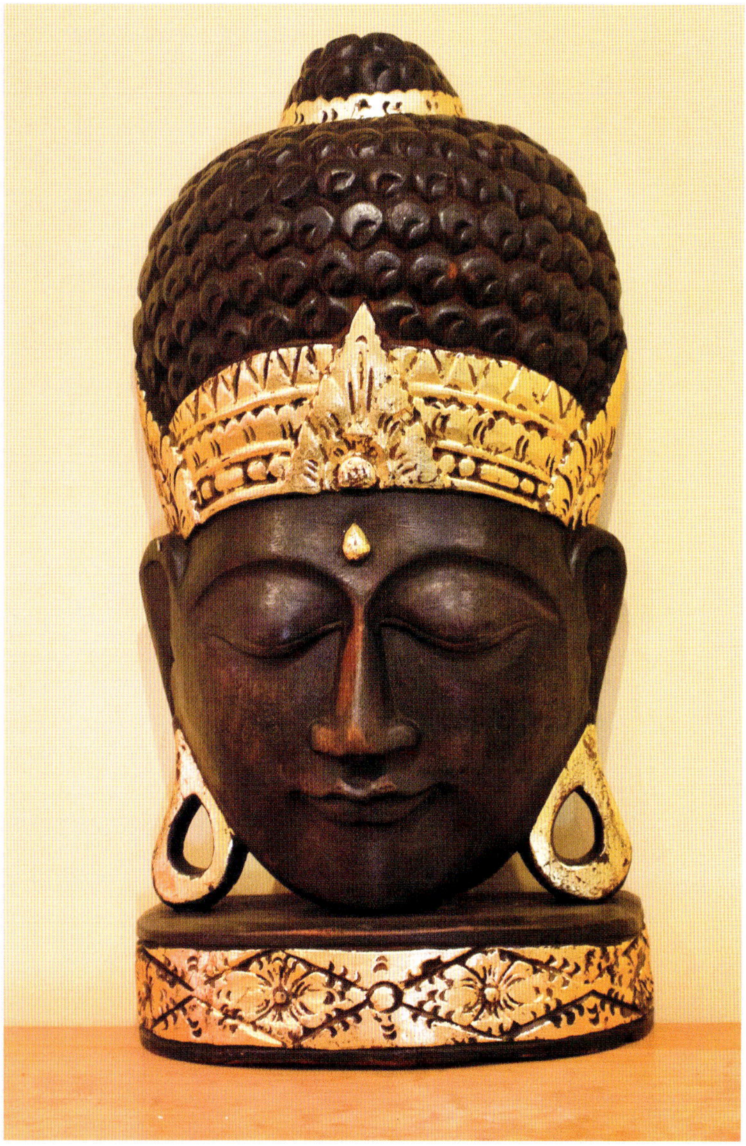

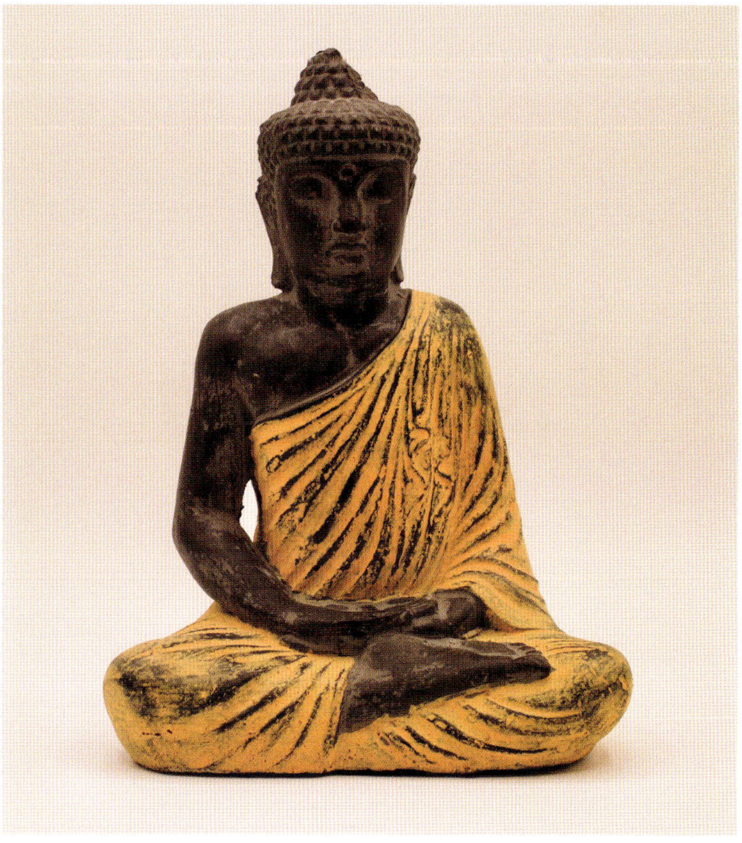

Artist unknown, *Enlightened Buddha* (Indonesia), 2010. Wood. *Photo: Myrah Brown Green*

Artist unknown, *The Sitting Buddha* (Singapore), 1991. Stone on an antique stone. *Photo: Myrah Brown Green*

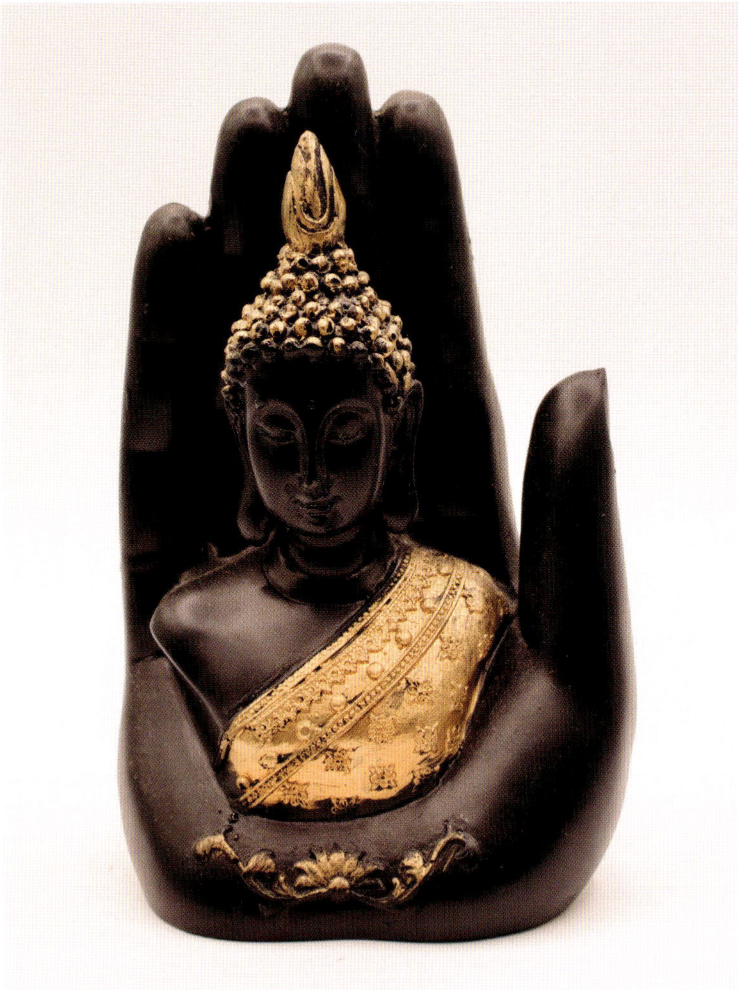

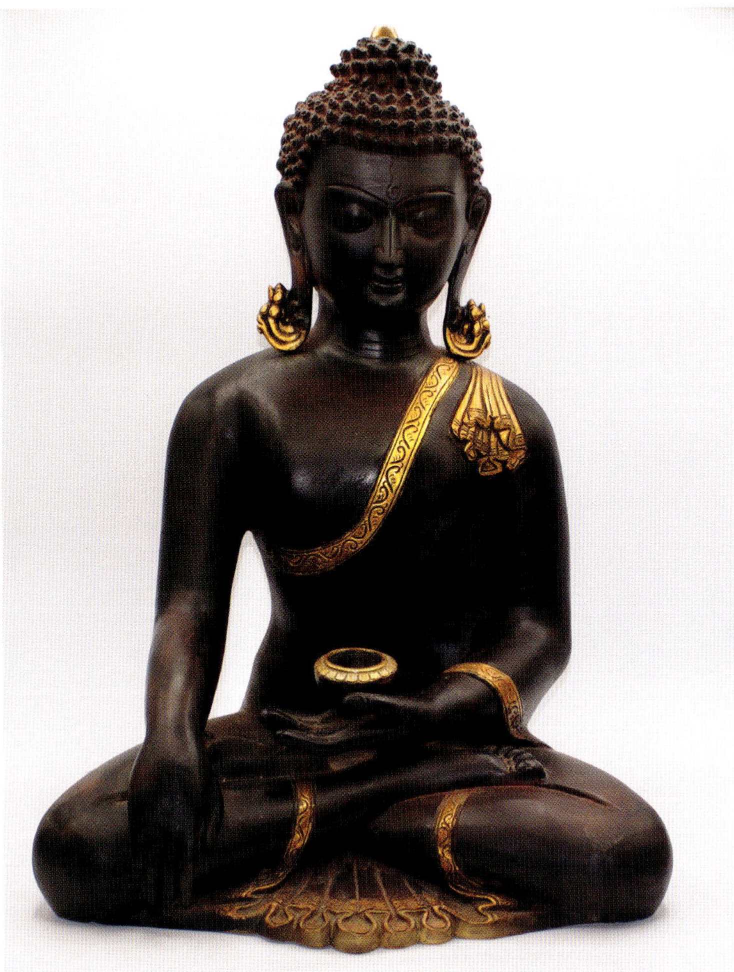

Artist unknown, *Meditative Buddha* (Bali), 2001. Resin.
Photo: Myrah Brown Green

Artist unknown, *Enlightened Buddha*, 1995. Cast iron.
Photo: Myrah Brown Green

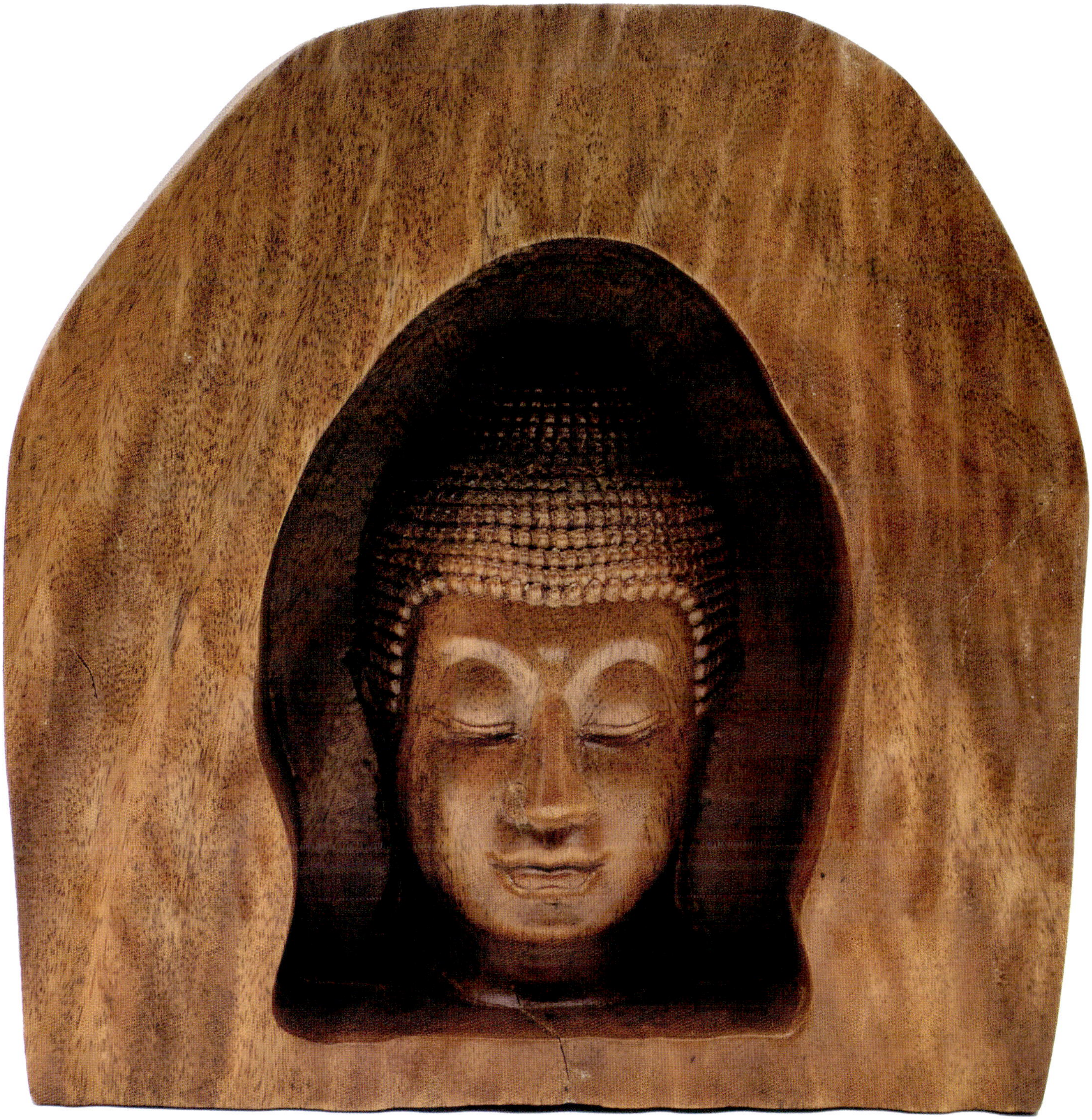

Artist unknown, *Meditative Buddha*, 2021. Wood.
Photo: Myrah Brown Green

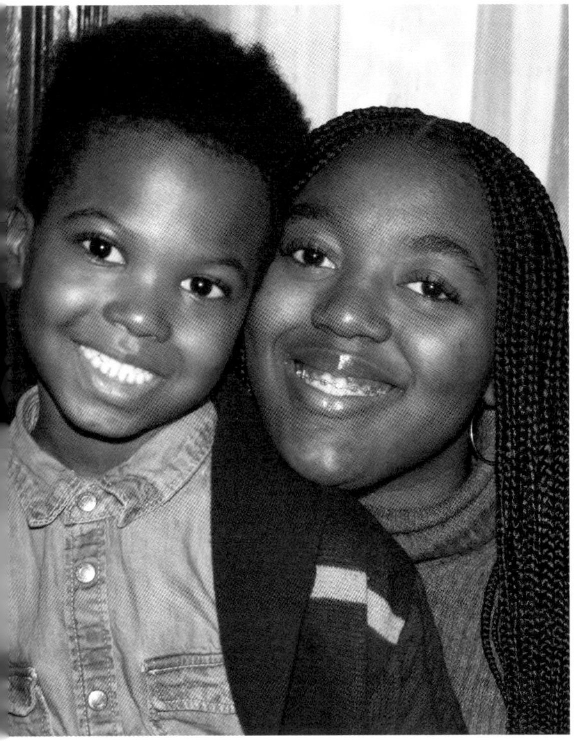

Photo: Myrah Brown Green

SUMMER-ZAIRE BELL AND CYRIE RICHARD WILLIAMS

NANA'S GIFTS

DR. MYRAH: What was the first piece of art that you collected and when?

CYRIE RICHARD WILLIAMS: The first piece of art that I collected was a quilt that Nana made for me when I was a baby.

SUMMER-ZAIRE BELL: The very first art piece that I collected was one of my grandmother's quilts. It was a goddess symbol that she later turned into a quilt, and it was gifted to me when I was a baby.

DR. MYRAH: Why are you a Keeper of Nana's Gifts?

CYRIE RICHARD WILLIAMS: I am a Keeper of Nana's Gifts because they are beautiful and remind me of life.

SUMMER-ZAIRE BELL: I am a Keeper of my Nana's Gifts and legacy through my own journey as an artist, and by honoring the art-filled world she created around me. Growing up, Nana's collection of art and her own creations shaped my love for creativity. Every piece tells a story, and her passion for art became mine. Nana taught me that art is more than beauty—it's a way to navigate life, express truth, and connect with others.

Nana always told me that when I was ready, I could choose from her quilts and other cherished works in her collection. That promise is a tangible way I connect to her legacy, but what she's given me goes even deeper. It's in the lessons she's shared: to stay authentic in my work, to never compromise my vision, and to find strength in a competitive art world.

Nana's legacy is my foundation and my inspiration, a gift I'll continue to nurture and share with the world.

Dr. Carolyn L. Mazloomi, *Untitled*, 1996. Cotton fiber appliqué, 24" × 17". *Photo: Myrah Brown Green*

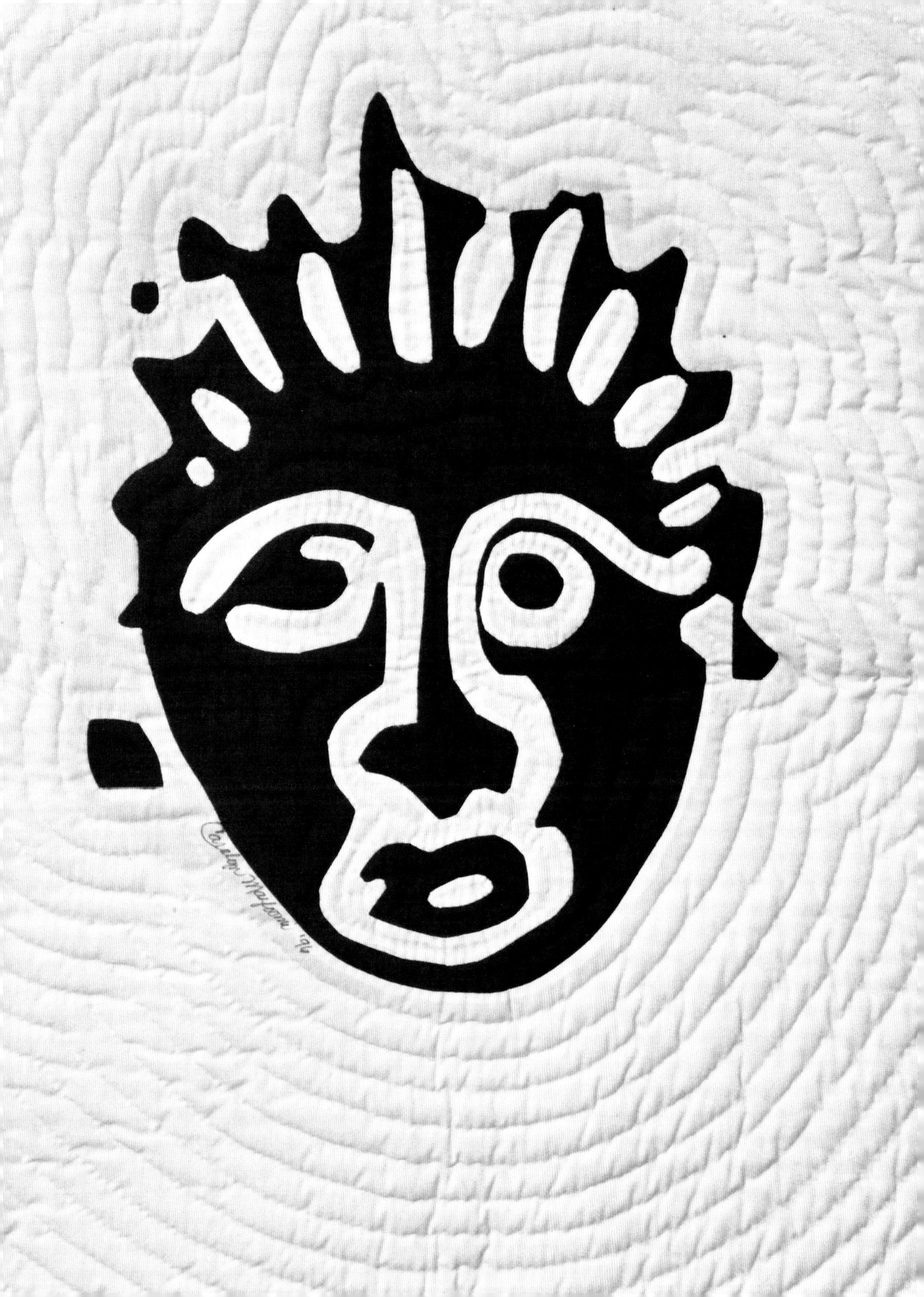

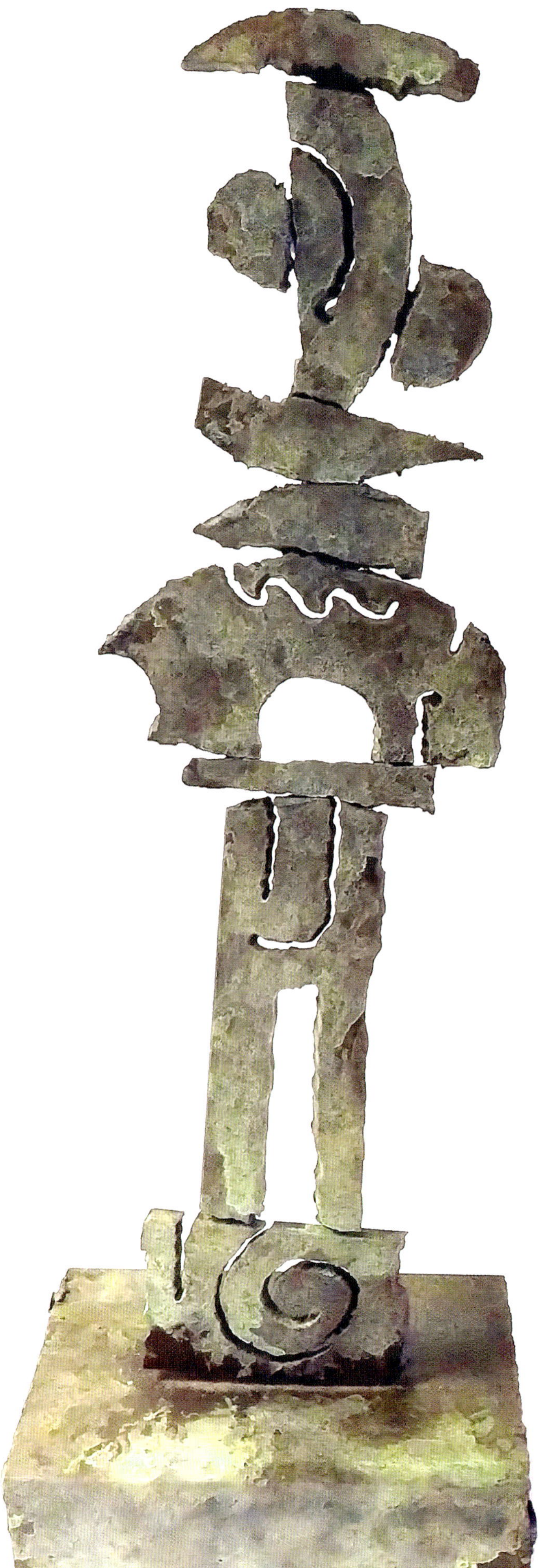

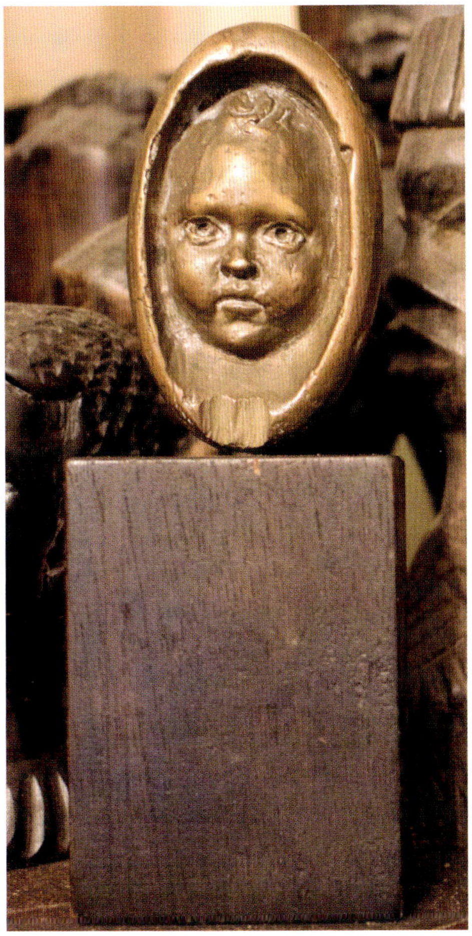

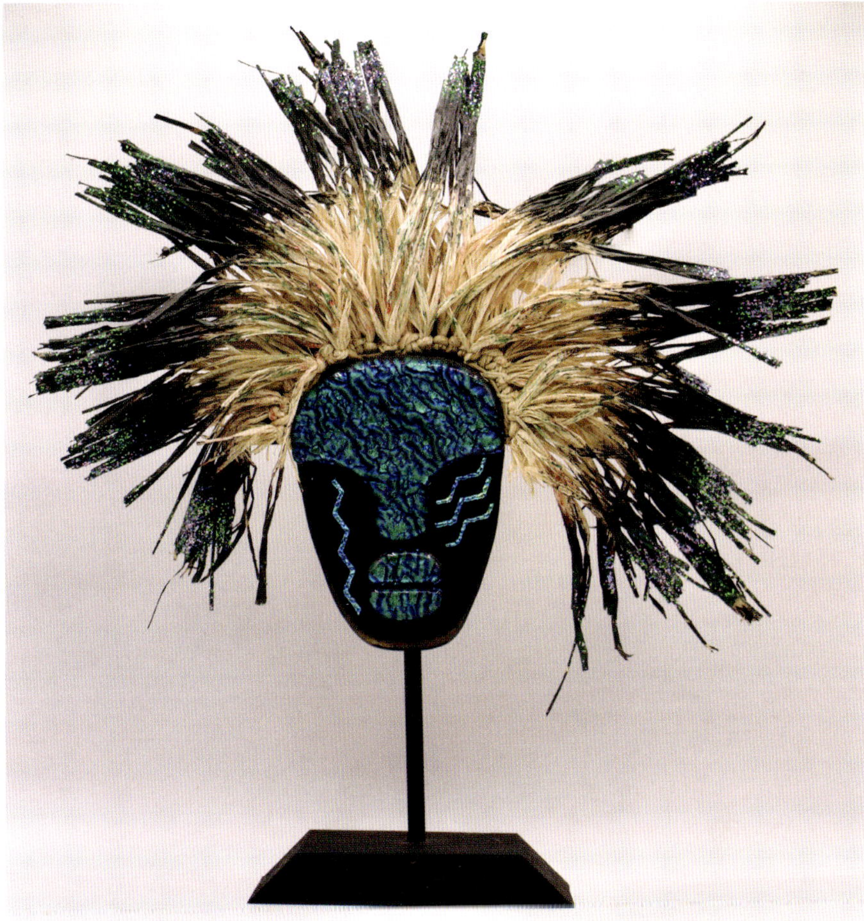

Opposite: Jerome China, *Soulful Stance*, 2024. Welded steel, 21" × 6". *Photo: Courtesy of the artist*

Augusta Savage, *To the Youngest Delegate*, 1936. N.N.C. #38, bronze, 3" × 1.74". *Photo: Myrah Brown Green*

Ken Wright, *Mask*, 2018. Kiln-formed fused glass and raffia, 21" × 17". *Photo: Myrah Brown Green*

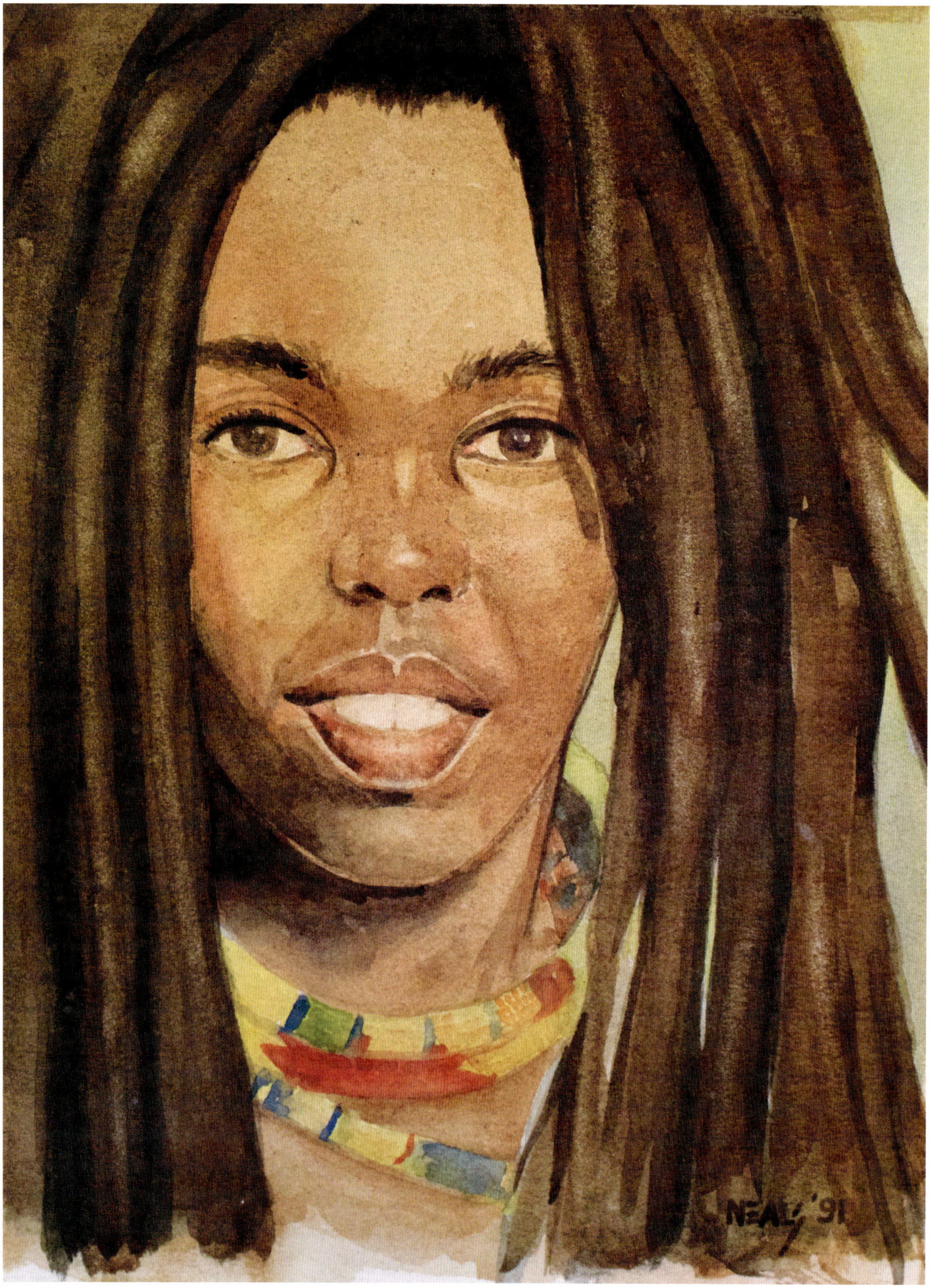

Above: Otto Neals, *Mama Myrah*, 1991. Watercolor on watercolor paper, 11" × 9". *Photo: Myrah Brown Green*

Vanessa Greene, *Nightingale*, 2003. Mixed media, 14" × 11".

Emmet Wigglesworth, *Innocent Bystanders*, 2003. Pen and ink, 9" × 16". *Photo: Myrah Brown Green*

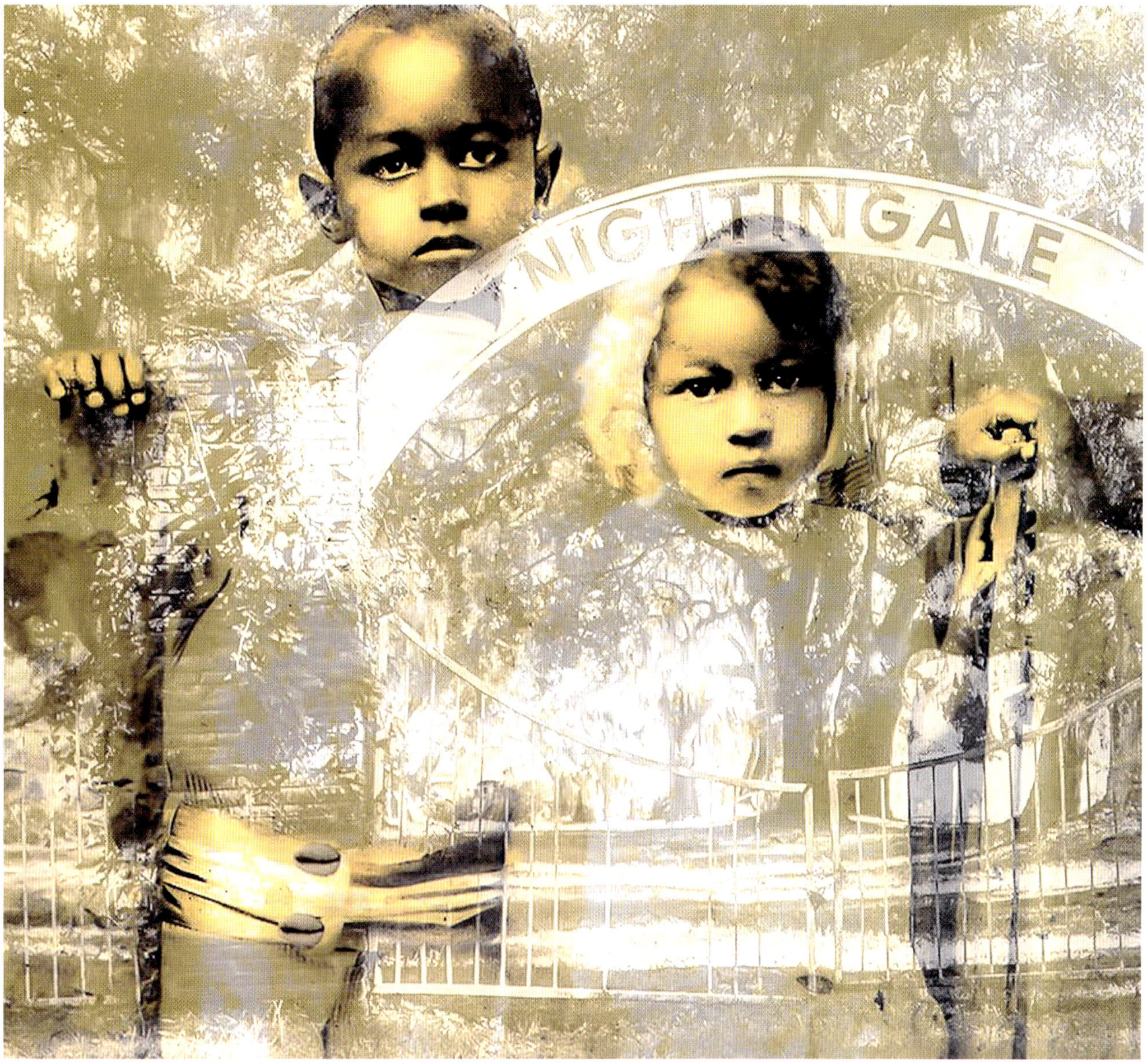
NIGHTINGALE

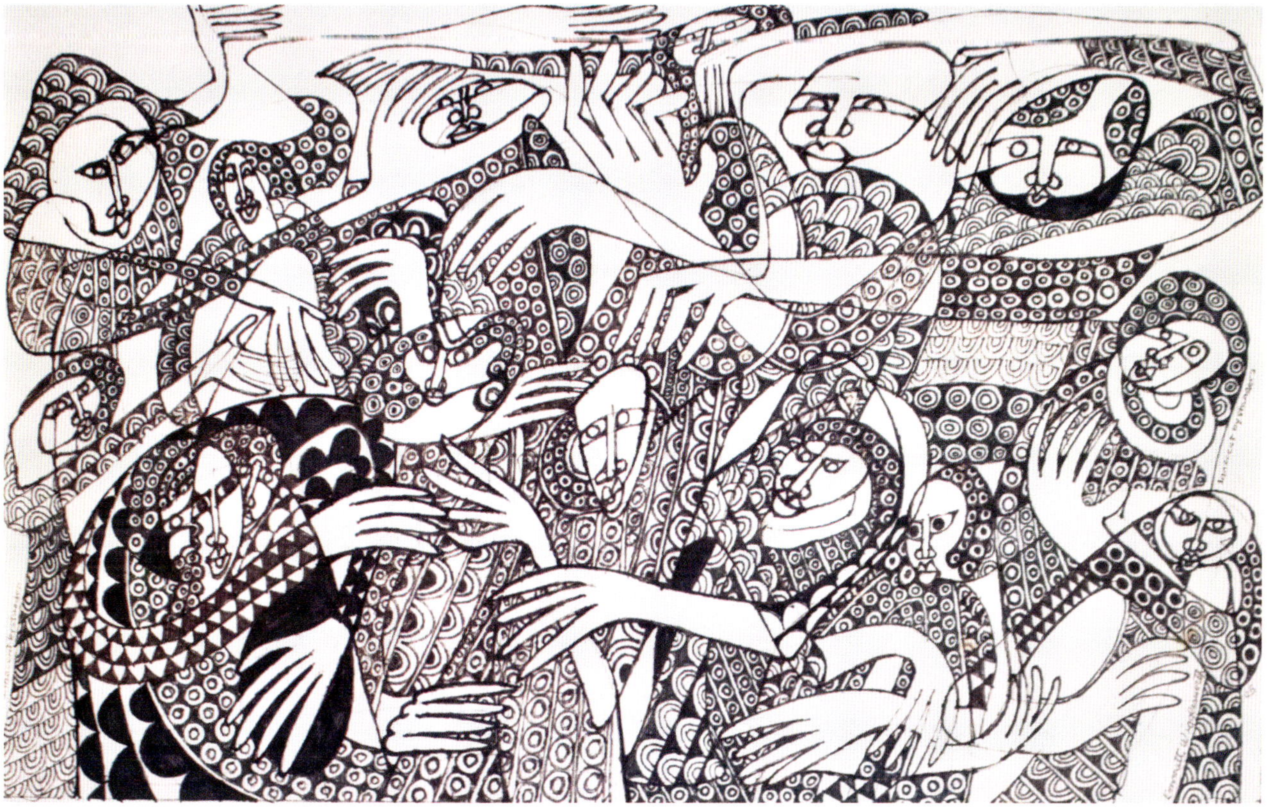

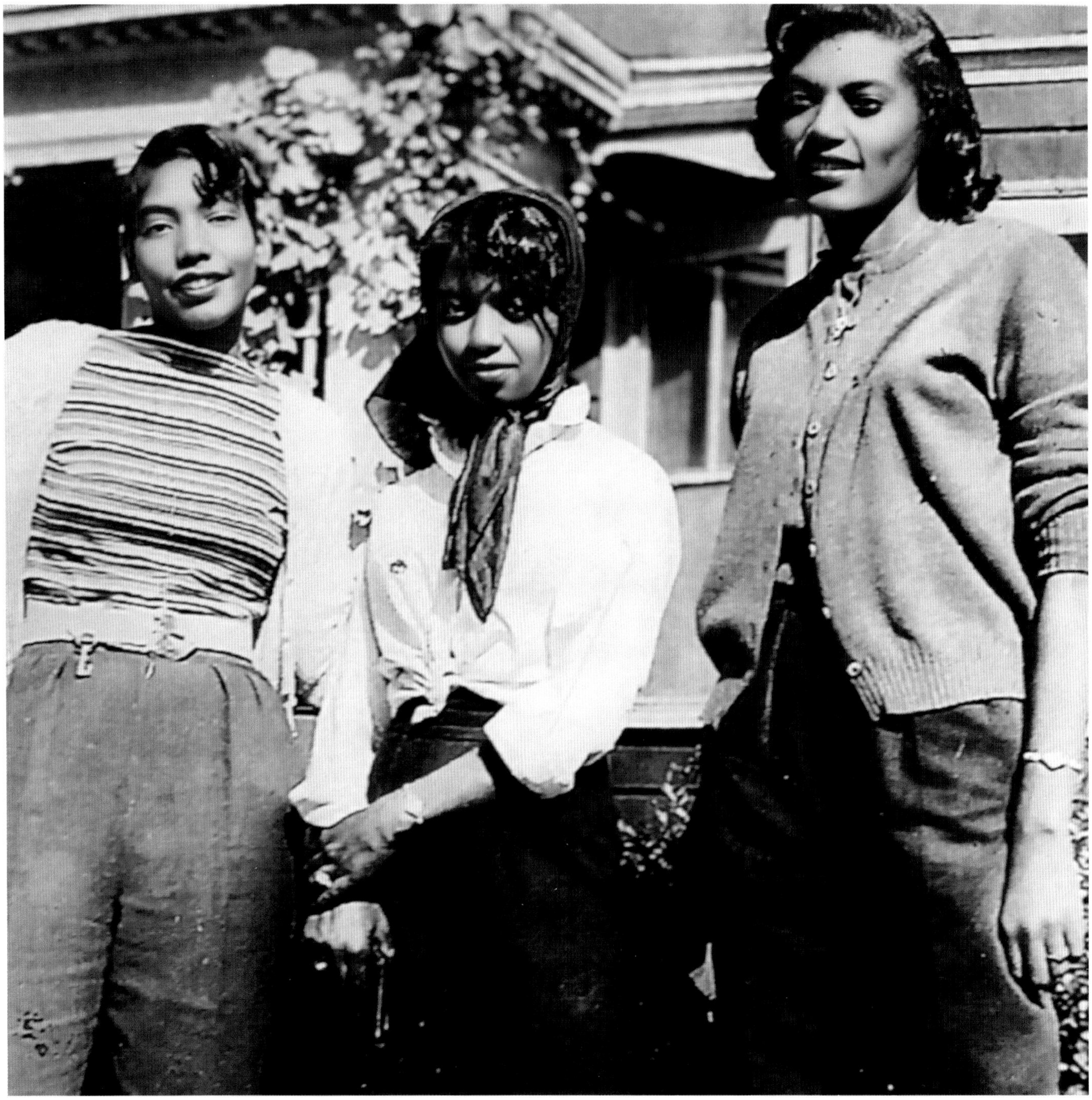

Hodges Brown Sr., *Parallel Mothers*, 1957. Black-and-white film, 14" × 11".

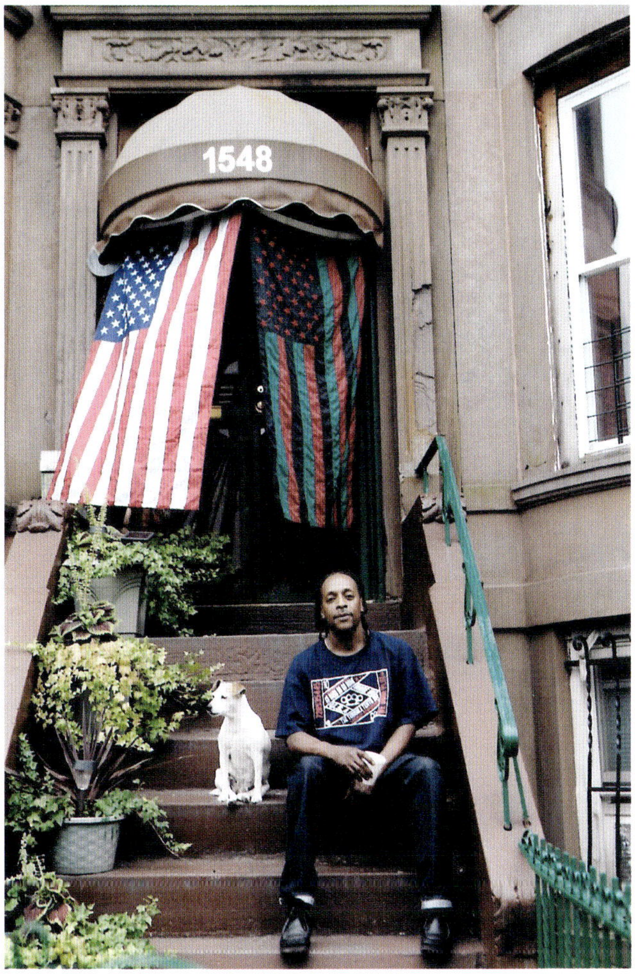

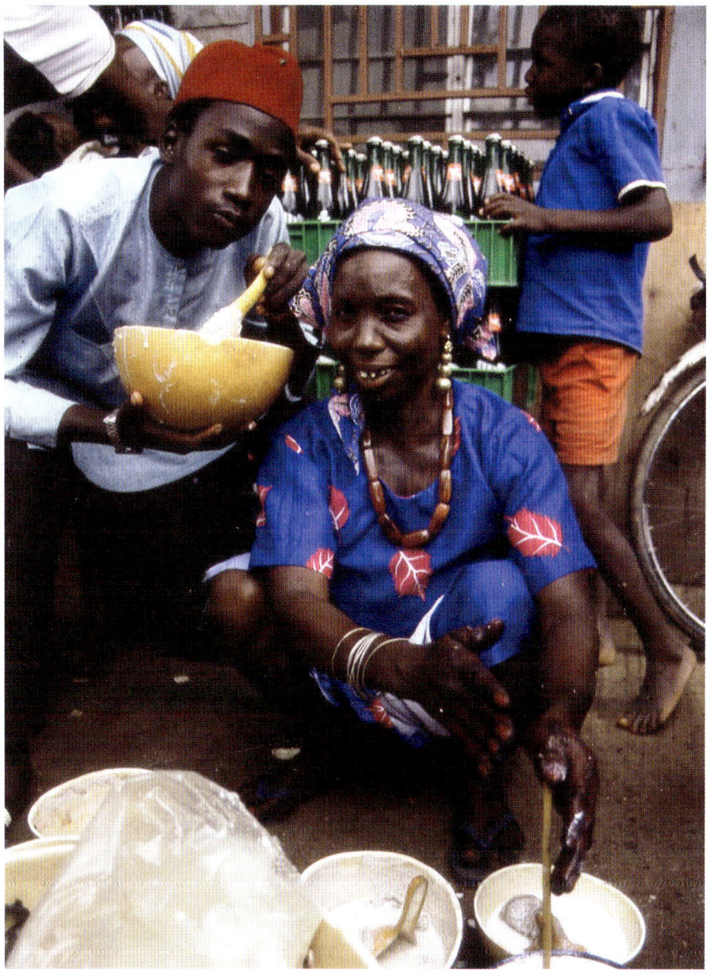

Jamel Shabazz, *Black in America*, 1980. C-print, 14" × 11".

Richard E. Green, *Yogurt Vendor* (Mali, West Africa), 1990. Slide film, 14" × 11".

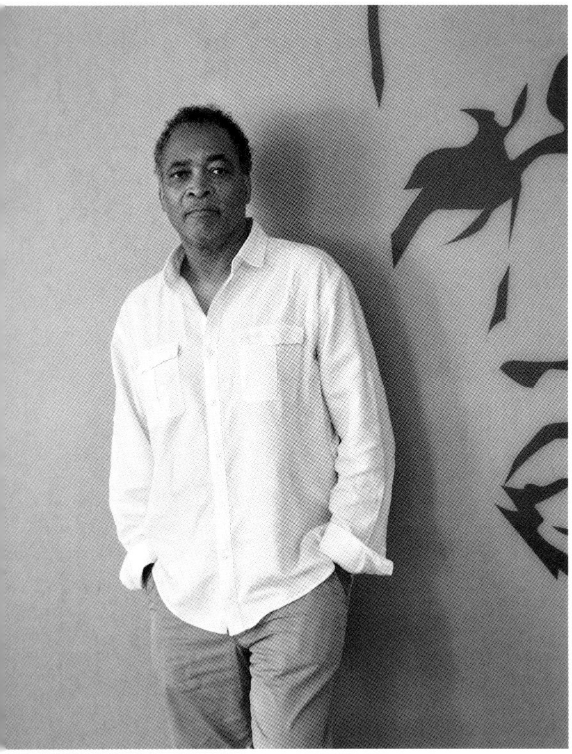

Photo: Myrah Brown Green

MICHAEL BRADLEY
CONTEMPORARY ABSTRACT ART

DR. MYRAH: What was the first piece of art that you collected and when?

MICHAEL BRADLEY: The first piece of art that I ever collected is by Doris Price, called *Speaking in Jazz*. It's called a *pour quoi* original, which is a French term. It's a form of a limited edition, and I purchased it from [the] Savacou Gallery in about 1988. I never really met her. I know that she was affiliated with a collective that worked out of the Jamaica Art Center. It was like a who's who that was a part of that collective, with artists like Ann Tanksley, Otto Neals . . . I believe she ultimately moved to or lived in Delaware.

DR. MYRAH: Why are you a Keeper of Contemporary Abstract Art?

MICHAEL BRADLEY: It's all part of my evolution as a collector. Initially I was always interested in certain imagery. I was a part of the CUNY educational system in the seventies. I always drifted toward imagery that made a political or social statement. As I evolved as a collector and my interest became a little bit more divergent, I started looking at imagery that was more than just two dimensional . . . and I've always been attracted to art where form and function was an issue and how the artists used various elements, as opposed to just a canvas and a paintbrush, or a piece of paper and a paintbrush. But it was found objects; various elements on how they created their image beyond just painting it. So as time went on and I became a more seasoned collector, twenty years into the process my eye started drifting toward these types of images. It was always about what element did the artist use to create that finished product, and that was always a major attraction for me. I think it is reflected in the works that you've selected that speak to that need. When you look at the Charlotte Ka and you see all of the elements in her piece that are just beyond an imagery that we would call *encaustic*. But there's other elements that she's using, and those other elements create an image, and a feeling, and emotion that goes simply beyond just a painting.

Eric Pryor, *Big Al's Rhythm*, 1997. Oil on wood, 36" × 12". *Photo: Myrah Brown Green*

Phillipe Dodard, *In the Mood*, 1989. Acrylic on wood, 8" × 8". *Photo: Myrah Brown Green*

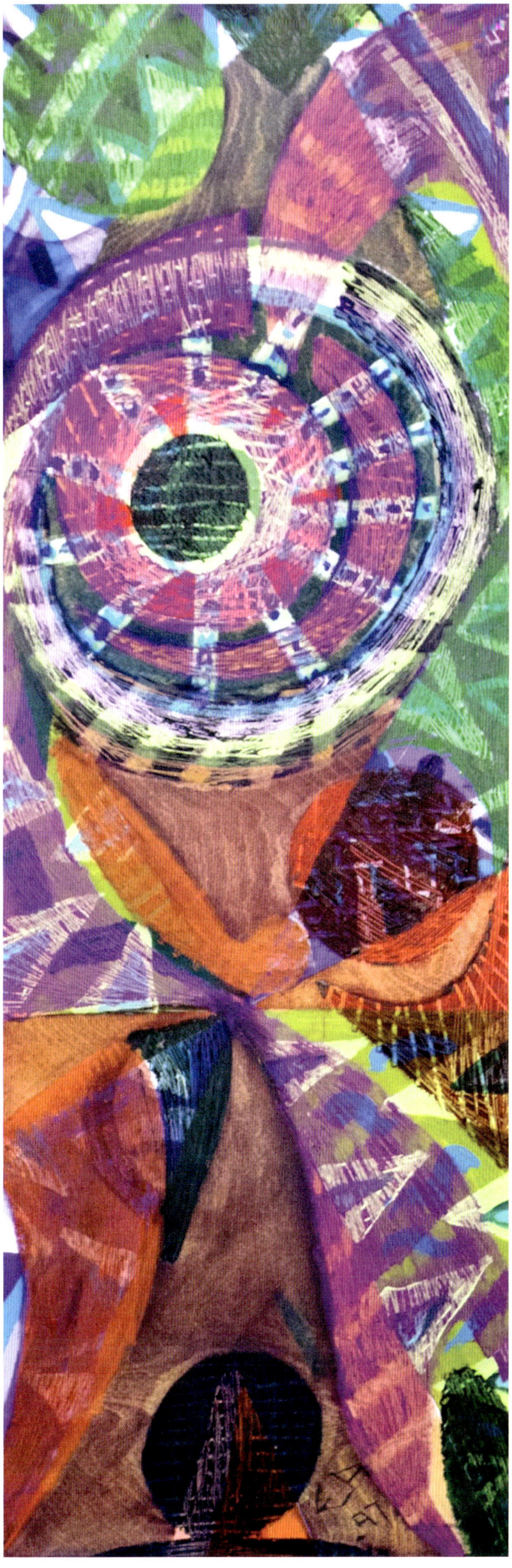

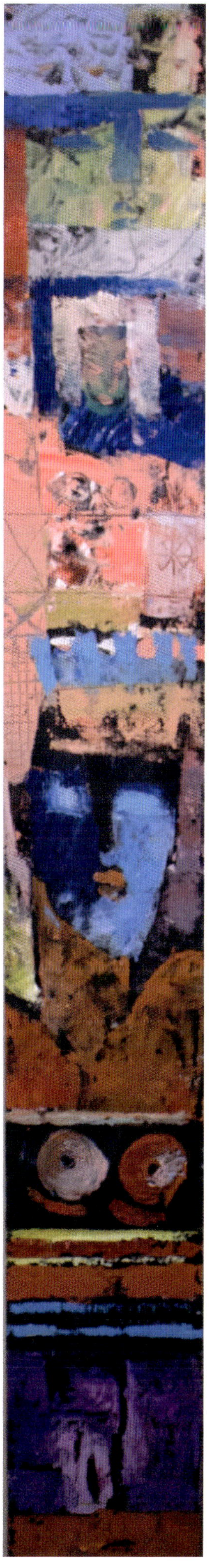

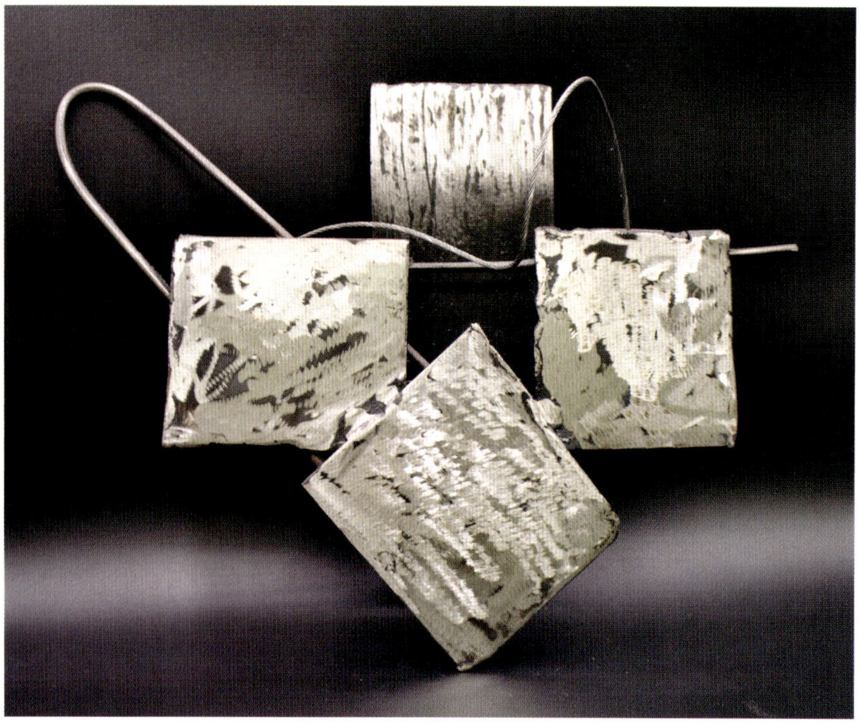

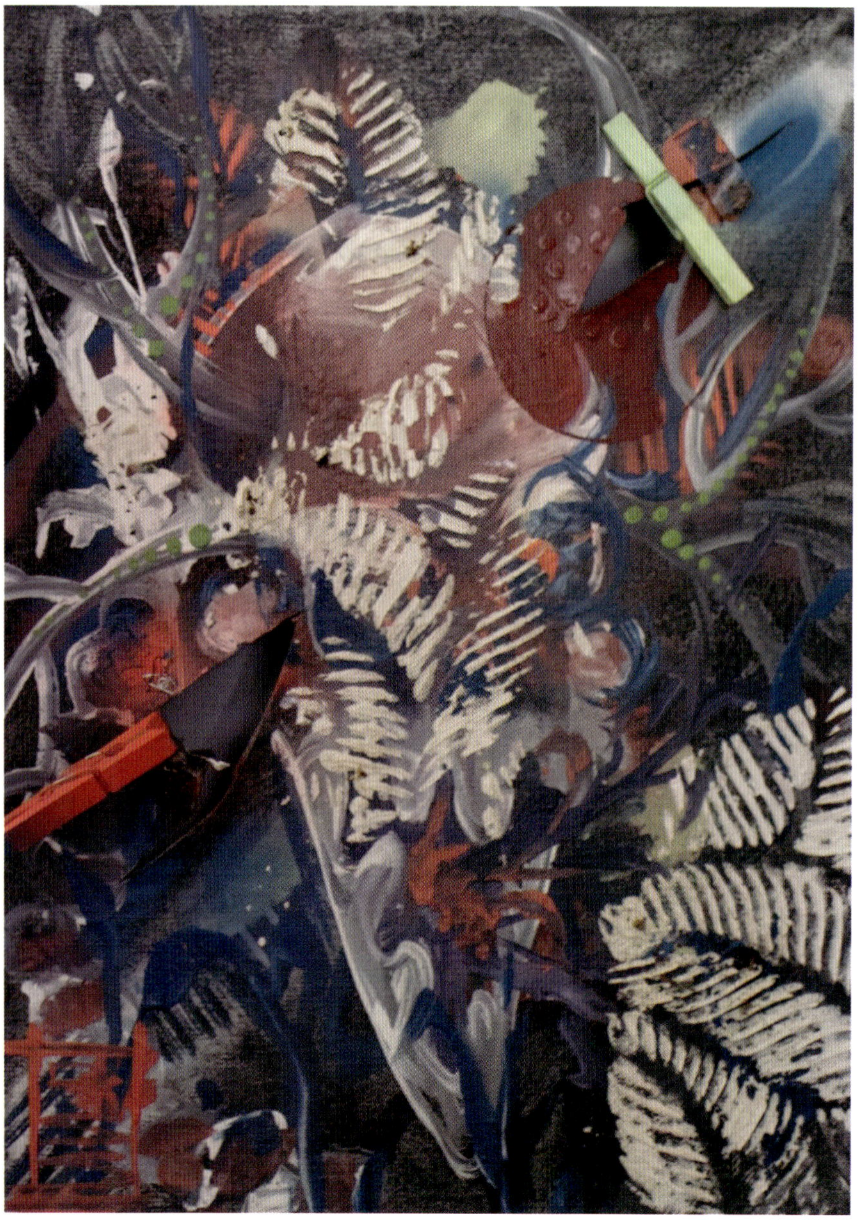

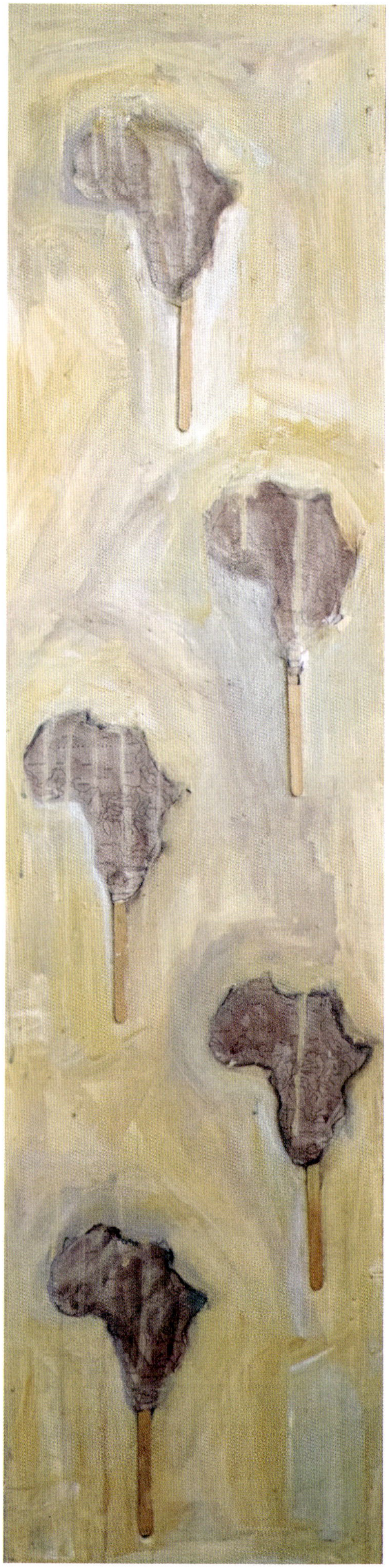

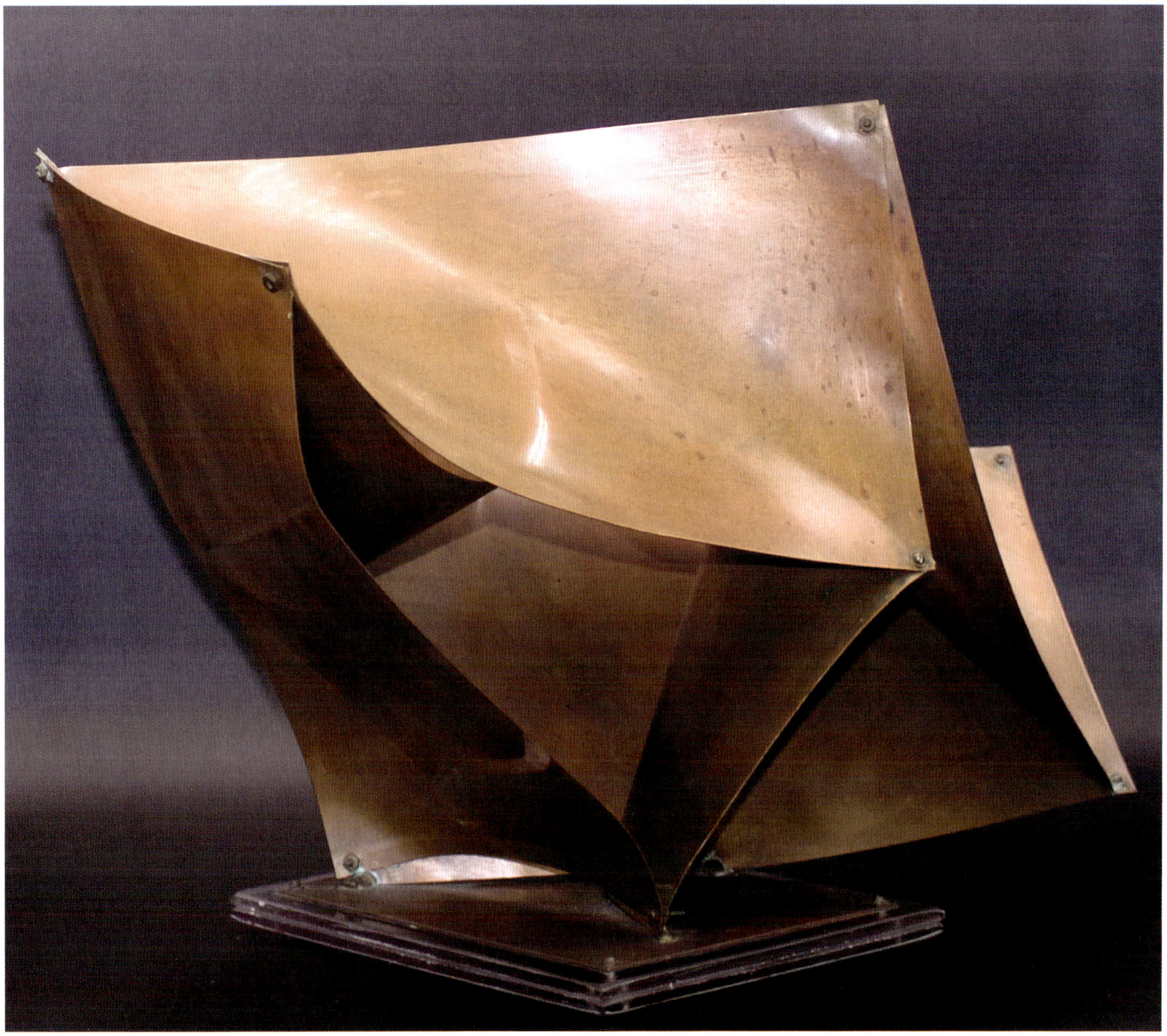

Opposite, top left: John McDaniel, *Abstraction Veve #3*, 2007. Steel, 15"x 12". *Photo: Myrah Brown Green*

Opposite, bottom left: Rachel Smith Sepulveda, *Untitled*, 2023. Mixed media, 16" × 12". *Photo: Myrah Brown Green*

Opposite, right: Derrick Adams, *Africa on a Stick*, 1994. Mixed media, 48" × 12". *Photo: Myrah Brown Green*

Valeria Cray-Dihaan, *Firebird*, 2002. Heated brass and copper sheets (Plexiglas stand, nuts, and bolts), 12" × 20" × 10". *Photo: Myrah Brown Green*

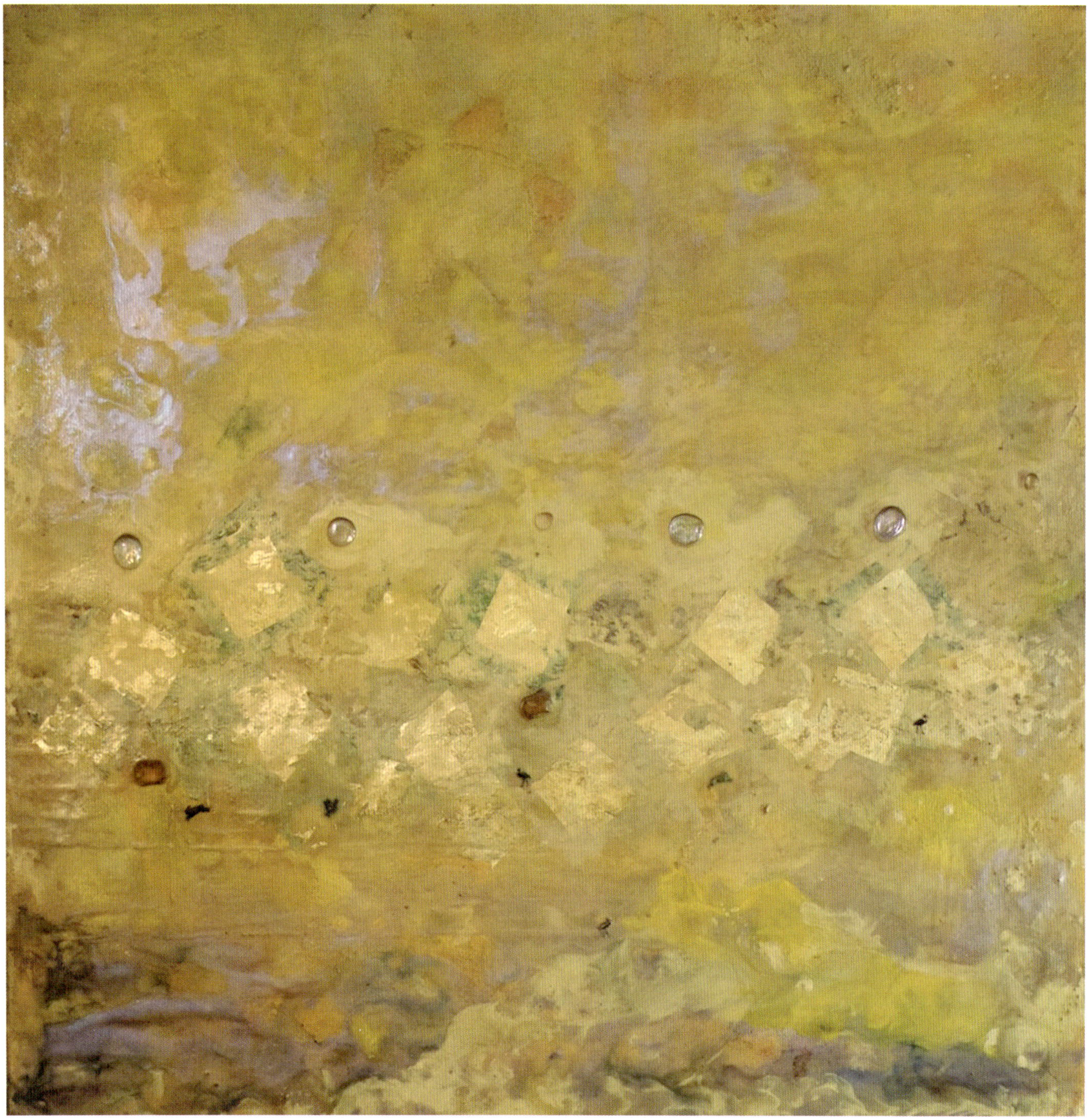

Above: Charlotte Ka, *Untitled*, 2005. Encaustic, 48" × 48". *Photo: Myrah Brown Green*

Gregory Coates, *Fence*, 2005. Mixed-media wall sculpture, 16" × 18". *Photo: Myrah Brown Green*

Adger Cowans, *Open Way*, 2003. Acrylic on wood, 8" × 8". *Photo: Myrah Brown Green*

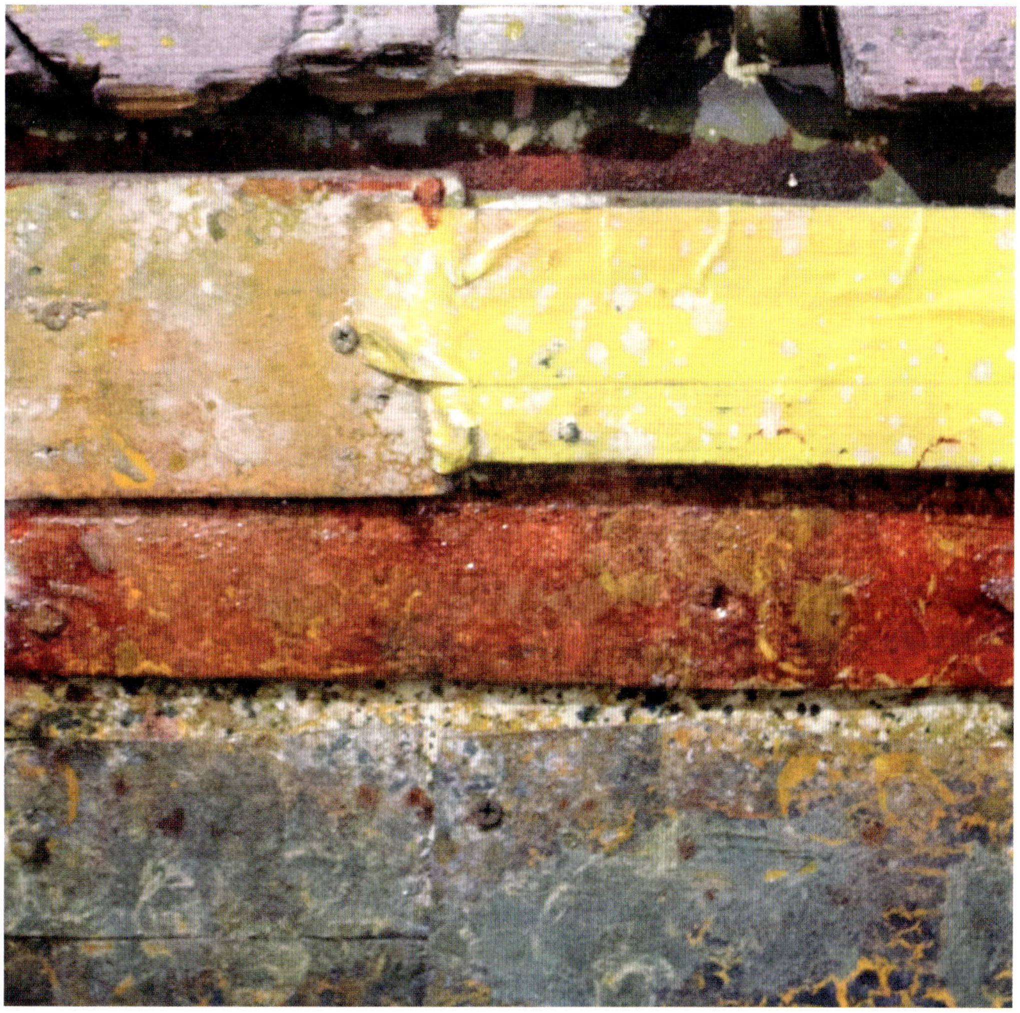

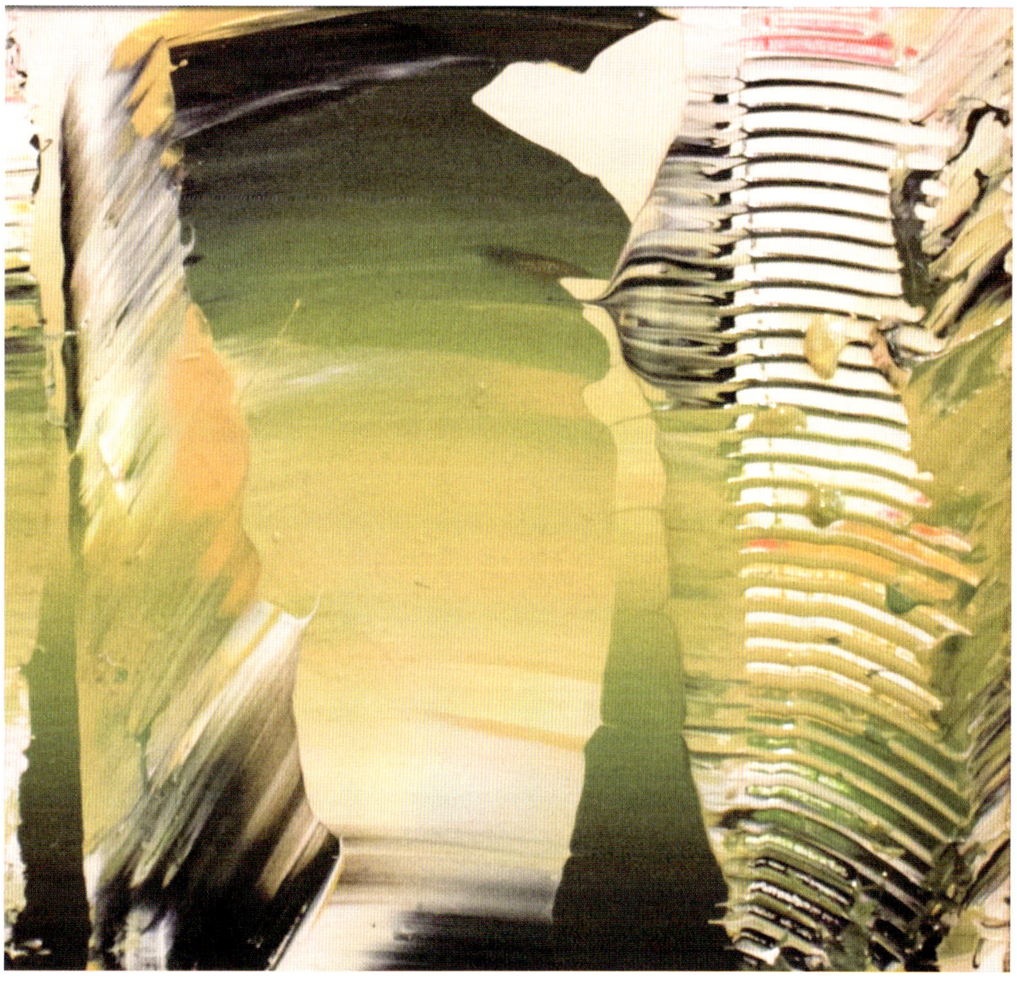

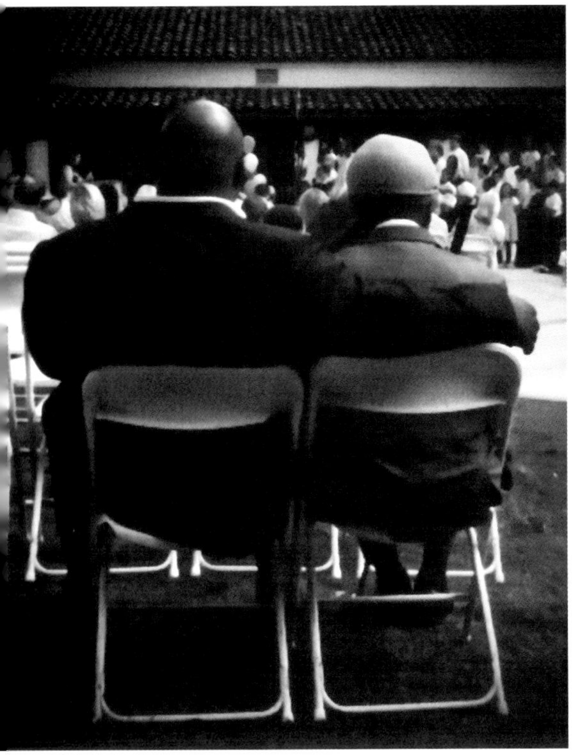

Photo: Courtesy of the collector

KWAME BRATHWAITE II
WORKS BY MY FATHER

DR. MYRAH: What was the first piece of art that you collected and when?

KWAME BRATHWAITE II: When I was four years old, a family friend who was a commercial artist drew a picture for me of my favorite superhero: the Incredible Hulk. For years I attempted to re-create that image until my senior year in high school, when I finally illustrated my own version of the image. At age five, when I was asked about my profession as an adult, I responded with "I want to be an artist when I grow up." When asked, "What kind of artist?," I responded "a colorer."

DR. MYRAH: Why are you a Keeper of your father's photographs?

KWAME BRATHWAITE II: When I look back, I realize that there are many moments that have brought me to this role as the second "Keeper of the Images"; for instance:

Working alongside my Baba in the darkroom and witnessing his sheer joy as his images came to life as his apprentice at age sixteen. Discussions with my father about organizing and archiving his work helped me truly understand the importance of his work and the passion that fueled him.

When I think of the birth of this project to ensure the preservation of his work, I can't help but think about how it all began. My mother and father were visiting my wife and family in Pasadena around 2013. My father had a manila envelope which contained two incredible photographs. The first was an image of the Righteous Brothers, David Bowie, Yoko Ono, John Lennon, and Roberta Flack backstage at the Grammys in 1975. The second image was one of Muhammad Ali sitting on a bench on the Congo River in Kinshasa in 1974. This was a couple of days before the Rumble in the Jungle, the iconic fight with Ali versus George Foreman. This image stood out, particularly because Ali wasn't being photographed while entertaining the crowd. He was in what seemed to be a pensive mood. I said to my father, "Why haven't I seen these pictures before?" His reply was "I've got plenty of pictures you've never seen before." My wife, Robyn, and I looked at each other and knew that we had to do something to preserve this incredible body of work.

Around that same time, my mom also reminded my sister and me that Baba had done what he was supposed to do, and that it was now up to us to ensure that his work would continue and move to the next level.

This legacy is why I am now a "Keeper of the Images" . . . and it's why I must both honor and continue to reveal our truth.

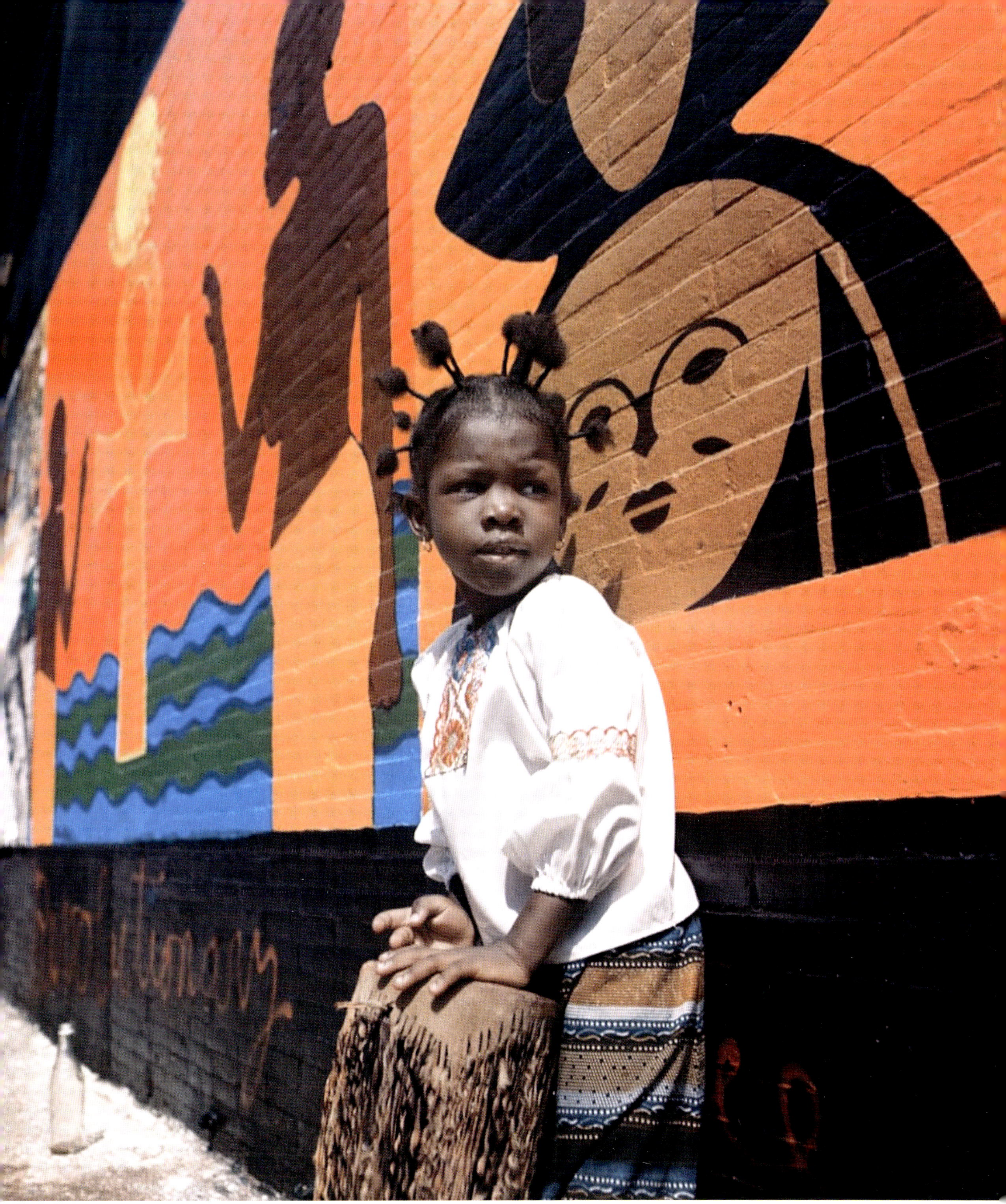

Kwame Brathwaite, *Untitled* (Ndola Brathwaite in front of a community mural. Harlem, New York), 1972. Archival pigment print.

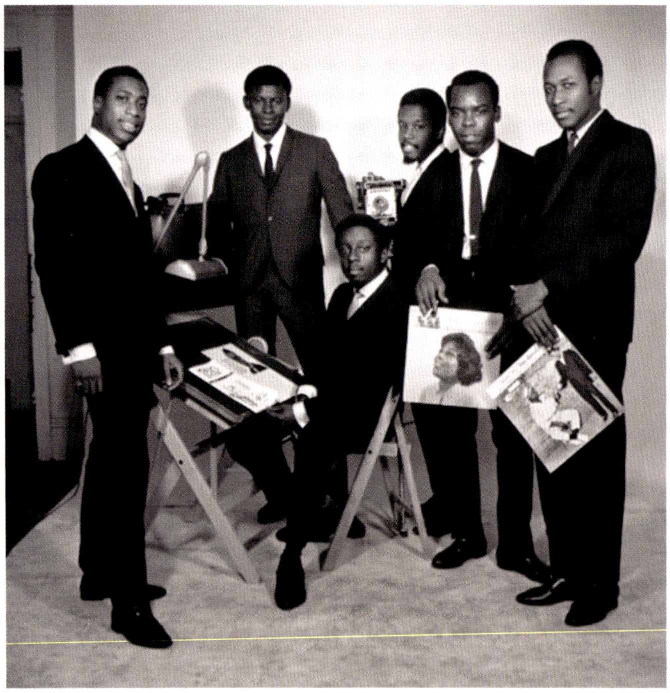

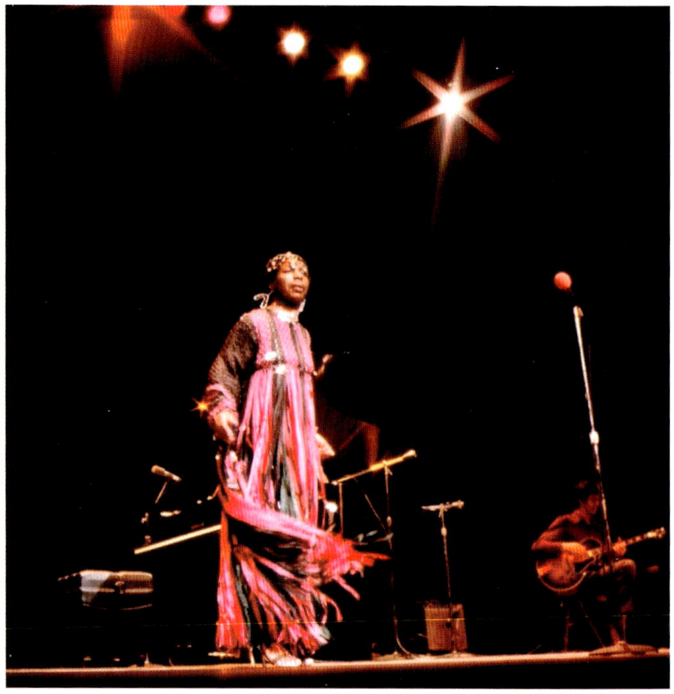

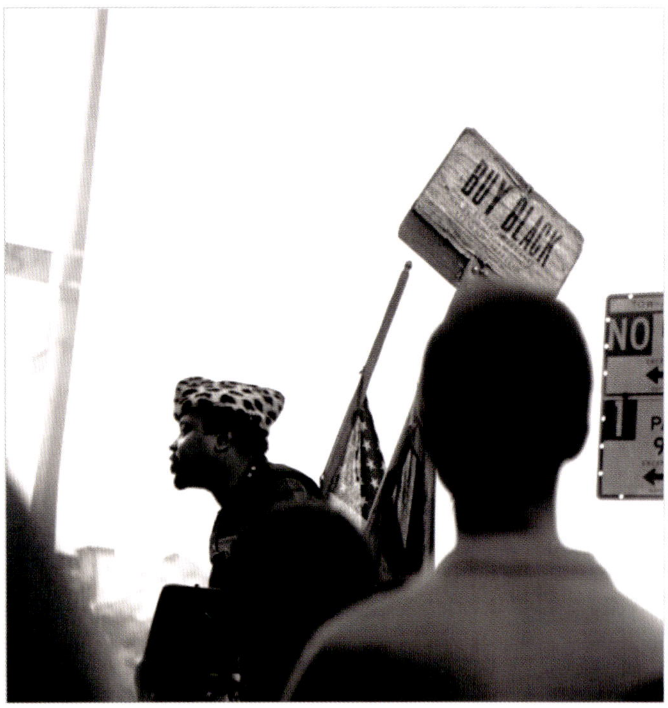

Top left: Kwame Brathwaite, *Untitled* (original AJAS members. *left to right*: Robert Gumbs, Frank Adu, Elombe Brath, *(seated)* Kwame Brathwaite, Ernest Baxter, and Chris Hall), 1965. Archival pigment print, 30" × 30".

Top right: Kwame Brathwaite, *Untitled* (Nina Simone at the Beacon Theatre), ca. 1974. Archival pigment print, 30" × 30".

Kwame Brathwaite, *Untitled* (Charles Peaker Street Speaker, Head of ANPM After Carlos Cookes passed away, on 125th Street), 1968. Archival pigment print, 15" × 15".

Opposite: Kwame Brathwaite, *Untitled* (crowd at Human Kindness Day), 1974. 40" × 27.5".

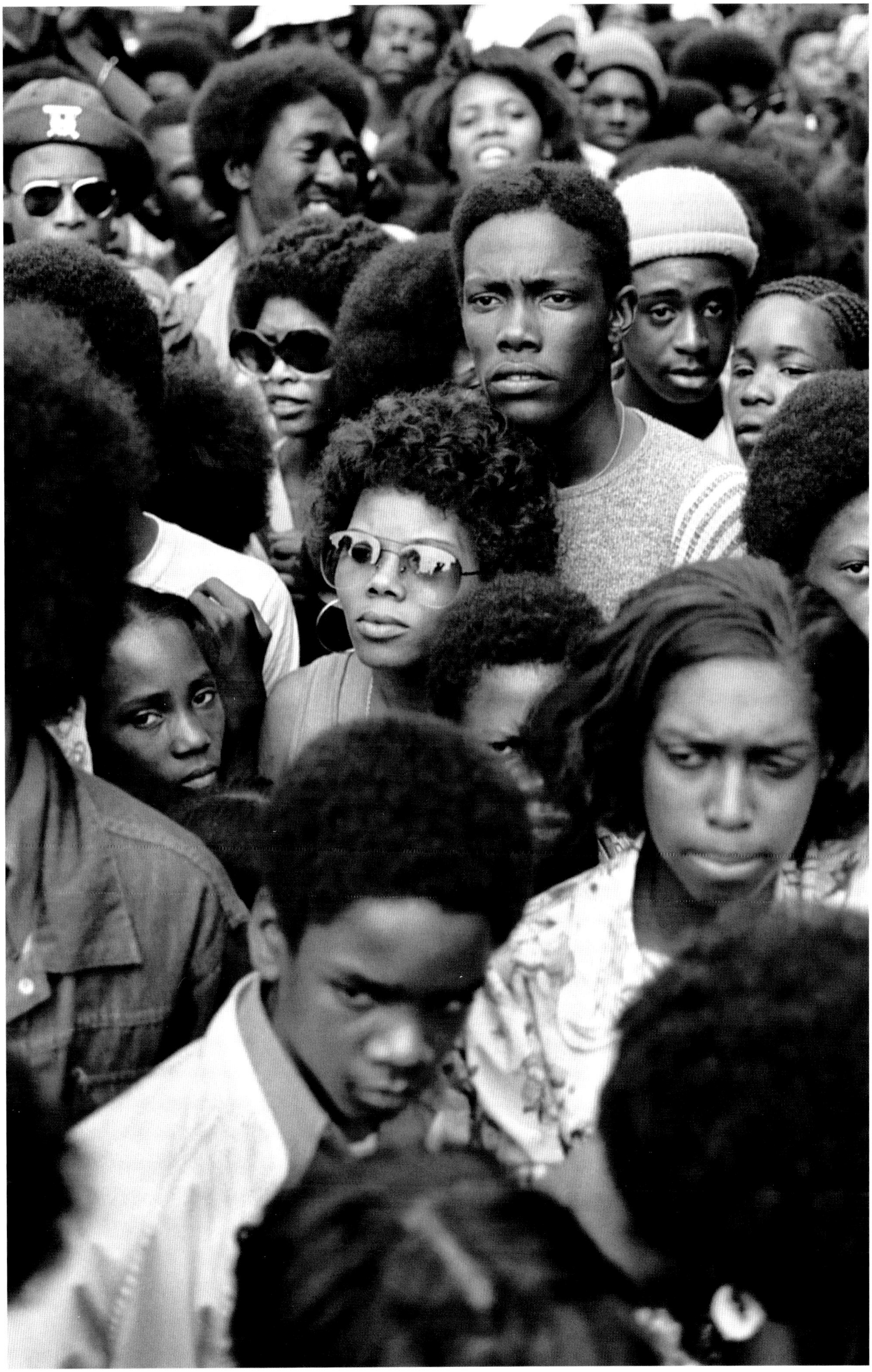

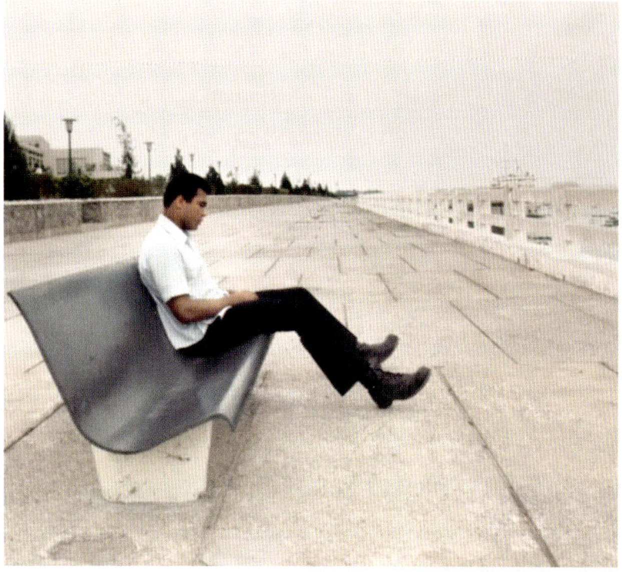

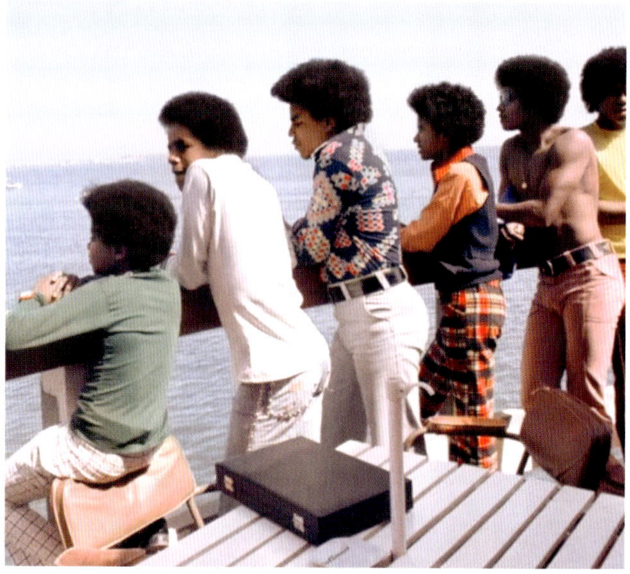

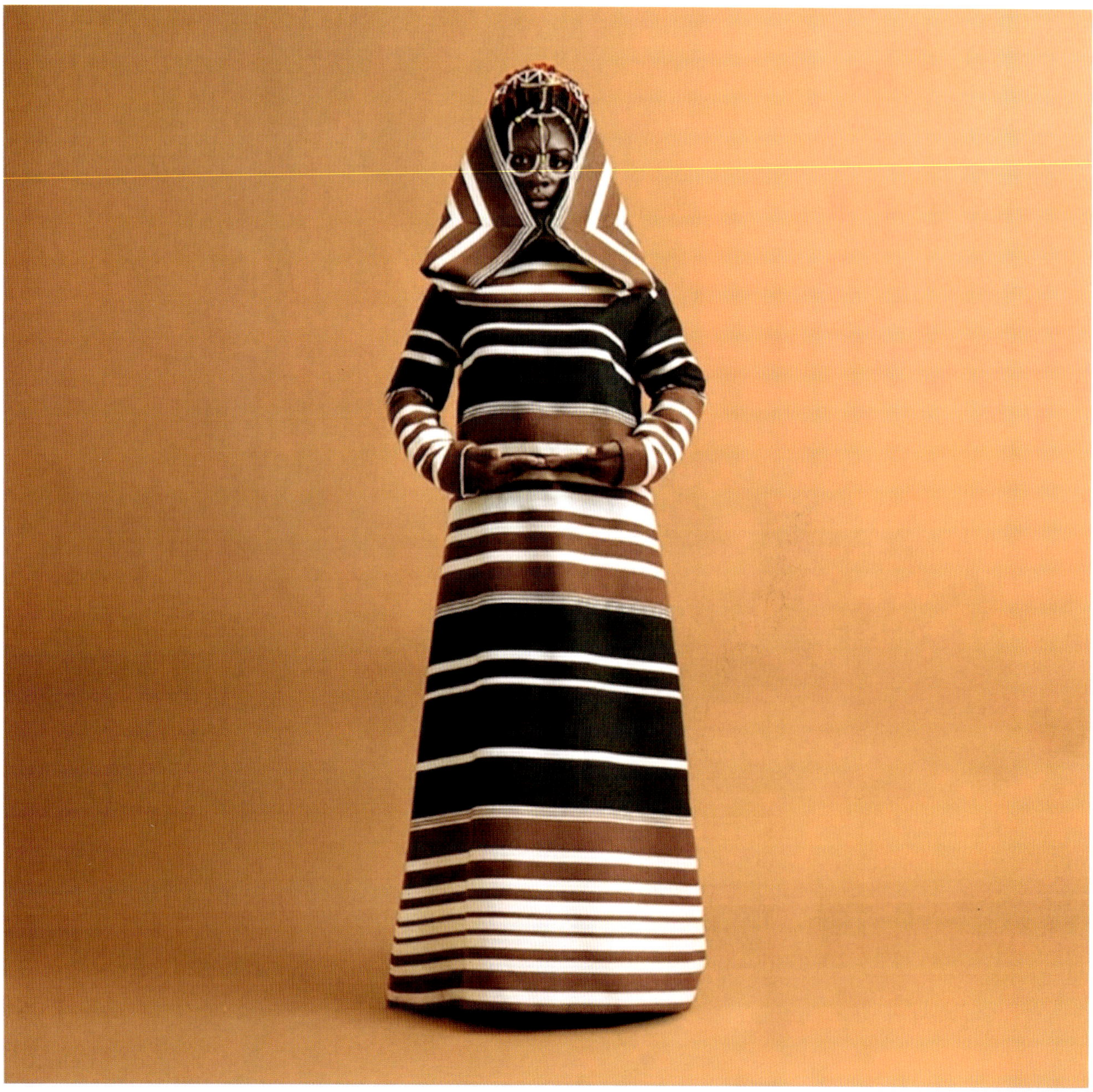

Top left: Kwame Brathwaite, *Gray Day on the Congo*, 1974. Archival pigment print, 40" × 60".

Top right: Kwame Brathwaite, *Untitled* (Jacksons on boat from Goree Island), 1974. Archival pigment print, 40" × 60".

Kwame Brathwaite, *MER*, 1968. Archival pigment print, 40" × 60".

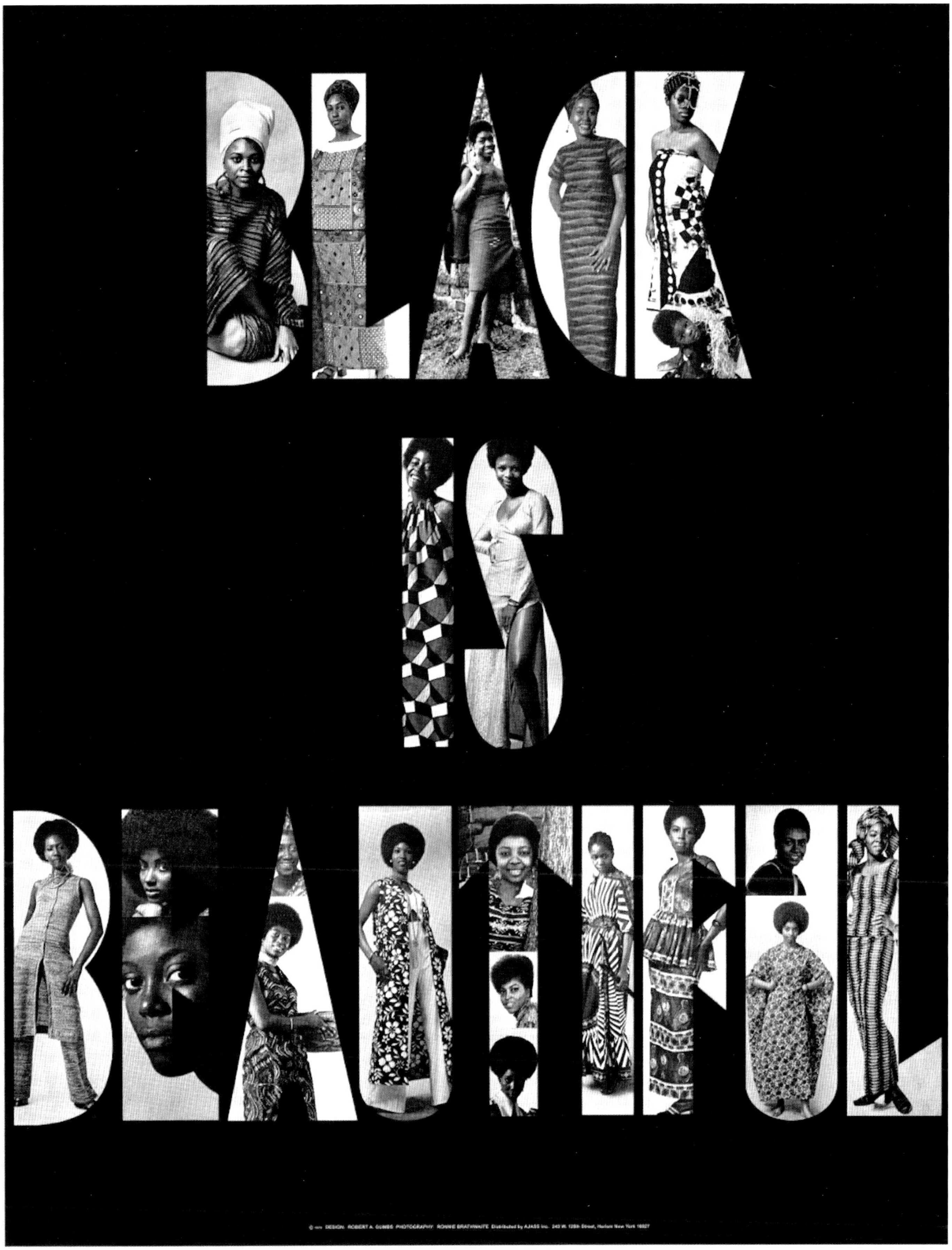

Kwame Brathwaite, *Untitled* (Black Is Beautiful poster from 1970).
Archival pigment print, 60" × 47.5".

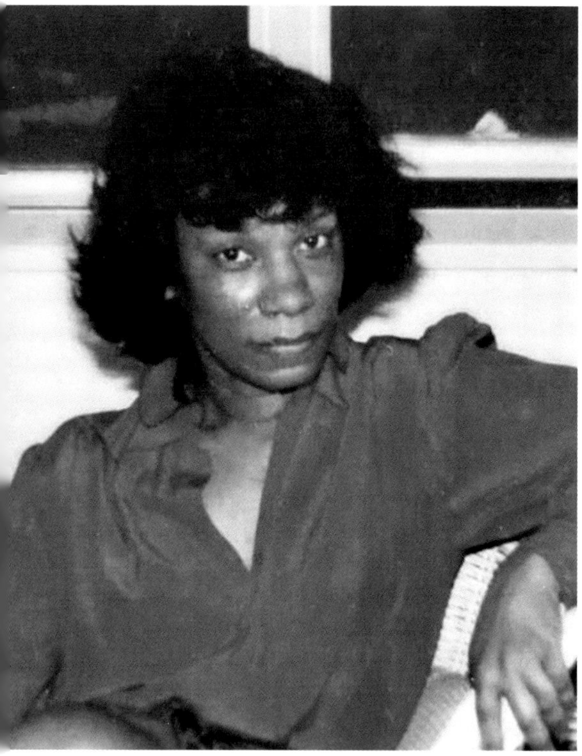

Photo: Courtesy of the estate

PATRICIA SCIPIO-BRIM (1947–2023)
COLORS

DR. MYRAH: What was the first piece of art that you collected and when?

JENNIFER STEWART-HUTCHINSON ON BEHALF OF HER DEAR FRIEND: Patricia Brim's first art purchase was *Seated Woman* by James Denmark. The piece, which was featured on the gallery invitation and displayed on an easel in the window of Spiral Gallery on Vanderbilt Avenue, caught her eye as she entered the gallery in the early 1980s. Immediately drawn to it, Patricia asked for a red dot to be placed on it, claiming it as her own.

DR. MYRAH: Why are you a Keeper of images full of rich colors?

JENNIFER STEWART-HUTCHINSON ON BEHALF OF HER DEAR FRIEND: For over forty years, Patricia was a devoted keeper of African American art and art from the African diaspora. She was particularly drawn to vibrant, colorful pieces—a reflection of the vivid landscapes of her homeland, Trinidad & Tobago. For Patricia, art was more than a collection; it was her solace, [her] meditation, and a refuge from the rigorous world of law, where her daily attire often consisted of somber gray and black suits. Pieces like Romare Bearden's *Man Seated with Red Rooster* brought back cherished memories of chickens roaming in her childhood yard, evoking the warmth and exuberance of Carnival—the heart and soul of Trinidad & Tobago.

Patricia took immense pride in her role as the steward of this remarkable art collection, dedicating her life to celebrating and preserving the rich stories of her culture. Her passion for art, its colors, and the memories it evoked was an essential part of her identity, and a gift she shared with those around her.

Romare Bearden, *Man Seated with Red Rooster*, 1980. Watercolor on paper, 41" × 33". *Photo: Myrah Brown Green*

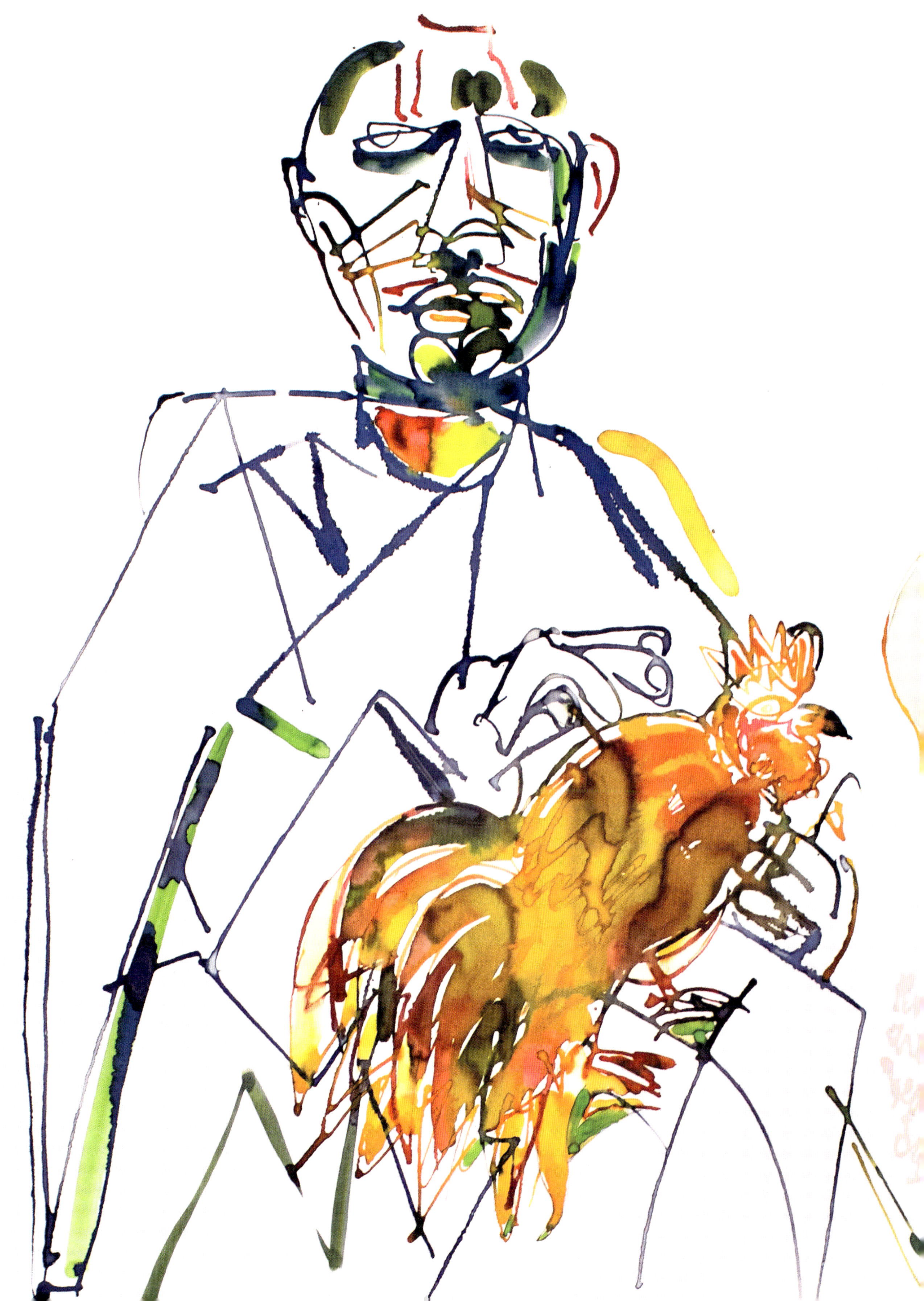

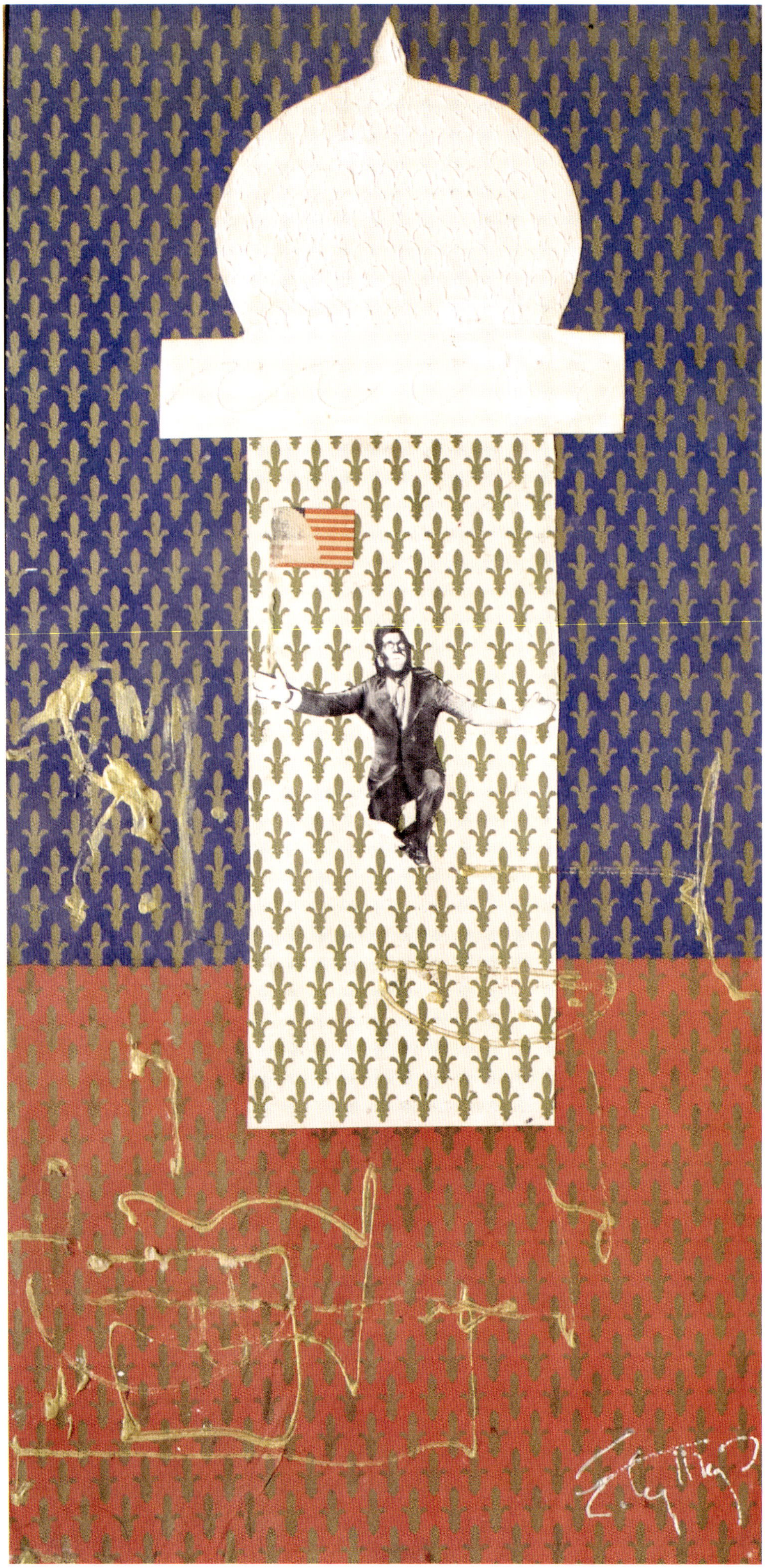

Ealy Mays, *Untitled*, 2007. Mixed media on panel, 6.25" × 13.25". *Photo: Myrah Brown Green*

Opposite top: Ealy Mays, *Untitled*, 2006. Mixed media on panel, 24" × 12.5". *Photo: Myrah Brown Green*

Opposite bottom: David Hammonds, *The Man Nobody Killed: Michael Steward*, 1985. Red and black spray paint on cardboard (limited edition 100/200), 10.75" × 8.50". *Photo: Myrah Brown Green*

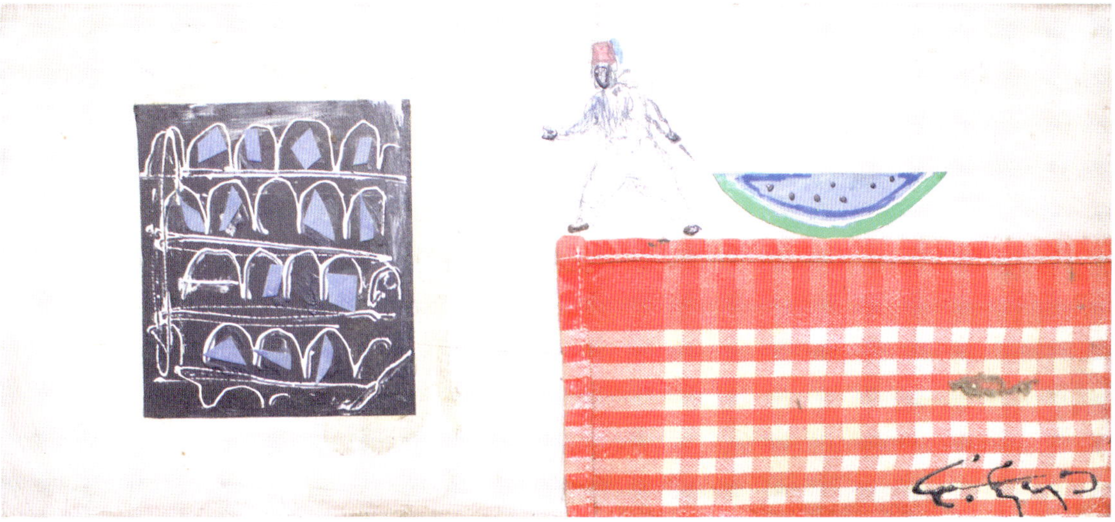

MICHAEL
STEWART
1958–
1984

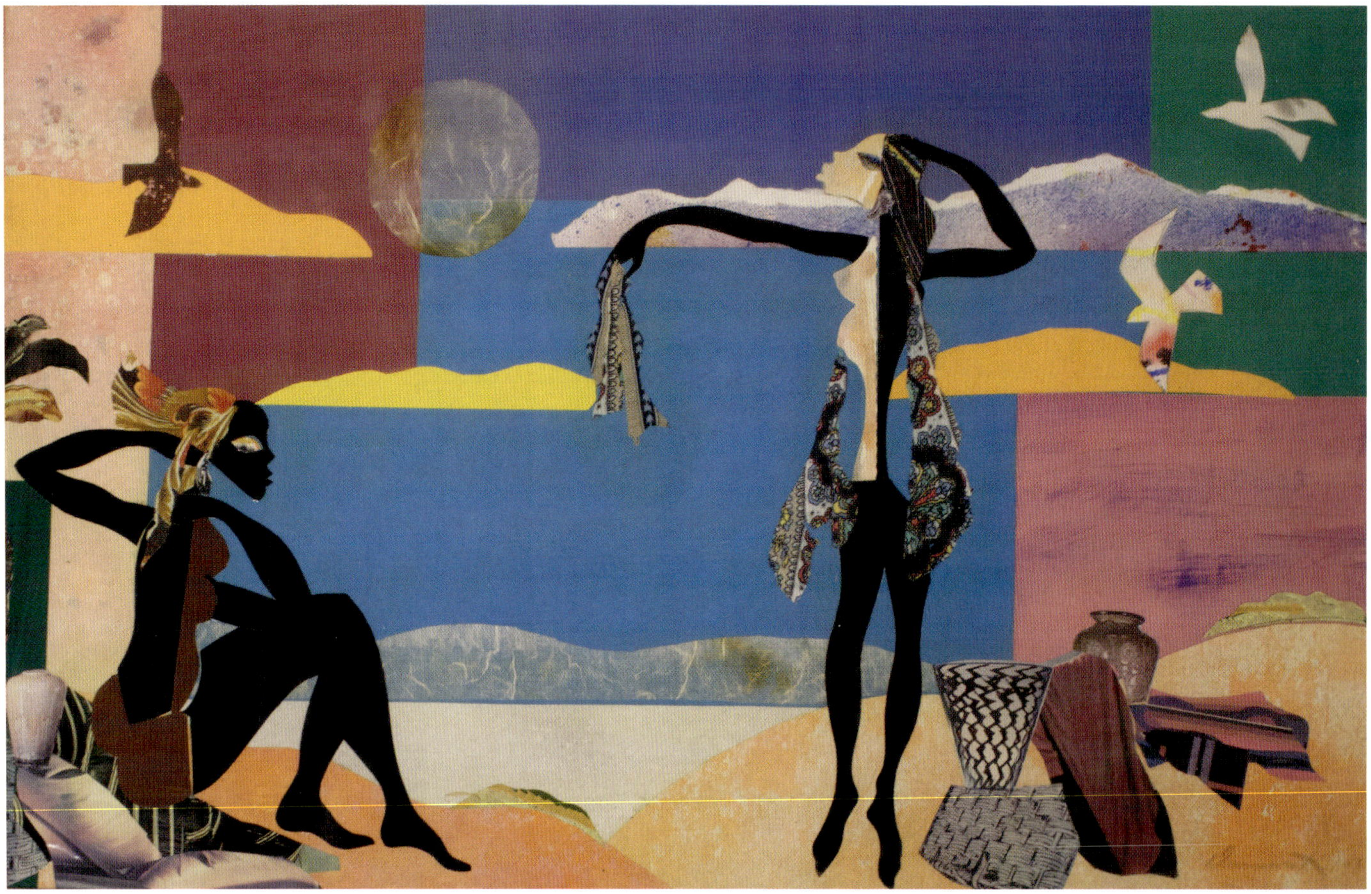

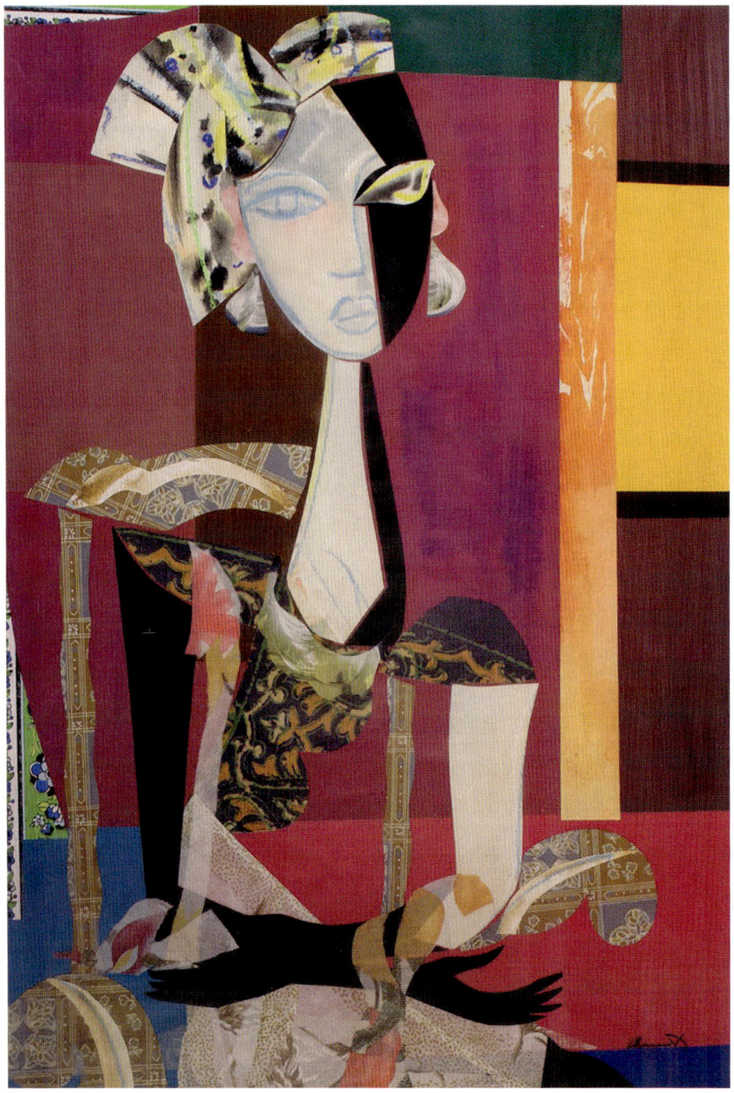

James Denmark, *The Female Figures at the Beach*, 1987. Collage of mixed media on paper and fabric on Masonite board, 19" × 31". *Photo: Myrah Brown Green*

James Denmark, *Woman Seated*, 1980. Collage of mixed media on paper and fabric on Masonite board, 40.5" × 30.5". *Photo: Myrah Brown Green*

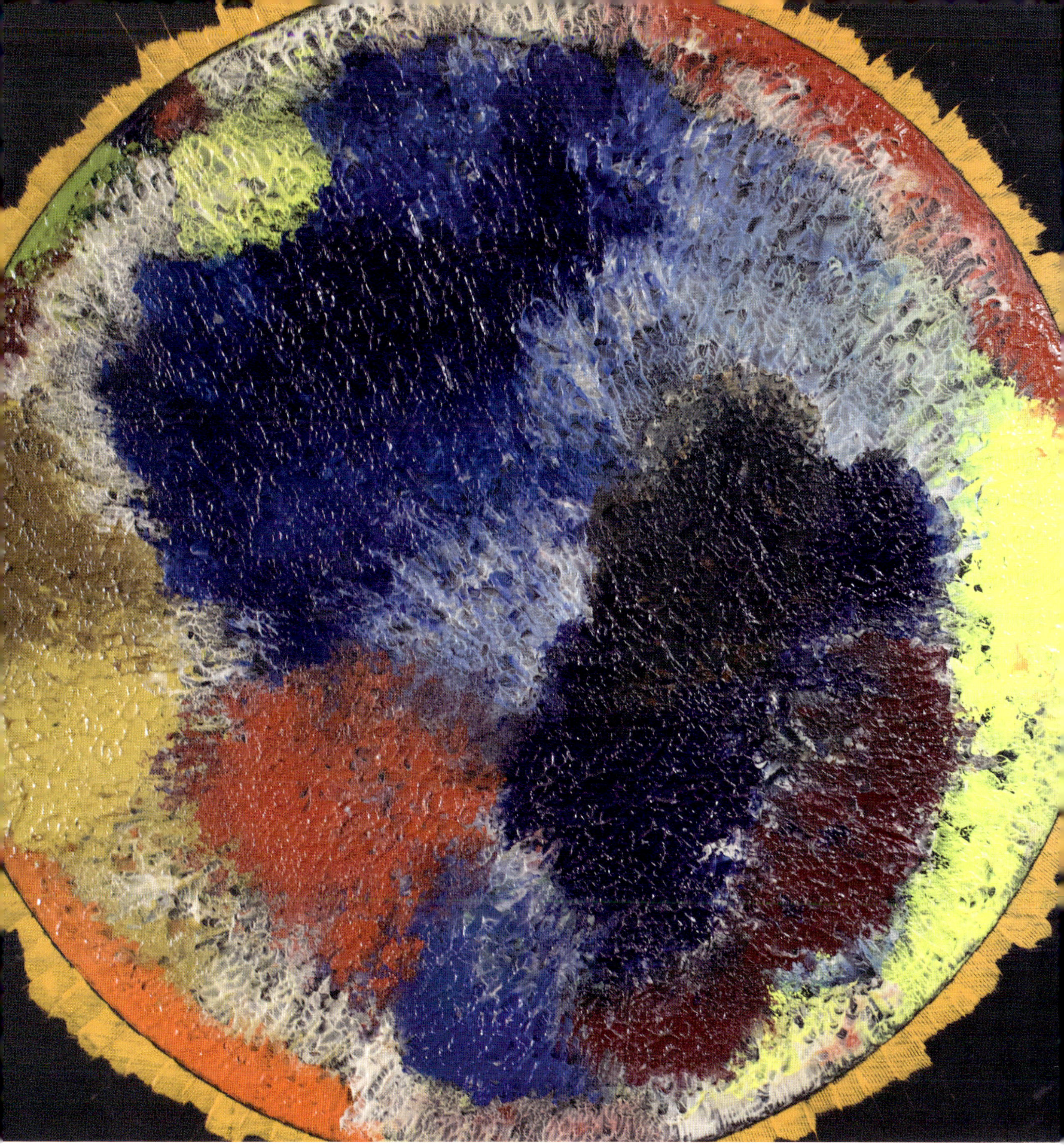

Leon Meeks, *The Abstract Beauty of Earth*, 1969. Latex and acrylic polymer on wood panel, 41" × 33". *Photo: Myrah Brown Green*

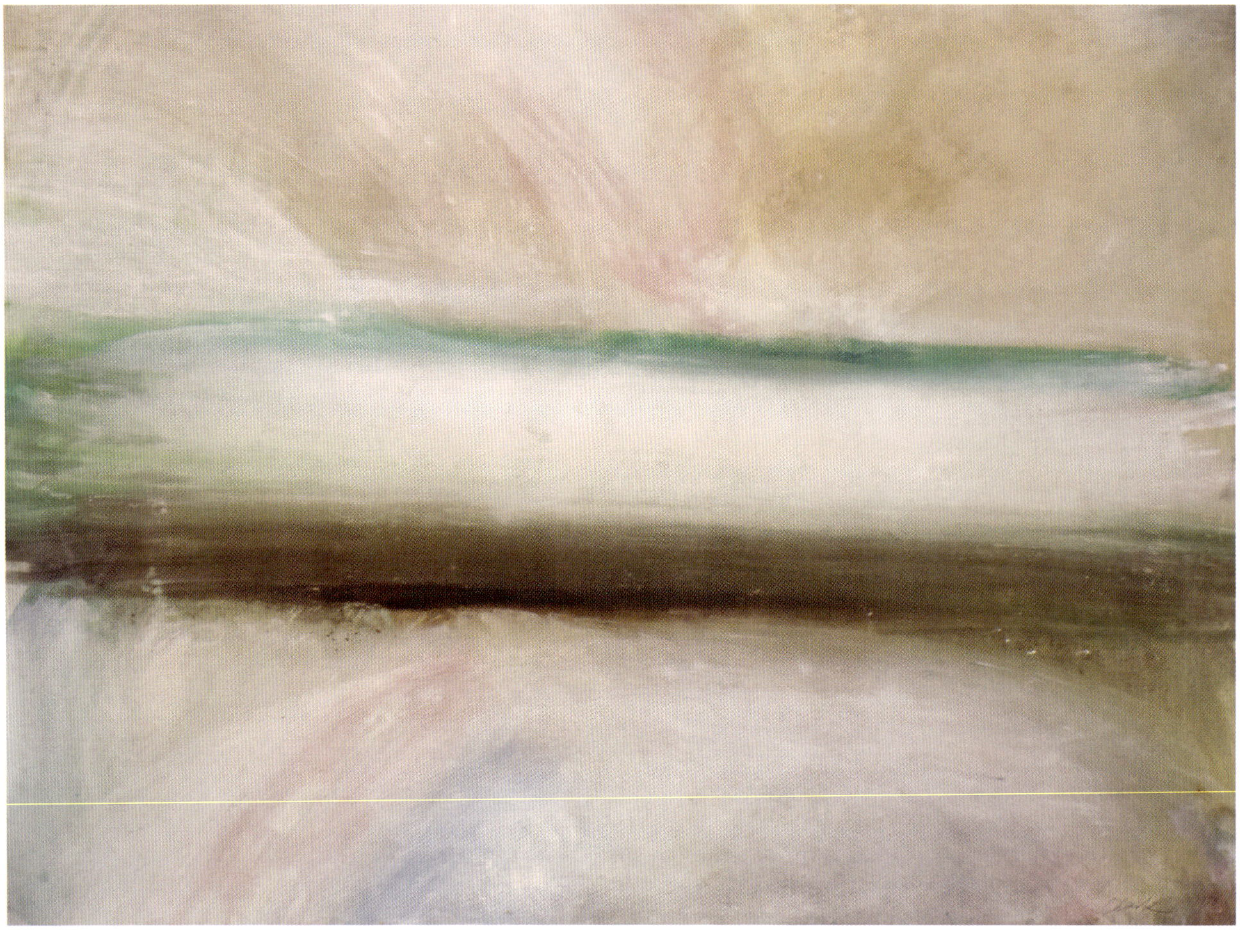

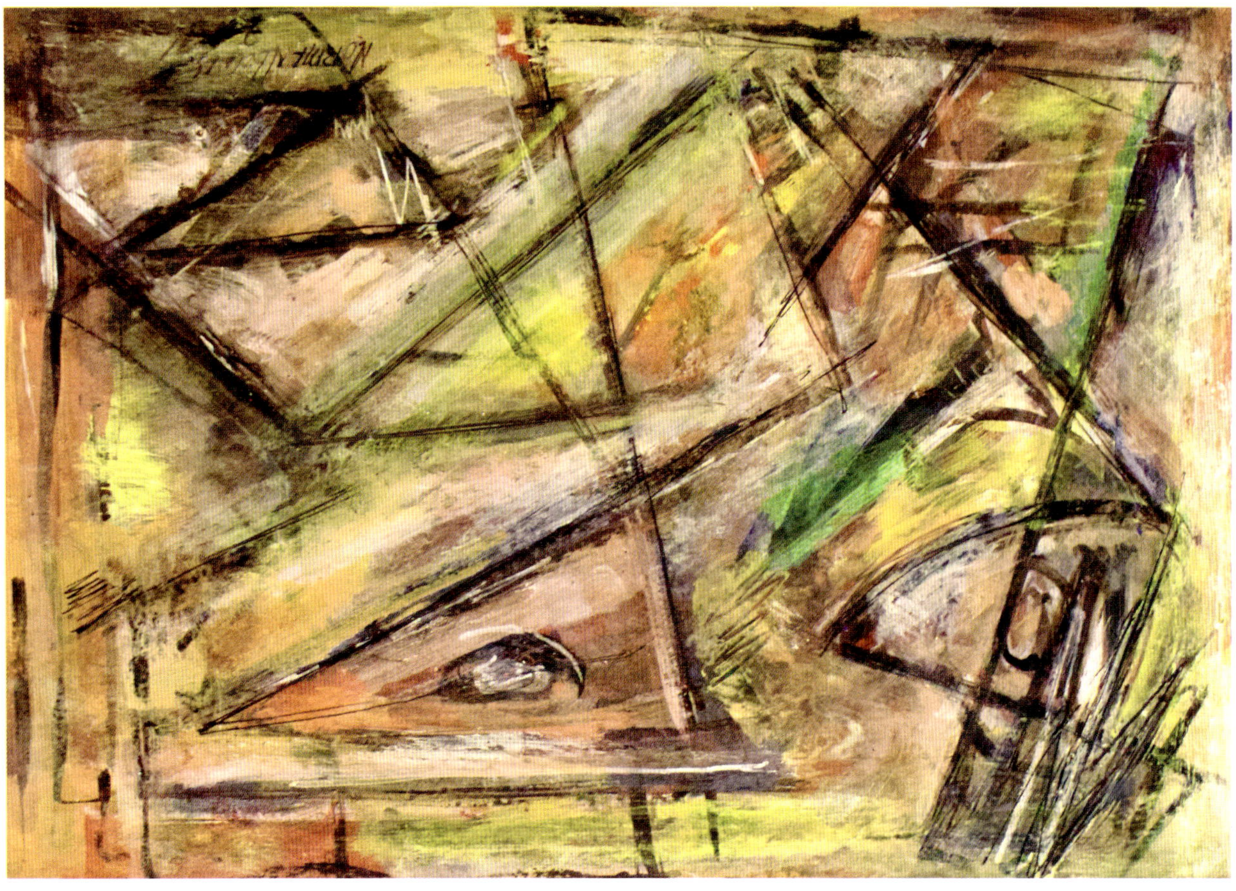

Ed Clarke, *Abstract in White, Green, and Grey*, 1990. Pigment on paper, 38" × 50". *Photo: Myrah Brown Green*

Norman Lewis, *Untitled*, 1946. Oil on Masonite, 10" × 14". *Photo: Myrah Brown Green*

Opposite: Sir Frank Bowling, *Ben Woodick*, 2002. Acrylic on canvas in red and blue, 28" × 20". *Photo: Myrah Brown Green*

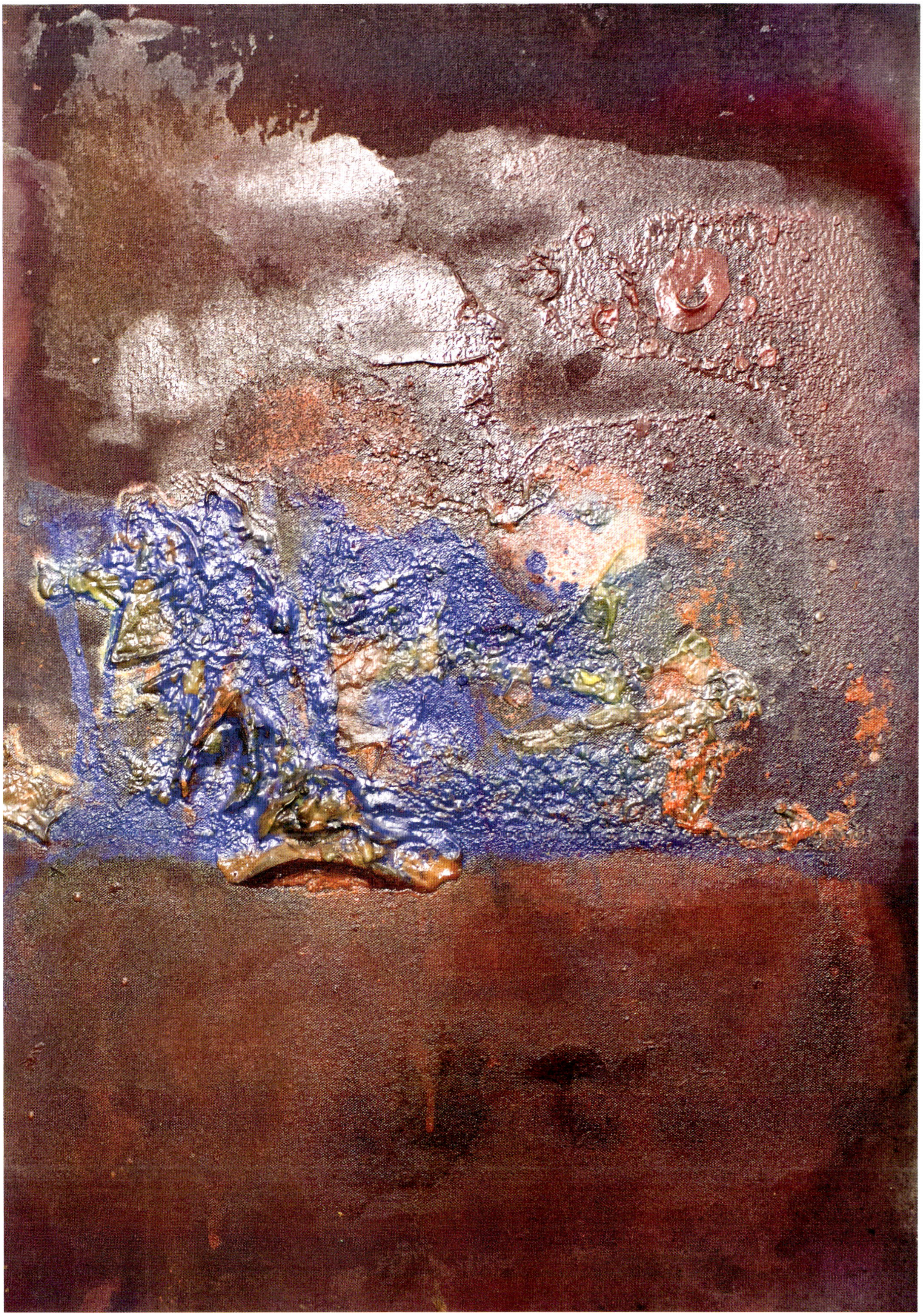

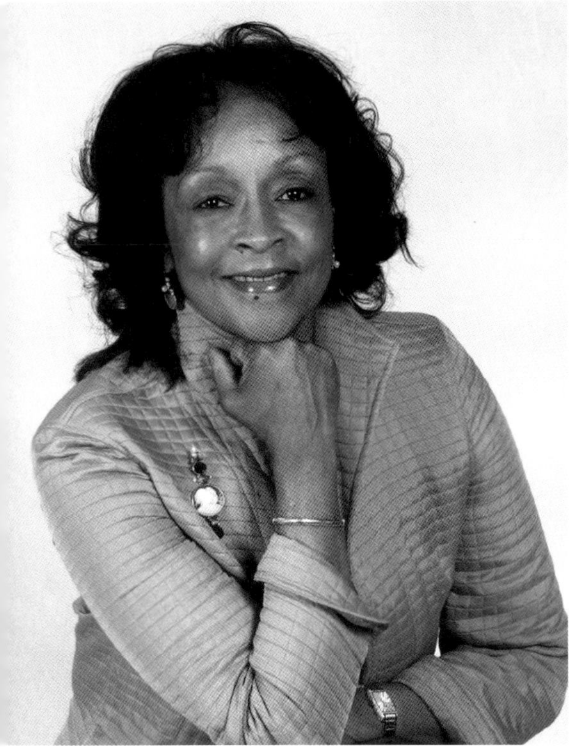

Photo: Ralph Gabriner

DONNA CHAMBERS

VINTAGE BLACKAMOORS AND BLACK CAMEO JEWELRY

DR. MYRAH: What was the first piece of art that you collected and when?

DONNA CHAMBERS: It was a piece made of painted, weathered slats of wood, with a group of kids playing during a parade, and the kids were Black and white. I bought it in 1973 in Greenwich Village on LaGuardia Avenue, where artists had booths on summer days like Memorial Day and the Fourth of July. I was visiting another artist and saw this piece by Robert Carter, and at the time I didn't know I was collecting, but I love it so much it is still hanging in my bedroom—three apartments and fifty years later.

DR. MYRAH: Why are you a Keeper of Vintage and Black Cameo Jewelry?

DONNA CHAMBERS: For over four decades I have been a goldsmith and jewelry designer. My creative eye began to develop with an after-school job with midcentury modern artist Vera Neuman. During my college years at Pratt Institute in the late 1960s, my cultural awareness significantly increased. My passion for Blackamoor and Black Cameos began while attending jewelry trade and antique shows, where I was captivated by their beauty and historical significance. As they were small pieces of art that could be housed in little shadow boxes, I focused on gold and jeweled Blackamoors, recognizing their artistic inspiration for me as a jeweler and investment potential. As a woman of color, I was deeply drawn to these figures, which reflect a complex history of cultural fascination rarely seen by most. I believe it is my responsibility to preserve and share these pieces, ensuring they are appreciated by those who understand their historical and cultural importance.

Artist unknown, *Othello Moro di Venezia*, 1870. 18-karat gold, engraved yellow-gold locket, enamel with three small diamonds, 1.5" × 1.25". *Photo: Ralph Gabriner*

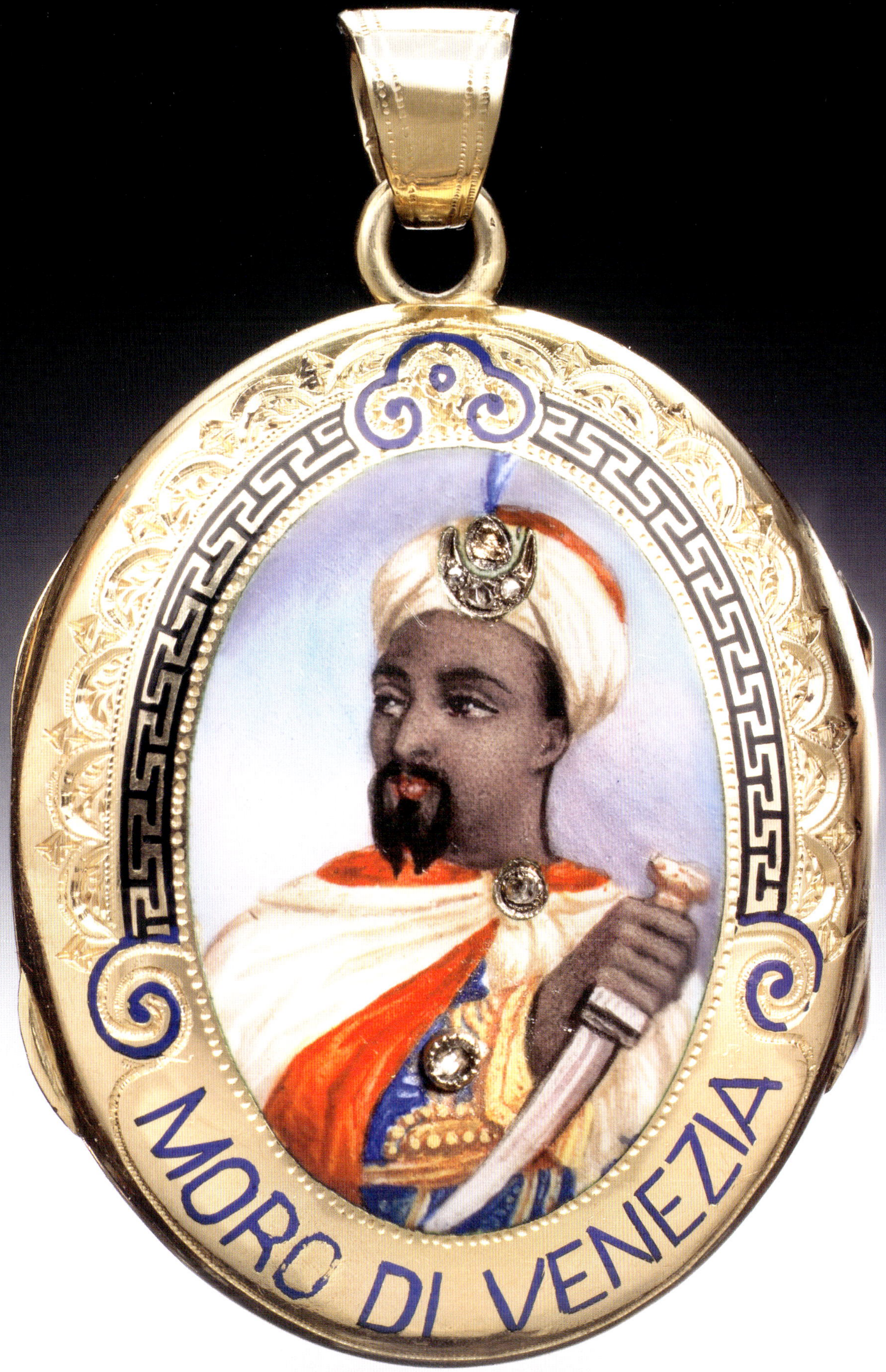
MORO DI VENEZIA

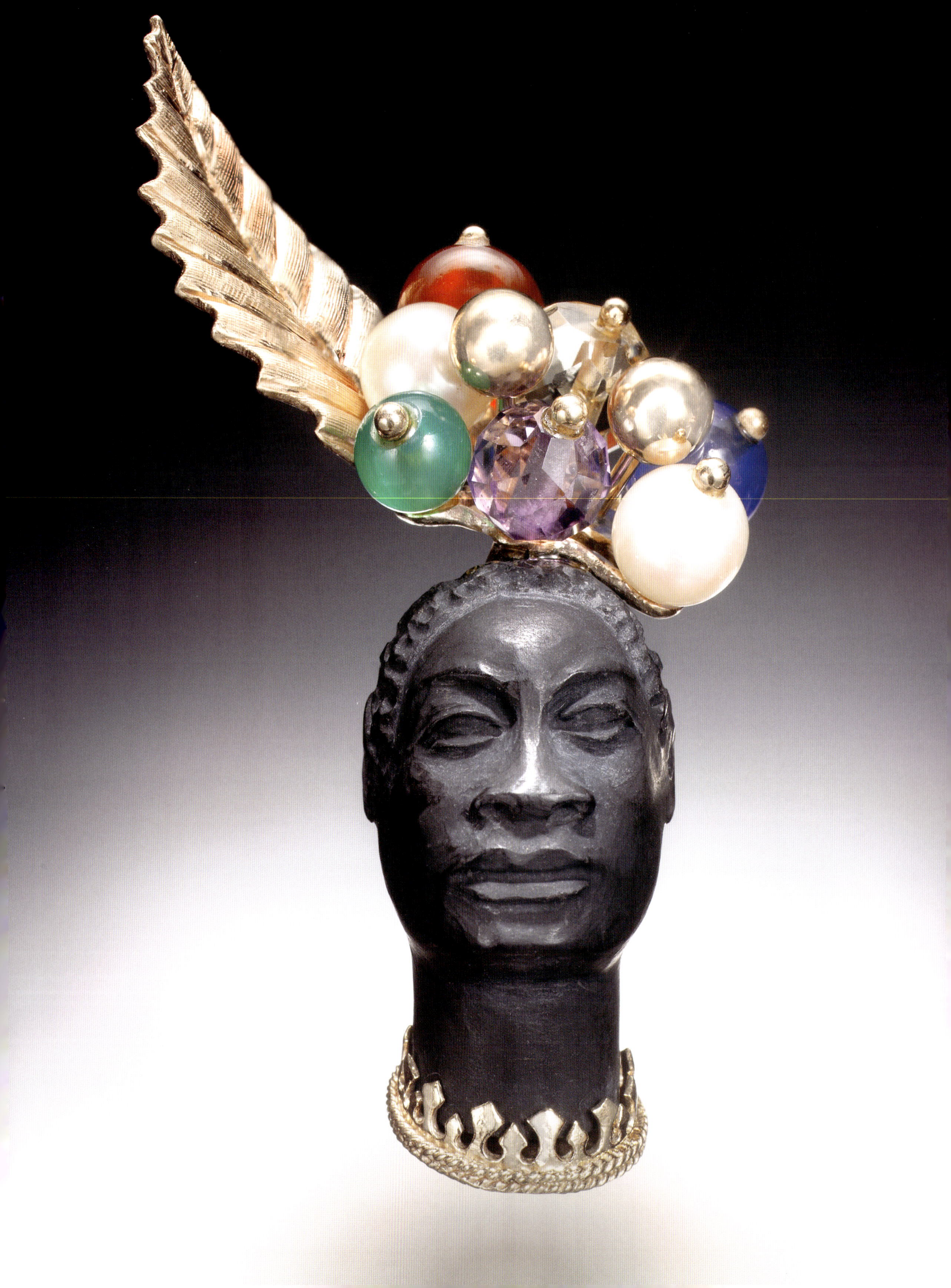

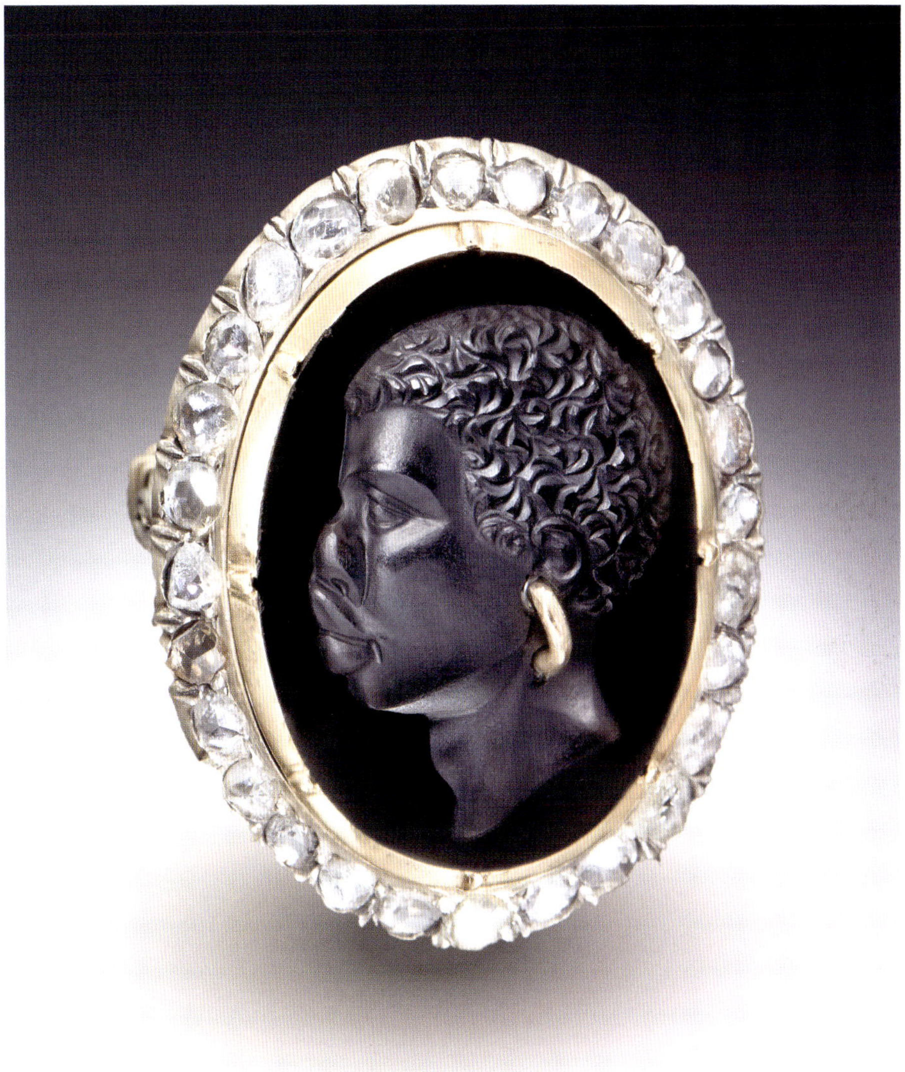

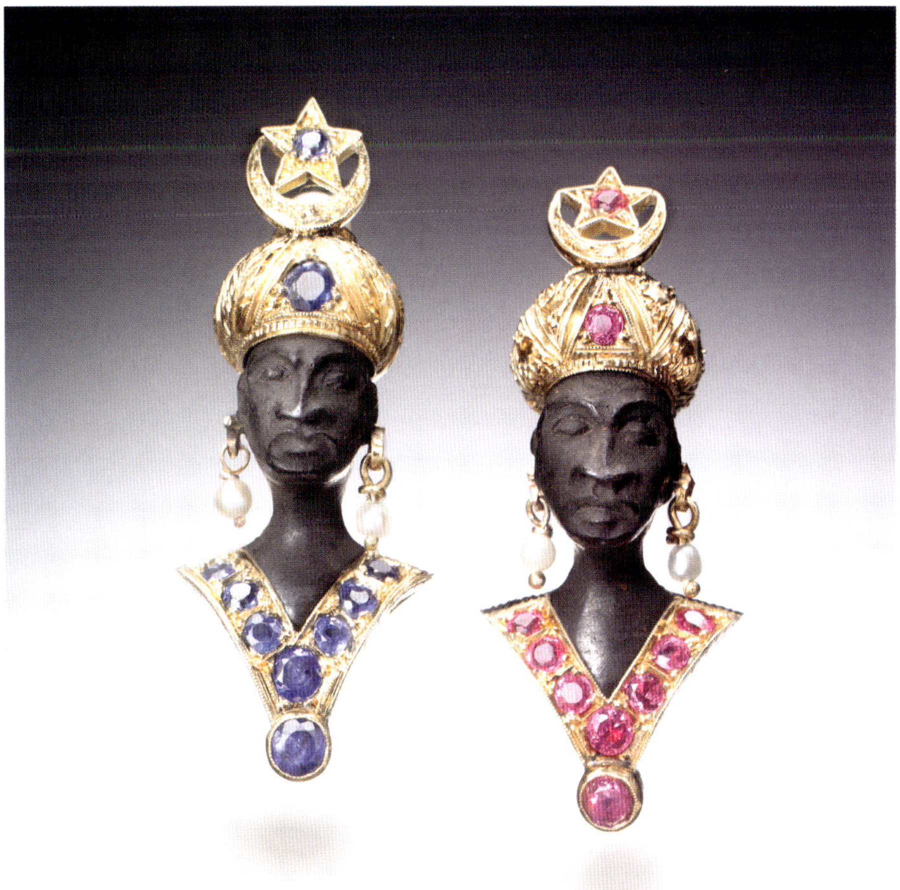

Opposite: Artist unknown, *Blackamoor Brooch with Fascinator*, 1960. Vintage carved head adorned with a gold crown collar and plume of colorful gemstones and pearls, 2.25". *Photo: Ralph Gabriner*

Artist unknown, *Black Cameo Ring*, 1860. 18-karat gold, 23 rose-cut diamonds and center profile carved from onyx, 1½". *Photo: Ralph Gabriner*

Artist unknown, *Twin Nardi Brooches*, 1900. Italian Nardi, one trimmed with sapphires and the other with rubies, both with star and crescent and pearl earrings, 1.5" × 1.5". *Photo: Ralph Gabriner*

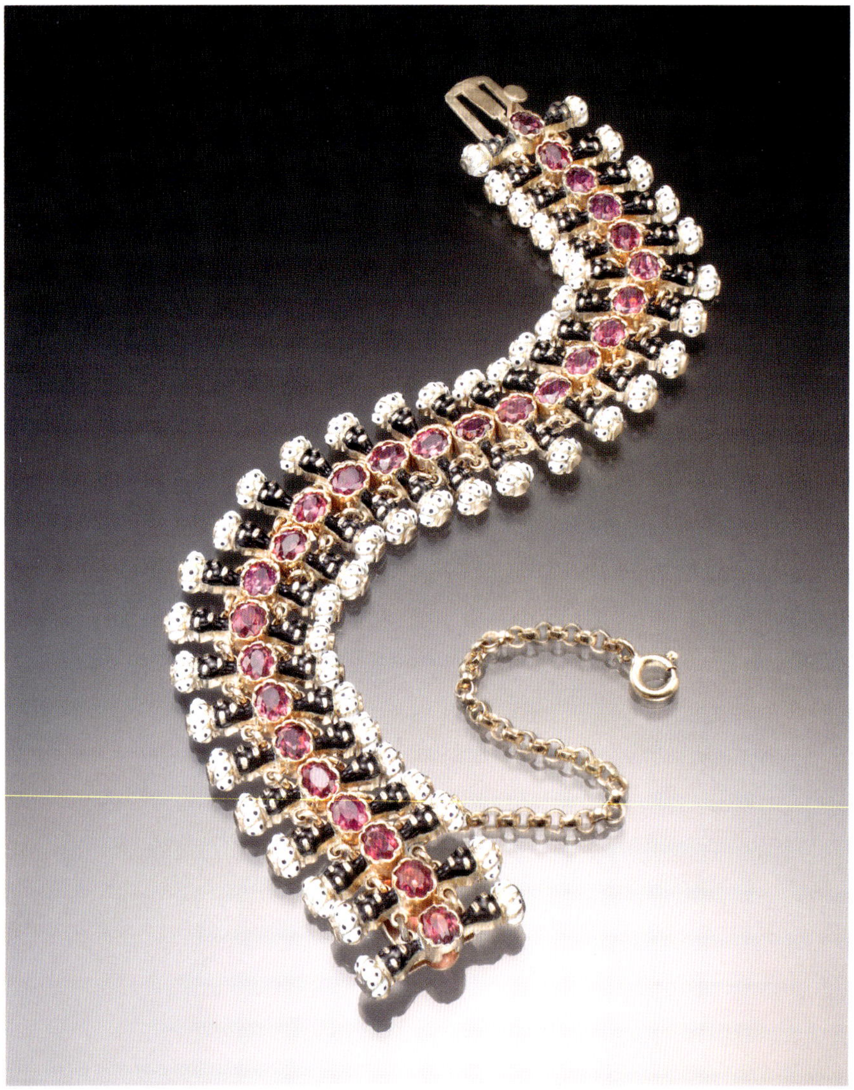

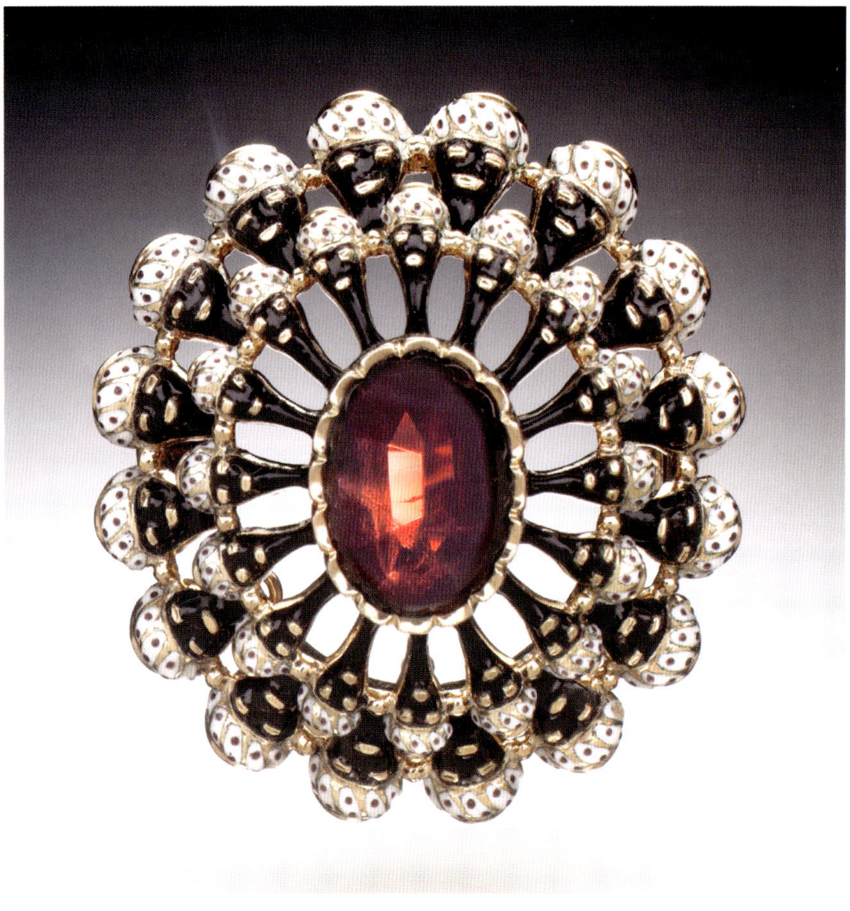

Artist unknown, *Enamel Blackamoor Bracelet*, 1880. 18-karat gold, rose-cut pink garnets, enamel Blackamoor figures, 6.5" × .75". *Photo: Ralph Gabriner*

Artist unknown, *Blackamoor Brooch*, 1880. 18-karat gold, rose-cut pink garnet in a scalloped setting with double row of enamel Blackamoor figures, 1.75" × 1.5". *Photo: Ralph Gabriner*

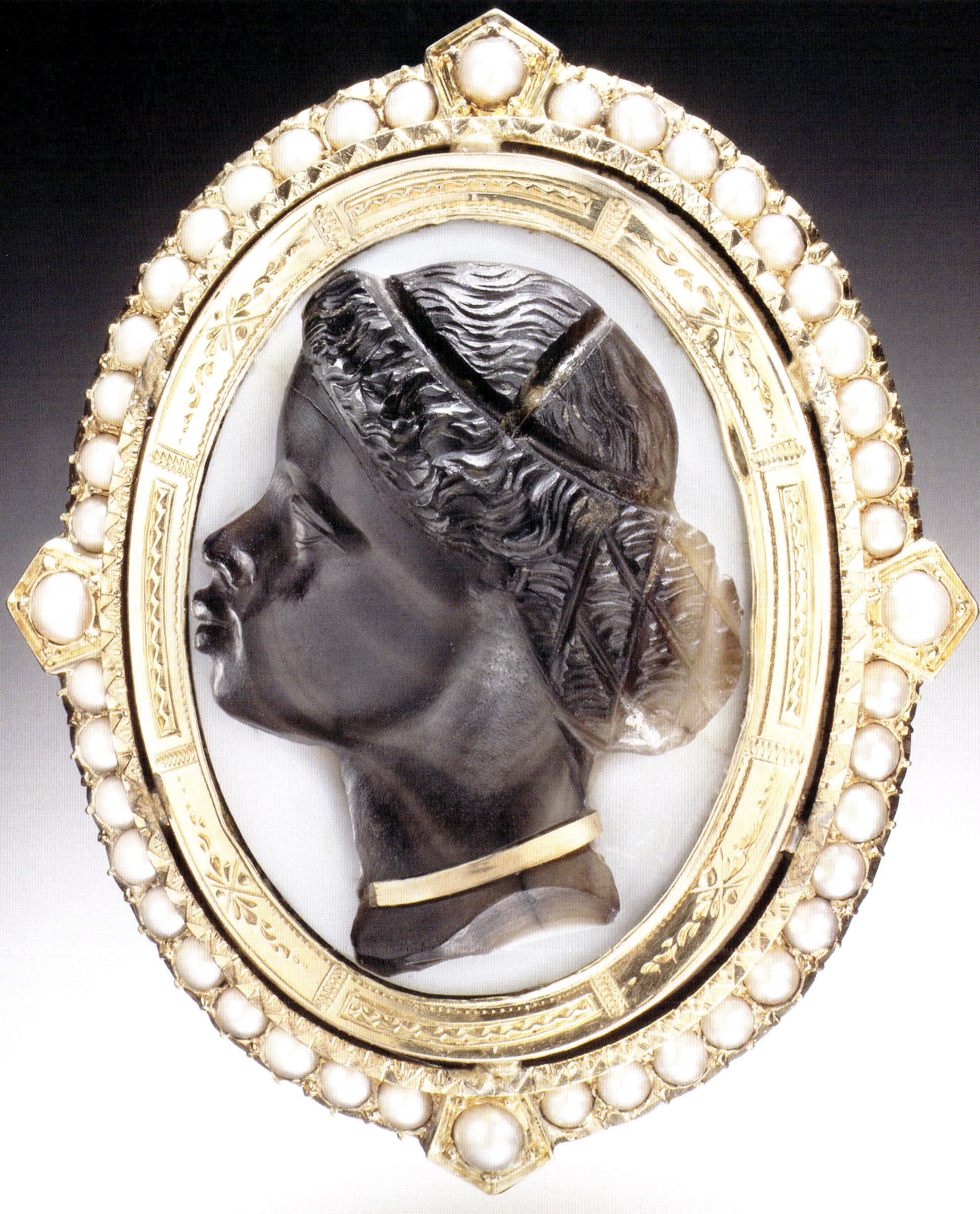

Artist unknown, *Black Cameo*, 1850. 18-karat yellow gold with engraving around the inner rim, trimmed with white pearls (face is carved from agate), 2" × 1.75". *Photo: Ralph Gabriner*

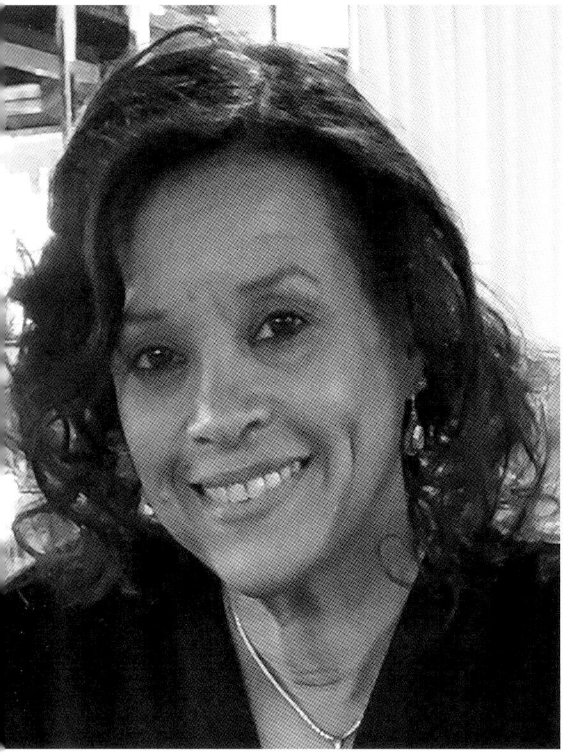

Photo: Courtesy of the collector

MEREDITH CHANDLER
MY MOTHER'S ART

DR. MYRAH: What was the first piece of art that you collected and when?

MEREDITH CHANDLER: The first piece of art I collected was at the Fulton Art Fair in the early eighties. It was a mixed-media image illustrated by Jimmy James Greene. The image was of a young girl in a white dress, wearing brown boots [and] carrying an infant also dressed in white. The girl had two braids resting on her shoulders. It gave the feeling of young innocence. The background showed an African woman holding a child. The painting gave an overall feeling of paying homage to our ancestors.

DR. MYRAH: Why are you a Keeper of your Mother's art?

MEREDITH CHANDLER: My mother, Violet Hewitt Chandler, told her life's story through her artwork, and I'd like to think of myself as a guardian of my mother's life story and legacy. The artwork is a tangible connection to my mother, a reflection of her creative spirit and personality. Having the pieces allows me to preserve and honor her legacy, while also sharing her story with future generations, especially now that she is gone. Preserving her artwork also allows me to continue to promote my mother's reputation as a painter and contributor to the Black/Caribbean culture as well as perpetuate the importance and significance of Black art, especially by a Black female artist.

The artworks are now cherished heirlooms, which will be passed down through our family. It serves as a link between generations, reminding my family of where we came from and the creative talents that run in our genes. My mother's paintings generally showed her love of children and family. She had a vision of children as angels. My mother did not like how Black children were depicted, which started her desire to paint children as she remembered in her childhood as being happy, playing, and taking care of each other.

There is a strong sense of pride having artwork made by someone close to us. My mother's art, and that of her father and siblings, have certainly been an influence in my early years. My mother's paintings have certainly deepened my appreciation for her creativity and are a source of inspiration for my own art journey.

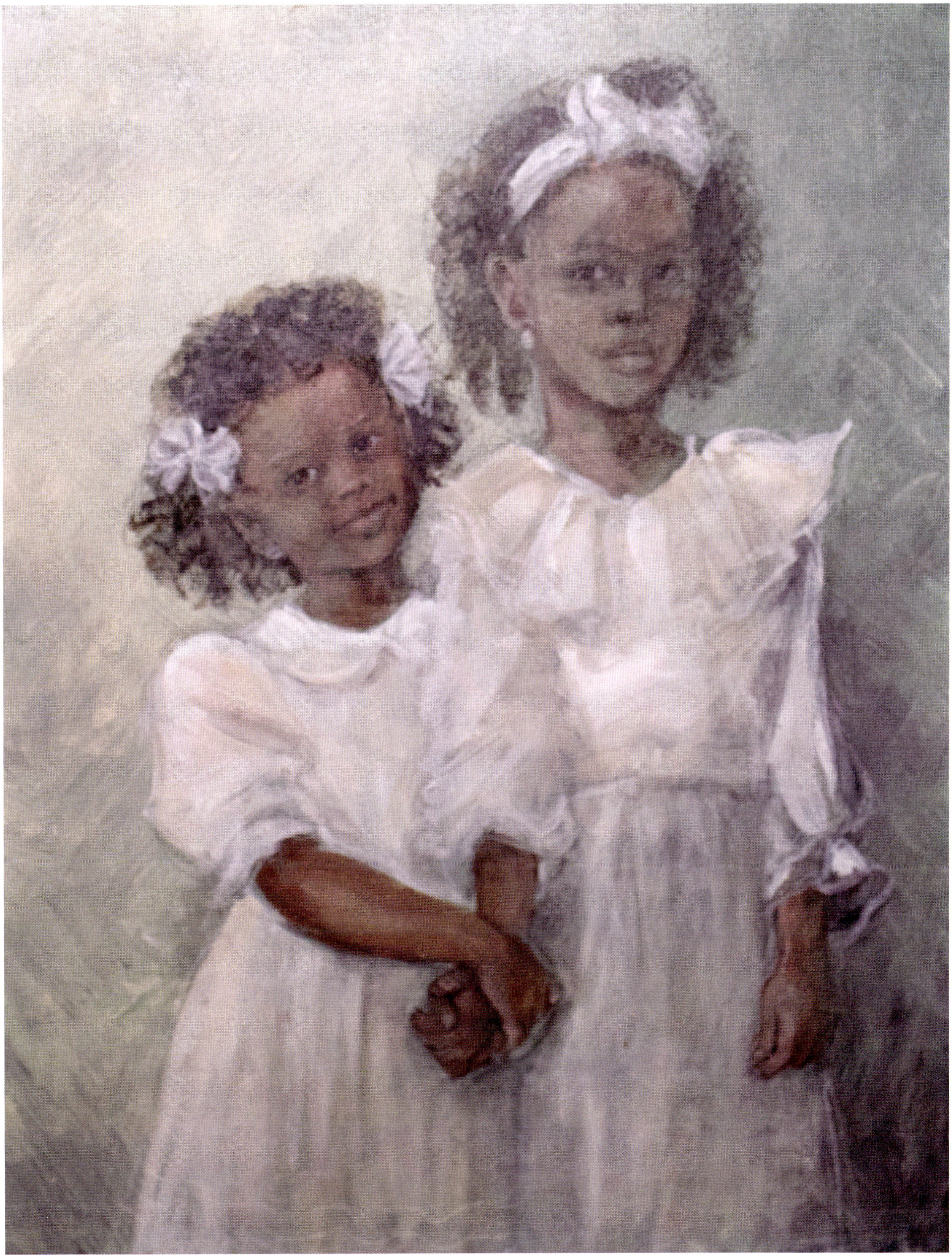

Violet Hewitt Chandler, *Girls in Pink Pastel*, 1990. Acrylic on canvas, 28" × 22". *Photo: Myrah Brown Green*

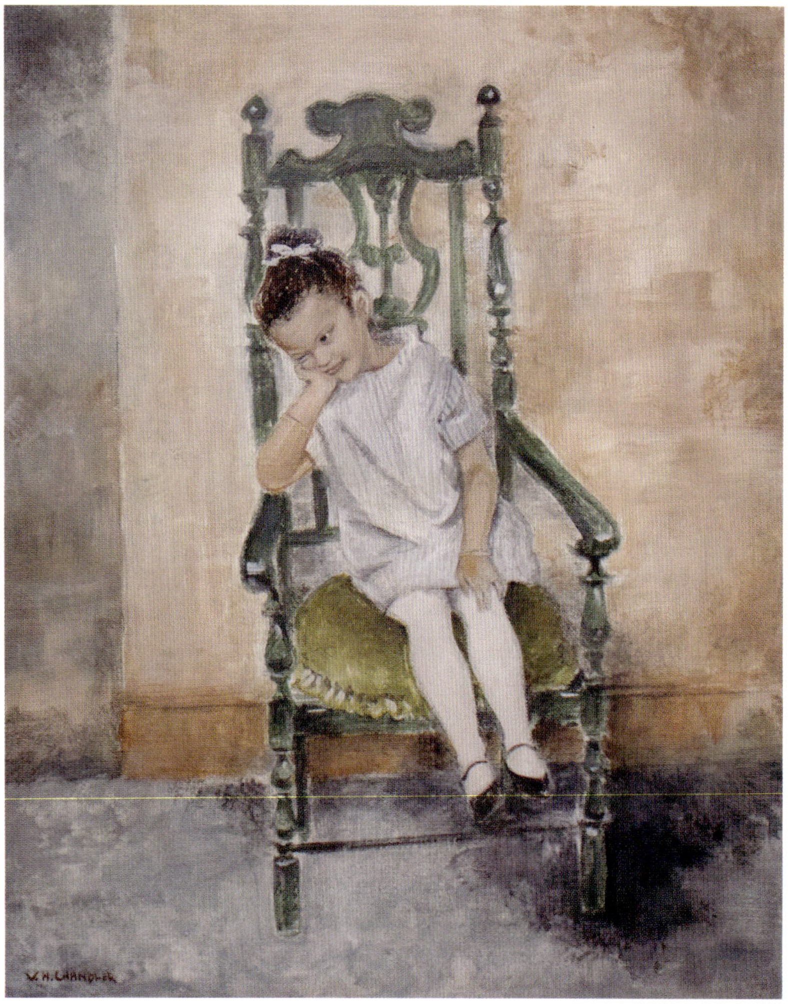

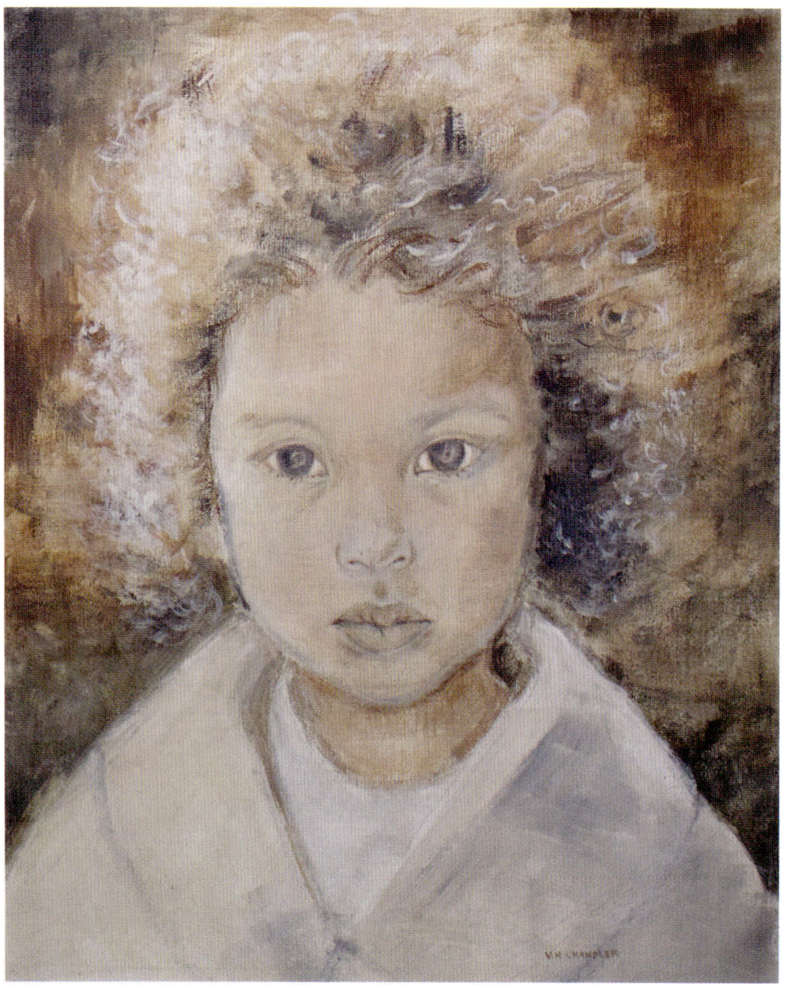

Violet Hewitt Chandler, *Mimi*, 1981. Acrylic on canvas, 24" × 24". *Photo: Myrah Brown Green*

Violet Hewitt Chandler, *Tired of Posing*, 1980. Acrylic on canvas, 24" × 20". *Photo: Myrah Brown Green*

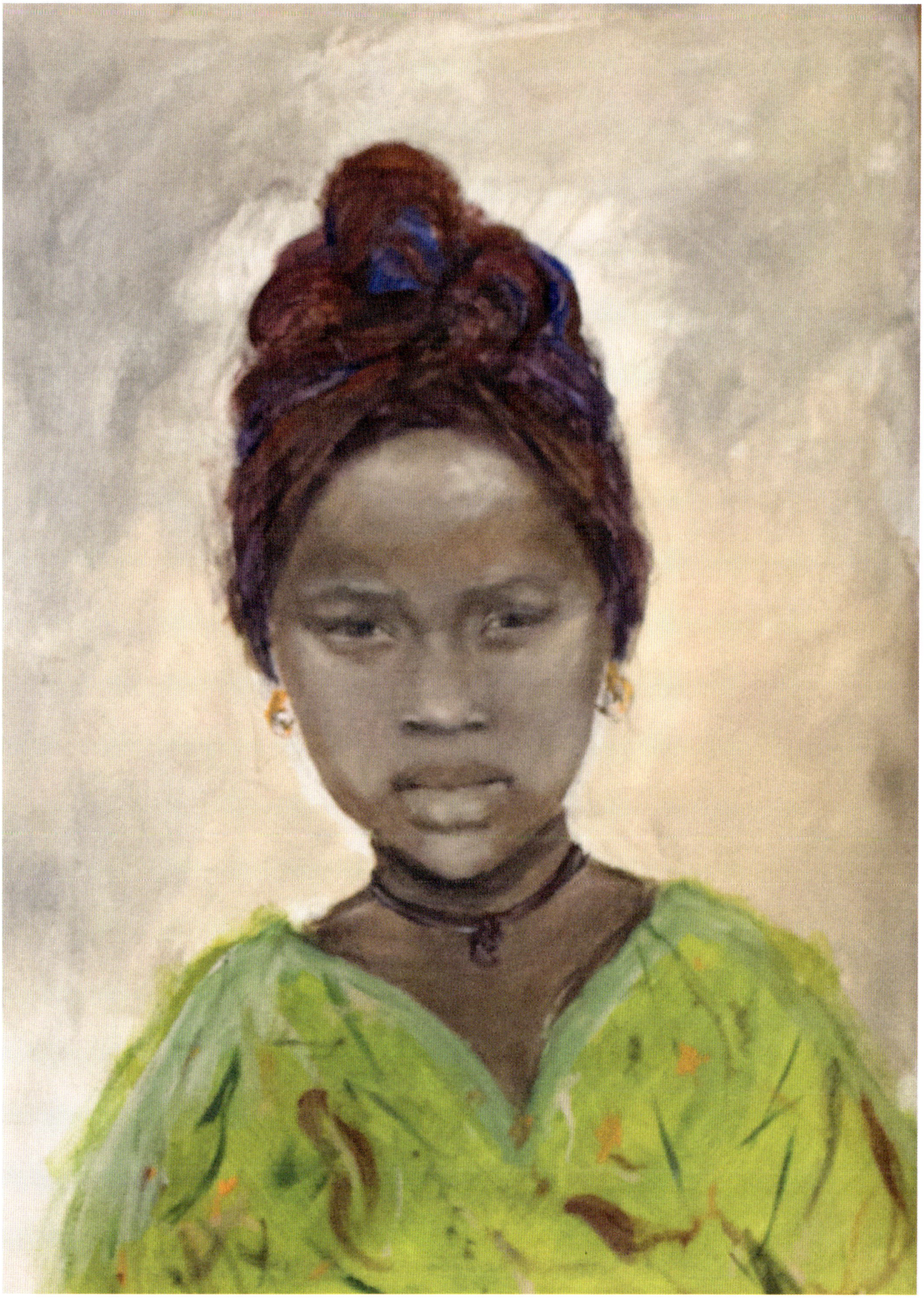

Violet Hewitt Chandler, *Girl in Turban*, 2000. Acrylic on canvas, 24" × 20". *Photo: Myrah Brown Green*

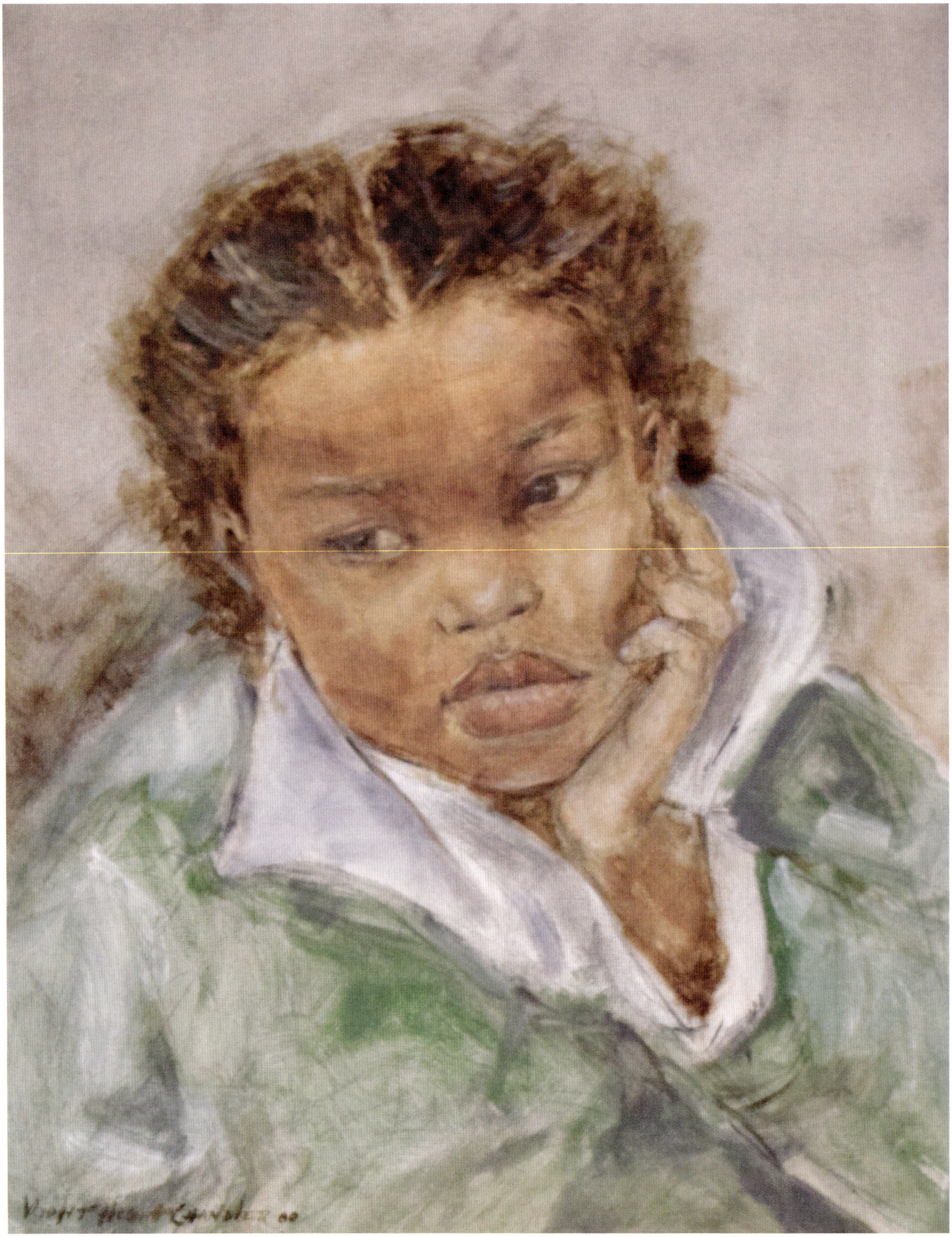

Violet Hewitt Chandler, *Thinking*, 2000. Acrylic on canvas, 20" × 16". *Photo: Myrah Brown Green*

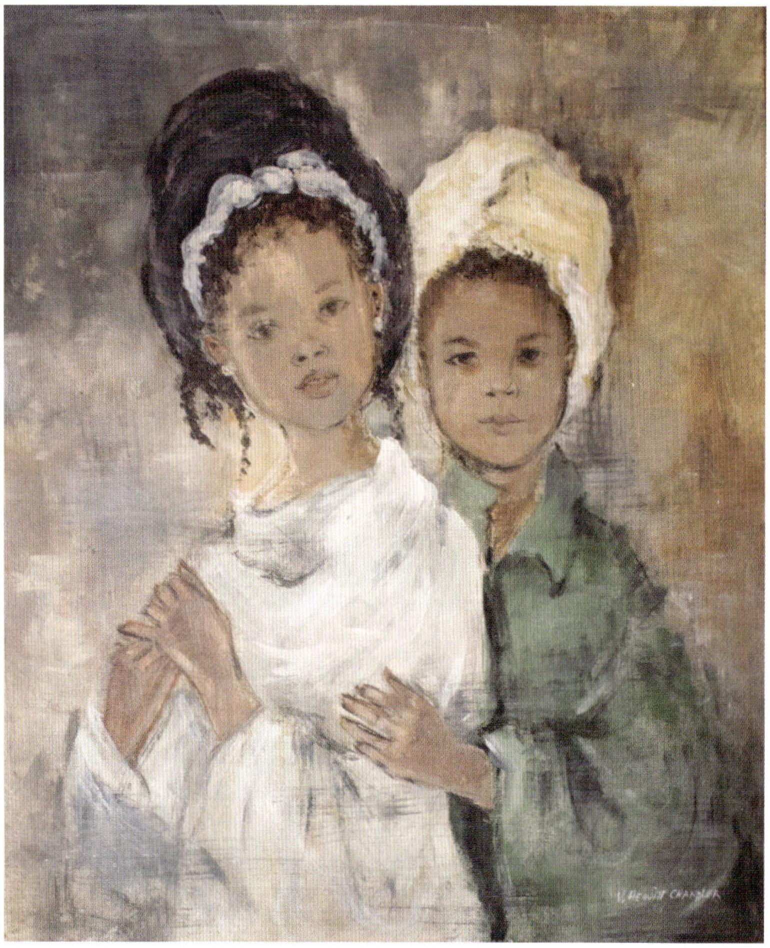

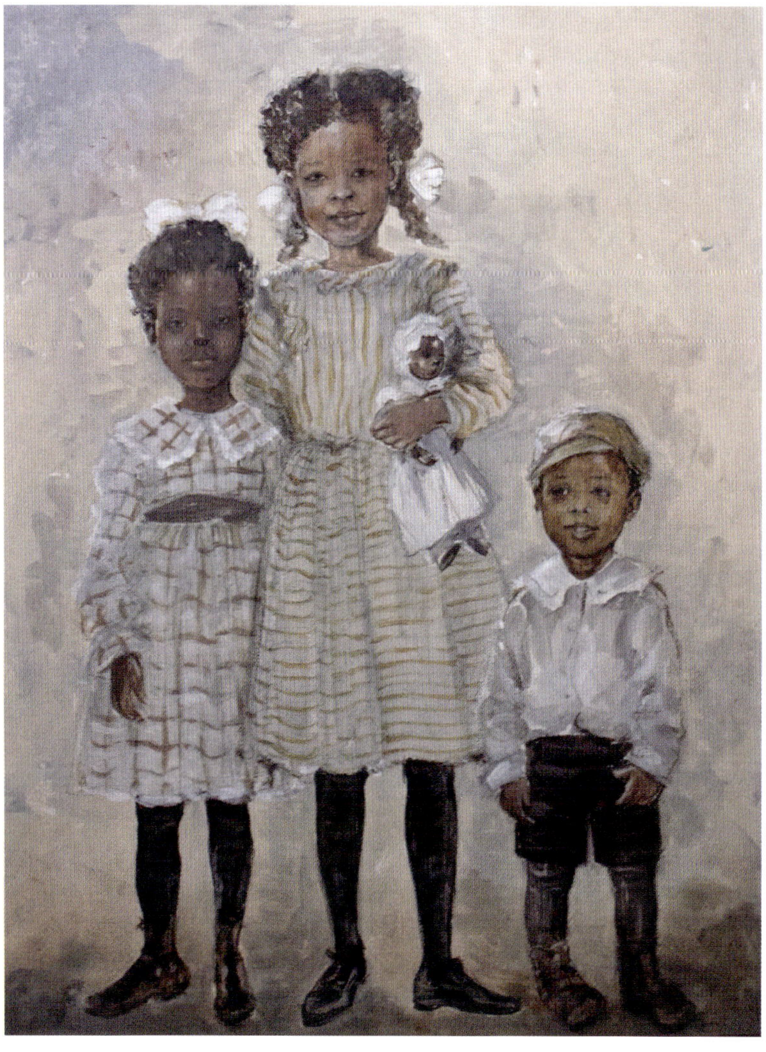

Violet Hewitt Chandler, *Friends*, 1990. Acrylic on canvas, 24"x 20". *Photo: Myrah Brown Green*

Violet Hewitt Chandler, *Siblings*, 1980. Acrylic on canvas, 20" × 16". *Photo: Myrah Brown Green*

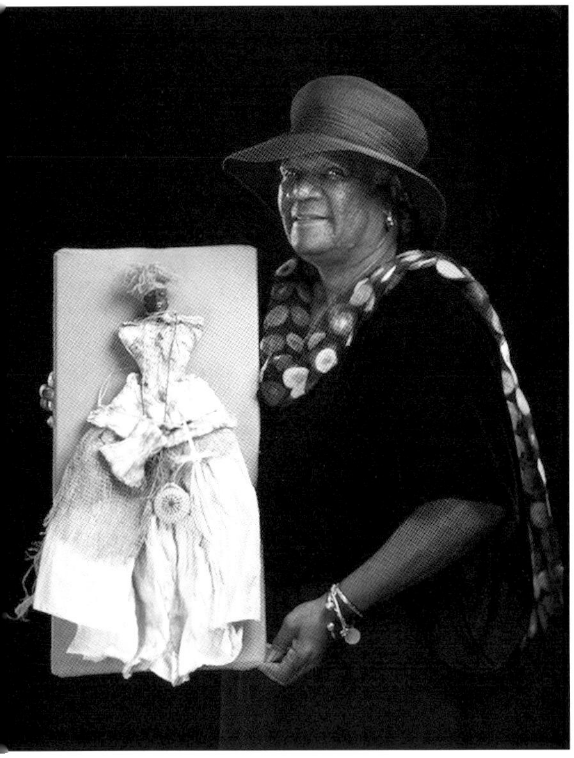

Photo: Aisha Butler

TAMBRA CHISOLM
TALISMAN*

DR. MYRAH: What was the first piece of art that you collected and when?

TAMBRA CHISOLM: The first piece of art I "acquired" began as a favor for a friend. In 1981, my daughter's godfather asked me to hold a piece of his artwork for him. *Carnival* by Peter Giscombe (1980) has been with me for forty-three years; I suppose it is part of my collection now.

DR. MYRAH: Why are you a Keeper of Talisman?

TAMBRA CHISOLM: When I was baptized in 1966, my paternal aunt gifted me a sterling silver necklace with a cross. I still have that cross today. I suppose it was then that I would have been identified as a keeper of talisman.

Over the years, I have collected items one would classify as talismans. My collection is diverse. It includes items that represent healing, protection, comfort, and sentimental value. As a quilter, I integrate talismans in my work. Examples include using a slight layer of crushed lavender and sage with the batting before closing my bed quilts; this symbolizes the offering of comfort and healing, or placing the Gye Nyame on the label of my quilts as an offering of spiritual protection. Additionally, my art quilts are embellished with talismans for the properties and beauty they hold.

When I encountered and purchased my first piece from Paula Whaley, I was enamored by her use of the Gye Nyame (see *Untitled Piece #4*). Her use of talismans captures my attention, adoration, and appreciation for not only the work itself, but the purposeful use of the actual talisman. My collection of Sister Paula's works reflects who I am, a Keeper of Talisman.

*Collector is holding Oneeki's *Daughters of the Dust* series, ca. 2017. Air-dried clay, open-weave burlap, tea-stained paper, stiffener, brass wire, and ivory, 24" × 12".

Paula Whaley, *Attalah's Twists*, 2019. Polymer clay, leather suede scraps, brass wire, 4.25" × 5". *Photo: Aisha Butler*

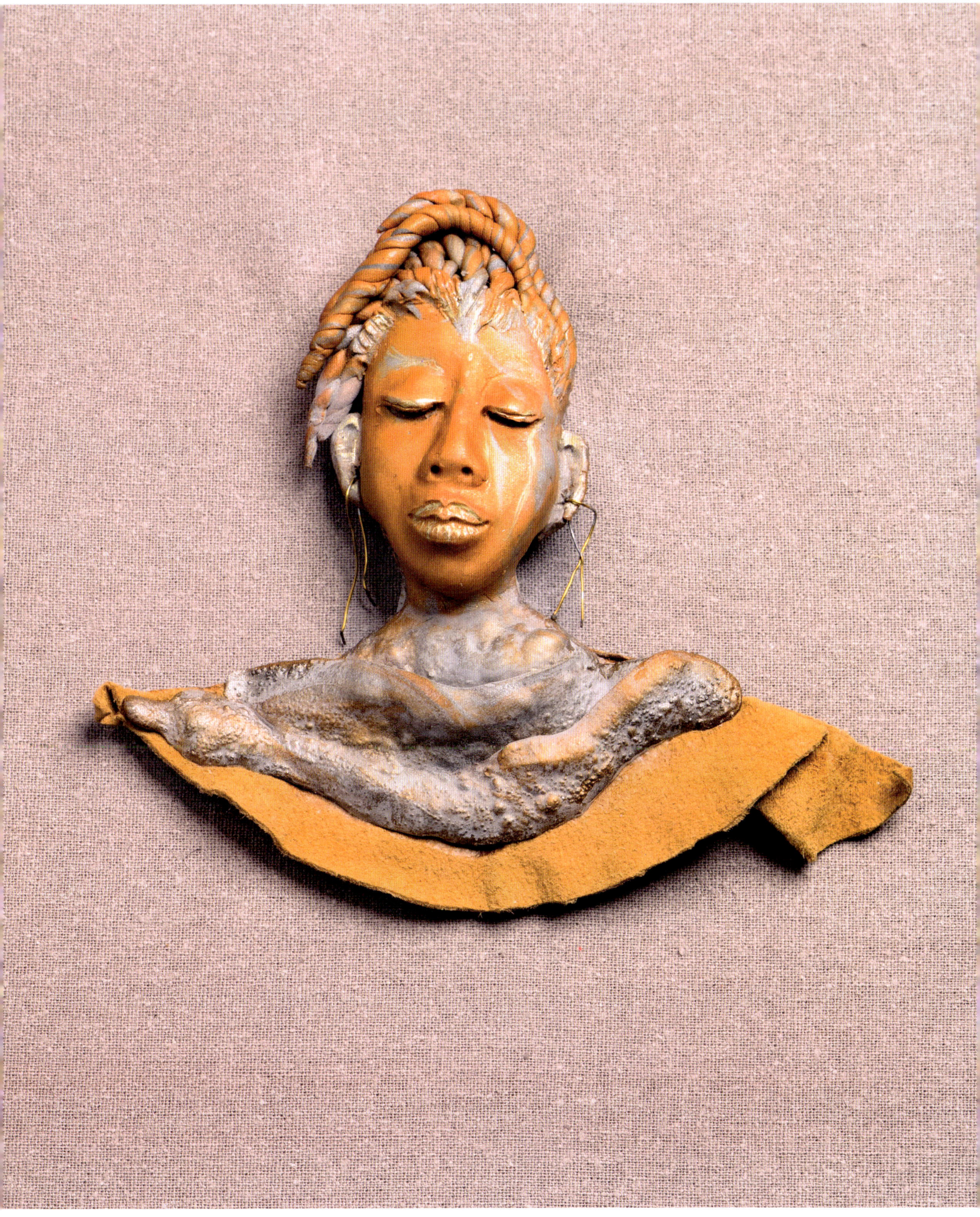

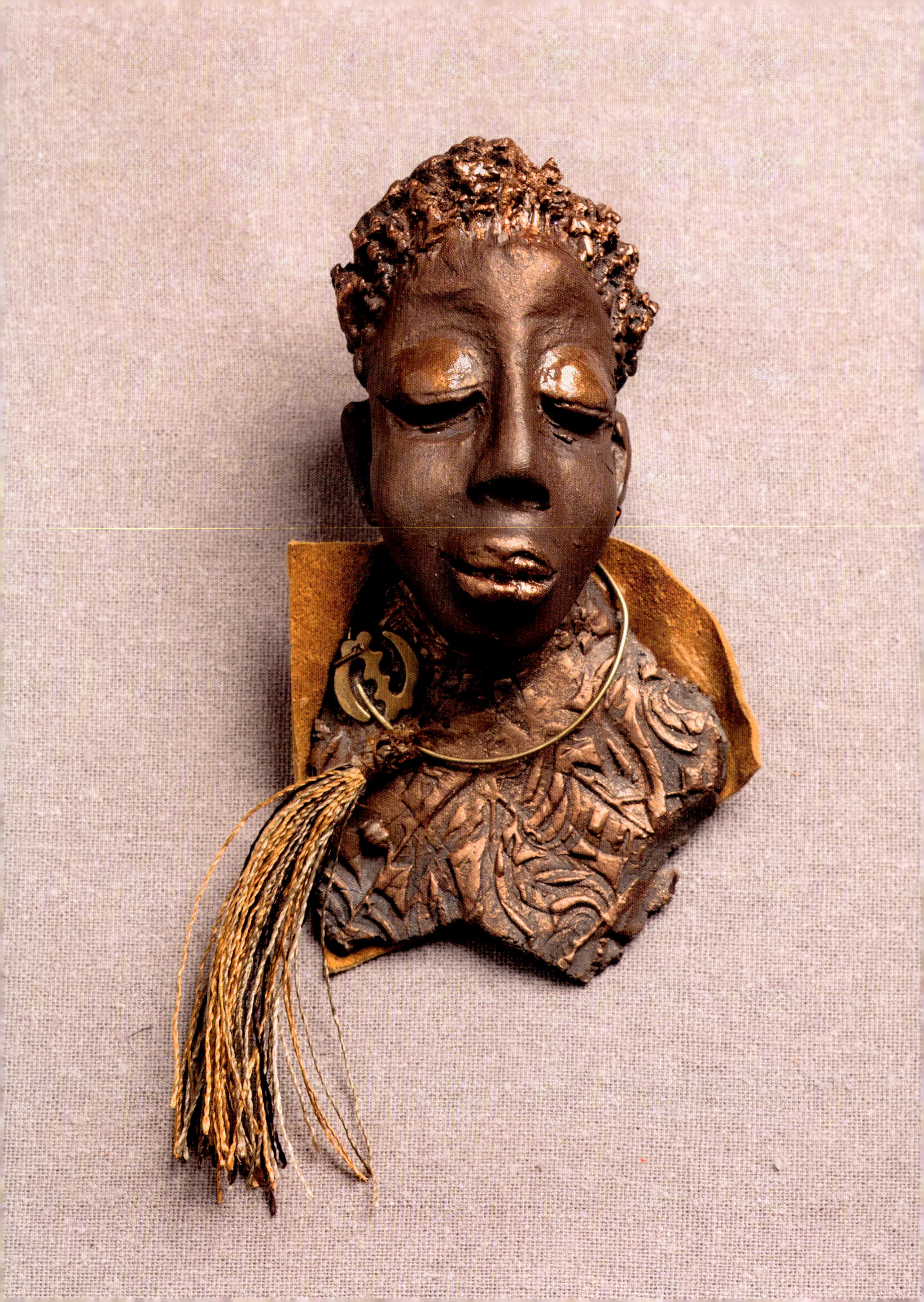

Opposite: Paula Whaley, *GyeNayame*, 2015. Air-dried clay, brass gye nyame, polyester, beads, leather suede scraps, and acrylic paint, 2.5" × 3.5". *Photo: Aisha Butler*

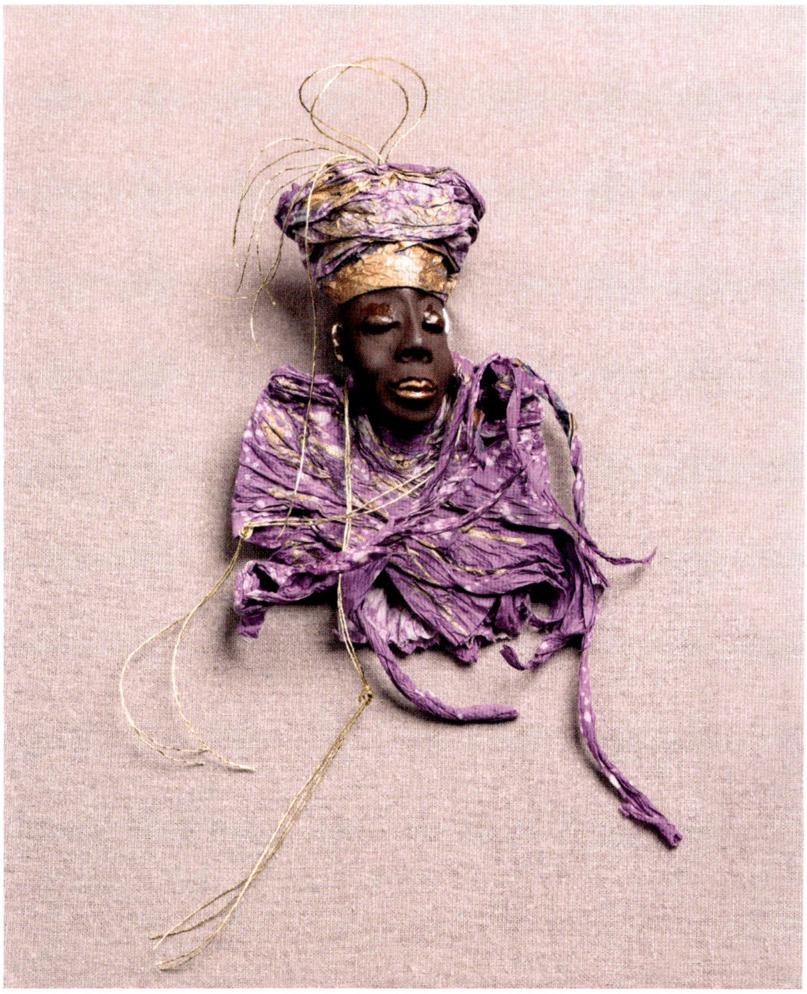

Paula Whaley, *Crowned*, 2018. Air-dried clay, tissue paper, gold thread, and acrylic paint, 3.25" × 5.5". *Photo: Aisha Butler*

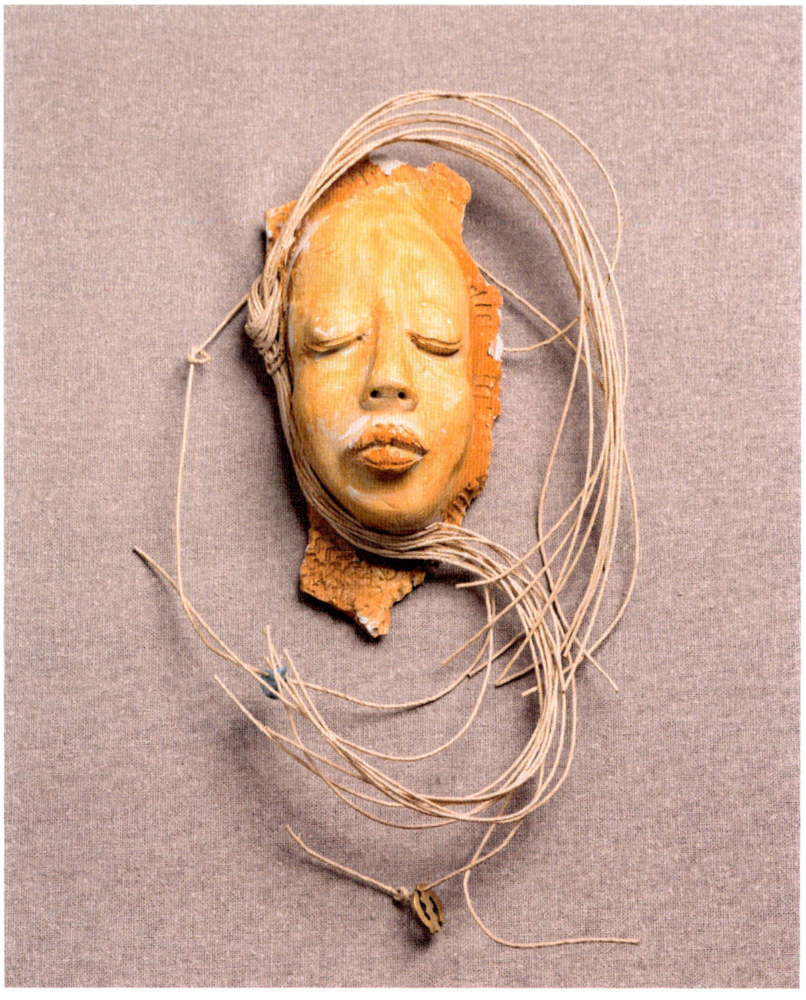

Paula Whaley, *Meditation*, 2019. Air-dried clay, watercolor, turquoise gemstone, gemstone, brass string, and brass gye nyame, 2.25" × 4.5". *Photo: Aisha Butler*

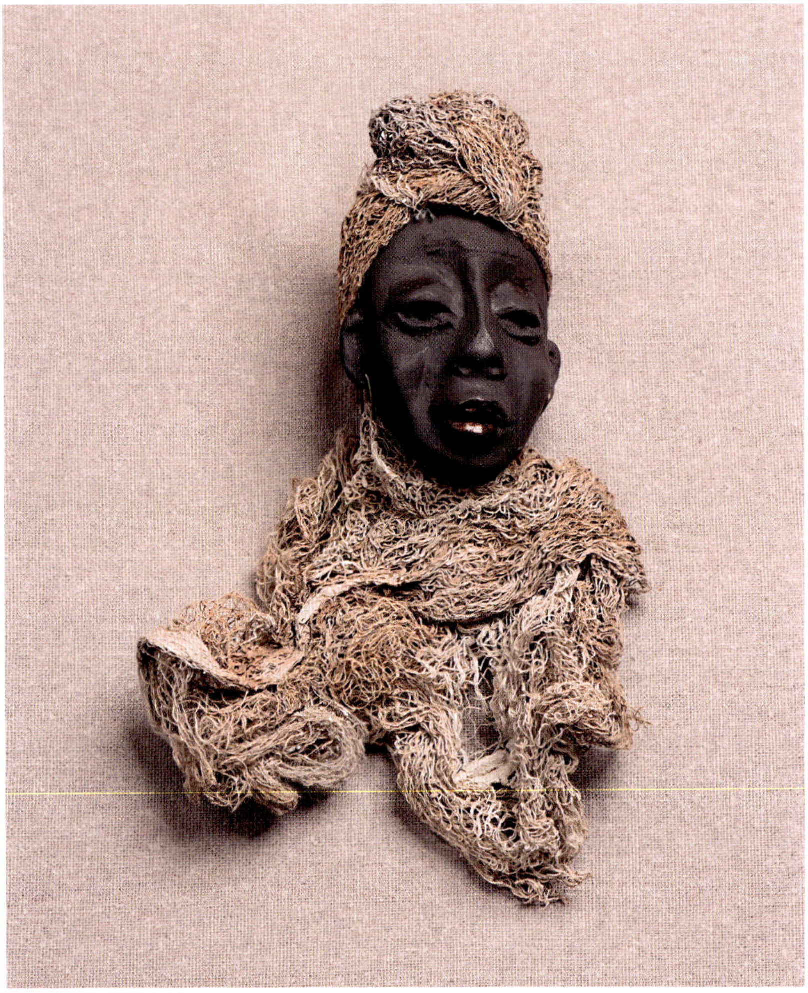

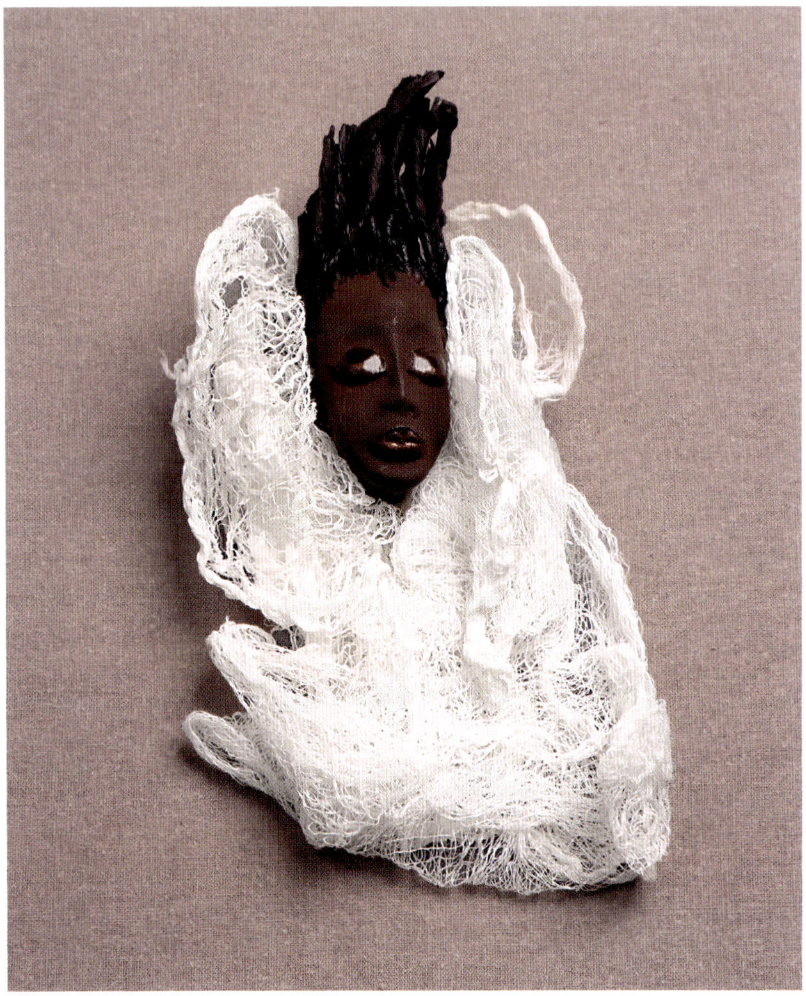

Paula Whaley, Oneeki's *Harriet Tubman-Walking in Her Footsteps*, 2021. Air-dried clay, tea-stained surgical gauze, and acrylic paint, 3.25" × 5". *Photo: Aisha Butler*

Paula Whaley, *Angel*, 2020. Air-dried clay, tissue paper, surgical gauze, stiffener, and acrylic paint, 4" × 7". *Photo: Aisha Butler*

Opposite: Paula Whaley, *Classy Silk Butterfly Woman*, 2020. Air-dried clay, dupioni silk, silk ribbon, brass wire, and acrylic paint, 5" × 5". *Photo: Aisha Butler*

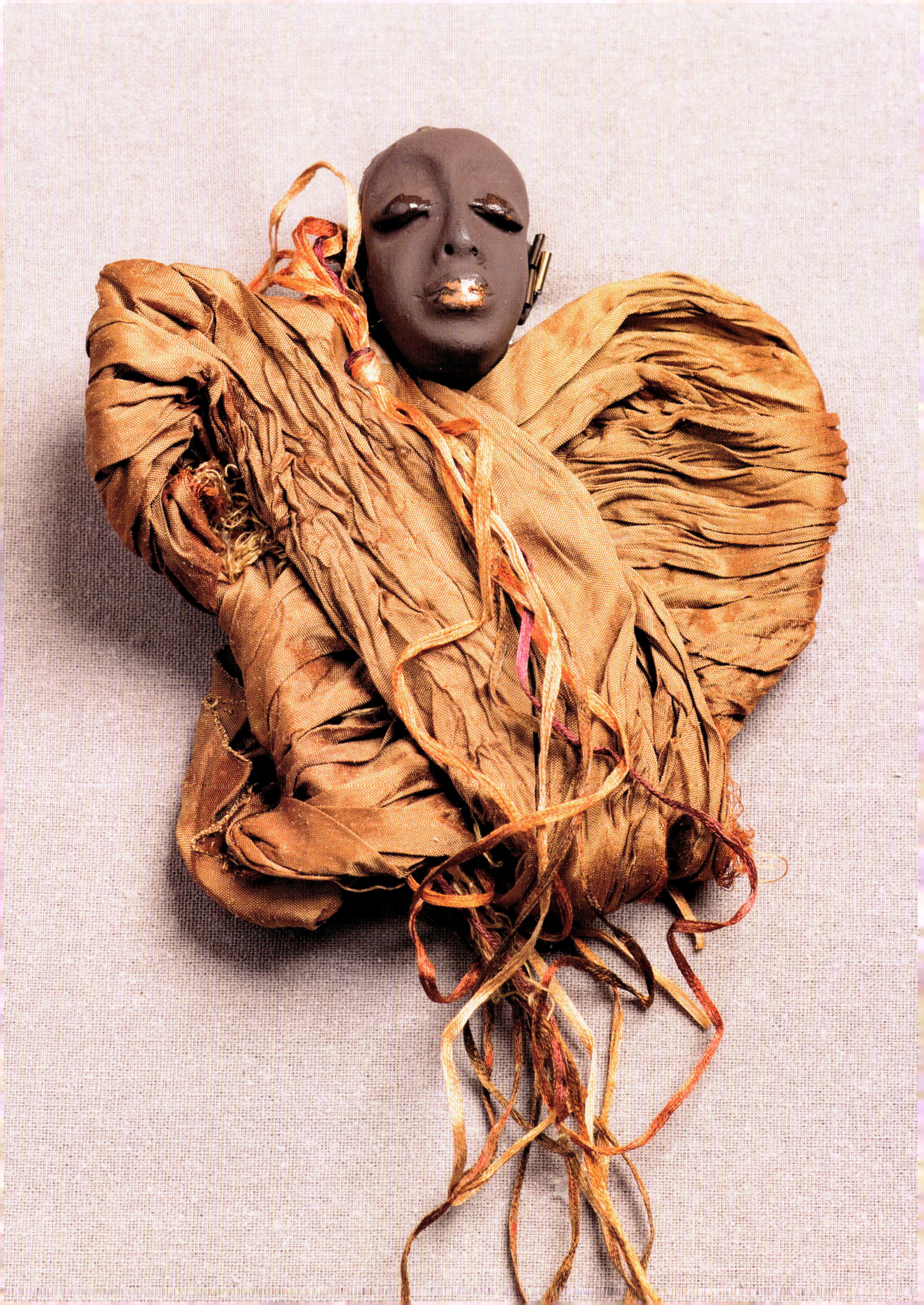

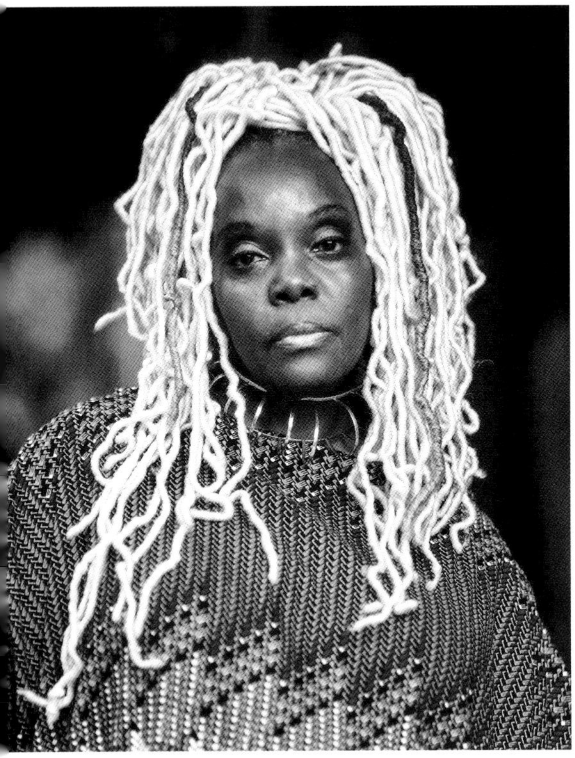

Photo: Zamani Feelings

VASHTI DUBOIS
YOUNG WOMEN'S PORTRAITS

DR. MYRAH: What was the first piece of art that you collected and when?

VASHTI DUBOIS: When I was in college, I bought some posters, but my first intentional art purchase was a doll made by a Black woman who was losing her sight. Her collection was called *Fiddlesticks*. She had so many beautiful dolls that it was difficult to choose—it felt like they were all speaking to me at once, "Pick me," but I could only afford the one. I call her my mama doll.

DR. MYRAH: Why are you a Keeper of Young Women's Portraits?

VASHTI DUBOIS: I was very self-conscious as a girl, and I think it had something to do with how I perceived others "seeing" me. What, who, and how did they see as they looked at me. I don't recall encountering images of Black girls around me, especially not in portraits. I did not see portraits of ordinary Black girls in museums, galleries, or even homes, except for maybe a school photograph.

These portraits I began collecting are evidence of Black girlhood, of our existence; they are our visual stories. I wanted to be able to see these stories for myself, and I wanted to share these visual stories with anyone else who entered the spaces where I lived or worked. Whenever I see a Black girl, I always see a part of myself that may be hidden, even from me. If the world stops turning tomorrow, there is a record of ordinary Black girlhood through these portraits.

Tara Pearson, a.k.a. MistySol, *Aya*, 2020. Textile, beads, and acrylic on canvas, 48" × 54". *Photo: Zamani Feelings*

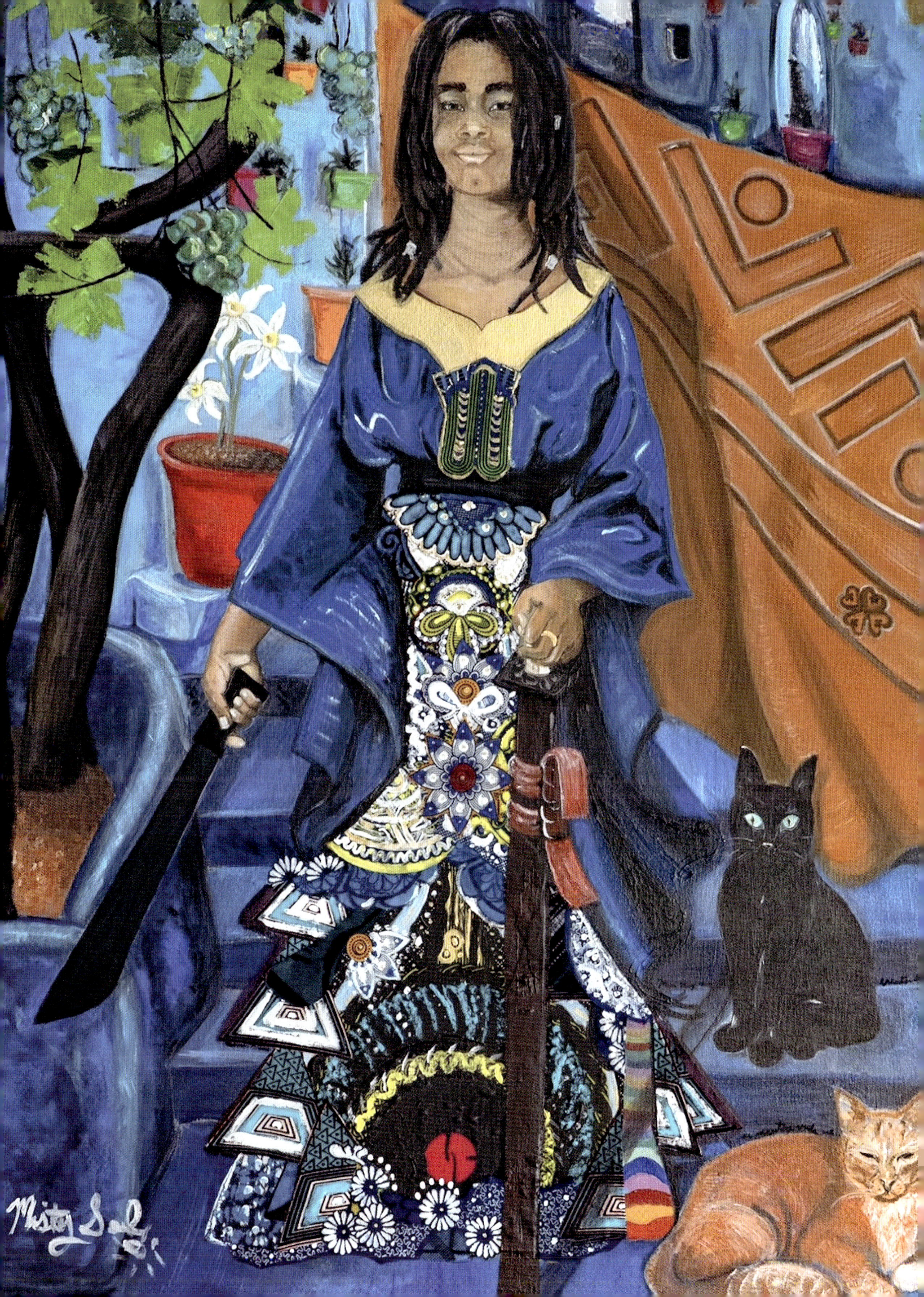

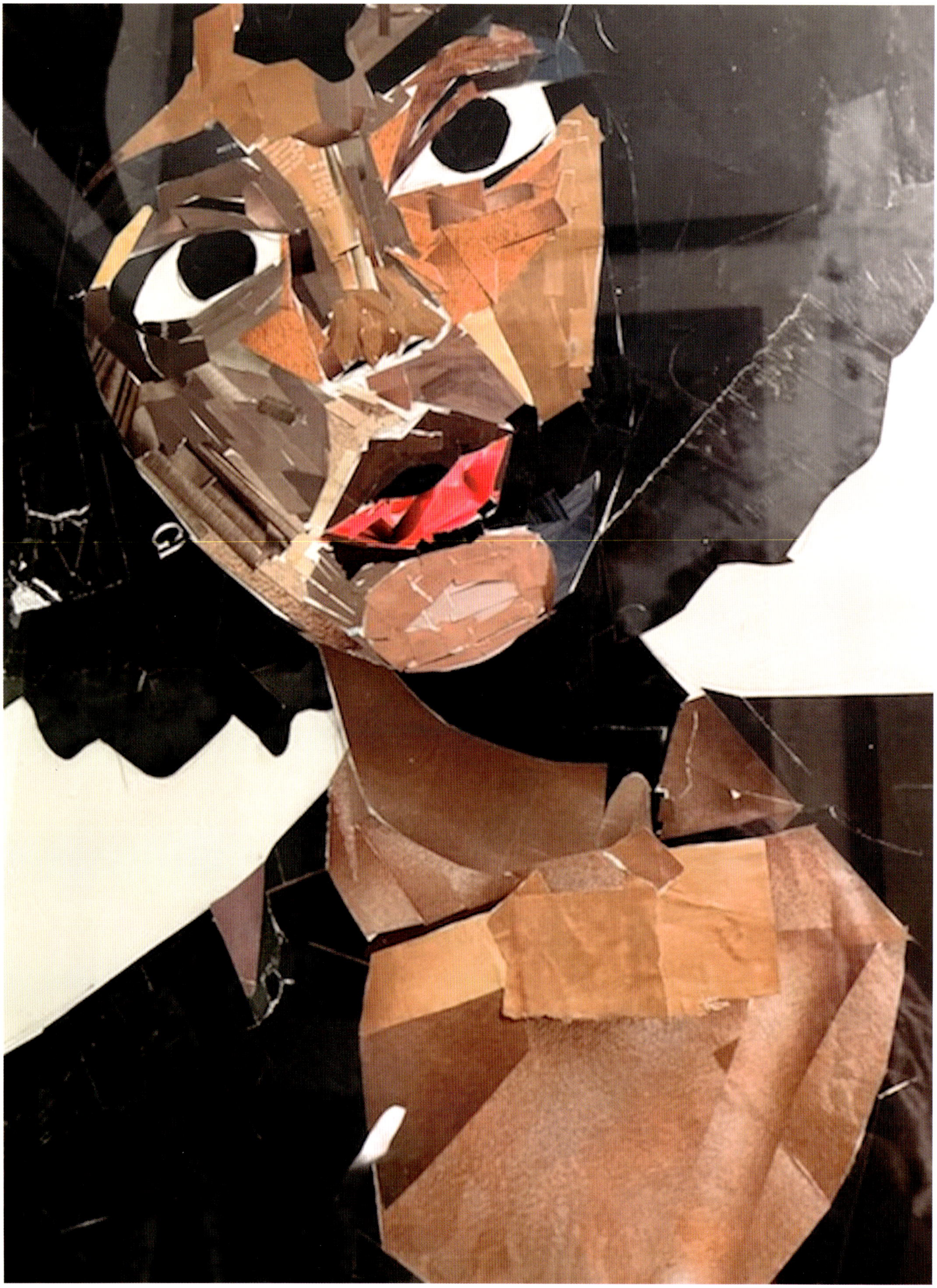

Simone Gilbert, *Muse Adelei*, 2019. Collage, 34" × 28". *Photo: Zamani Feelings*

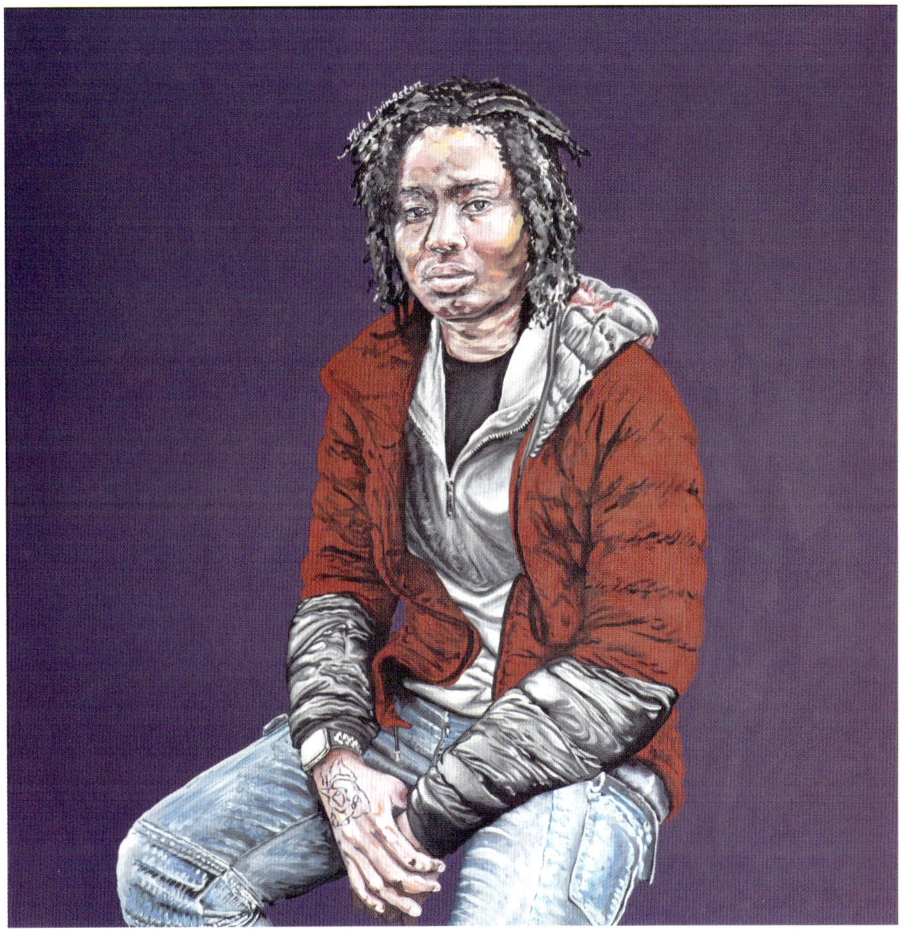

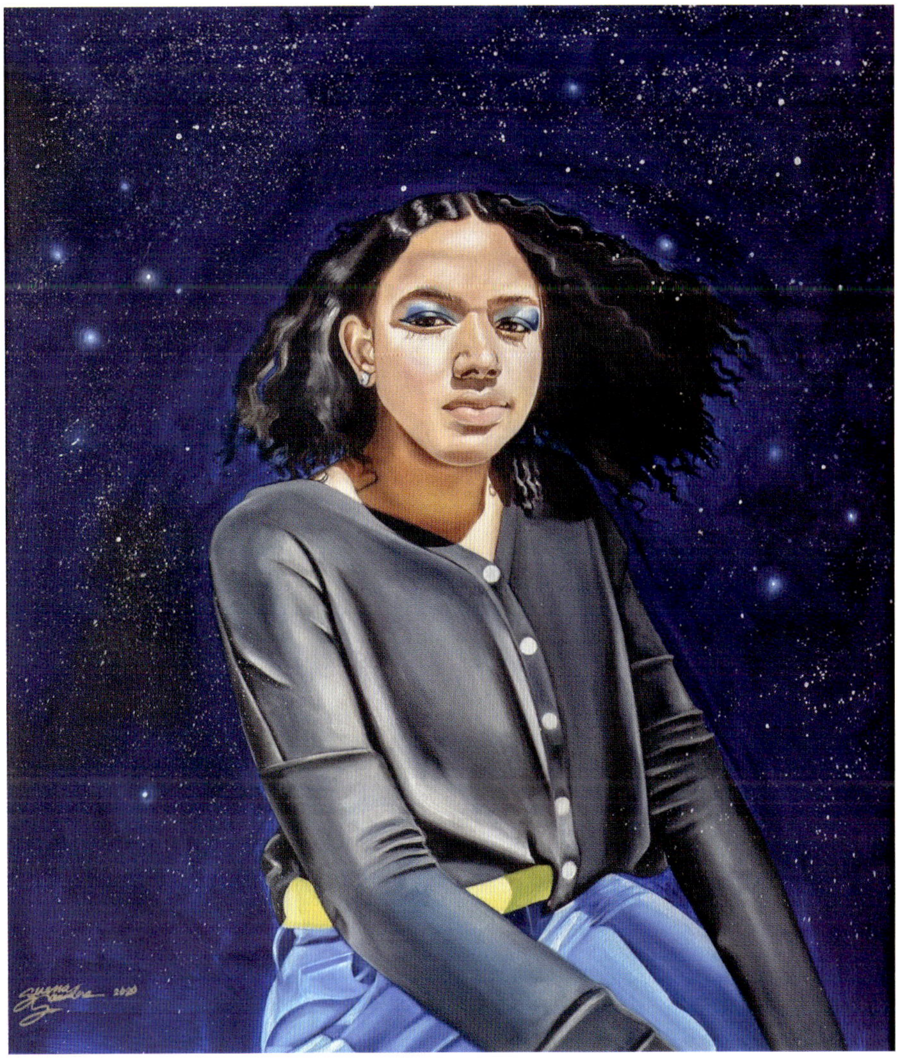

Nile Livingston, *Tyjanea Williams*, 2020. Acrylic on canvas, 48" × 48". *Photo: Zamani Feelings*

Serena Saunders, *Myka Ollison*, 2020. Acrylic on canvas, 52" × 58". *Photo: Zamani Feelings*

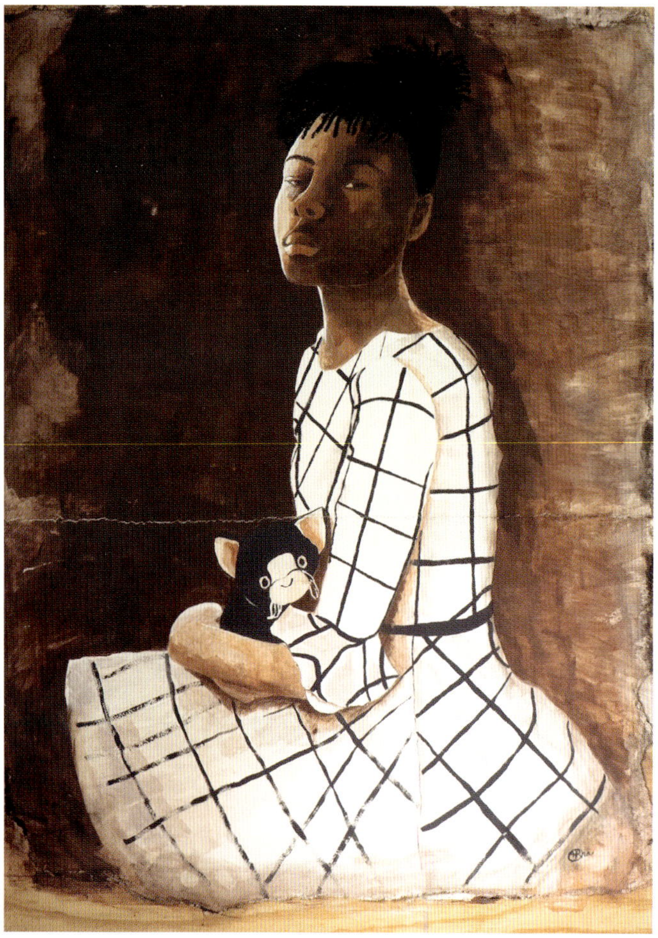

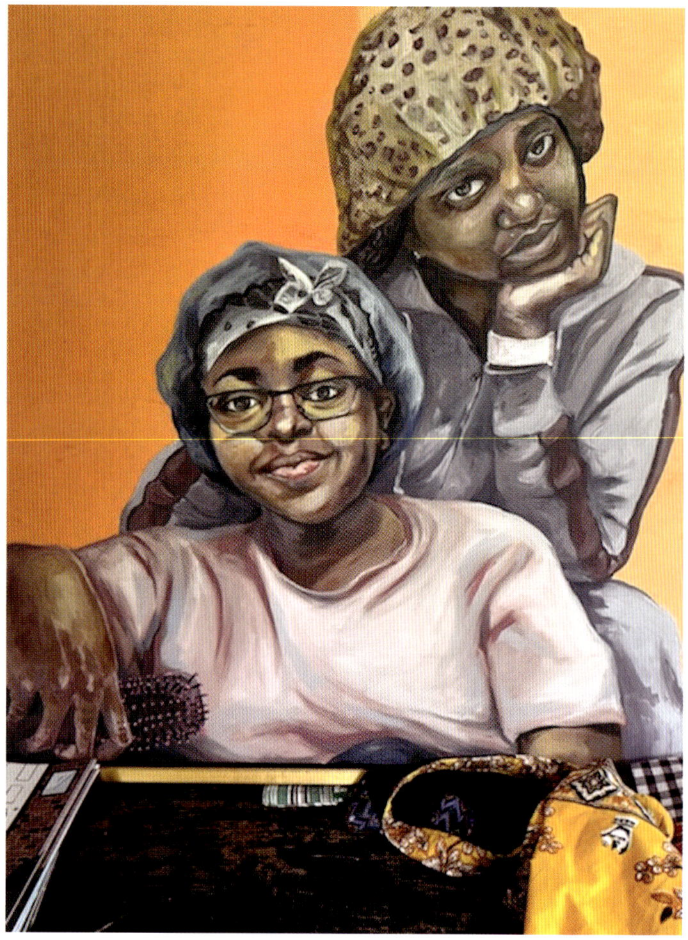

Chanell Phillips, *Cristine Harvey*, 2020. Acrylic on paper and wood panel, 34" × 42". *Photo: Zamani Feelings*

Ebony Smith, *My Sisters*, 2018. Acrylic on canvas, 38" × 38". *Photo: Zamani Feelings*

Opposite: Misha McGlowen, *Madison*, 2020. Acrylic on canvas, 58" × 60". *Photo: Zamani Feelings*

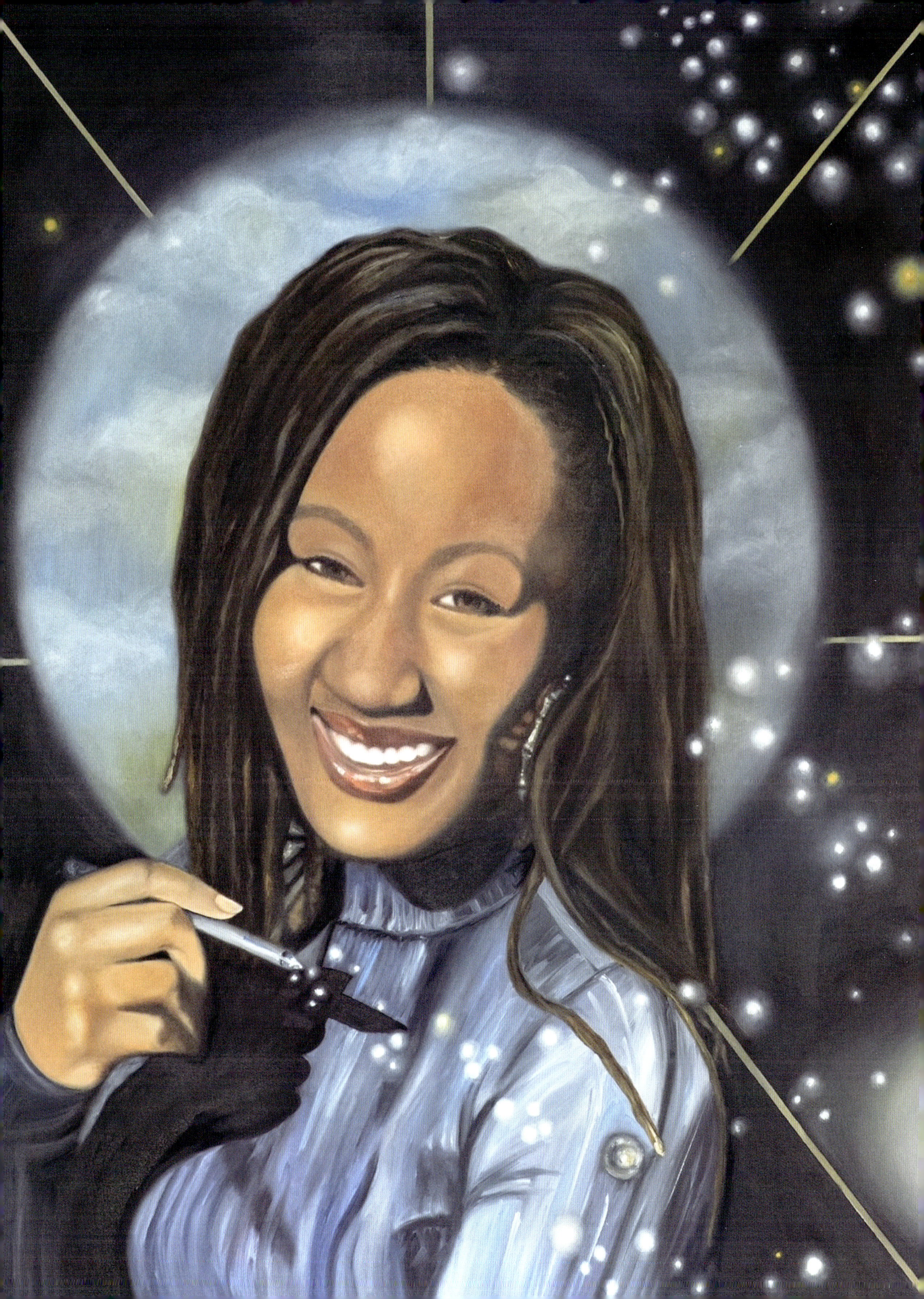

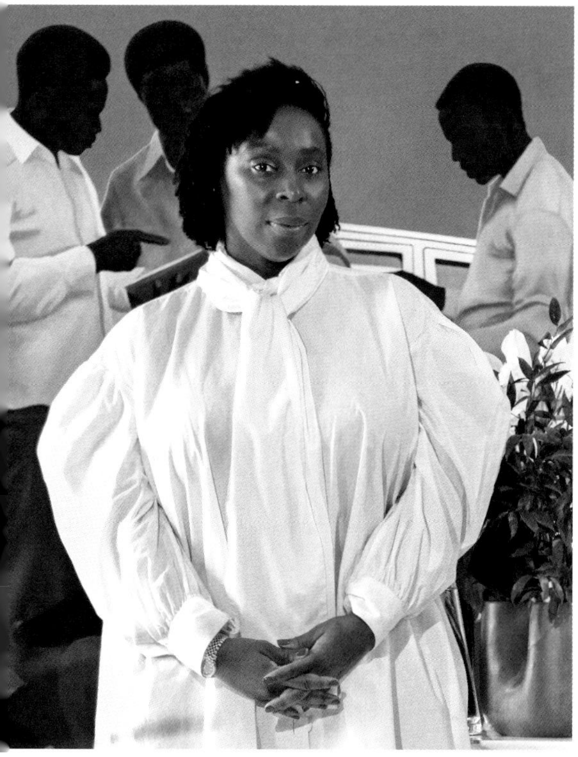

Photo: Adeyinka Akingbade

UGOMA EBILAH
NIGERIAN ARTISTS

DR. MYRAH: What was the first piece of art that you collected and when?

UGOMA EBILAH: The first piece of art I collected was in 2011, by a Nigerian artist named Gerald Chukwuma. I do not recall what the work is titled, but it is a wood-based relief work with hopeful bursts of grounding earth tones that is eternally beautiful and calming to look at but is also a precious memoir of my days as a budding curator and hopeful collector . . . the days when I was discovering fresh, courageous, and independent ways to feel, to look, and to see art.

DR. MYRAH: Why are you a Keeper of Nigerian Art?

UGOMA EBILAH: Art has a magical way of helping us better understand who we are, who we were, and who we wish to be as a people. I am passionate about preserving, promoting, and elevating the rich aesthetic, cultural, and spiritual heritage of my beloved country, Nigeria. Nigerian art is a mirror into Nigerian history, tradition, hope, and identity. By collecting works by Nigerian artists, I am doing my part to augment the conversations about Nigerian cultural posterity and to immortalize the unique Nigerian self-gaze as expressed through various visual art forms. While my collection is centered on art from Nigeria, I am interested in *all* art and have also collected art from Angola, Morocco, Kenya, Zimbabwe, South Africa, Australia, Jamaica, Ghana, Venezuela, USA, and the United Kingdom, to name a few. I believe that all forms of art are a window into self. My life and work are dedicated solely to elevating beauty and staying in that beauty—so art is a sort of appendage of my being. I collect art to gather and place totems around me that remind me about who I am and who I want to be. I collect art that moves me, excites me, and even challenges me. I collect art to honor my heritage and my role as a custodian of emotions, stories, and cultures.

Richard Ovbiebo, *Clan*, 2020. Mixed media (fiberglass and bicycle wheel), 20" diameter. Nigeria. *Photo: Adeyinka Akingbade*

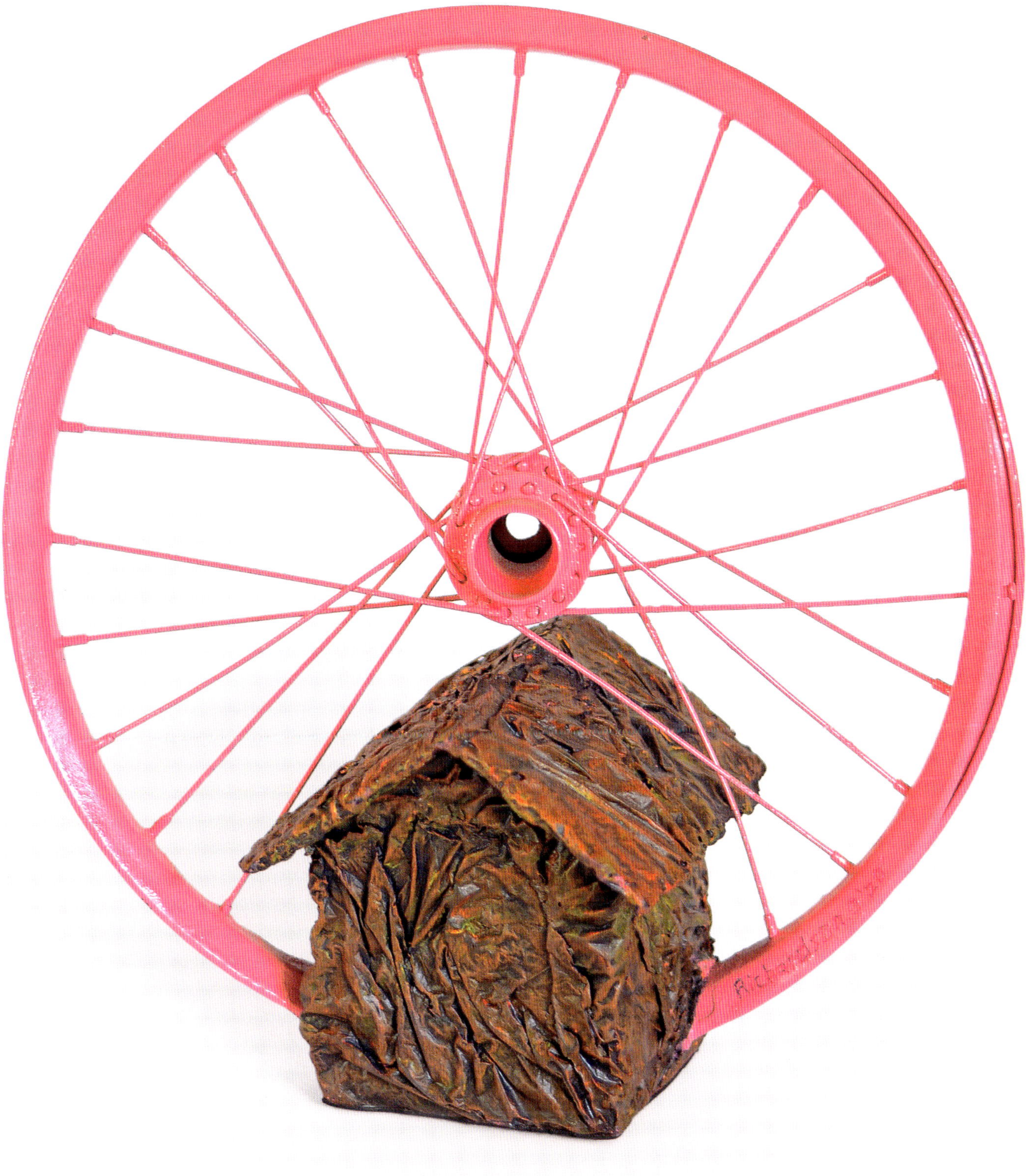

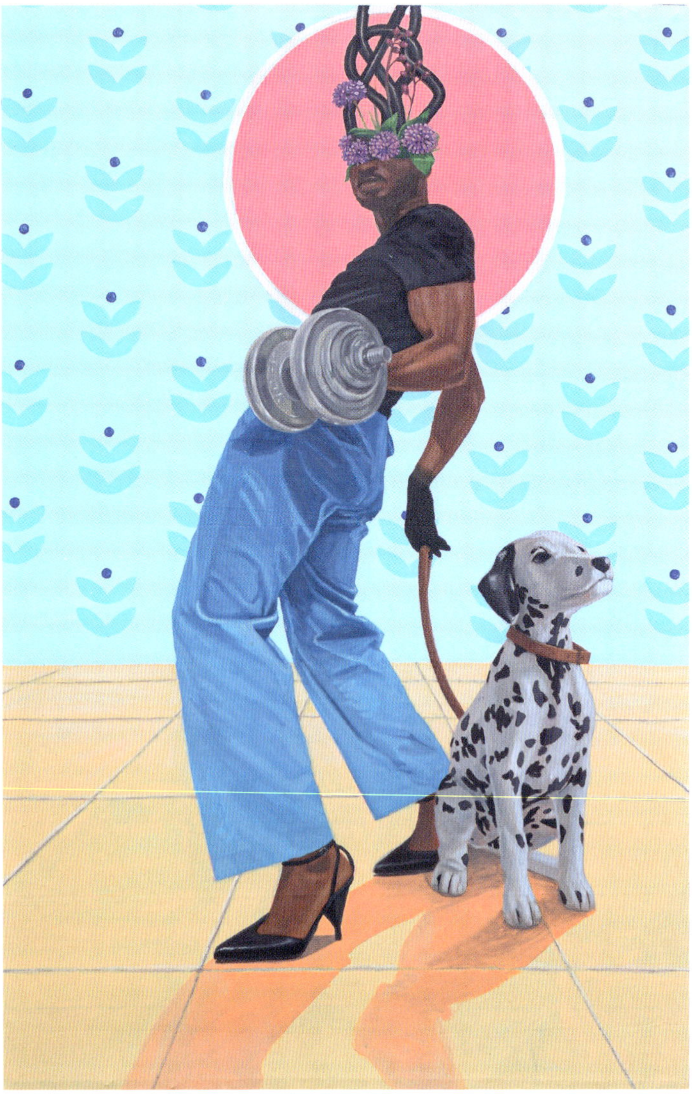

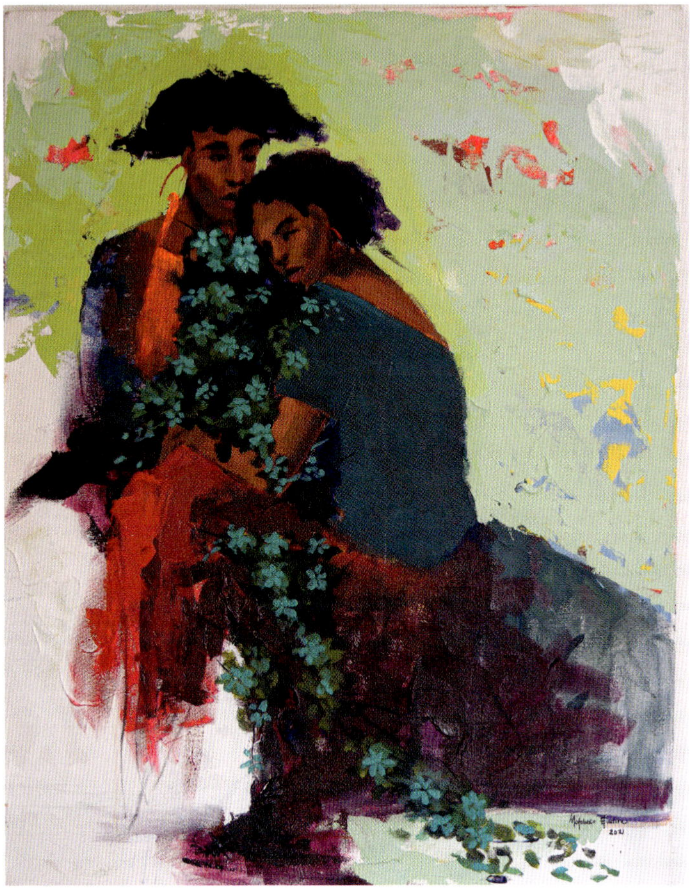

Julius Agbaje, *The Paradox*, 2022. Acrylic on canvas, 72" × 48". Nigeria. *Photo: Adeyinka Akingbade*

Mofoluso Eludire, *Safe in Solace II*, 2021. Acrylic on canvas, 38" × 30". Nigeria. *Photo: Adeyinka Akingbade*

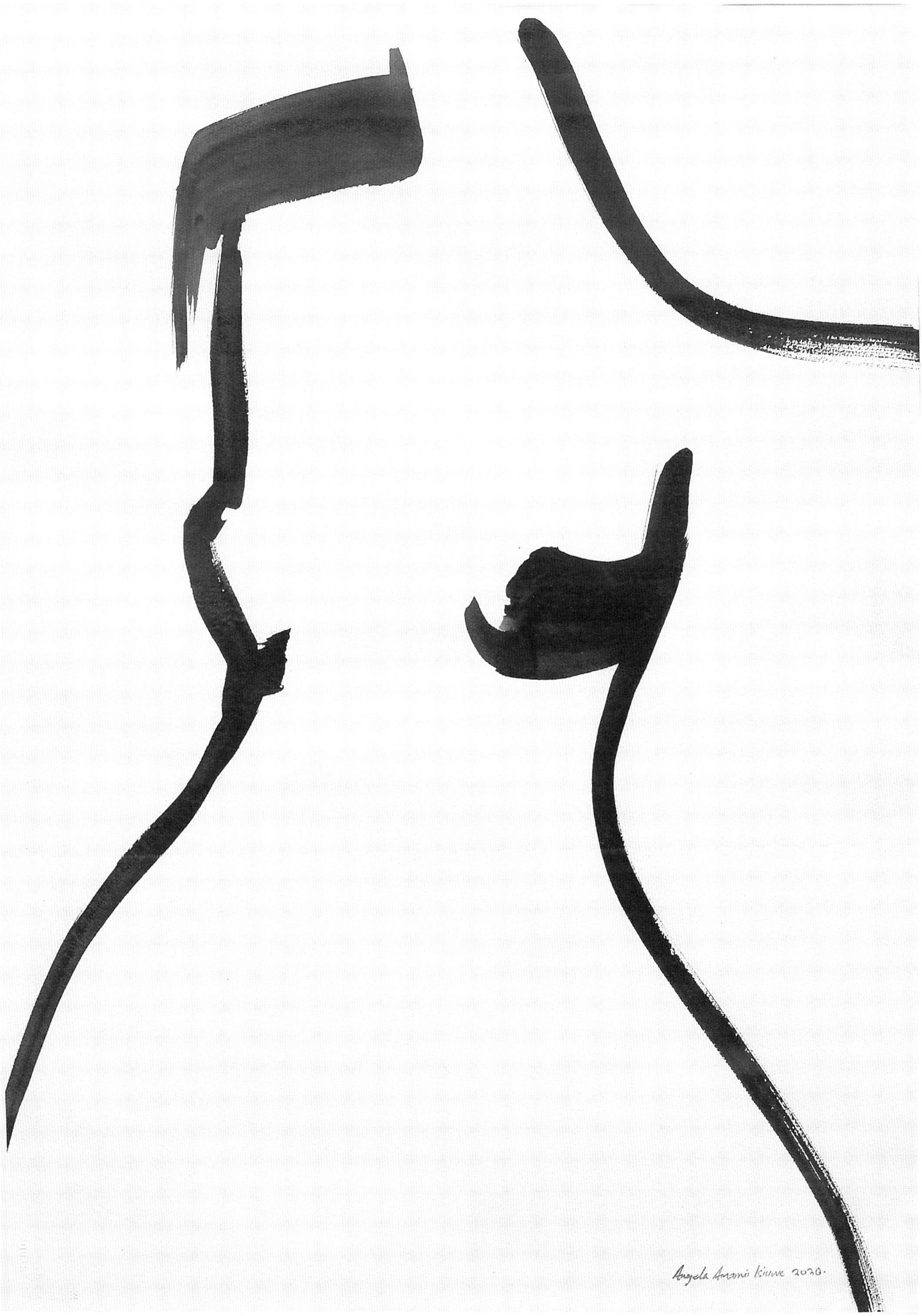

Angela Isiuwe, *Mystique*, 2020. Acrylic on paper, 30" × 22". Nigeria. *Photo: Adeyinka Akingbade*

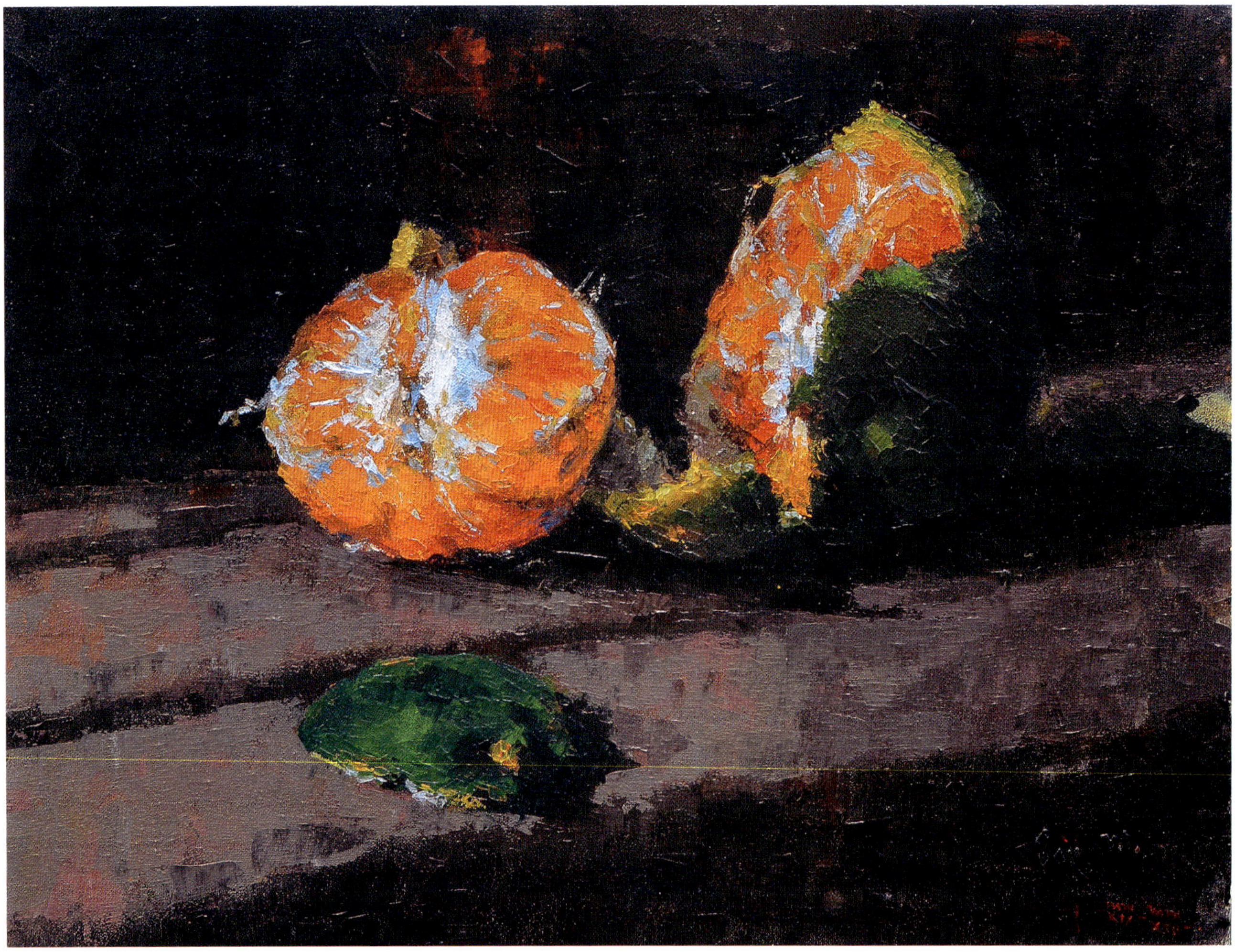

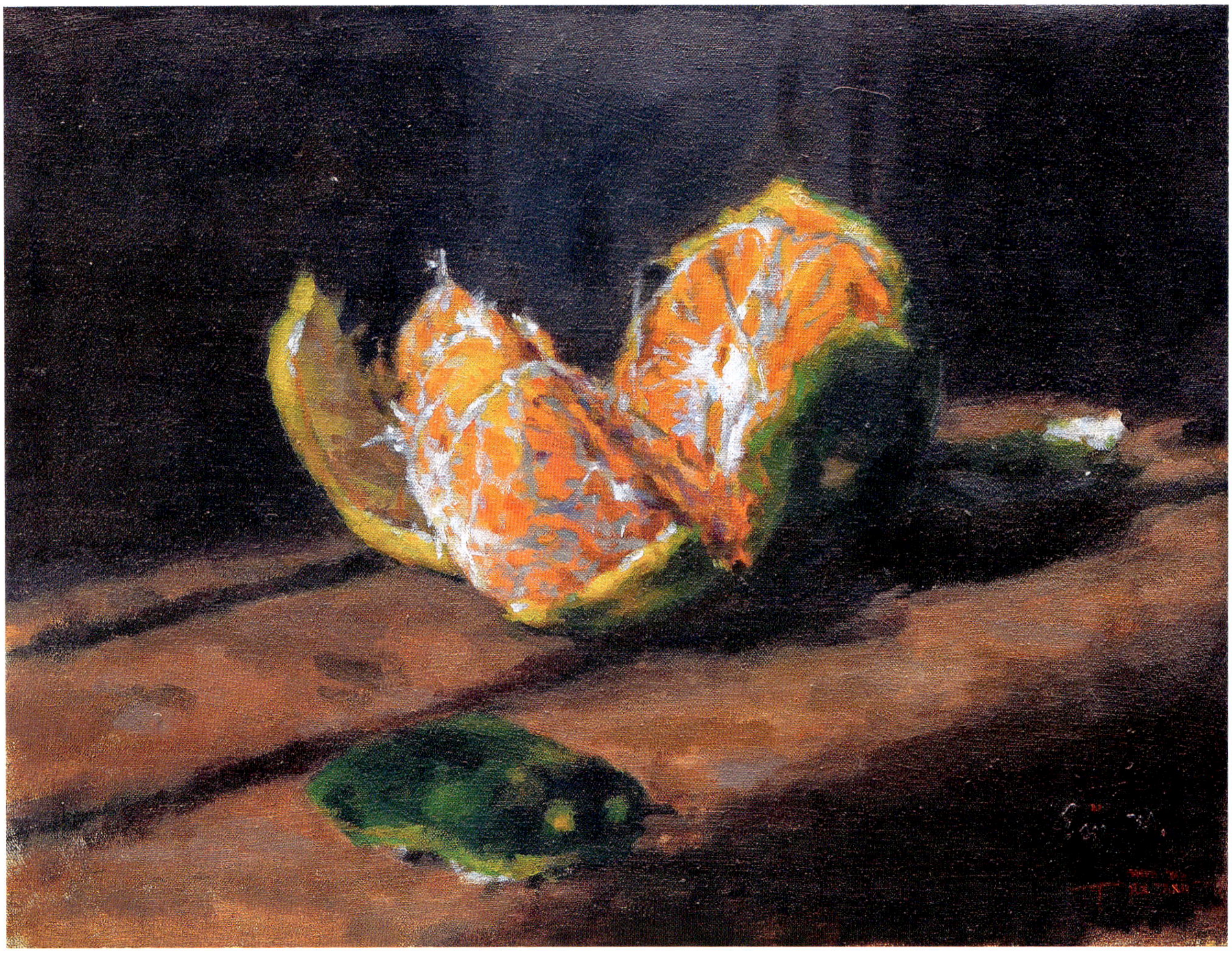

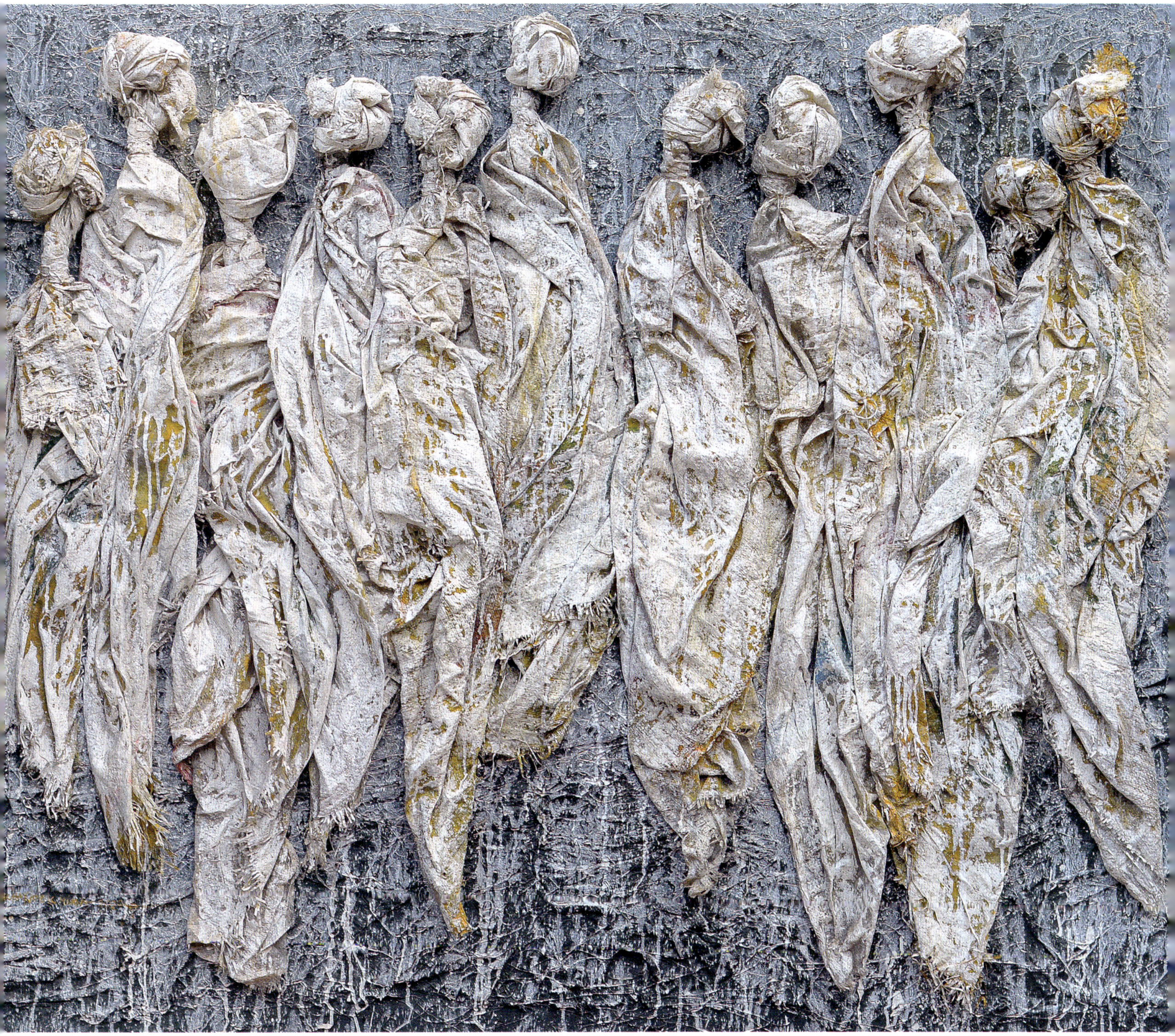

Raji Babatunde, *Evening Night V*, ca. 2020–2022.
Acrylic on canvas, 18" × 24". Nigeria. *Photo: Adeyinka Akingbade*

Raji Babatunde, *Evening Night VI*, ca. 2020–2022.
Acrylic on canvas, 18" × 24". Nigeria. *Photo: Adeyinka Akingbade*

Above: Uchay Joel Chima, *Elders Forum*, 2020. Mixed media (sacks, strings, acrylic on canvas), 54" × 66". Nigeria. *Photo: Adeyinka Akingbade*

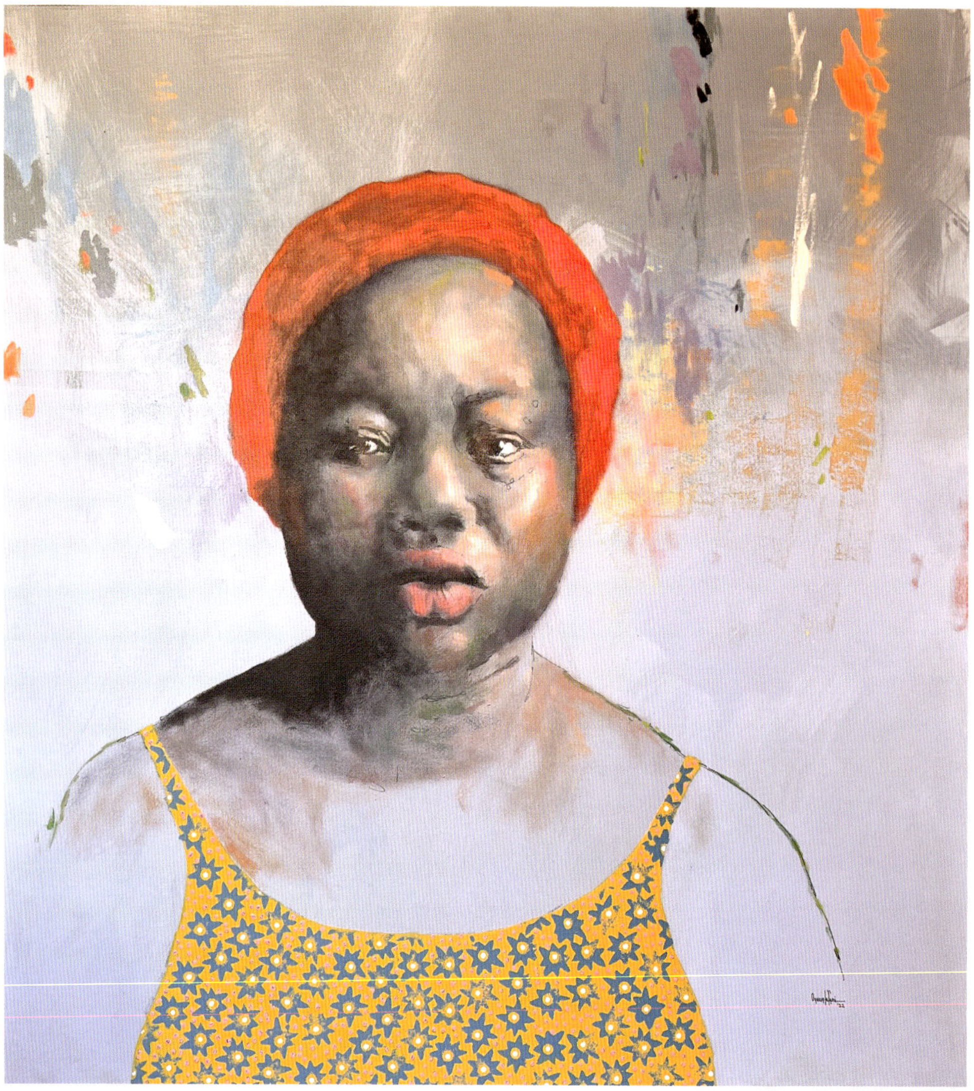

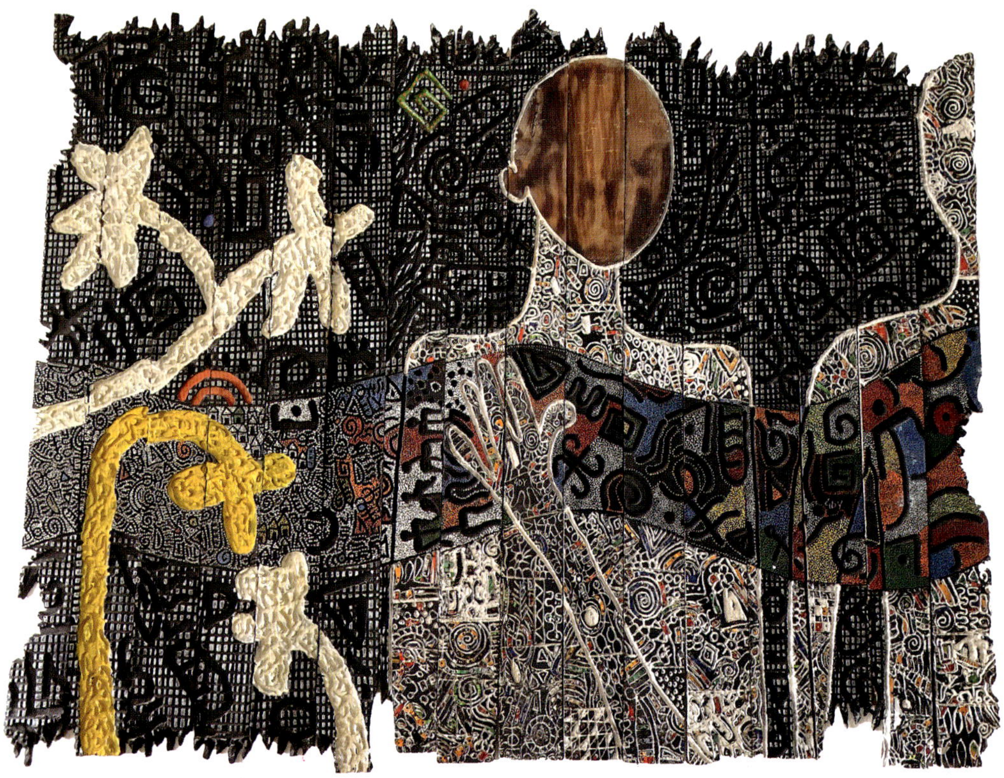

Olufemi Oyewole, *Untitled*, 2022. Acrylic on canvas, 72" × 72". Nigeria. *Photo: Adeyinka Akingbade*

Gerald Chukwuma, *Colored Road*, 2016. Mixed media (wood, acrylic, and tin cans), 60" × 72". Nigeria. *Photo: Adeyinka Akingbade*

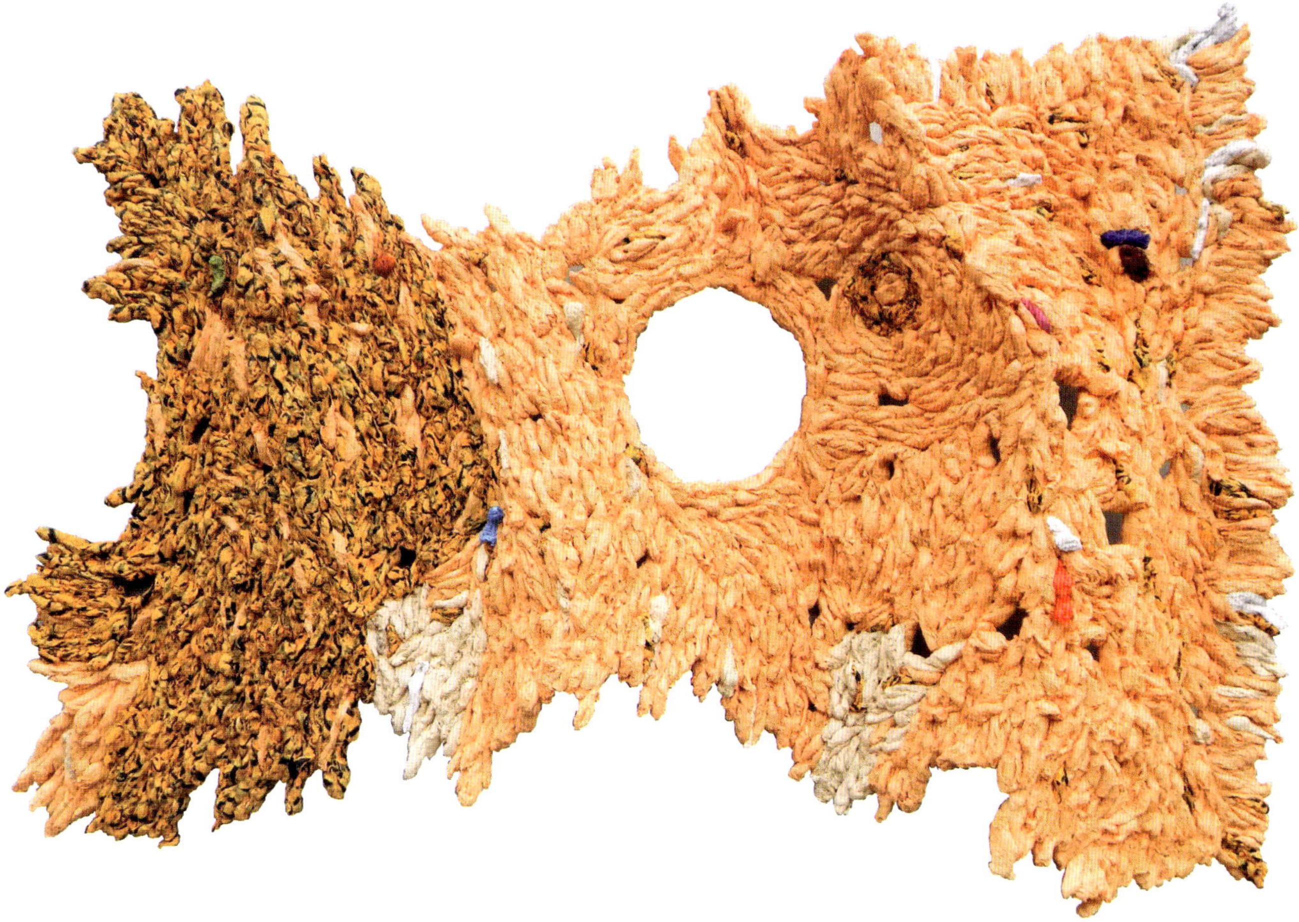

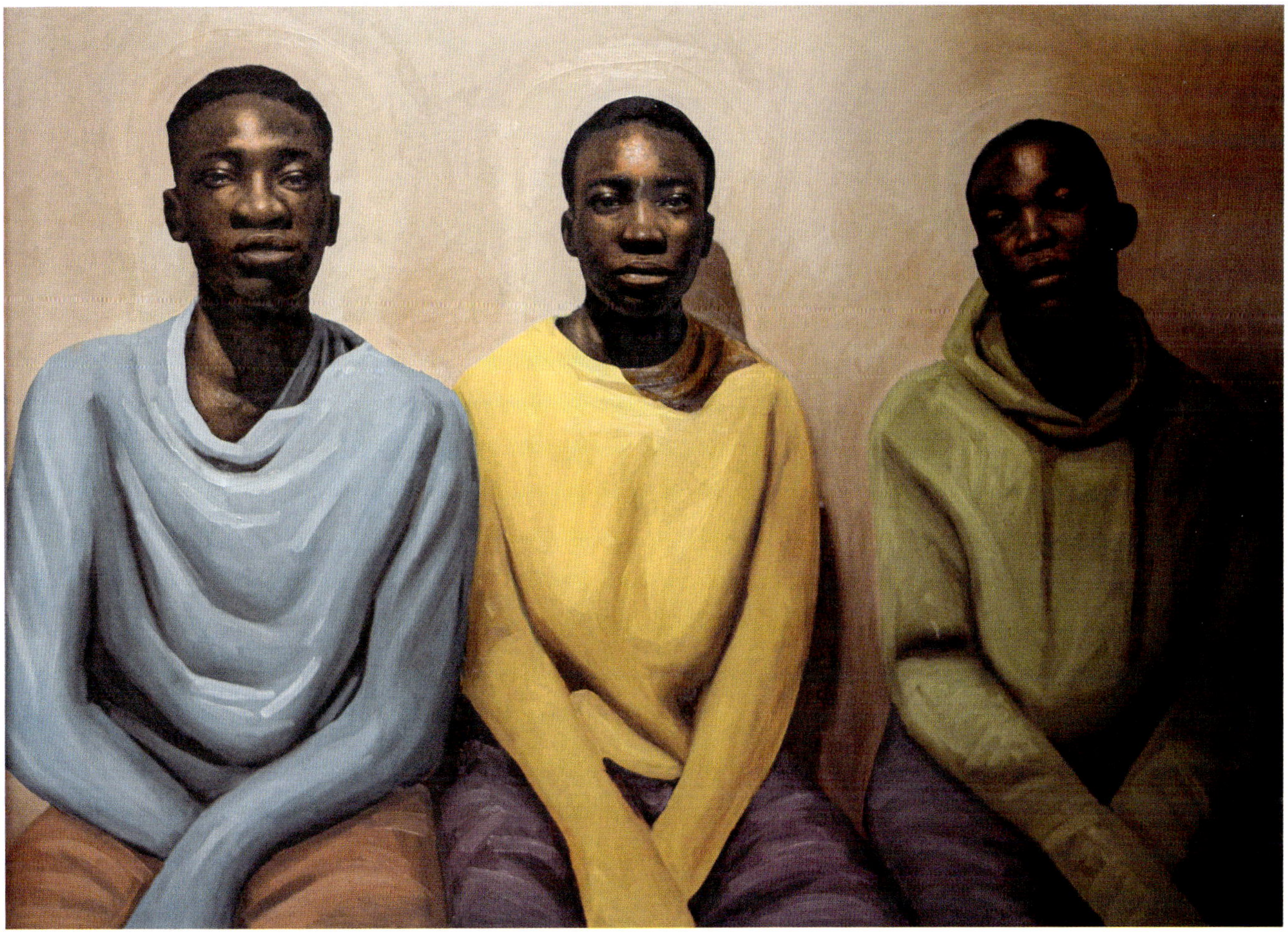

Olumide Onadipe, *The Orbit*, 2020. Plastic bags, 50" × 81". Nigeria. *Photo: Adeyinka Akingbade*

Oliver Okolo, *Bandits*, 2021. Oil on canvas, 48" × 60". Nigeria. *Photo: Adeyinka Akingbade*

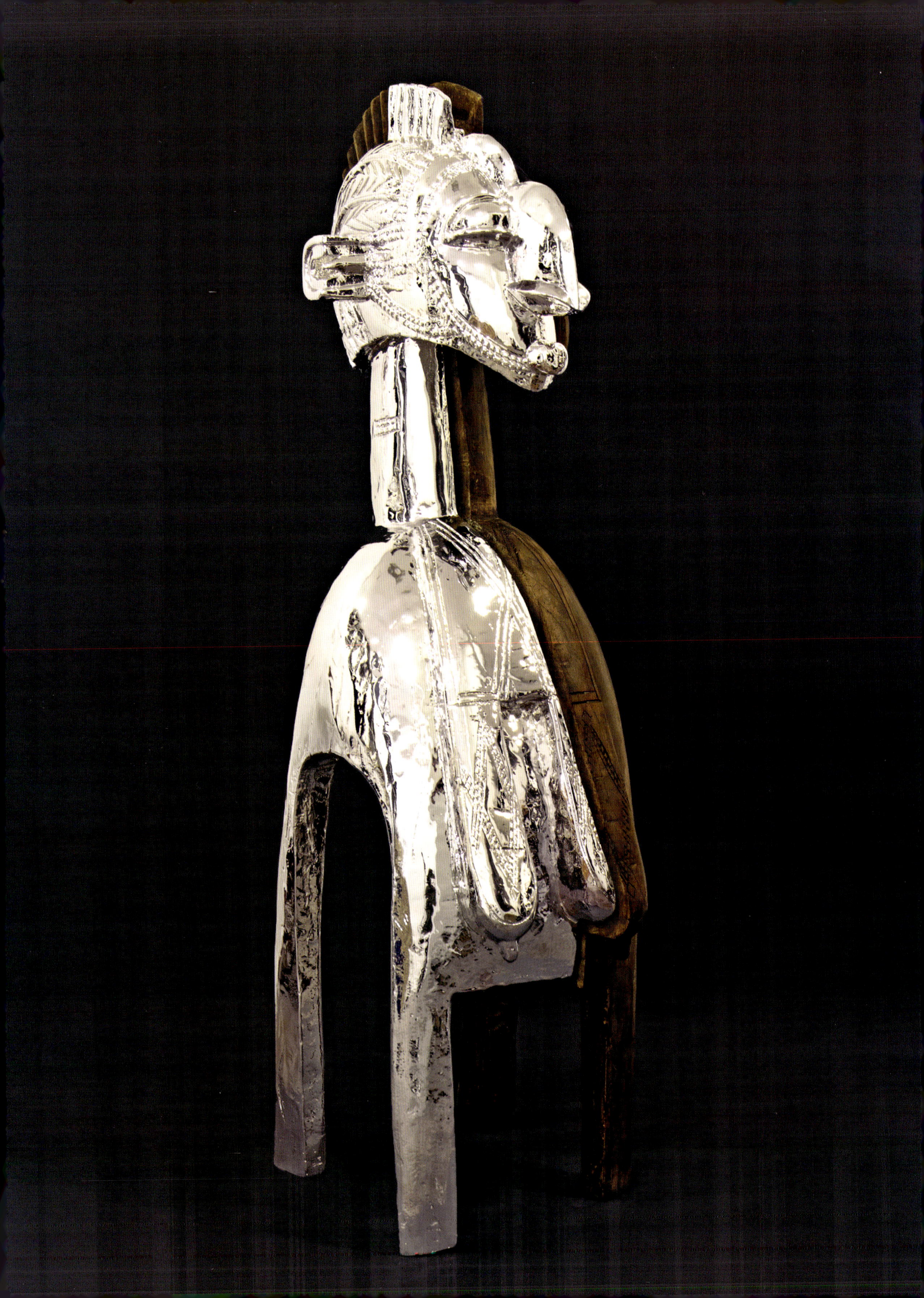

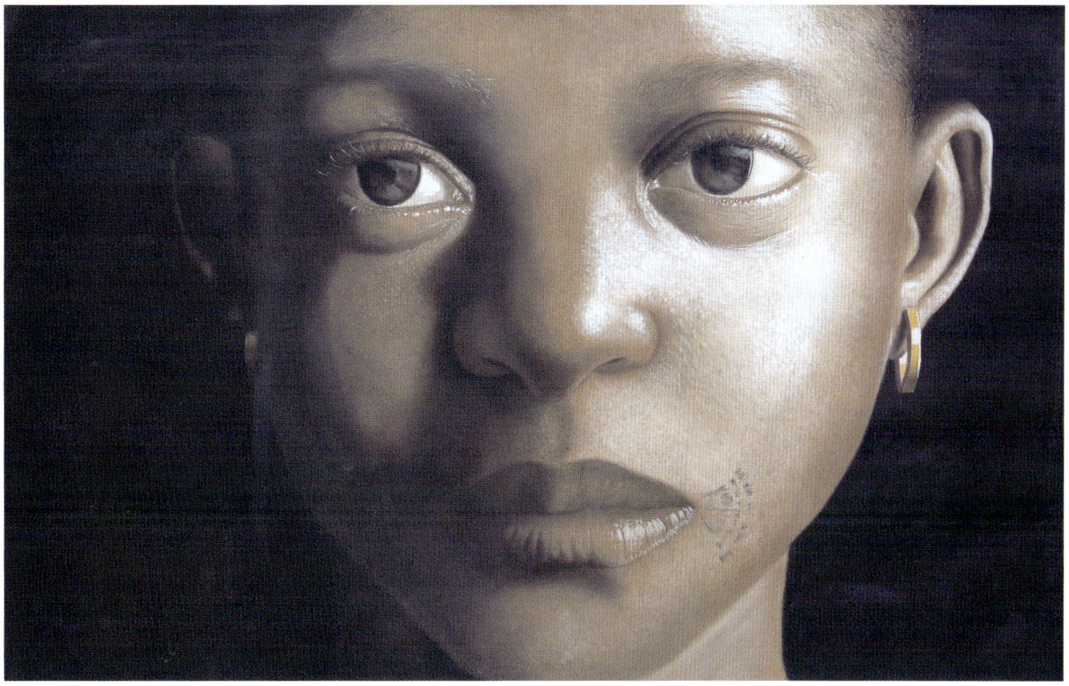

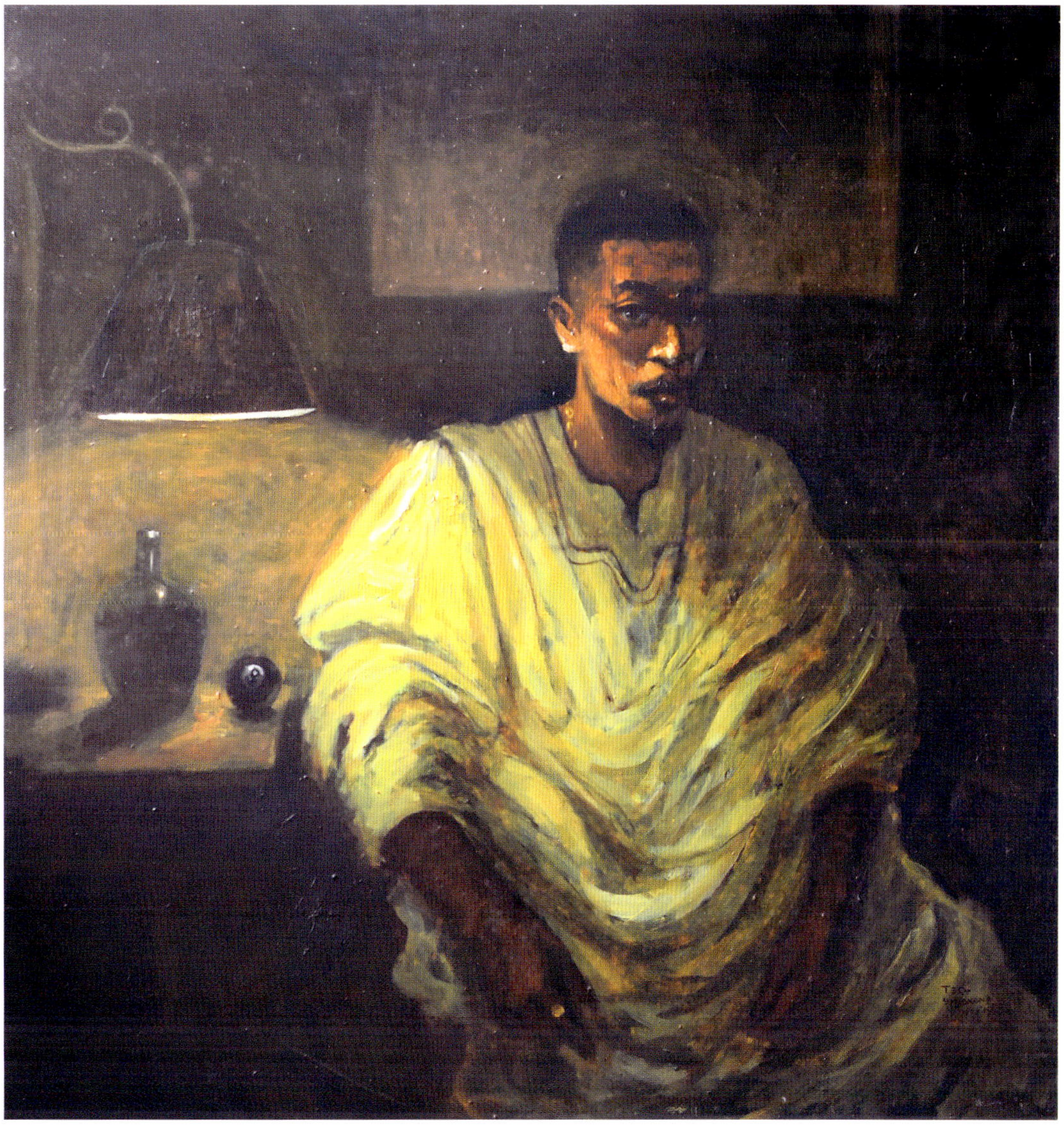

Opposite: Niyi Olagunju, *Baga Nimba*, 2020. Sculpture (chrome and wood), 48" height. Nigeria. *Photo: Adeyinka Akingbade*

Babajid Olatunji, *Tribal Mark Series III*, 2017. Acrylic, oil, charcoal, and pen, 36" × 48". Nigeria. *Photo: Adeyinka Akingbade*

Tega Akpokona, *Babatunde*, 2020. Oil on canvas, 60" × 60". Nigeria. *Photo: Adeyinka Akingbade*

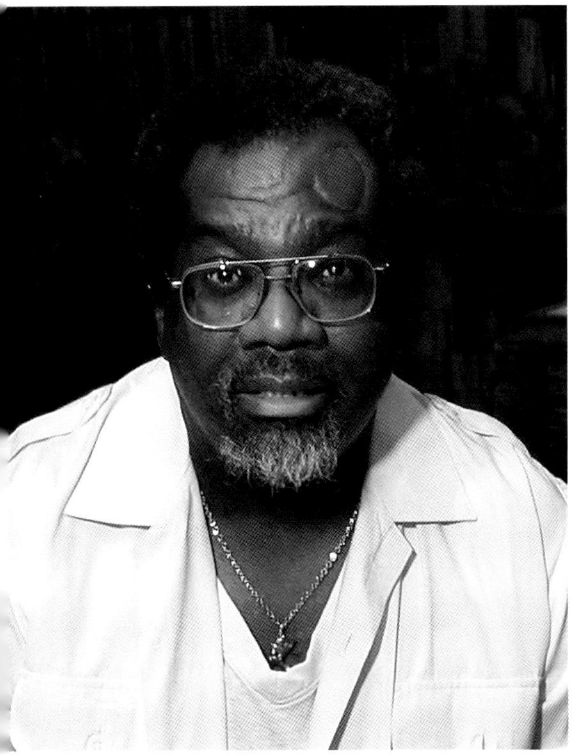

Photo: Mark Blackshear

DR. ERIC EDWARDS
AFRICAN SCULPTURE

DR. MYRAH: What was the first piece of art that you collected and when?

DR. ERIC EDWARDS: The first piece of African Art that I collected was a Senufo Maternity Figure indigenous to Mali, West Africa, in March 1971.

DR. MYRAH: Why are you a Keeper of African Art?

DR. ERIC EDWARDS: I started collecting African Art because I knew that I was collecting my past and shared ancestry, with the hope of better understanding who I was and the contributions to man and womankind which people of color gave. My museum, the Cultural Museum of African Art (CMAAINC.ORG), has the artifacts that tell the stories of true history, which is not taught in public schools.

Artist unknown, *Mende Helmet Mask-Sande Society-Ceremony* (Sierra Leone), nineteenth century. Wood. *Photo: Leslie Jean Bart*

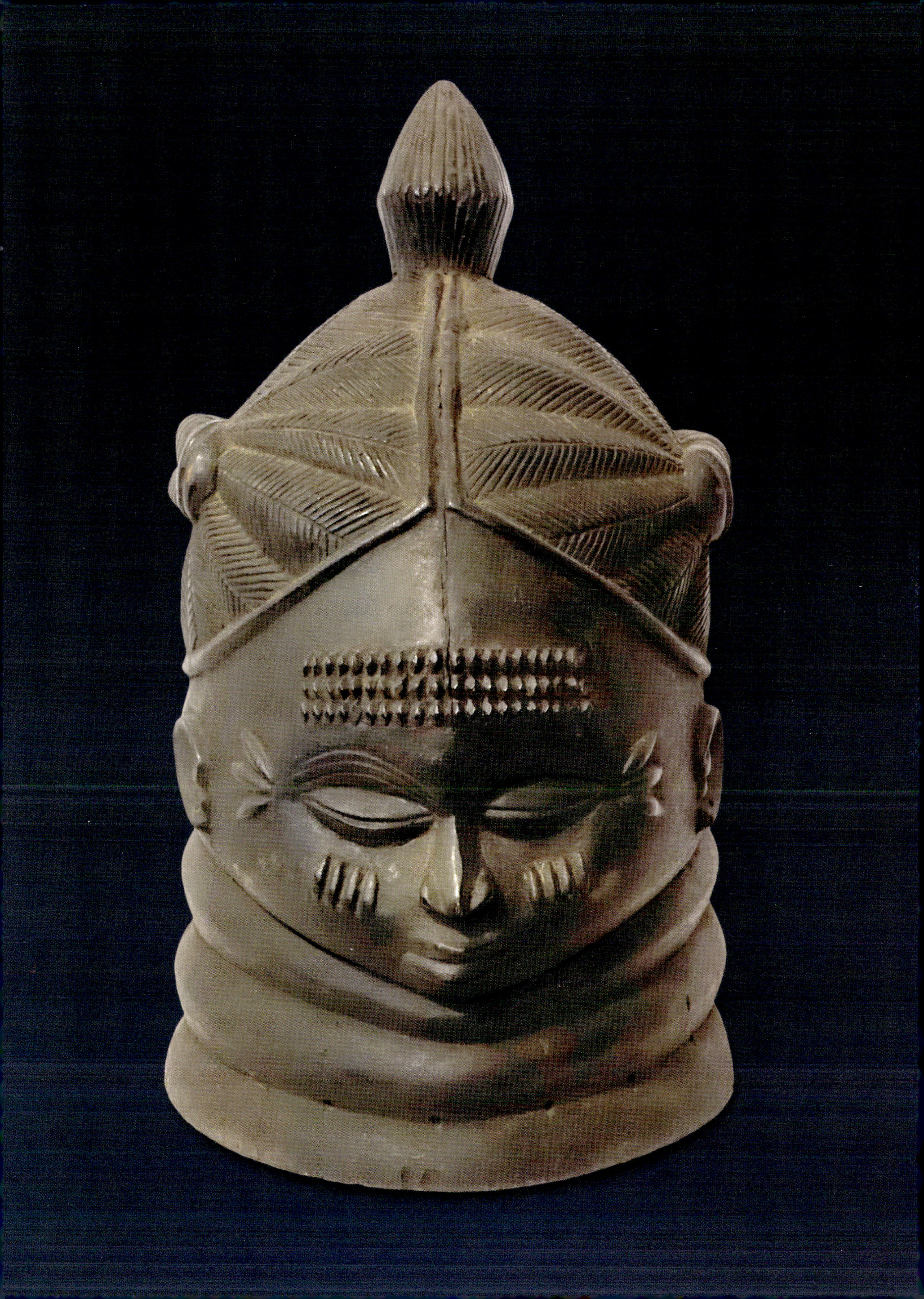

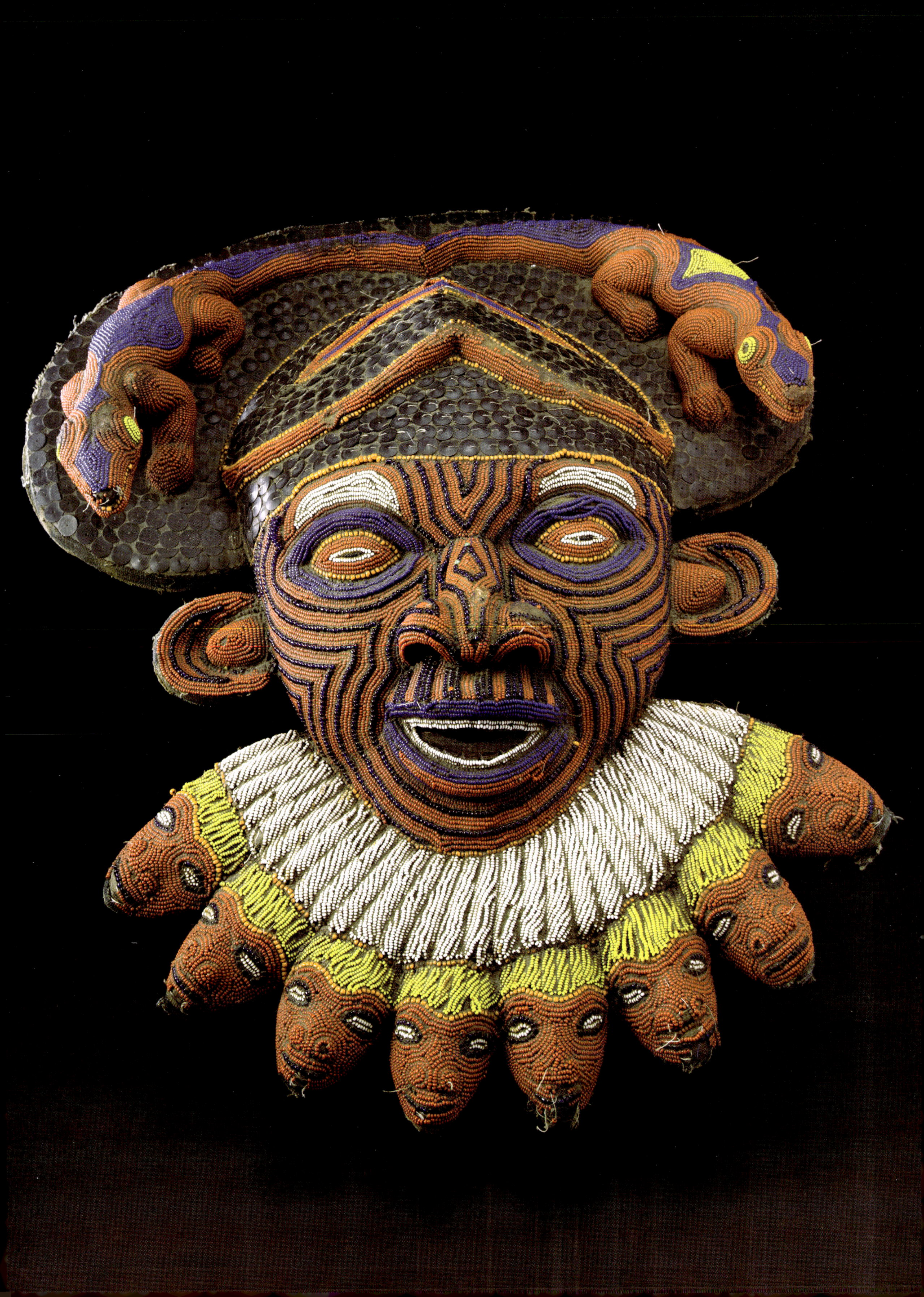

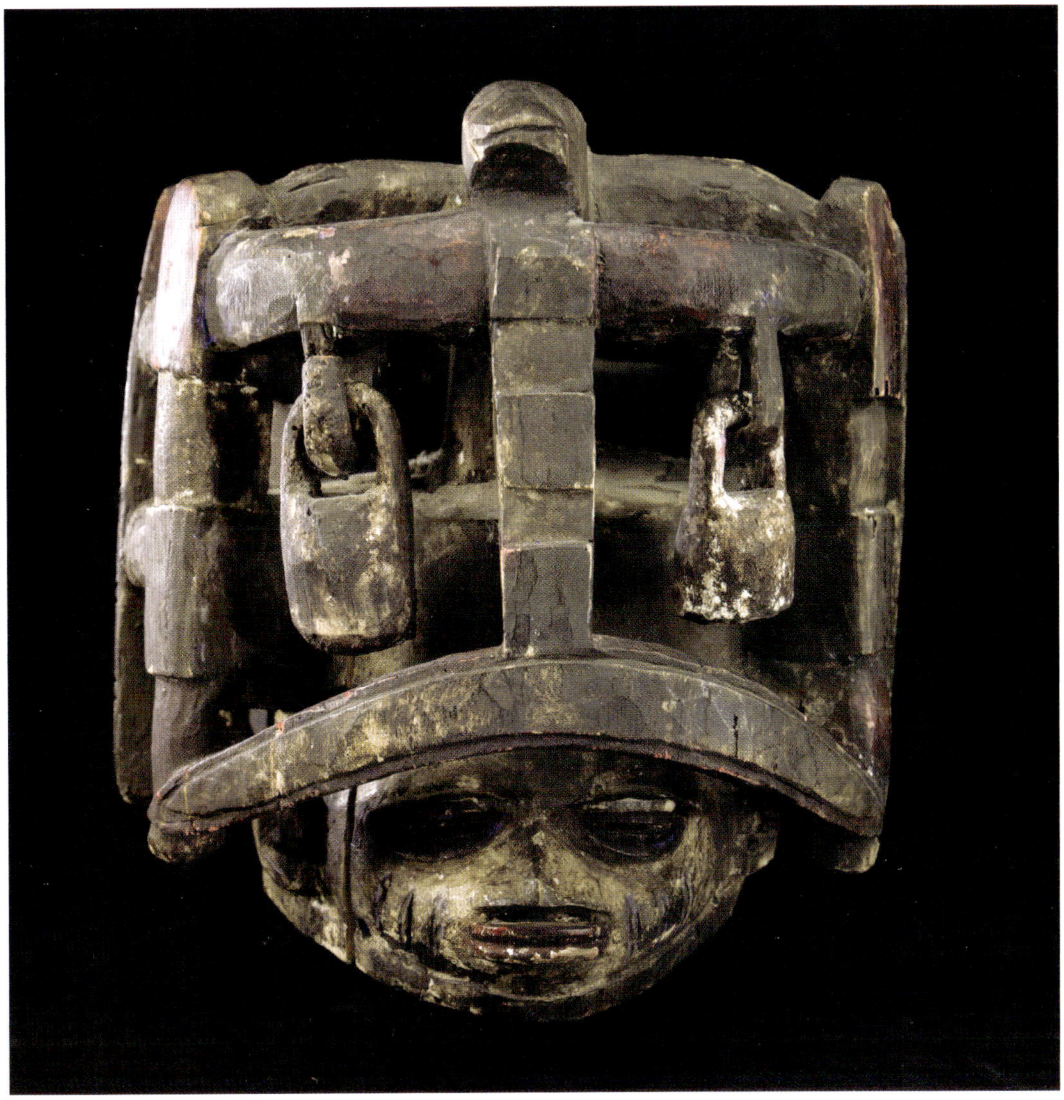

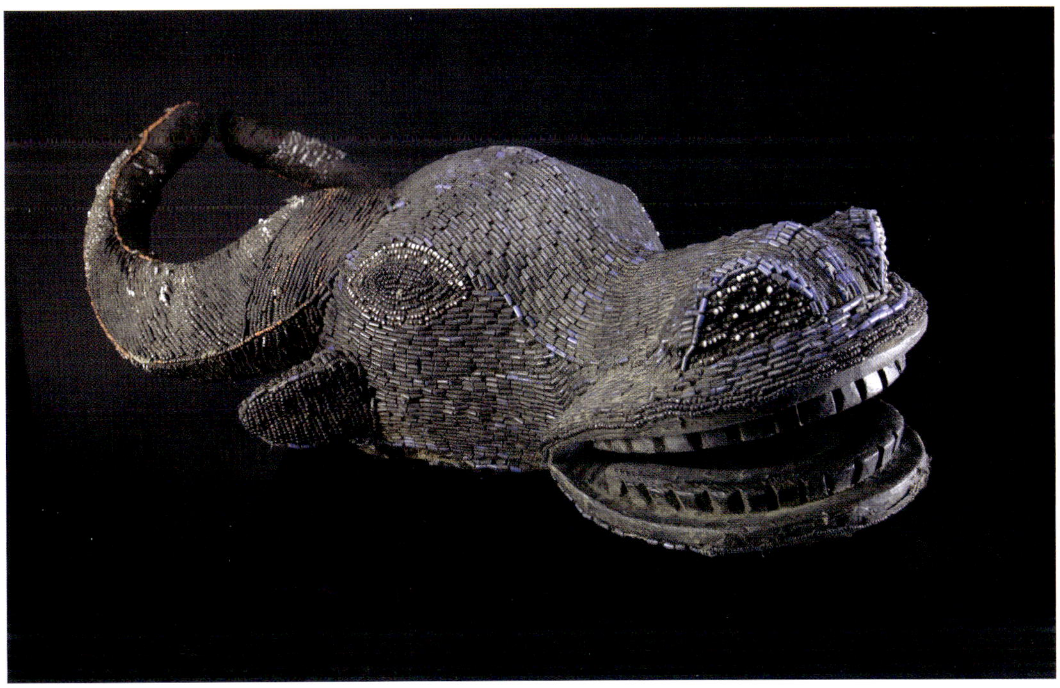

Opposite: Artist unknown, *Tikar Chief Royal Protective Mask* (Cameroon), late nineteenth century. Ancient beads, wood, woven fabric, and earth pigments. *Photo: Leslie Jean Bart*

Artist unknown, *Gelede Secret Society Helmet* (Nigeria), nineteenth century. Wood and earth pigments. *Photo: Leslie Jean Bart*

Artist unknown. *Bamileke Buffalo Helmet* (Cameroon), late seventeenth century. Wood, ancient beads, and woven cloth. *Photo: Leslie Jean Bart*

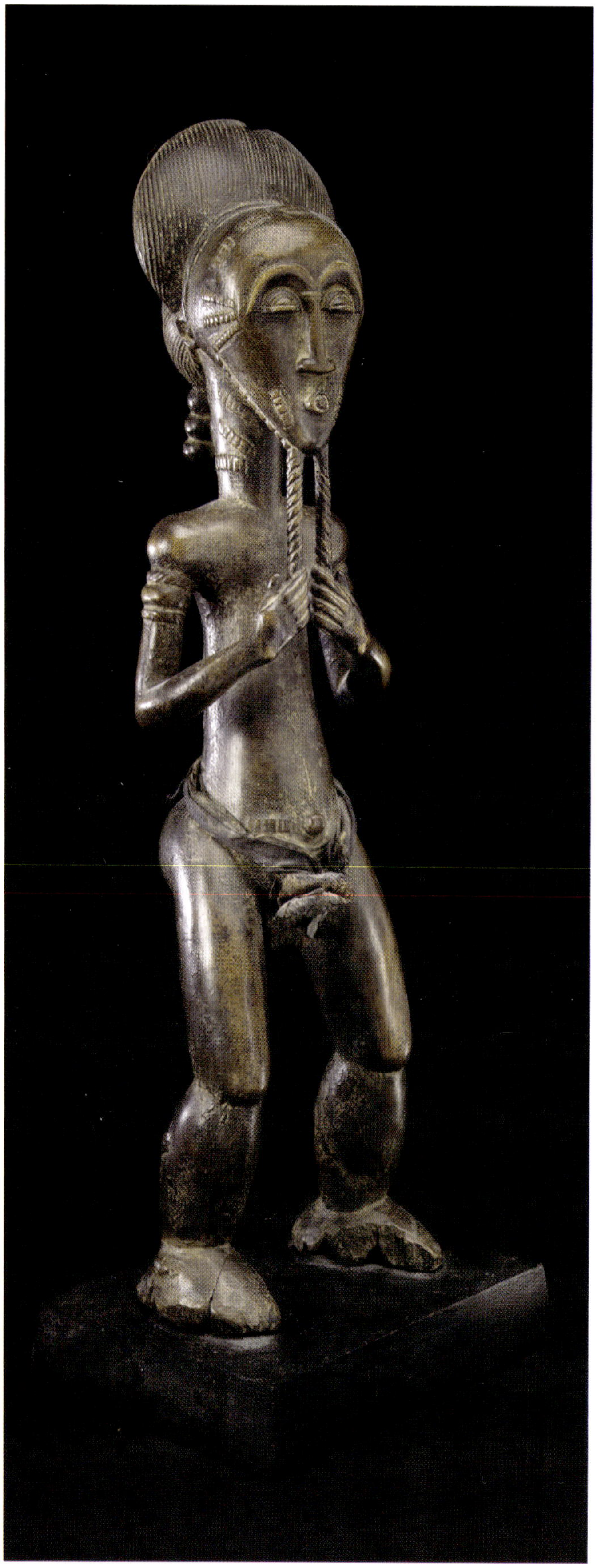

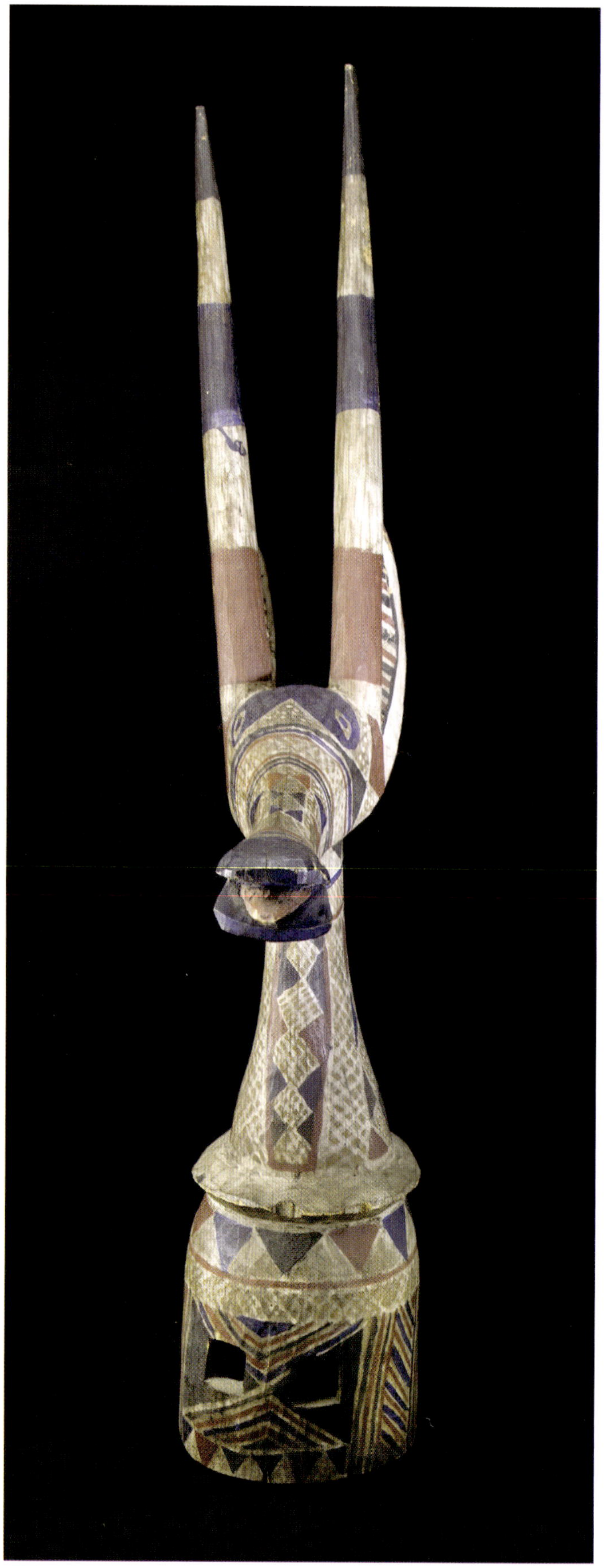

Artist unknown, *Baule Chief Figure* (Ivory Coast), nineteenth century. Wood. *Photo: Leslie Jean Bart*

Artist unknown, *Karenga Bobo Helmet* (Burkina Faso) mid-nineteenth century. Wood and earth pigments. *Photo: Leslie Jean Bart*

Opposite: Artist unknown, *Songye Healing Protective Figure-Fetish Figure* (Congo), late eighteenth century. Wood. *Photo: Leslie Jean Bart*

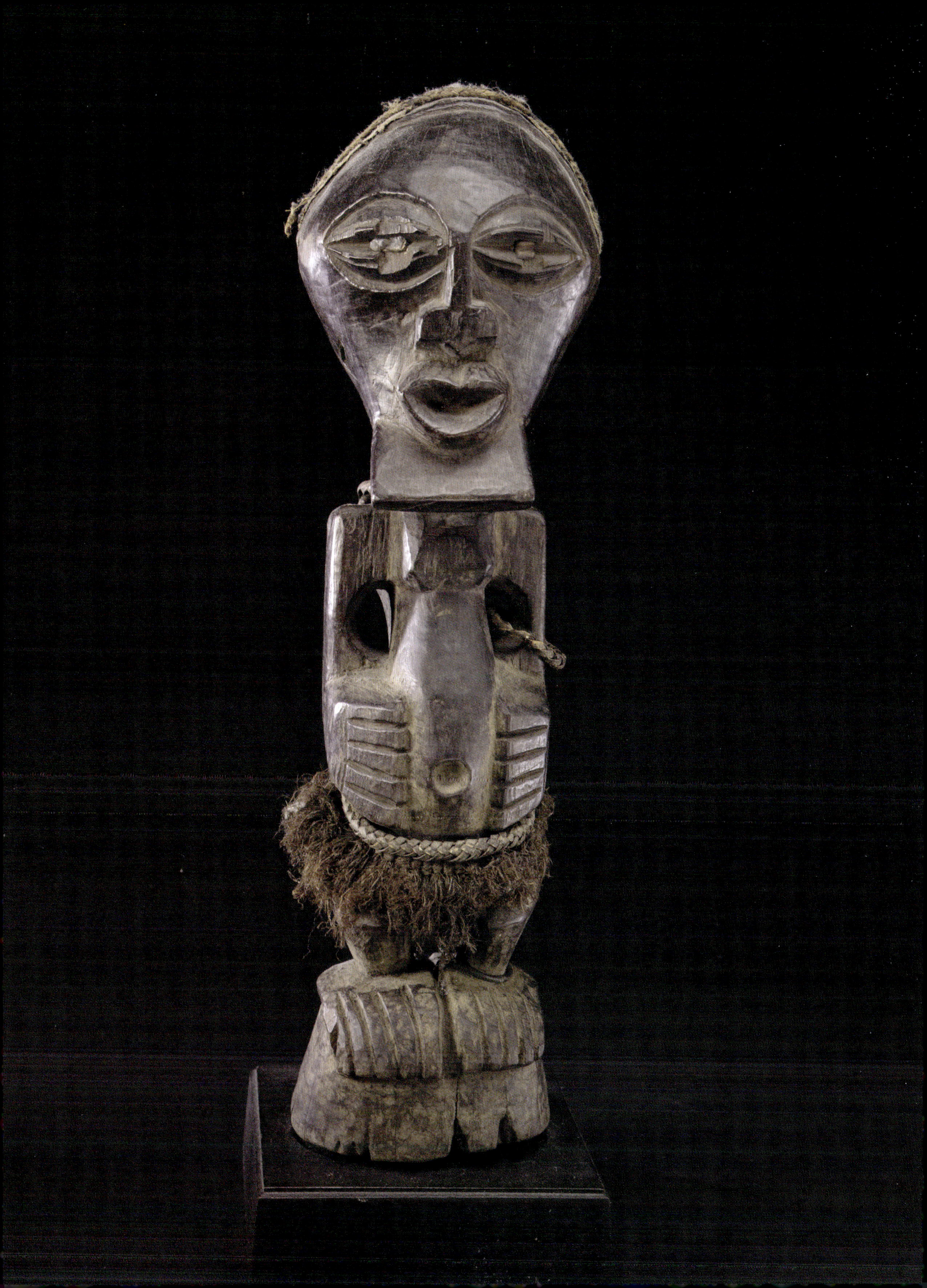

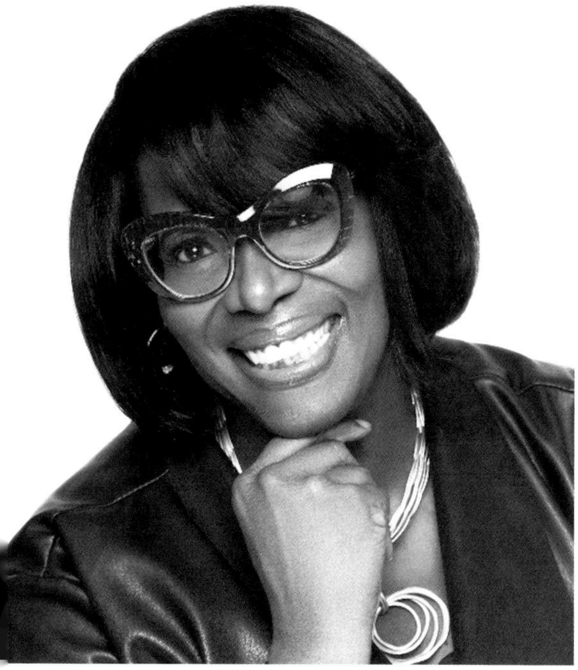

Photo: Tyquane Bates

SAUNDRA ALEXIS HEATH

VISIONARY ART

DR. MYRAH: What was the first piece of art that you collected and when?

SAUNDRA ALEXIS HEATH: The first piece of art that I collected was a metal print of vintage advertising featuring a Black man. This was in the early eighties.

DR. MYRAH: Why are you a Keeper of Visionary Art?

SAUNDRA ALEXIS HEATH: I am a keeper of Visionary Art because of its unfettered beauty and truth. I am drawn to it over and over again. I find visionary artists to be some of the most intriguing. I admire their commitment to their work and their art practice, which often exists off the radar of the traditional gallery system and art market. I resonate with their otherness and their confidence in their particular style of expression. Their work carries an authenticity that does not seek approval from external systems of validation. There is a purity in the art, even when the pieces are very complex, layered, or simple but not easily discerned. I've met visionary artists who describe themselves as teachers and messengers, channeling spirit through their art. This intuitive process, in which the artist allows the work to unfold organically, unmediated by convention, destination, or expectation, creates a rawness that I deeply appreciate and a message that I'm always curious to explore. This work excites me, and I believe it should be shown, celebrated, and collected. Given the commitment to erasure and revision in our current political climate, I believe visionary art presents a compelling opportunity.

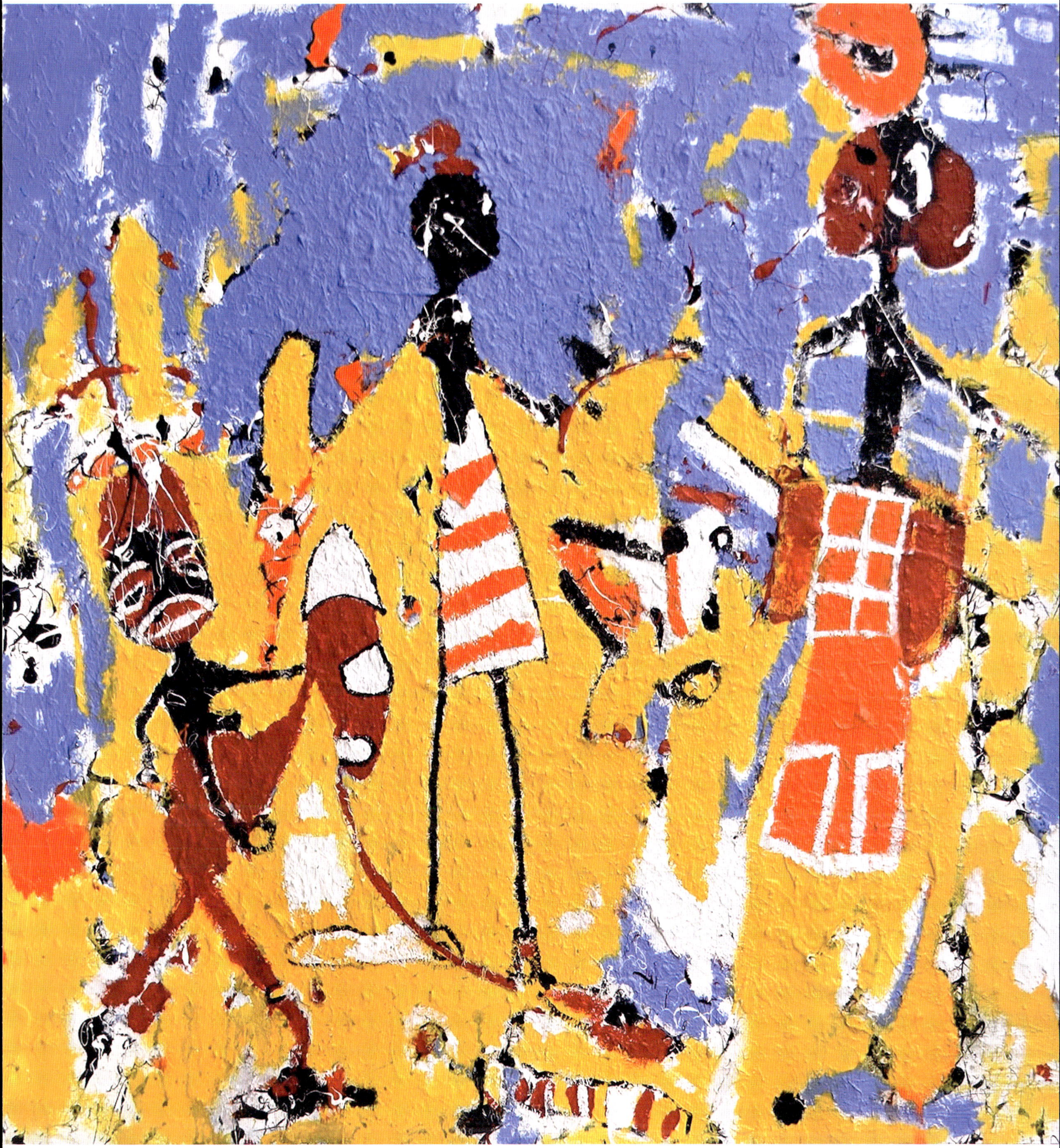

Thomas E. Heath, *The Red Giraffe*, 2020. Acrylic on wood, 48" × 48". *Photo: Saundra Alexis Heath*

Thomas E. Heath, *Earth and Gold*, 2005. Acrylic on wood, 40" × 40". *Photo: Saundra Alexis Heath*

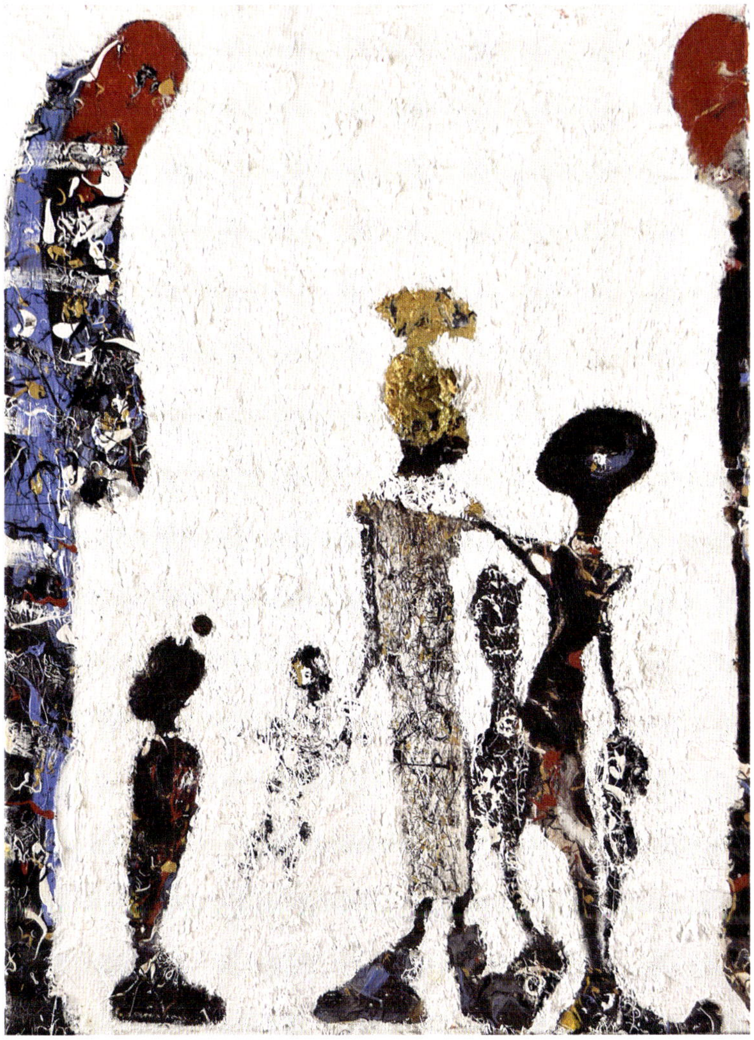

Thomas E. Heath, *First Village*, 2014. Acrylic on canvas, 31" × 25". *Photo: Saundra Alexis Heath*

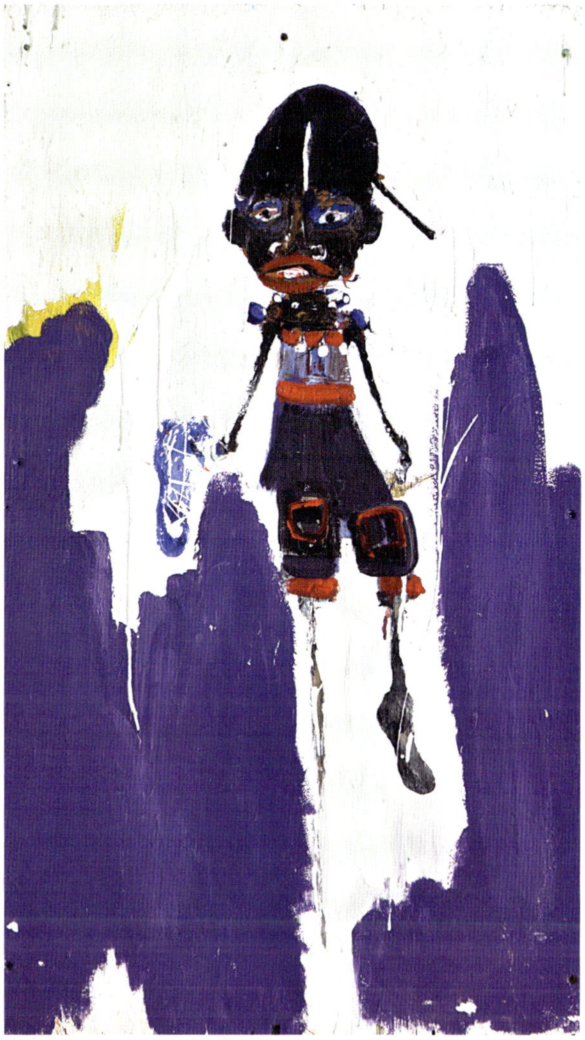

Thomas E. Heath. *Blue Sneaker*, [year]. Acrylic on wood, 20" × 34". *Photo: Saundra Alexis Heath*

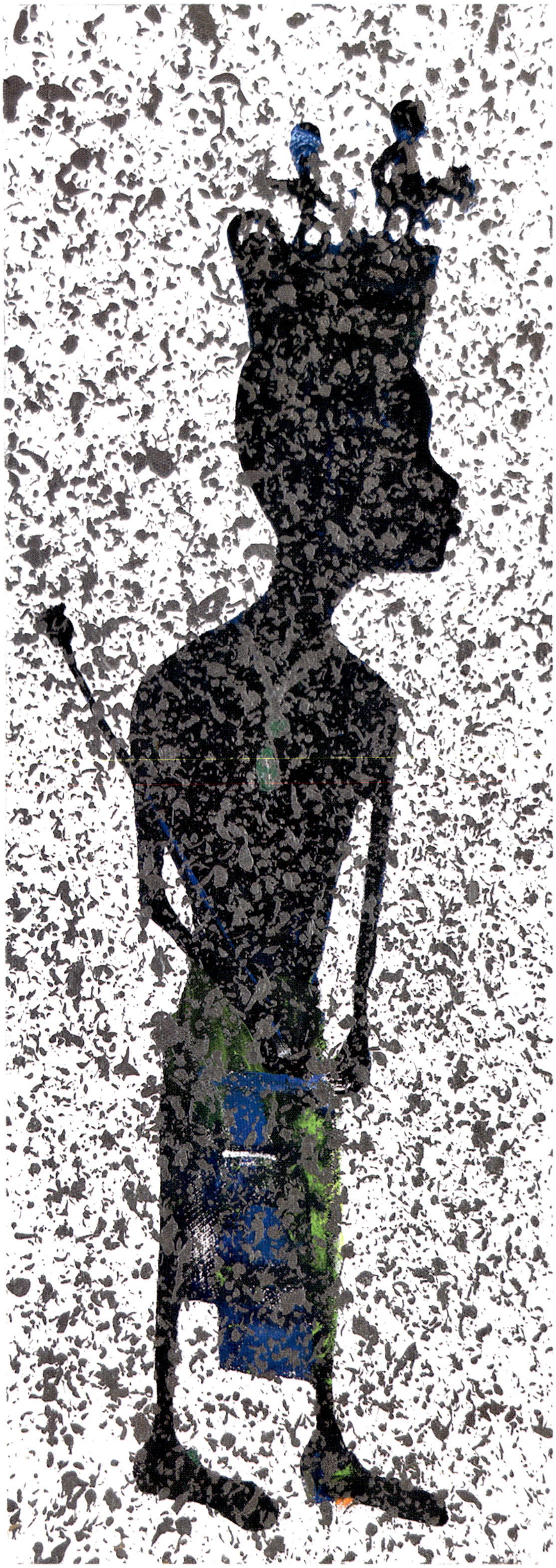

Left: Thomas E. Heath, *The Bishop's Son*, 2003. Acrylic on panel, 47" × 17". *Photo: Saundra Alexis Heath*

Thomas E. Heath, *Family Inclusion*, 2021. Acrylic on wood, 40" × 40". *Photo: Saundra Alexis Heath*

Thomas E. Heath, *The Chosen One*, 2017. Acrylic on wood, 24" × 24". *Photo: Saundra Alexis Heath*

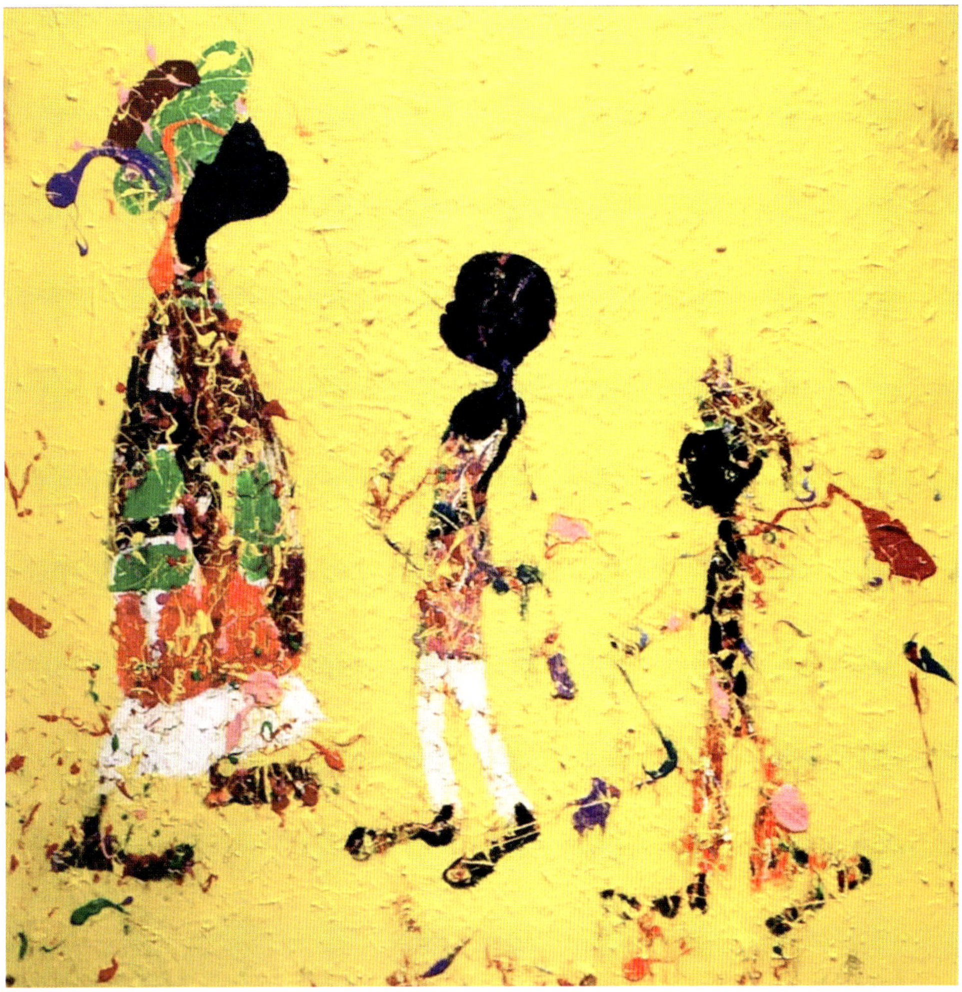

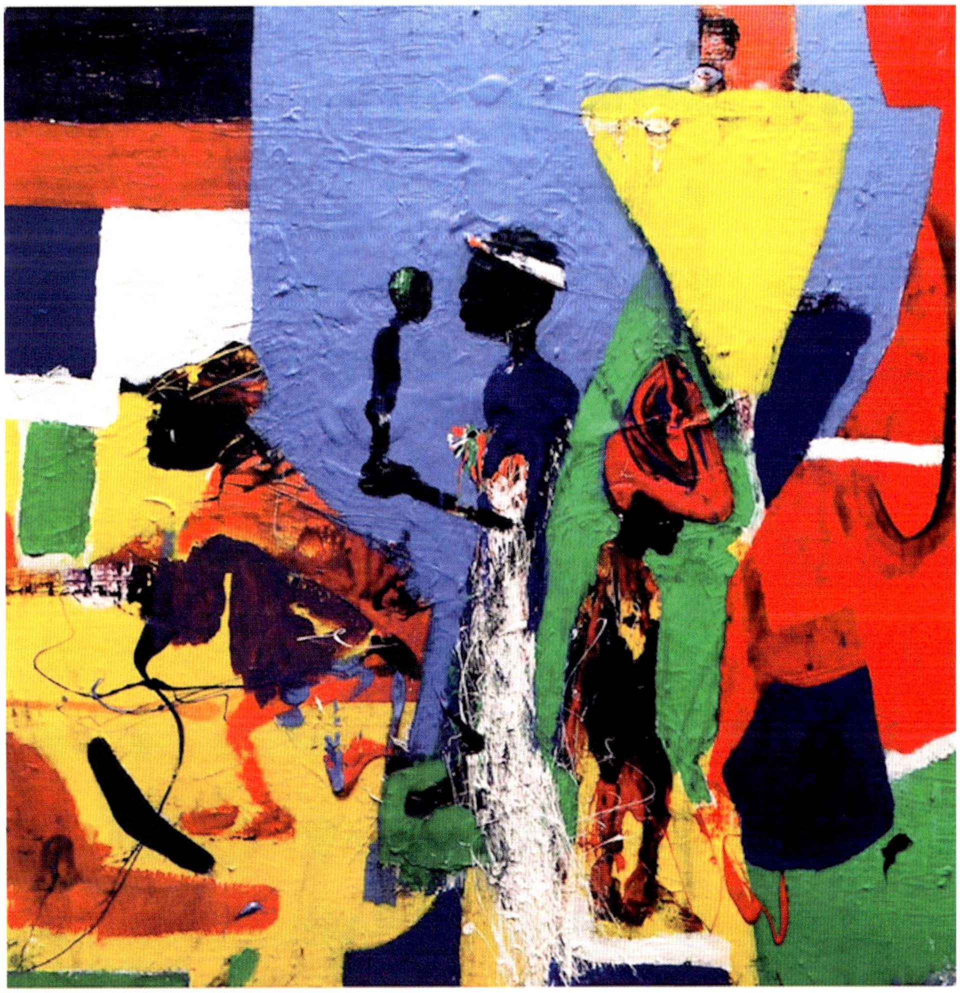

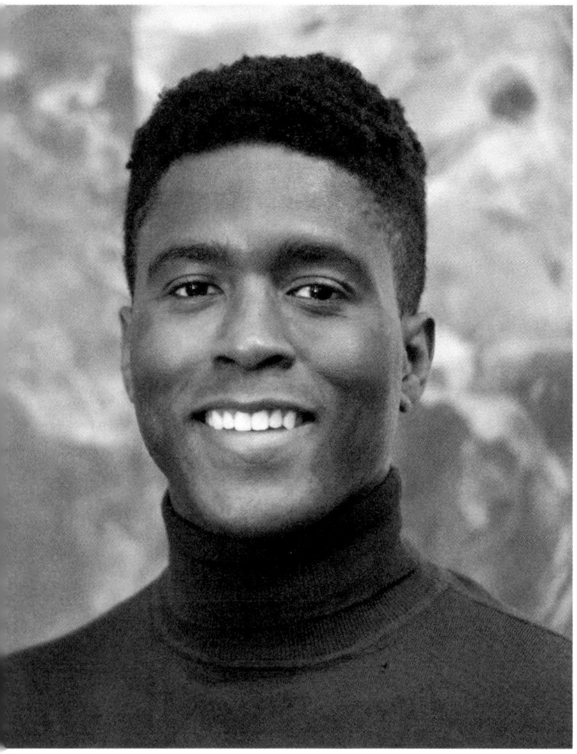

Photo: Kameron Hutchinson

TRAVIS HUTCHINSON
SCULPTURE

DR. MYRAH: What was the first piece of art that you collected and when?

TRAVIS HUTCHINSON: The first piece of art I collected was *The Fighter* by David Catlett Mora. I discovered it at Dorsey's Art Gallery and was immediately drawn to it. The piece captures the intensity of the fighter's approach to life, yet it is imbued with a cool color palette—a quiet reminder to always stay composed under pressure. It was a powerful moment that resonated deeply with me, setting the stage for my journey as a collector.

DR. MYRAH: Why are you a Keeper of Sculpture and other images?

TRAVIS HUTCHINSON: As a child I was surrounded by art. I always had pieces in my room, including a Charles White print that hung over my bed. I remember one day breaking the glass on that cherished piece. My mom was understandably upset, but when I proudly declared that I knew it was a Charles White print, she chose not to discipline me. That moment planted a seed of appreciation and reverence for art that would stay with me forever.

In a world consumed by excess and relentless consumption, I find solace in curating and cherishing a few truly beautiful things. My collection, whether sculpture or paintings, reflects this intentionality. The sculptures we collect, for instance, embody both form and function, much like beautiful architecture—marrying practicality with elegance and artistry.

Being a keeper of sculpture and other images is also a way of preserving stories and perspectives. Years later, when applying to Yale, I wrote my admission essay about Jacob Lawrence's *Confrontation at the Bridge*, highlighting how art has shaped my perspective and understanding of the world. Art has always been more than an object to me—it's a dialogue, a connection, and a mirror of identity. Through my collection, I celebrate craftsmanship and ensure these narratives endure, creating a legacy of beauty and meaning for generations to come.

Oniway Millar, *Little Scholar of Mali*, 1980. Rock sculpture.
Photo: Kameron Hutchinson

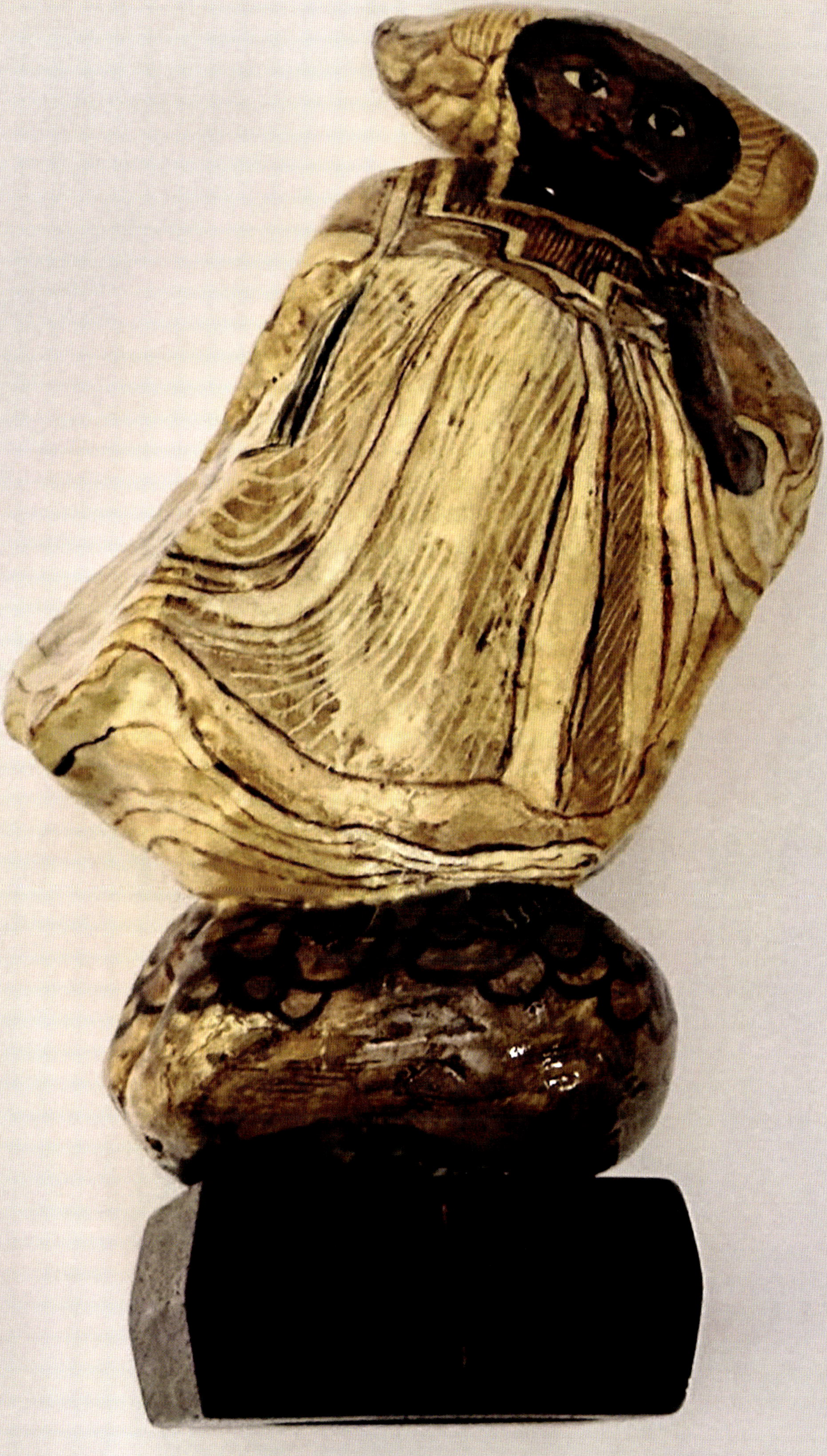

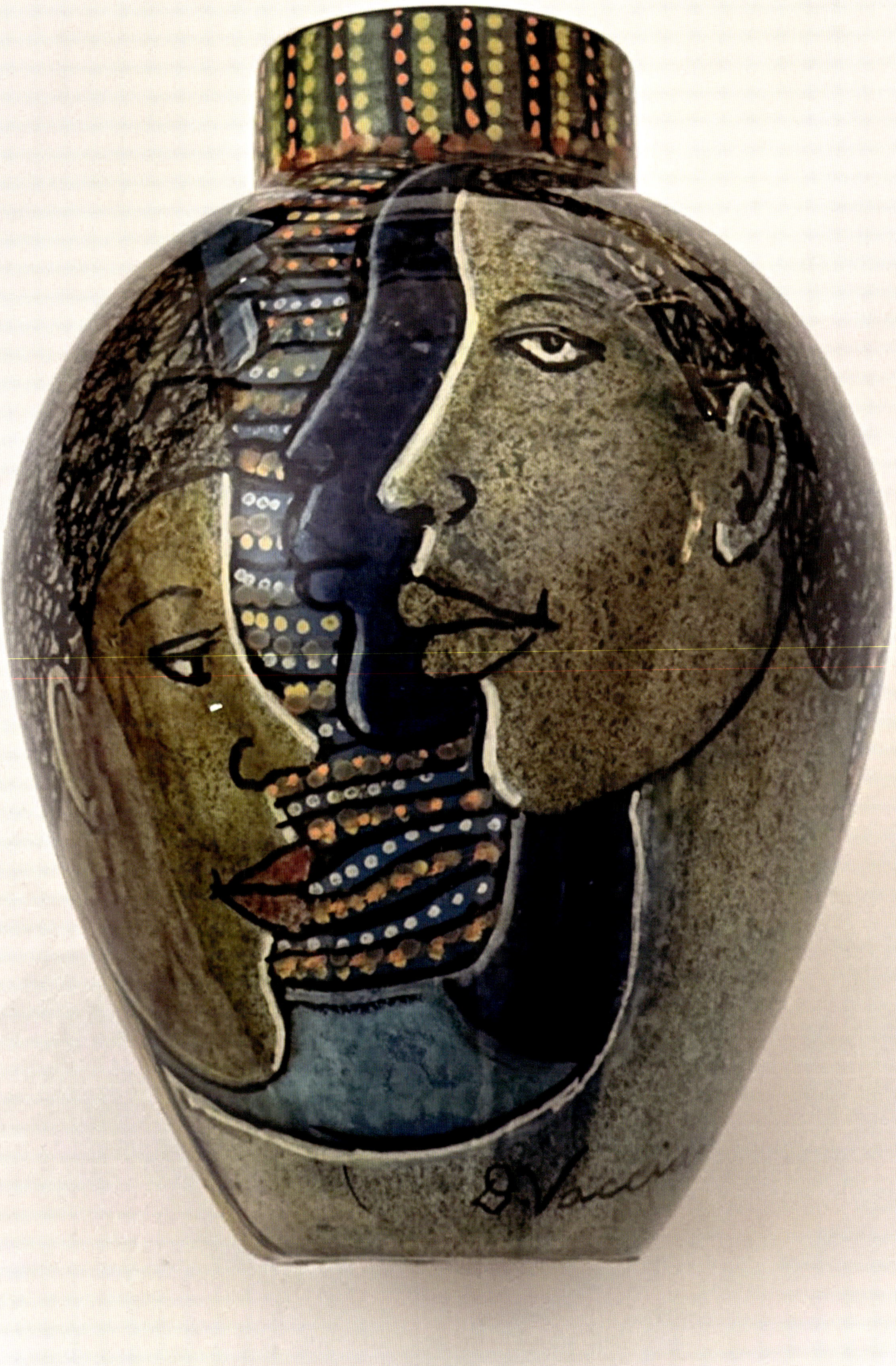

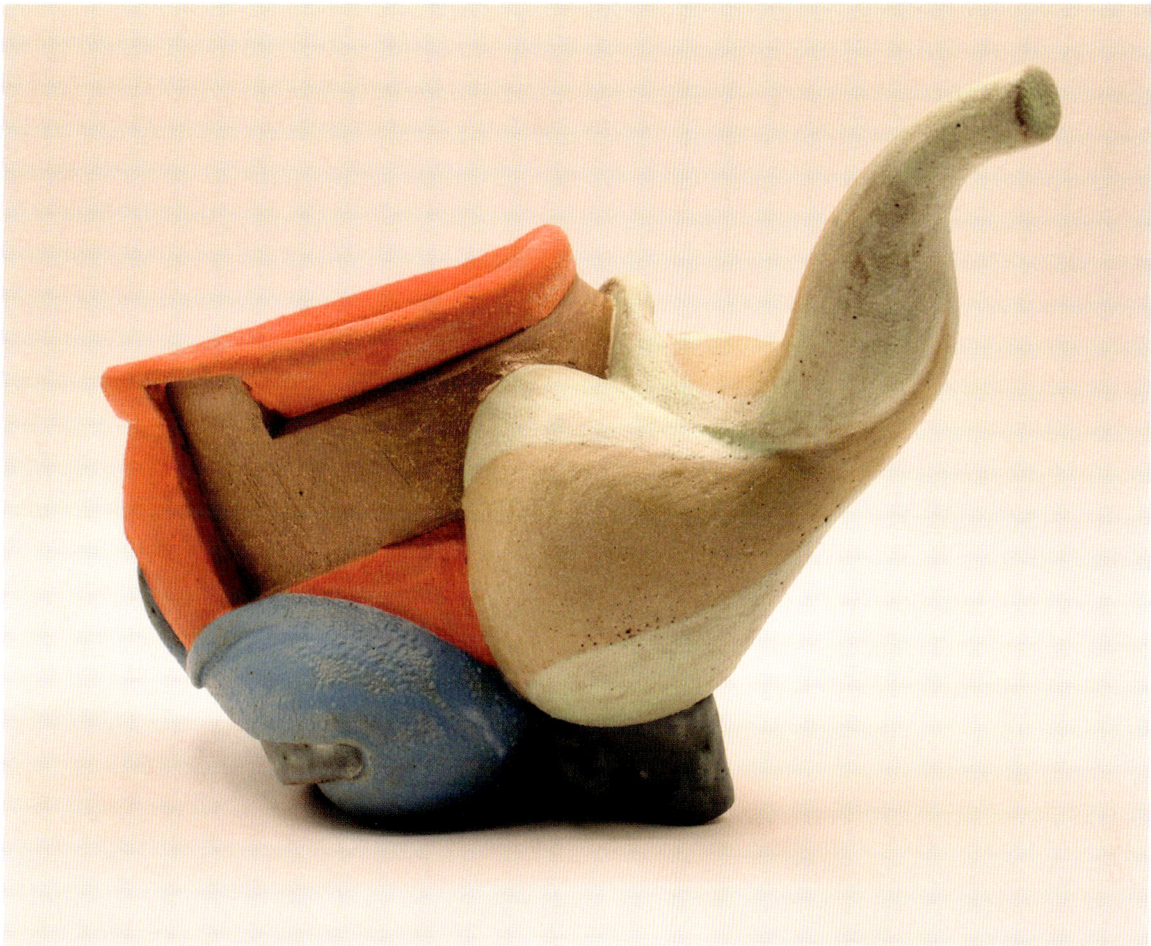

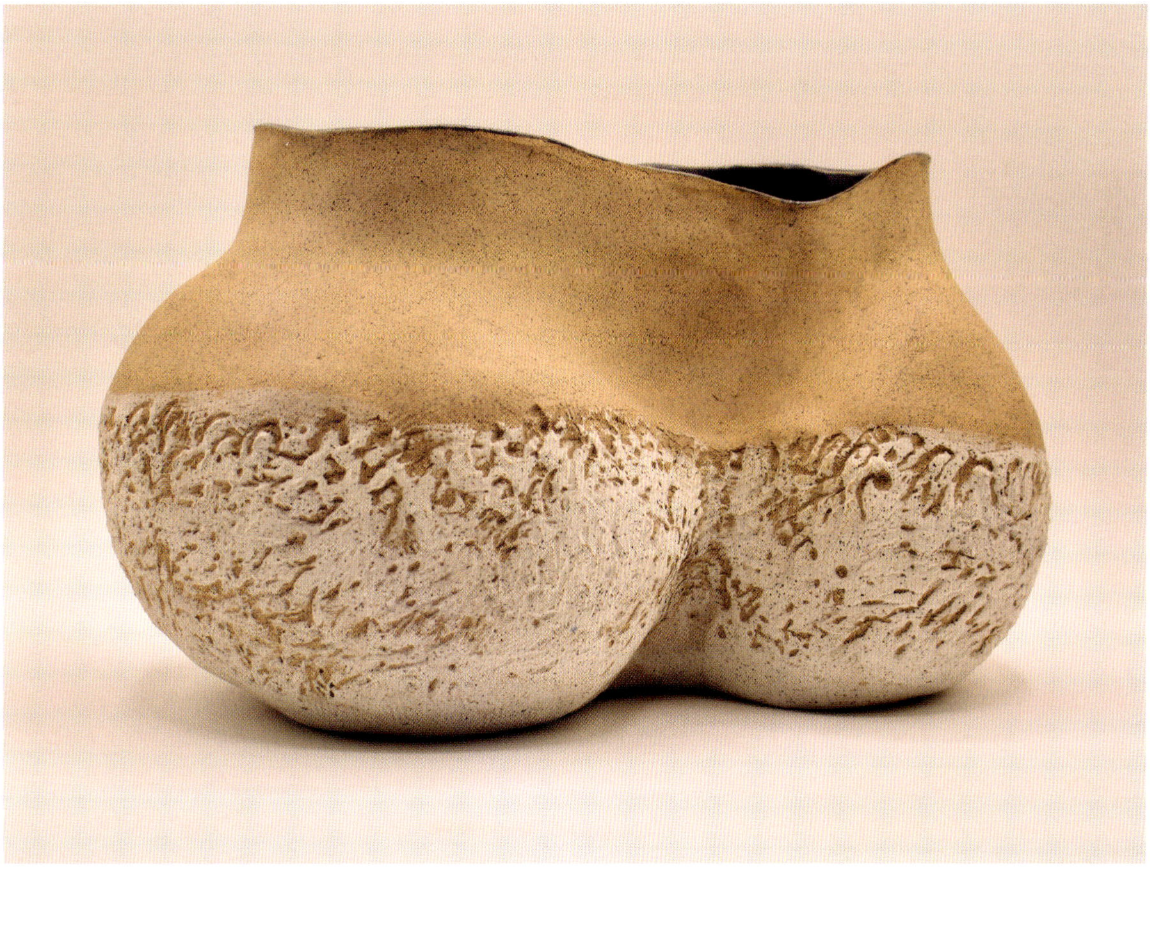

Opposite: Dudley Vaccianna, *Untitled*, 2000. Glass, 13" × 6". *Photo: Kameron Hutchinson*

Malcolm Mobuto Smith, *Scoop*, 2020. Stoneware thrown and altered, 5" × 11.5". *Photo: Myrah Brown Green*

Helen Ramsaram, *Untitled*, 2011. Stoneware. *Photo: Myrah Brown Green*

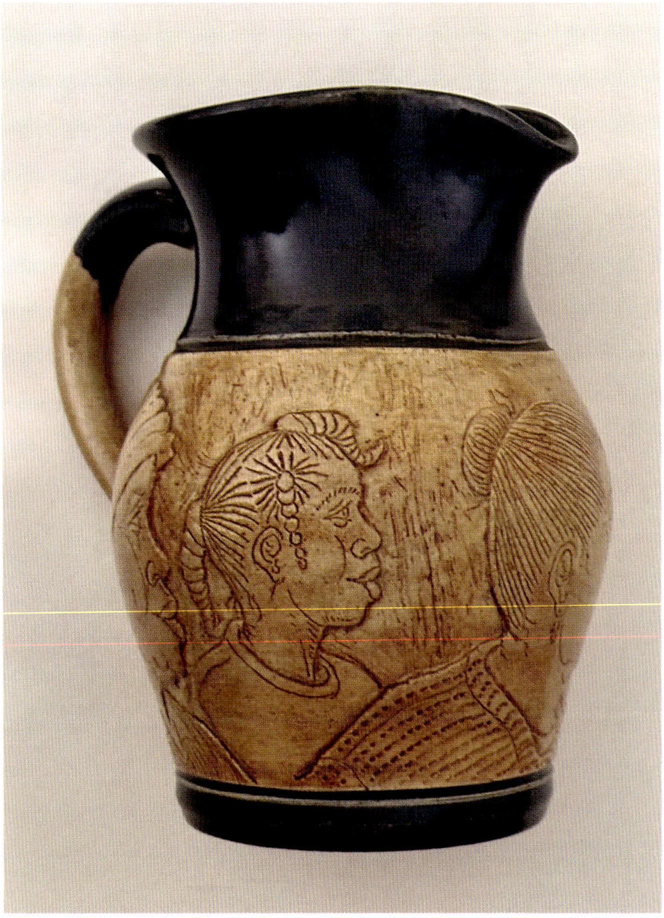

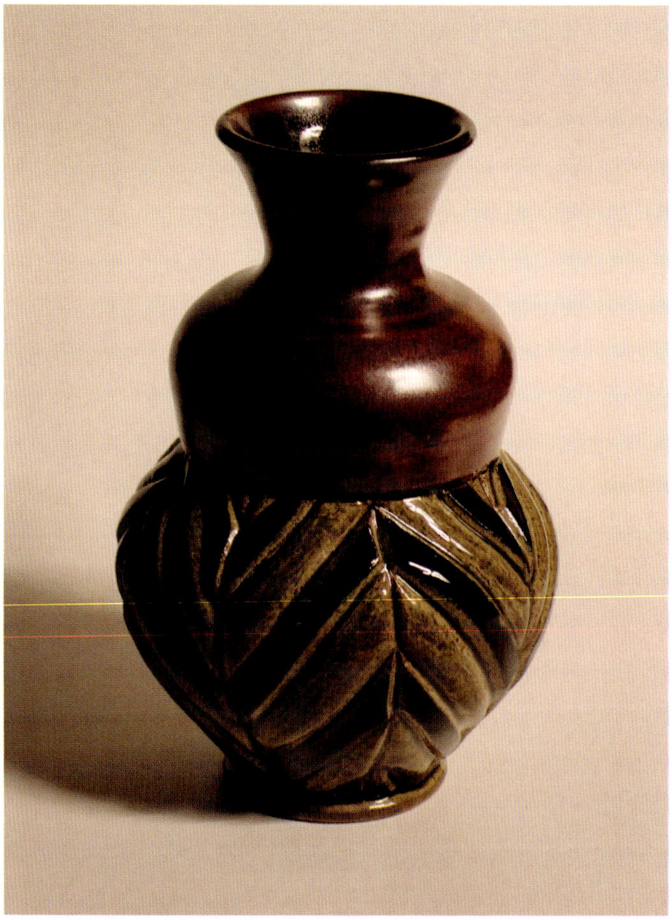

Winston and Rosa Eugéne, *Untitled*, 1997. Stoneware, 8" × 8". *Photo: Myrah Brown Green*

David R. MacDonald, *Vase*, 2017. Stoneware, 9" × 7". *Photo: Myrah Brown Green*

Opposite: Roberto Lugo, *Water Tower*, 2024. Mixed media, 7.5" × 6". *Photo: Myrah Brown Green*

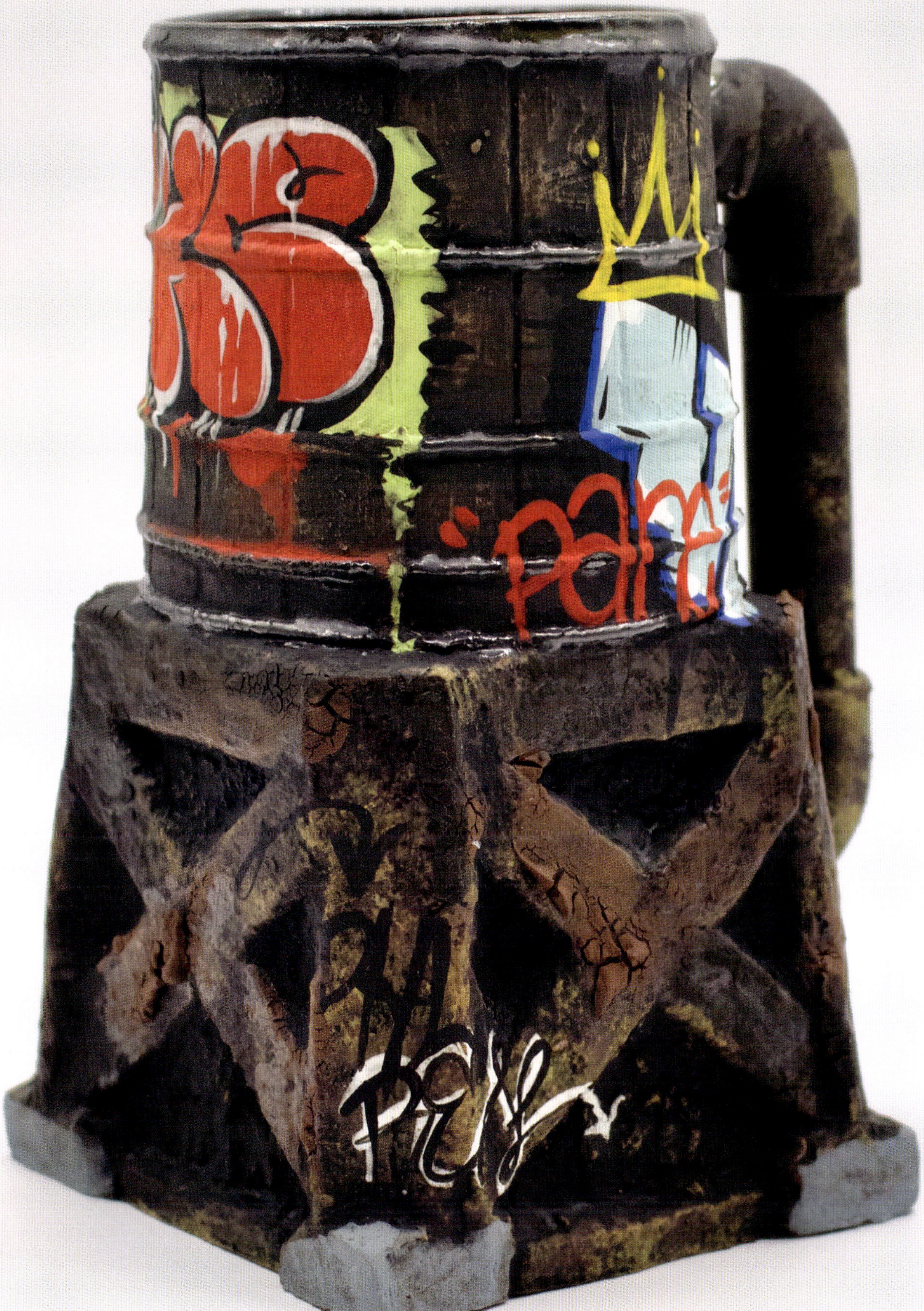

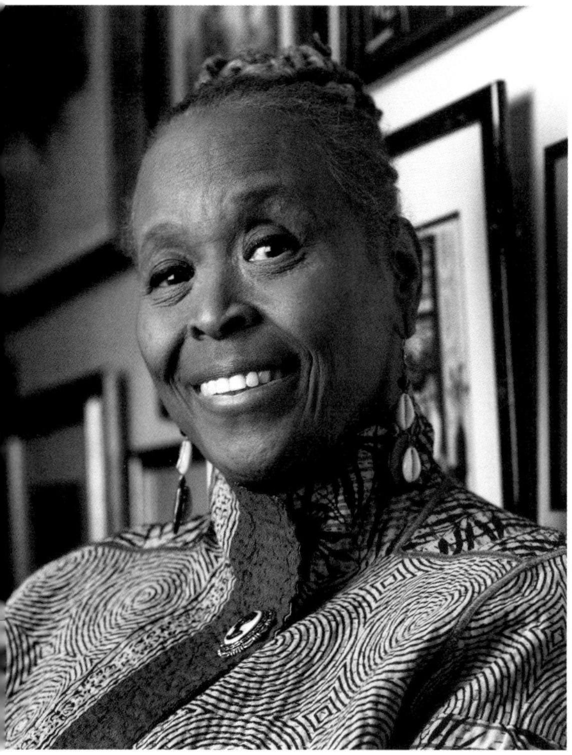

Photo: Michael Young

SHELLEY INNIS
WEUSI ARTIST COLLECTIVE

DR. MYRAH: What was the first piece of art you collected and when?

SHELLEY INNIS: The first piece of art that I collected was more than fifty years ago, and that was in 1974. Actually I was with Ronald, my husband; we were on a date. We had just started going out together around that time. He took me down to the Village and said, "I want to take you to this house because these women have all of this African art." We went to the house, and believe me, they had tons of African art in there. I picked up a batik that was purple and black with an African theme of people in the community doing chores. I still have it.

DR. MYRAH: Why are you a Keeper of works by the Weusi Artist Collective?

SHELLEY INNIS: Because those brothers and sisters were very important to the Black Arts Movement. They came together during the Black Arts Movement. Actually they were probably, I believe, one of the initial carriers of the Black Arts Movement in Harlem, which ultimately gained creative momentum; then the movement moved clear across the country, pollinating with other Black art organizations. Many of the brothers were members of the 20th Century Artists group, then they broke away from that organization and started the Weusi Art Collective. My husband, Ronald "Okoe" Pyatt, was the archivist for the organization. In fact, his papers, from as early as the sixties, documenting the activities of the group, were acquired by the Driskell Center Archives. The collection is called the *Oko Pyatt and Shelley Innis Archive of the Weusi Collective*. Art is very important to me. Besides being beautiful, it shows the creativity of our people. Many of the Weusi artists, including my husband, are self-taught. Especially Otto. Otto is an artist that does everything. There's nothing he can't do.

Rudy Irwin, *Untitled* (gallery sign), 1970. Oil on terry cloth, 36" × 23". *Photo: Myrah Brown Green*

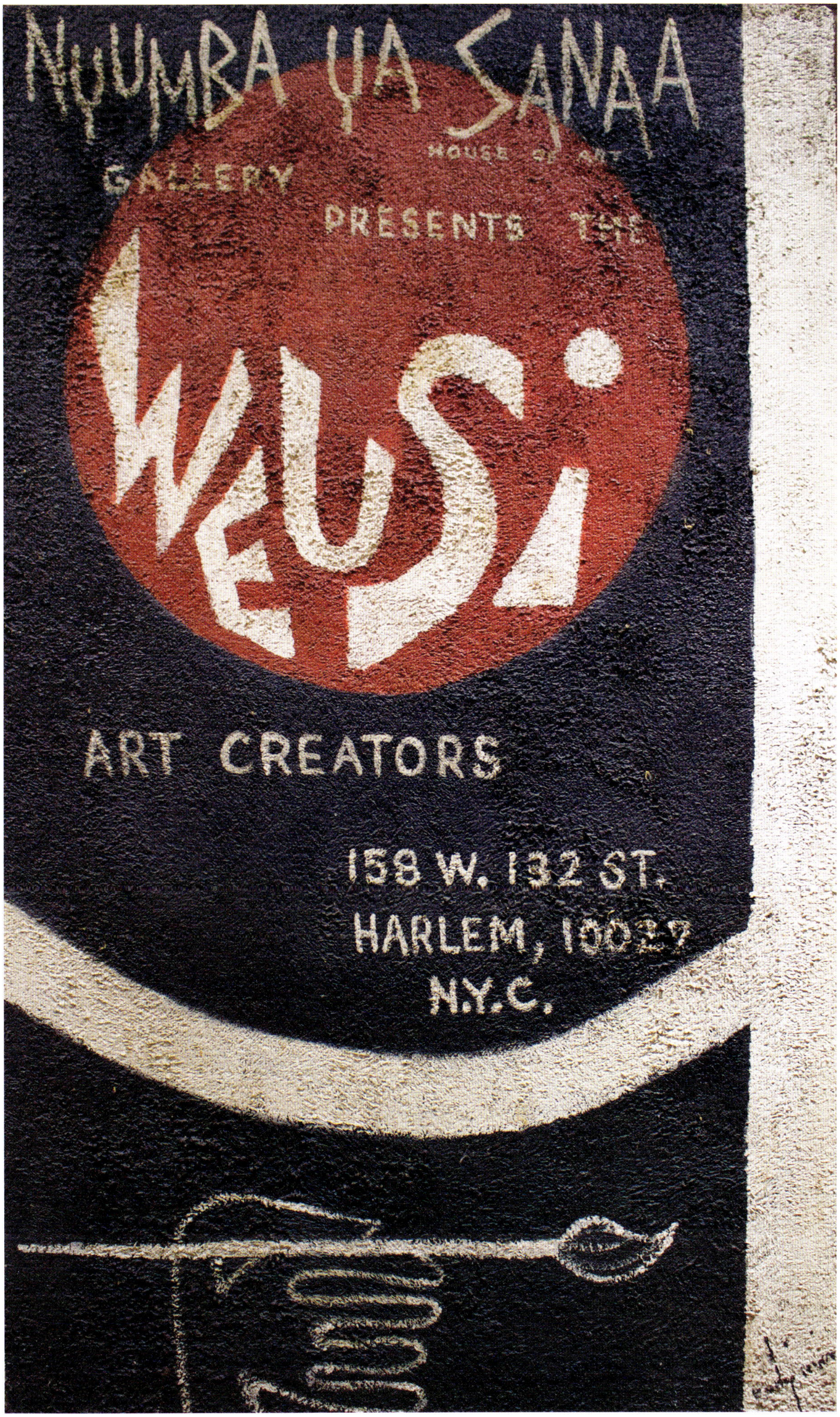
NYUMBA YA SANAA
HOUSE OF ART
GALLERY
PRESENTS THE
WEUSI
ART CREATORS
158 W. 132 ST.
HARLEM, 10027
N.Y.C.

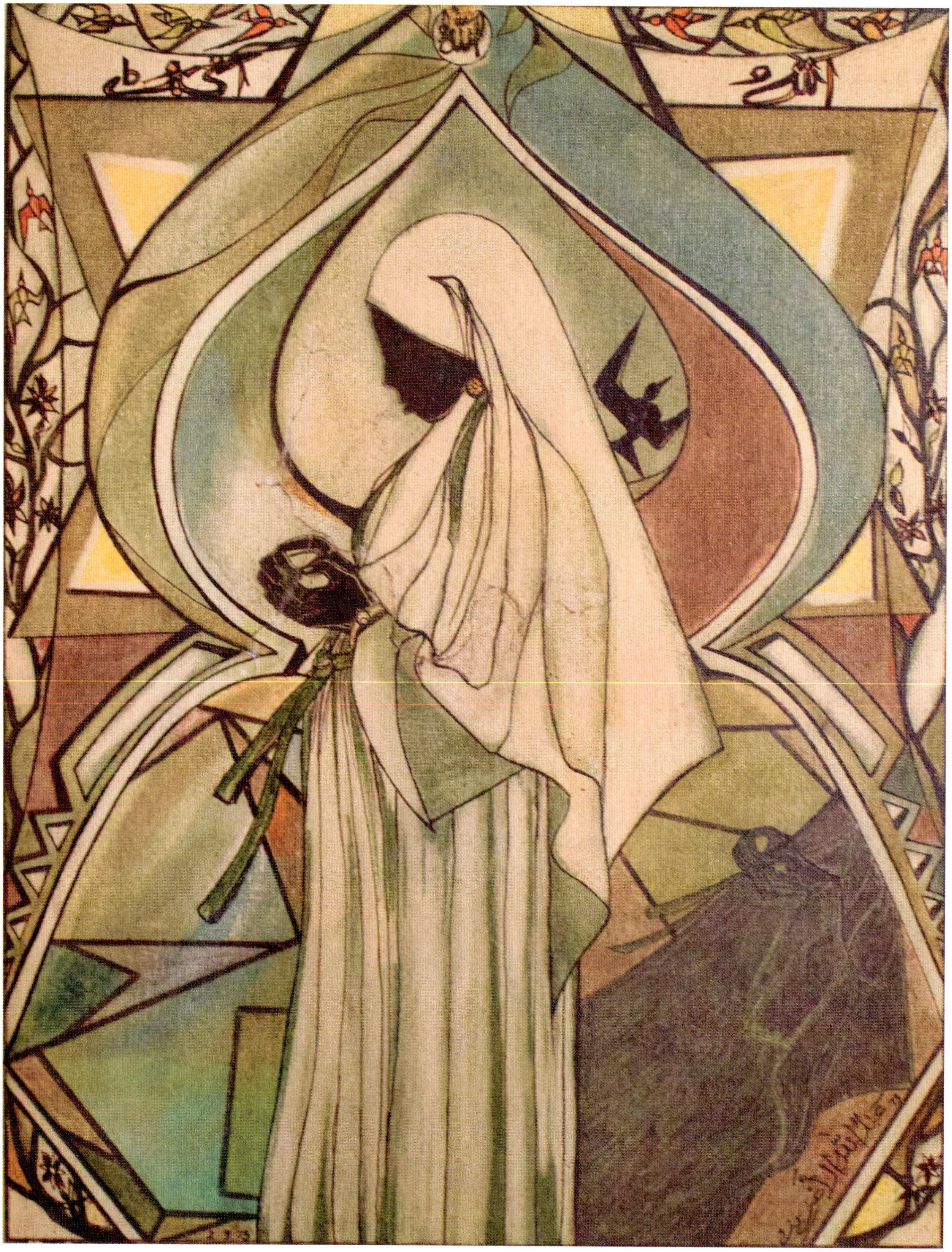

Above: Abdullah Aziz, *Mother with Child*, 1973. Oil on canvas board, 20" × 16". *Photo: Myrah Brown Green*

Kay Brown, *Sister with Braids*, 1974. Color etching and aquatint on créme woven paper, 14" × 11". *Photo: Myrah Brown Green*

Dindga McCannon, *Monet's Garden: Yellow Flowers*, 2014. Felt, 12" × 18". *Photo: Myrah Brown Green*

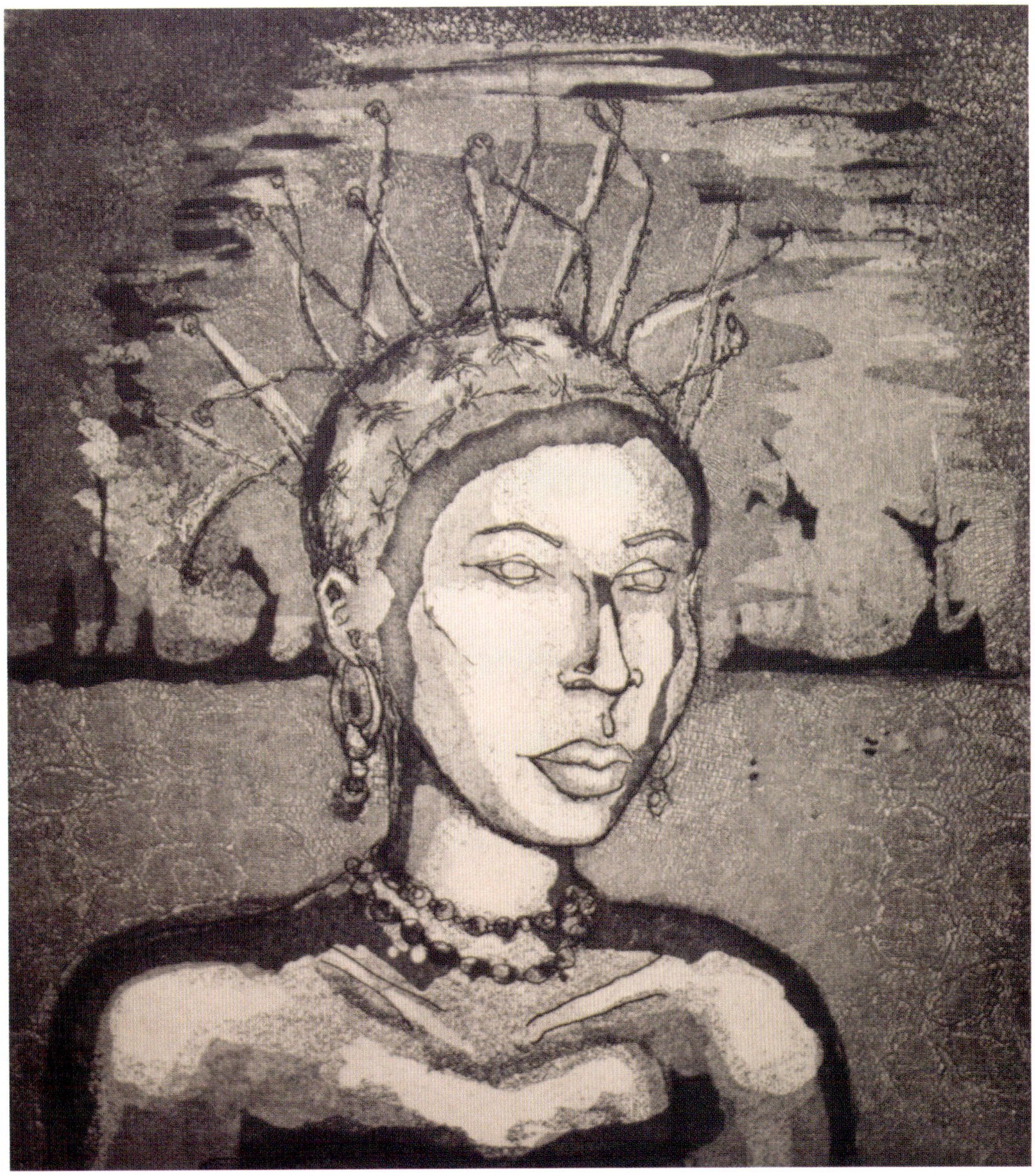

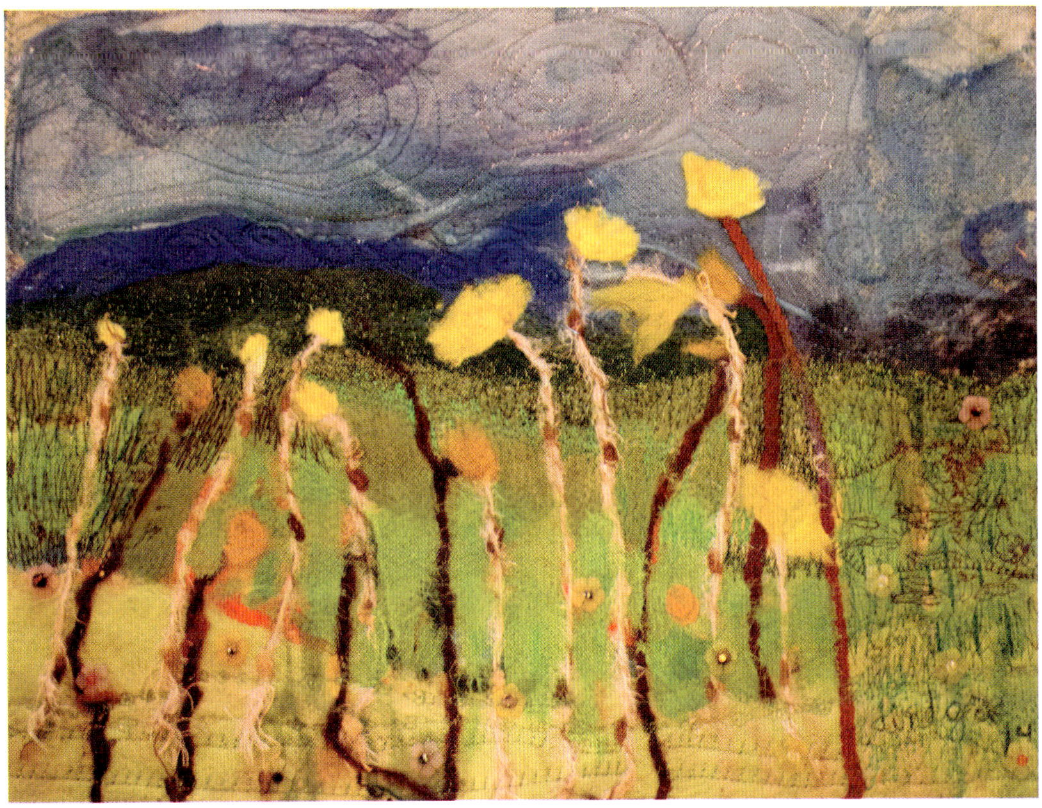

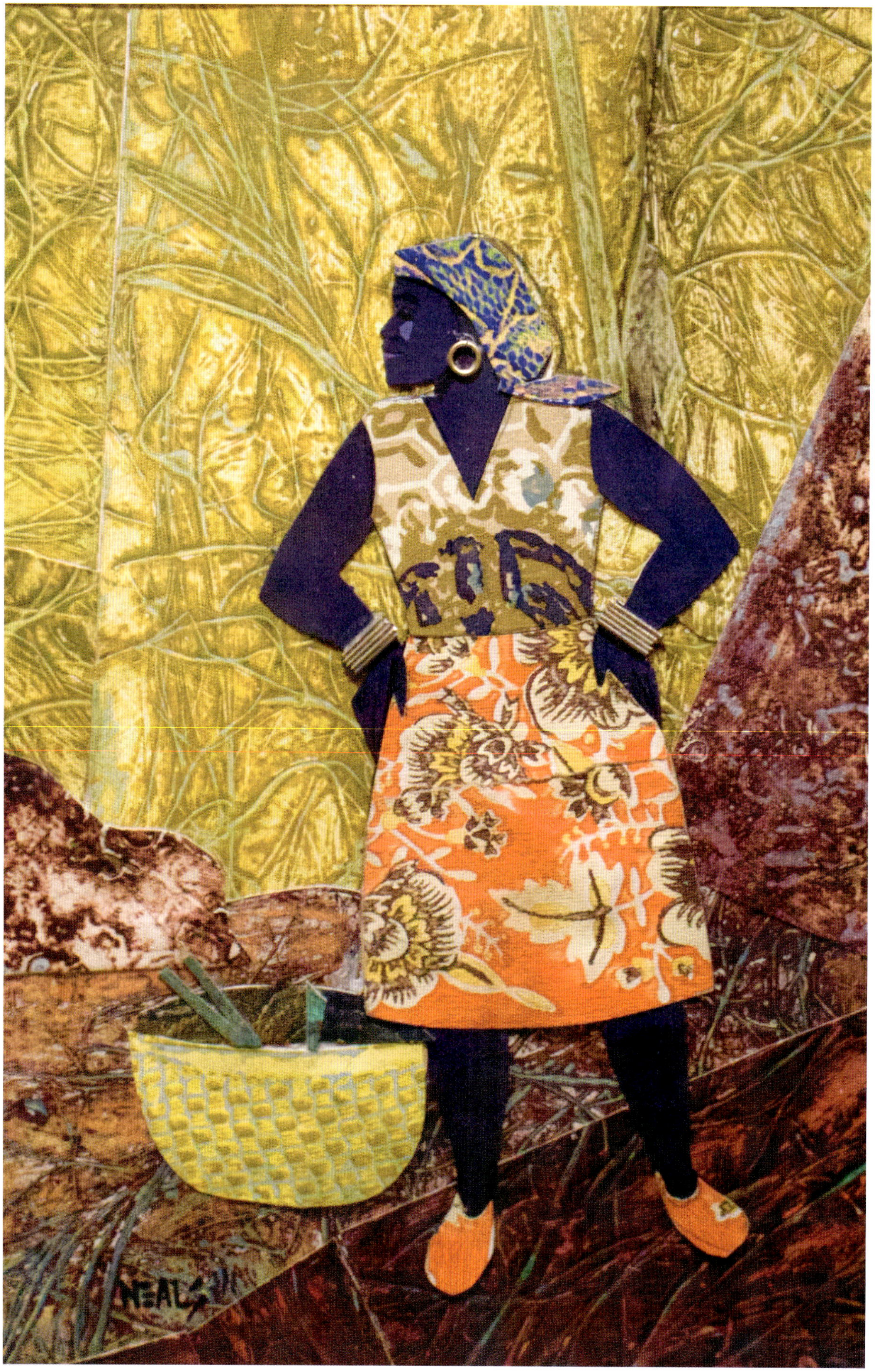

Otto Neals, *Untitled*, 2015. Collage, 13" × 9".
Photo: Myrah Brown Green

Opposite: Taiwo Yusuf Balogun (Taiwo DuVall), *Africa*, 1963.
Hand-pulled print (A/P), 15" × 12". *Photo: Myrah Brown Green*

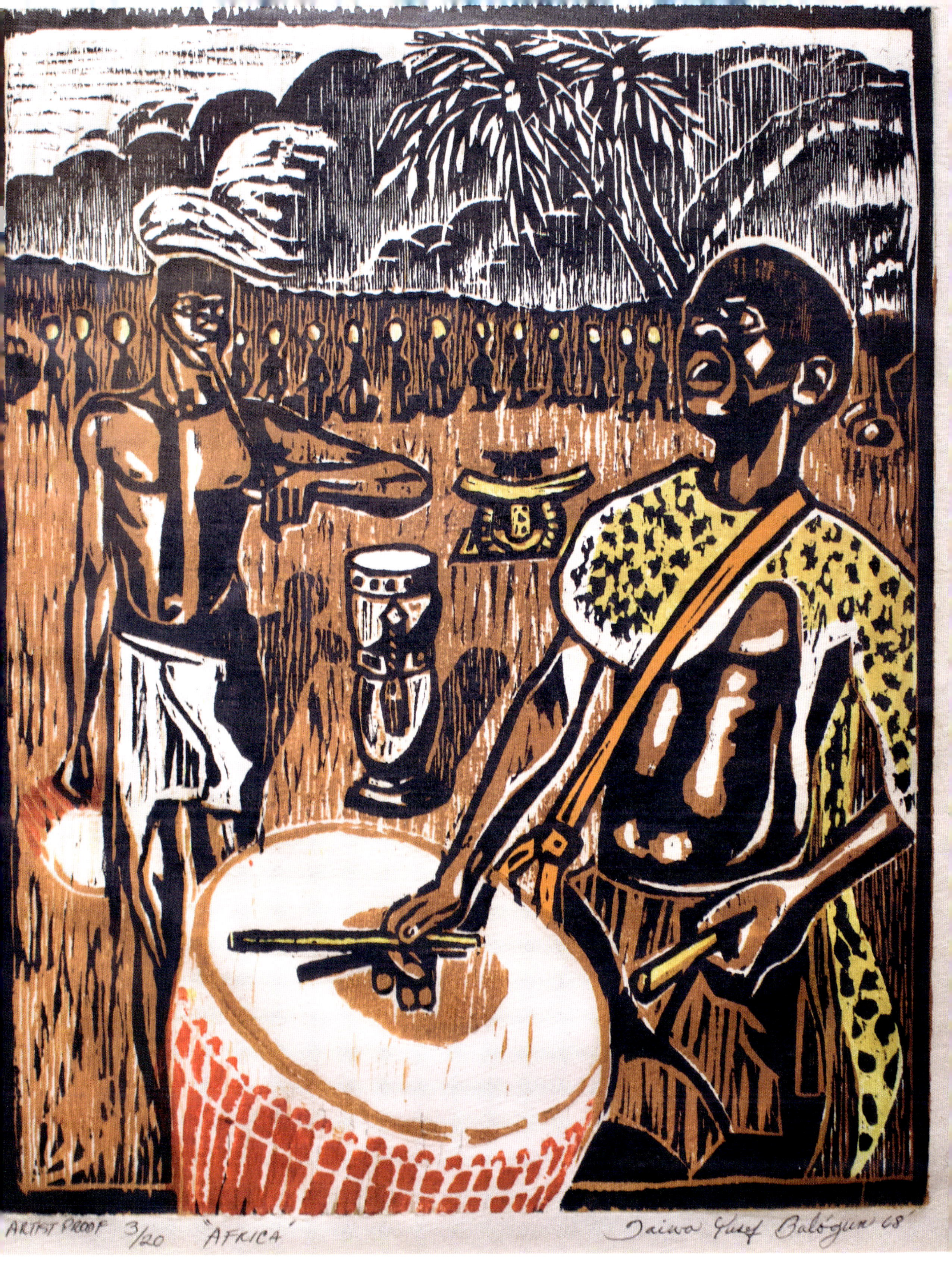
ARTIST PROOF 3/20 "AFRICA"

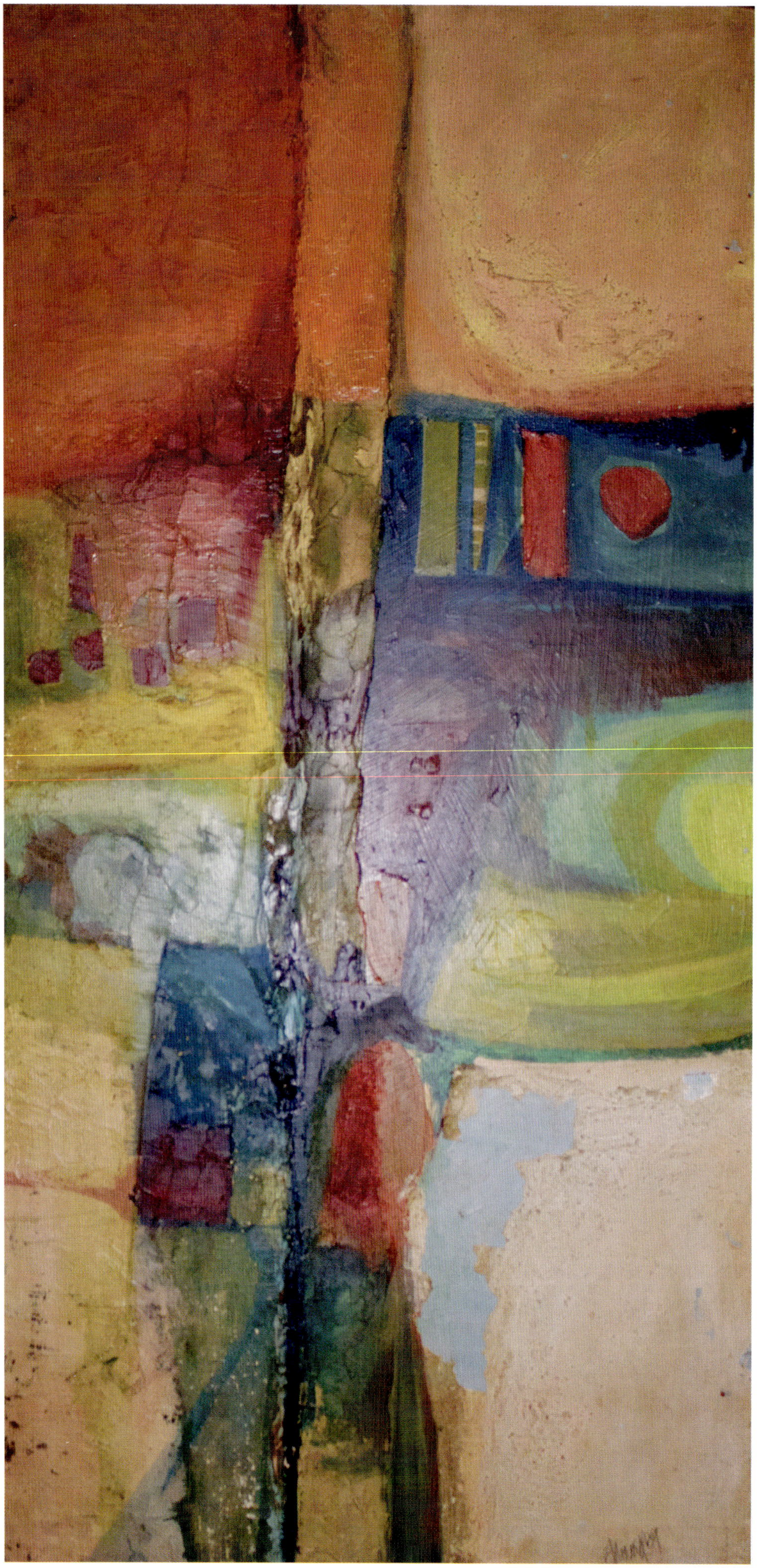

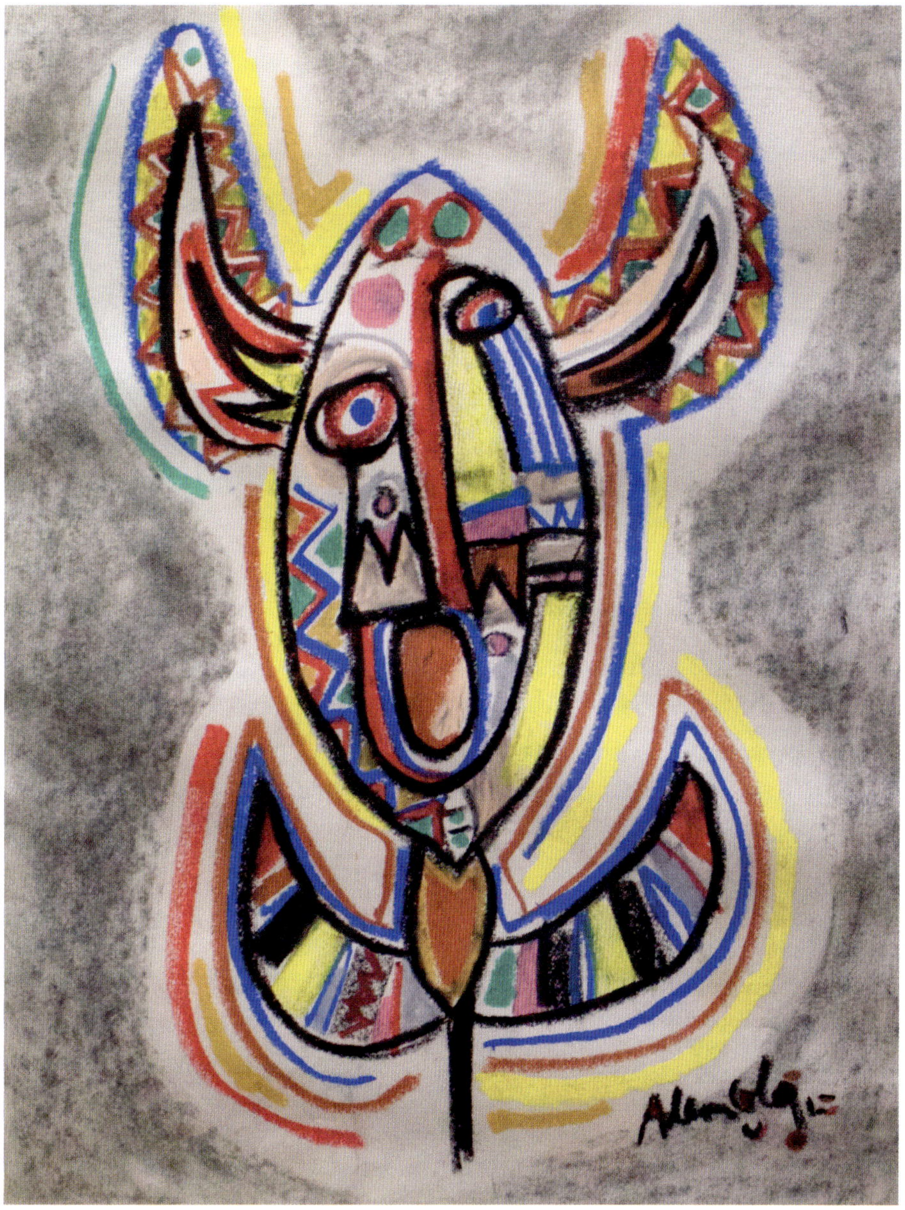

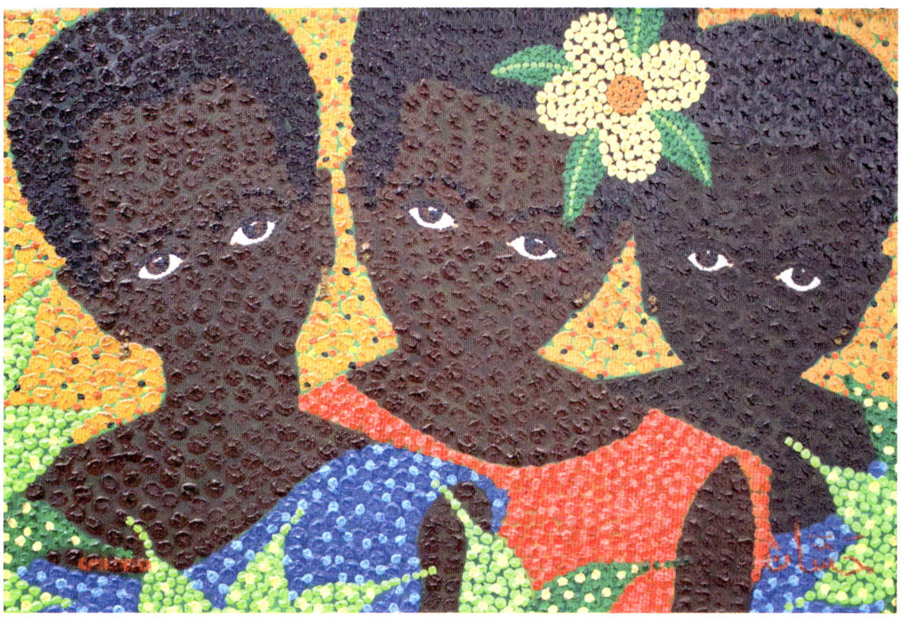

Opposite: Bill Howell, *Untitled*, 1960. Acrylic on wood, 36" × 24". *Photo: Myrah Brown Green*

Ademola Olugebefola, *Untitled*, 2015. Oil crayon on paper, 16" × 13". *Photo: Myrah Brown Green*

Gaylord Hassan, *They Shall Have Power in the Future*, 1986. Acrylic pointillism, 18" × 25". *Photo: Myrah Brown Green*

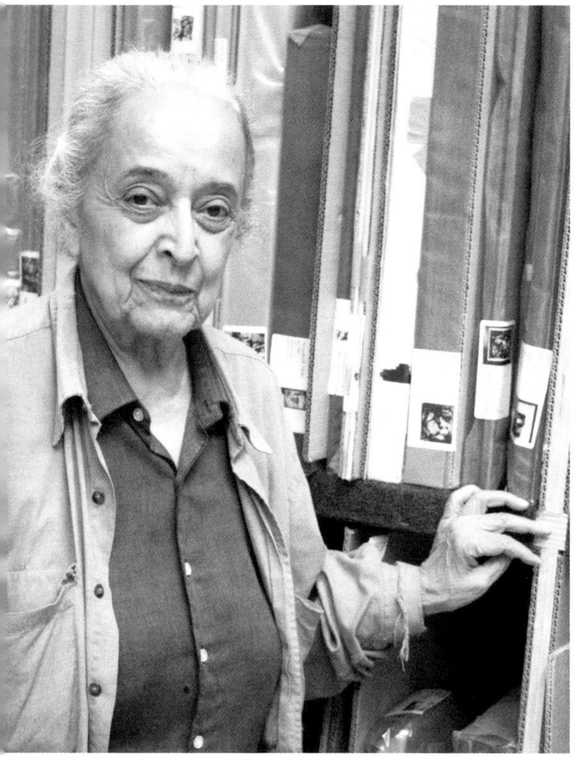

Photo: Myrah Brown Green

CORRINE JENNINGS
NINETEENTH CENTURY

DR. MYRAH: What was the first piece of art you collected and when?

CORRINE JENNINGS: In the mid-1960s I was studying in California and went to a friend's house to a party. Her parents had the Charles White drawing, *Juba*, hanging on their wall. I thought it was so beautiful. I knew some artists but did not know anything about Charles White. A while later, I was walking around exploring in Los Angeles and saw the Heritage Gallery. Immediately I went in, and Charlotte Sherman let me buy two of White's offset lithograph portfolios that he made for folks with little income. They let me pay for them over time, and that got me started as a collector. I bought the "I Have a Dream" series and the "Wanted Posters." I still have them.

DR. MYRAH: Why are you a Keeper of Nineteenth-Century Art?

CORRINE JENNINGS: I was born in Rhode Island, near where the Bannisters had lived. I read about Edward and Christiana Bannister's work as abolitionists. I knew they were friends with Frederick Douglass. I didn't understand the peaceful, pastoral scenes, seascapes, and landscapes. Then I discovered that Bannister often painted places where terrible things had happened. Then I understood his vision and determination. His works are often like signposts, narratives of deeply held histories—equivalent to the oral tradition. With these guiding ideas, I have also collected James Presley Ball, Duncanson, James Bolivar Needham, Patrick Reason, and Tanner. I have been learning history in a different way.

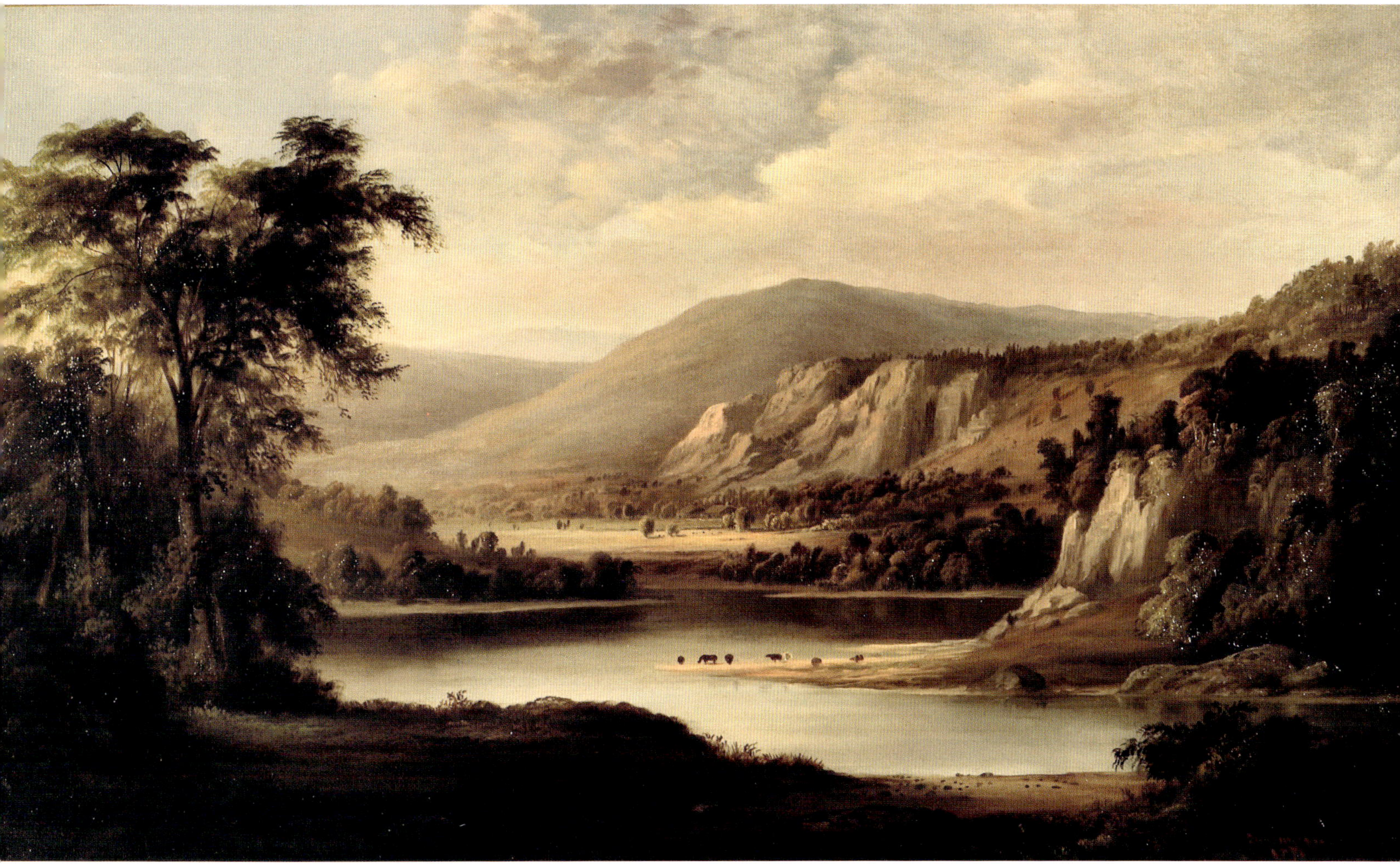

Robert Seldon Duncanson, *Untitled*, 1871. Oil on canvas, 26.5" × 39.5". *Photo: Courtesy of Kenkeleba House*

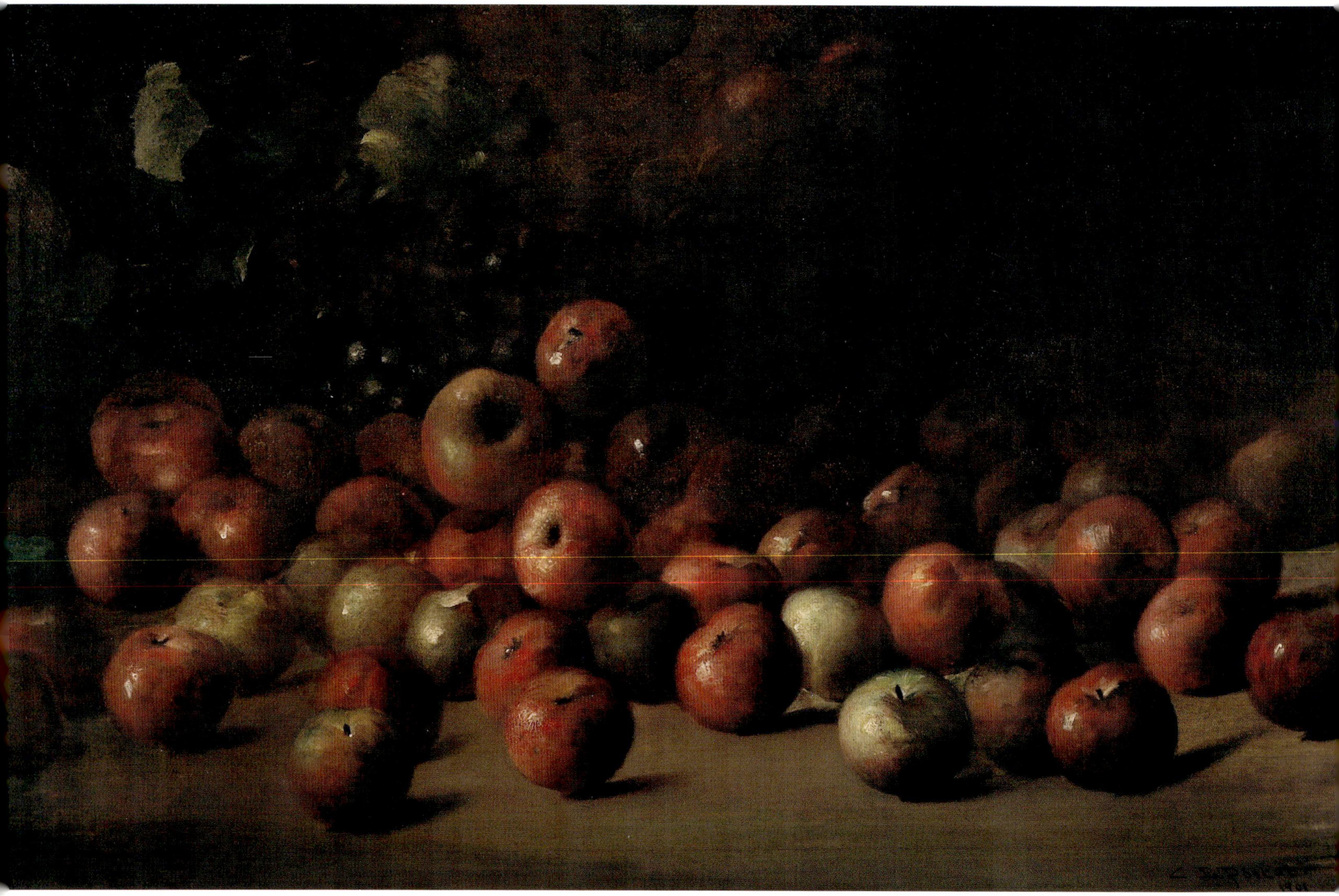

Charles Ethan Porter, *Untitled* (apples), 1901. Oil on canvas, 25.75" × 37". *Photo: Courtesy of Kenkeleba House*

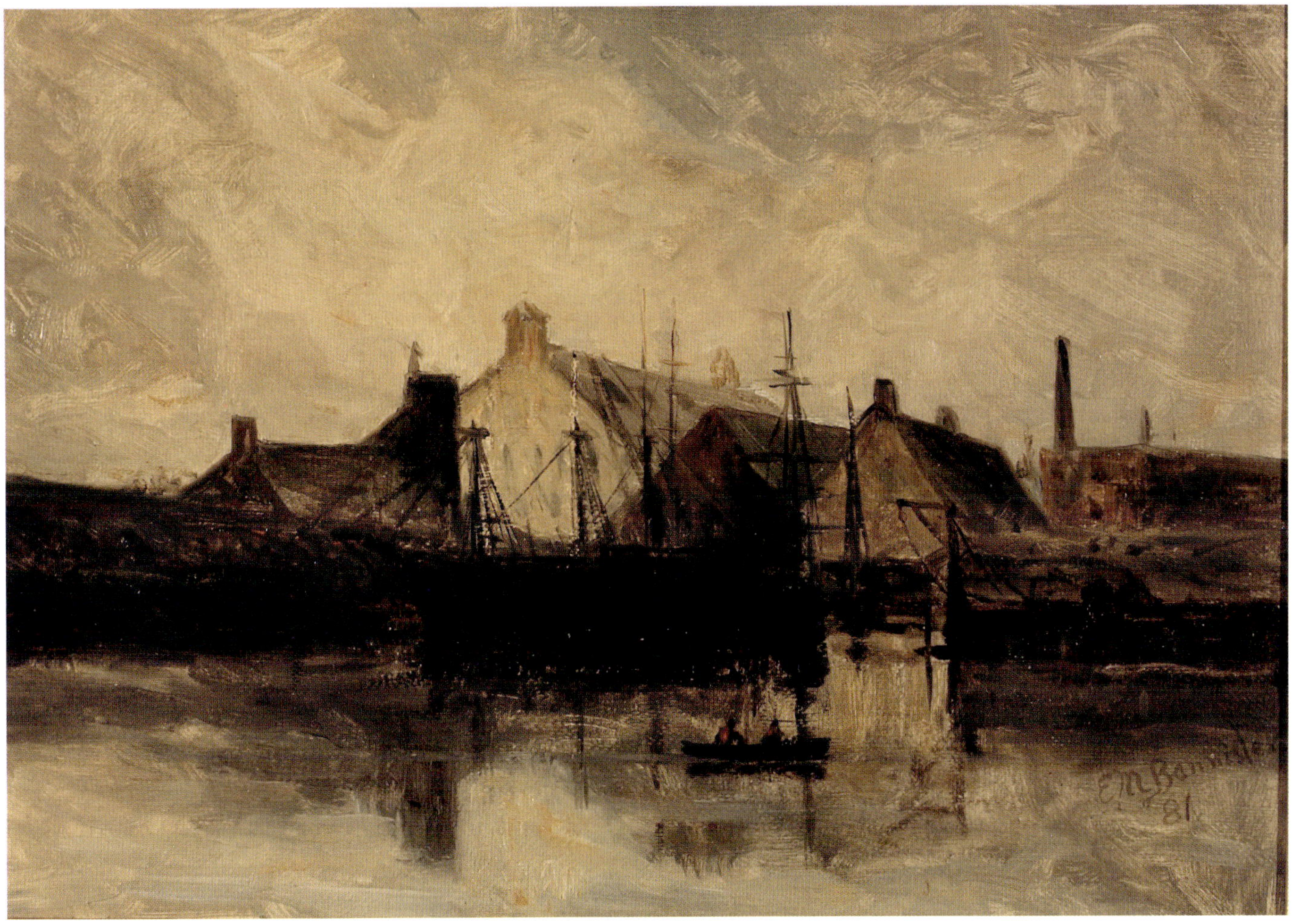

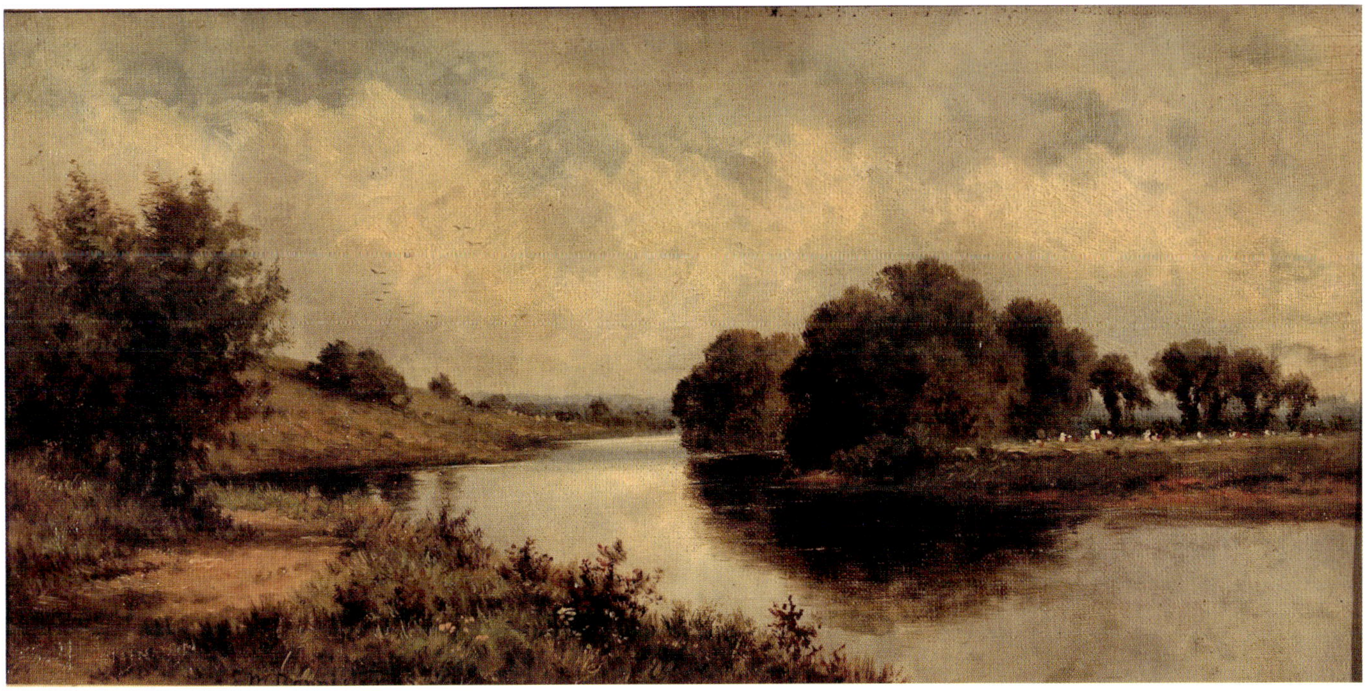

Edward Mitchell Bannister, *Providence River*, 1881. Oil on canvas, 21.75" × 27.875". *Photo: Courtesy of Kenkeleba House*

Edward Mitchell Bannister, *Providence River*, 1881. Oil on canvas, 21.75" × 27.875". *Photo: Courtesy of Kenkeleba House*

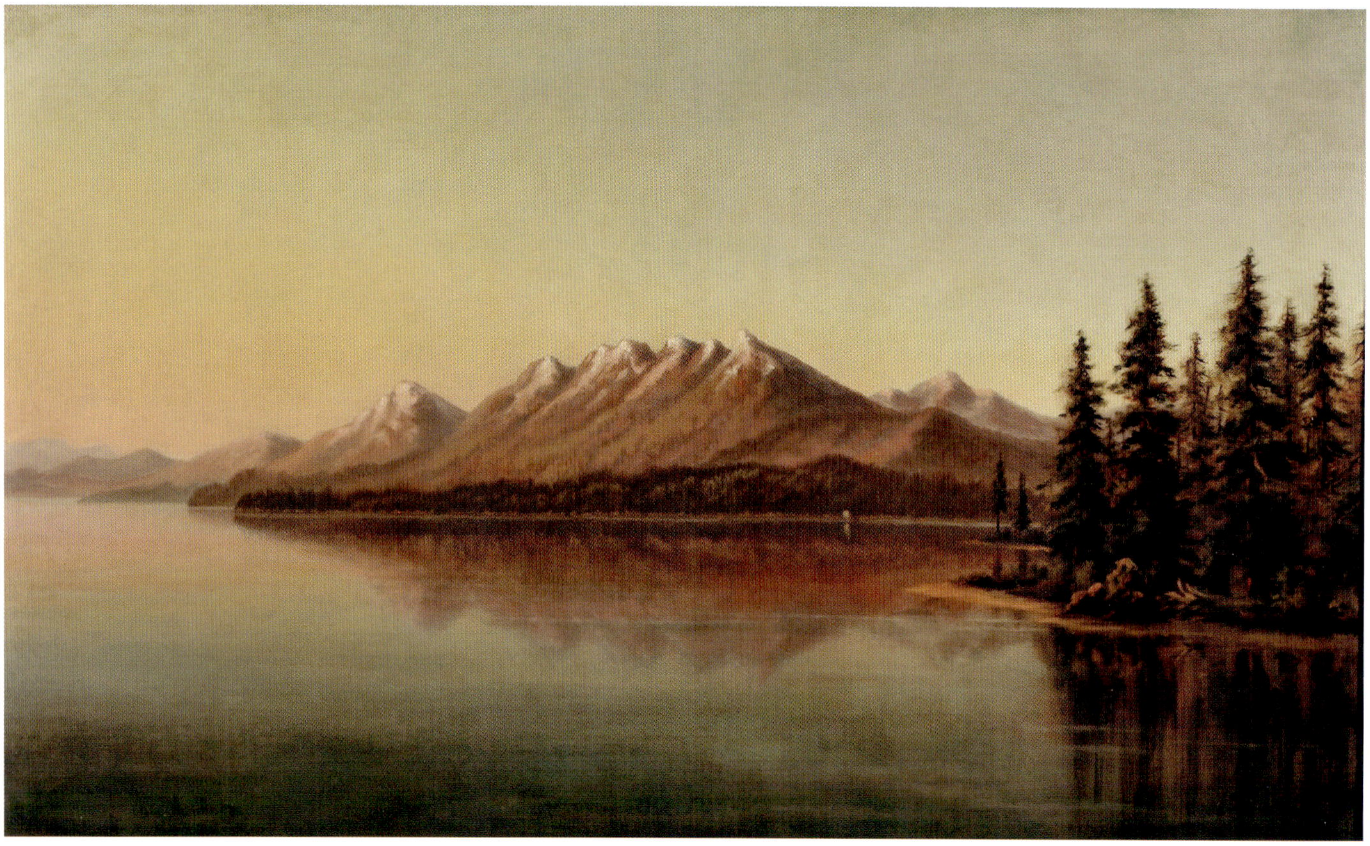

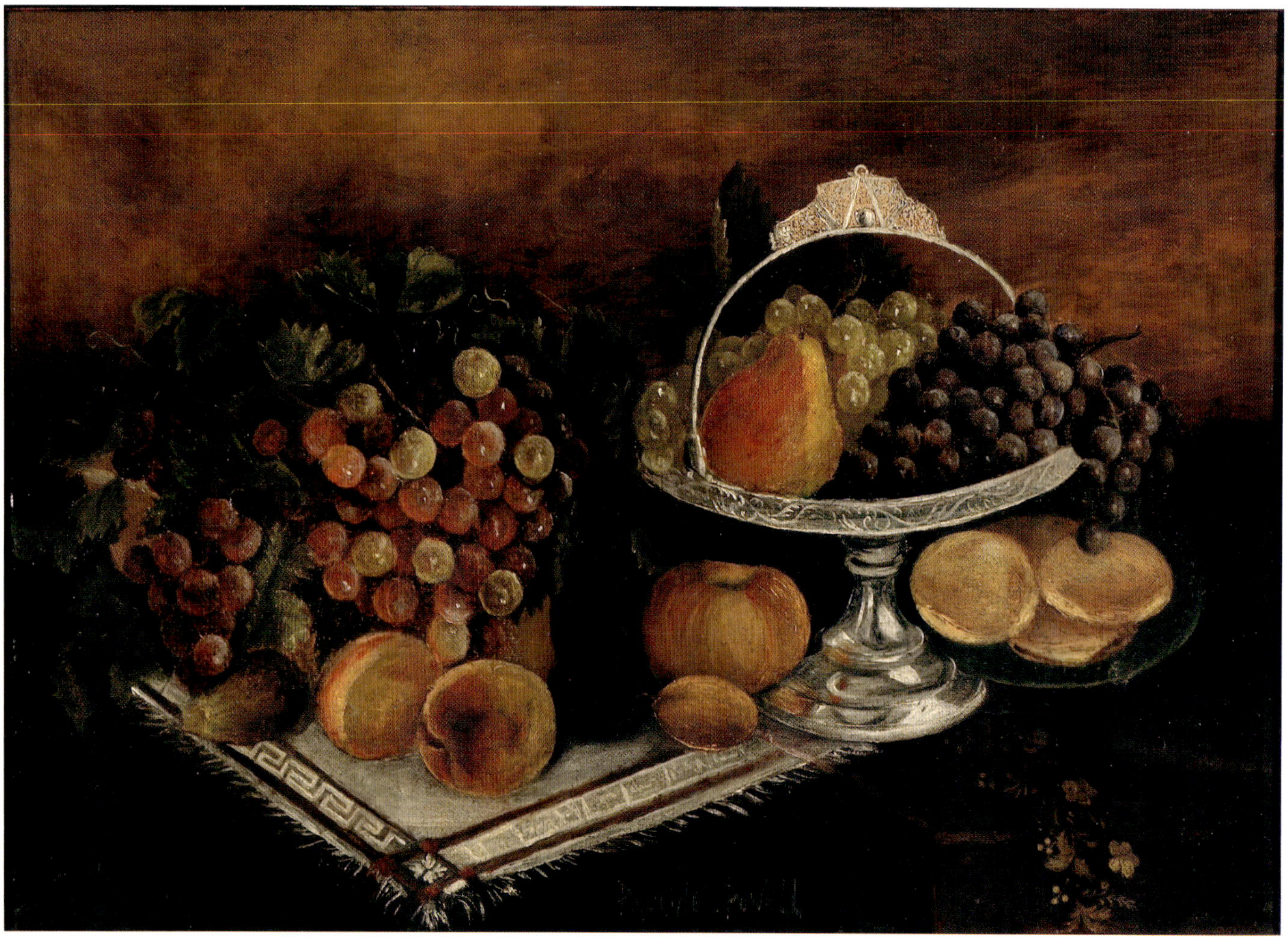

Grafton Tyler Brown, *Lake Tahoe, CA*, 1882. Oil on canvas, 21" × 31.5". *Photo: Courtesy of Kenkeleba House*

Pauline Powell Burns, *Still Life with Fruit*, 1890. Oil on canvas, 23" × 30.25". *Photo: Courtesy of Kenkeleba House*

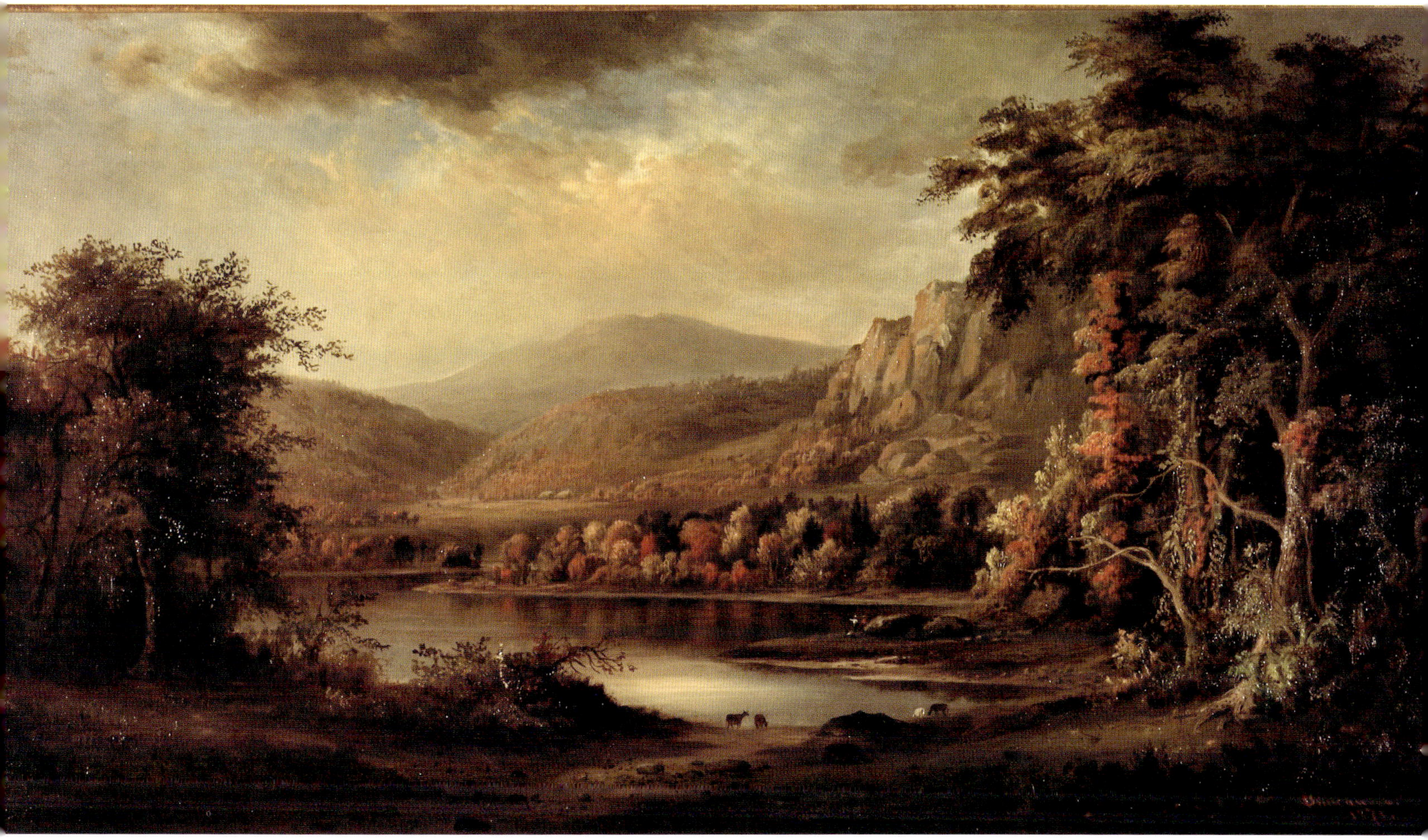

Robert Seldon Duncanson, *Autumn Landscape*, 1871. Oil on canvas, 26.5" × 38.5". *Photo: Courtesy of Kenkeleba House*

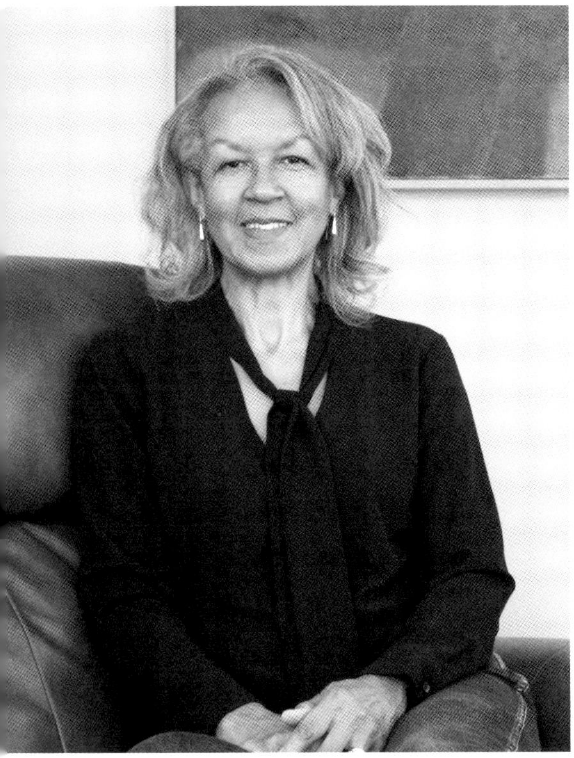

Photo: Myrah Brown Green

WENDY JONES
FRIENDS

DR. MYRAH: What was the first piece of art you collected and when?

WENDY JONES: I attended the Nubian Women's Art Circle awards and exhibition at Cinque Gallery in Soho in 1997. There I was introduced to the work of Ann Tanksley, among others. I have always been attracted to two types of images: either depictions of the human face or abstract works. That day, I purchased a silk aquatint by Ann Tanksley titled *Mary*. The subject represents Jesus's mother, which I later realized. The lush colors and the subject's gentle depiction drew me in. It remains one of my favorite works of art to this day.

DR. MYRAH: Why are you the Keeper of art by friends?

WENDY JONES: I did not intend to be a keeper, so to speak. My collecting unfolded organically and blossomed as I became more involved with artists who were already friends or later became friends through working together. I formally represented artists in my home at art salons and in other larger venues, such as art fairs, cultural institutions, and churches. My desire is to share the beauty and significance of the work, which in turn could help to spread a greater understanding of what compels the creative process.

The true gift to me has been getting to know the artists, learning their stories and what has propelled them throughout their lives. I have learned there is no one way, and that most artists absolutely must create. Like oxygen to life, creating work is a necessity. Looking at art, like listening to music, is basically food for the soul, and I believe it is important to be surrounded by beauty in its myriad forms.

Opposite: Sonia Lynn Sadler, *A Good Foundation*, 2008. Scratchboard, 7" × 5". *Photo: Myrah Brown Green*

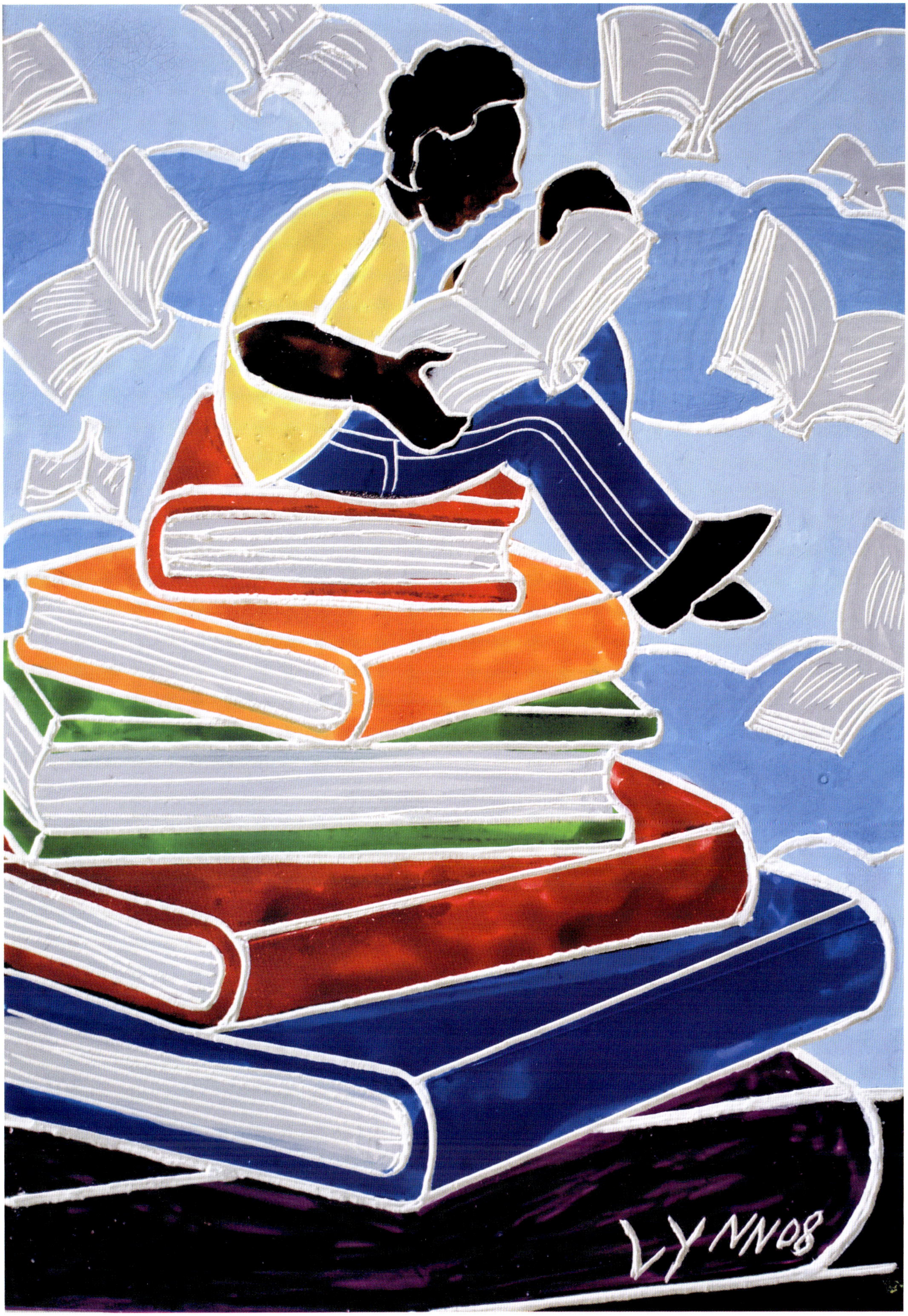
LYNN08

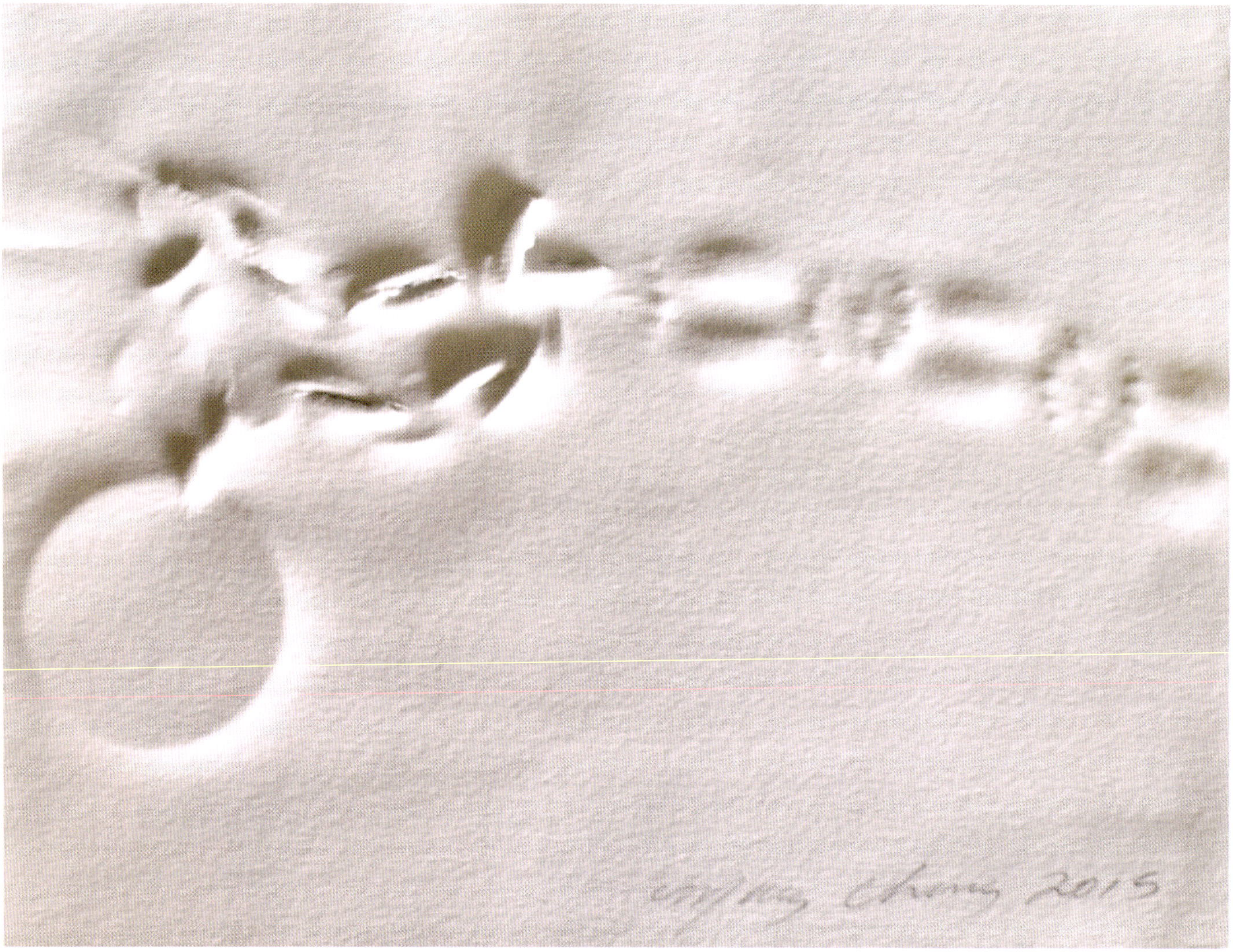

Mary Chang, *Time and Space*, 2015. Embossment, 5.5" × 7.5". *Photo: Myrah Brown Green*

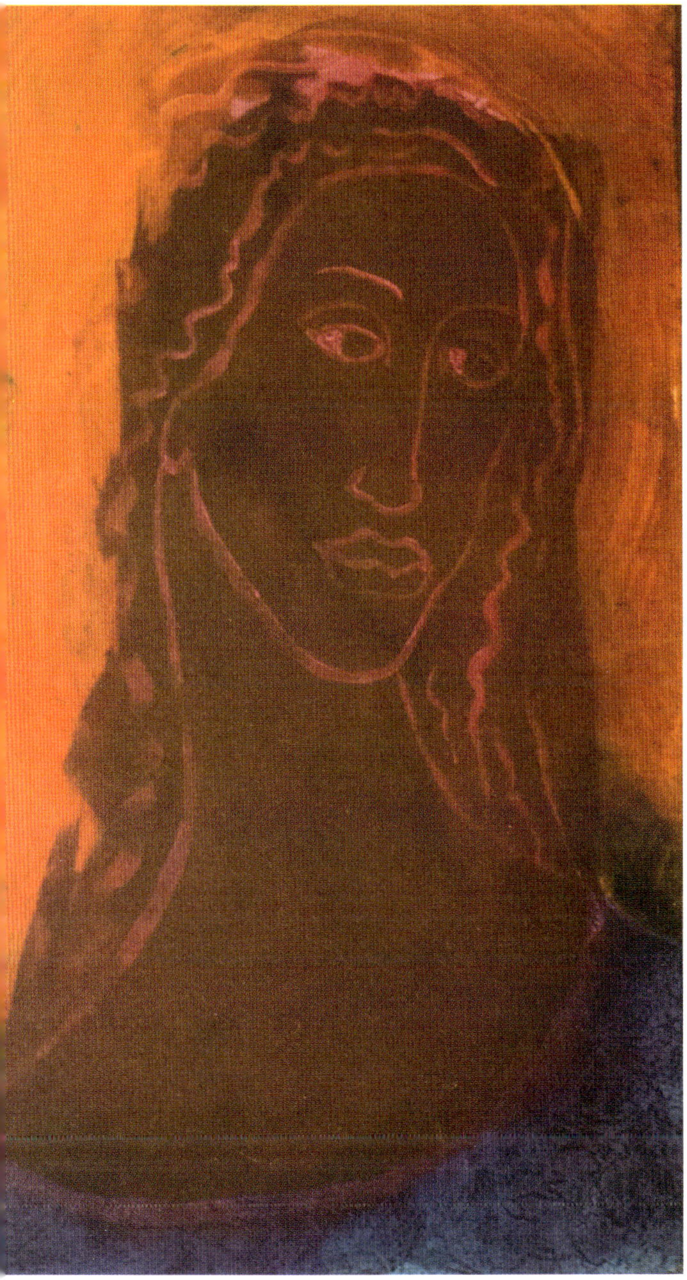

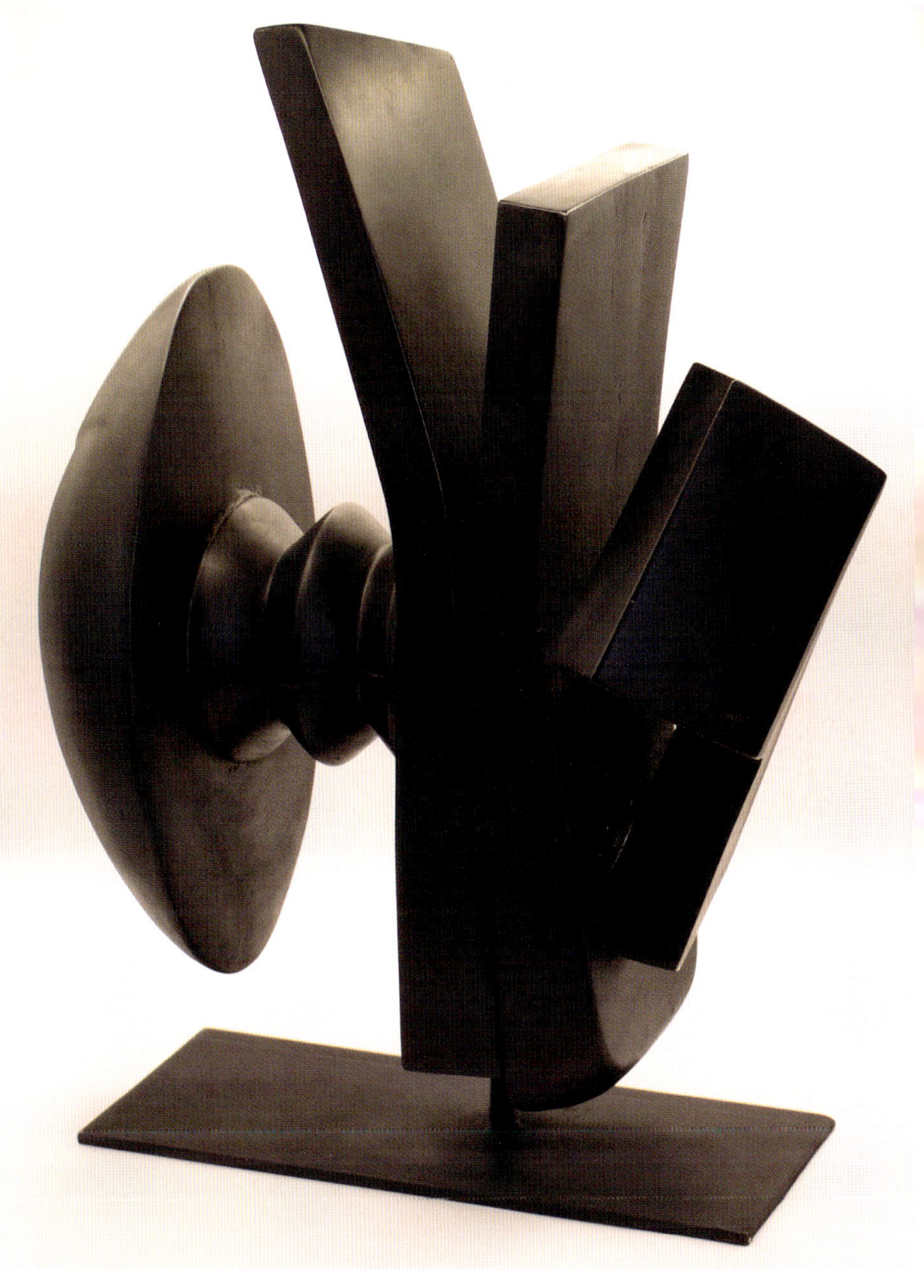

Ann Tanksley, *Mary*, 2003. Silk aquatint, 14.5" × 8.5". *Photo: Myrah Brown Green*

Edward Martin, *Needlepoint II*, 2006. Ebony wood, 21" × 17". *Photo: Myrah Brown Green*

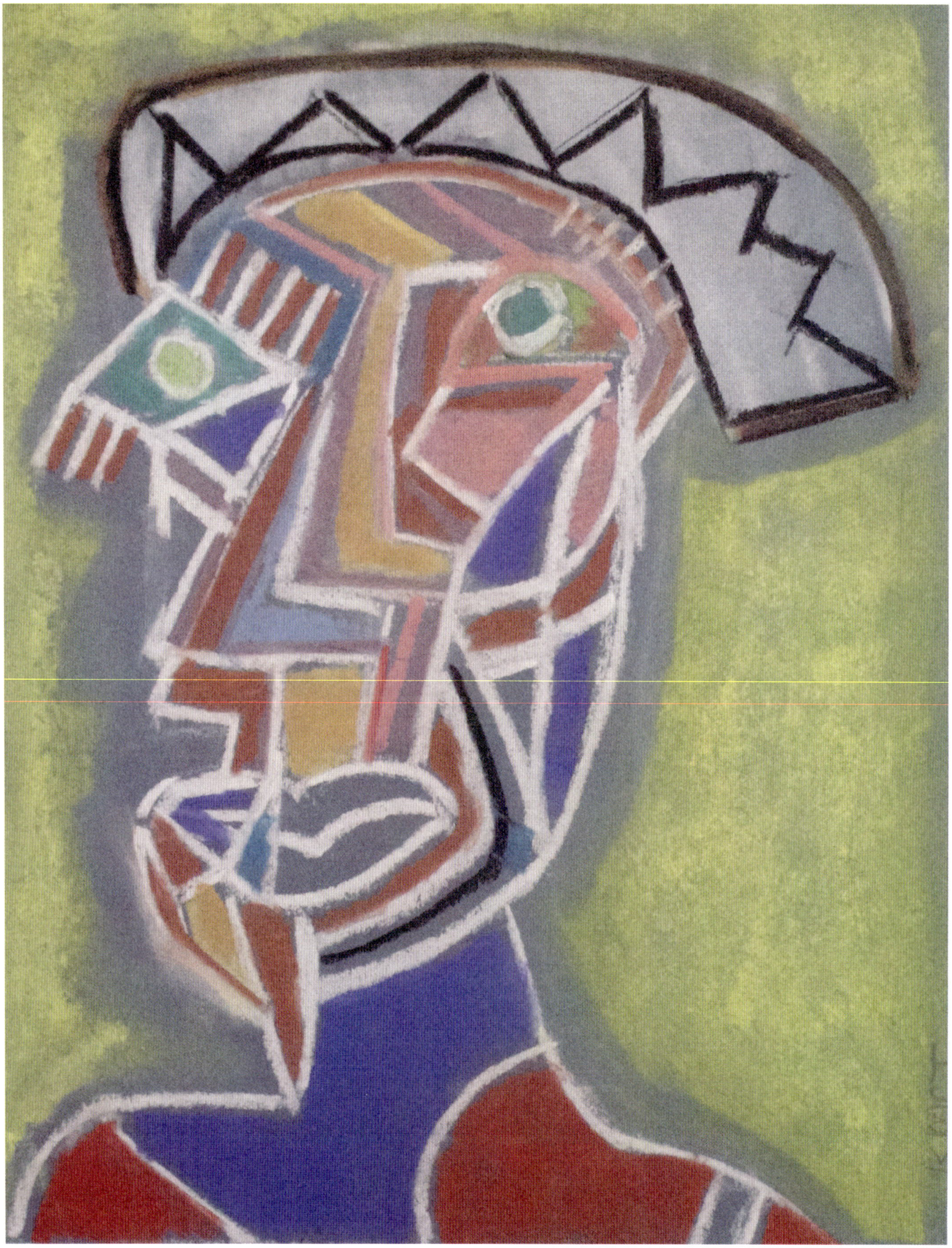

Karl A. McIntosh, *That Face*, 2000. Oil stick on board, 9.5" × 7.5". *Photo: Myrah Brown Green*

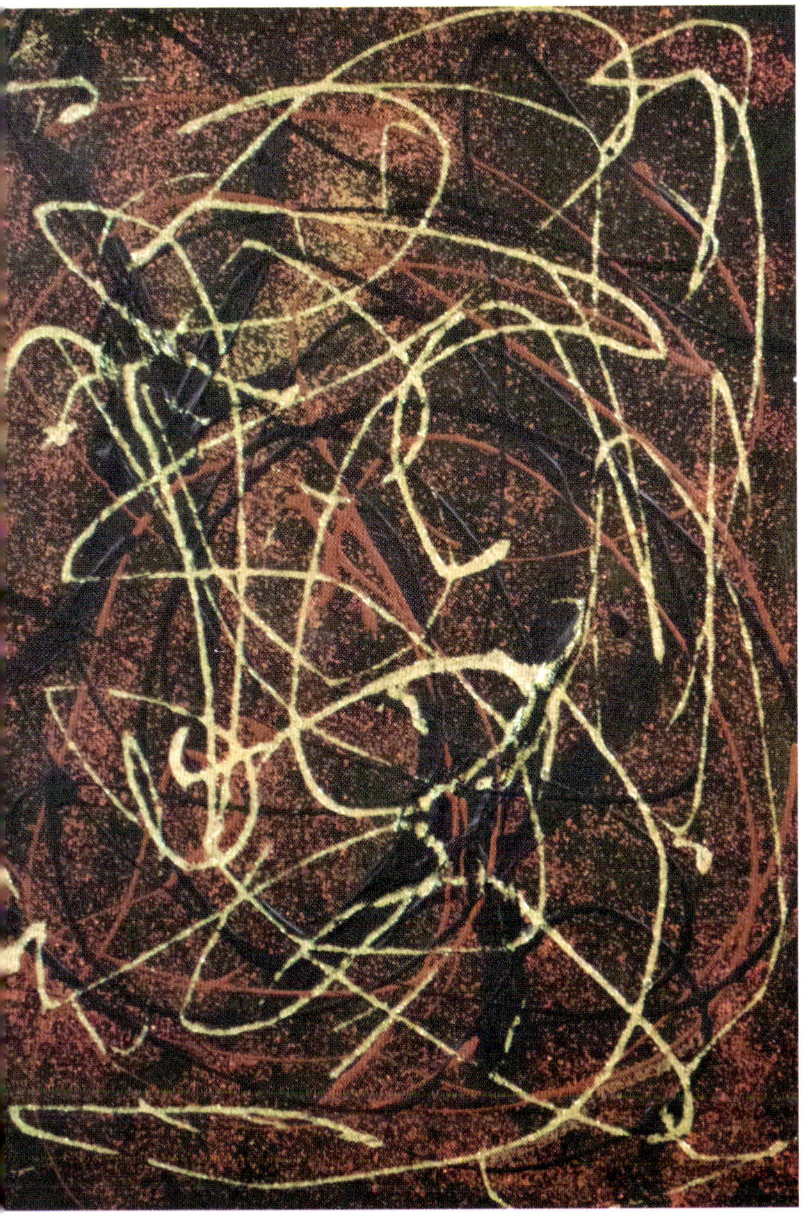

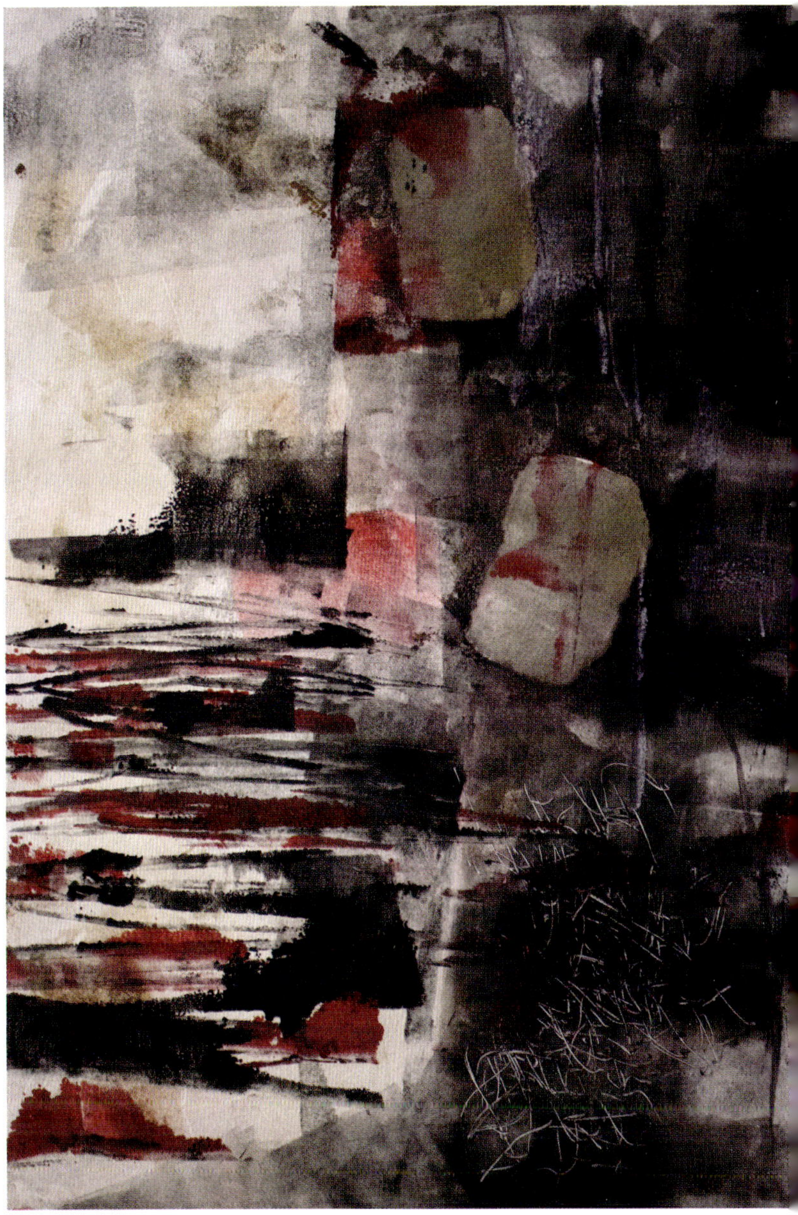

Joseph S. Bell-Bey, *Untitled*, 2000. Mixed media on board, 23.75" × 17.5". *Photo: Myrah Brown Green*

Ramona Candy, *Untitled*, 2008. Monotype, 10.75" × 16". *Photo: Myrah Brown Green*

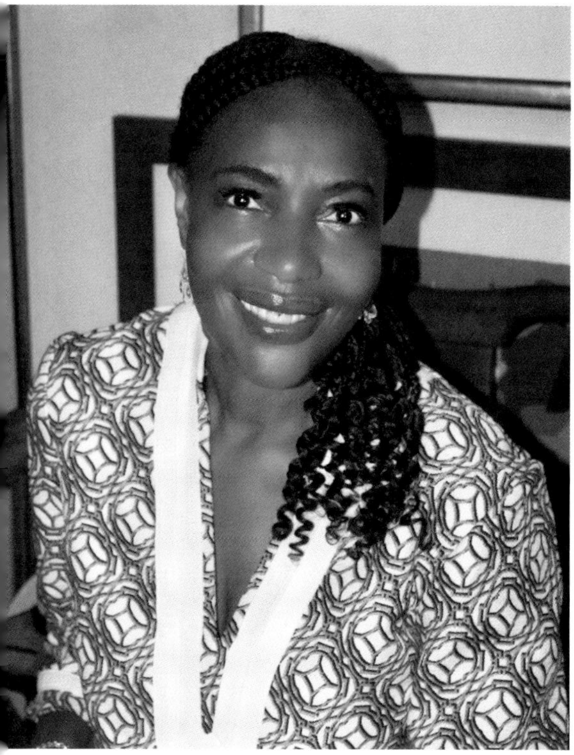

Photo: Myrah Brown Green

DIANA LAMONT

CHILDREN

DR. MYRAH: What is the first piece of art you collected and when?

DIANA LAMONT: In 1997, I set out to find a piece of art to bring into my home, but I knew I wanted it to be special—something created by an artist of color. At the time I didn't realize this decision would mark the beginning of a life-changing journey. The piece I chose was *Mother and Daughter*, a beautiful collage by James Denmark. This artwork became the anchor of my collection, the piece that opened my eyes to the vibrant art community around me. Since then, *Mother and Daughter* has filled my life with joy, happiness, and love, and it continues to remind me of the power art has to connect us to our own stories, and to others.

DR. MYRAH: Why are you the Keeper of children's images?

DIANA LAMONT: I am the keeper of children's images because of the deep sense of family that has shaped my life. Growing up in Manchester, England, as the child of Jamaican parents, I was surrounded by the love, safety, and spiritual nurturing they provided for me and my five siblings. In many ways, being the keeper of these children's images is a continuation of those values—a gift I've embraced. Each piece of art I collect reflects my life experiences and personal journey. I gravitate toward children's art because, to me, children represent endless possibilities. They are symbols of change, creativity, boundless imagination, innocence, and perseverance. I see in them the hopes of our past and the promises of our future—carrying us forward as a people with infinite potential to fulfill our dreams.

Every day I open my door to see Elizabeth Catlett's *Madonna*, my favorite work of art, which depicts a mother lovingly embracing her children. Catlett, with her intimate portrayals of mothers and children, takes me back to the days of my young adulthood when I taught children's religious education at my church. Those memories, like the art itself, lift me up. The children's art in my home reflects dancers, athletes, thinkers, artists, knowledge seekers, and the simple joy of children at play.

My parents always taught me that children are our future, and with that belief comes the responsibility to protect, nurture, and encourage them. The artists who have captured children and families in their work have inspired me deeply. Their art celebrates the strength and love within our communities and has sparked my own passion for collecting art. I am forever grateful to them.

Opposite: Elizabeth Catlett, *Madonna*, 1982. Lithograph, 20" × 15.5". *Photo: Myrah Brown Green*

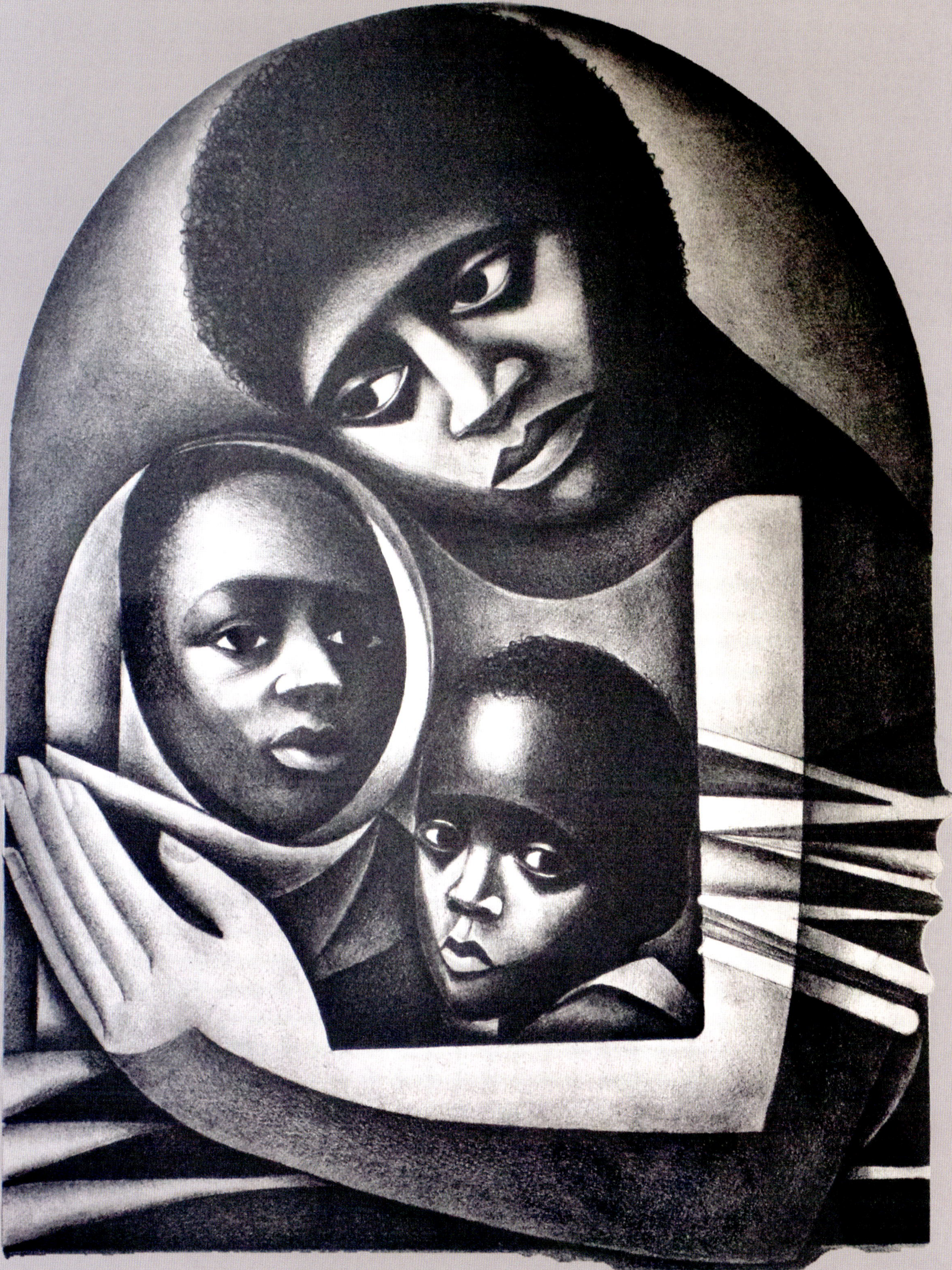

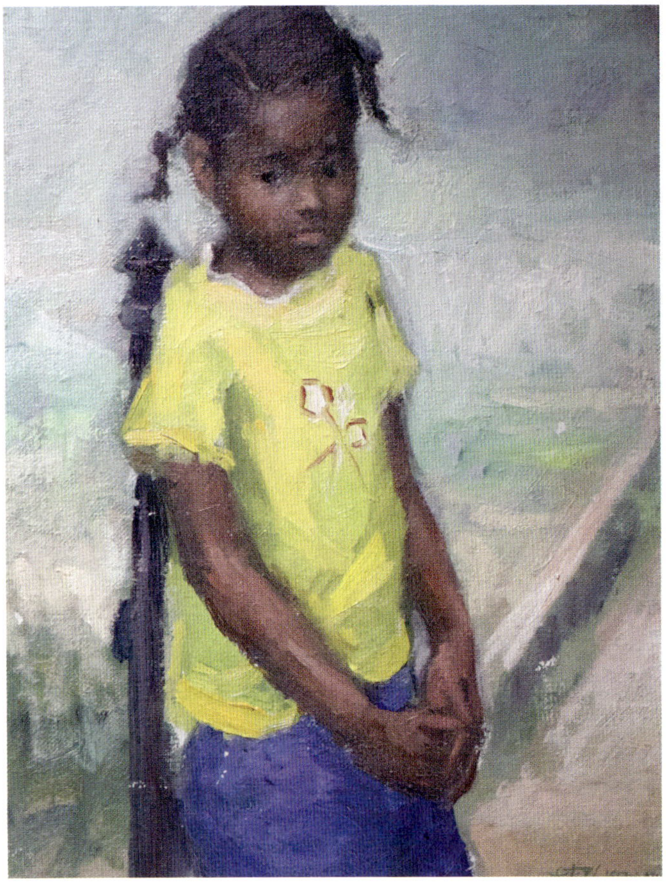

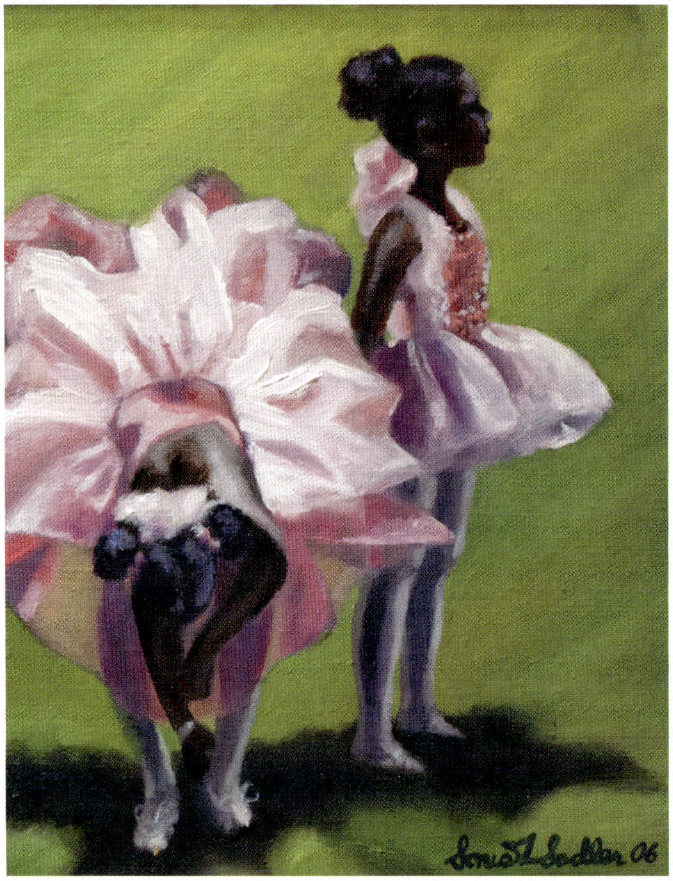

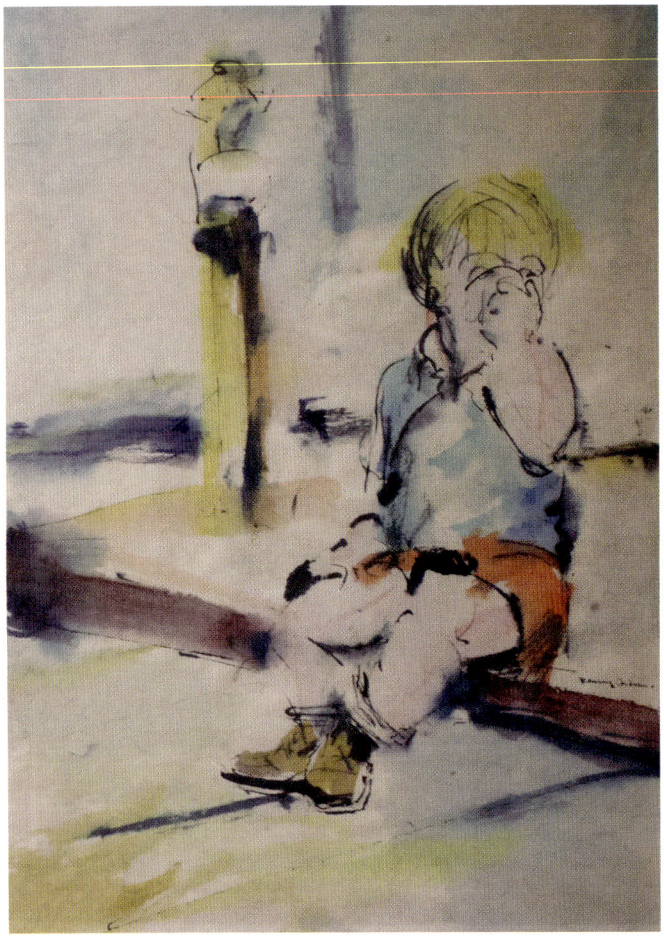

Top left: George Wilson, *Solitude (Girl in Yellow Dress)*, 1980. Oil on canvas, 13" × 10.5". *Photo: Myrah Brown Green*

Top right: Sonya Lynn Saddler, *Ballerina*, 2006. Oil on canvas, 17" × 11". *Photo: Myrah Brown Green*

Benny Andrews, *Young Boy on Curb*, 1960. Watercolor, 12" × 16". *Photo: Myrah Brown Green*

Opposite: Tamara Madden, *Untitled*, 2010. Mixed media, 11.5" × 8.5". *Photo: Myrah Brown Green*

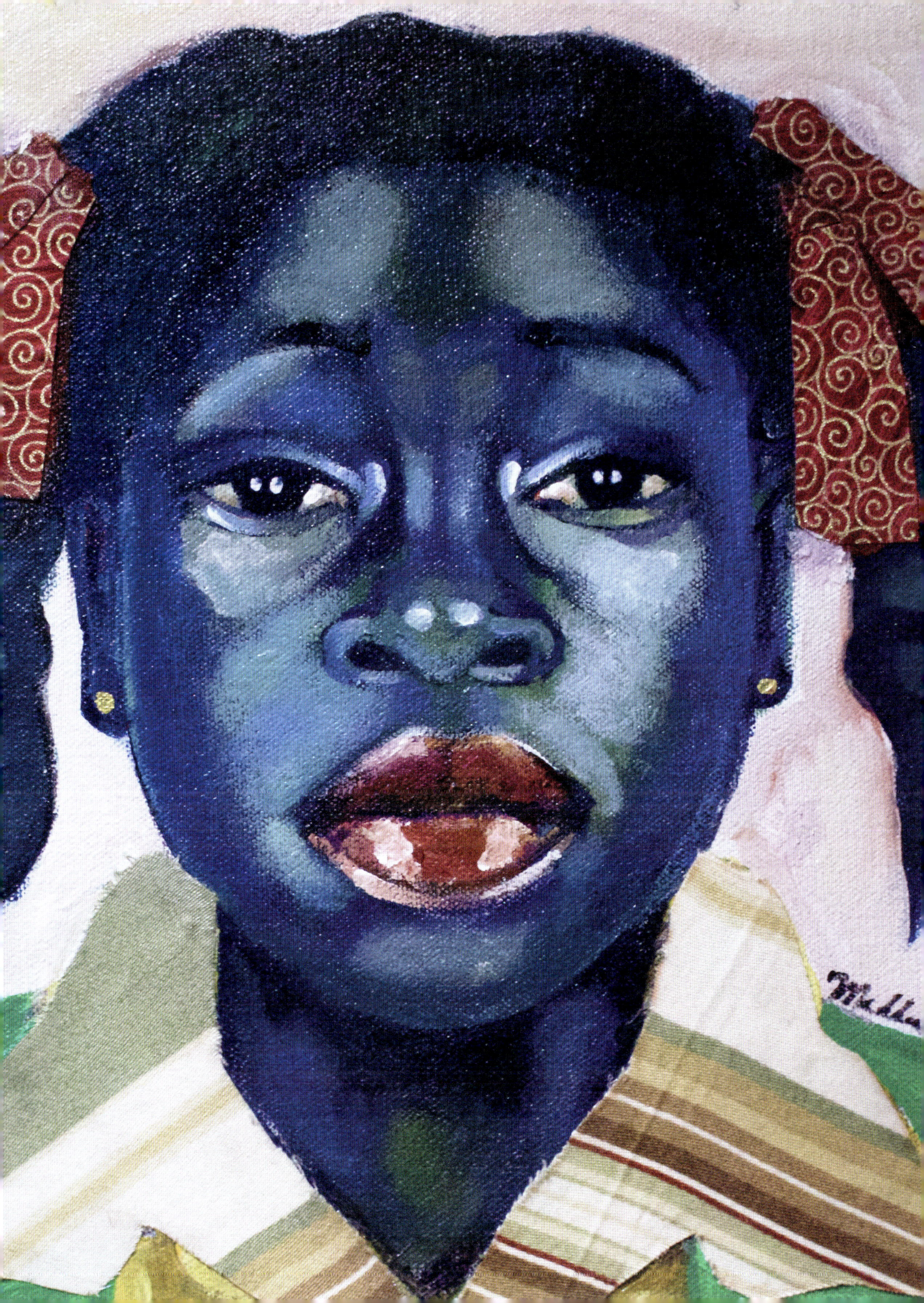

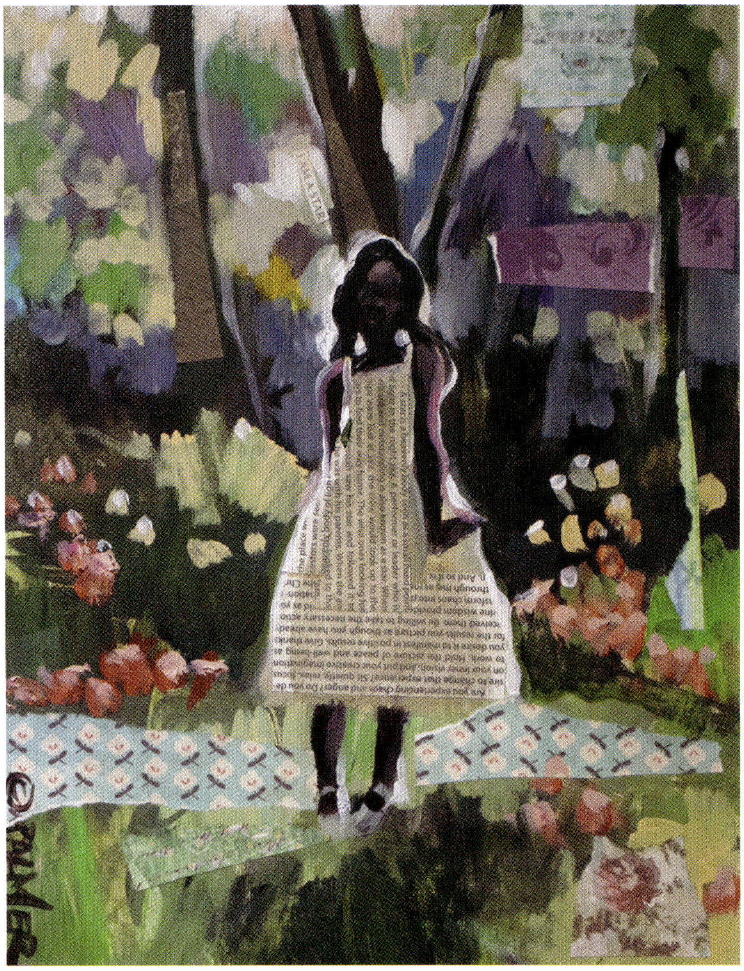

Charlie Palmer, *Lauren*, 2014. Collage, 13.5" × 10.5". *Photo: Myrah Brown Green*

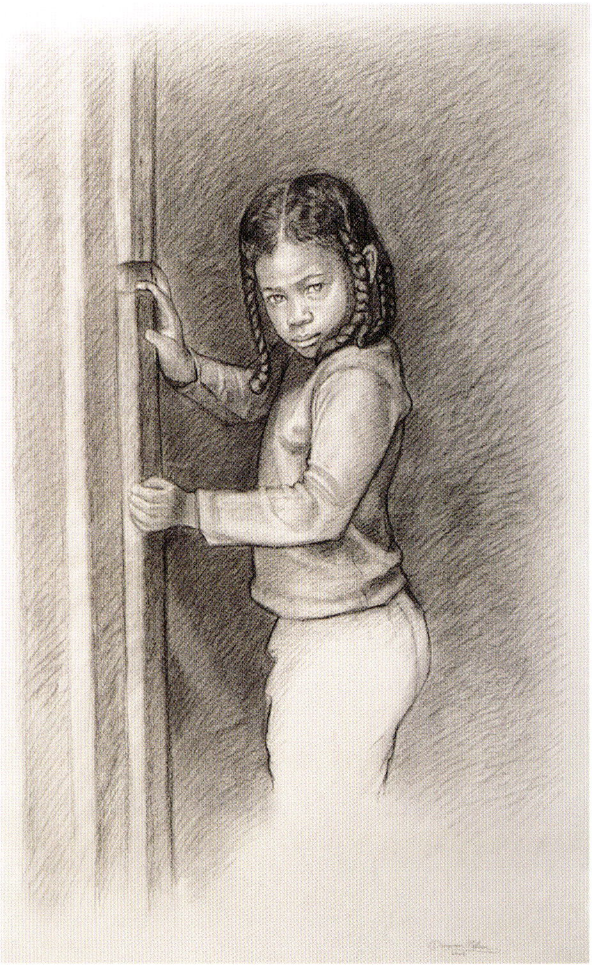

Donovan Nelson, *Girl in Doorway*, 2005. Charcoal, 50" × 32". *Photo: Myrah Brown Green*

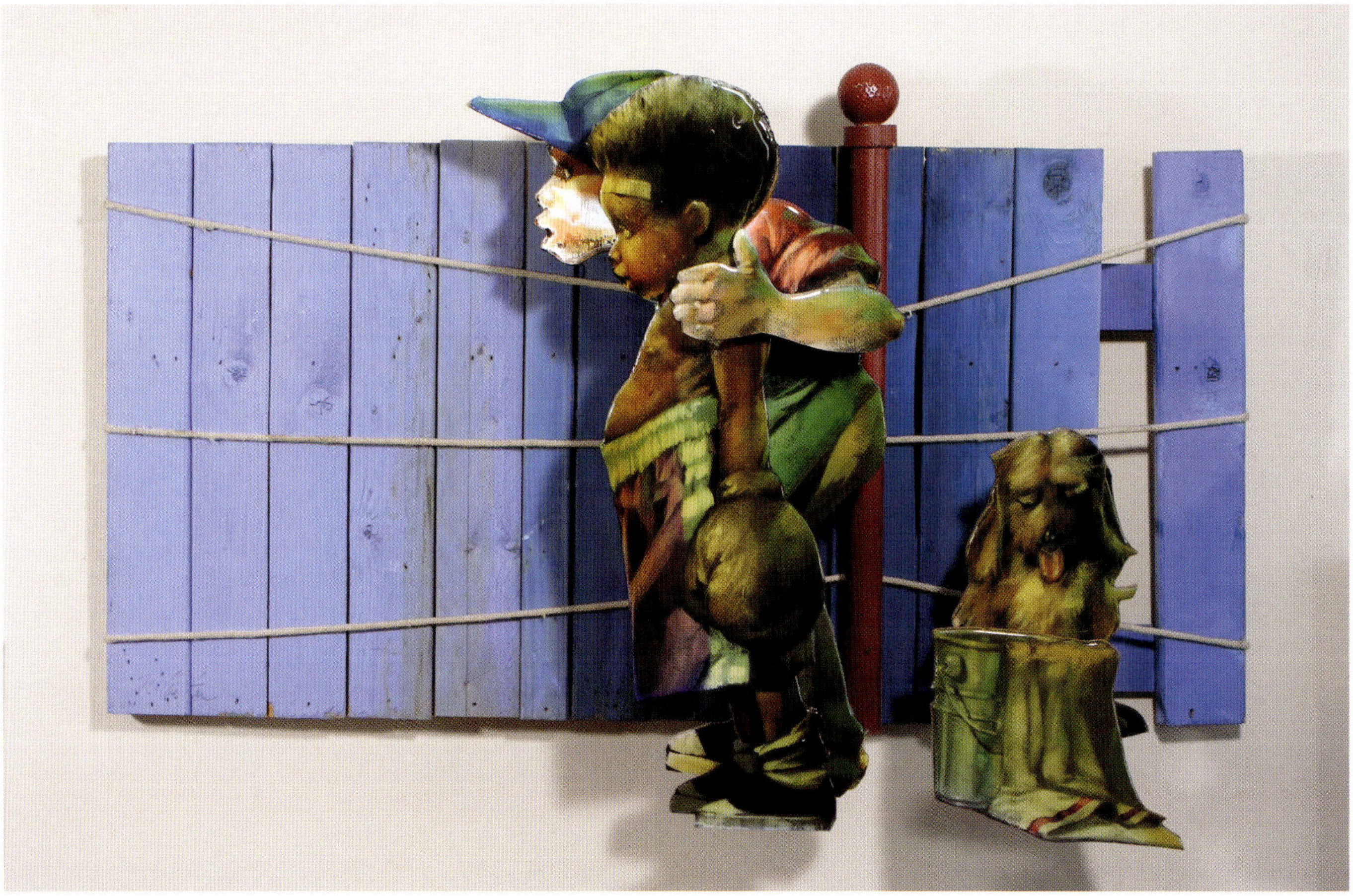

Robert Carter, *Untitled* (year unknown). Mixed media (wood, paint, paper), 32" × 15.5". *Photo: Donovan Nelson*

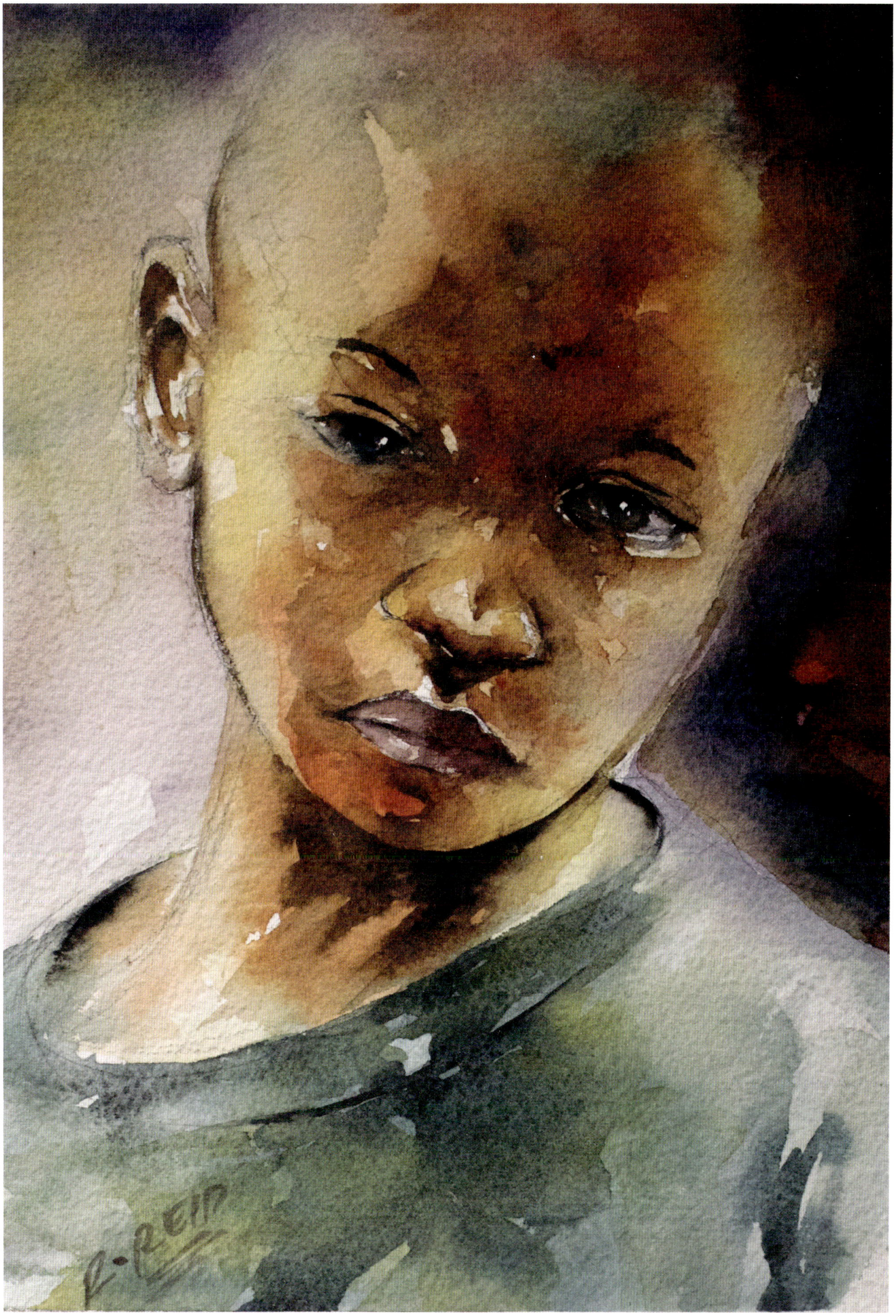

Robert Reid, *There is a Child in Me*, 2021. Watercolor, 17" × 11". *Photo: Myrah Brown Green*

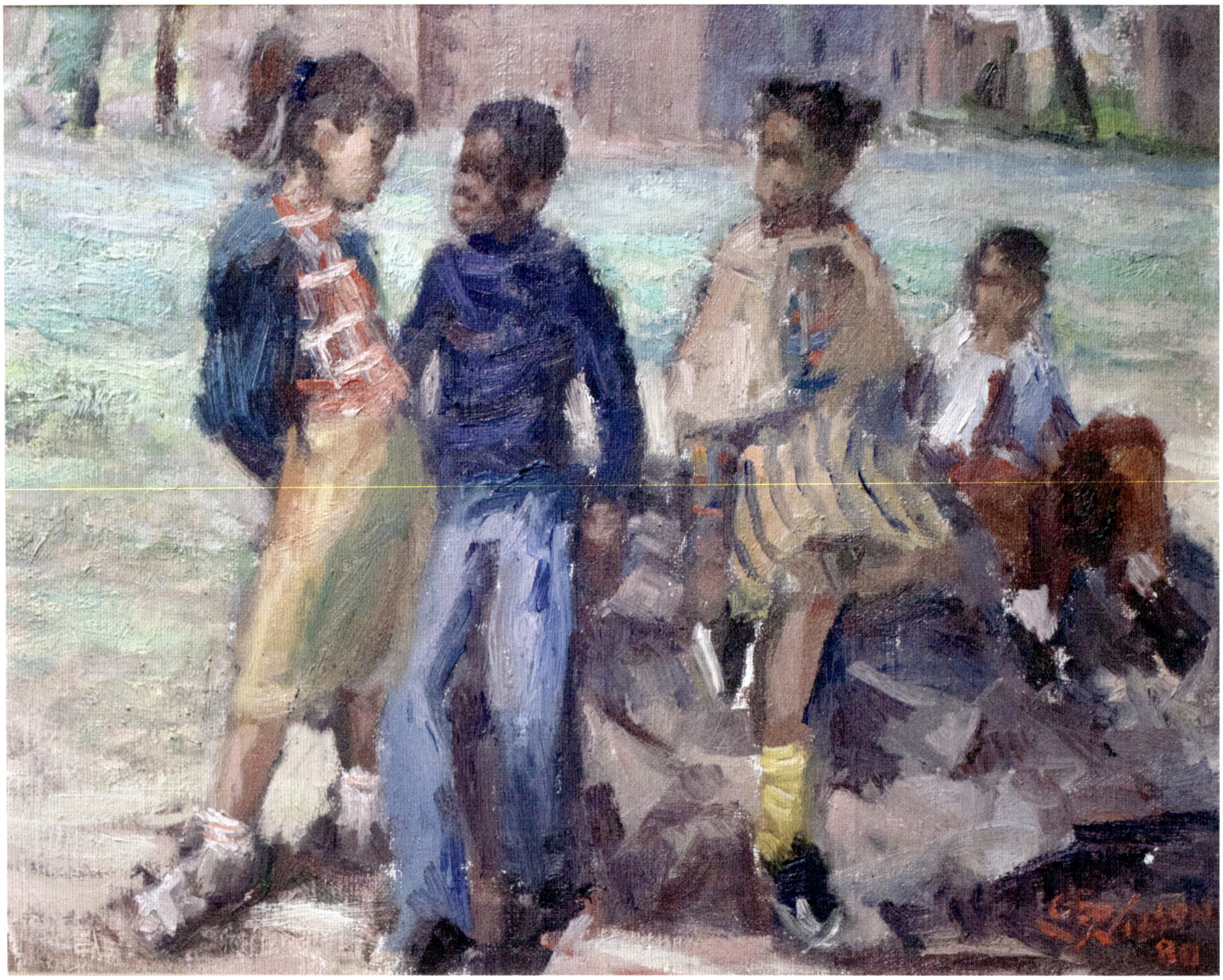

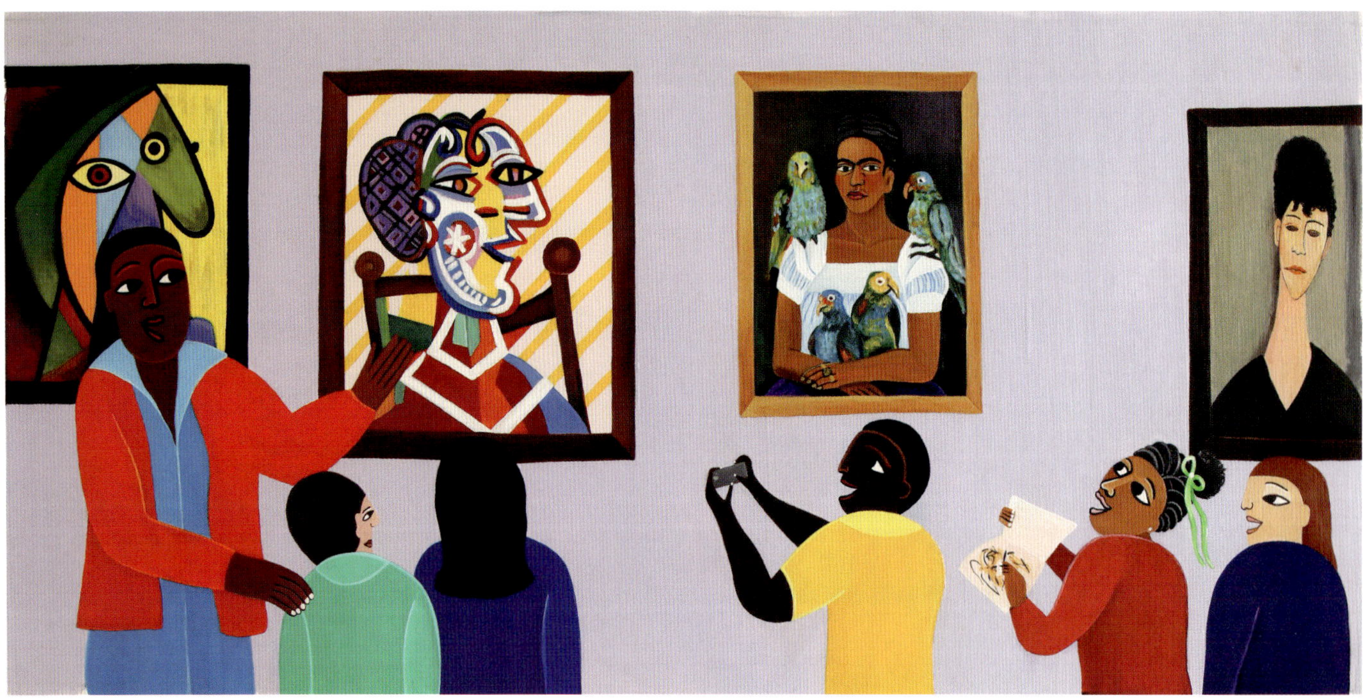

George Wilson, *Let's Get Together* (1980). Oil on canvas, 11" × 14". *Photo: Myrah Brown Green*

Laura James, *The Museum*, 2018. Acrylic on canvas, 9" × 21". *Photo: Myrah Brown Green*

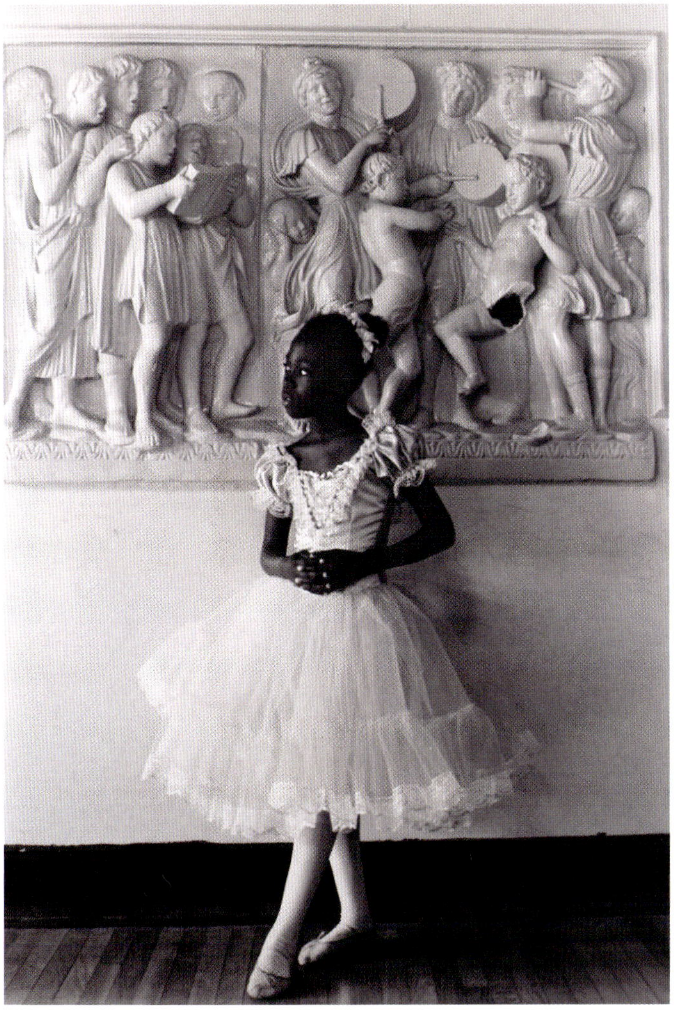

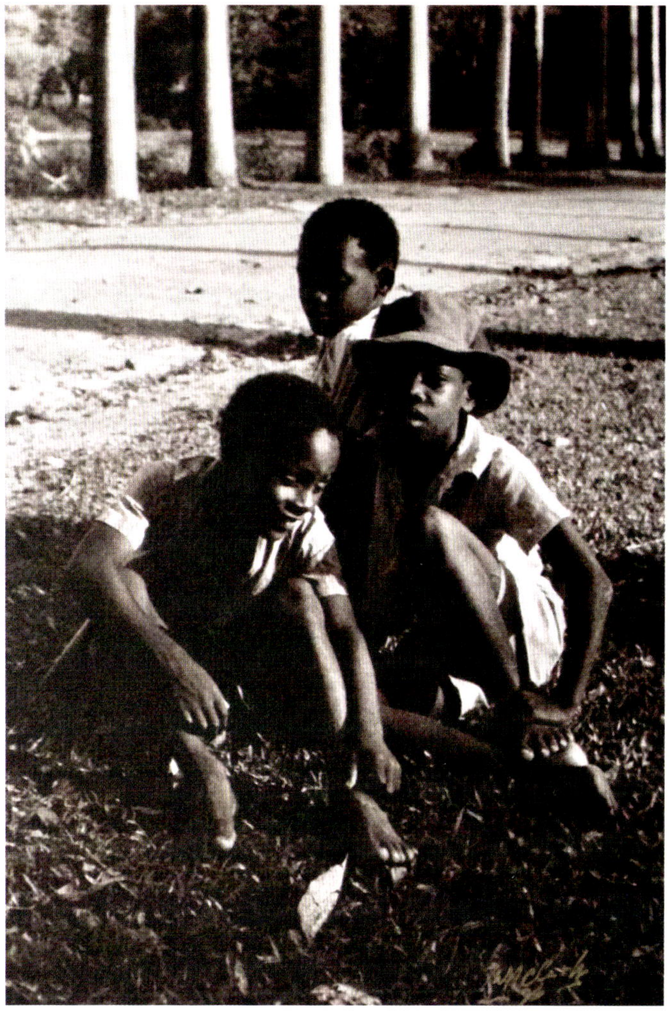

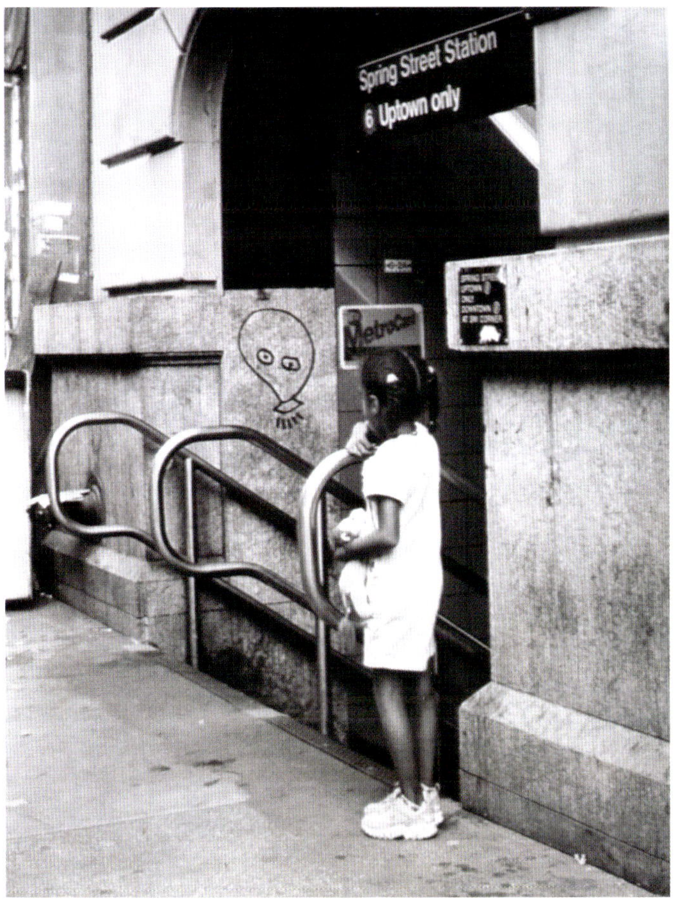

Top left: Leroy Henderson, *Ballerina*, ca. 1992–1994. Silver gelatin print, 21" × 14".

Top right: Wayne Clarke, *Next Move* (year unknown). Silver gelatin print, 14" × 9.5".

Beuford Smith, *My Friend* (NYC) (year unknown). Silver gelatin print, 14" × 11".

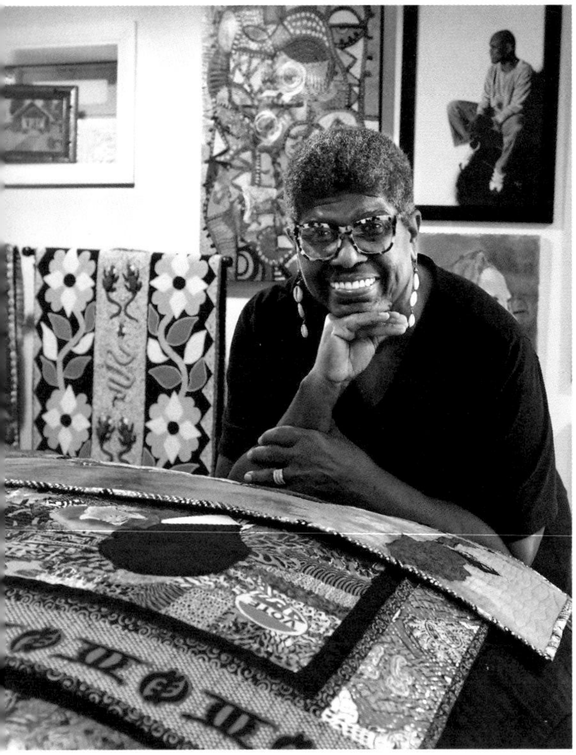

Photo: Tom Pich

DR. CAROLYN MAZLOOMI
QUILTS

DR. MYRAH: What was the first piece of art that you collected and when?

DR. CAROLYN MAZLOOMI: The first quilts I collected were made by Faith Ringgold. She traded me two quilts of hers for two of mine. The quilts were *Tar Beach II* and *Coming to Jones Road*. How fortunate for me!

DR. MYRAH: WHY ARE YOU A KEEPER OF QUILTS?

DR. CAROLYN MAZLOOMI: I am a collector of African American story quilts that deal with Black history and social justice issues. It is very important for me to place the quilts in museum collections so people can see them. It is critical, at this time in our nation's history, that these quilts be preserved. At this time, there are over thirty states in America which have legislated laws against the teaching of Black history in public schools. Viewing the story quilts in museums is an alternative and nonthreatening approach to topics of social issues about people, places, and events that are embedded in the American memory as sensitive cultural parameters of race, class, and gender . . . the tough stuff of American history most white folks don't want to hear.

Quilts hold a very special place in Black culture. No other artistic form is more closely associated with African Americans than quilt making, representing skill, aesthetic beauty, and utilitarian need. The art form was historically one of the few mediums accessible to marginalized groups to tell their own story, to provide warmth for their families, and to empower them with a voice. Moreover, for African Americans, the quilt became a covert expression of resistance with the context of storytelling. In this way, quilters found an outlet for their emotions, adversities, and triumphs.

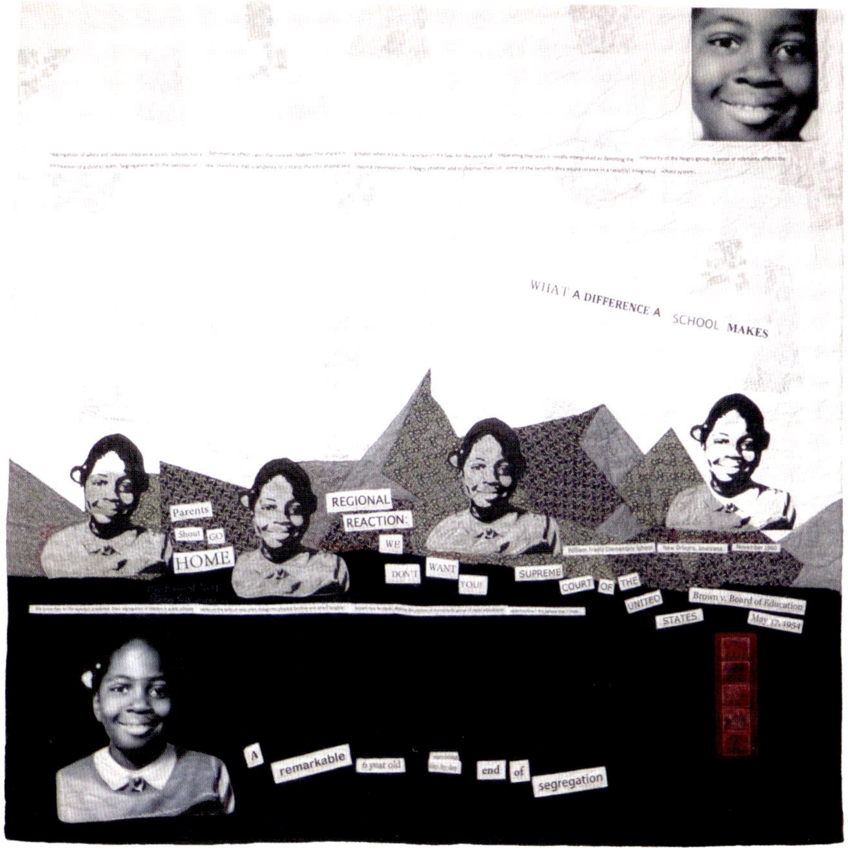

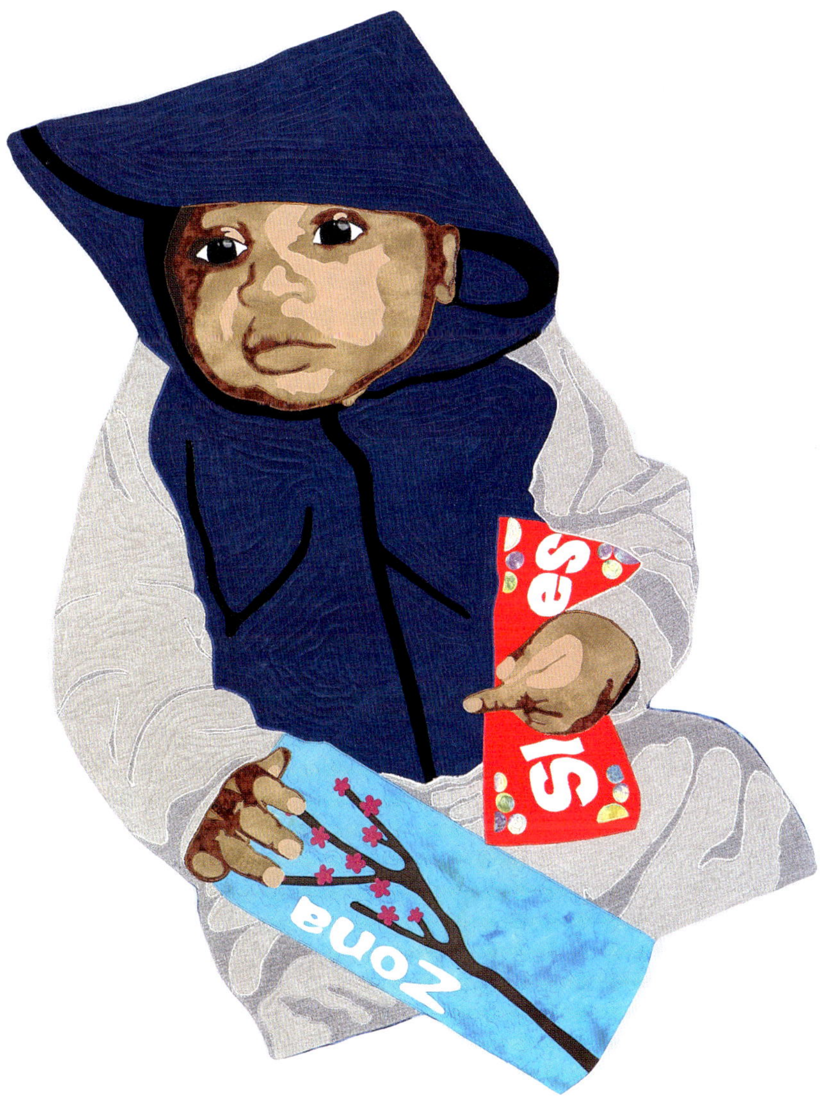

Marion Coleman, *Ruby Nell Bridges*, 2012. Textile, 50" × 50". *Photo: Chas. E. Martin*

Dorothy Burge, *Trayvon Could Have Been My Son*, 2012. Textile, 48" × 30". *Photo: Chas. E. Martin*

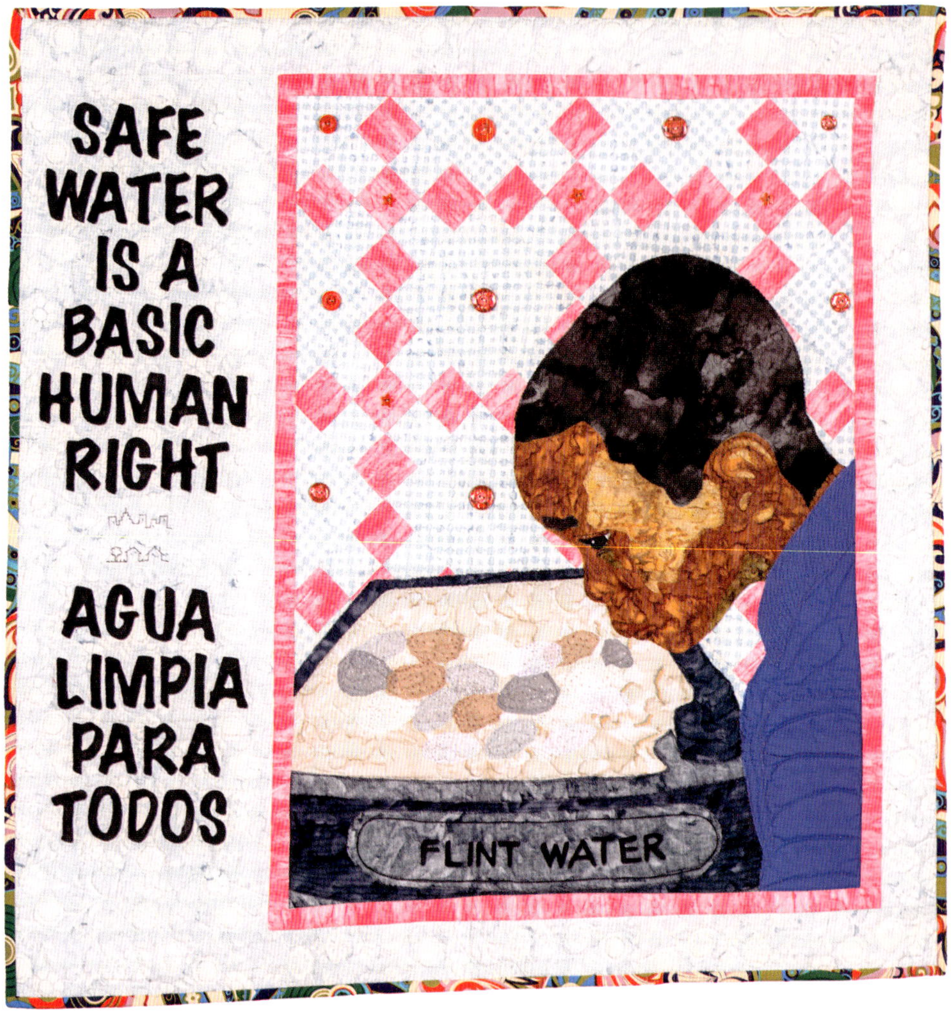
SAFE WATER IS A BASIC HUMAN RIGHT
AGUA LIMPIA PARA TODOS
FLINT WATER

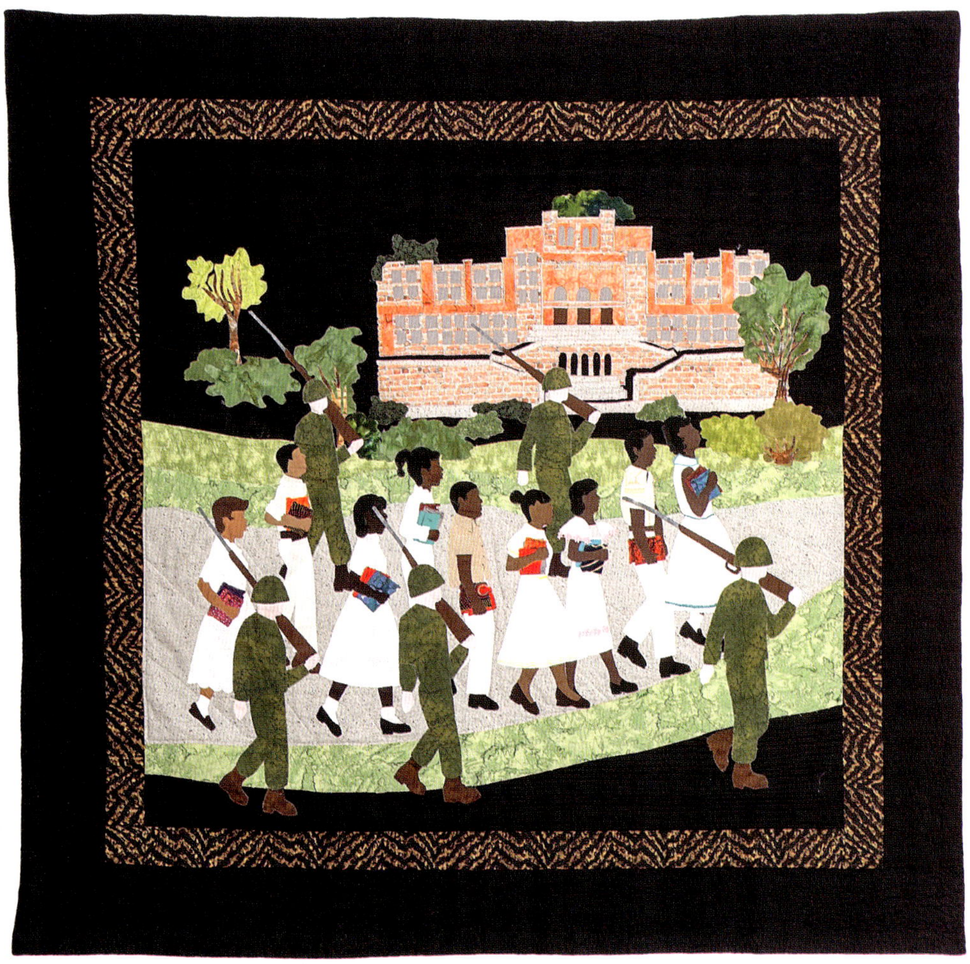

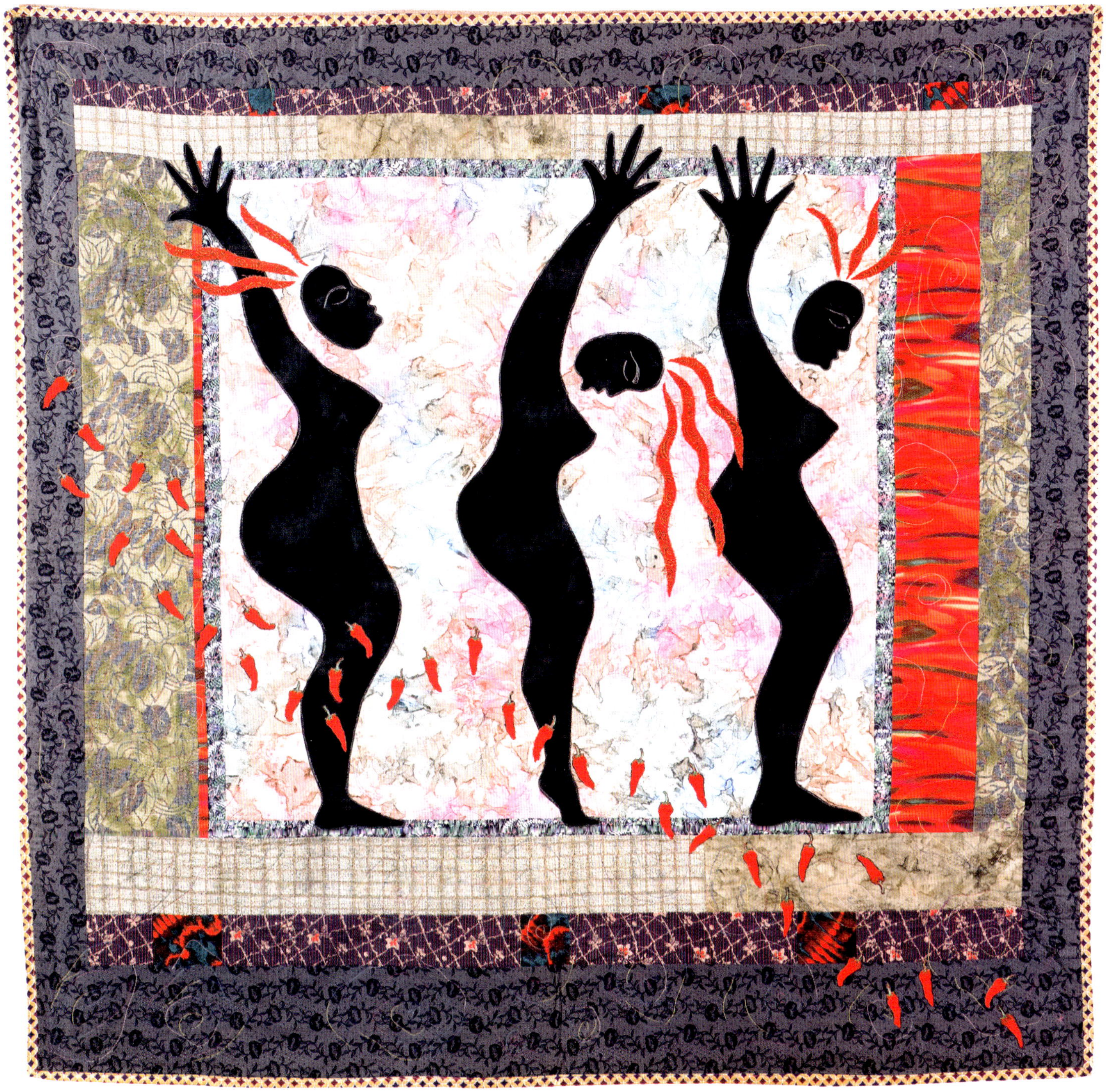

Sylvia Hernandez, *Flint Water*, 2014. Textile, 50" × 50". *Photo: Carolyn L. Mazloomi*

Sandra Noble, *Little Rock Nine*, 2012. Textile, 50" × 50". *Photo: Chas. E. Martin*

Above: Myrah Brown Green, *Heat*, 2004. Textile, 62.5" × 66.5". *Photo: Myrah Brown Green*

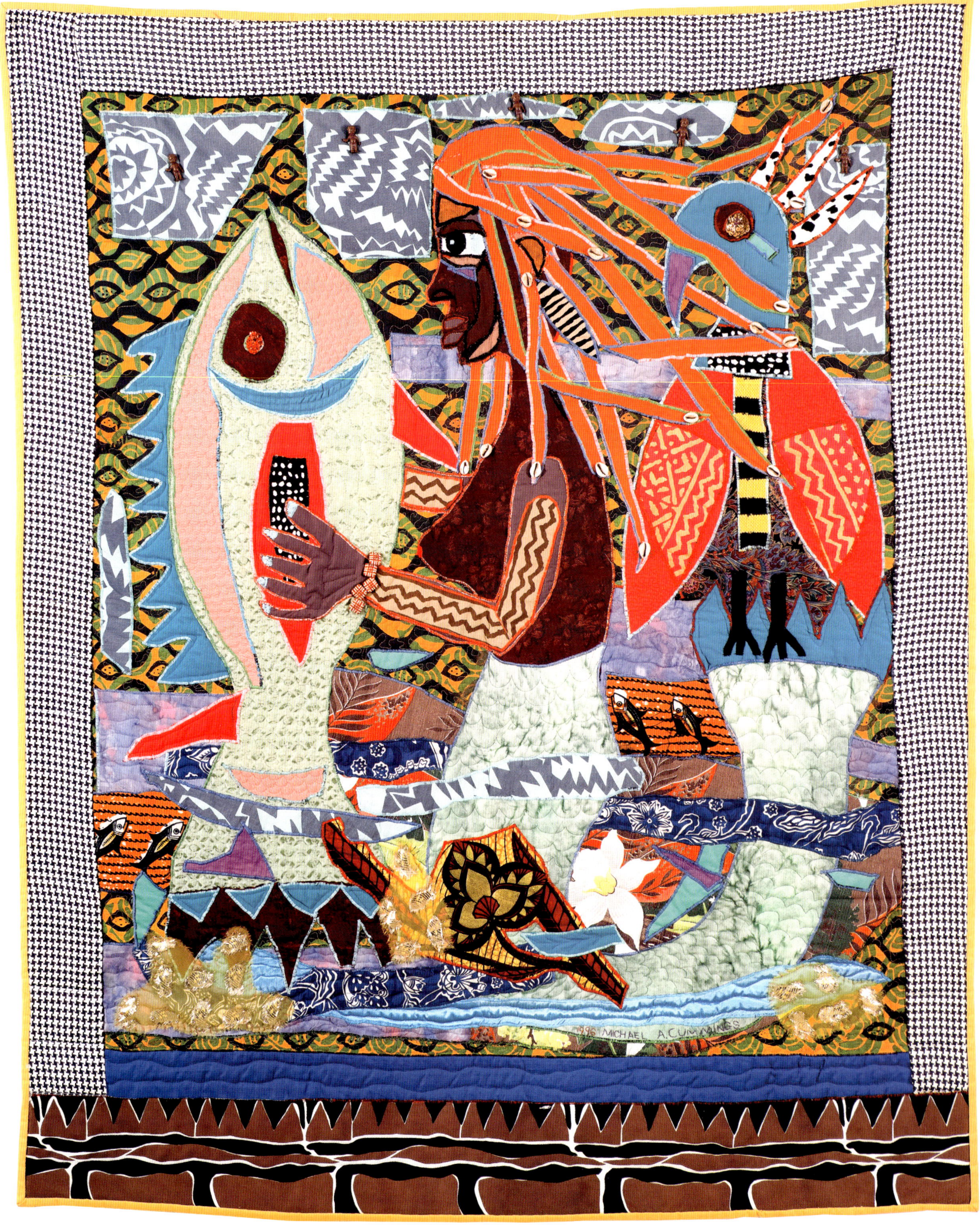

Above: Michael Cummings, *Haitian Mermaid*, 1996. Textile, 67" × 51". *Photo: Carolyn L. Mazloomi*

Carolyn Crump, *Cracked Justice*, 2020. Textile, 66" × 78". *Photo: Carolyn L. Mazloomi*

Lauren Austin, *Instruments of His Justice*, 2012. Textile, 45.5" × 35". *Photo: Chas. E. Martin*

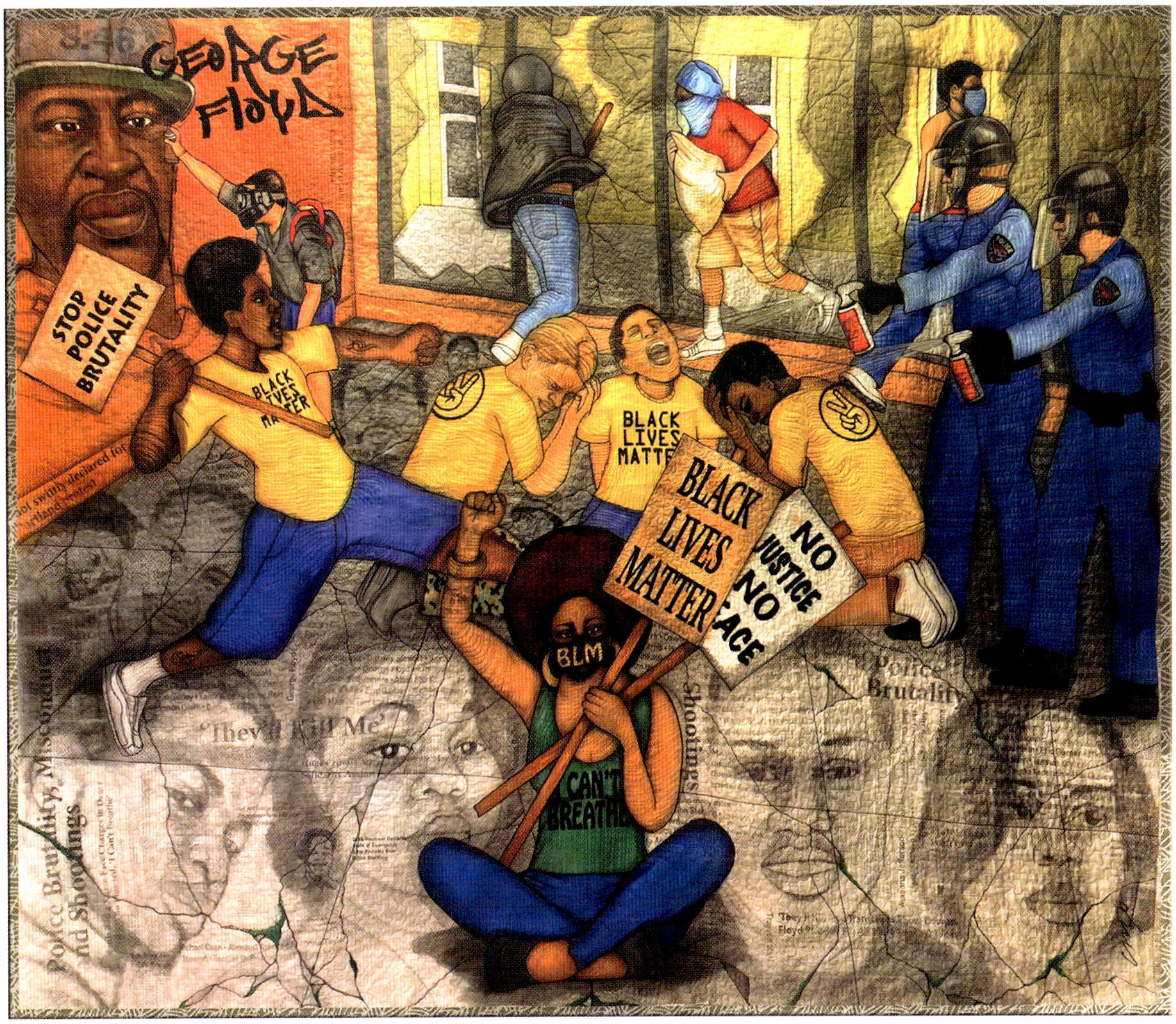
GEORGE FLOYD
STOP POLICE BRUTALITY
BLACK LIVES MATTER
BLACK LIVES MATTER
BLACK LIVES MATTER
BLM
Police Brutality
'They'll Kill Me'
Shootings

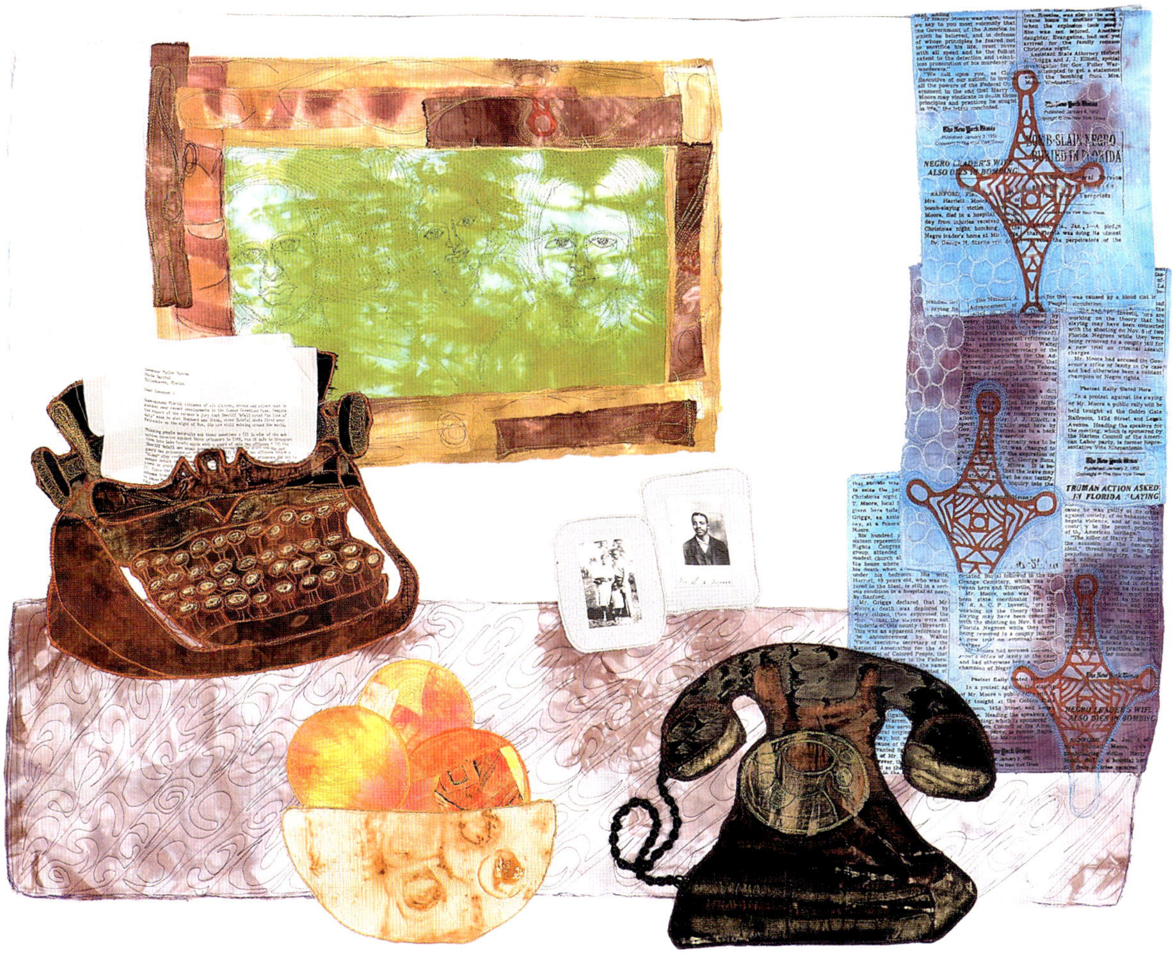

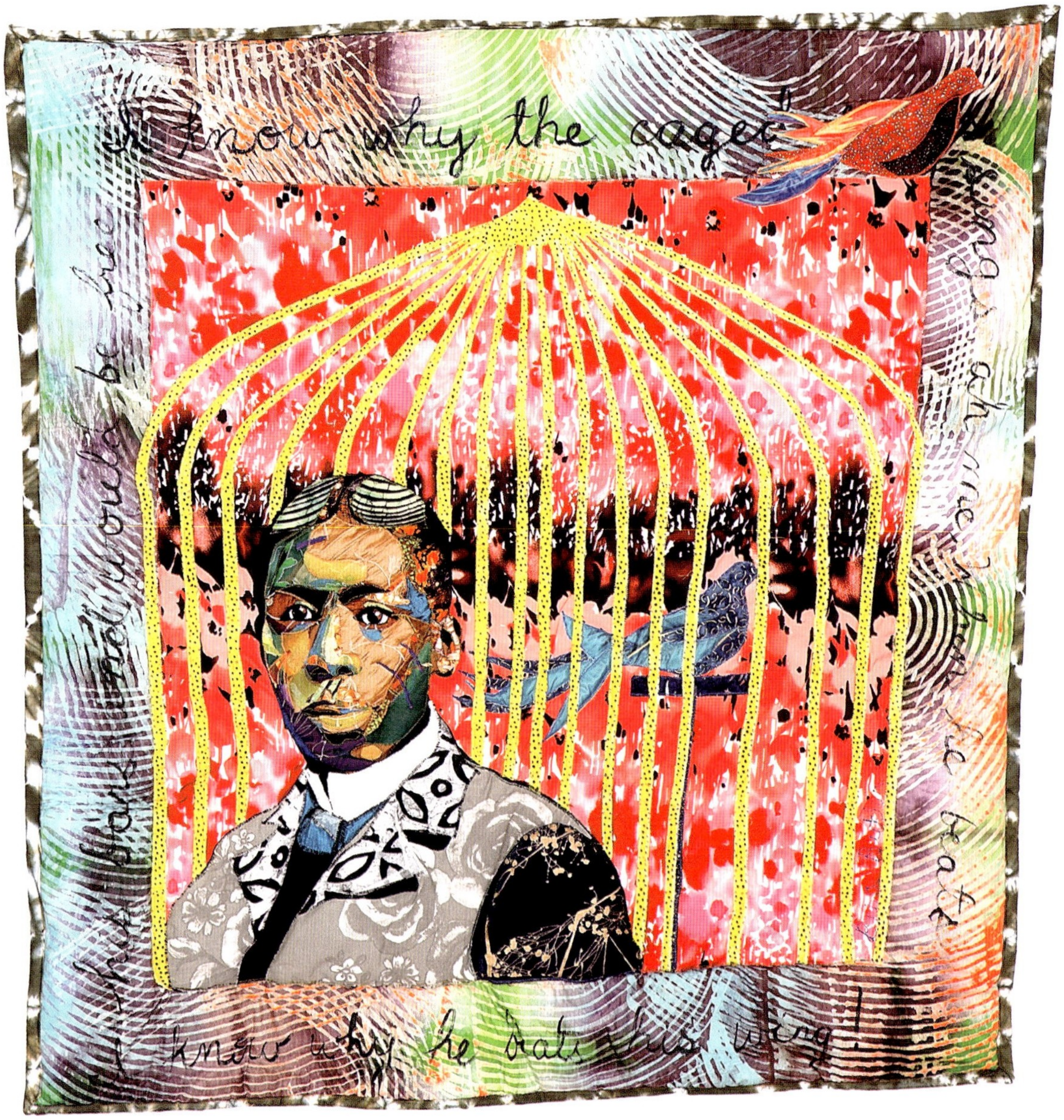
know why the caged

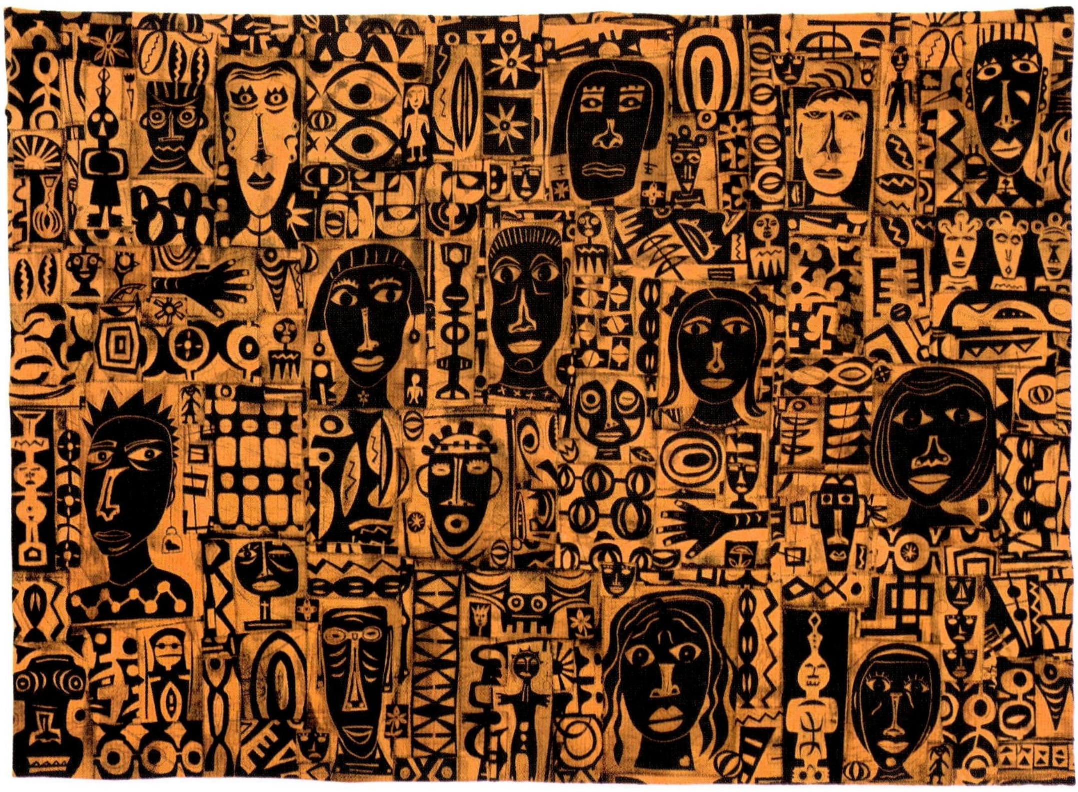

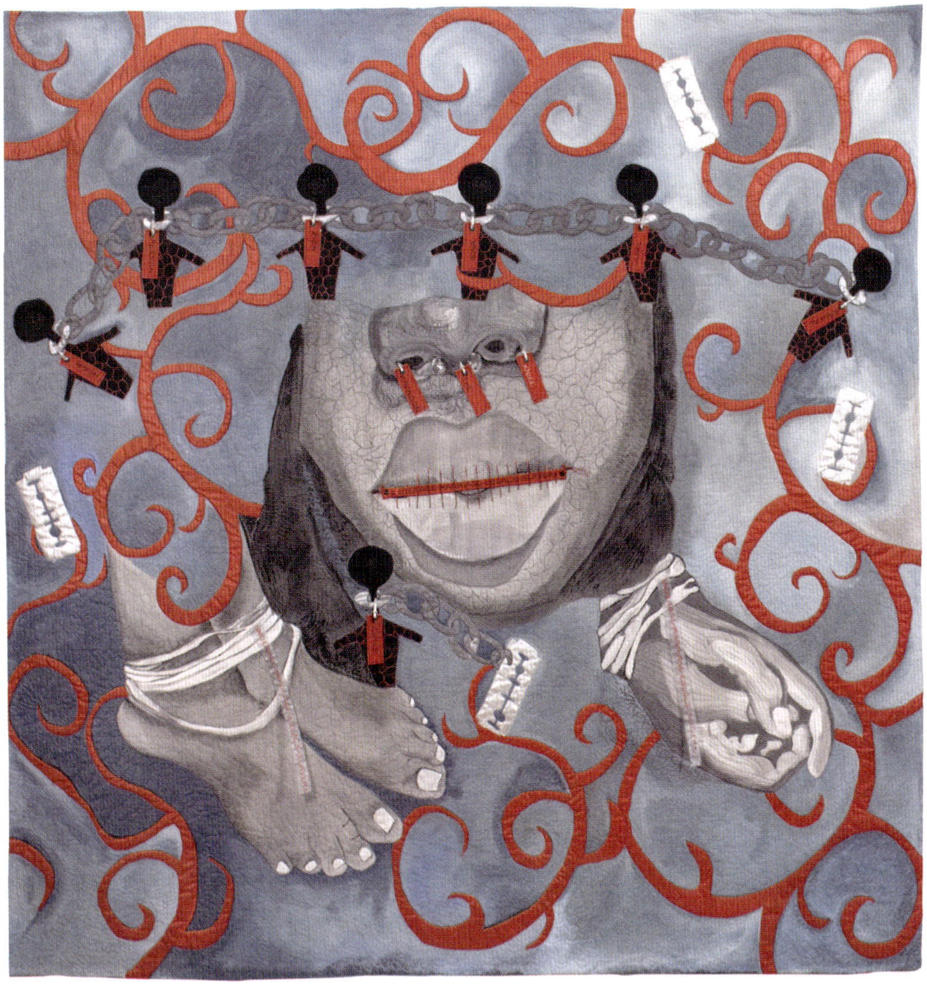

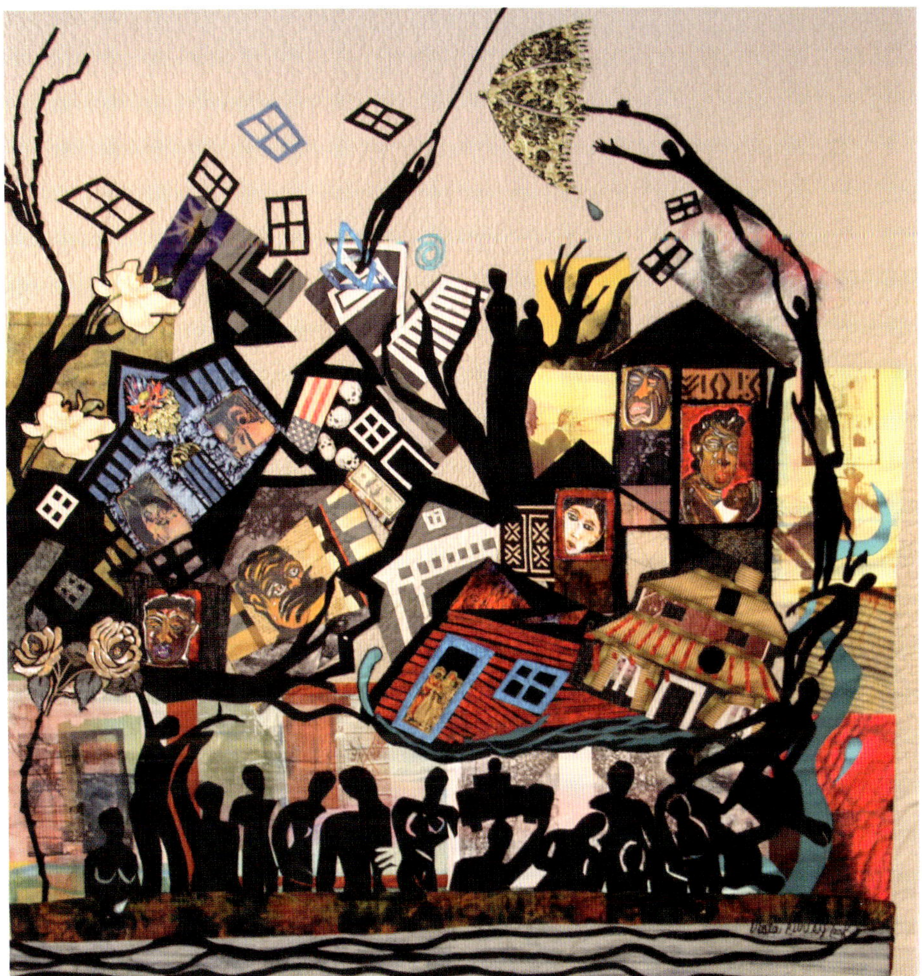

Opposite: Bisa Butler, *I Know Why the Caged Bird Sings*, 2012. Textile, 50" × 50". *Photo: Chas. E. Martin*

Opposite: Sharon Kerry-Harlan, *On the Face of it All*, 2016. Textile, 72" × 102". *Photo: Sharon Kerry-Harlan*

Sandra Scott, *Blood Ties*, 2016. Textile, 50" × 50". *Photo: Carolyn L. Mazloomi*

Viola Burley Leak, Katrina *Wreckage and Tears*, 2012. Textile, 76" × 69". *Photo: Chas. E. Martin*

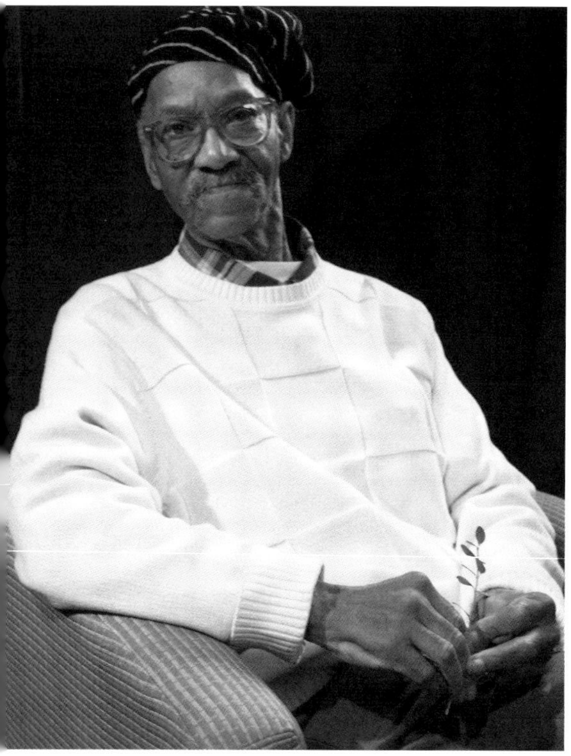

Photo: Myrah Brown Green

KARL A. MCINTOSH
MY COMMUNITY

DR. MYRAH: What was the first piece of art that you collected and when?

KARL A. MCINTOSH: The first piece of art that I collected was by Marion Griffith in the early seventies. She taught me to print at Restoration's print shop, along with the artist MLJ. When Marion painted, we used to trade artwork. She often painted woods and farmlands, using a magnifying glass. Much of her work depicts very small images that seem to be hidden within the composition. In the midst of her depiction of flowers, trees, and other forms of nature, she painted little people too.

DR. MYRAH: Why are you a Keeper of Community Art?

KARL A. MCINTOSH: I live in a community and was associated with Dorsey's Art Gallery, which was the community gallery. I had no choice but to connect with other artists from the community. I learned from these artists. And so, obviously, it was easier to collect art from the community where I was from and where I lived.

Many people who were a part of the community actually came from outside the community. I remember Elizabeth Catlett and Mr. Dorsey being good friends. Whenever Catlett came to New York, he would visit her, and she would come and visit the gallery. That is when I collected some of her work.

The culture of Dorsey's Gallery was not just community; it was like a family.

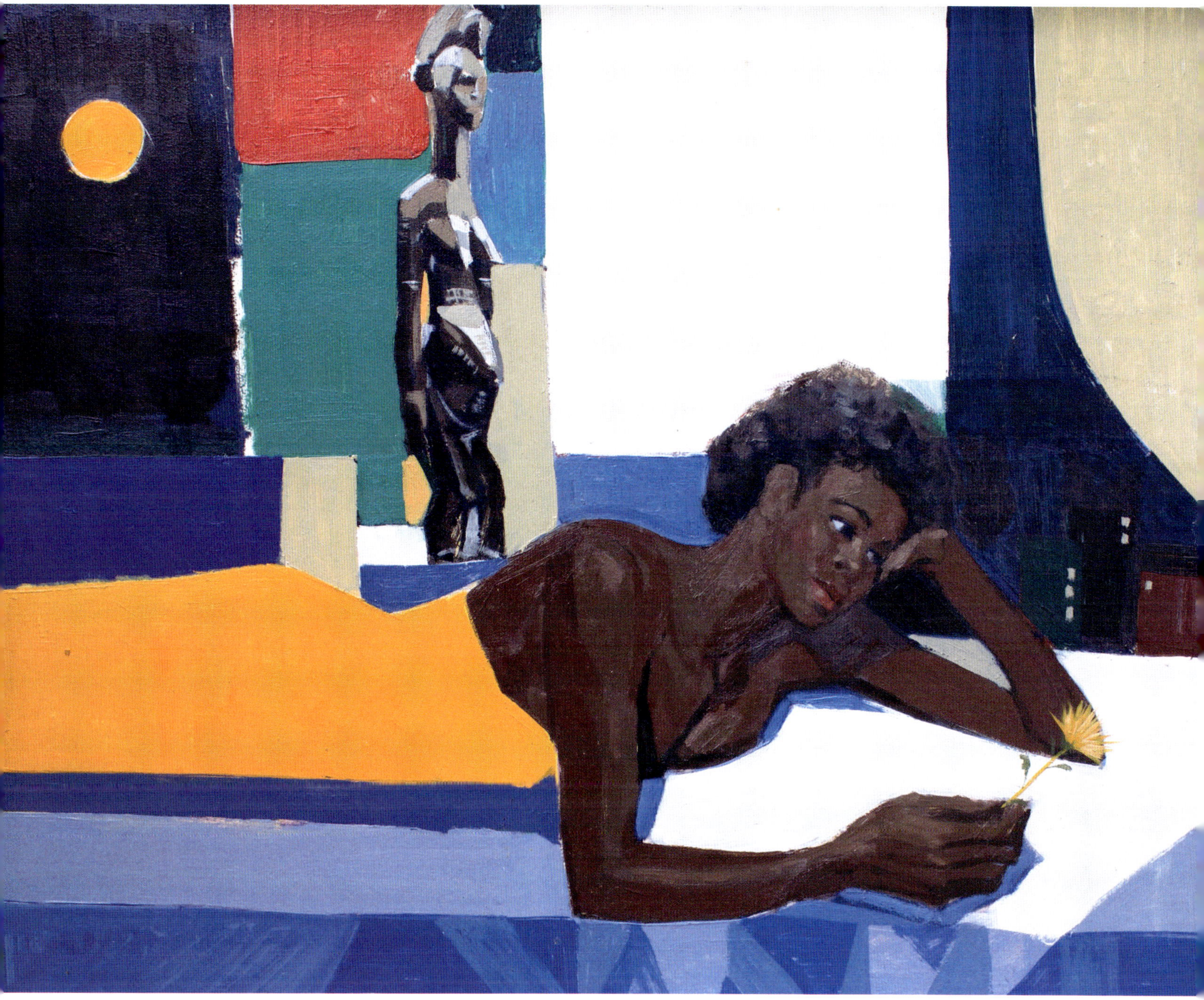

Ernest Crichlow, *Untitled* (date unknown). Acrylic on board, 35" × 24". *Photo: Myrah Brown Green*

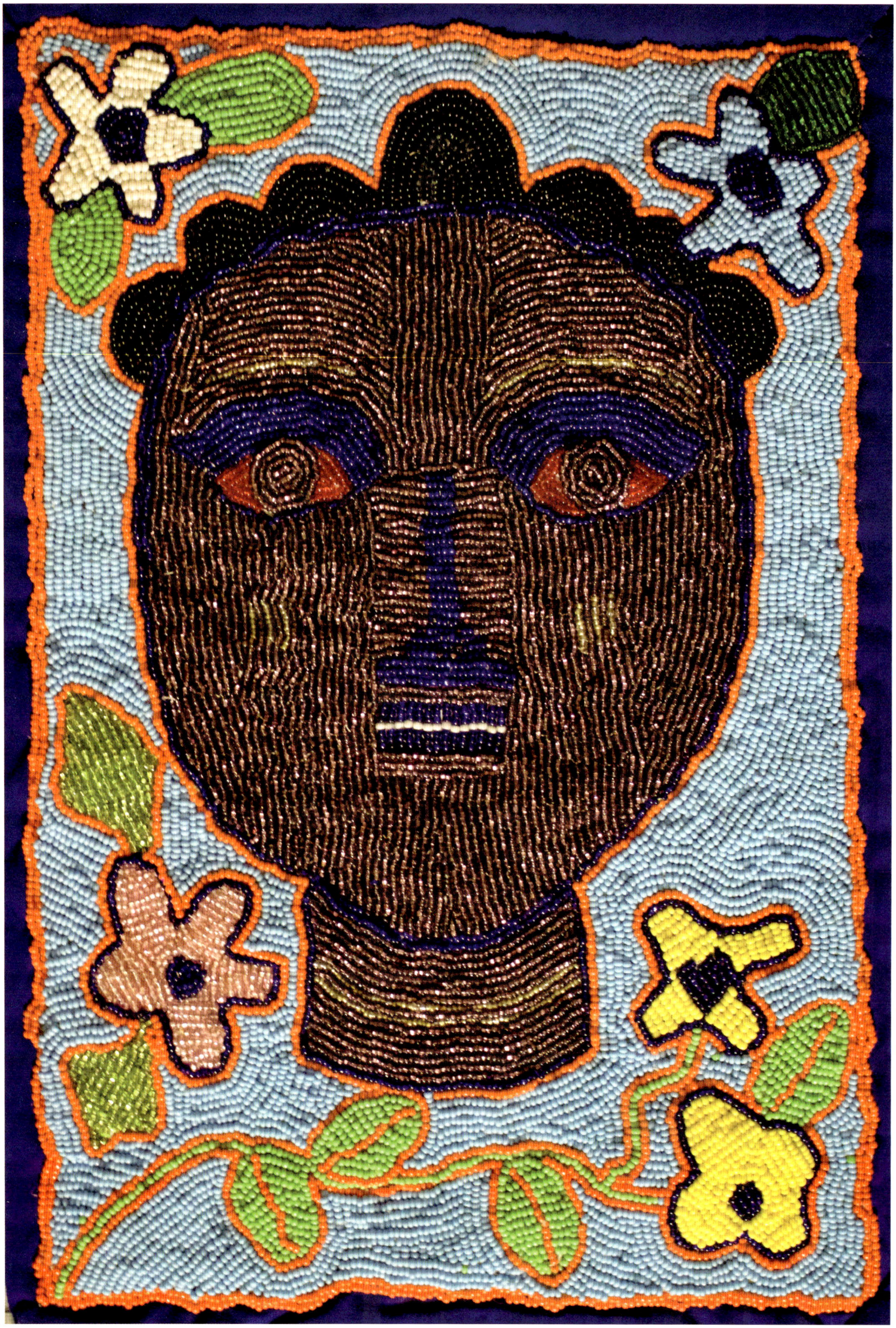

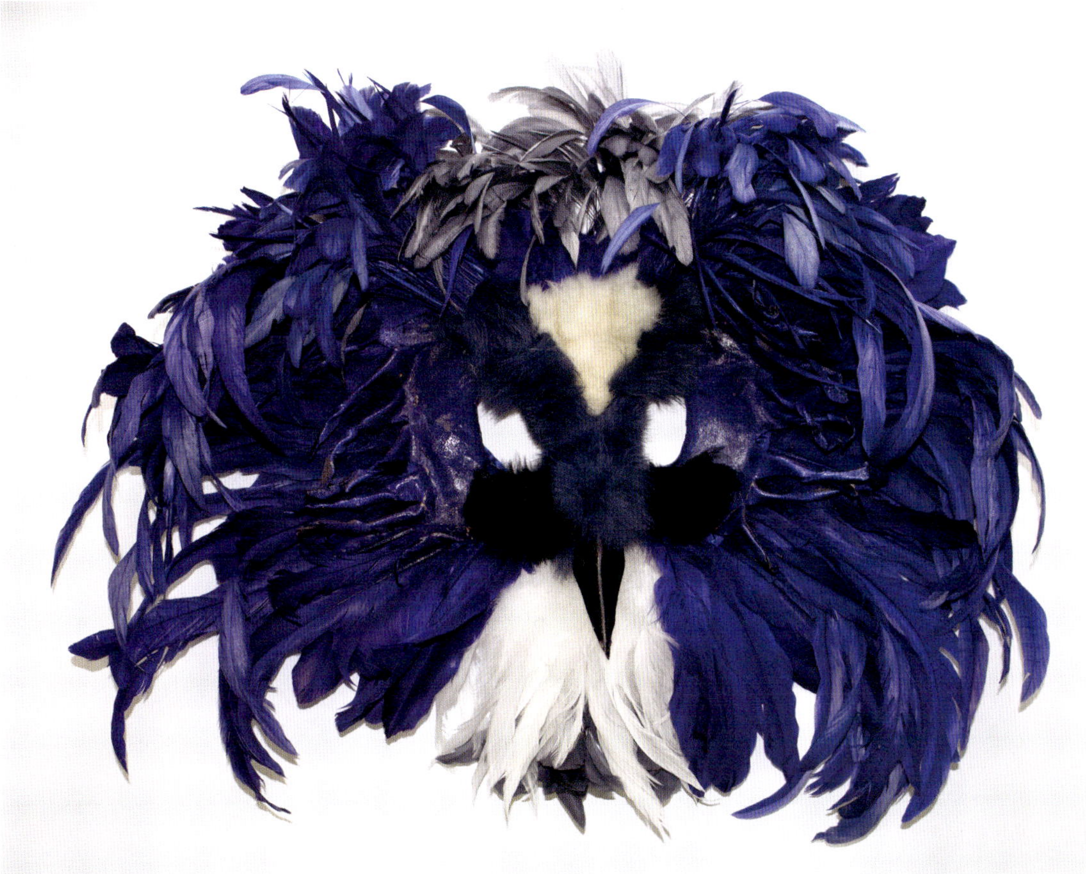

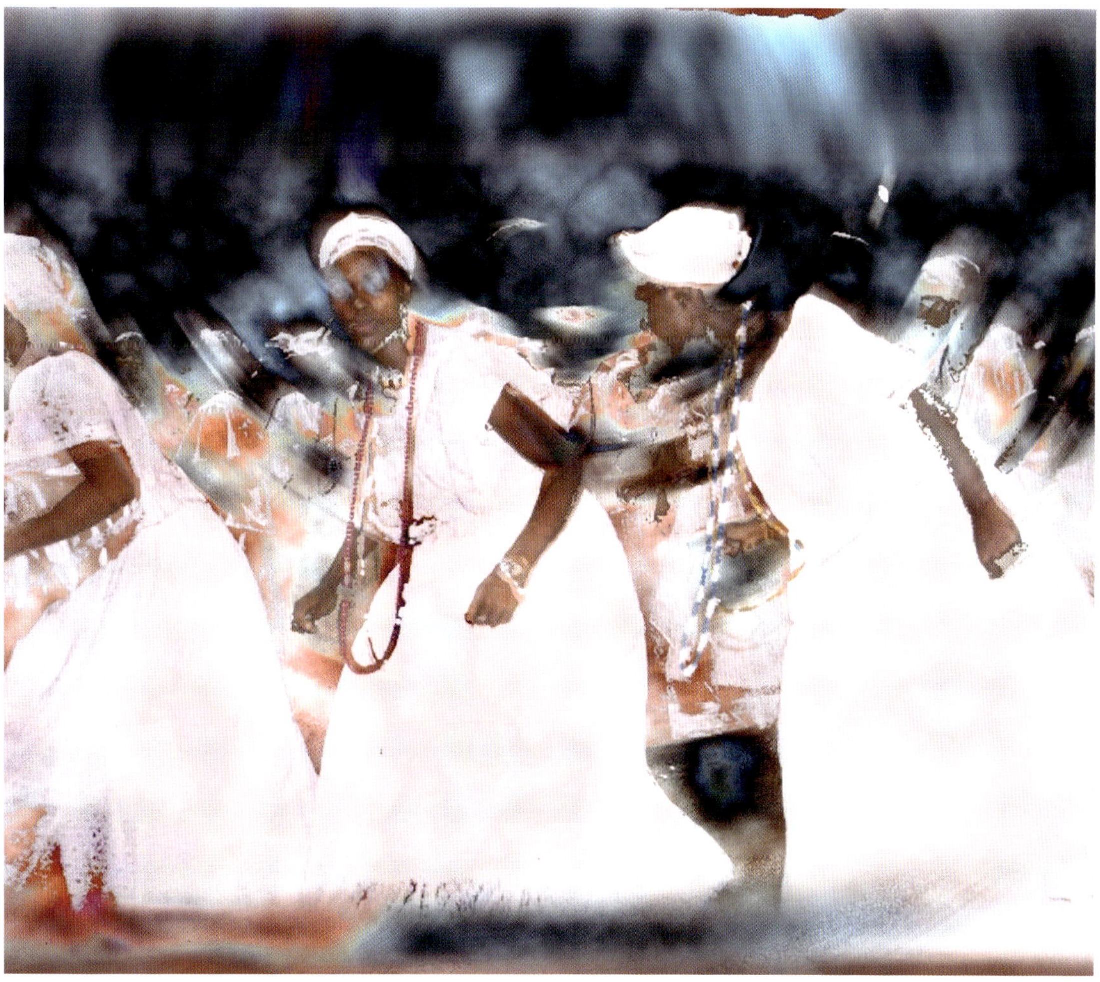

Opposite: Femi Turpin, *Untitled*, 2020. Beads on fiber, 20" × 14". *Photo: Myrah Brown Green*

Roman Mitchell, *Blue Bubo* (American great horned owl), 2024. Leather, fur, and feathers, 16" × 21.5". *Photo: Myrah Brown Green*

House of Life (Bahia, Brazil), ca. 1995. Metallic silver c-print, 16" × 20". *Photo: William Jones*

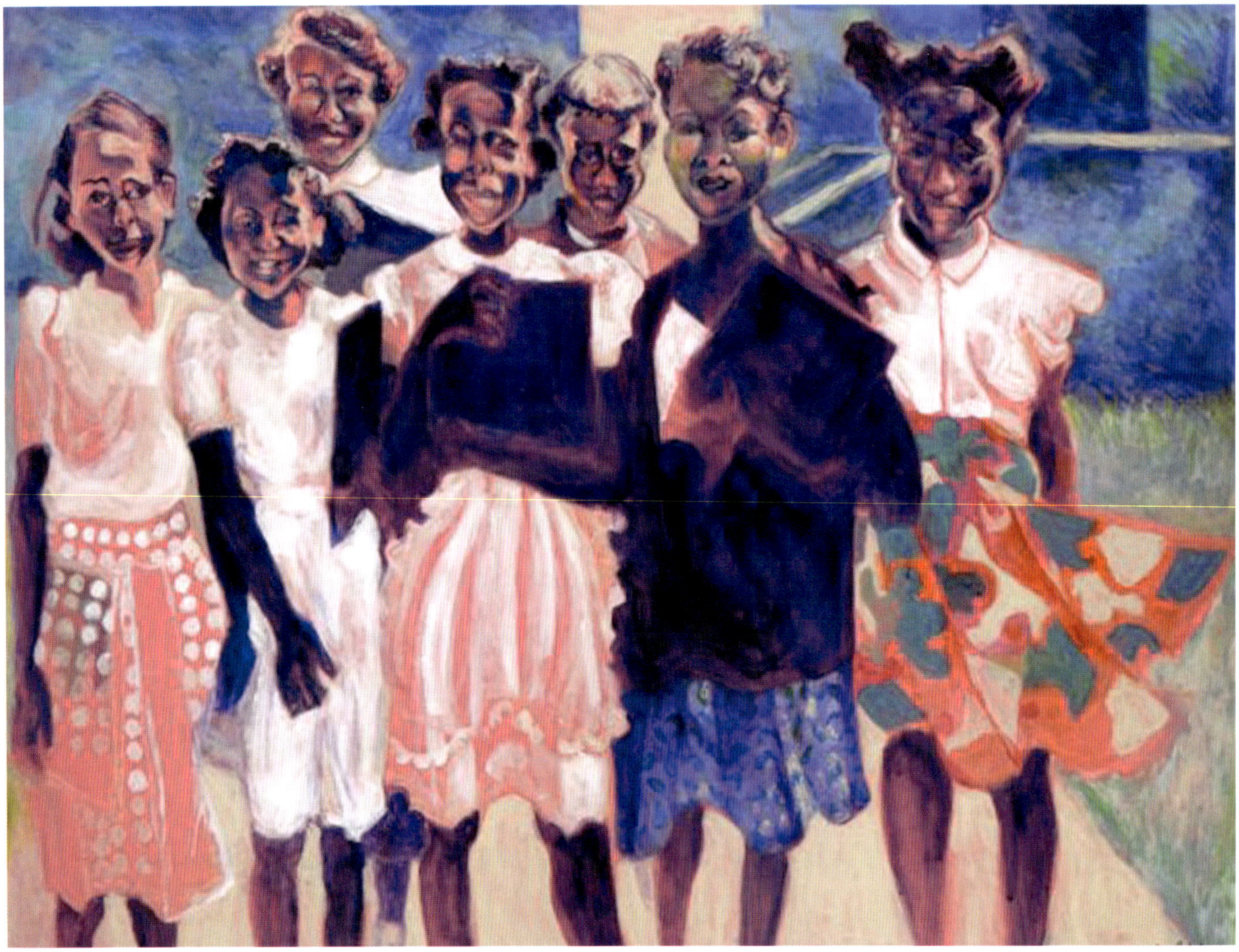

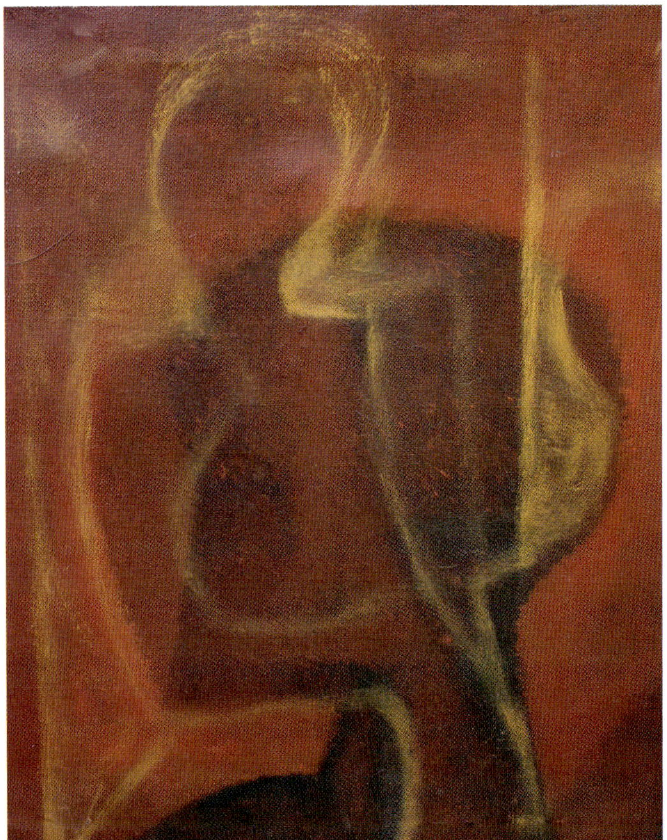

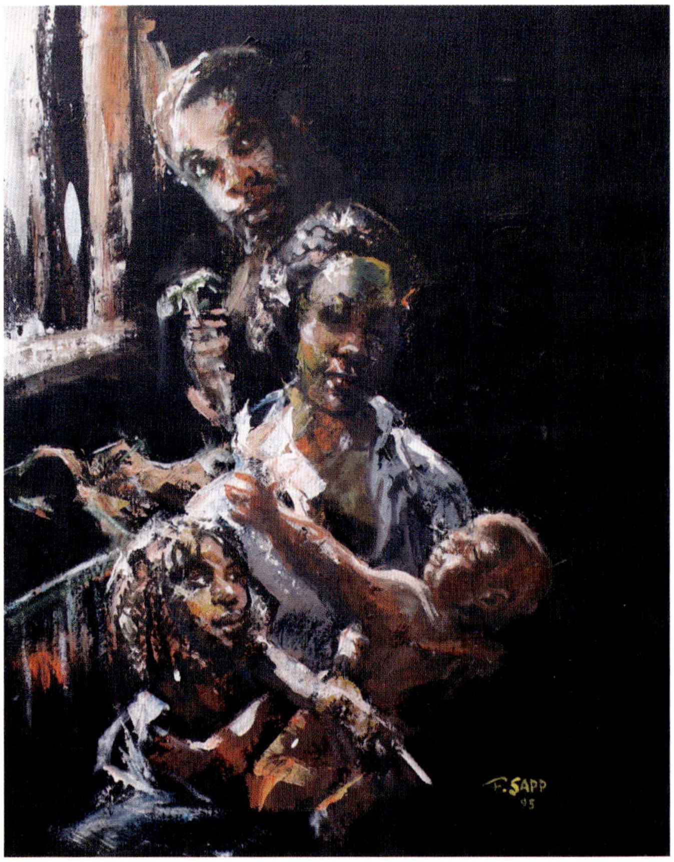

Top: Debra Ambush, *Encircling Angles* (Moton High School), 2023. Acrylic on canvas, 18" × 24". *Courtesy of the artist*

Leroy Clarke, *Untitled*, 1982. Acrylic on canvas, 24" × 20". *Photo: Myrah Brown Green*

Floyd Sapp, *Untitled*, 1995. Acrylic on canvas, 24" × 17". *Photo: Myrah Brown Green*

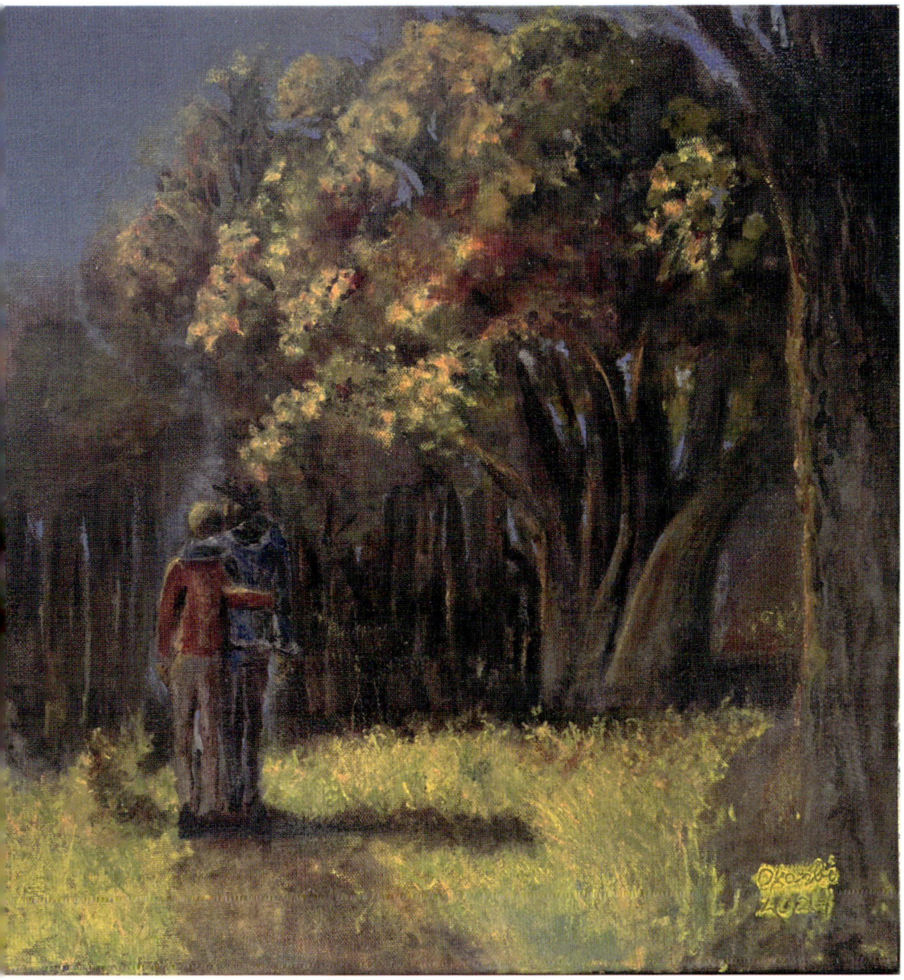

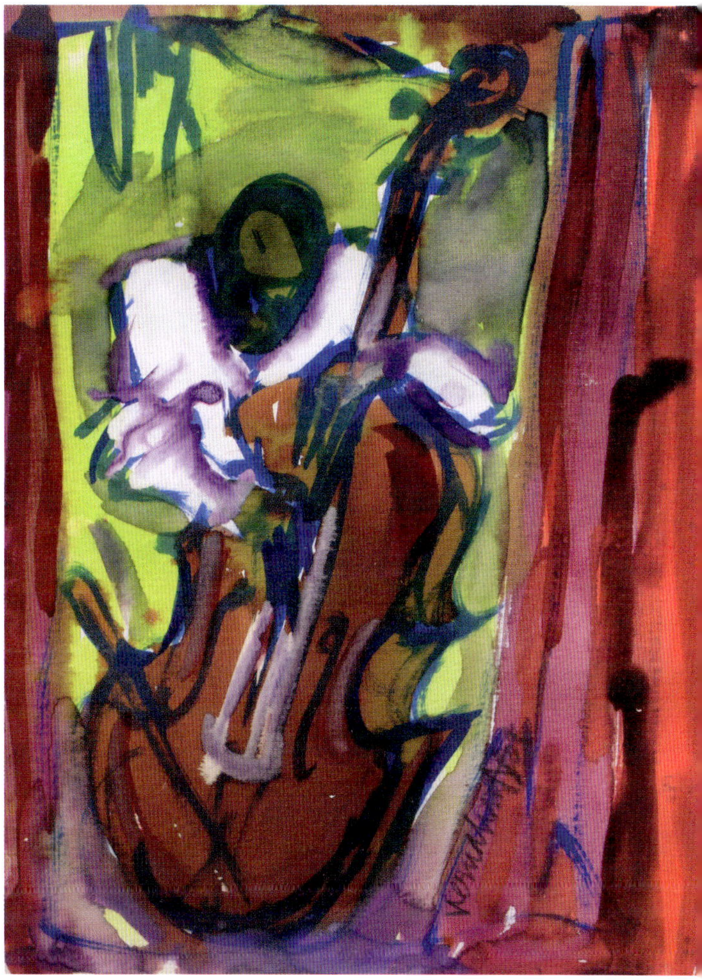

Okanbi Pound, *Walking in the Park*, 2024. Oil on canvas, 18" × 18". *Photo: Myrah Brown Green*

Verna Hart, *Crimson Base Blues II* (date unknown). Gouache on paper, 14" × 11". *Photo: Myrah Brown Green*

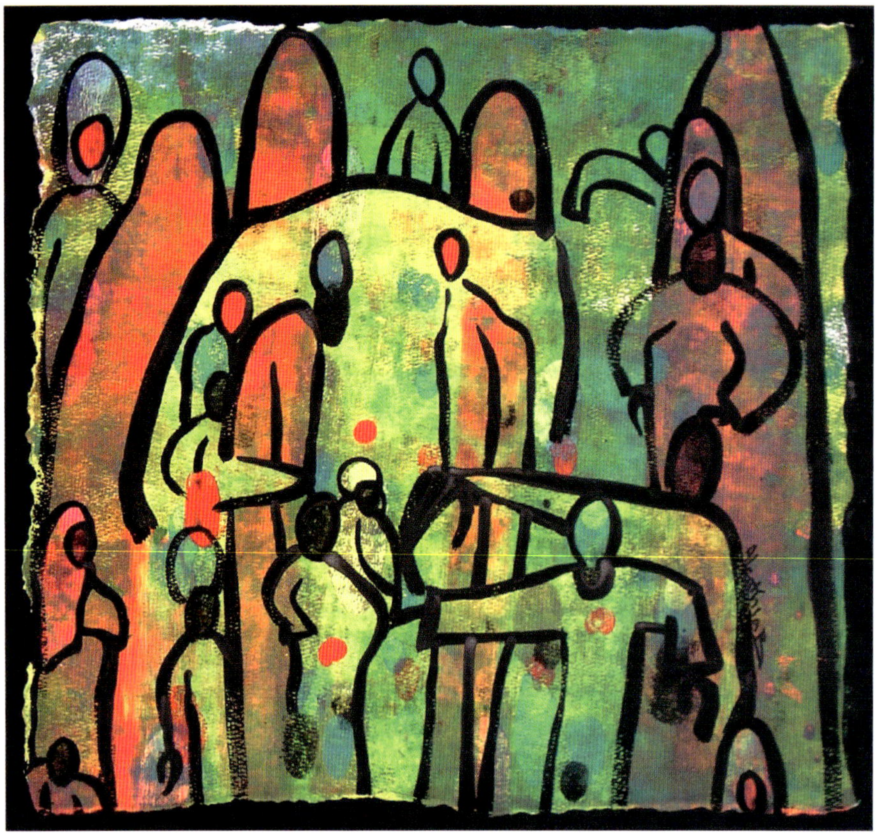

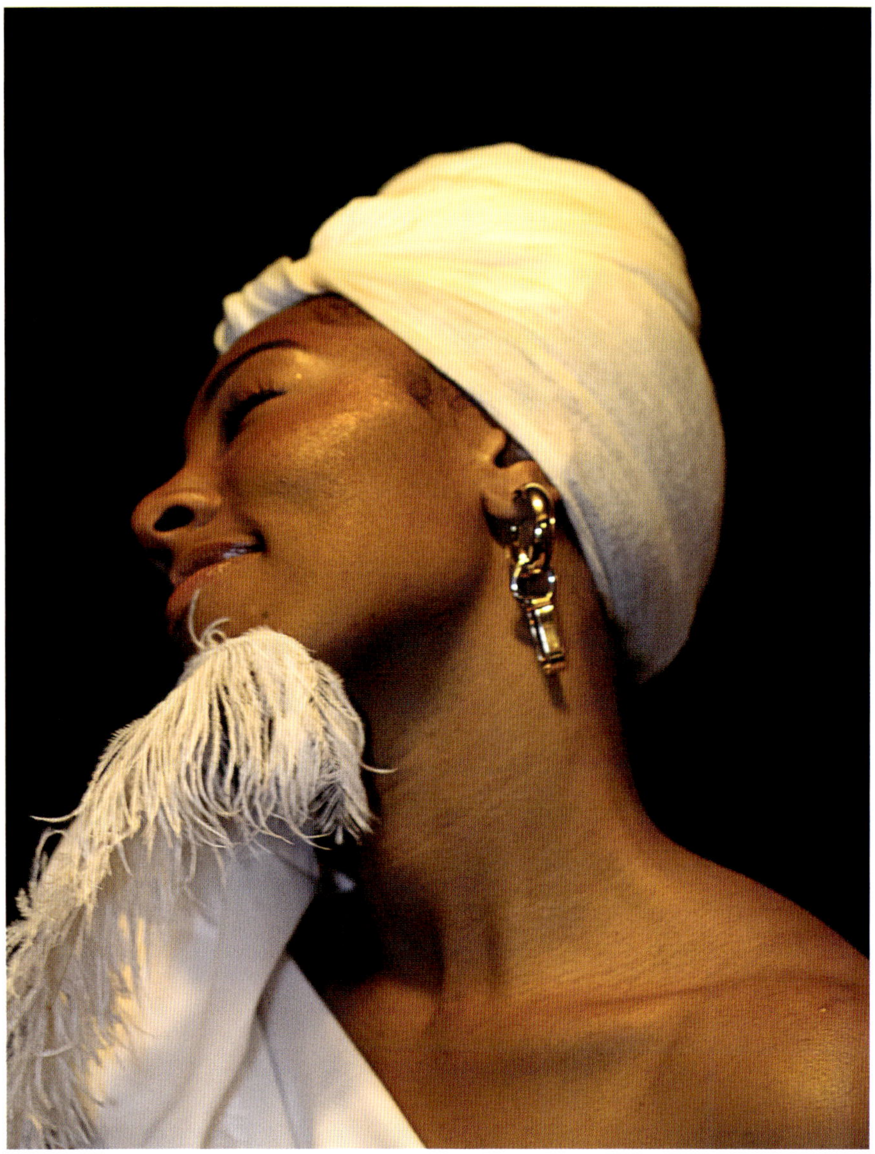

Aleathia Brown, *Community*, 2022. Acrylic on hand-torn fine-art paper (limited edition), 20" × 20".

Sannii Crespina-Flores, *Lovingly*, 2019. Archival pigment print, 11" × 8".

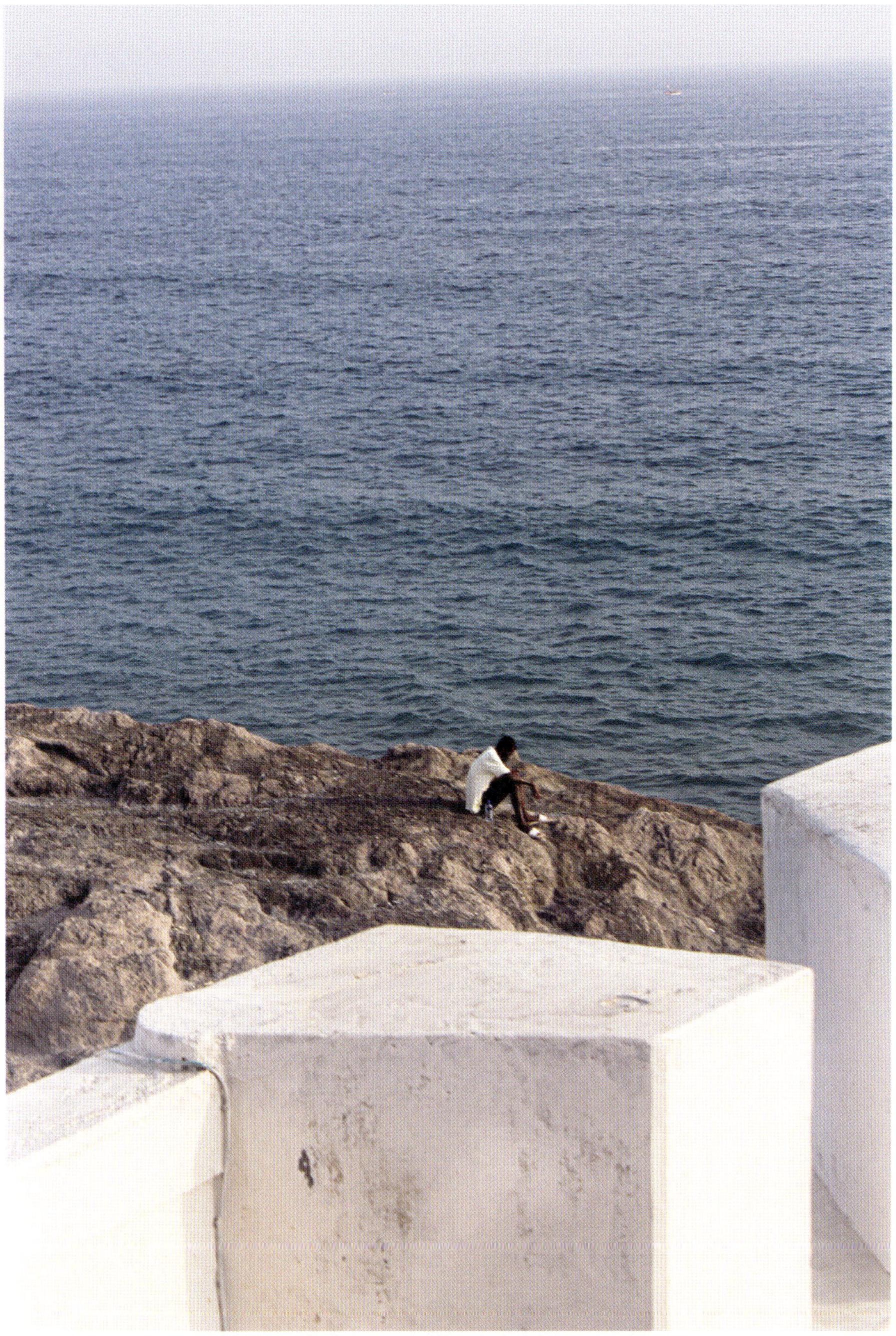

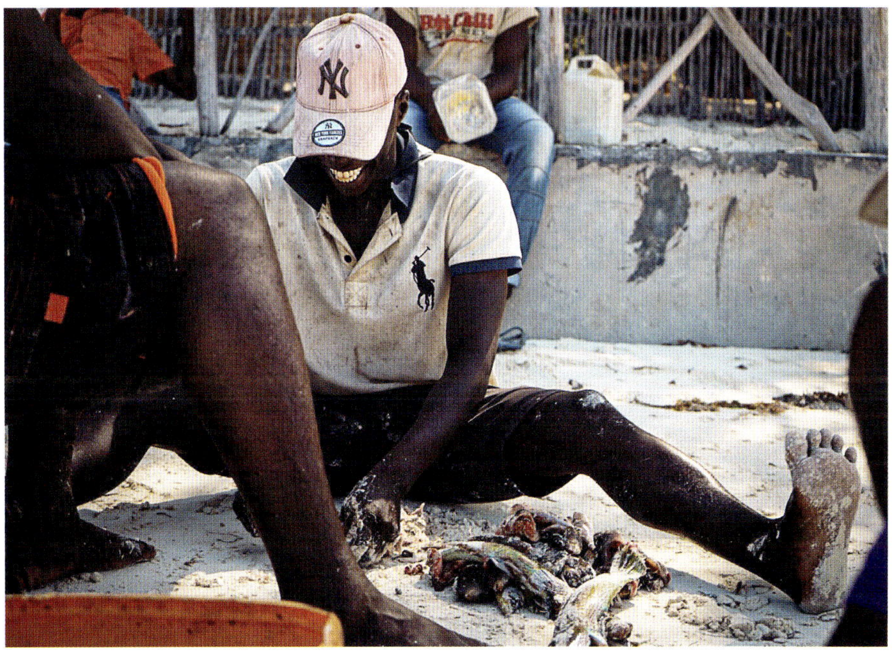

Summer-Zaire Bell, *In Thought* (Liberia), 2023.
Archival pigment print, 19" × 13".

Ryin Baskin, *Catch of Day: Red Snapper*, 2019.
Archival pigment print, 11" × 14".

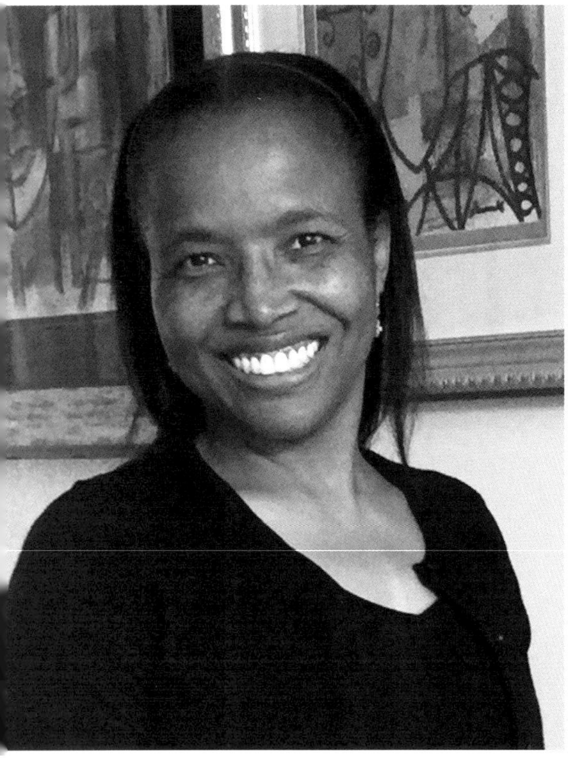

Photo: Courtesy of the collector

DUNA MENOS
IN HER SPACE

DR. MYRAH: What was the first piece of art that you collected, and when?

DUNA MENOS: One never forgets the first piece of art acquired at the start of an incredible journey. For me, it began over twenty years ago with two stunning collages by James Denmark: *Wanda* and *The Princess*. These works became the foundation of what is now my collection and sparked a lifelong appreciation for art that uplifts and celebrates Black culture and heritage.

DR. MYRAH: Why are you a Keeper of images featuring Black women in their personal spaces?

DUNA MENOS: The artistic depiction of Black women, whether in painting, drawing, collage, photography, or sculpture, is a marvel in its own right. These images capture moments of quiet beauty, strength, and individuality—expressions of a grace and power that defy words.

Seeing these women in their personal spaces offers a window into their essence. Whether it is a woman braiding her hair (Ernest Crichlow), reclining in the nude (Louis Delsarte), resting in stillness (Leo Carty), walking in thoughtful reflection (Betty Blayton), or singing under a spotlight (Karl McIntosh), each image tells a story of resilience and self-possession.

At first I didn't consciously recognize myself as a keeper of these images. Yet, as I reflect on my collection, I see how these depictions have woven themselves into a tapestry of identity and representation. They are reflections of me, of us, and of the many layers of Black womanhood: complex, diverse, and endlessly inspiring.

In cherishing these works, I hold space for these narratives to endure and resonate, ensuring that their beauty and meaning are preserved for future generations. Through this I am reminded of the power of art to affirm, celebrate, and connect.

Opposite: Leo Carty, *At Rest*, ca. 1990. Acrylic on paper, 16" × 12". *Photo: Myrah Brown Green*

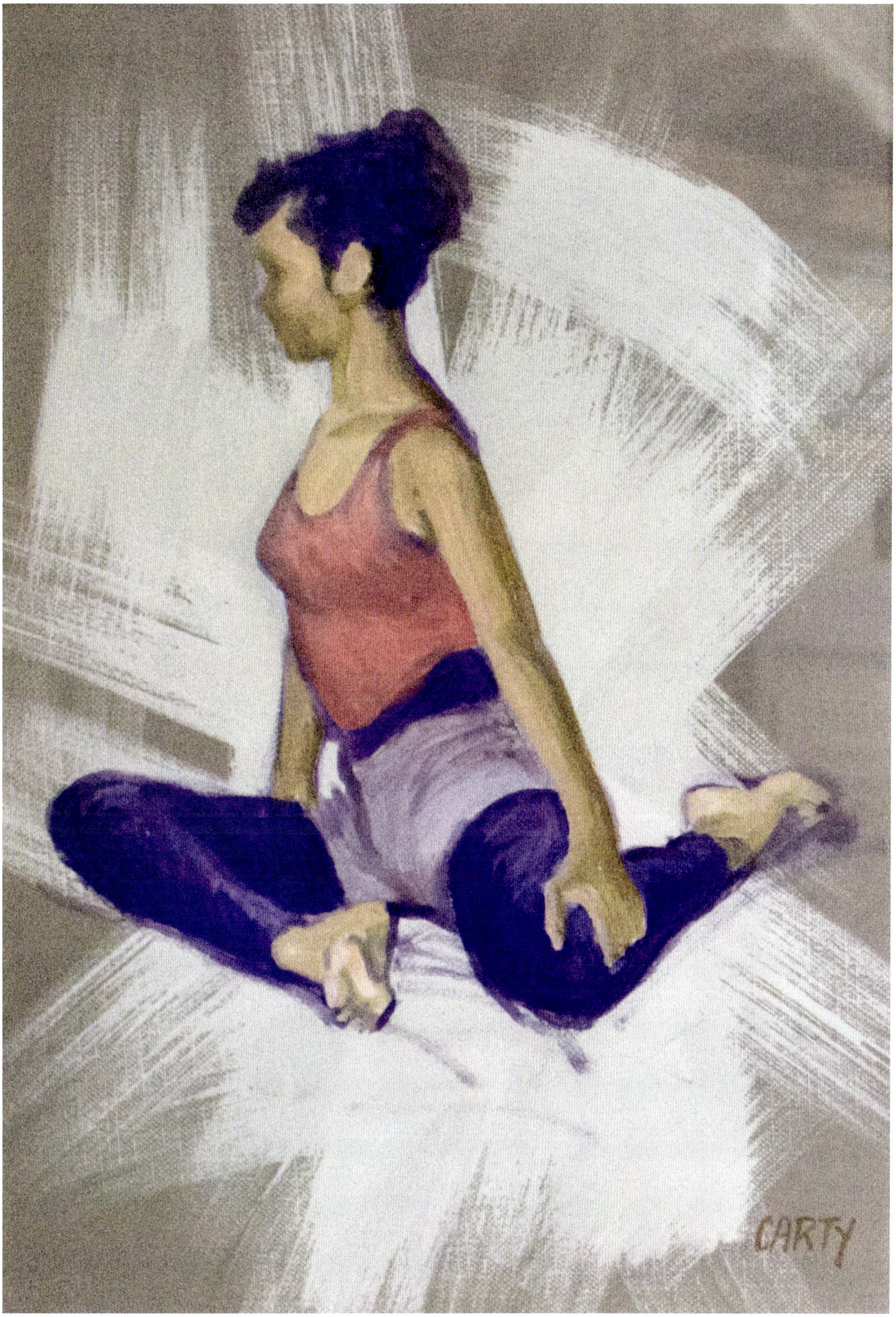
CARTY

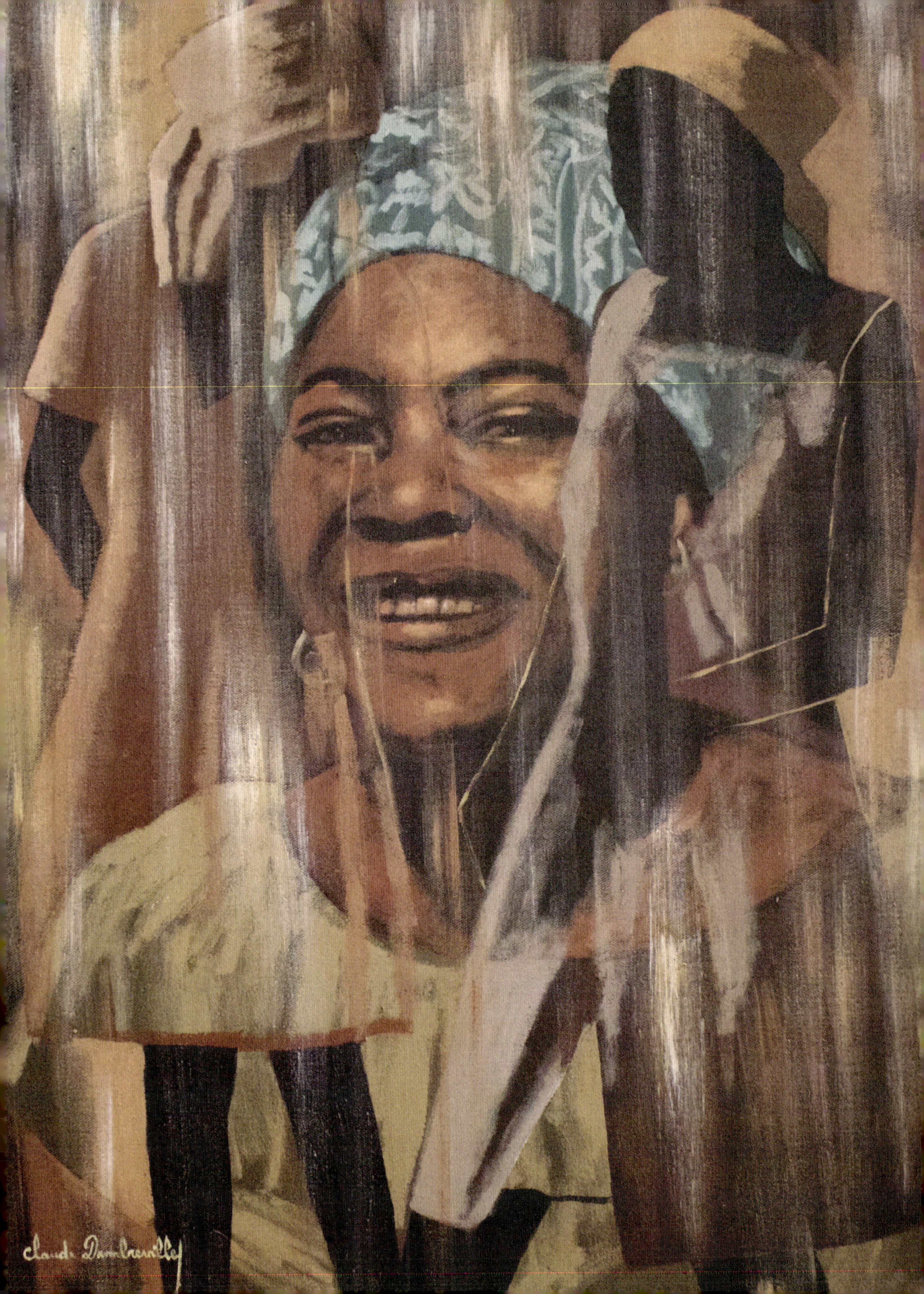
Claude Dambreville

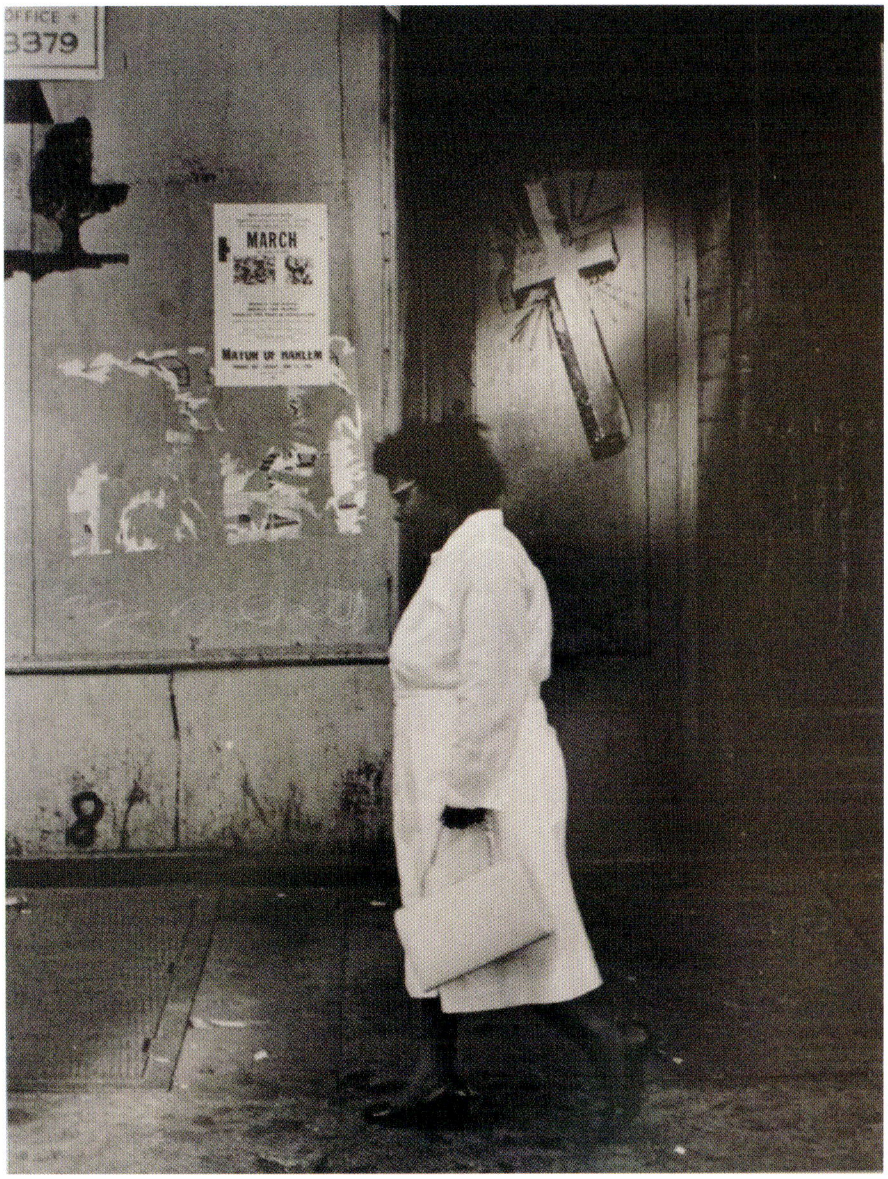

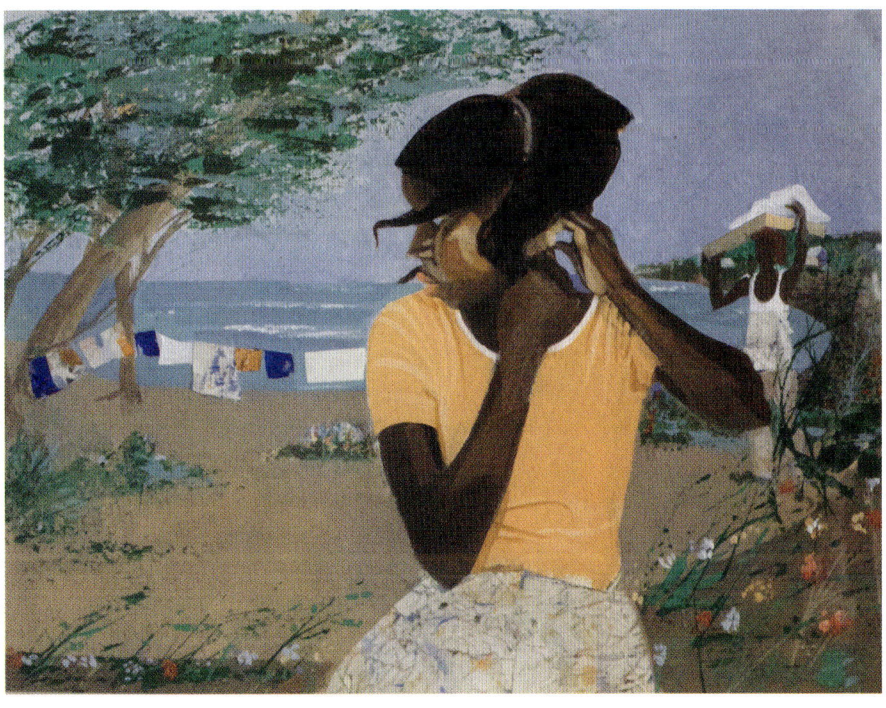

Opposite: Claude Dambreville, *Marchades* (date unknown). Oil on canvas, 32" × 24". *Photo: Myrah Brown Green*

Beuford Smith, *Sunday Morning*, 1968. Silver gelatin print, 14" × 11".

Ernest Crichlow, *Untitled* (date unknown). 14.5" × 19.5". *Photo: Myrah Brown Green*

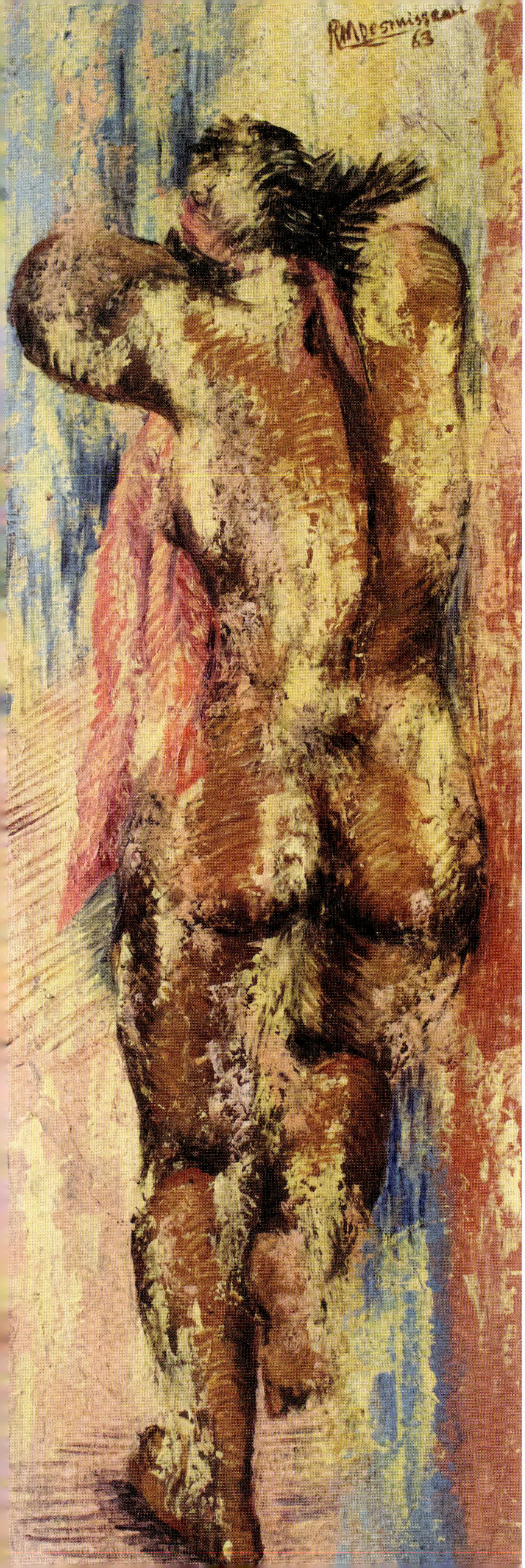

Rose-Marie Desruisseau, *Untitled*, 1963. Oil on canvas, 39" × 14". *Photo: Myrah Brown Green*

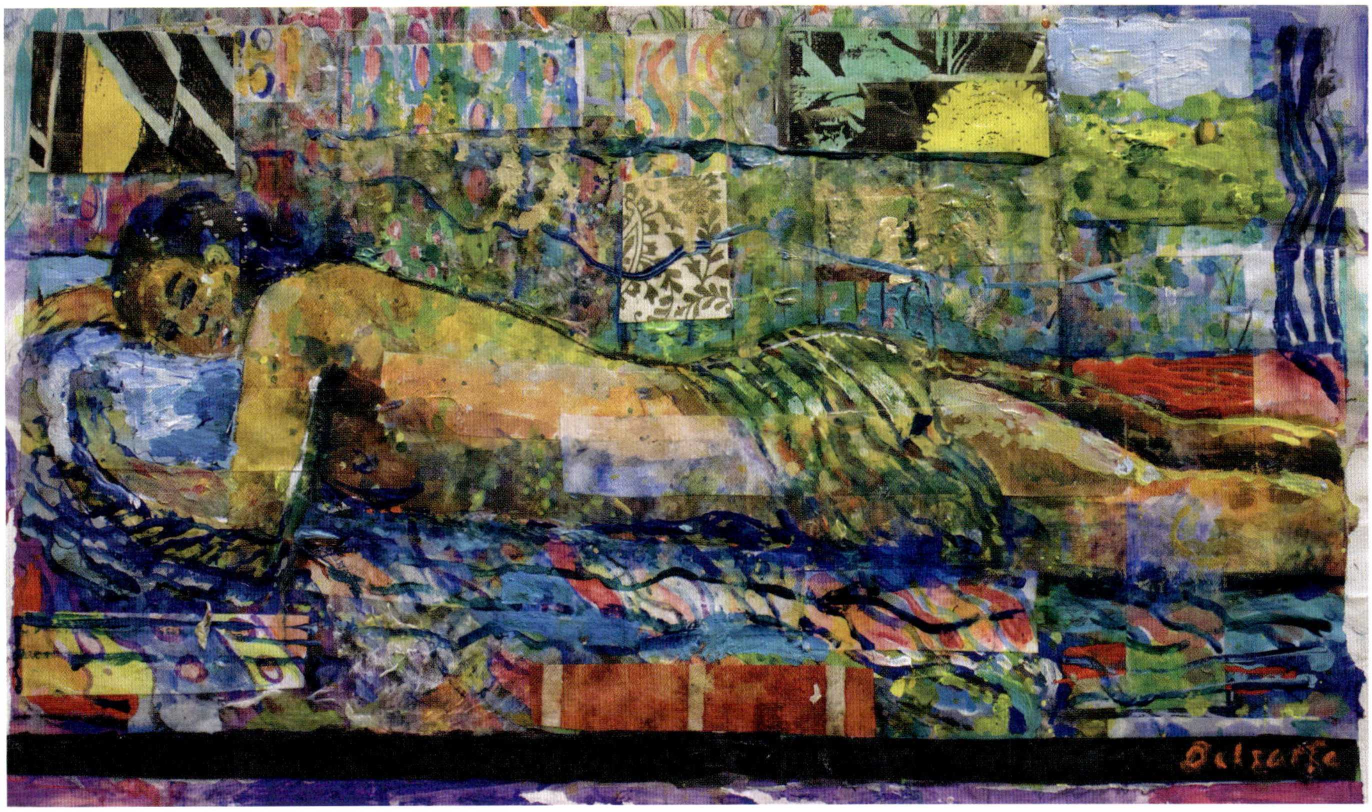

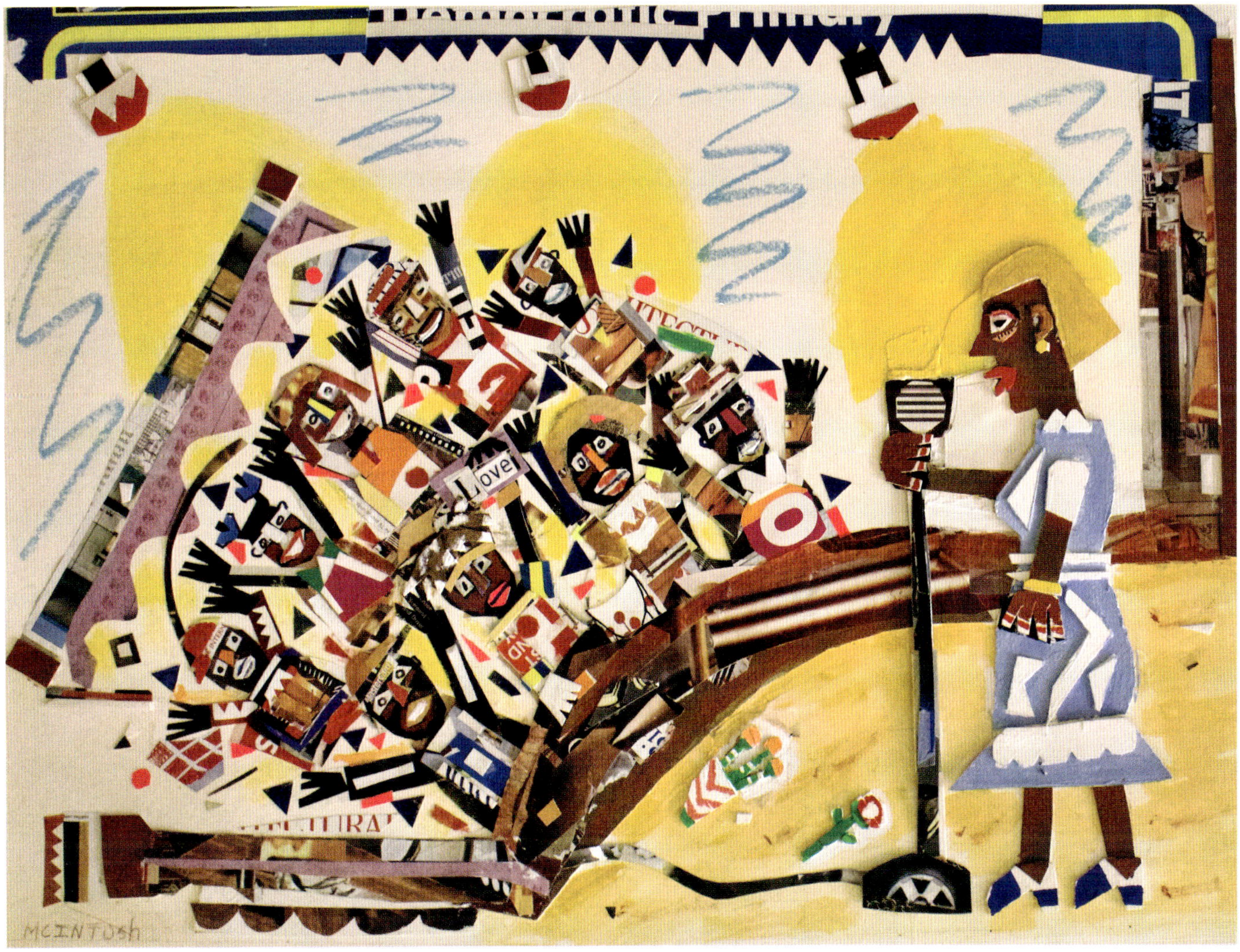

Louis Delsart, *Reclining Nude*, 2014. Mixed-media collage, 11" × 20". *Photo: Myrah Brown Green*

Karl A. McIntosh, *Diva*, ca. 2020. Collage, 20" × 27". *Photo: Myrah Brown Green*

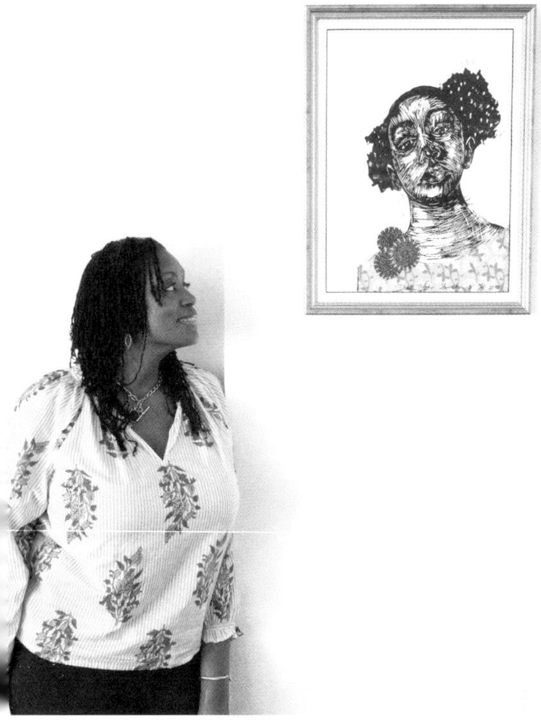

Photo: Colin Czerwinski

TARA MHELLA
CONTEMPORARY WOMEN

DR. MYRAH: What was the first piece of art that you collected and when?

TARA MHELLA: I started collecting art while studying in Zimbabwe. My first pieces were small Shona sculptures depicting families. These pieces, which were fashioned out of soapstone and serpentine, spoke to me with their powerful narratives.

DR. MYRAH: Why are you a Keeper of the art of Contemporary Black Women?

TARA MHELLA: Contemporary Black women artists speak for and to our community through their artwork. Their art documents the struggle and accomplishment of the Black community and tells the story of Black people through the transatlantic slave trade, in the diaspora, and on the African continent. This art connects us and keeps us rooted through our ancestry. These artists bind us together with narratives that depict our history of resistance and modern-day stories of resilience and love. As a collector, I serve as a vessel showcasing our stories past, present, and future. I am a keeper of contemporary Black women artists in honor of their artistic skill and cultural relevance. My work as a collector is a necessary act of cultural preservation.

Evita Tezeno, *Date Night*, 2018. Mixed-media collage on paper, 11" × 8". *Photo: Colin Czerwinski*

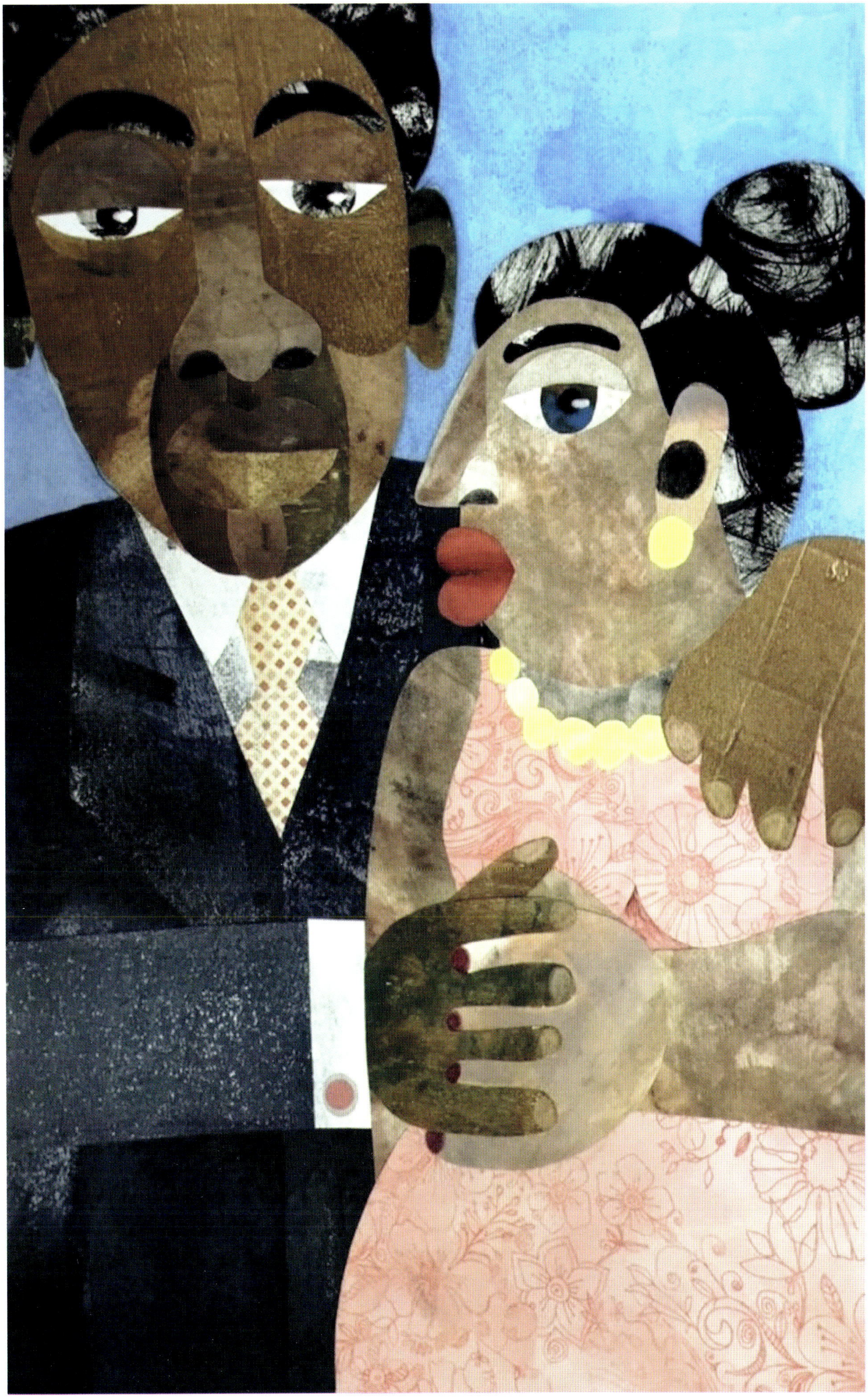

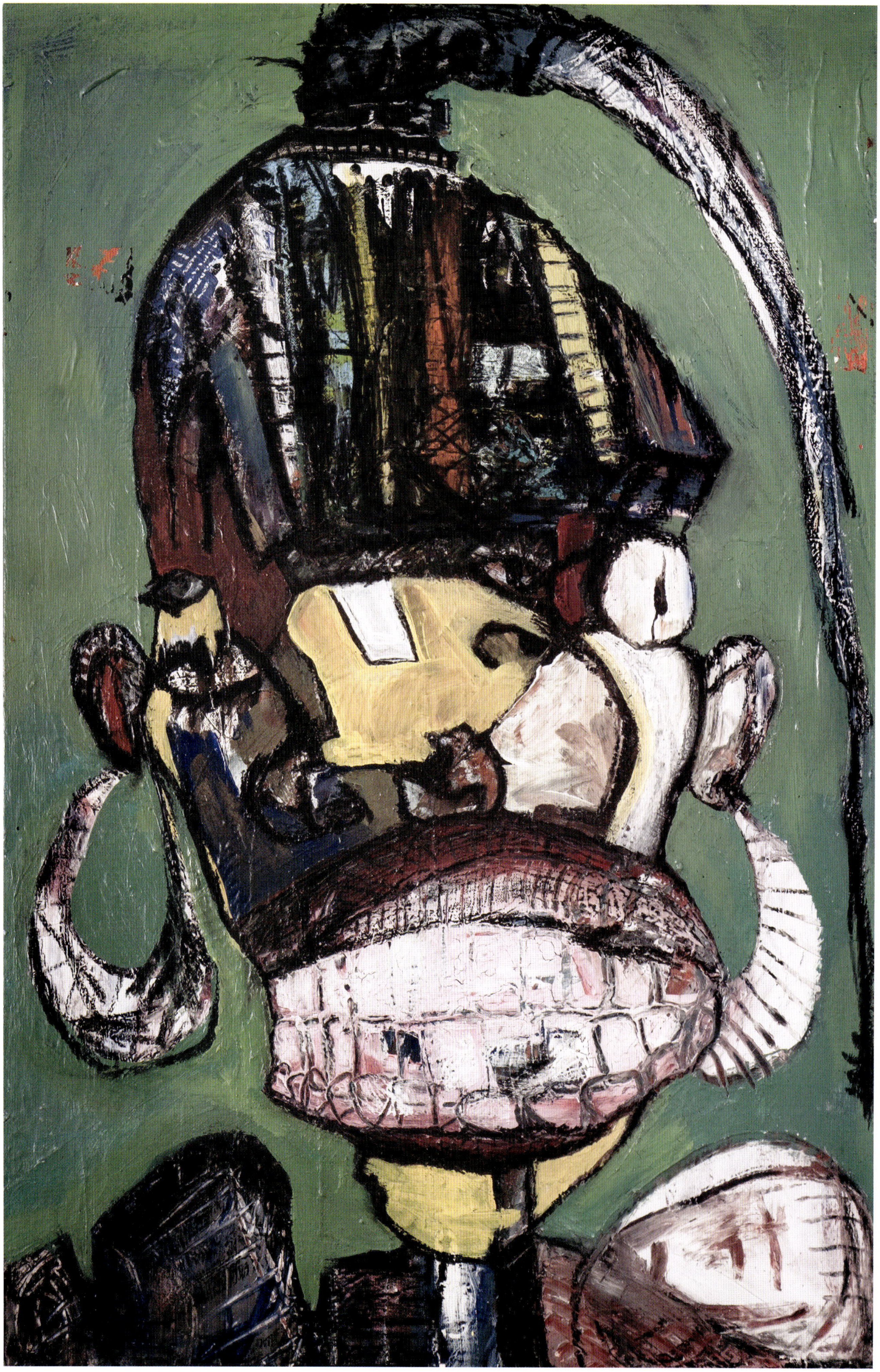

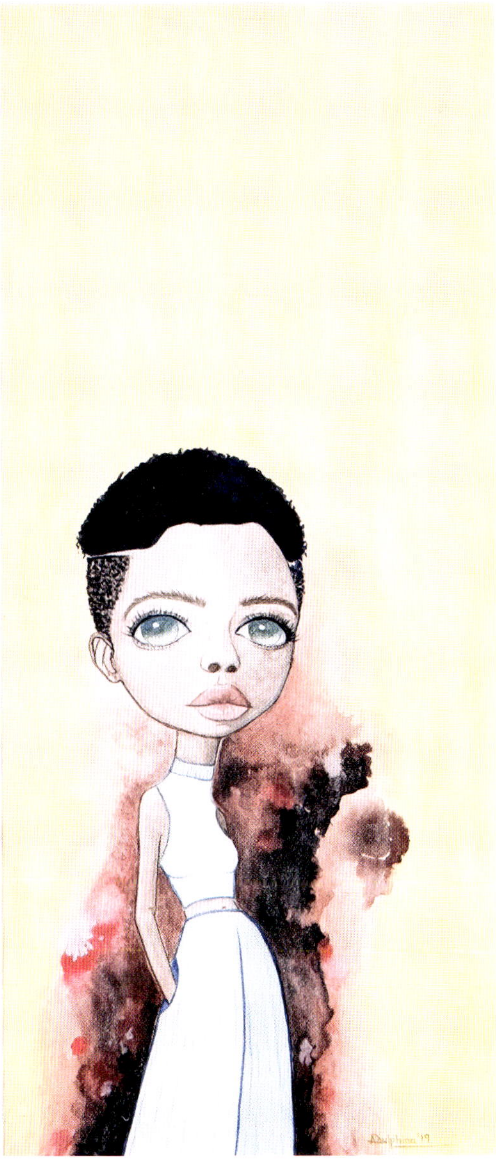

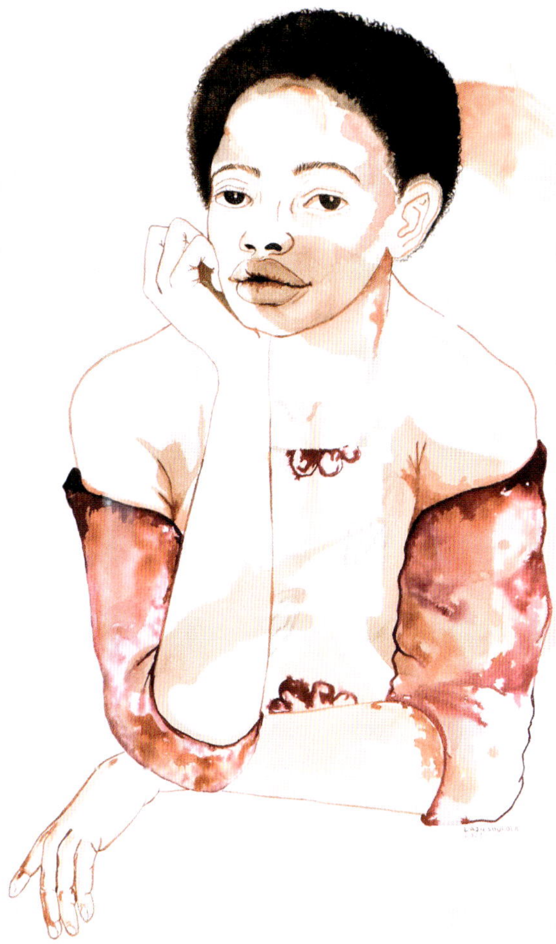

Opposite: Genesis Tramaine, *Around the Way Girl*, 2018. Acrylic, spray paint, gouache, pain sticks, and oil on canvas, 24" × 18". *Photo: Colin Czerwinski*

Adulphina Imuede, *Daydreaming*, 2019. Watercolor, acrylic, and ink on paper, 10" × 20". *Photo: Colin Czerwinski*

Laju Sholoa, *In My Feelings*, 2021. Tea, acrylic, and ink on paper, 22" × 30". *Photo: Colin Czerwinski*

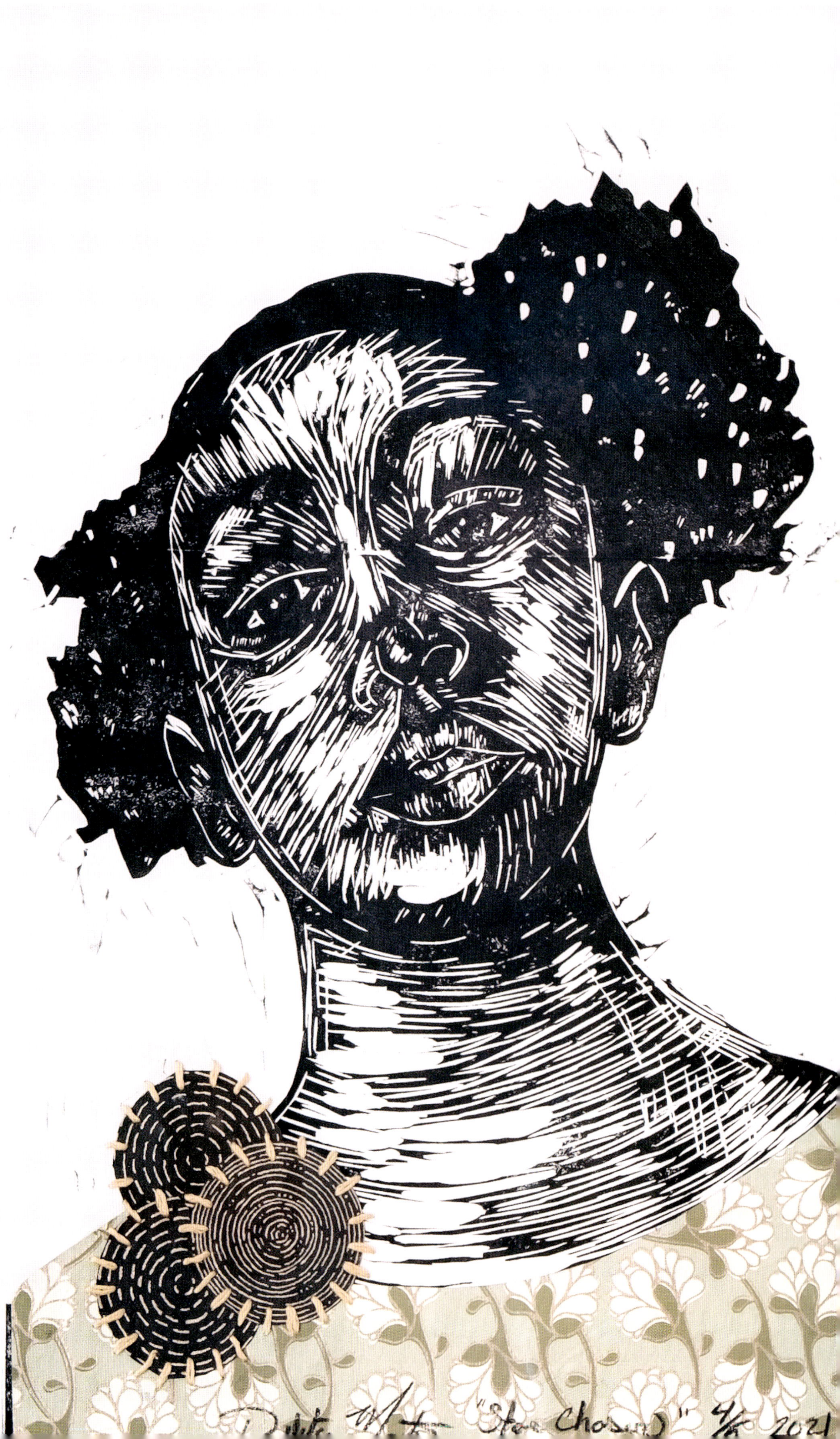

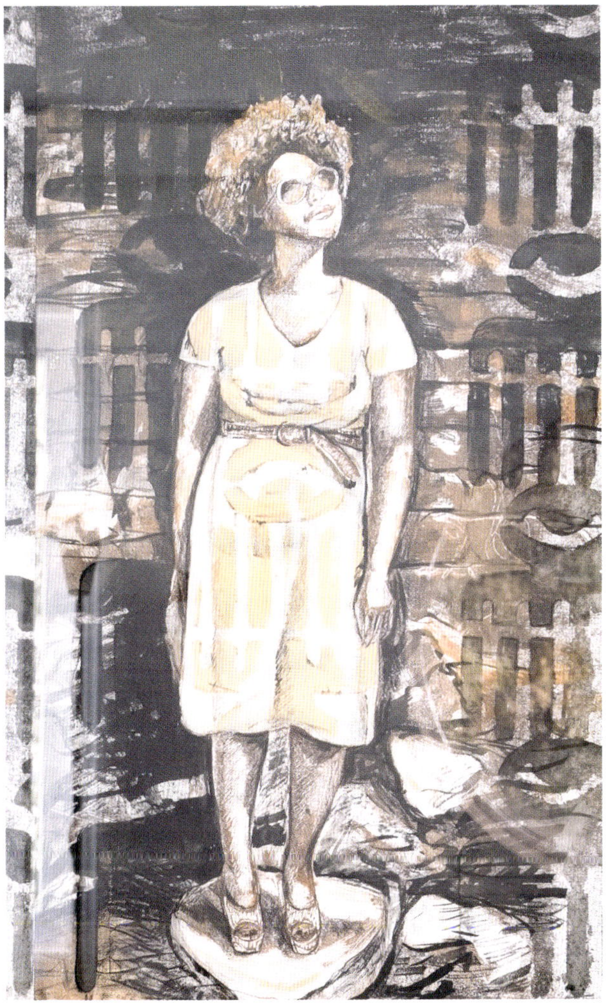

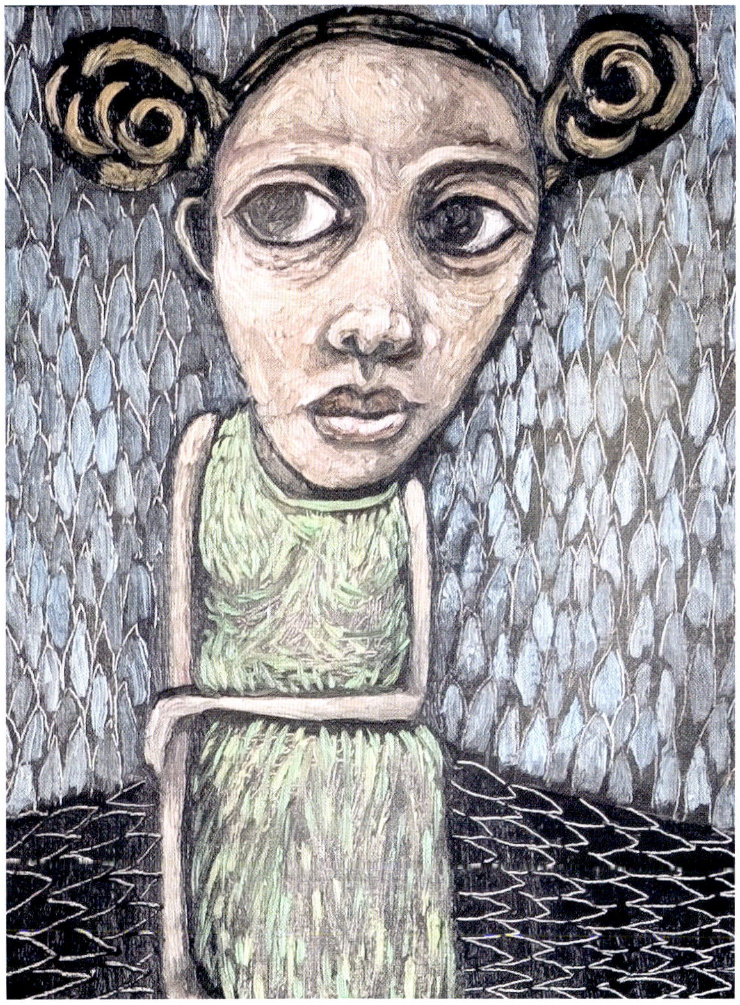

Opposite: Delita Martin, *Star Chaser* (four of five, varied editions), 2021. Relief, hand stitching, and decorative papers on handmade Abaca paper, 15" × 20". *Photo: Colin Czerwinski*

LaToya Hobbs, *Crystal Study #1*, 2013. Monotype and collage on paper, 23" × 14". *Photo: Colin Czerwinski*

Zoya Taylor, *Girl on the Corner*, 2020. Oil on canvas, 11" × 9". *Photo: Colin Czerwinski*

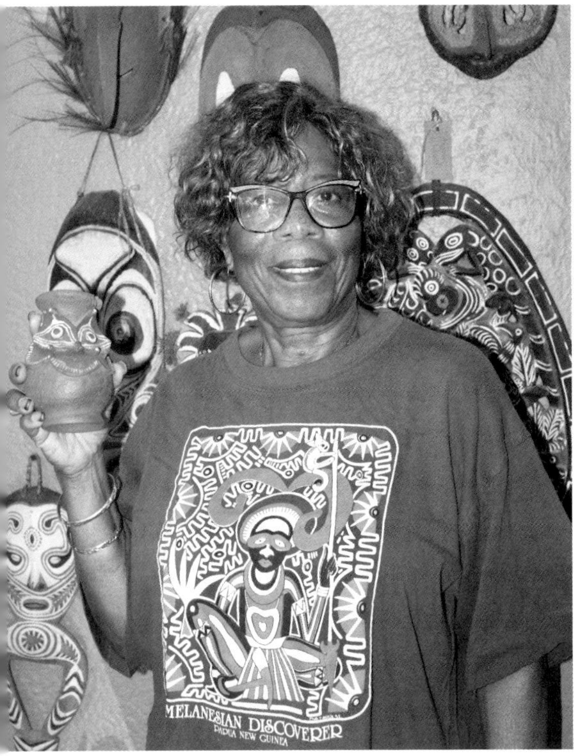

Photo: Myrah Brown Green

LORRAINE D. MITCHELL
PAPUA NEW GUINEA

DR. MYRAH: What was the first piece of art that you collected and when?

LORRAINE D. MITCHELL: The first piece of art that I collected was around 1991 or '92. It's by Jewel Golden; a collage piece titled *Born of Pain*. I was very impressed when I saw it at an art exhibit. I didn't think I had the money for it at the time. What I didn't know was that artists would sometimes accept payment in installments.

That's how I paid for my first piece of expensive art. It was about $1,500. She let me pay over time, and I was so happy. That piece still hangs in my dining room to this day.

DR. MYRAH: Why are you a Keeper of Art from Papua New Guinea?

LORRAINE D. MITCHELL: I am a Keeper of art and cultural treasures from Papua New Guinea. My journey there left a lasting imprint on my spirit, and my home reflects that experience. Once you set foot in Papua New Guinea, one witnesses the incredible artistry. Then, once speaking with the people, and truly seeing them, you recognize the undeniable connection to Africa. And so do they.

One unforgettable moment took place the night we flew into Mount Hagen, after leaving Port Moresby. Local villagers boarded a bus just to see us. Their faces told stories. Their expressions were powerful. They rubbed their skin against ours and said, "Wantok, wantok"—a word that means "one skin," "one talk," or "same language." It was a moment of deep connection. An unspoken recognition of shared origin.

Later, we traveled up the Sepik River to a remote region called Timbuktu and boarded the Melanesian *Discoverer*. When we arrived at the first village, the ship's Australian owner tried to lead us in. But the villagers rushed past her. They were trying to get to us. They saw themselves in us, the same way we saw ourselves in them.

These experiences were not fleeting. They were affirming. I remember a village chief who told us, had the Europeans arrived there, they too would have been enslaved, just as the brutal practice of blackbirding had been carried out in that region.

I've brought back objects—wood carvings, masks, ceremonial items—and I use them to teach. For those who may never travel as I did, I share these pieces so they too can see the world. So they can witness the many connections we have with others across the globe. There are more melanated people than we can ever imagine. And I've seen them. I've spoken with them. I've stood on their land. And I give thanks for that.

I also thank my Uncle John, a cook on a merchant marine ship. When he visited my mother, he would arrive with the biggest grin and his arms full of treasures from Africa—carved elephants and lions that I would play with as a child. Watching him, I knew: "When I grow up, I want to be just like him."

And now I am.

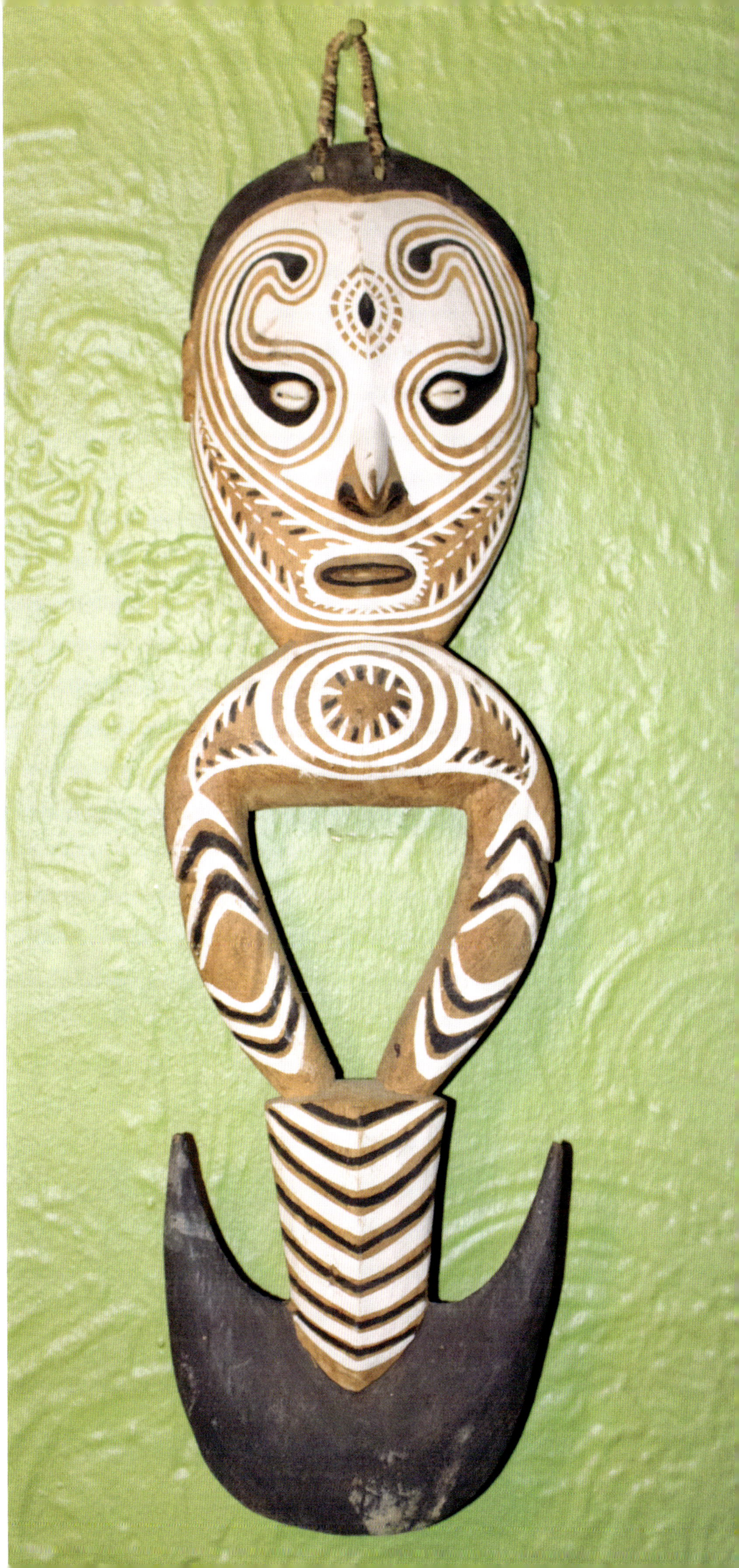

Papua New Guinea artist, *Untitled*, 1980.
Wood with black and white paint, 20" × 6".
Photo: Myrah Brown Green

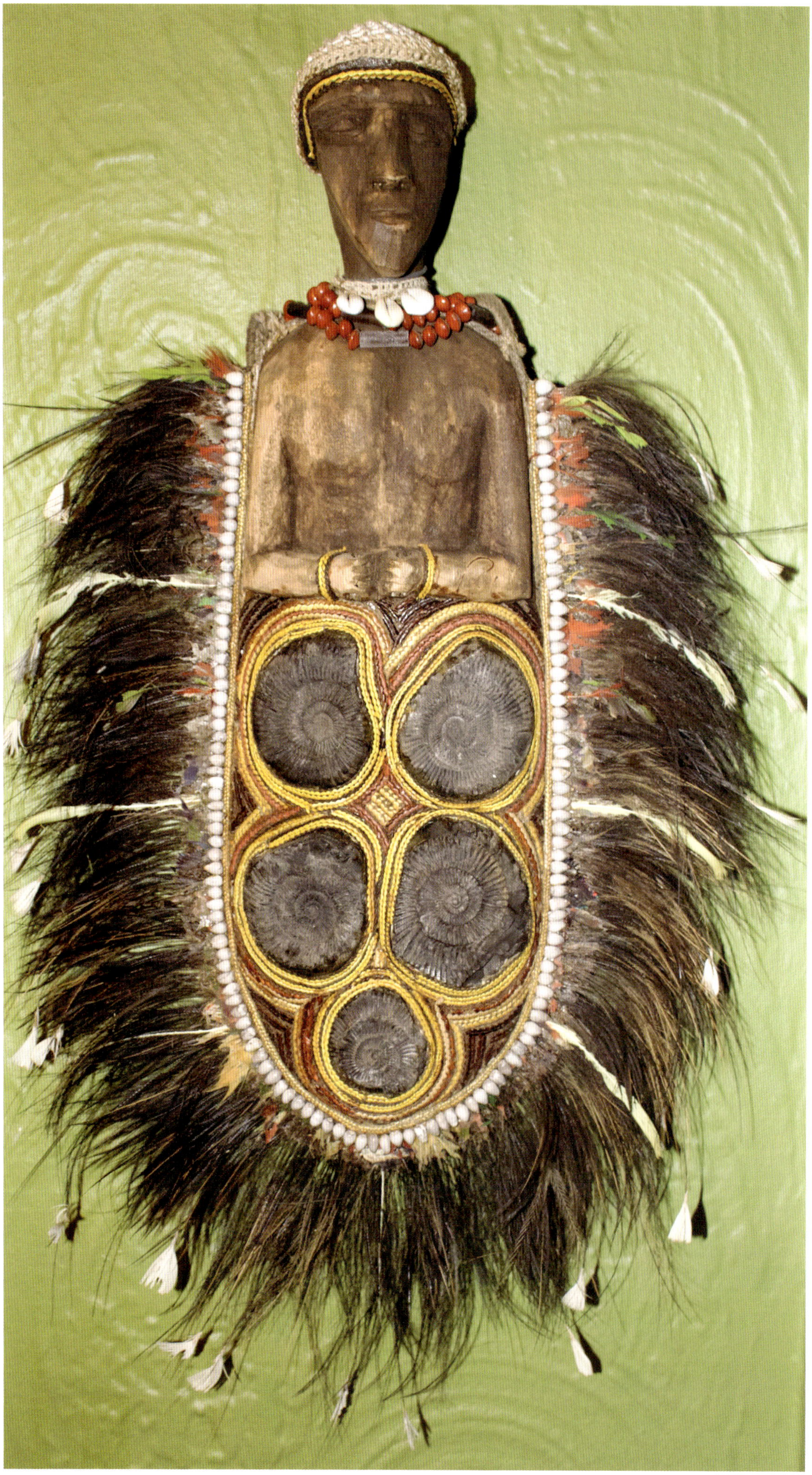

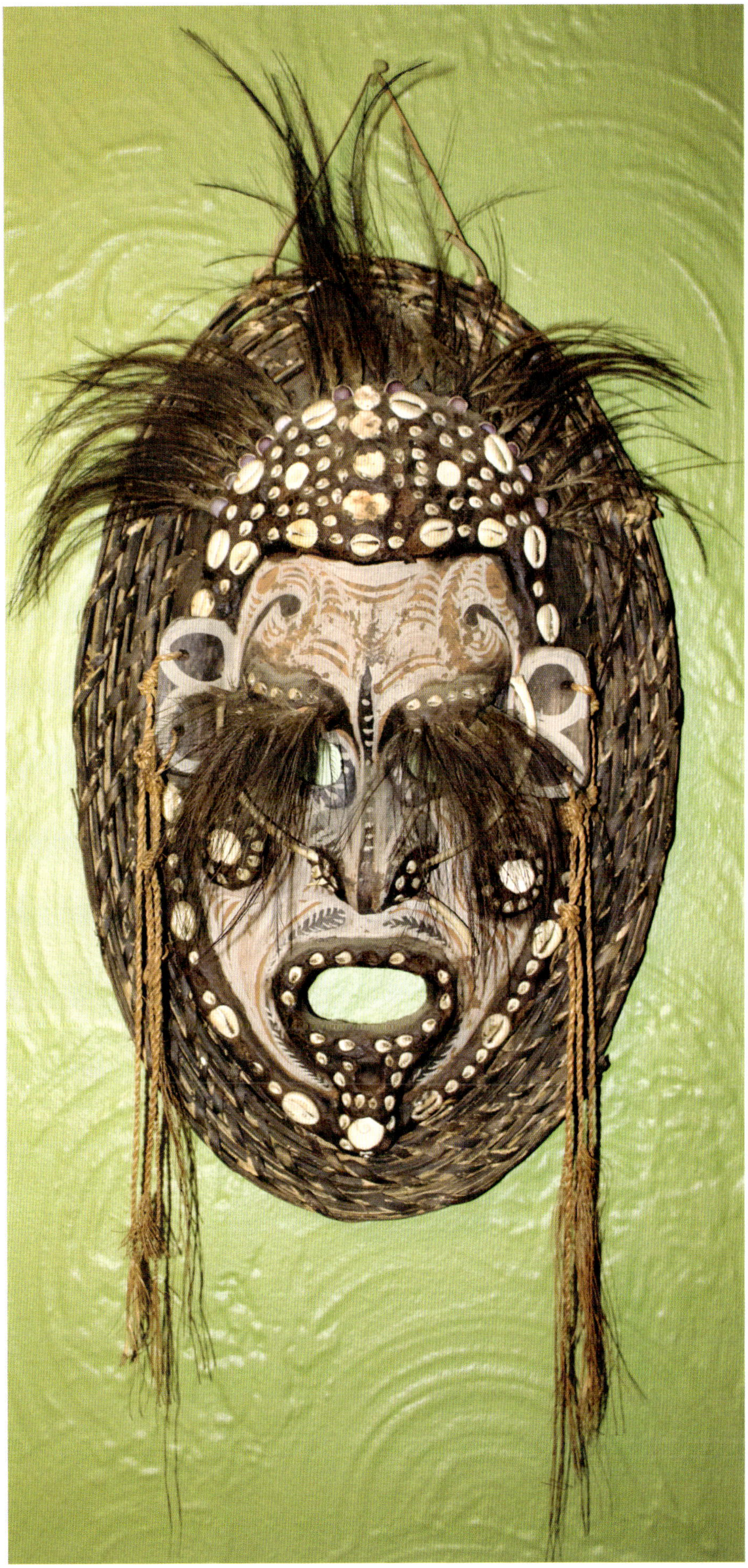

Opposite: Papua New Guinea artist, *Untitled*, 1980. Mixed media: feather, fossils, shells, and wood. 18" × 10". *Photo Myrah Brown Green*

Papua New Guinea artist, *Bride's Price*, 1980. Bone, shells, leather, feathers, and jute, 5" × 7". *Photo: Myrah Brown Green*

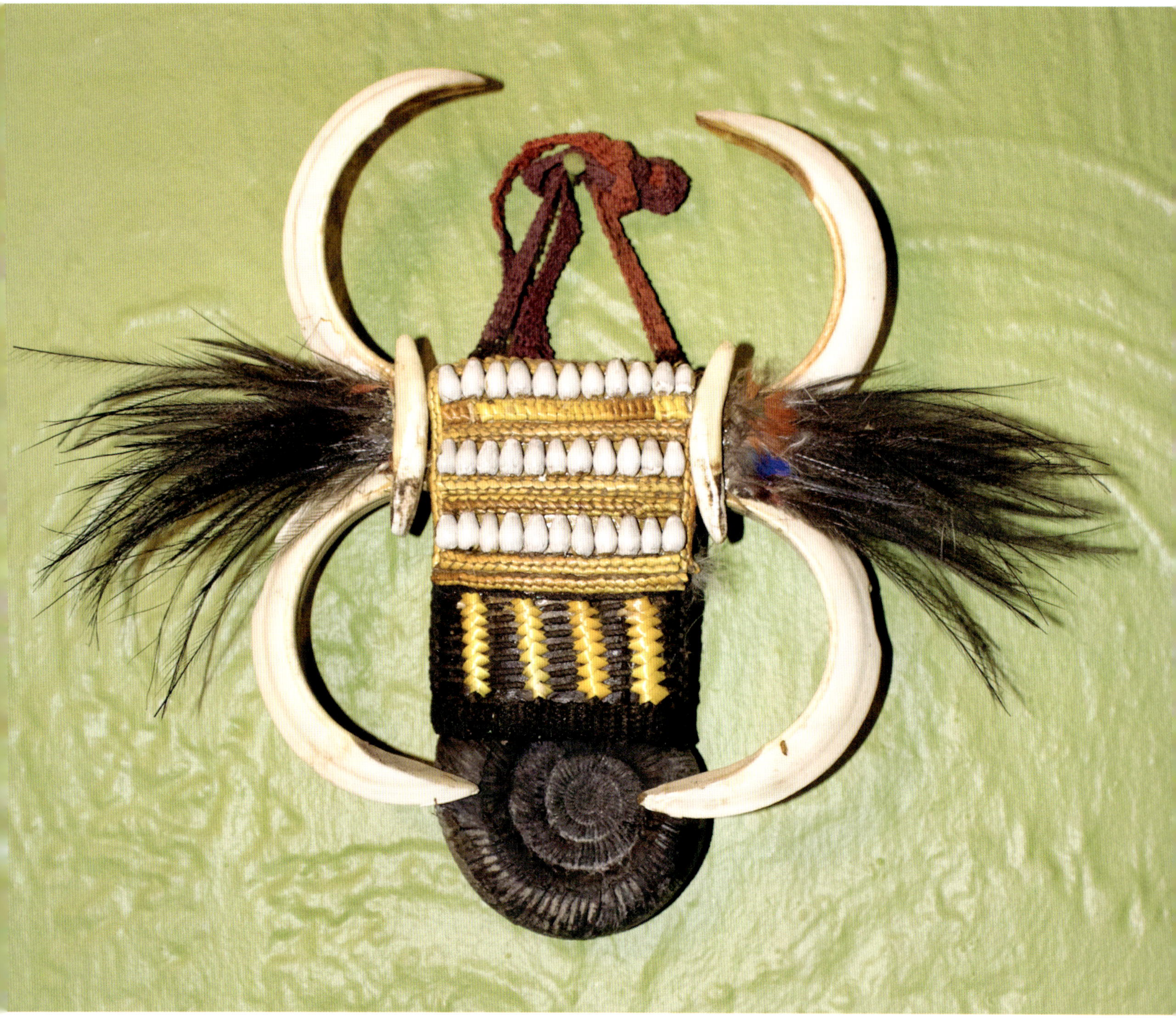

Papua New Guinea artist, *Mask*, 1980. Wood, shells, jute, feathers, and paint, 14" × 6". *Photo: Myrah Brown Green*

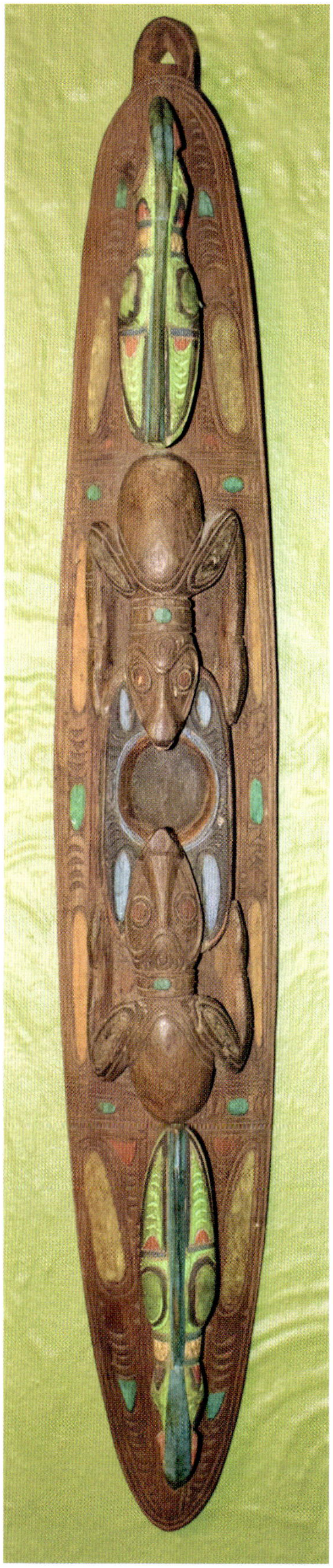

Papua New Guinea artist, *Untitled*, 1980. Wood and green paint, 23" × 4". *Photo: Myrah Brown Green*

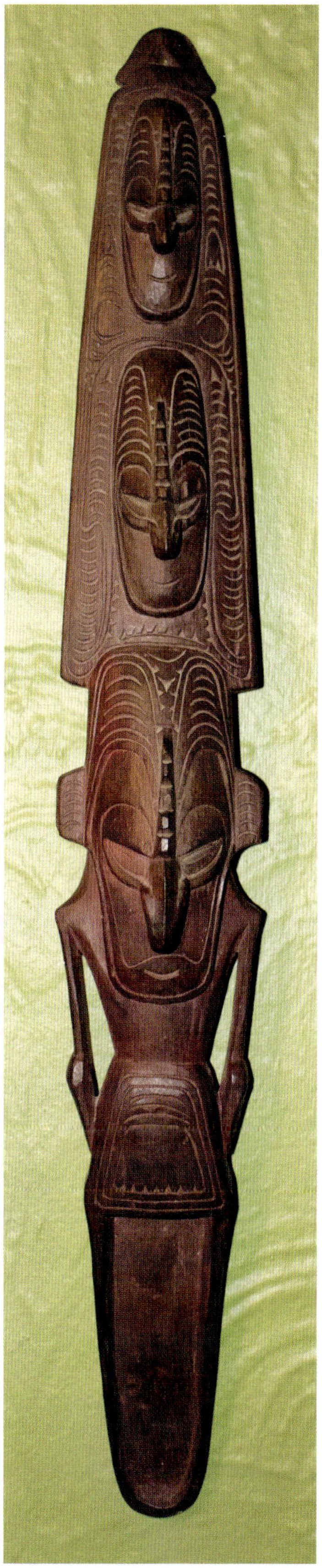

Papua New Guinea artist, *Untitled*, 1980. Wood, 23" × 4". *Photo: Myrah Brown Green*

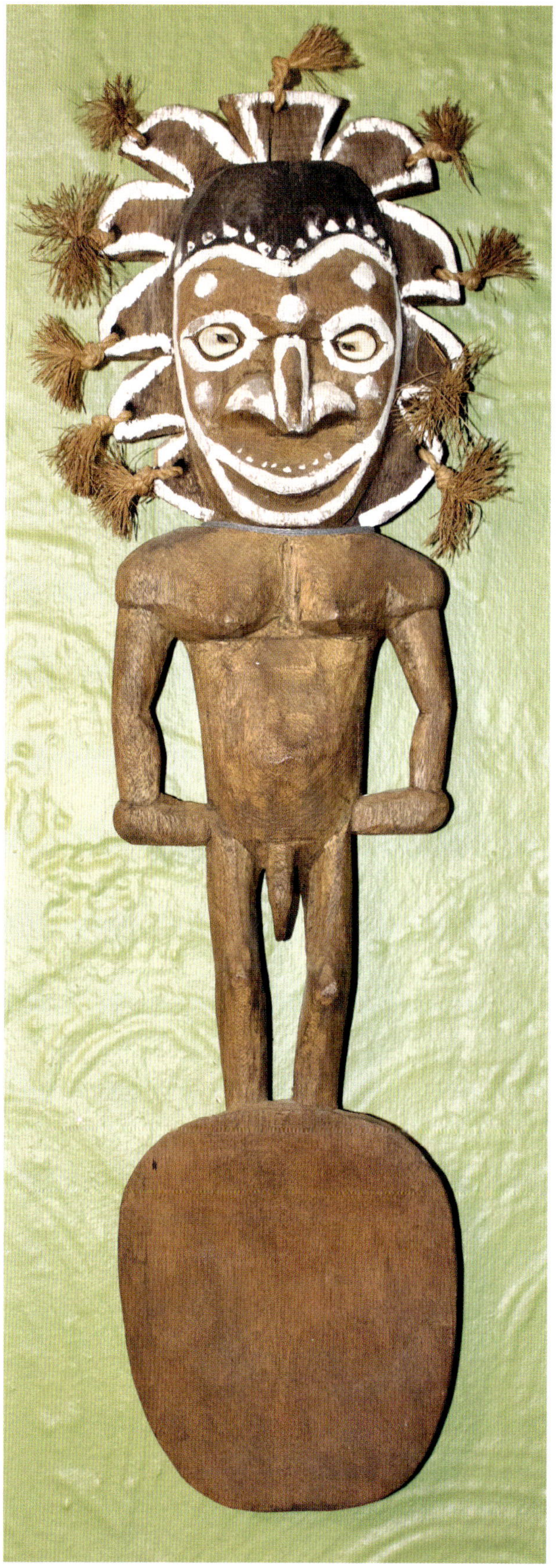

Papua New Guinea artist, *Spoon*, 1980. Wood and paint, 21" × 6". *Photo: Myrah Brown Green*

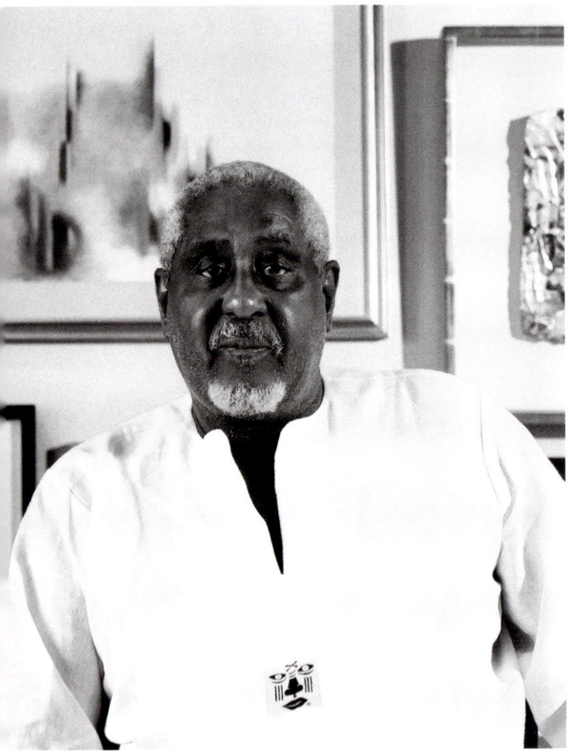

Photo: Corey Hughes

CLARENCE MOSLEY JR.
INNOVATIVE MALE ARTISTS

DR. MYRAH: What was the first piece of art that you collected and when?

CLARENCE MOSLEY JR.: The first piece of art that I collected was William Toliver's *Natural Beauty*. I purchased it in 1990. Prior to that, I had been drawn to a variety of narrative images. When I saw Toliver's work, I wanted it in my collection.

DR. MYRAH: Why are you a Keeper of works by Innovative Male Artists?

CLARENCE MOSLEY JR.: I collect overall to be a trustee for the positive images of our culture. Being a father myself, these men represent something that is very dear to my heart. As a collector, I hope to pass along my connection with these images to my children and grandchildren.

It gives me a great deal of pleasure when I come home and I am surrounded by all of this beautiful artwork. It keeps me calm, at peace, and gives me a sense of historical reference to our past, present, and future. I think about our culture, and it sustains me.

While I have been collecting for a very long time, it is still refreshing to look at this art. I appreciate it more and more each day.

Although I have a wide range of art created by both male and female artists, it is the works that speak to fathers, sons, and brothers that continue to grab my attention. Many of those pieces carry a quiet strength, whether expressed through abstract forms or figurative imagery.

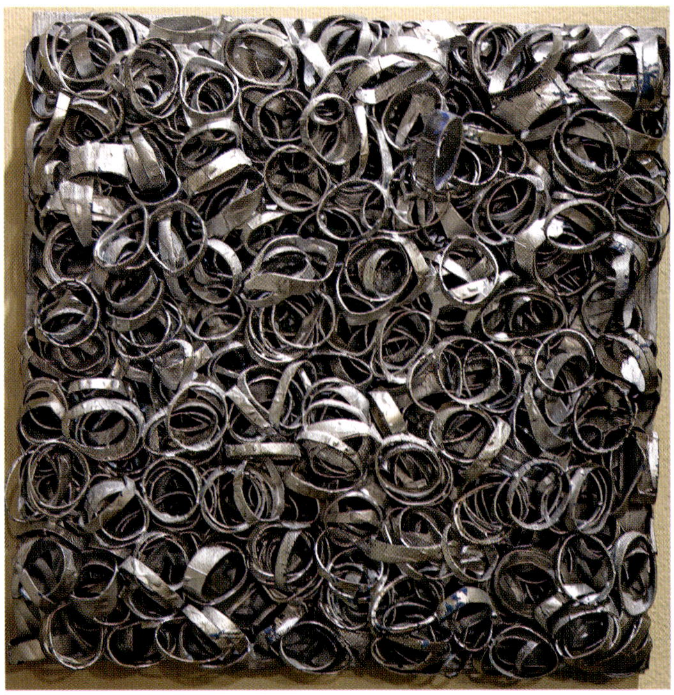

Gregory Coates, *Bubbles*, 2008. Rubber, jade glue, oil-base paint, 12" × 12". *Photo: Corey Hughes*

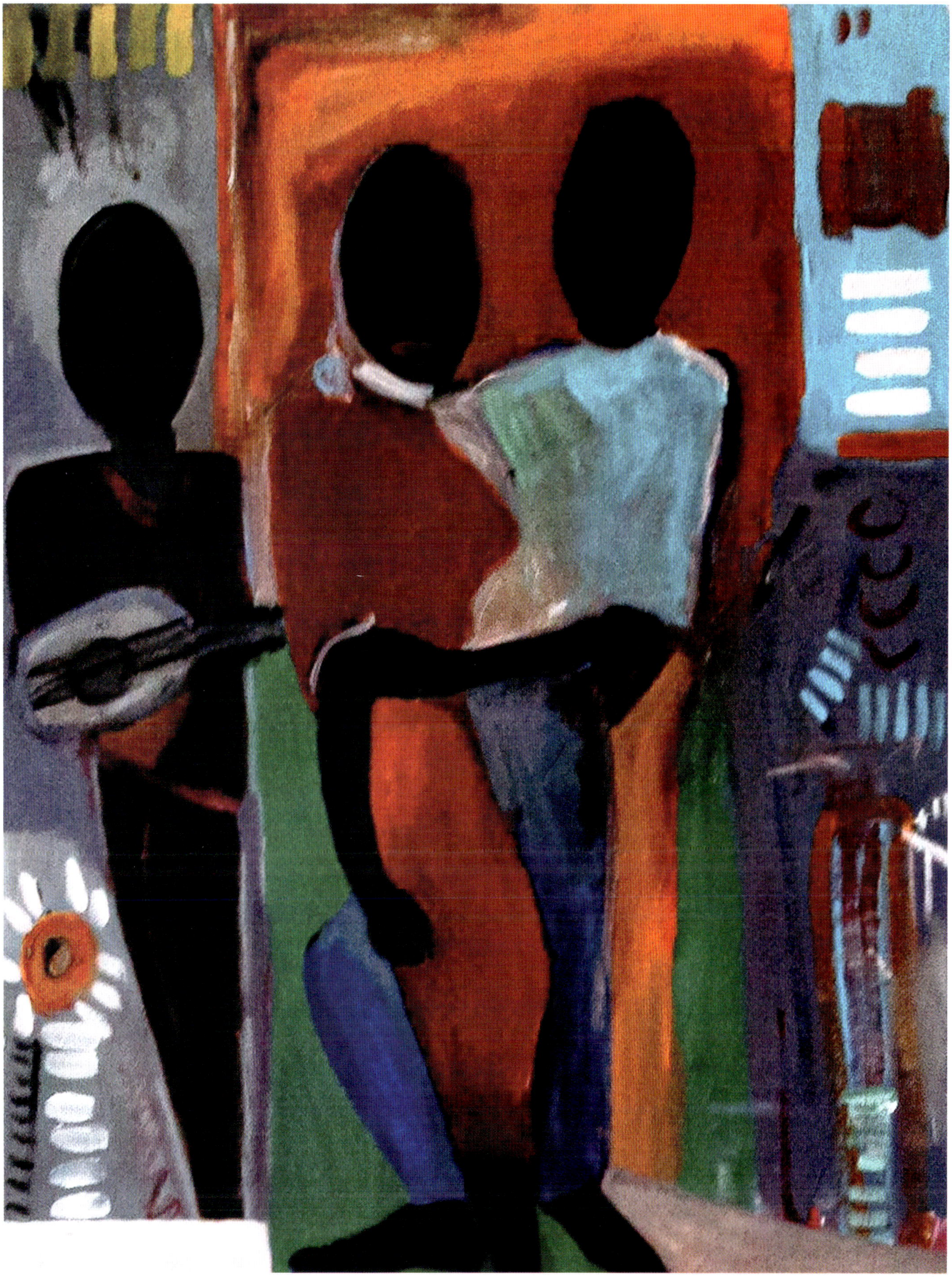

Ulysses Marshall, *Down Home Blues*, 2005. Acrylic on paper, 22" × 33". *Photo: Corey Hughes*

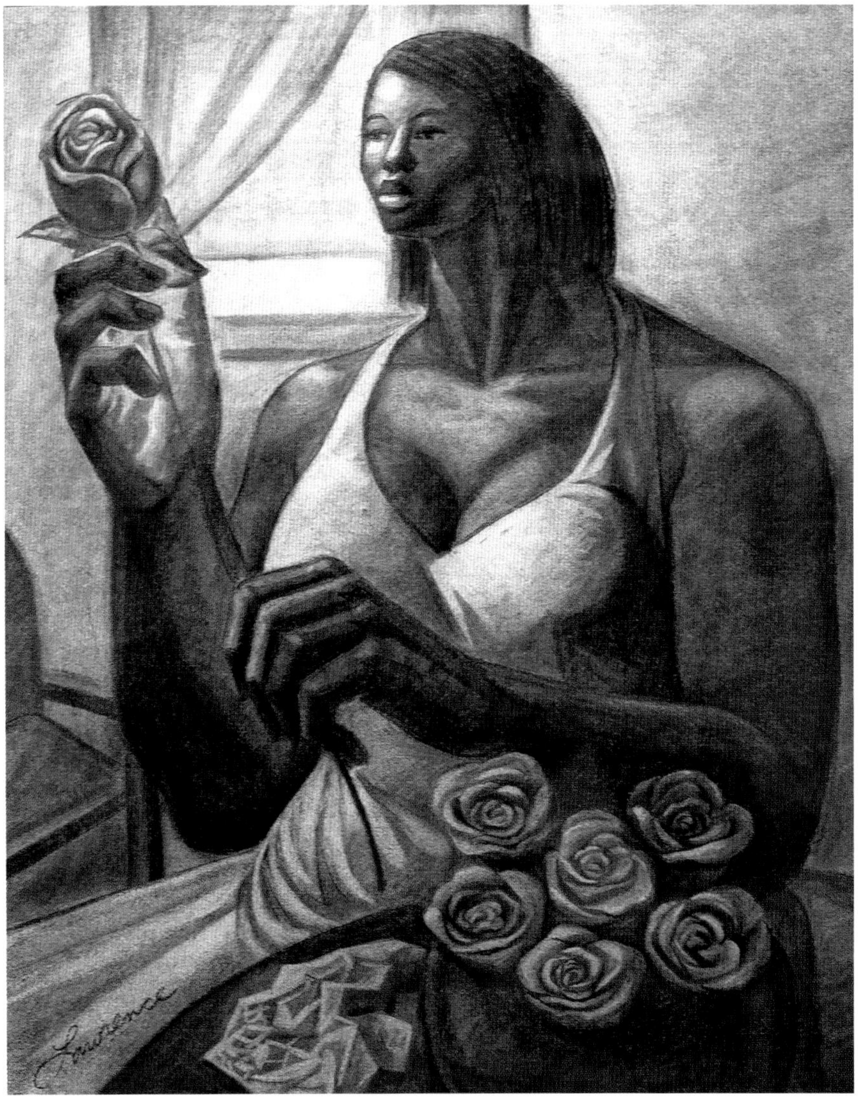

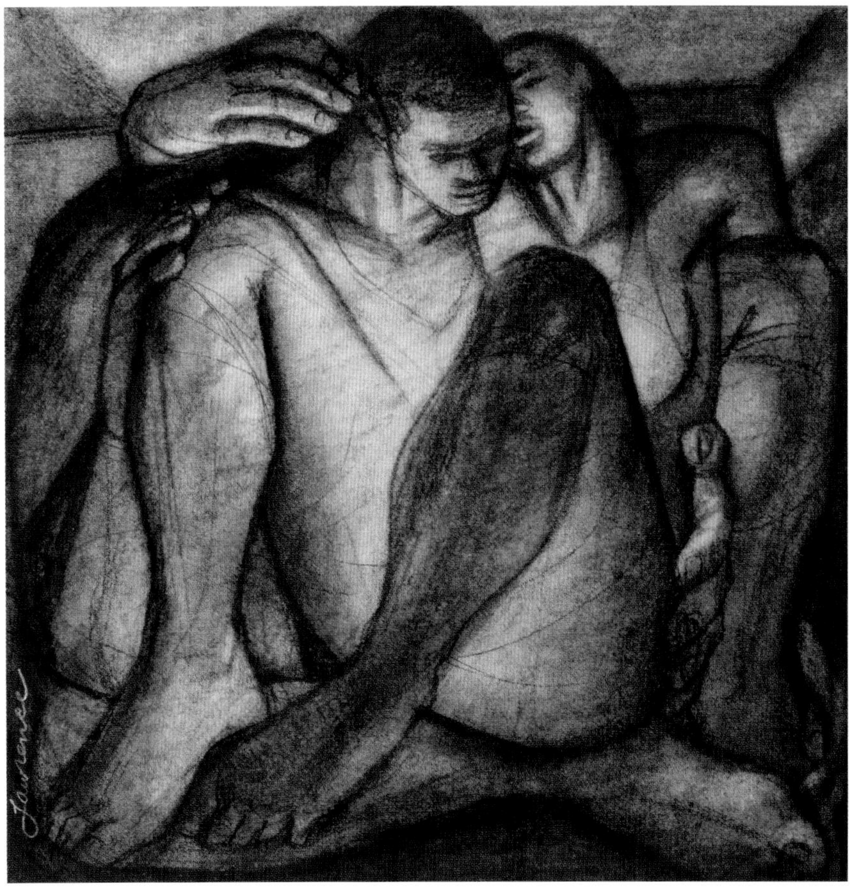

Lawrence Finney, *Seven Roses*, 2022. Charcoal on paper, 13.5" × 11". *Photo: Corey Hughes*

Lawrence Finney, *Whispers*, 2001. Charcoal on paper, 11" × 11". *Photo: Corey Hughes*

Opposite: Dox Thrash, *Nudes*, 1941. Watercolor and ink, 9.75" × 14". *Photo: Corey Hughes*

Opposite: Frank Wimberly, *One for Rashaan*, 2007. Pigment print, 21" × 27". *Photo: Corey Hughes*

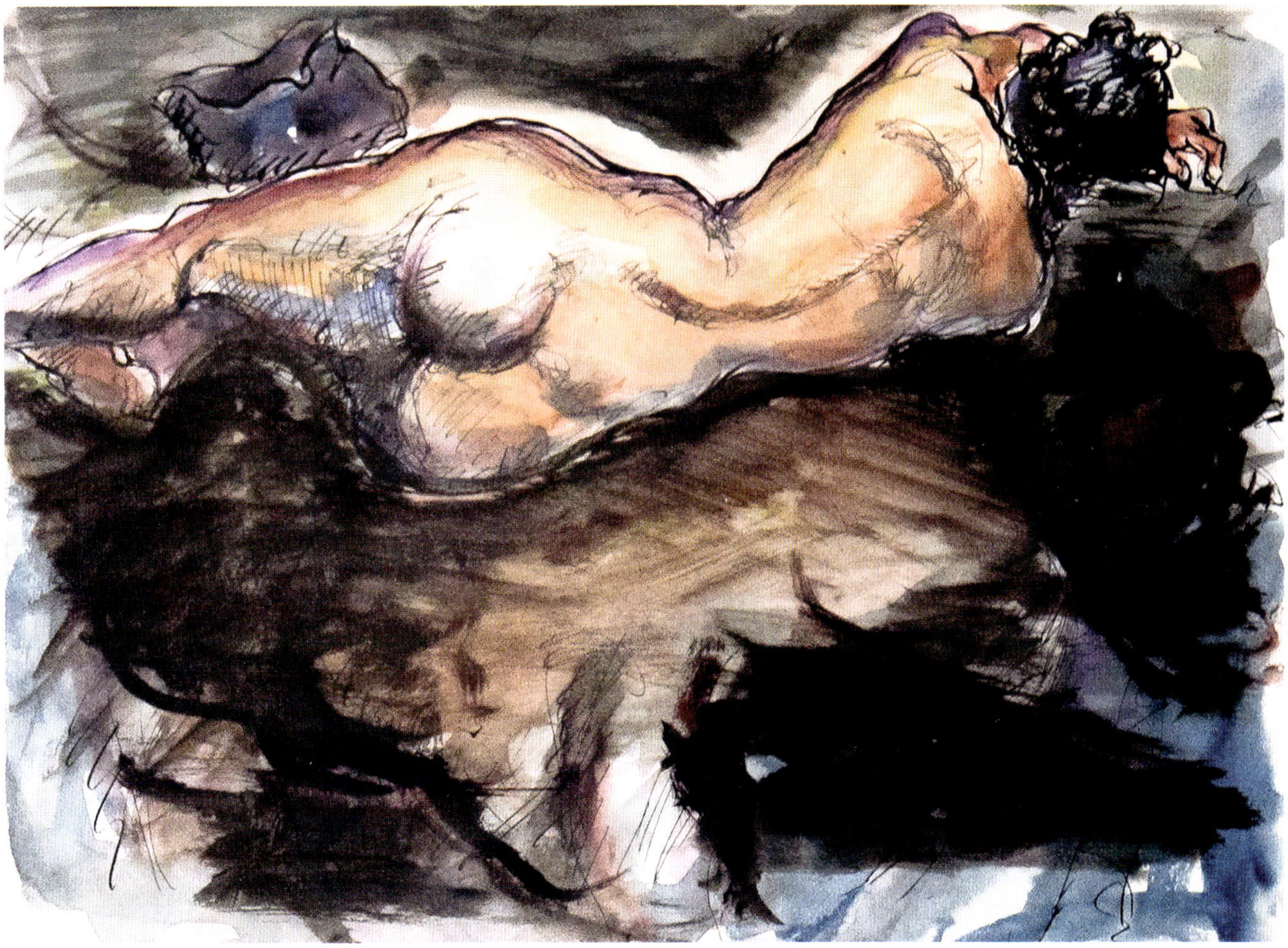

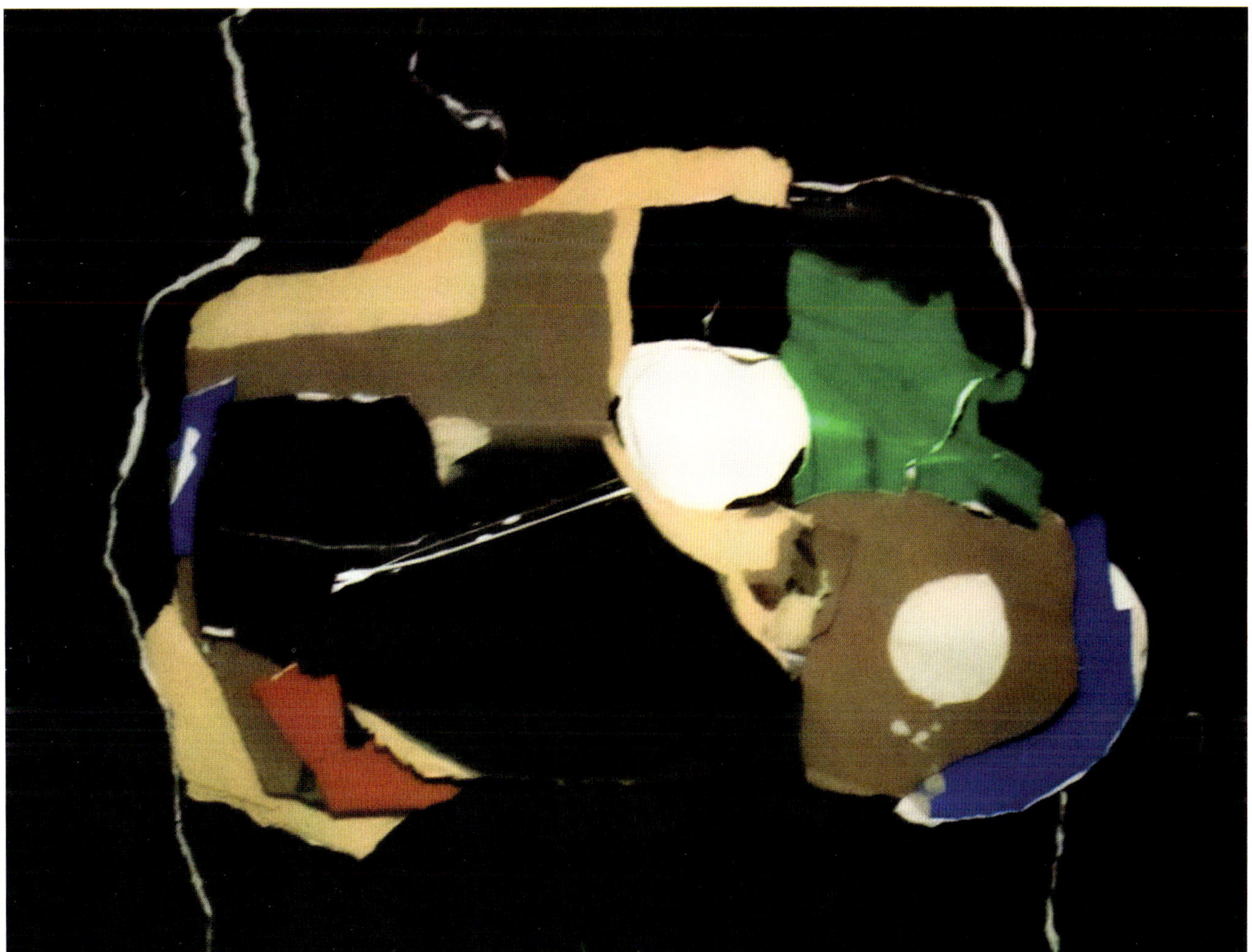

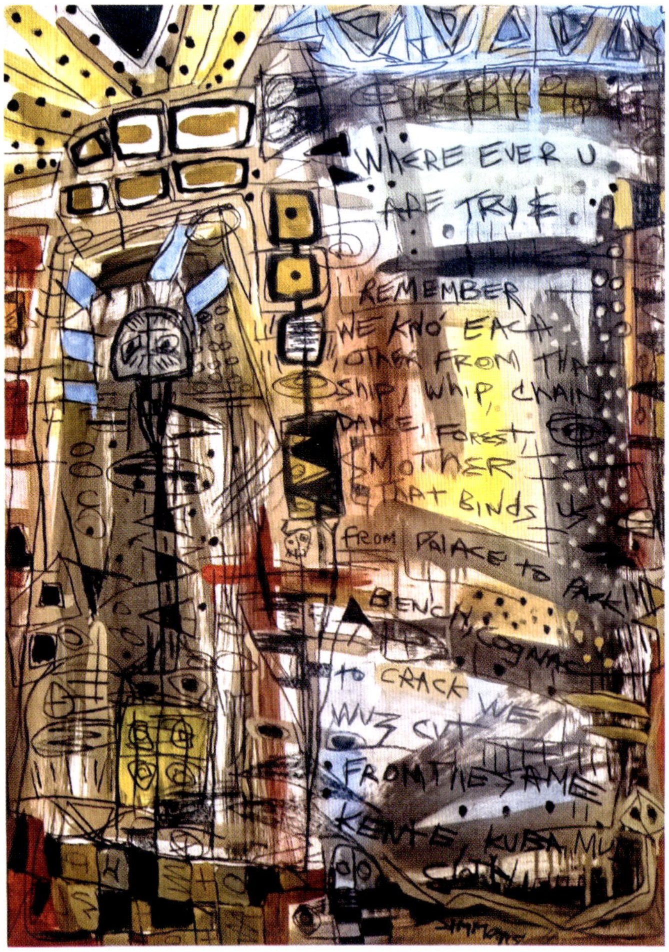

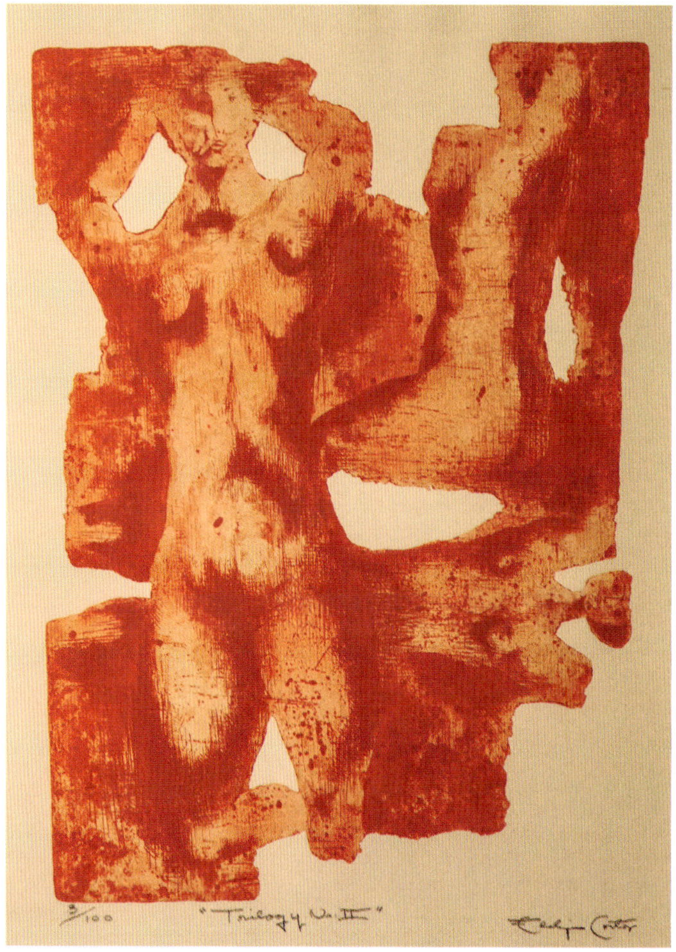

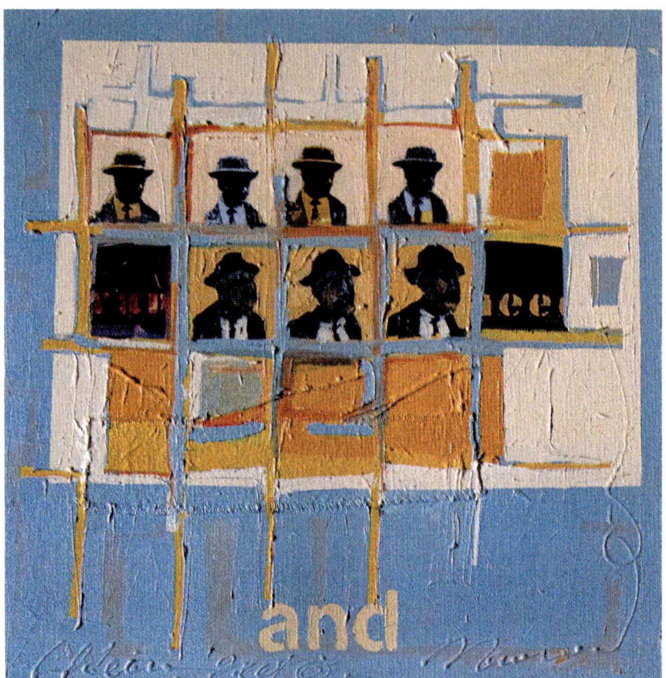

Top left: Danny Simmons, *Untitled*, 1994. Oil on paper, 27" × 22". *Photo: Corey Hughes*

Top right: Eldzier Cotor, *Trilogy No. II*, 1989. Sanguine intaglio, 22.25" × 15". *Photo: Corey Hughes*

Francks Deceus, *Want and Need*, 2001. Mixed media on canvas, 18" × 18". *Photo: Corey Hughes*

Opposite: John Biggers, *Balaphone*, 2000. Lithograph on rive paper, 19.25" × 13.25". *Photo: Corey Hughes*

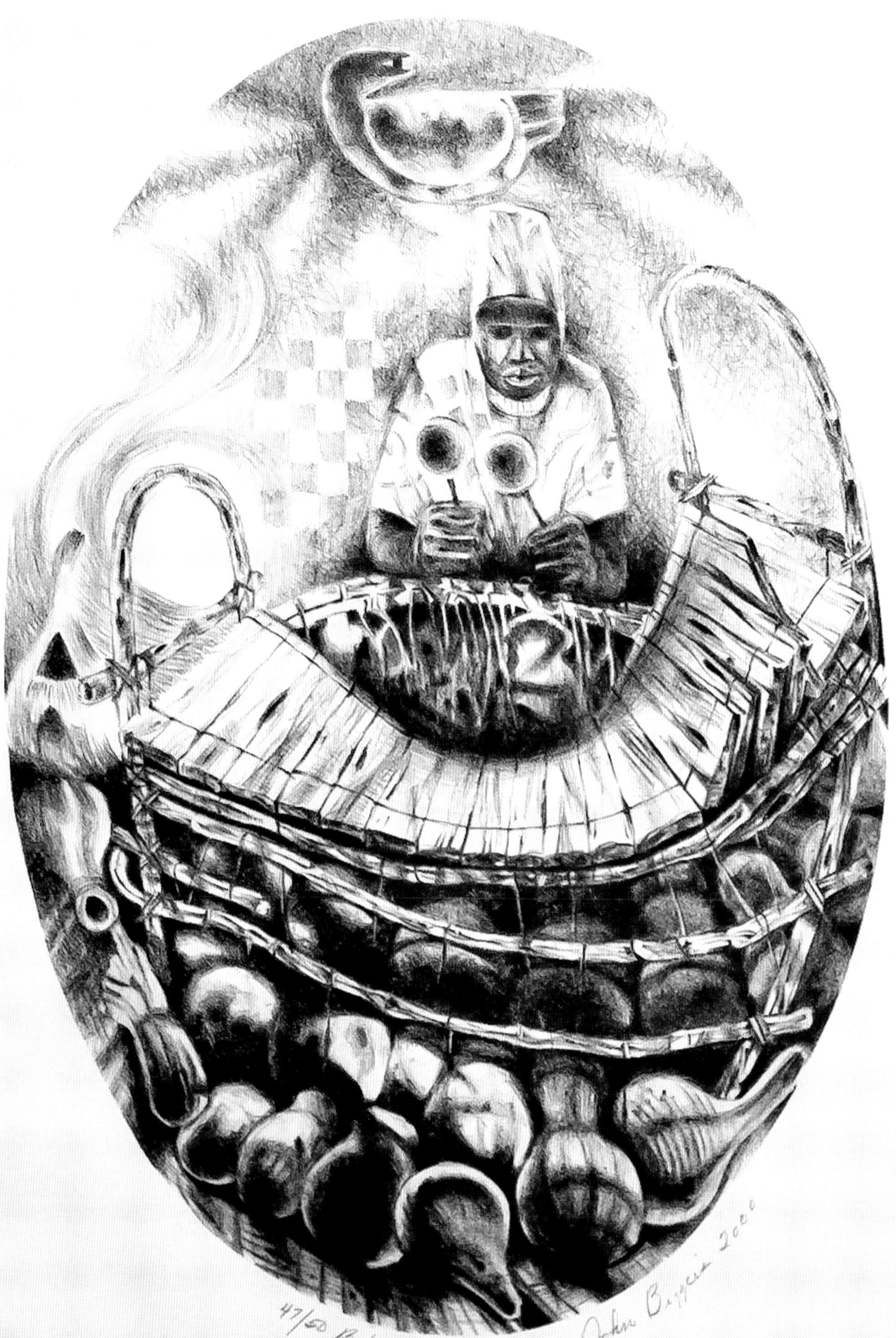
47/50 Balaphone
John Biggers 2000

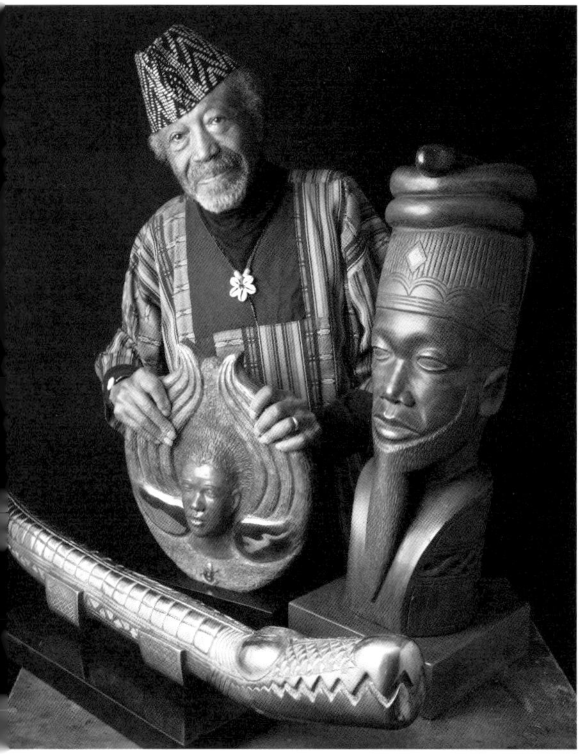

Photo: Randall Duchaine

OTTO NEALS
MOTHERS, DAUGHTERS, AND SISTERS

DR. MYRAH: What was the first piece of art that you collected and when?

OTTO NEALS: The first pieces I remember collecting were two works by Milton Caniff. Caniff was the illustrator for the *New York Daily News* and was best known for creating *Terry and the Pirates*. When he left the *Daily News*, the rights to *Terry and the Pirates* stayed with the paper, so Caniff started a new cartoon strip titled *Steve Canyon*, featuring a character by the same name and his lady friend, Capa Calhoun.

Caniff was one of my favorite cartoonists. I used to copy some of his works, especially his full-page illustrations of *Terry and the Pirates*. In fact, I still have some of those copies I made, and hope to show them to you one day.

At one point I sent some of my drawings to Caniff. To my surprise, he wrote back and he sent me two original pieces of art. One was *Capa Calhoun*. The other, *Steve Canyon*.

I was still in high school, just seventeen years old. I was proud of those pieces and treasured them for years.

DR. MYRAH: Why are you a Keeper of art by mothers, daughters, sisters, and friends?

OTTO NEALS: I wasn't thinking about them being women. I was moved by what they created.

Over time, Vivian Schuyler Key became one of the most important women artists in my life. I met her in 1958 at the Fulton Art Fair. Not long after, she invited me into a space she managed in a building on Hanson Place; what was then called the Hanson Place Diner.

That building became my creative home. My studio was there for about ten years.

Vivian was serious about her work. She had no patience for anything less than excellence. She loved painting and sculpture, and she excelled at both. One of her most powerful works, a piece honoring Dr. W. E. B. Du Bois, is now in Ghana, at the Du Bois House. She also created a larger-than-life bust of Langston Hughes. I don't know where that sculpture lives now, but it was monumental in every sense.

She was my mentor. From the late 1950s through the early 1980s, our studios were in the same building. She guided me. She challenged me. And she believed in me.

Miss Key was also the one who gave me my very first set of carving tools.

That moment and her presence shaped the artist I would become.

Archiving the history of forgotten women like Ms. Key and those that I have collected is the main reason why I am the keeper of their art.

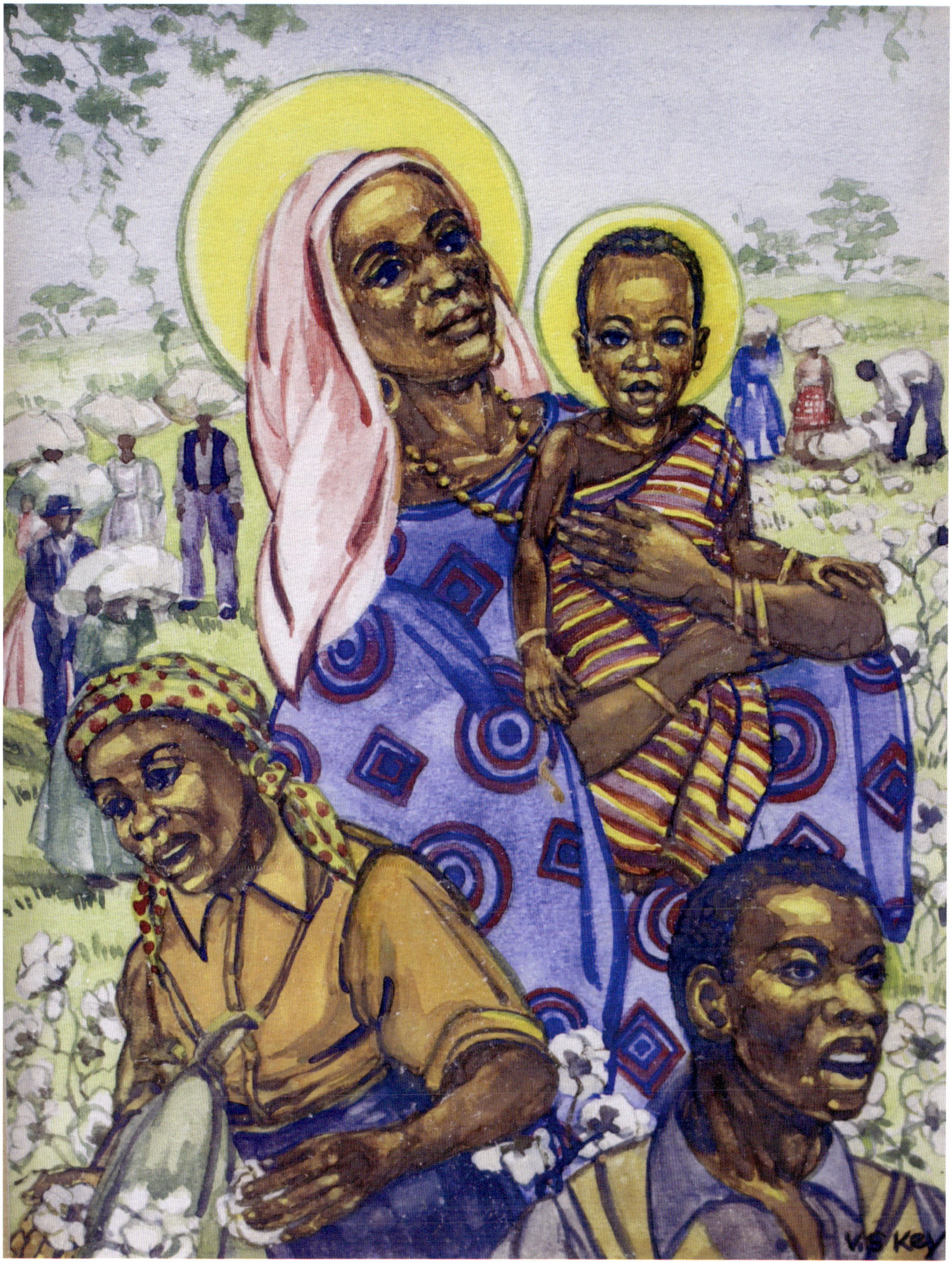

Vivian Schuyler Key, *God Bless the Child* (study), 1968.
Pencil, 14" × 11". *Photo: Myrah Brown Green*

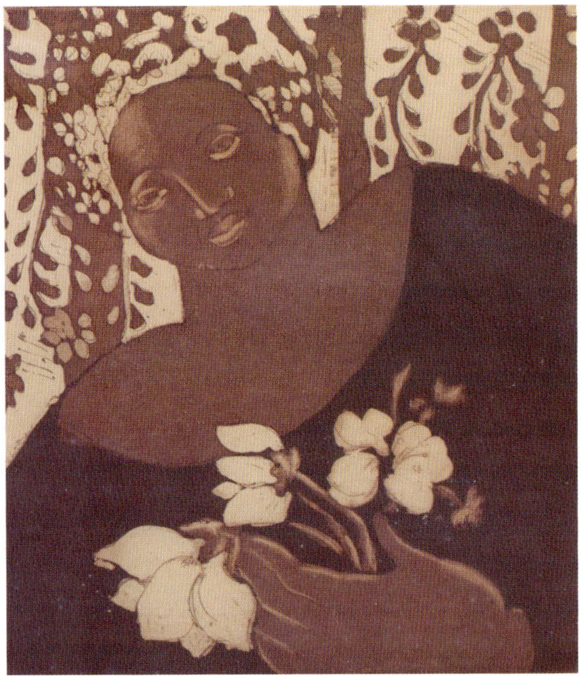

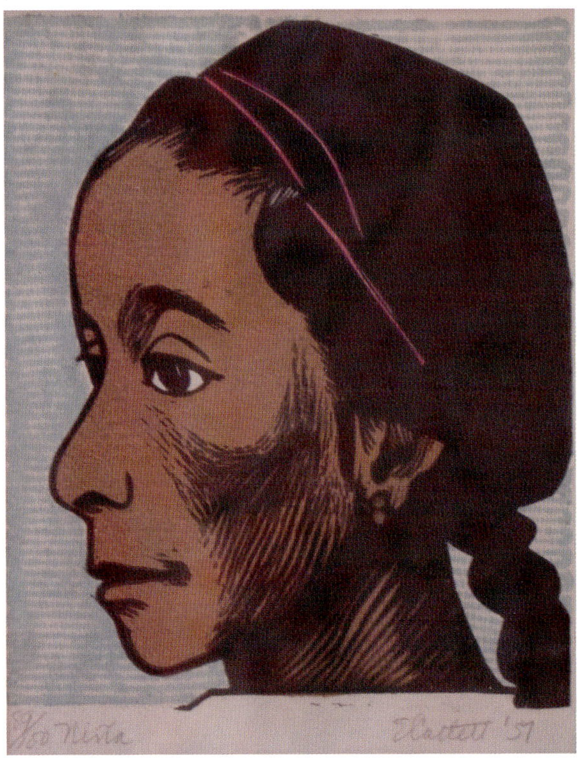

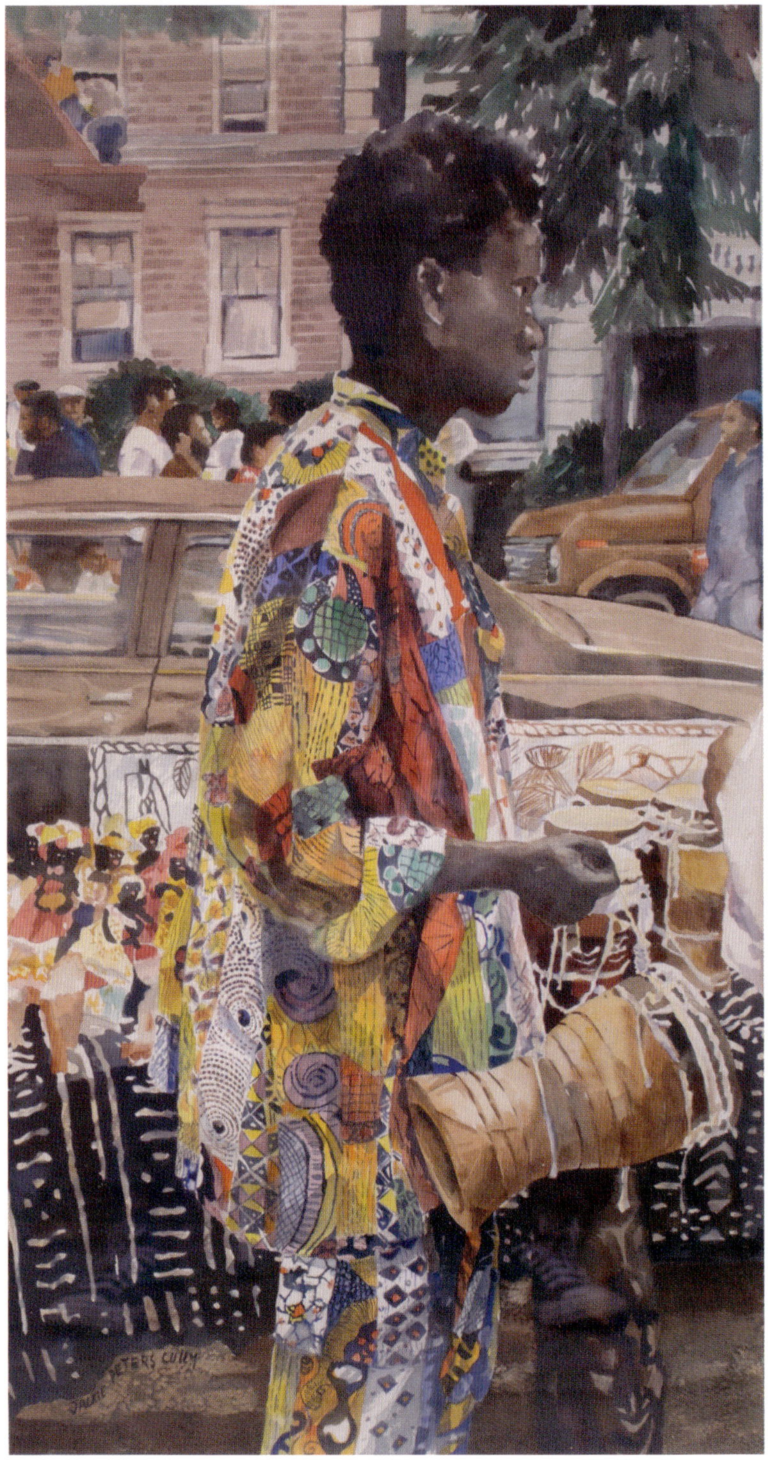

Top left: Nancy Brandon, *The Offering*, 1980. A/P etching, 14" × 13". *Photo: Myrah Brown Green*

Bottom left: Elizabeth Catlett, *Niña*, 1957. Linocut (89/100), 6" × 5.125". *Photo: Myrah Brown Green*

Jackie Peters Cully, *African Vendor*, 1989. Watercolor, 35" × 19". *Photo: Myrah Brown Green*

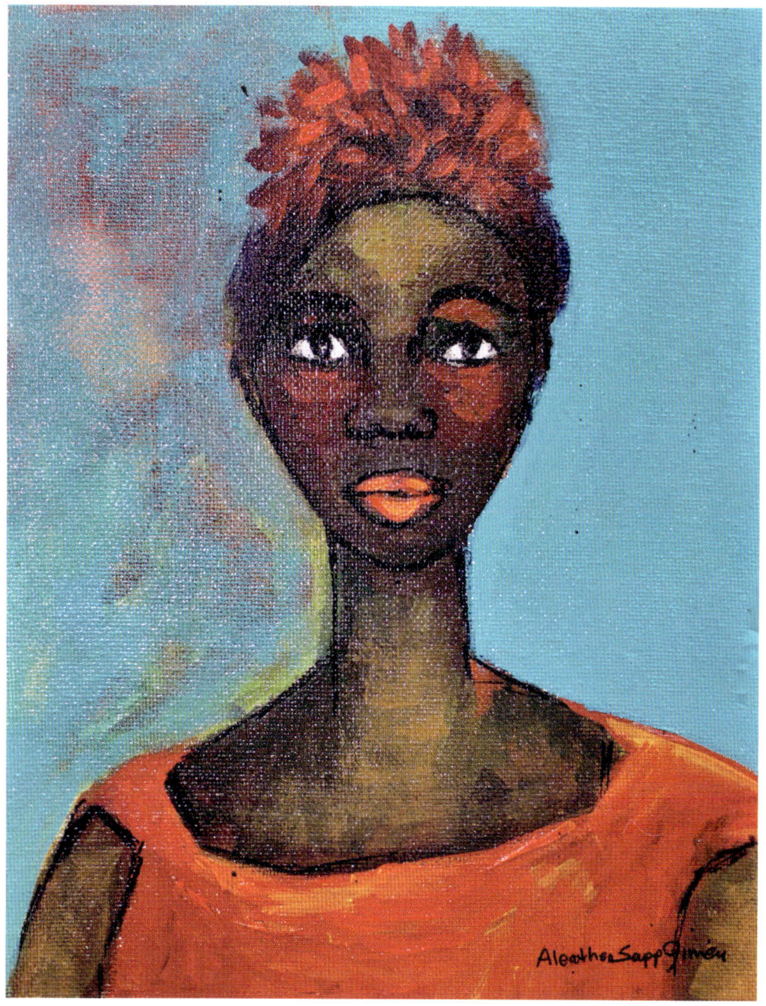

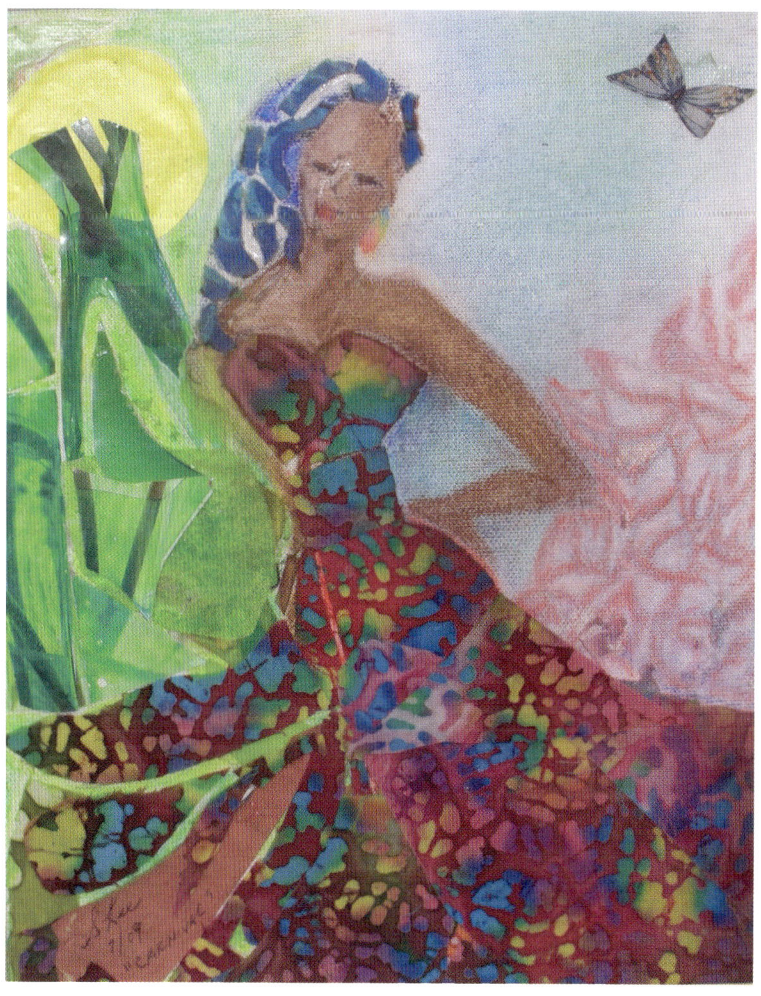

Aleathea Sapp-Jeminez, *Untitled*, 2021. Acrylic on canvas, 11" × 14". *Photo: Myrah Brown Green*

Scharalet Kee, *Carnival*, 2009. Collage, 13" × 12". *Photo: Myrah Brown Green*

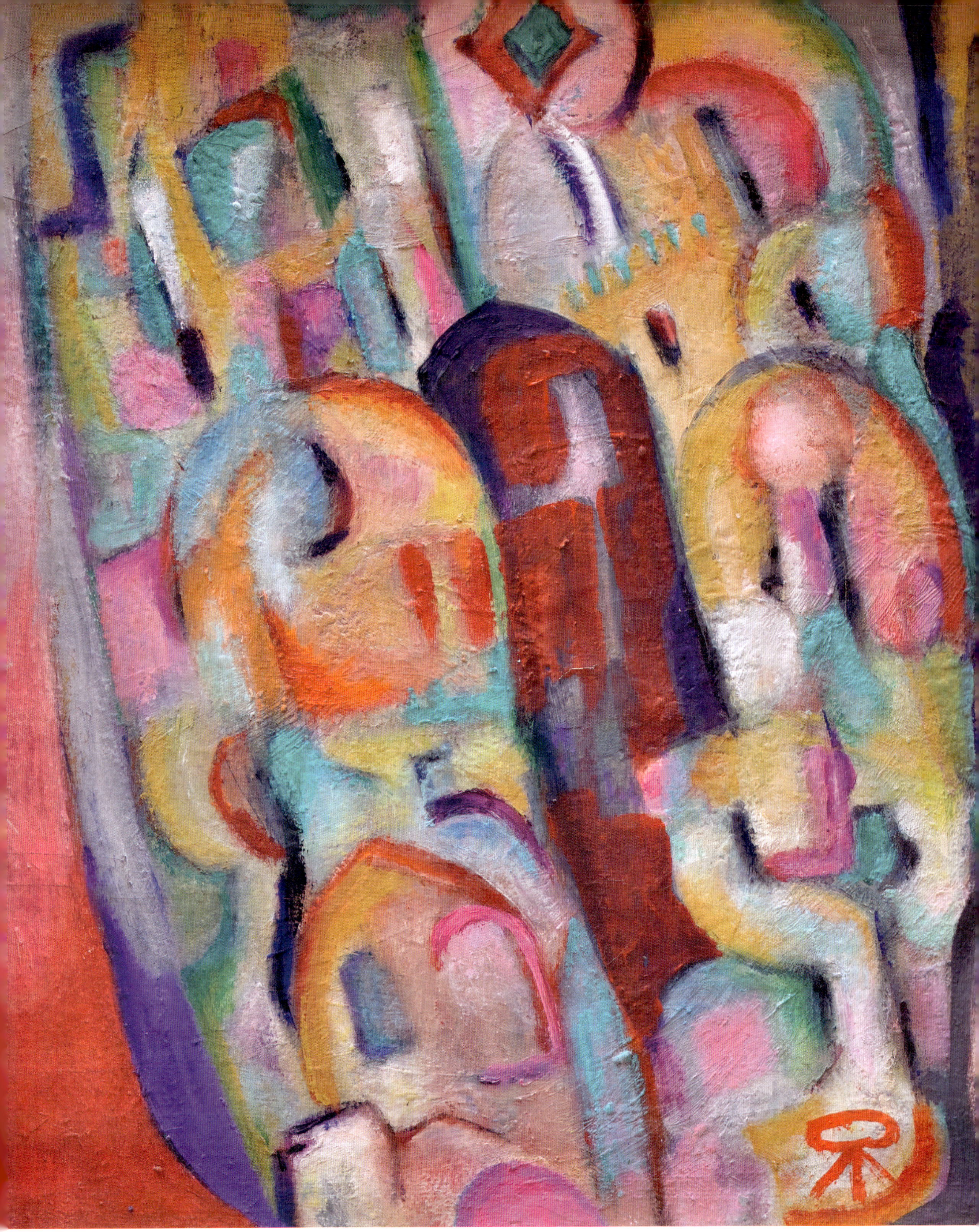

Rashonda Rhoden, *Before Dumbo*, 1960. Oil on canvas, 18" × 15". *Photo: Myrah Brown Green*

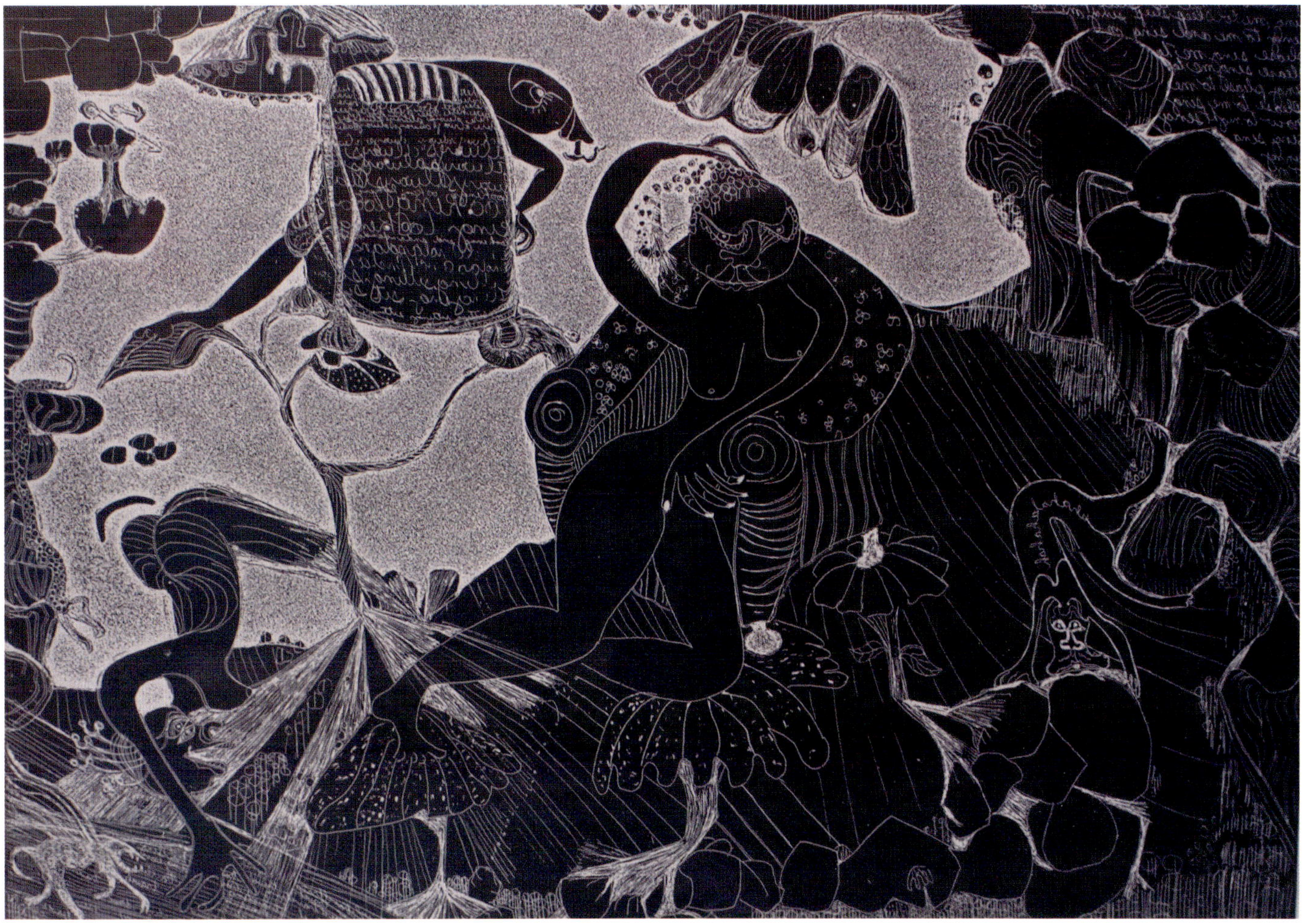

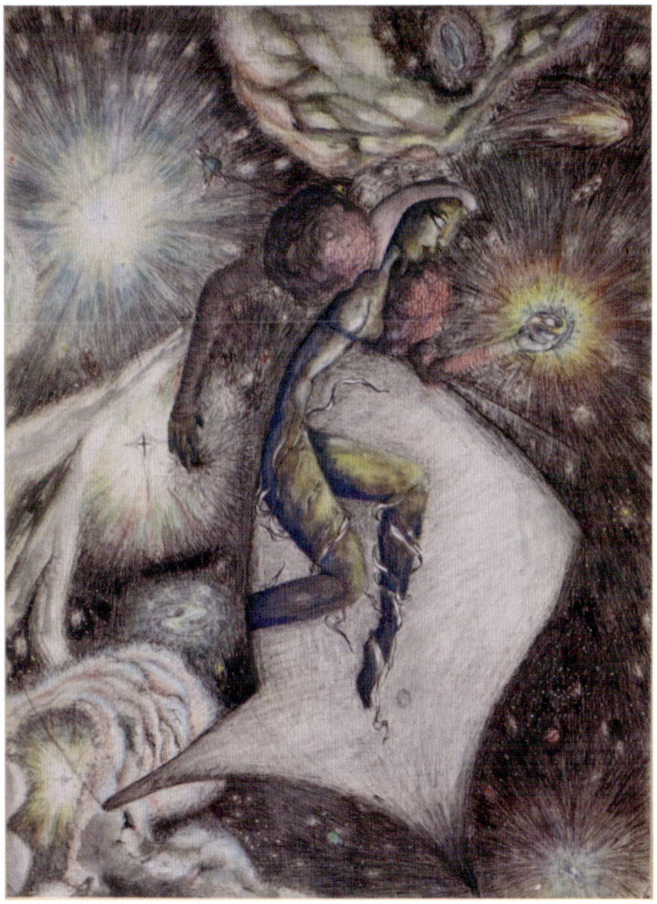

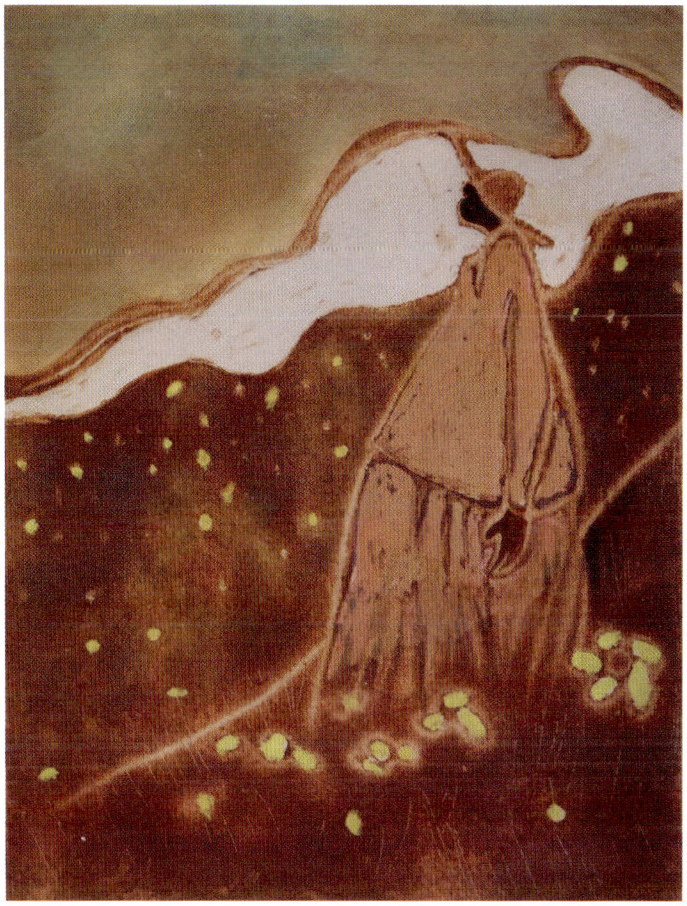

Top: Camille Billops, *I Am Black, I Am Black, I Am Dangerously Black*, 1974. Etching and aquatint relief printed, 11.875" × 17". *Photo: Myrah Brown Green*

Tabitha Theogene, *Orion*, 2017. Pen, ink, and colored pencil, 16" × 13". *Photo: Myrah Brown Green*

Ann Tanksley, *Blooming*, 2008. Monotype, 13" × 10". *Photo: Myrah Brown Green*

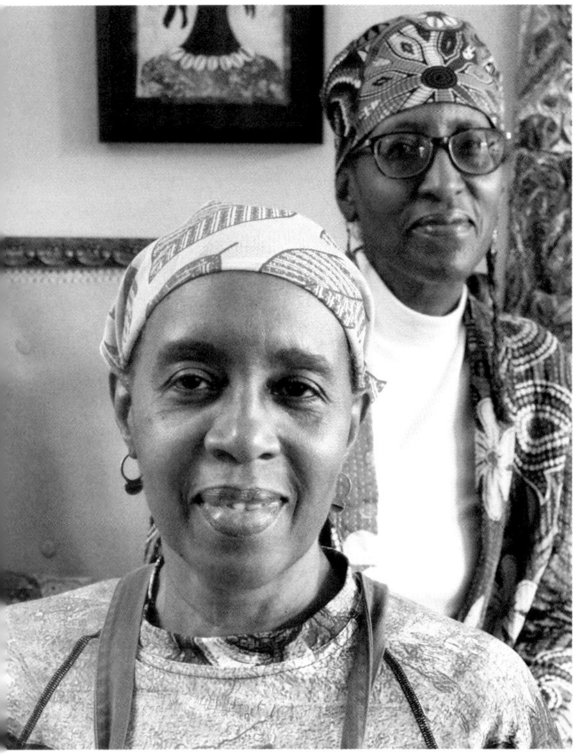

Photo: Myrah Brown Green

VERONICA NERO AND VALERIE NERO REID

STAINED GLASS

DR. MYRAH: What was the first piece of art that you collected and when?

VALERIE NERO REID: The first piece of art I ever collected was for my very first apartment. I bought it in the early eighties at Green Acres Mall. It was a picture of a sailboat floating on the water, and it just felt so relaxing.

VERONICA NERO: In the early eighties I bought a small piece from a street artist; a green fauna with a chicken. It reminded me of Haitian art. I loved the colors and the medium so much, I had it framed.

I also picked up a vibrant pastel drawing of an African marketplace around the same time. Both works were unplanned finds; simple, beautiful, and full of life.

DR. MYRAH: Why are you Keepers of Stained-Glass Art?

VERONICA NERO: There's something about the energy of a piece of stained-glass art that draws me in.

I remember seeing my first piece for purchase at the African Street Festival, held at Boys and Girls High School in Brooklyn. Ras was one of the artists set up at the festival. In his space, I saw a piece that immediately caught my attention. It was an ankh that was actually created by his aunt. I was so deeply moved by it and wanted to know more about the symbol, about the artist, and the story behind it. That moment at the festival stayed with me. It marked the beginning of my journey as a collector and my connection to the spiritual energy art can carry.

DR. MYRAH: Do you want to add anything, Valerie?

VALERIE NERO REID: When we were house hunting in Brooklyn, I was immediately struck by the stained glass in many of the homes we visited. There was something about the energy. It felt beautiful and peaceful.

I was grateful that the home we eventually chose had a small section of original stained glass in the upstairs parlor window. That one detail sparked something in us. After Veronica acquired our first stained-glass piece, I remember thinking, Wow, this is what the house was waiting for.

We became committed to bringing stained glass back into the home; not just as decoration, but as a way of restoring the home's spirit. It was about beauty, yes, but also about legacy. About keeping the history alive.

Opposite: Charles Ras Scott, *Heetep-Unshakeable State of Peace* (entrance door panel), 2015. Stained glass, 36.5" × 23.75". *Photo: Myrah Brown Green*

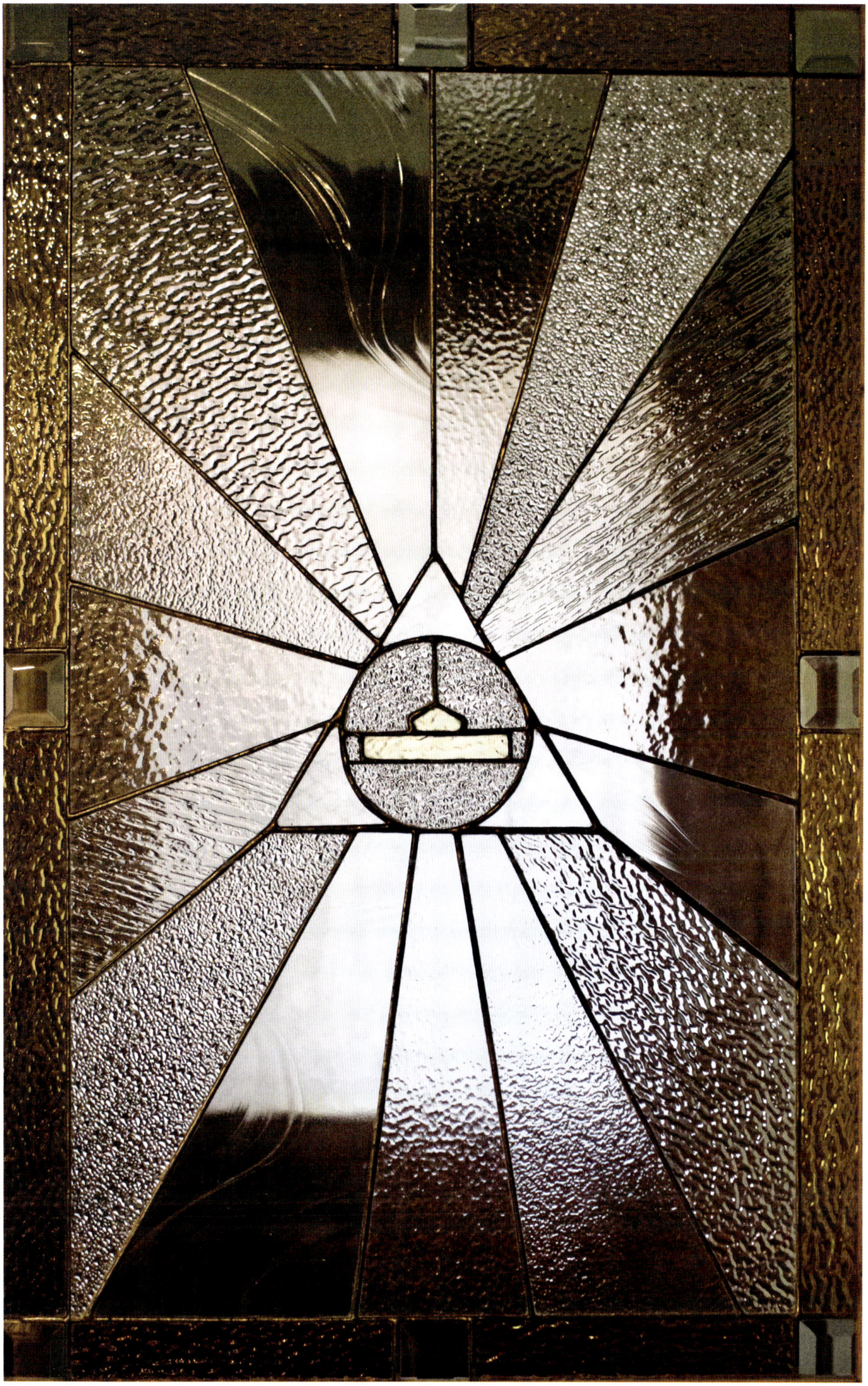

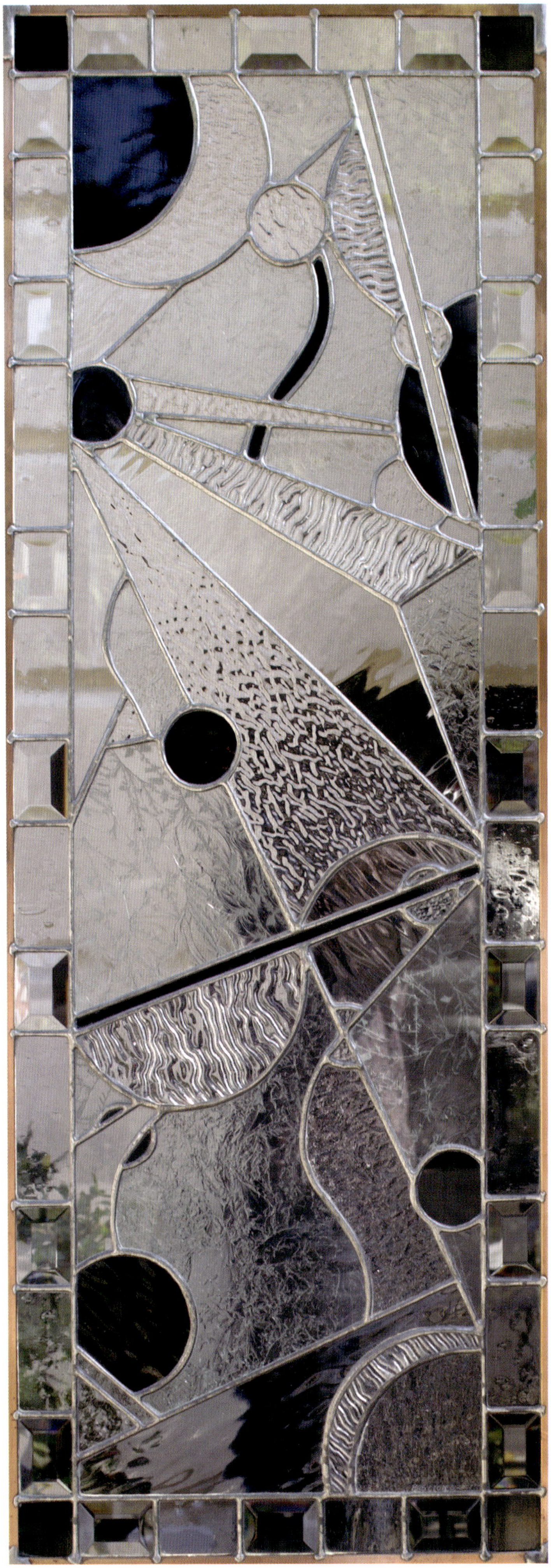

Left: Charles Ras Scott, *Clear Abstract with Black and Blue Shapes* (year unknown). Stained glass, 38" × 14". *Photo: Myrah Brown Green*

Charles Ras Scott, *Hapi-Festival Mask of West Africa*, 1999. Stained glass, 24.5" × 26.5". *Photo: Myrah Brown Green*

Charles Ras Scott, *Abstract Meditation*, 2018. Stained glass, 17" × 27". *Photo: Myrah Brown Green*

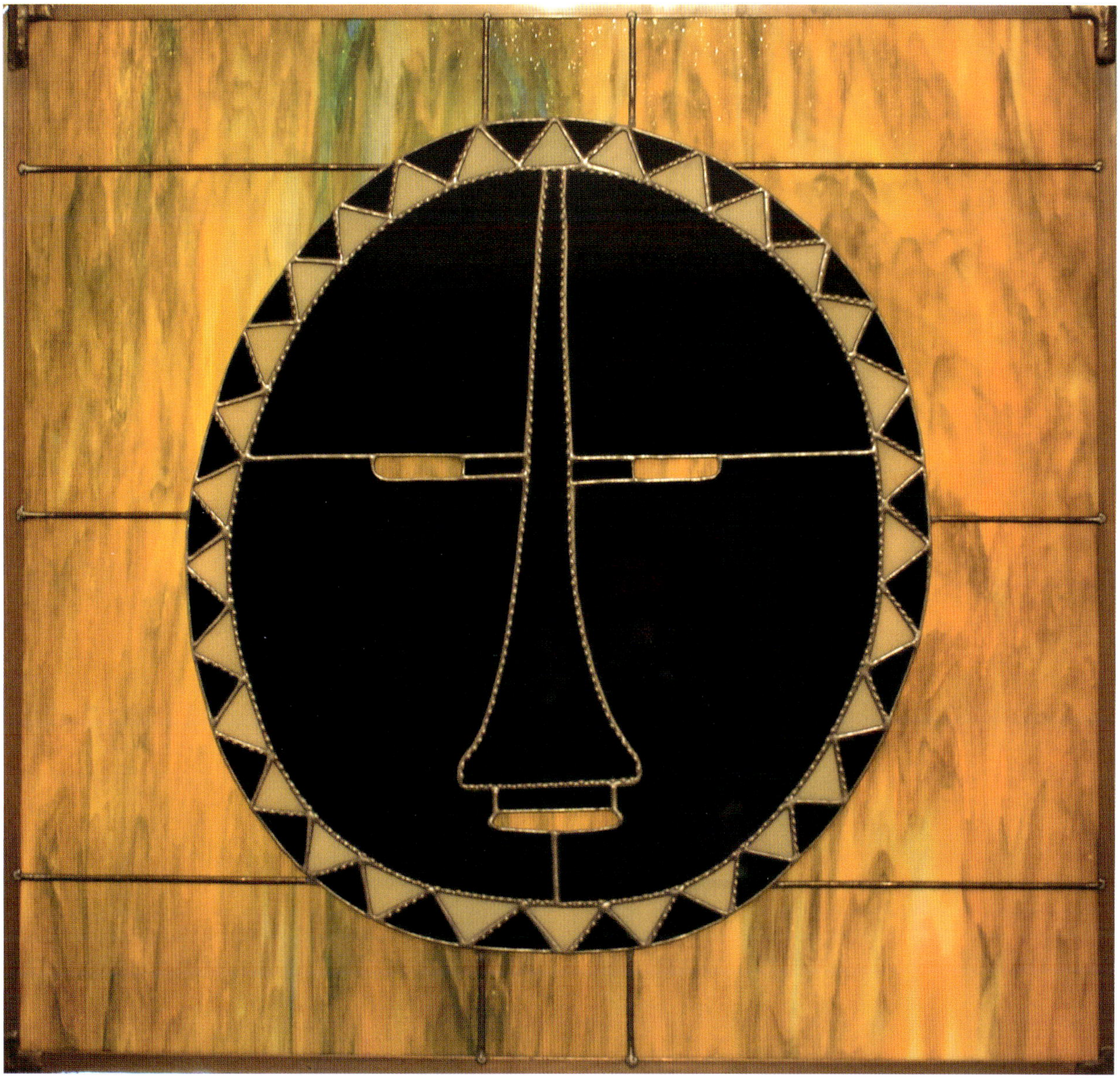

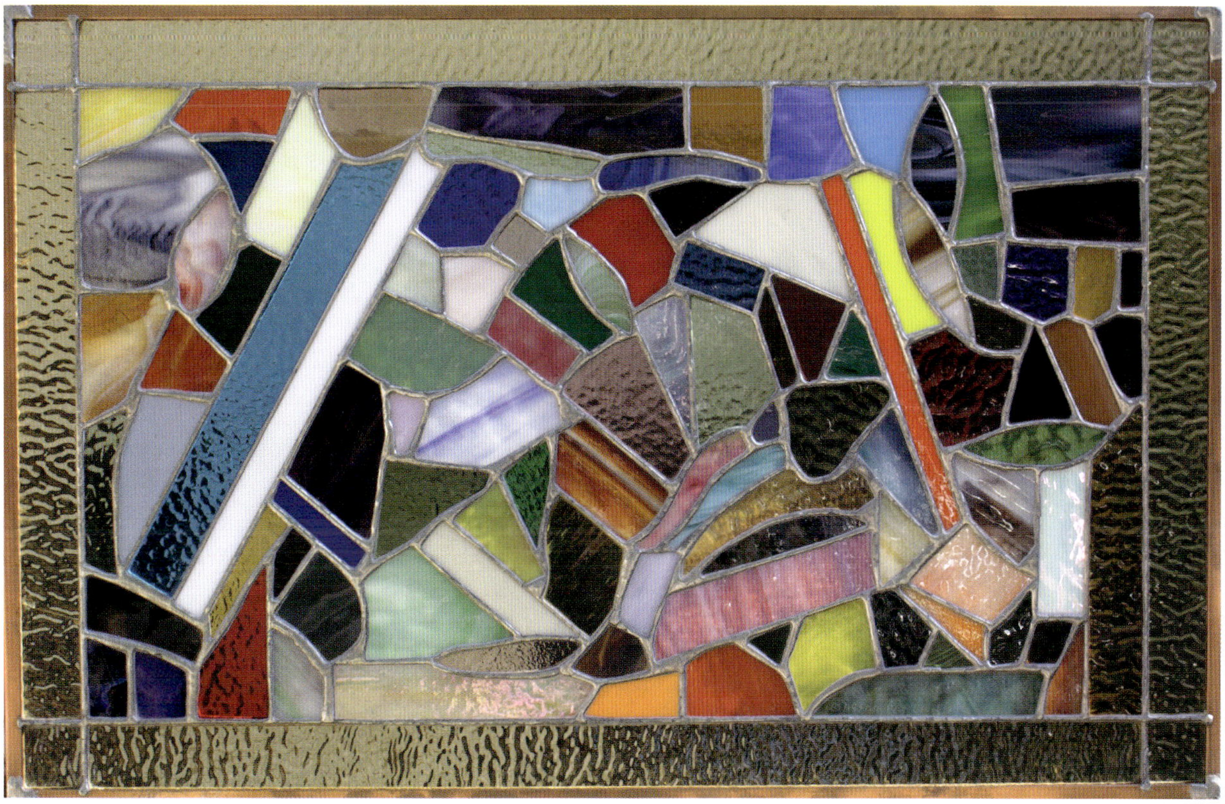

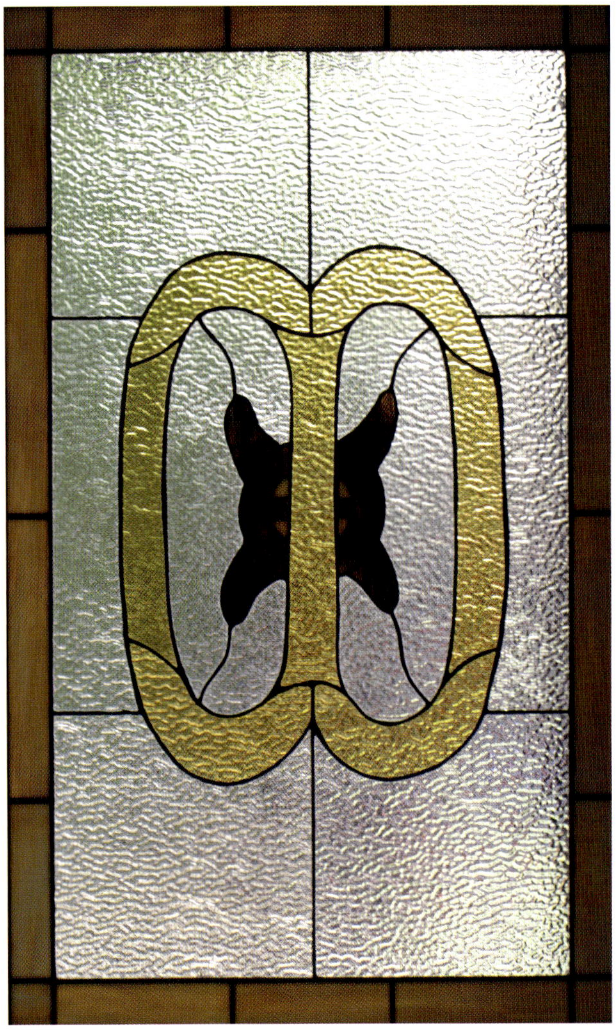

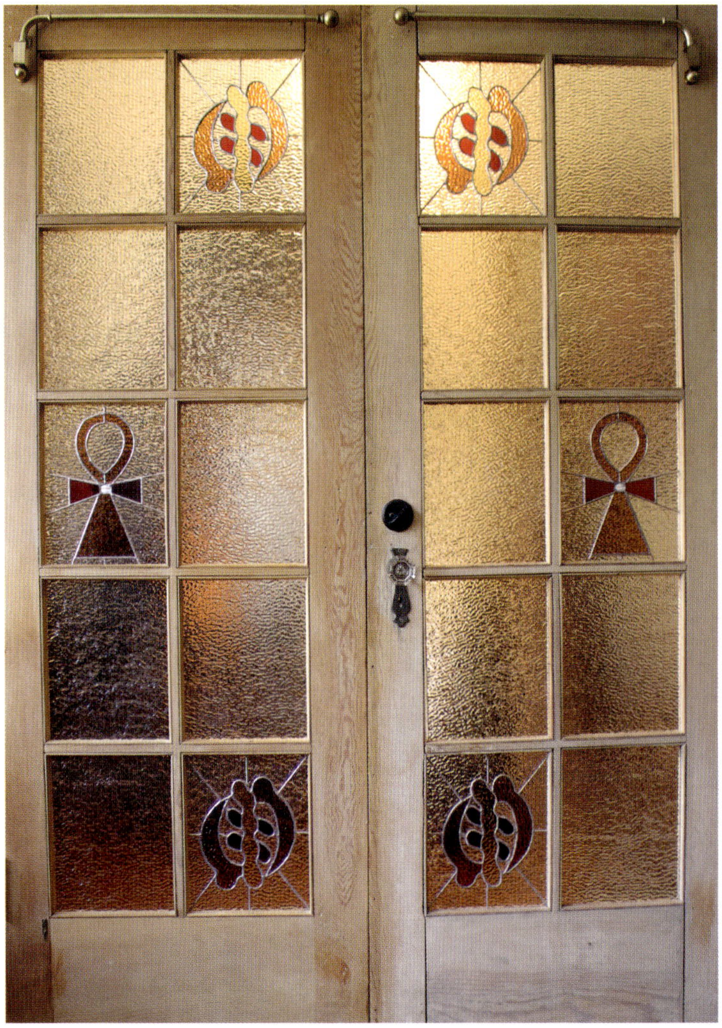

Charles Ras Scott, *Akwaaba* (entrance door panel), 2015. Stained glass, 36.75" × 23". *Photo: Myrah Brown Green*

Charles Ras Scott, *Ankh and Gye Nyame*, 2024. Stained glass; each door is 64" × 20". *Photo: Myrah Brown Green*

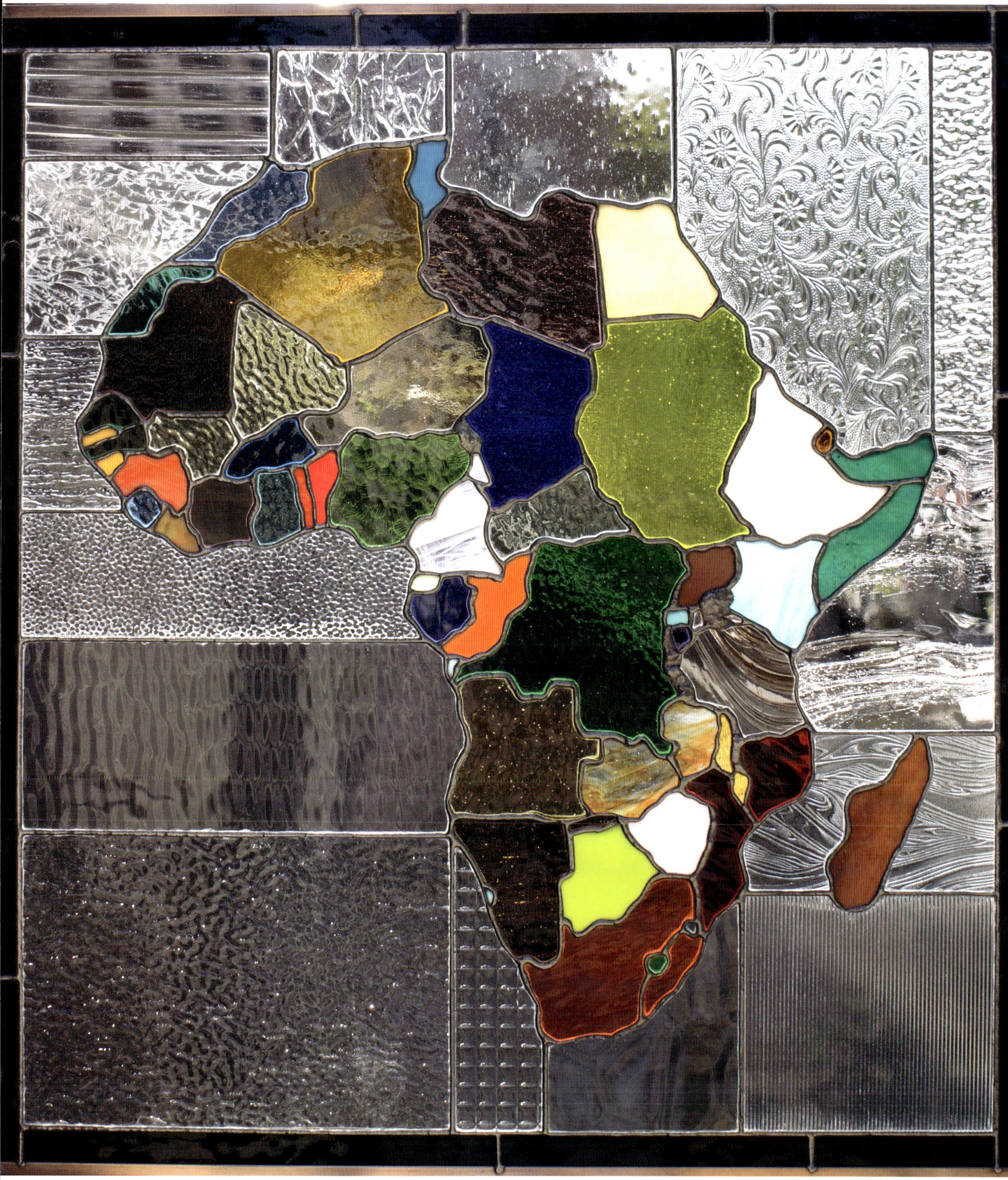

Charles Ras Scott, *Africa*, 2022. Stained glass, 18" × 18". *Photo: Myrah Brown Green*

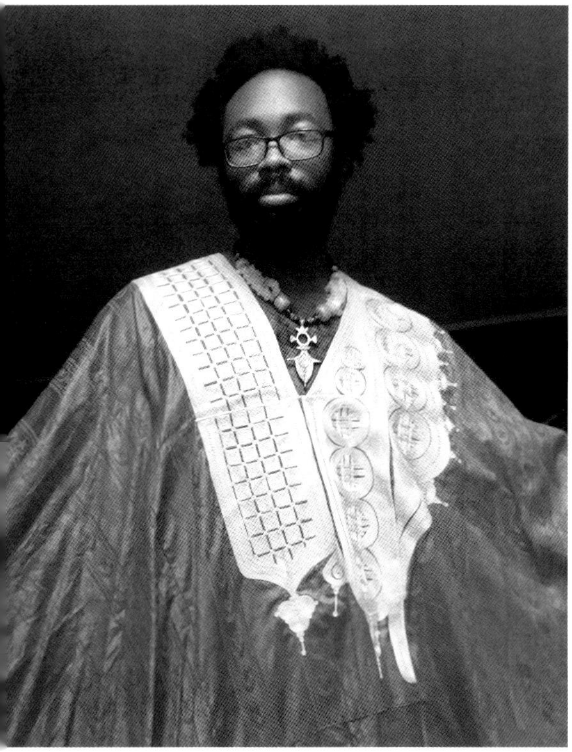

Photo: Courtesy of the collector

DEMANTI O'BRYANT
SURREALISM

DR. MYRAH: What was the first piece of art that you collected and when?

DEMANTI O'BRYANT: The first work of art that I collected through auction (September 2020) is a Woodrow Nash half-body sculpture. It was my eye-opening, and exciting, introduction to the reality of living with exceptional art by Black artists. In May 2021 I bought my first artwork directly from an artist . . . a portrait by Richard Mensah.

DR. MYRAH: Why are you a Keeper of art of African Diaspora Surrealism?

DEMANTI O'BRYANT: I've always had an affinity for unordinary art. My first surrealism piece, *Ancestral Embrace*, was purchased from Tim Short. I was over the moon that I could purchase something so extraordinary. After speaking with the artist, I realized what hurdles artists must overcome when they push the boundaries of what is traditionally appealing and comfortable. It was then that I wanted to champion Tim and the imaginative thinkers. During winter 2022, my art collector trajectory was affirmed and forever affected by Hayward gallery's exhibition *In the Black Fantastic*. I was motivated and realized that I wasn't the only Black art enthusiast that wanted to celebrate these types of voices. Furthermore, I was able to see Afro surrealist and Afro-futurist artists that were appreciated on a global scale.

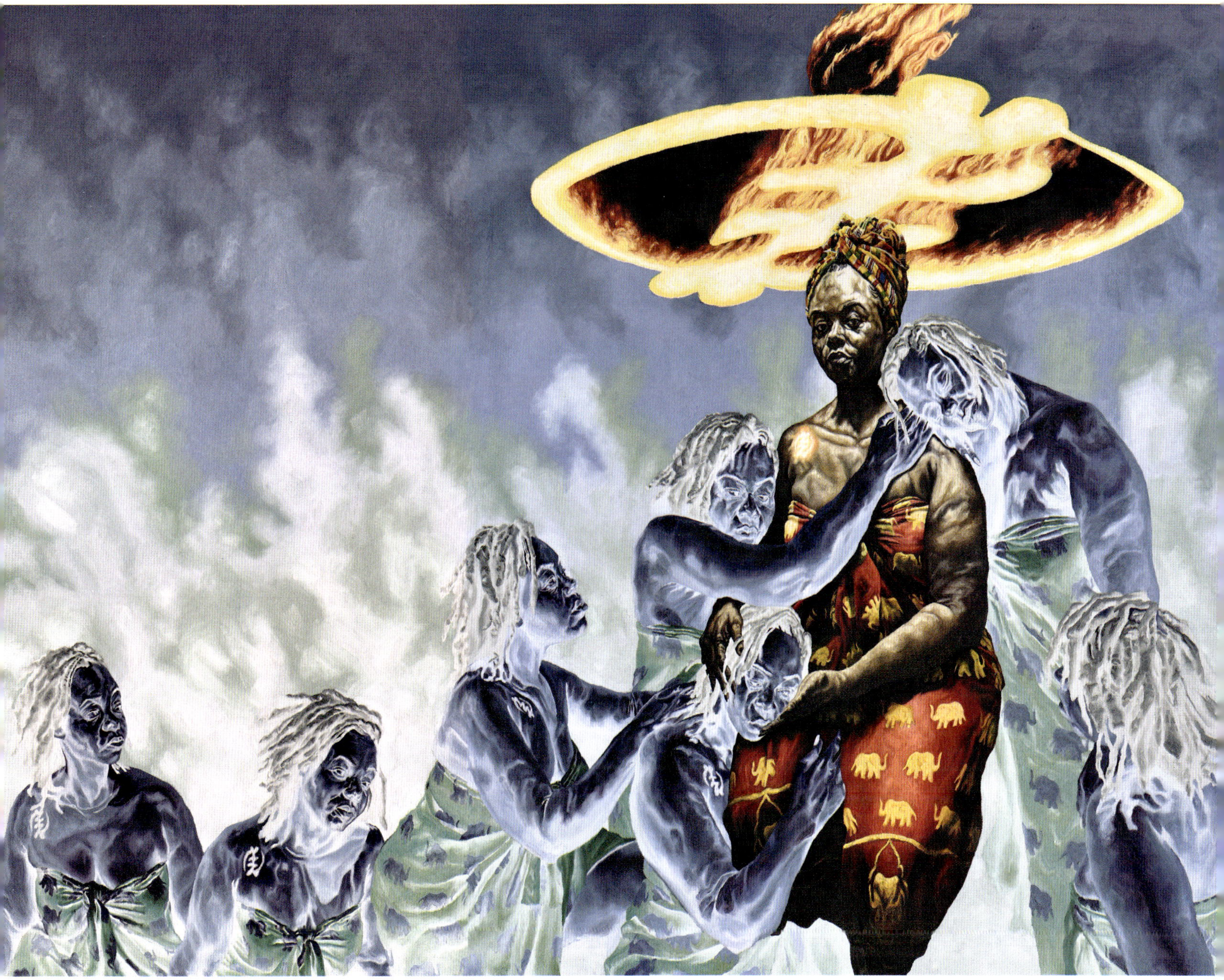

Tim Short, *Ancestral Embrace*, 2021. Oil on canvas, 46" × 62". *Photo: Courtesy of the artist*

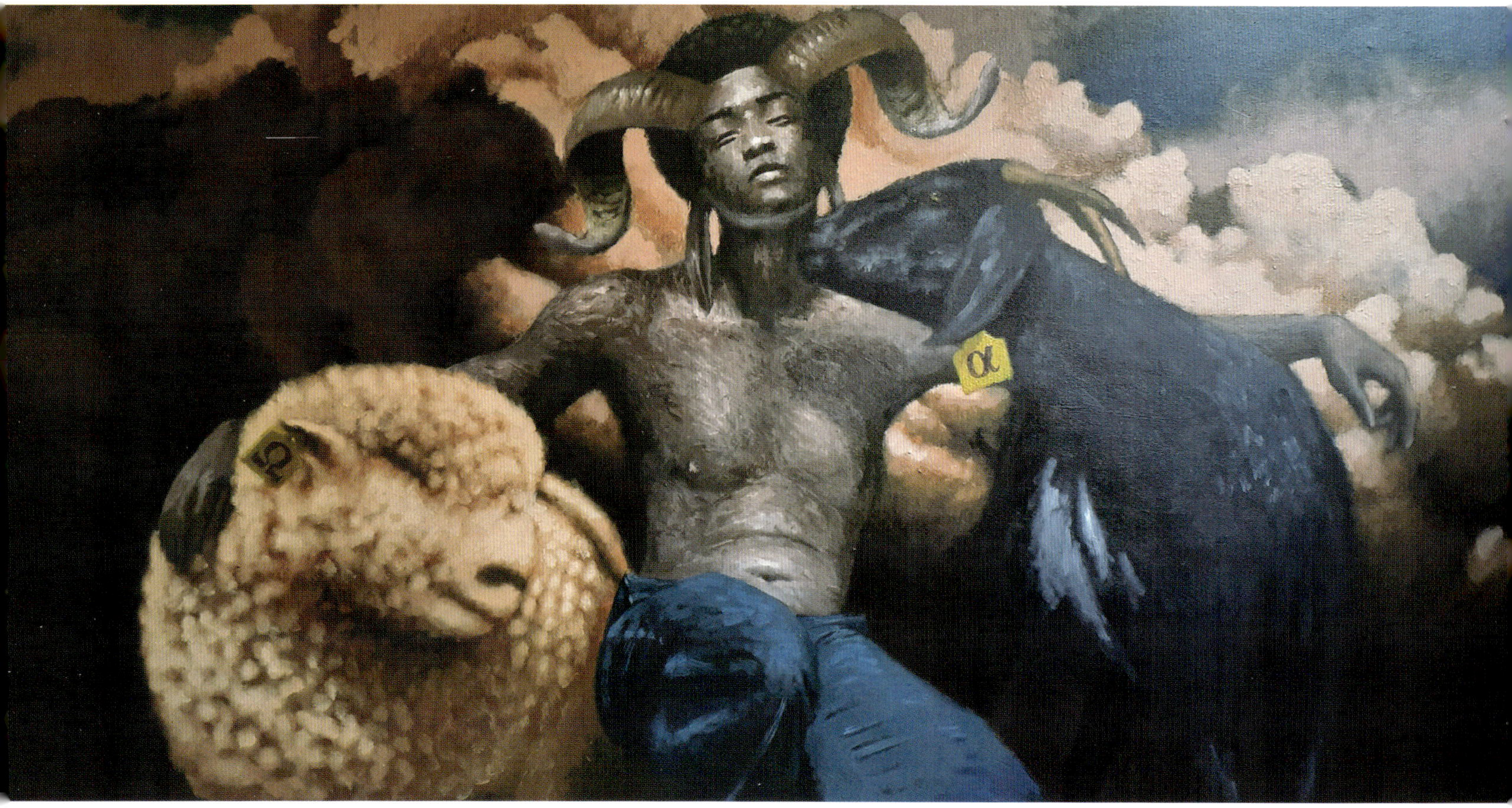

Ande Magoso, *Alpha and Omega*, 2023. Acrylic on canvas, 34" × 64". *Photo: Dacio Demo*

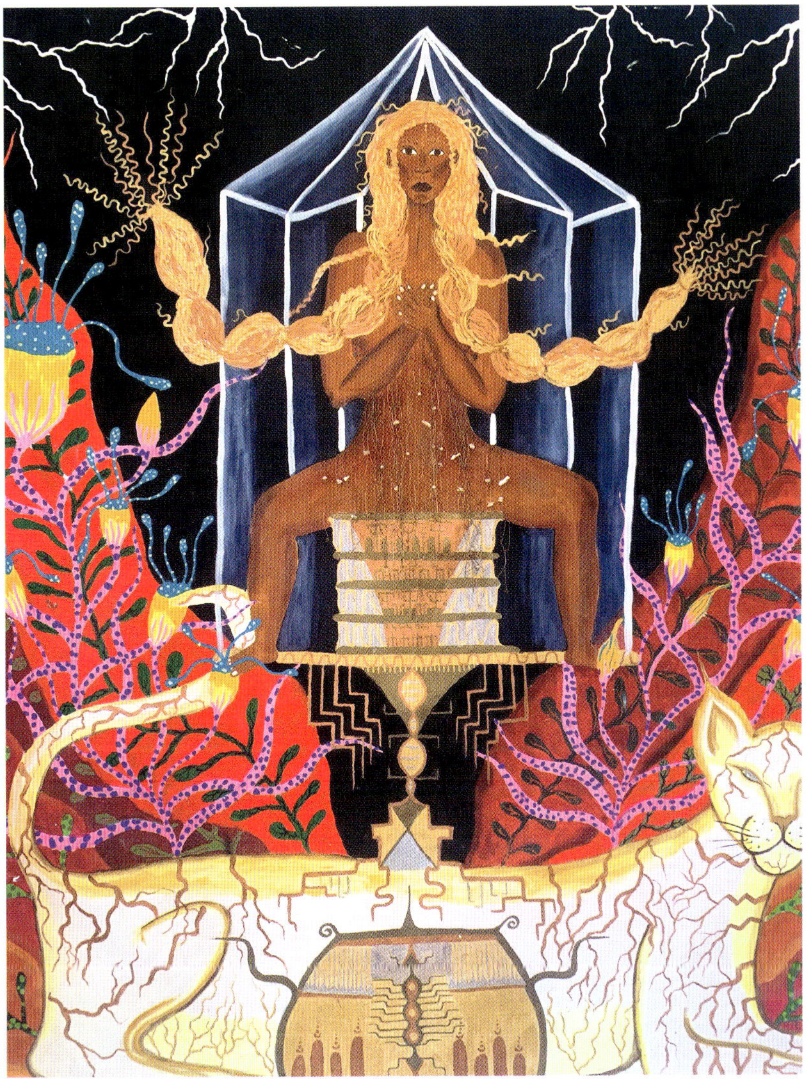

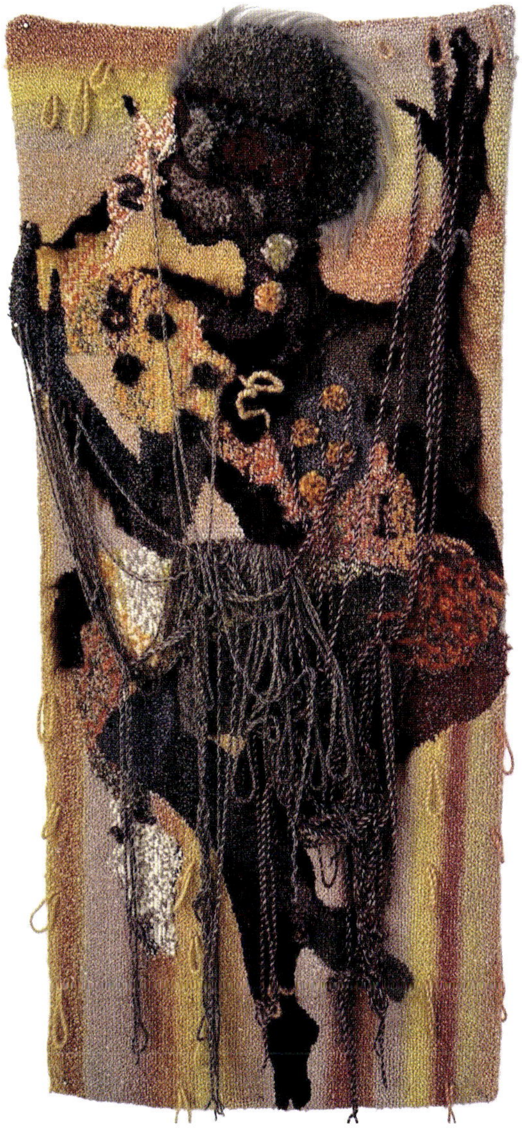

Lila Deva, *Nocturnal searches for the Key, the Spell and the Way to the Cat who Keeps the Secrets of the Heart*, 2022. Acrylic, oil, metals, and pearls on canvas, 71" × 79". *Photo: Courtesy of the artist*

Amani Quinnea Jackson. *Anxiety*, 2022. Faux fur, wool yarn, acrylic yarn, and chenille, 24" × 48". *Photo: Courtesy of the artist*

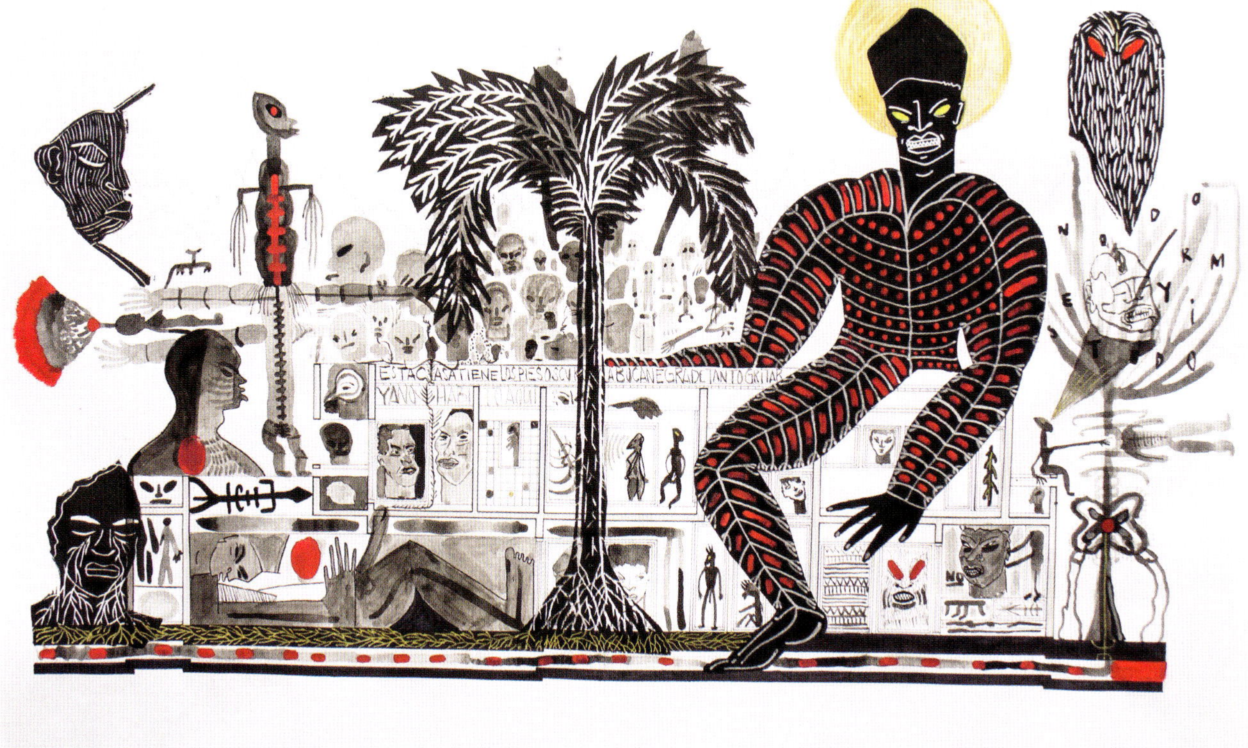

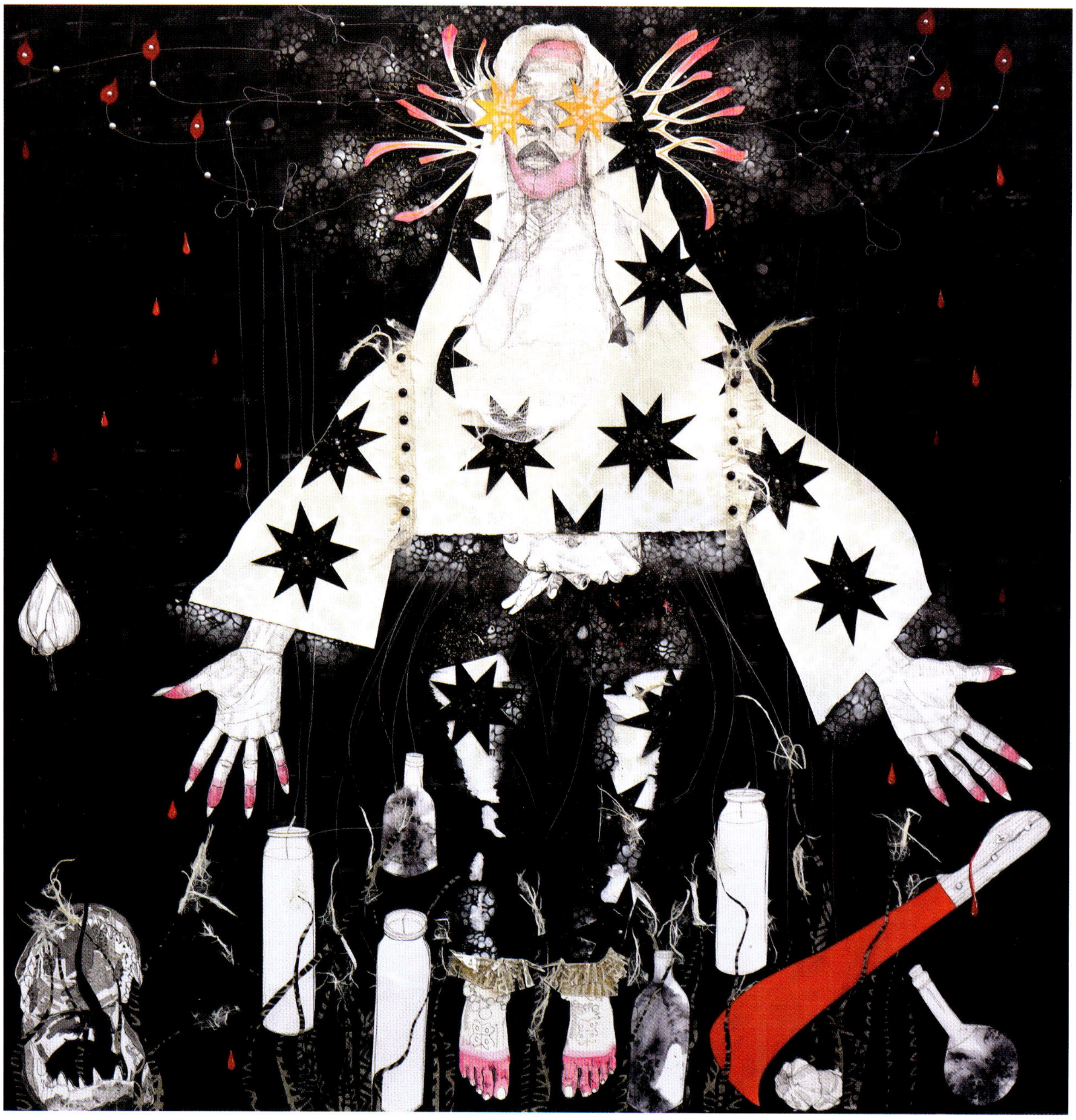

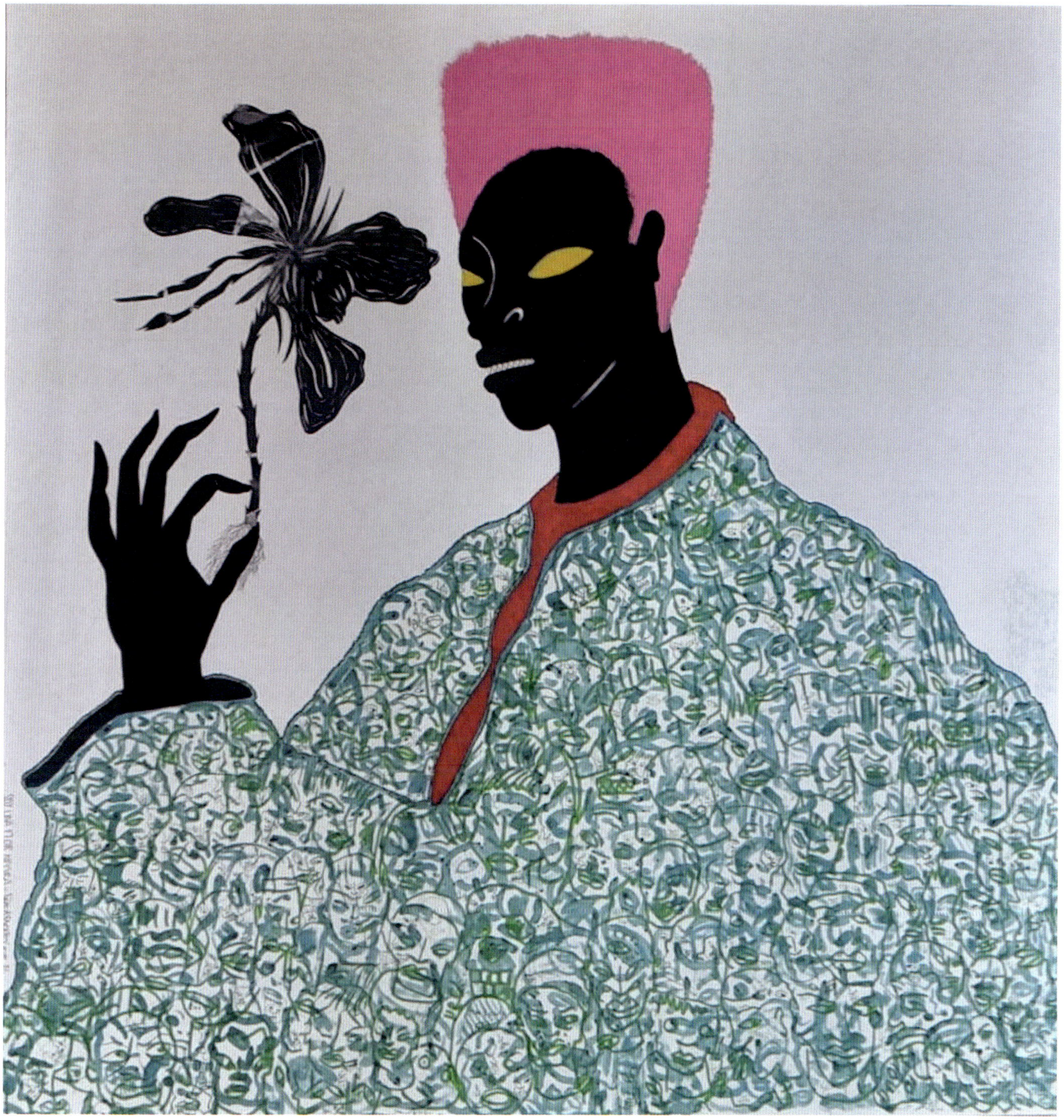

Frank Xarate, *This House has Dark Feet and a Black Mouth from Screaming so Much*, 2022. Woodcut; watercolor; black tempura; gold, white, and red posca marker on repurposed architectural plan, 9.69" × 27.56". *Photo: Courtesy of the artist*

Komikka Patton, *Channels of Communication*, 2023. Mixed-media collage: paper, watercolor, acrylic, spray paint, mica, pearls, india ink, and thread, 48" × 48". *Photo: Courtesy of the artist*

Above: Frank Xarate, *I am a Black Flower*, 2022. Green and red watercolor, pink posca marker, black tempera, and openwork marbled paper, 19.69" × 27.56". *Photo: Courtesy of the artist*

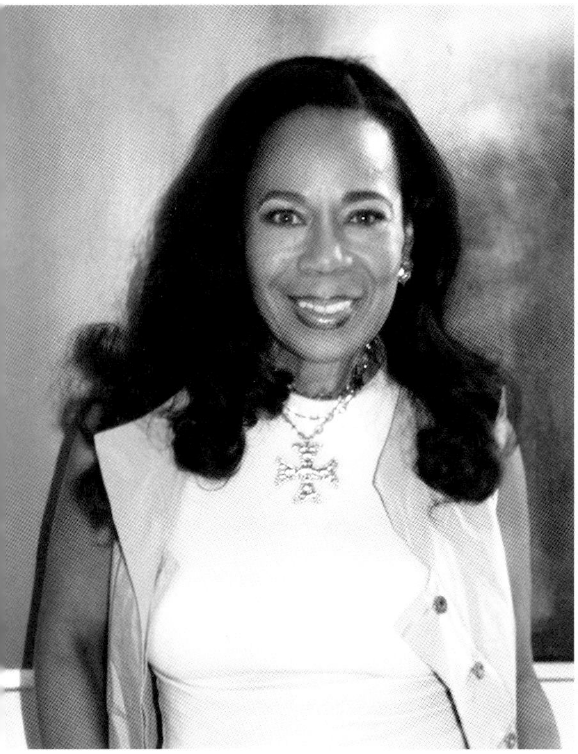

Photo: Dwayne Pierce

DENISE PIERCE
MOVEMENT

DR. MYRAH: What was the first piece of art that you collected and when?

DENISE PIERCE: The first piece of art that I ever purchased was by a man named Abe Wexler. He had an art studio in the basement of the co-op where we resided. Abe had a full-time job but pursued his love of painting with the dedication of an athlete. I would visit often with him, escaping within the colors, hues, and imagery created as he listened to classical music. The image purchased, *Boulangerie*, is a delicate watercolor and ink streetscape of a French bakery. Immersed in tones of pink, yellow, ocher, and green, it conjured imagery of possibility, beauty, and hope for its fourteen-year-old owner.

DR. MYRAH: Why are you a Keeper of art representing movement?

DENISE PIERCE: For as long as I can remember, I have been a visual person. I look at all sorts of things, important and unimportant. Art is life; it is personal. It creates and cements a visual memory of moments in time captured within a medium. Essentially the physical and emotional manifestation of the experience of one person at a particular time. It is history. The work in our collection embodies motion, movement, and a persistent resistance to censure, restriction, and constriction. Art often reflects the freedom and ability to be seen. As a people, there have been many obstacles in our path, forks in the road. Sacrifices and compromises are often made from the ashes we create. I am so honored to be able to journey into the visual memory of the artists and act as a caretaker of the work. The art is the creation of the artist and has a life of its own. It is meant to be experienced and grows, providing intimate and unique perspectives for each viewer. I am a Keeper because my commitment is to people, the human hand, and the intersection of thought and creation. We are fortunate to have museums, spaces where the experience of art can be egalitarian, to be enjoyed by many. Art, in visual and musical form, is the best of our humanity. It is a path to tolerance, empathy, understanding, and universality. Movement in the art is freedom.

Tafa (Fiadzigbe), *No Justice–No Peace–Harlem*, 2001. Oil on canvas, 32.75" × 26.75". *Photo: Dwayne Pierce*

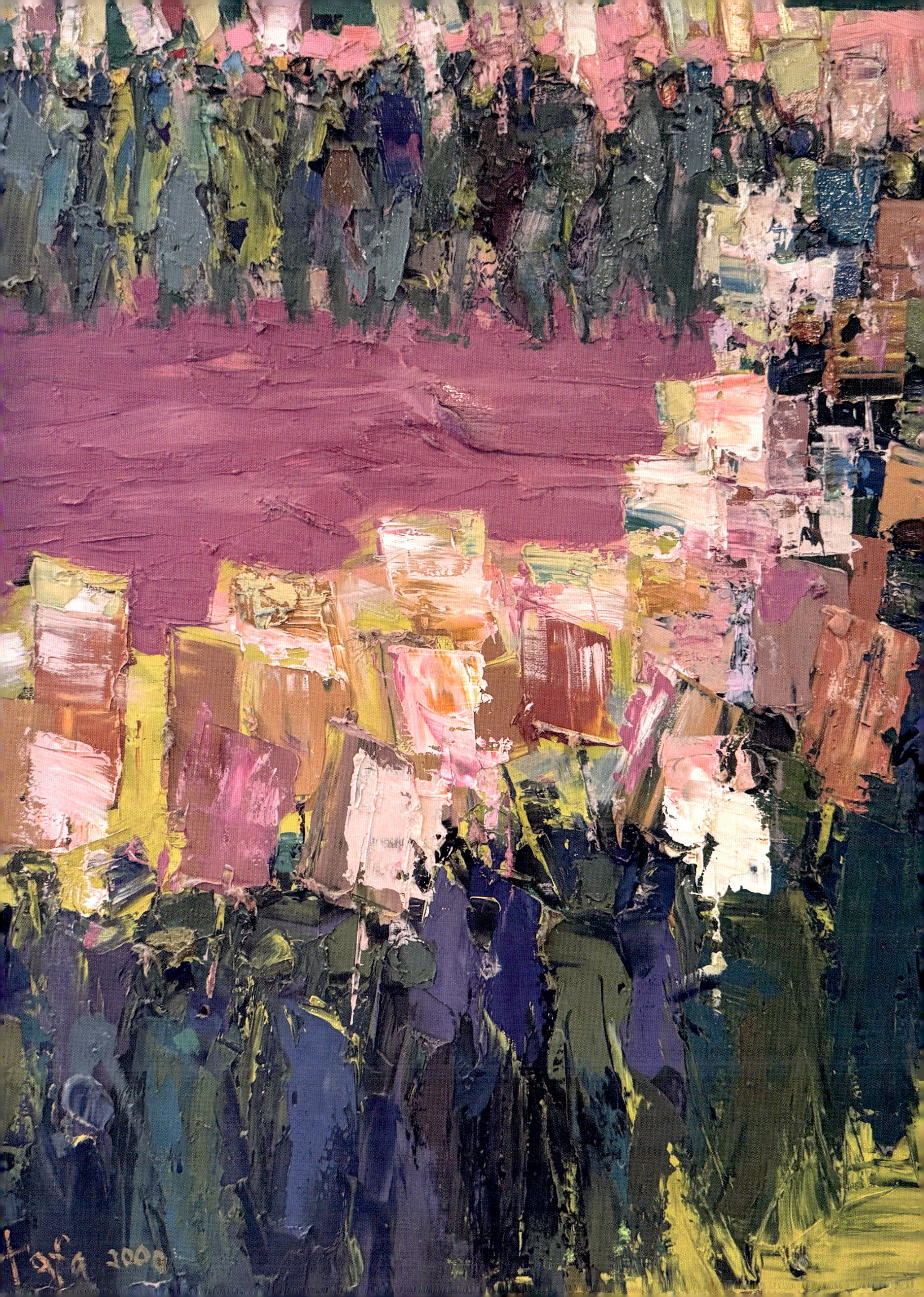

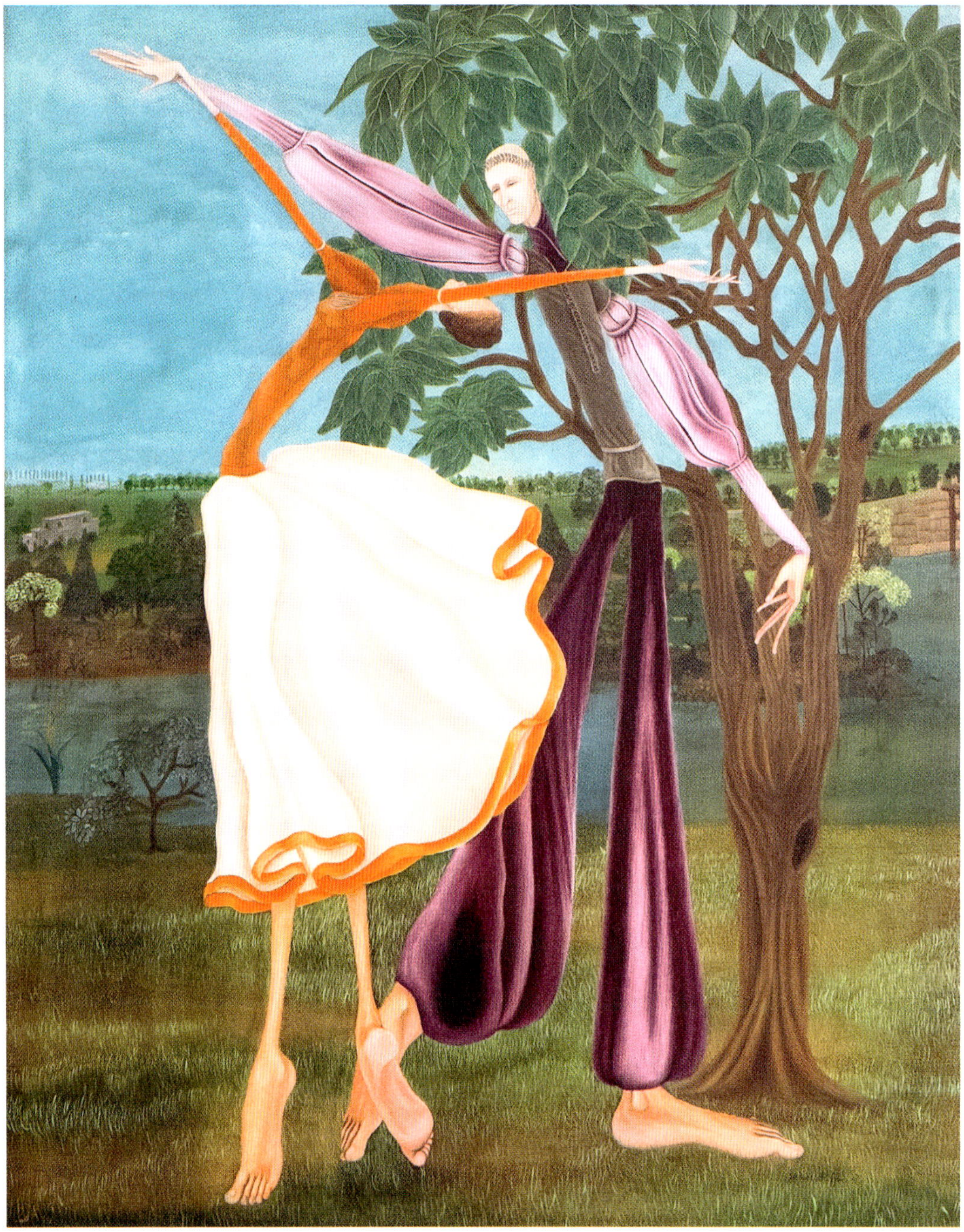

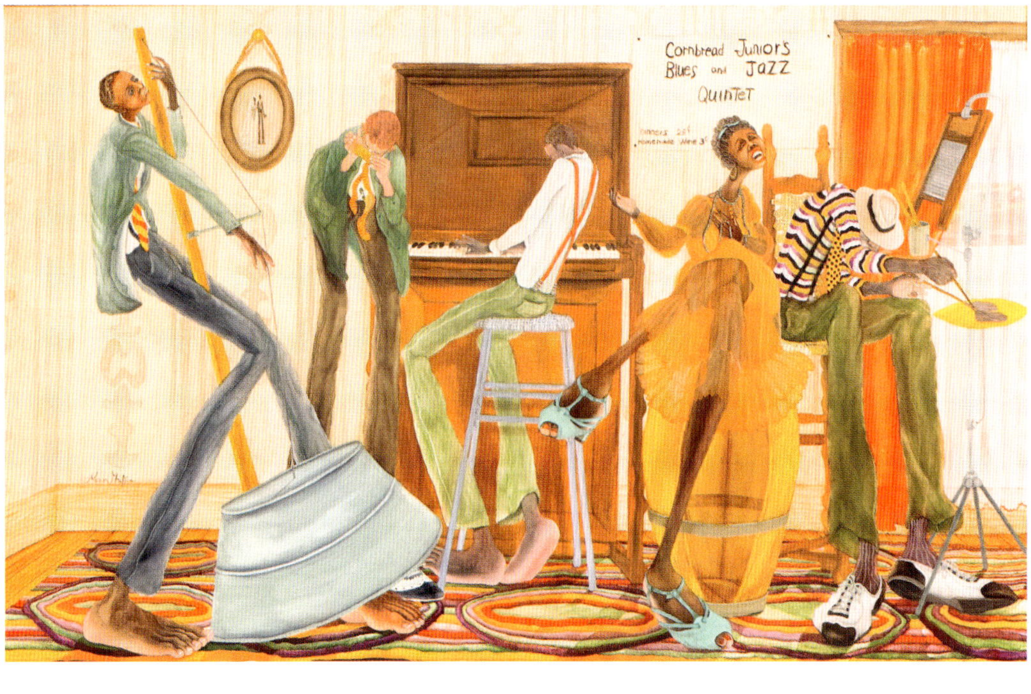
Cornbread Junior's
Blues and Jazz
Quintet

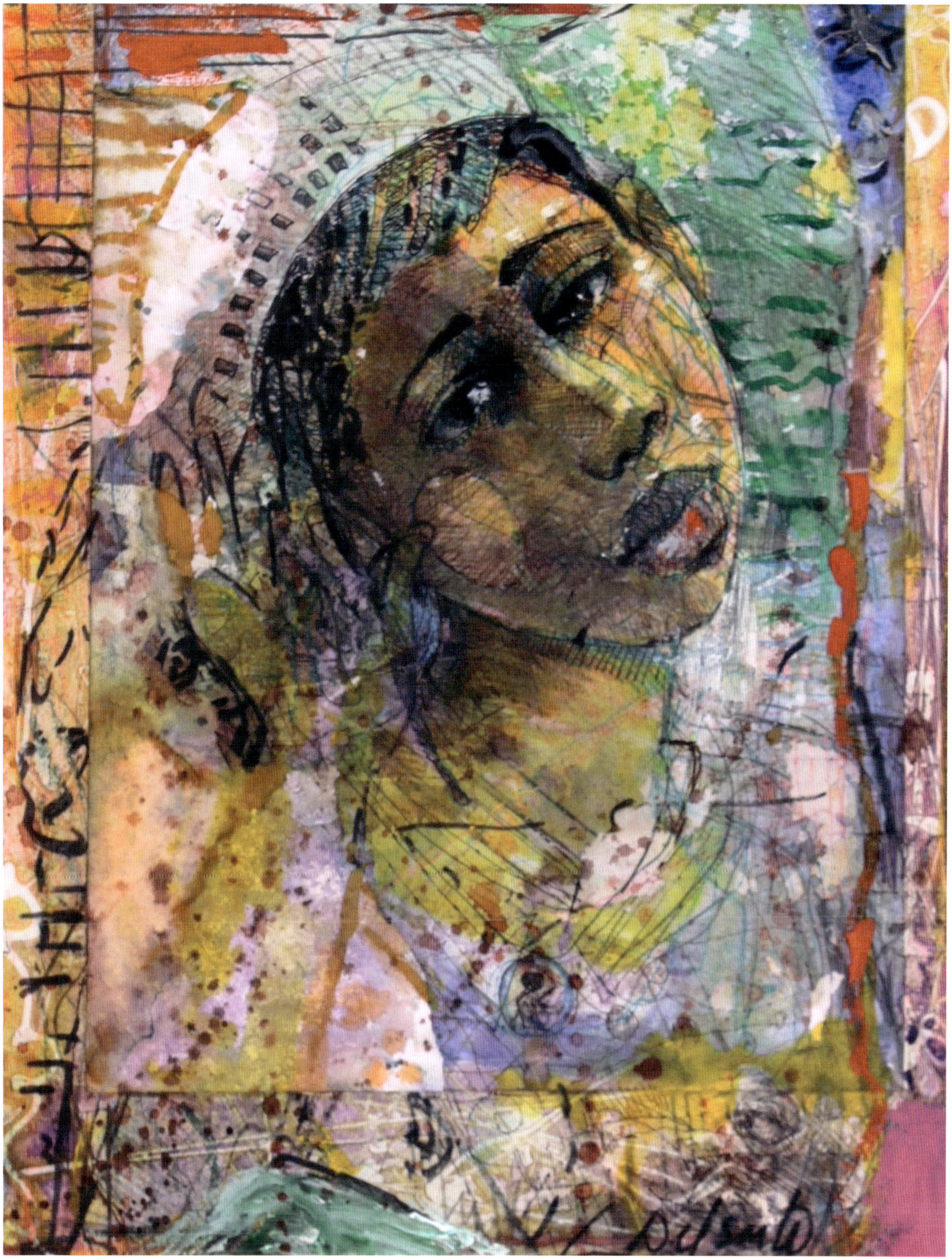

Marion Griffin, *Spanish Dancer*, 1996. Oil on canvas, 56" × 45.36". *Photo: Tyla Harrington*

Marion Griffin, *Rehearsal*, 1996. Oil on canvas, 33.5" × 51.75". *Photo: Tyla Harrington*

Above: Louis Delsarte, *Wavelengths*, 2004. Acrylic on watercolor paper, 25.25" × 17.25". *Photo: Dwayne Pierce*

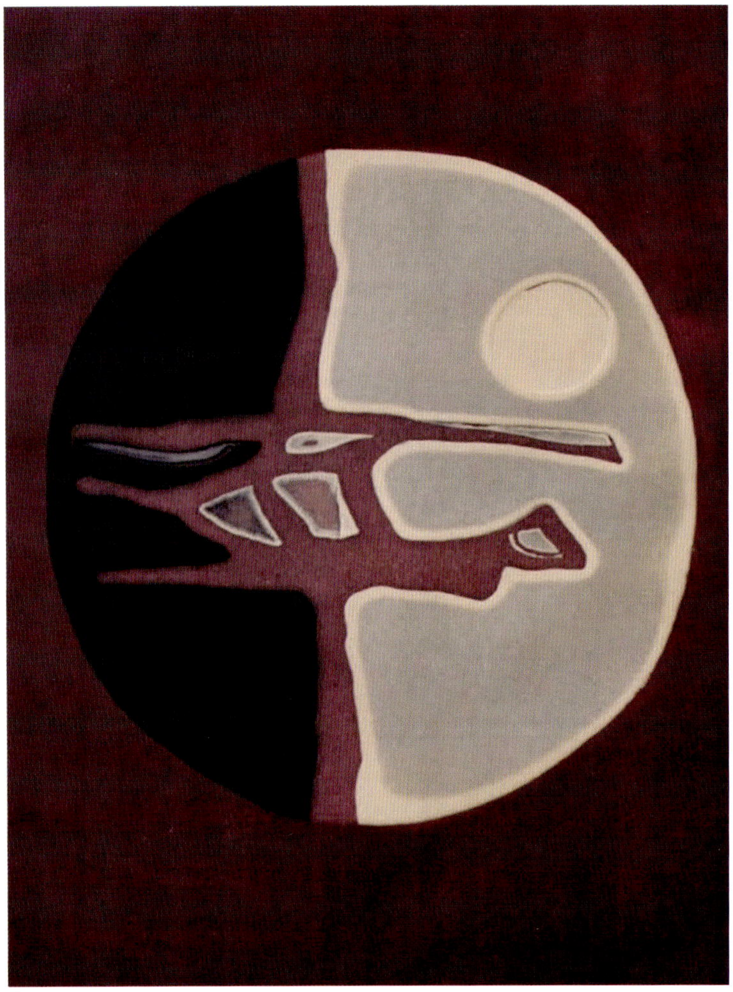

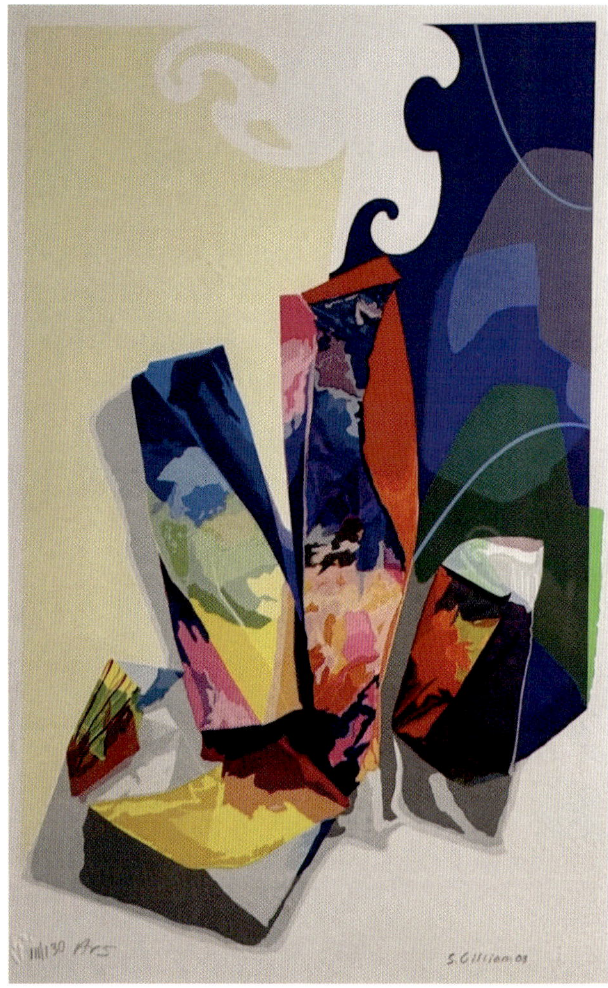

Betty Blayton, *Inner Synctal II*, 1974. Embossed lithograph, A/P, 32.5" × 25.25". *Photo: Dwayne Pierce*

Sam Gilliam, *ARS*, 2003. Color screen-print on woven paper, 28 5/16" × 20". *Photo: Dwayne Pierce*

Opposite: Christopher Gonzalez, *Madonna*, 1998. Acrylic on canvas, 20" × 17". *Photo: Dwayne Pierce*

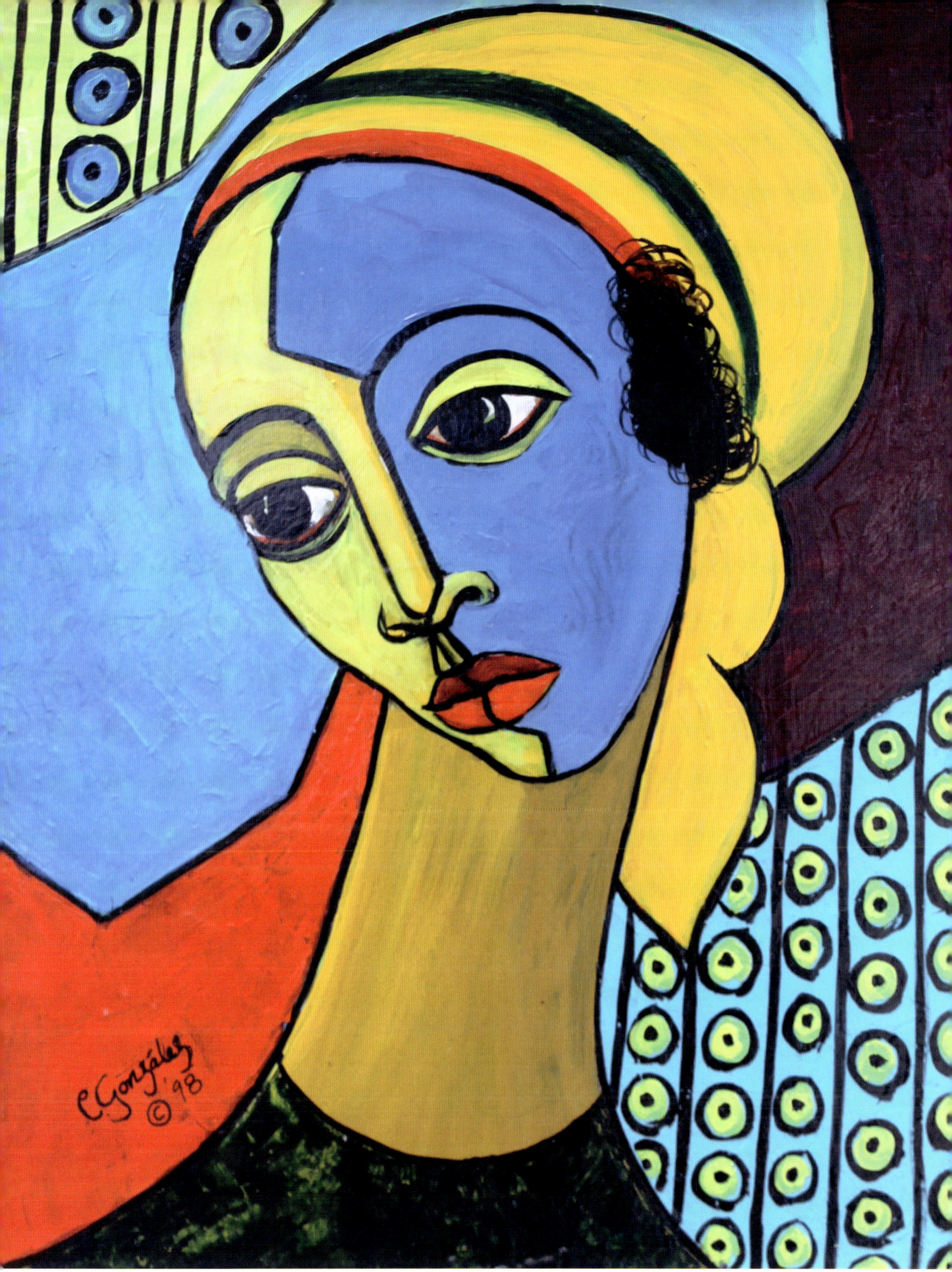
C. González
© '98

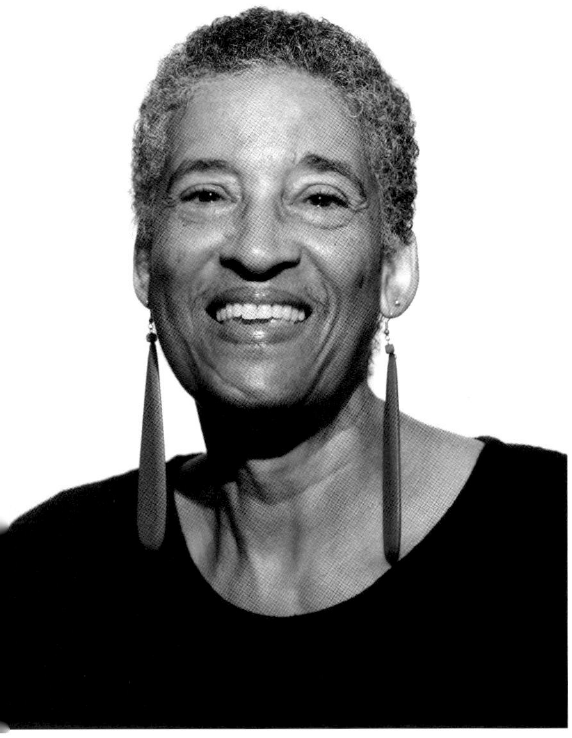

Photo: Foster Henry

VALERIE PILGRIM BELL-BEY
WATERCOLOR

DR. MYRAH: What was the first piece of art that you collected and when?

VALERIE PILGRIM BELL-BEY: The first piece of art that I collected was *Soul Searching*, a screen print by Sadikisha Collier, in 1988 at the Fulton Art Fair.

DR. MYRAH: Why are you a Keeper of Watercolor paintings?

VALERIE PILGRIM BELL-BEY: Watercolor is a very challenging medium. Perhaps that's why I find it so fascinating. It can flow with ease and grace and neatly stay within the confines of the artist's stroke or be strong willed and stubborn and go where it wants to go, defying the artist's direction. Some artists have allowed watercolor its independence and allowed it to meander and blend and define itself, while others have tamed the wandering medium to the point of photographic stillness. Each, with keenness of eye, deftness of hand, and respect for the medium, creates work, sometimes subtle and soothing, sometimes vibrant and powerful, that enchants and often mystifies the viewer. I am excited to have watercolor in my collection. I respect its uniqueness, versatility, and its ability to be magically transformed in ways that other mediums cannot. It is for all of the above reasons that I have been a keeper of watercolor images.

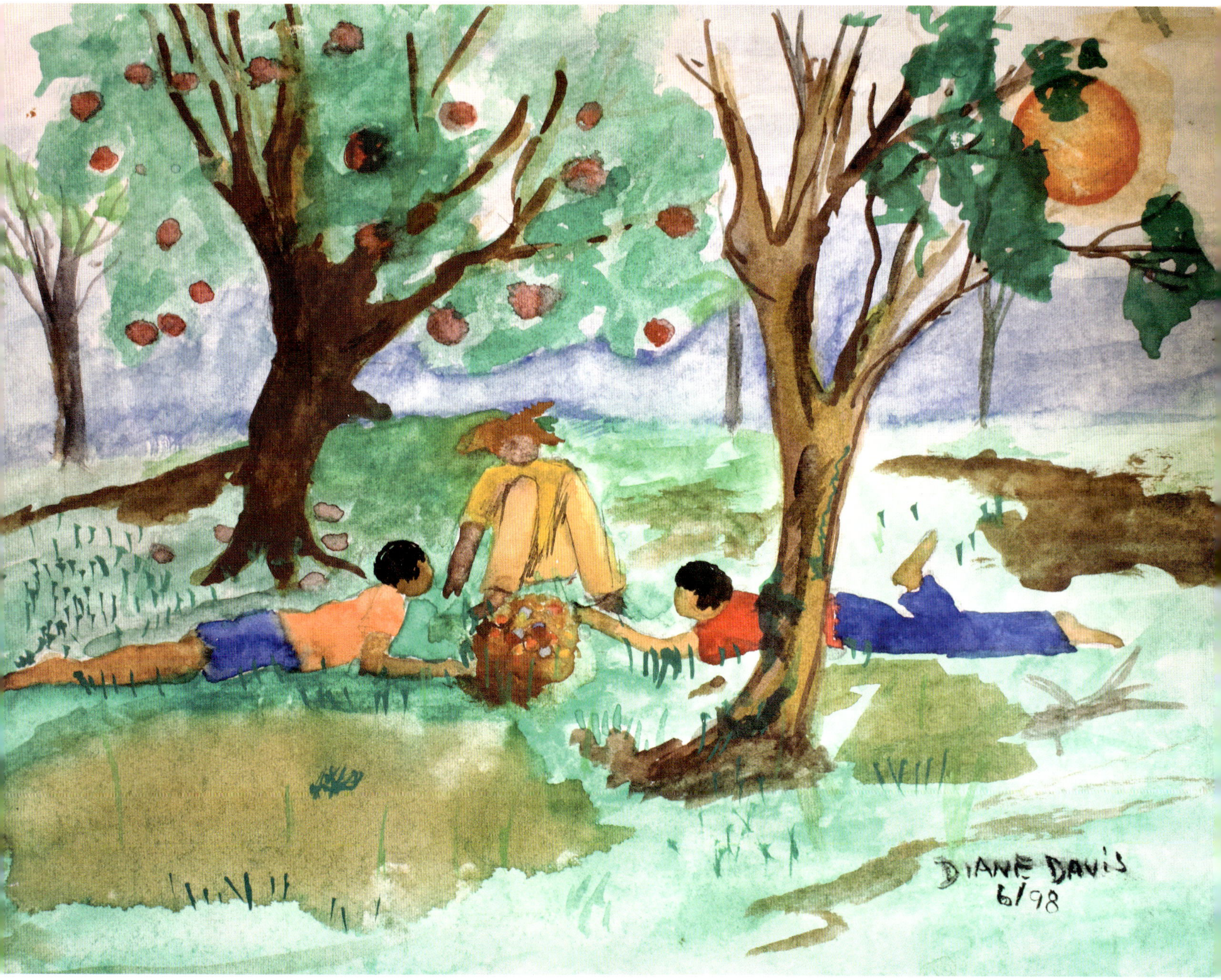

Diane Davis, *Shootin' Marbles*, 1988. Watercolor, 11" × 8". *Photo: Myrah Brown Green*

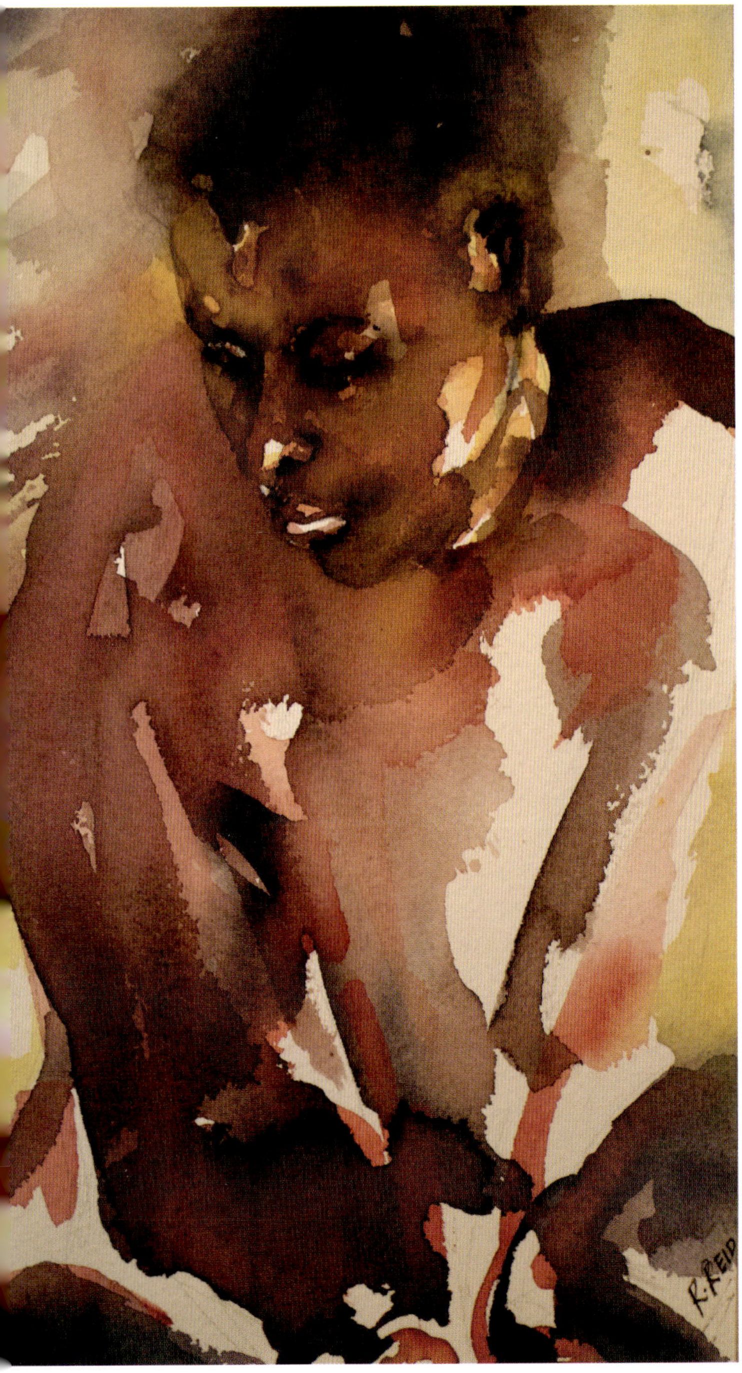

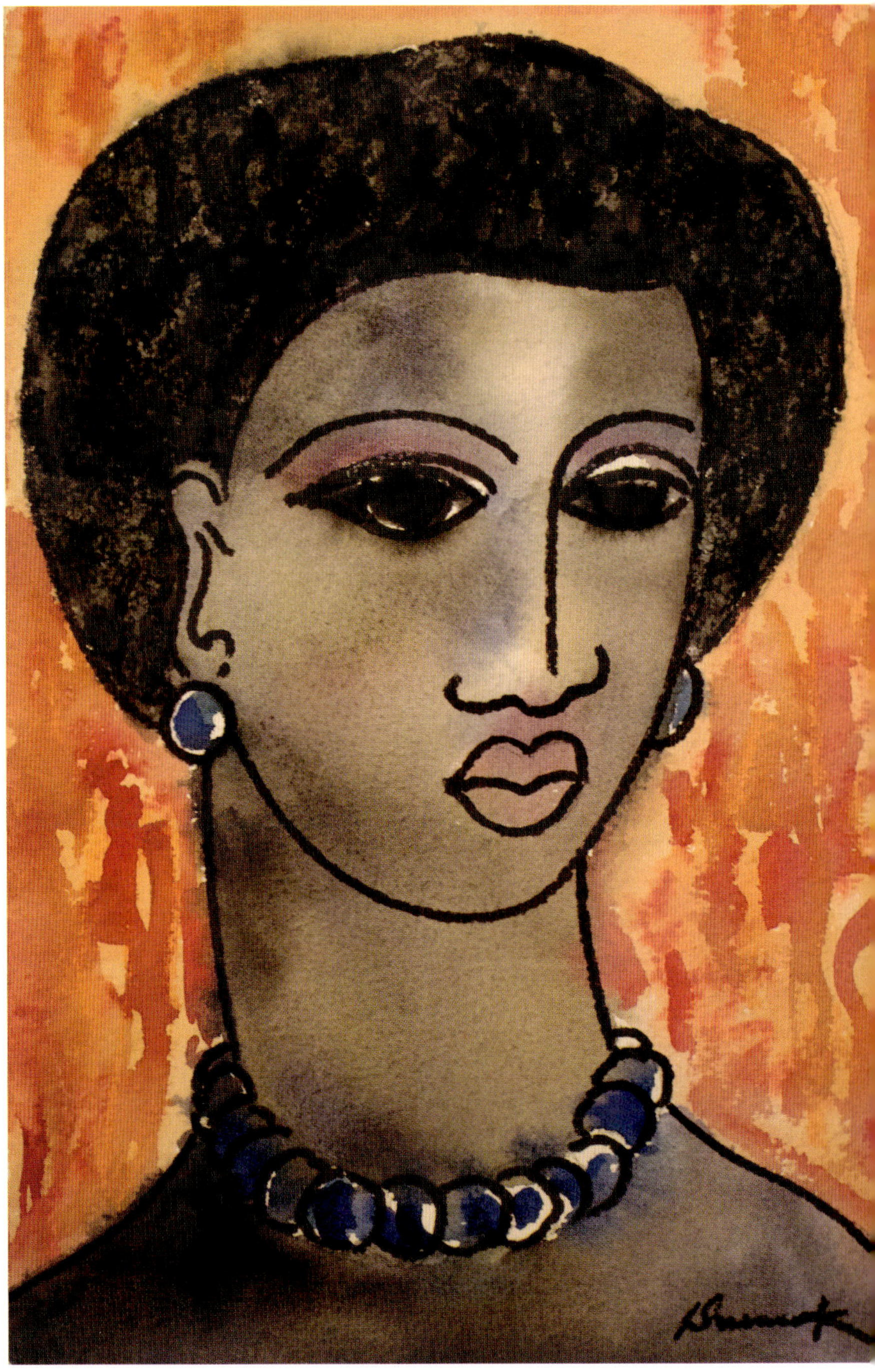

Robert Reid, *Untitled*, 1993. Watercolor, 7⅝" × 12". *Photo: Myrah Brown Green*

James Denmark, *Young, Black and Beautiful*, 1989. Watercolor, 7" × 10.125". *Photo: Myrah Brown Green*

Opposite: Cecil Cooper, *Untitled*, 1997. Watercolor, 9" × 12". *Photo: Myrah Brown Green*

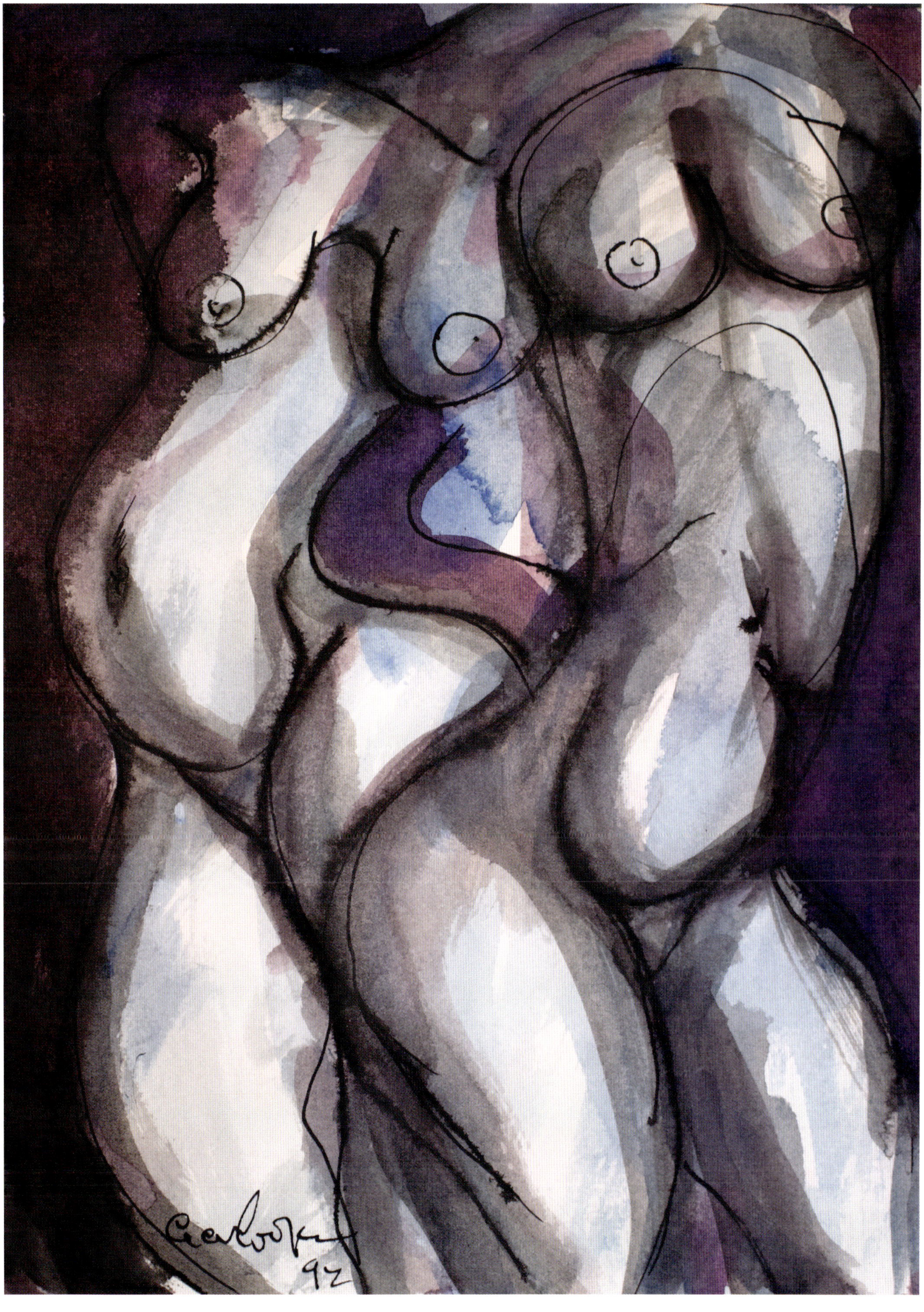

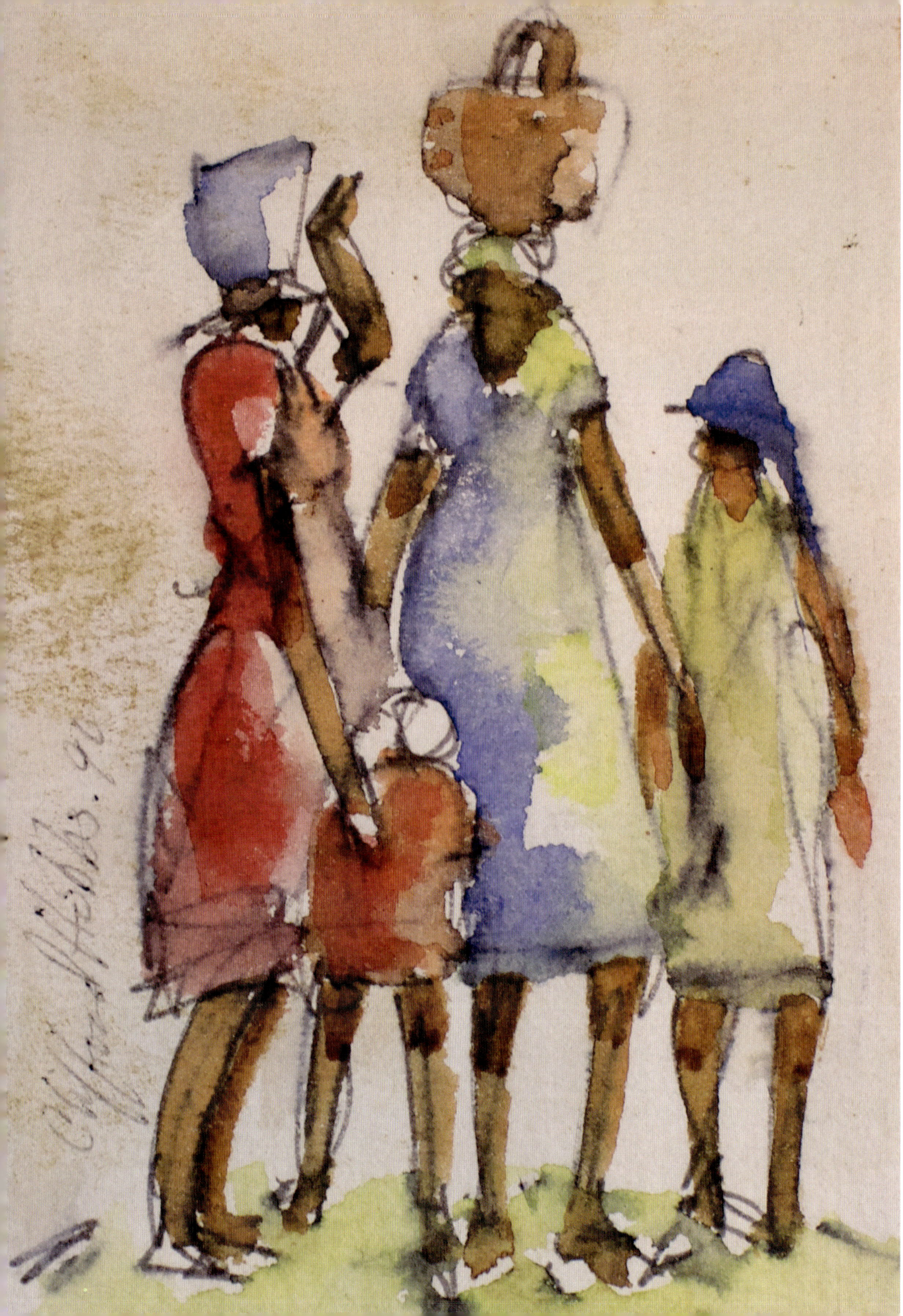

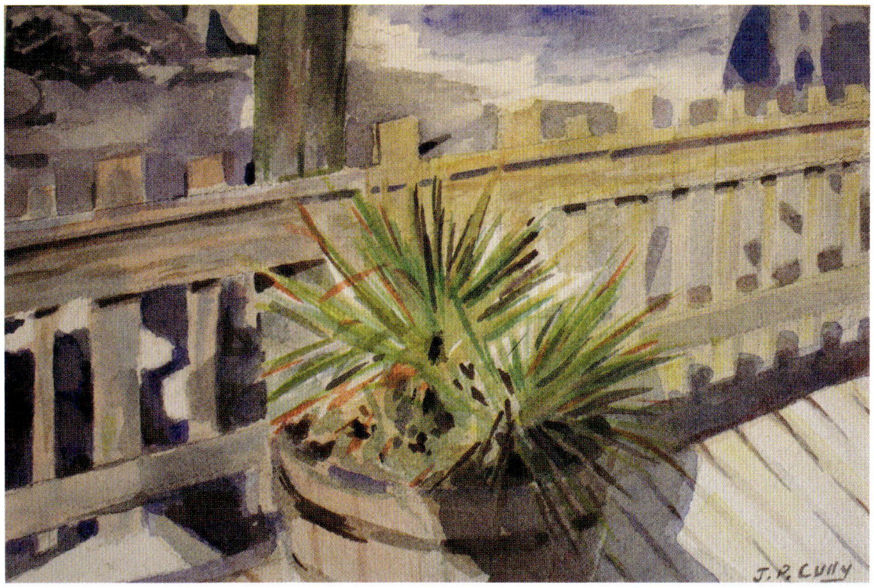

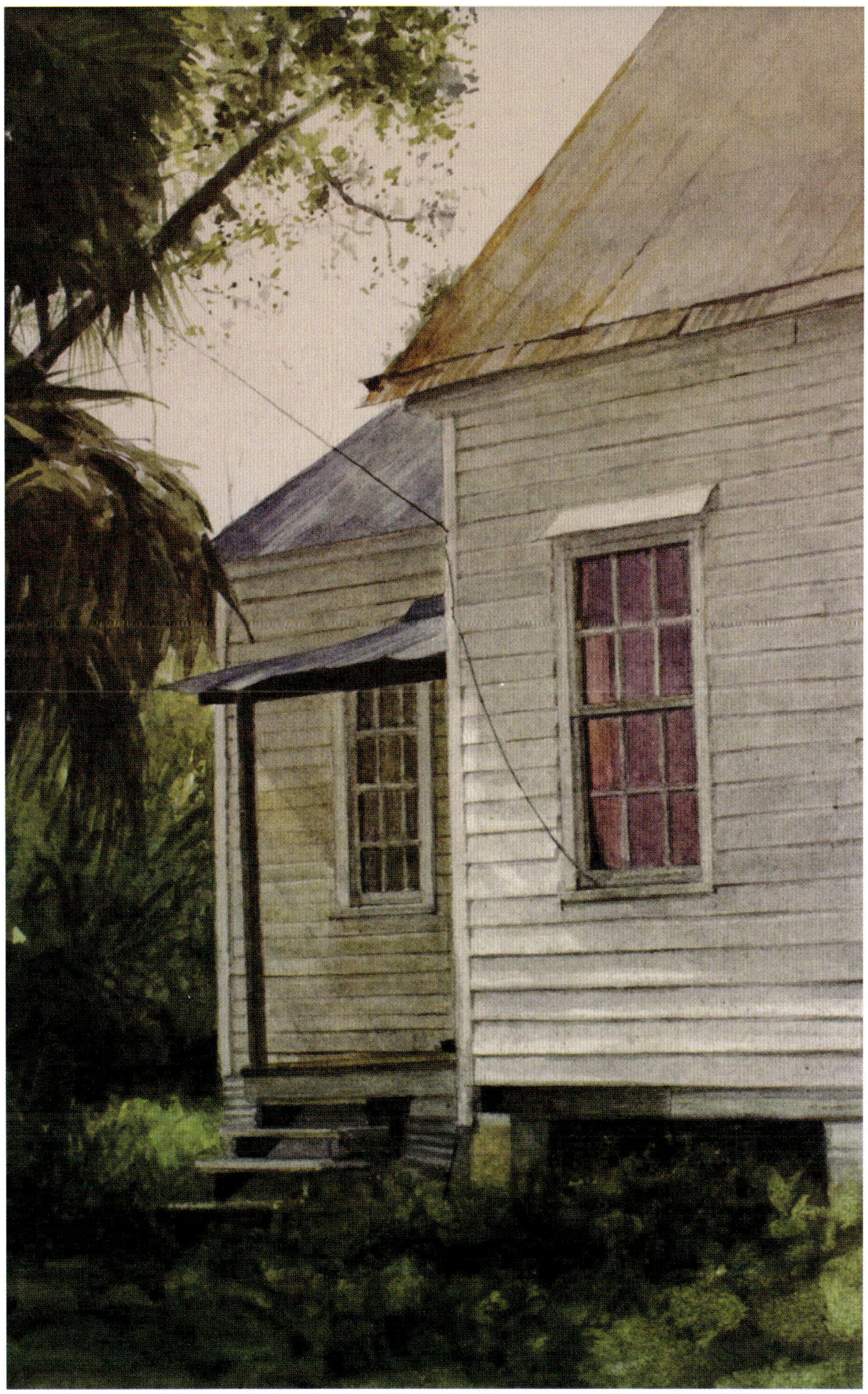

Opposite: Clifford Hobbs, *Village Women*, 1990. Watercolor, 4" × 5.75". *Photo: Myrah Brown Green*

Jackie Peters Cully, *Untitled*, 1989. Watercolor, 11" × 7.625". *Photo: Myrah Brown Green*

Dean Mitchell, *Pink Shade*, 2000. Watercolor, 4⅞" × 7.375". *Photo: Myrah Brown Green*

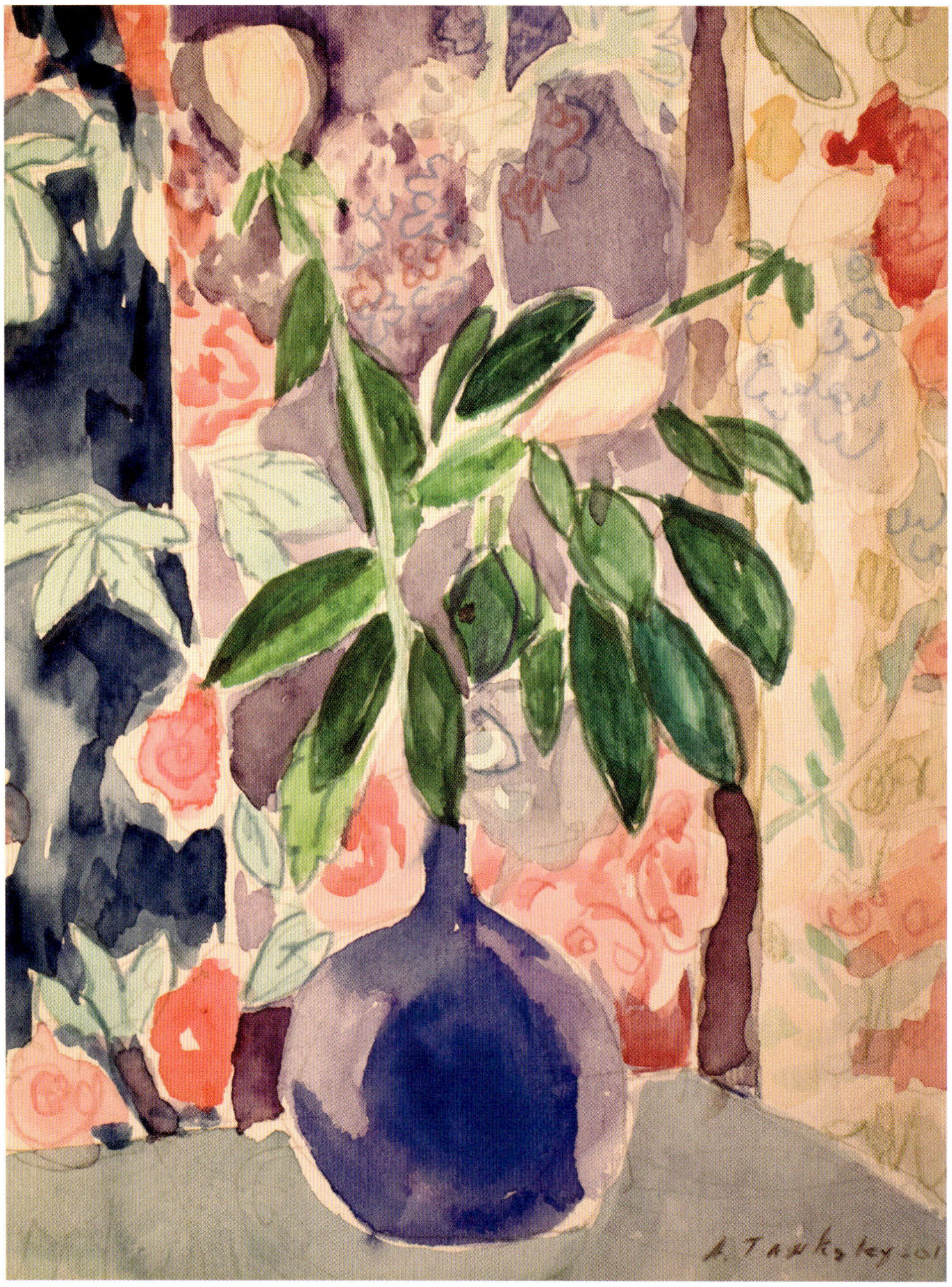

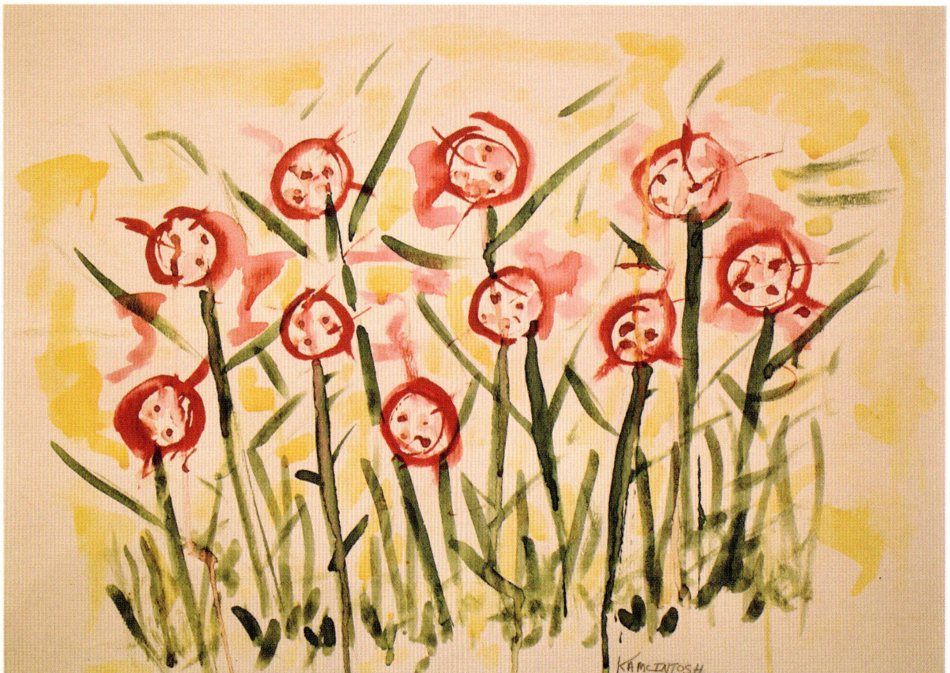

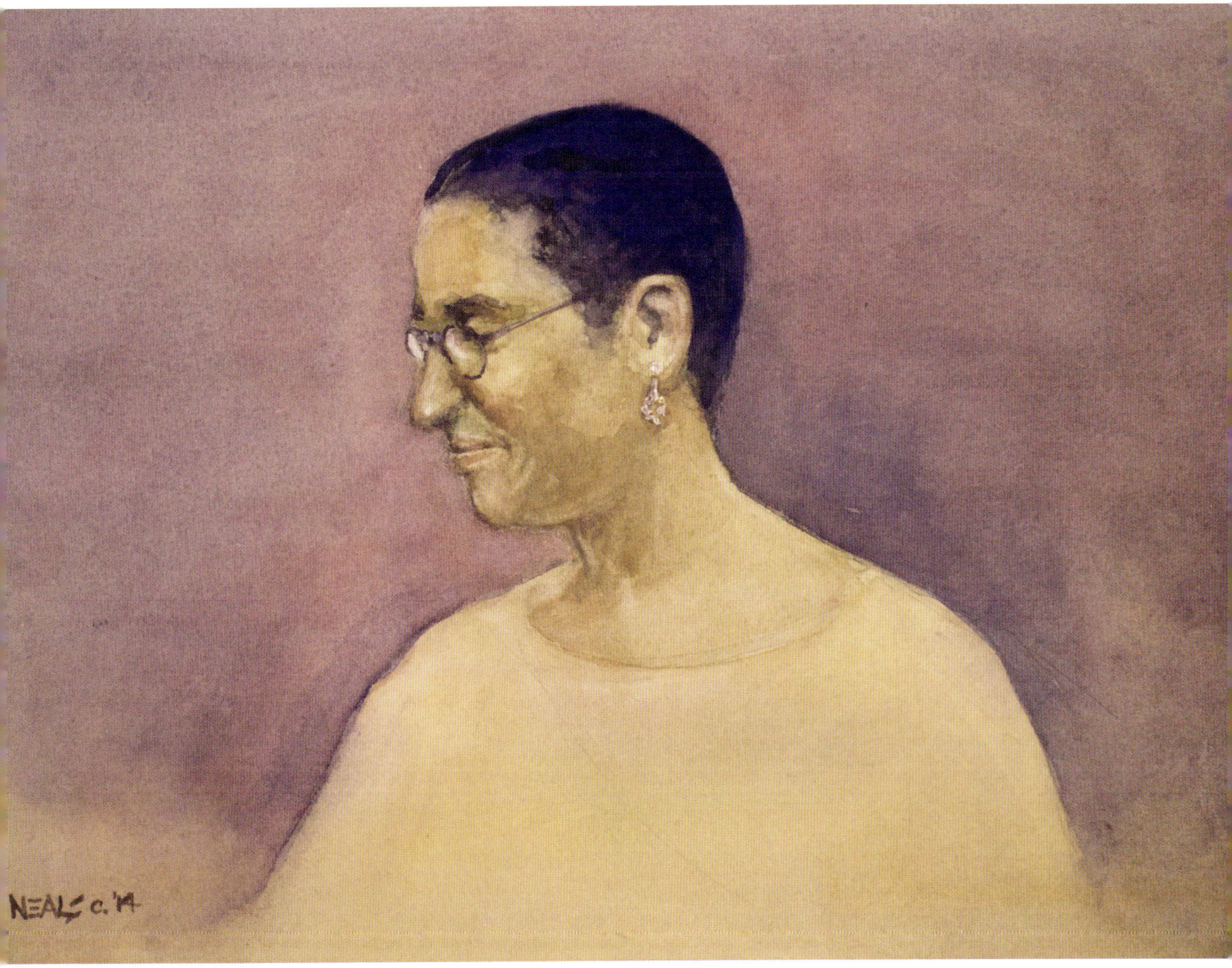

Ann Tanksley, *Untitled*, 2001. Watercolor, 6" × 7.5". *Photo: Myrah Brown Green*

Karl A. McIntosh, *Wild Flowers*, 1982. Watercolor, 24" × 18". *Photo: Myrah Brown Green*

Above: Otto Neals, *Untitled*, 2014. Watercolor, 12" × 9". *Photo: Myrah Brown Green*

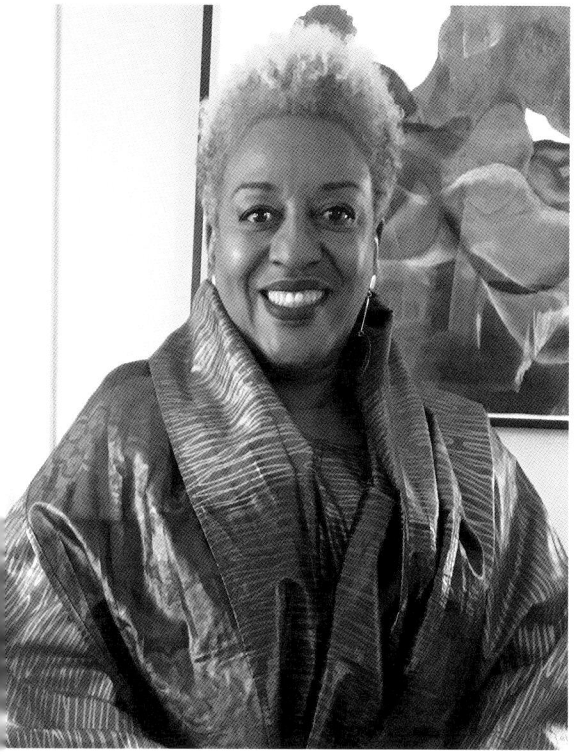

Photo: Yrneh Gabon Brown

CCH POUNDER
THE AFRICAN DIASPORA

DR. MYRAH: What was the first piece of art that you collected and when?

CCH POUNDER: Early in my acting career, I had a tight circle of friends—writers, poets, artists, chefs, musicians, actors—and we would have potluck dinners and share stories of our journeys, struggles, and successes. During that time, we began trading pieces of art as well, and it was then that began my passion for collecting art.

DR. MYRAH: Why are you a Keeper of art from the African Diaspora?

CCH POUNDER: In 1992, my late husband, Boubacar Koné, and I founded and built the Musée Boribana, the first contemporary art museum in Senegal. It was to show works from African artists and the African Diaspora. I became the museum procurer of Contemporary Art and, for the years following, disciplined myself in admiring but not purchasing pieces unless it was a fit for what the Musée required. When I retired from that role, I was able to broaden that scope and move forward in discovering and choosing whatever art spoke directly to me . . . but it was too late, I was hooked on purchasing African heritage art. Every now and then I came across a piece of art by other artists I just couldn't resist.

Carl Joe Williams, *Portrait of the Artists as an Essence, Clearance and Annie Williams*, The Early Years, 2019. Mixed media and collage on doors, 80" × 62". *Photo: Thom-Bennett Photographs*

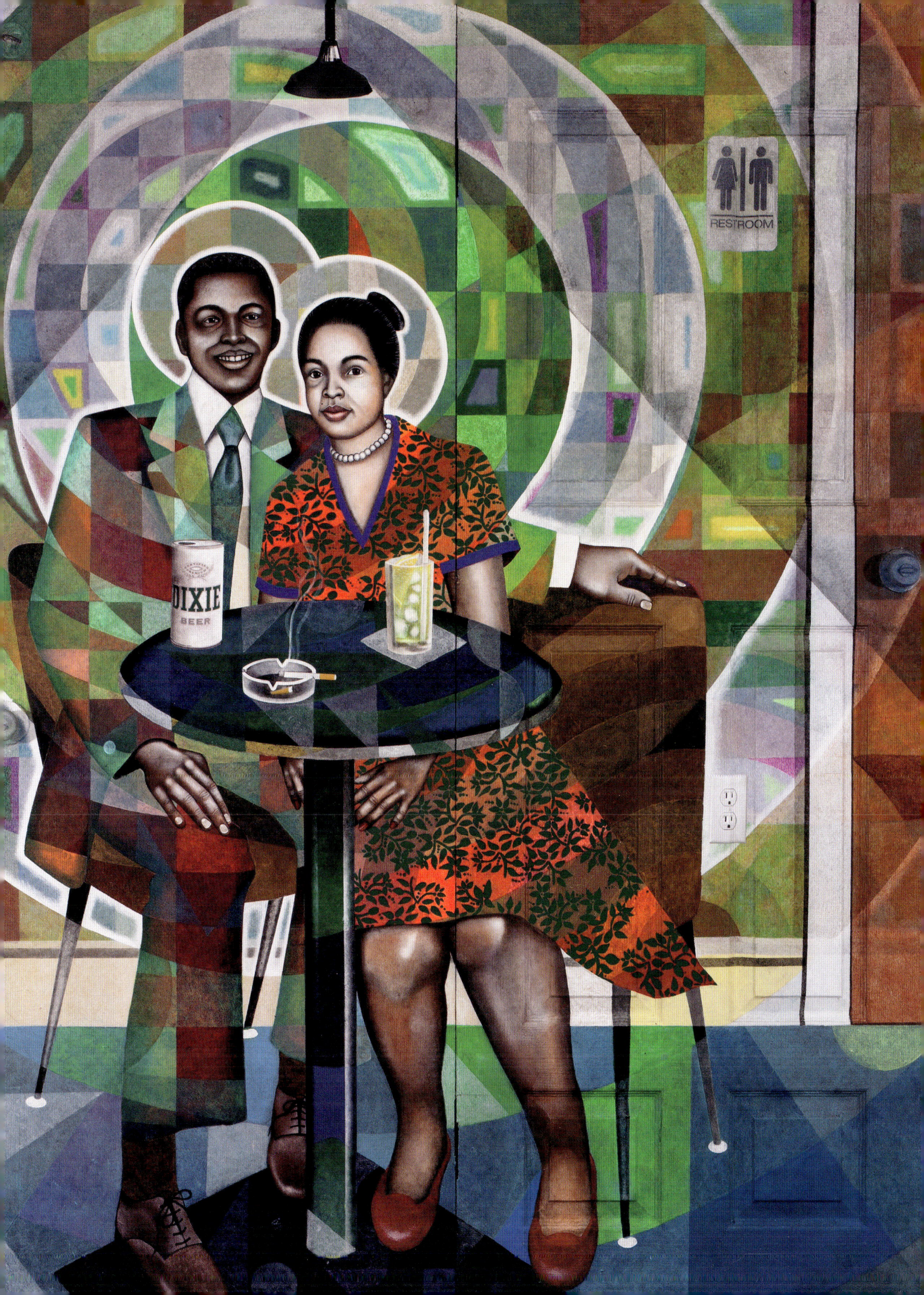
RESTROOM
DIXIE
BEER

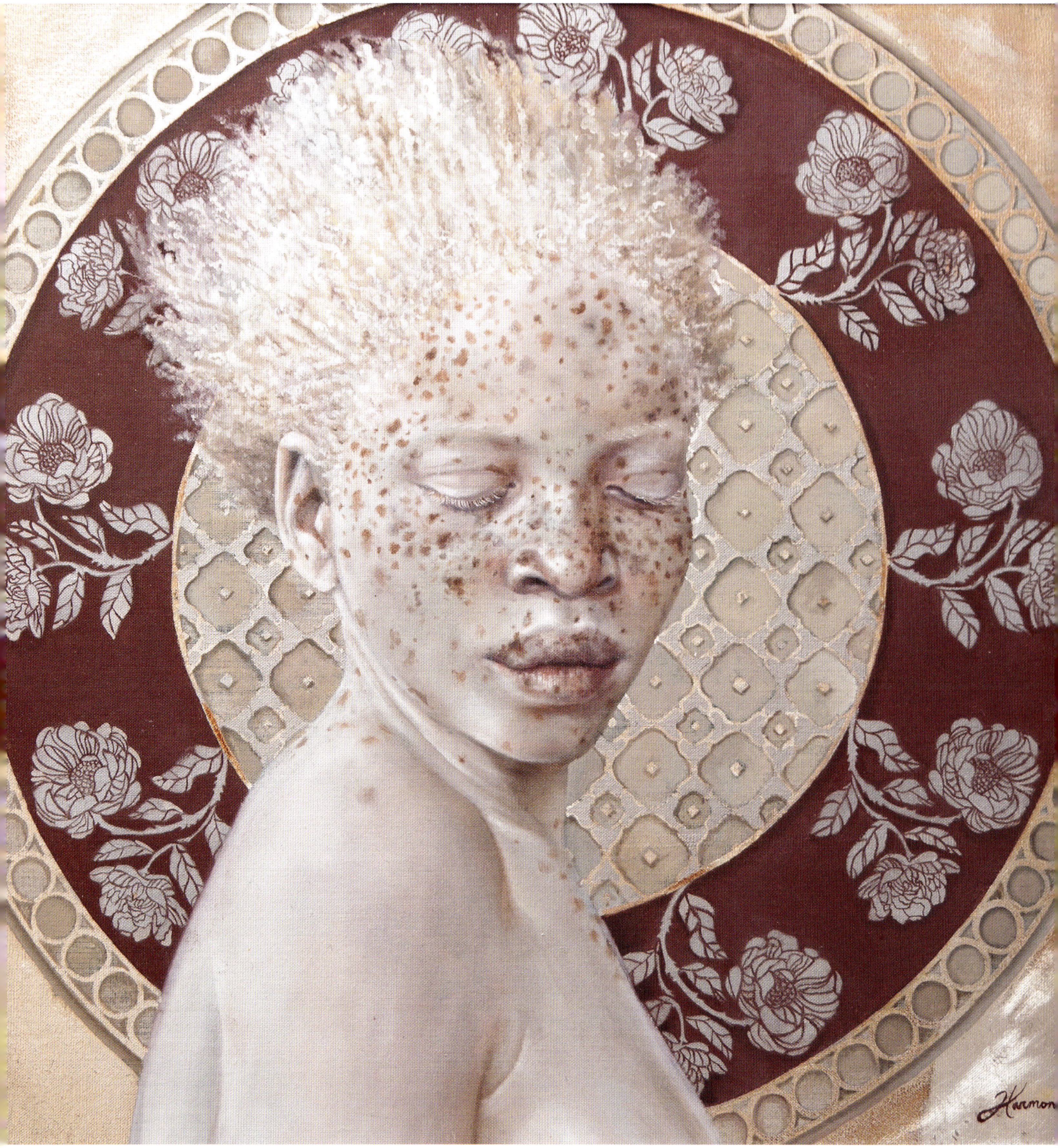

Harmonia Rosales, *Winter*, 2018. Oil on genuine silver on Belgian linen, 24" × 24". *Photo: Ashley Lorraine Photography*

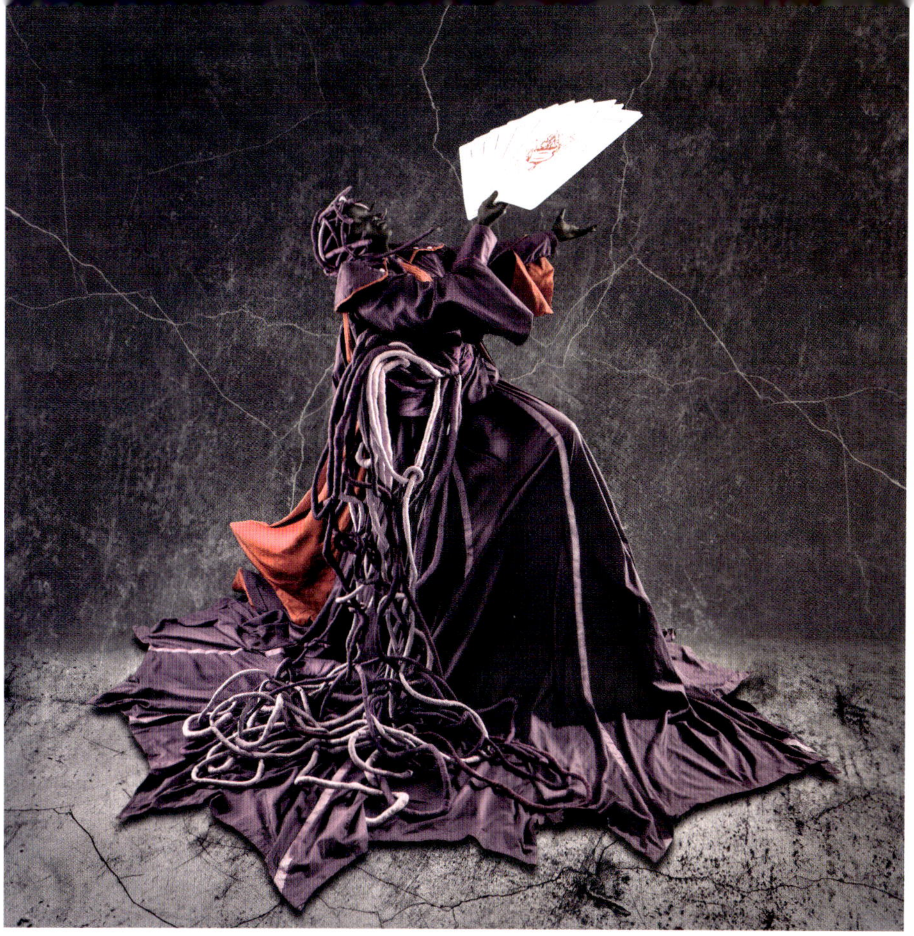

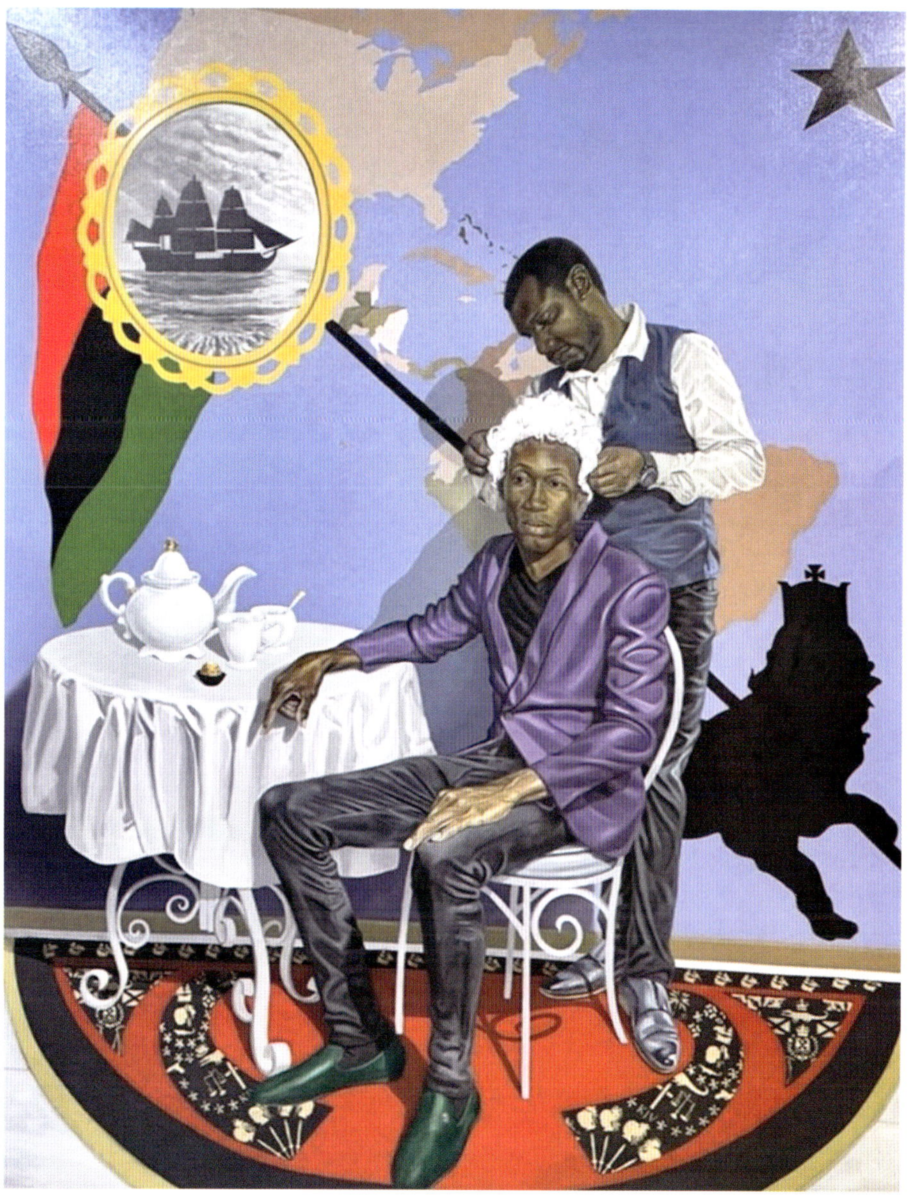

Mary Sibande, *Welding the Collision of the Past, Present, and Future*, 2017. Archival digital print (edition of ten), 43.5" × 43.75". *Photo: ©Mary Sibande, Courtesy of SMAC Gallery*

Greg Bailey, *Post-Colonial Paraphernalia*, 2021. Oil on canvas, 97" × 80". *Photo: Thom-Bennett Photographs*

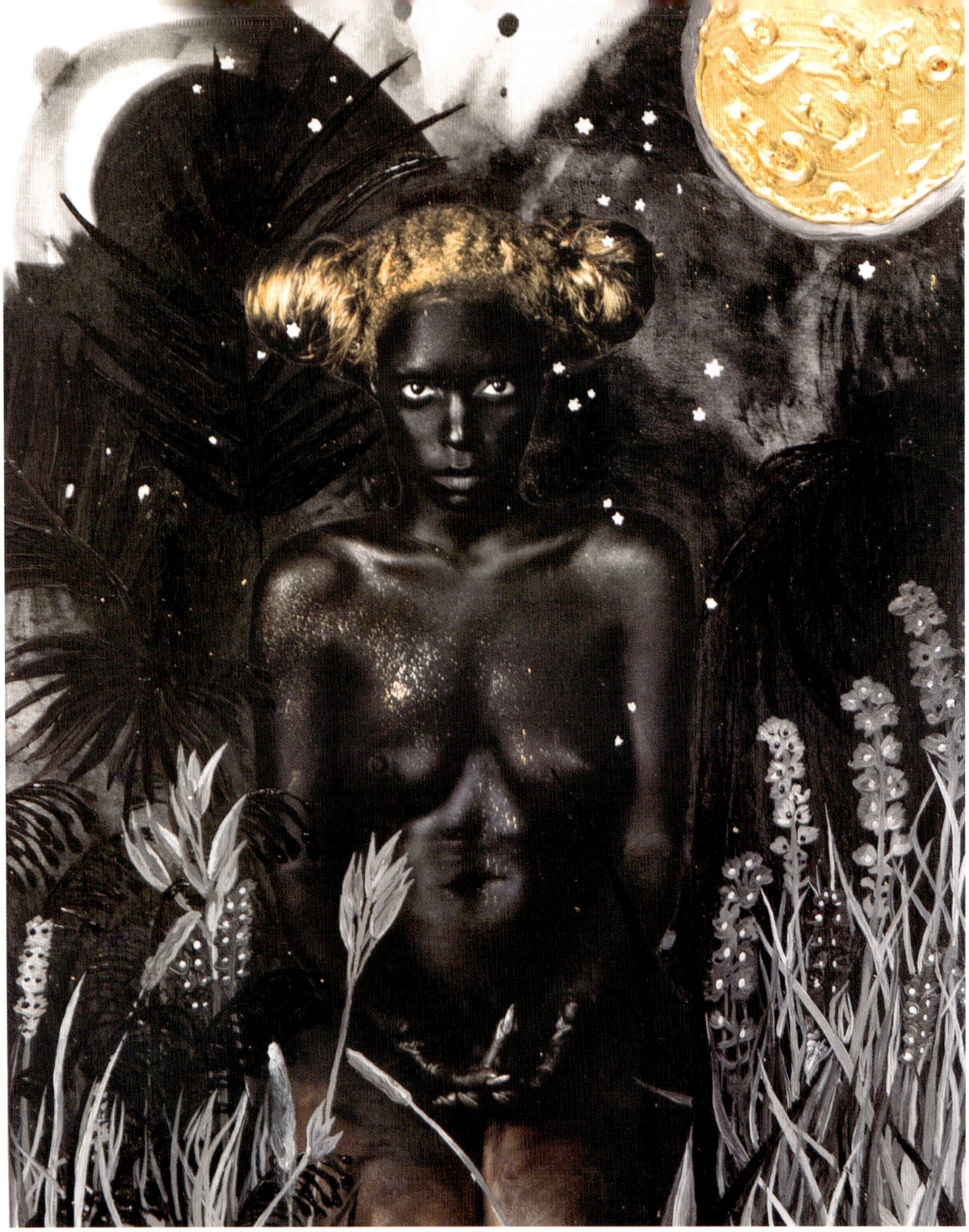

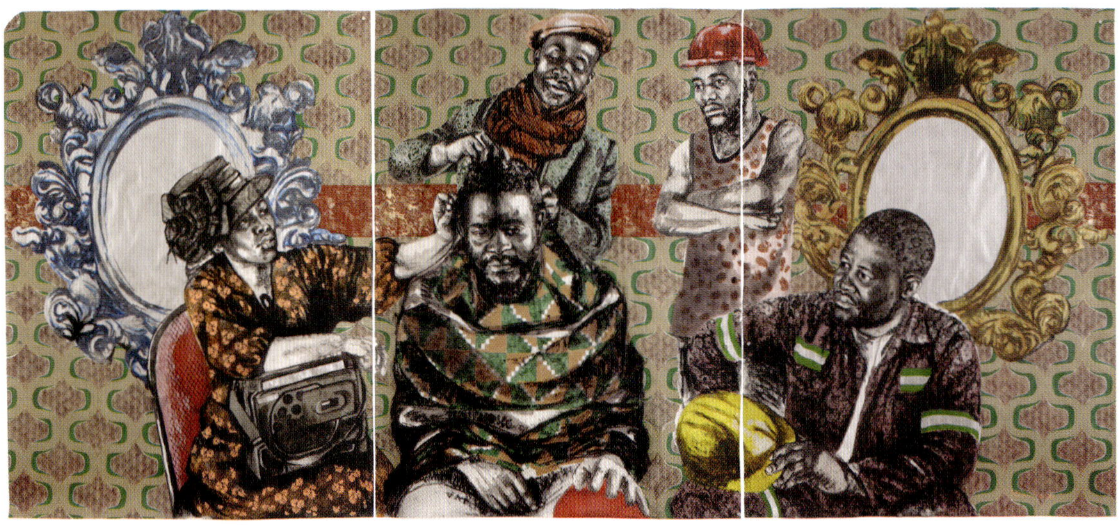

Lina Iris Victor, *The Dark Continent Series–No 9 (Massacre of the Innocents)*, 2017. 24-karat gold, acrylic, ink, and print on cotton rag paper, 9.8" × 7.8". *Photo: Ashley Lorraine Photography*

Bambo Sibiya, *Street Barbershop* (triptych), 2018. Acrylic and charcoal on paper, 78.25" × 177.25". *Photo: Khalifa Dieng*

Opposite: Loyiso Mkize, *Nomzomo*, 2019. Oil on canvas, 100" × 73". *Photo: Ashley Lorraine Photography*

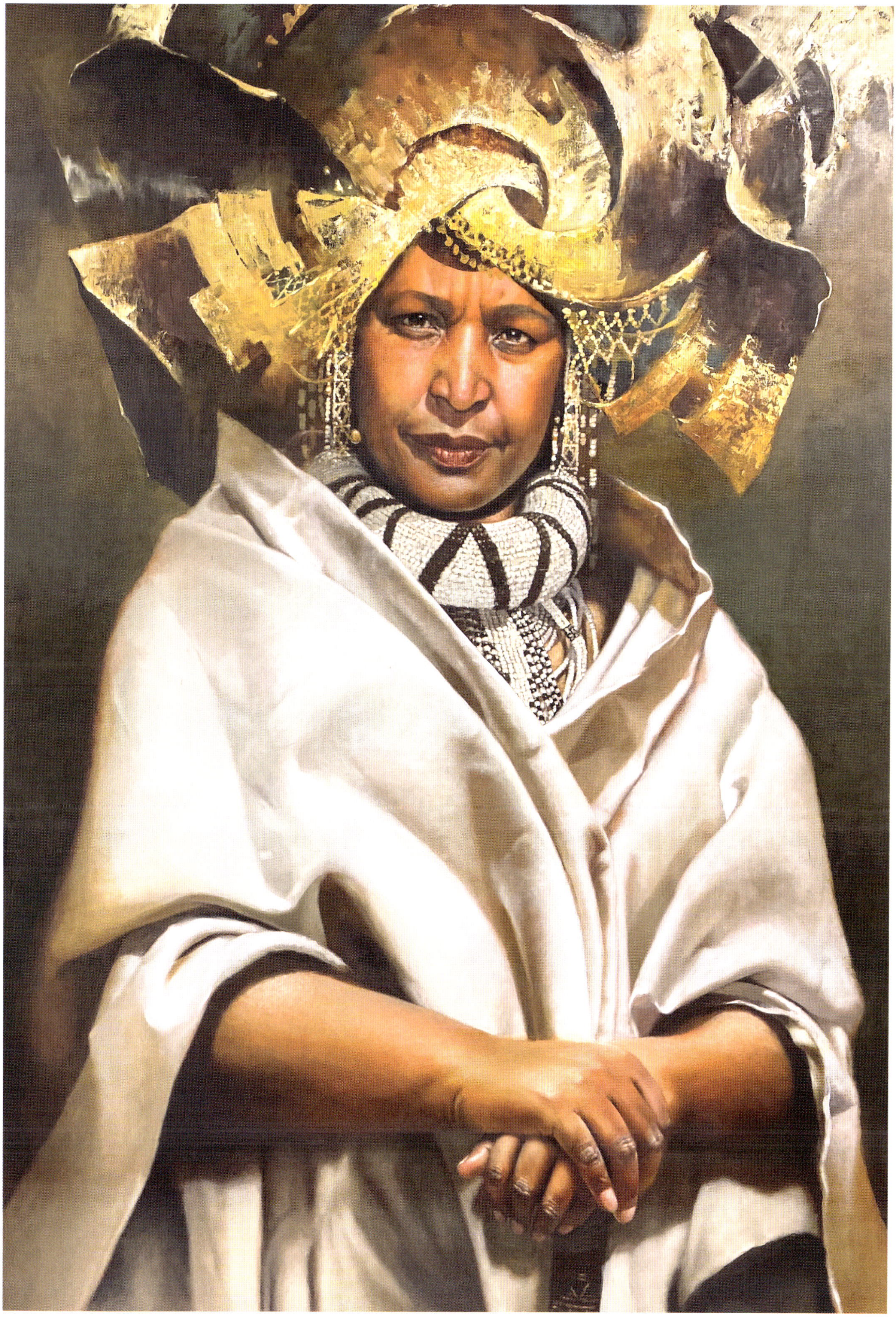

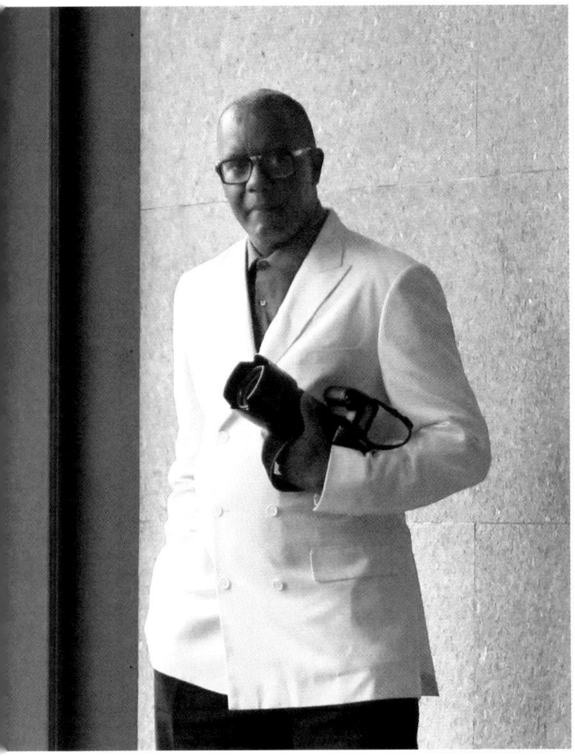

Photo: Tau Battice

JAMEL SHABAZZ
PHOTOGRAPHY

DR. MYRAH: What was the first piece of art you ever collected and when?

JAMEL SHABAZZ: I had just gotten my first apartment and wanted to decorate it with fine art. The very first piece I collected was an 11 × 14 color illustration of a mother breastfeeding her child in Kemet. The artist was Metu Deggkhet from Queens, New York. I met him at the African Street Festival in Brooklyn, New York, where I would go on to purchase not only this piece, but many others during the 1980s and 1990s.

DR. MYRAH: Why are you a Keeper of photographic images?

JAMEL SHABAZZ: I am a Keeper of images mainly because I am an artist and see the value in preserving history and culture for future generations. My interest in collecting also came from my father, who was an artist/photographer and avid collector himself. His appreciation for collecting started in the 1960s, in the form of family photo albums that were passed down from generation to generation, dating to the early 1900s. In addition, our home in Brooklyn always had paintings hanging on the walls, especially from painter Ernest Crichlow, who had close ties to the family. Living in such an artistic environment allowed me to see the value of collecting art and honoring those who made it.

Robert Abbott Sengstacke, *Saviors Day Prayer*, 1966. Digital c-print.

Zahir Muhammad, *Under the Gun*, ca. 1995. Silver gelatin print.

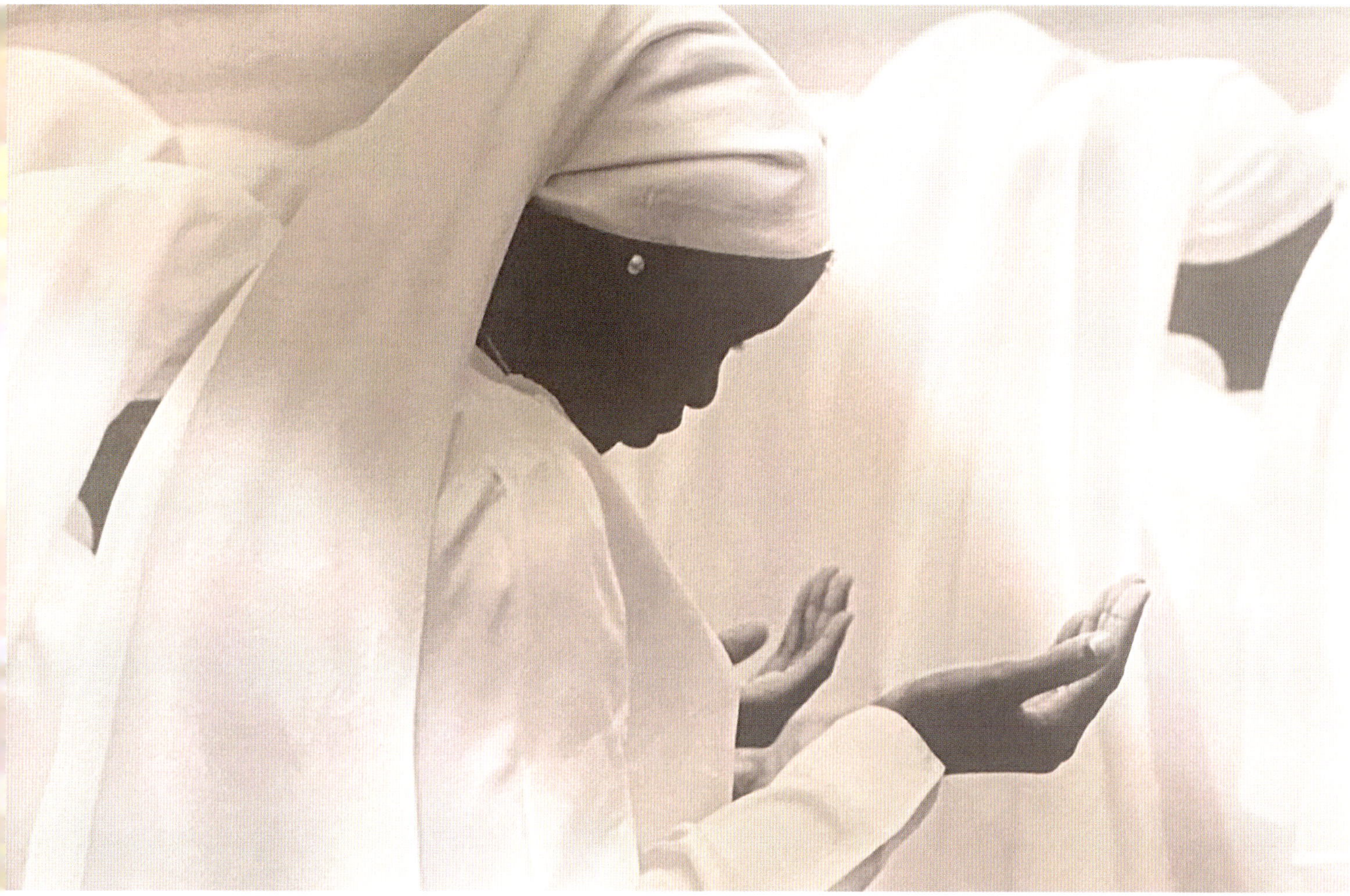

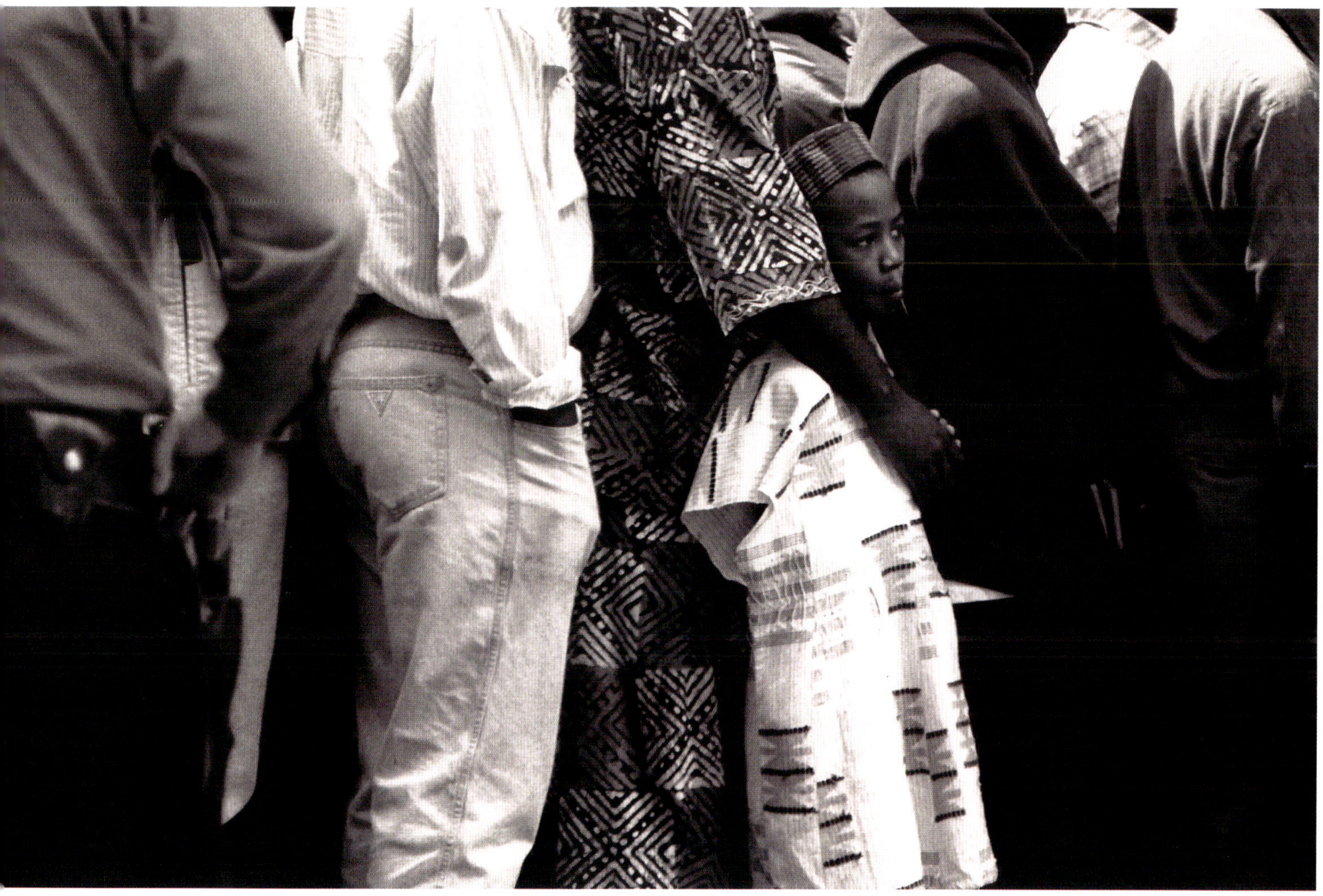

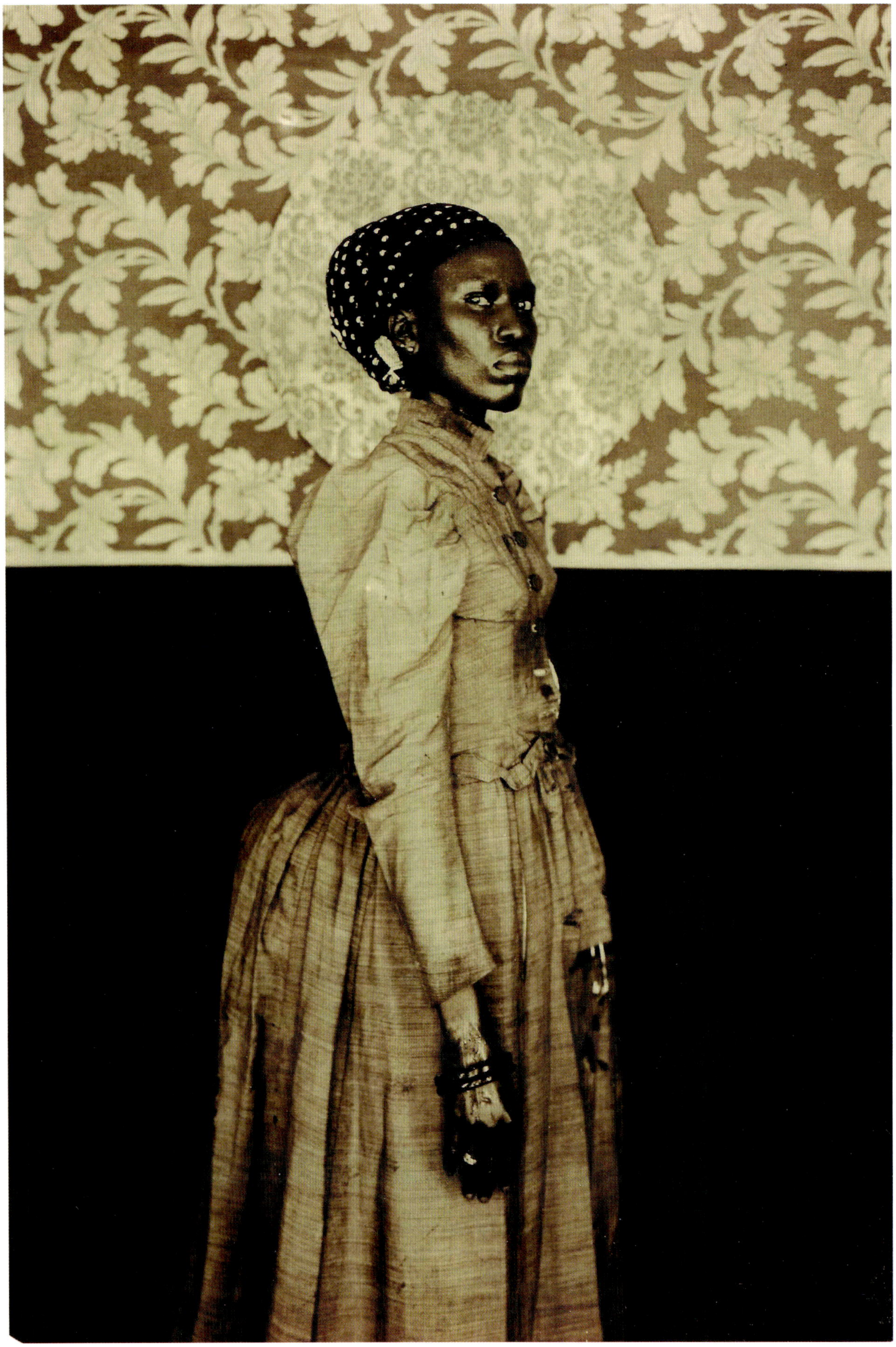

Above: Barron Claiborne, *Untitled*, ca. 2000. Mixed-media digital print.

Salimah Ali, *On the Water*, 2023. Archival pigment print.

Zahir Muhammad, *Untitled*, ca. 1995. Silver gelatin print.

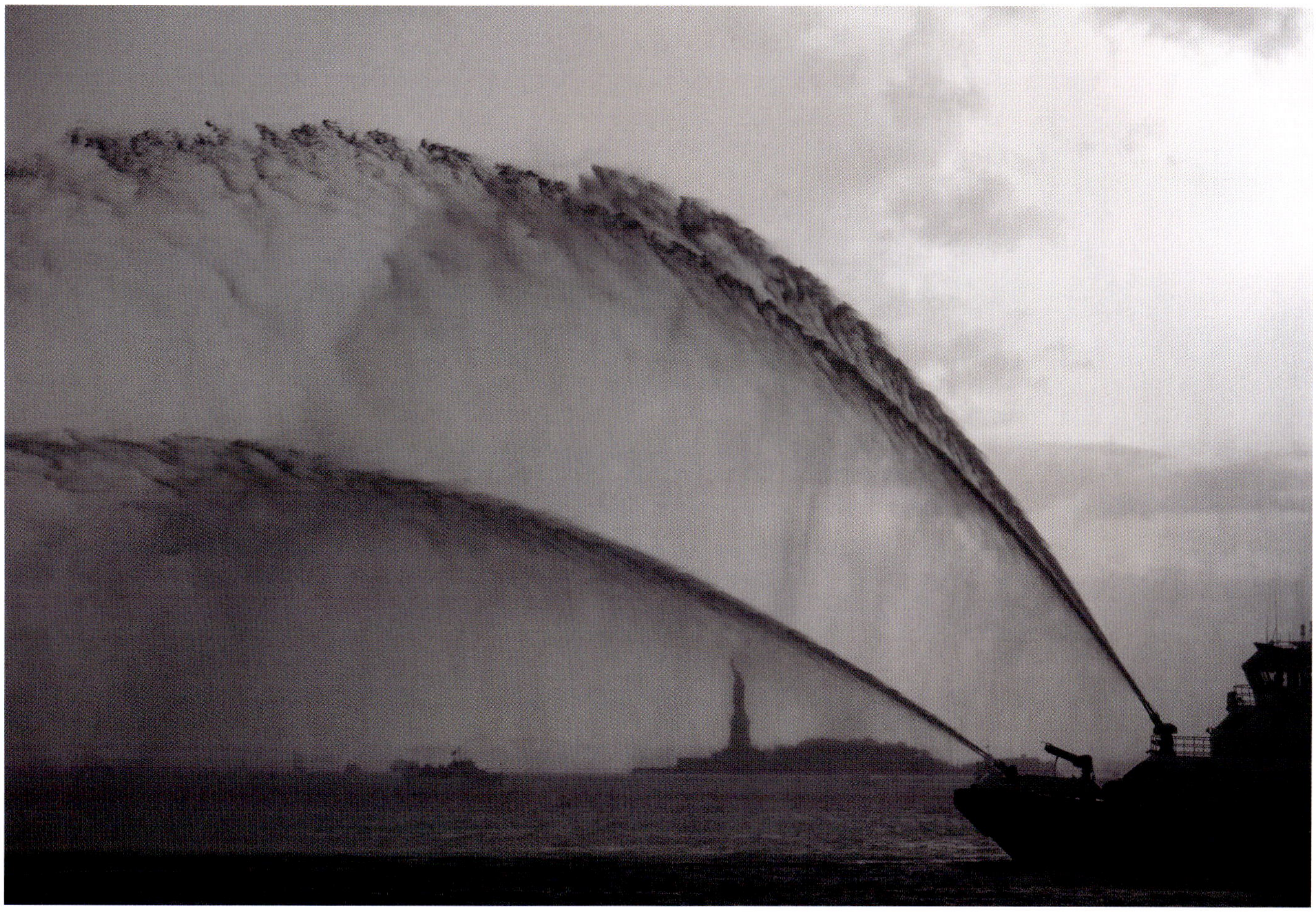

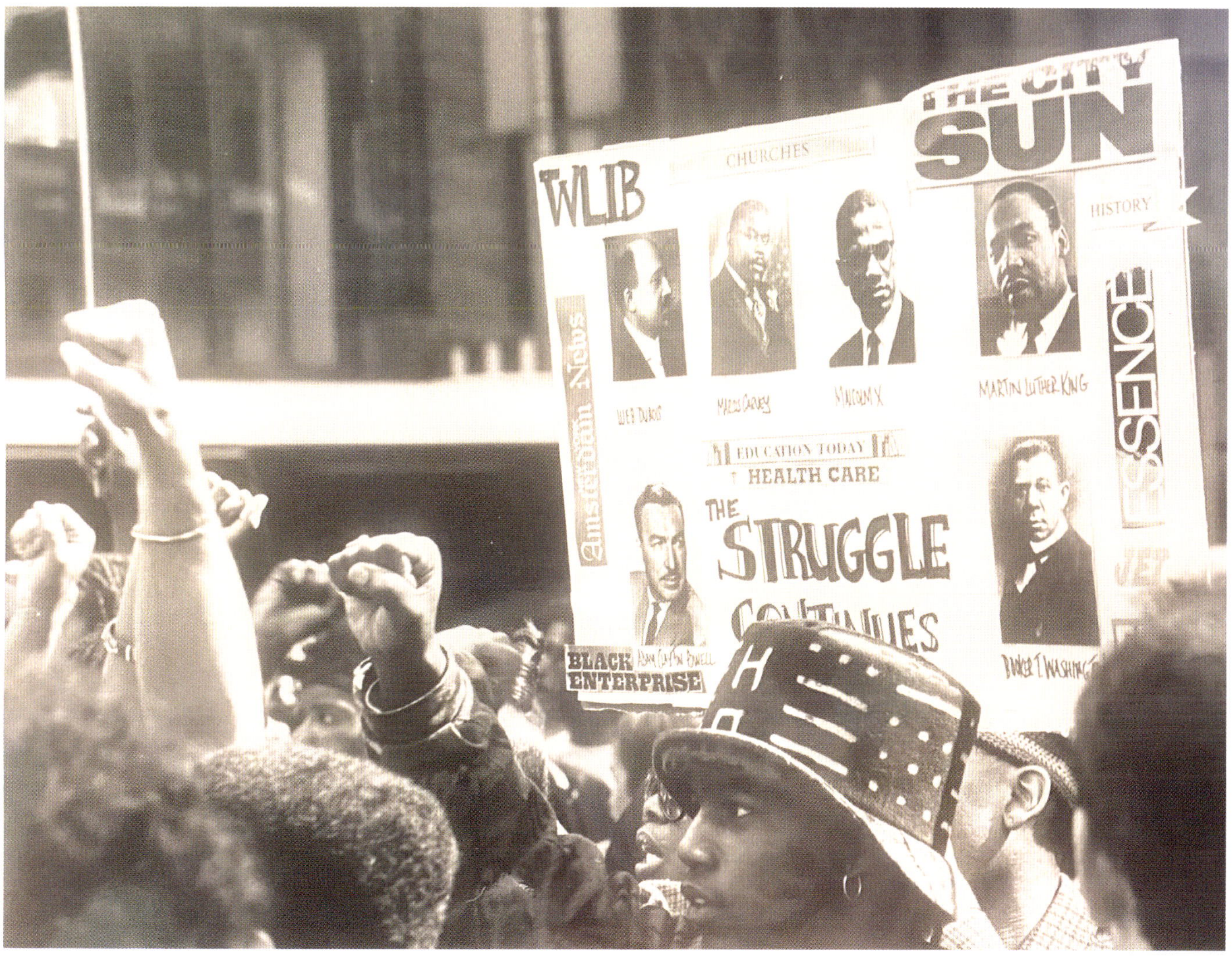

THE CITY SUN
CHURCHES
WLIB
HISTORY
Amsterdam News
MALCOLM X
MARTIN LUTHER KING
EDUCATION TODAY
HEALTH CARE
THE STRUGGLE
BLACK ENTERPRISE

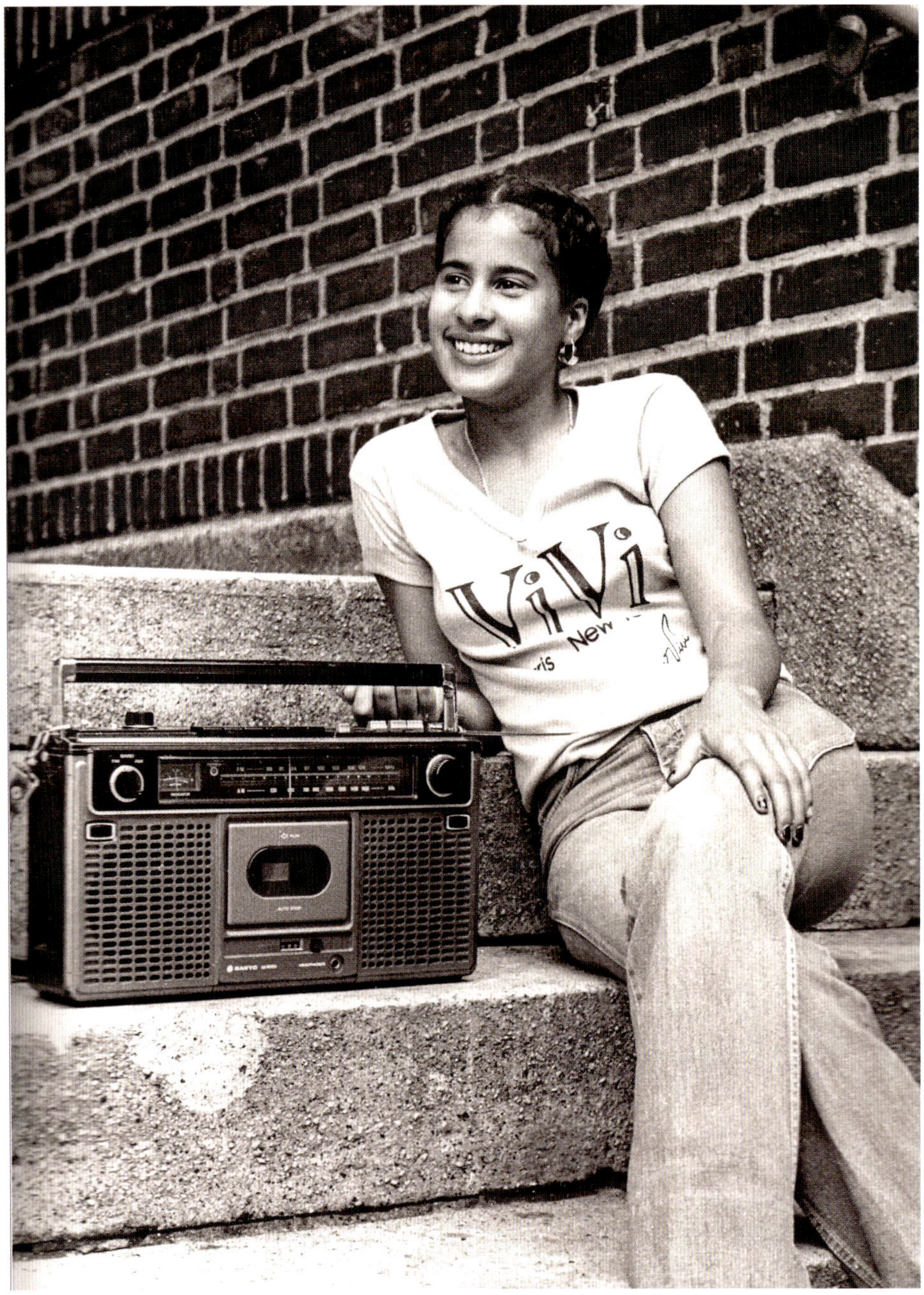

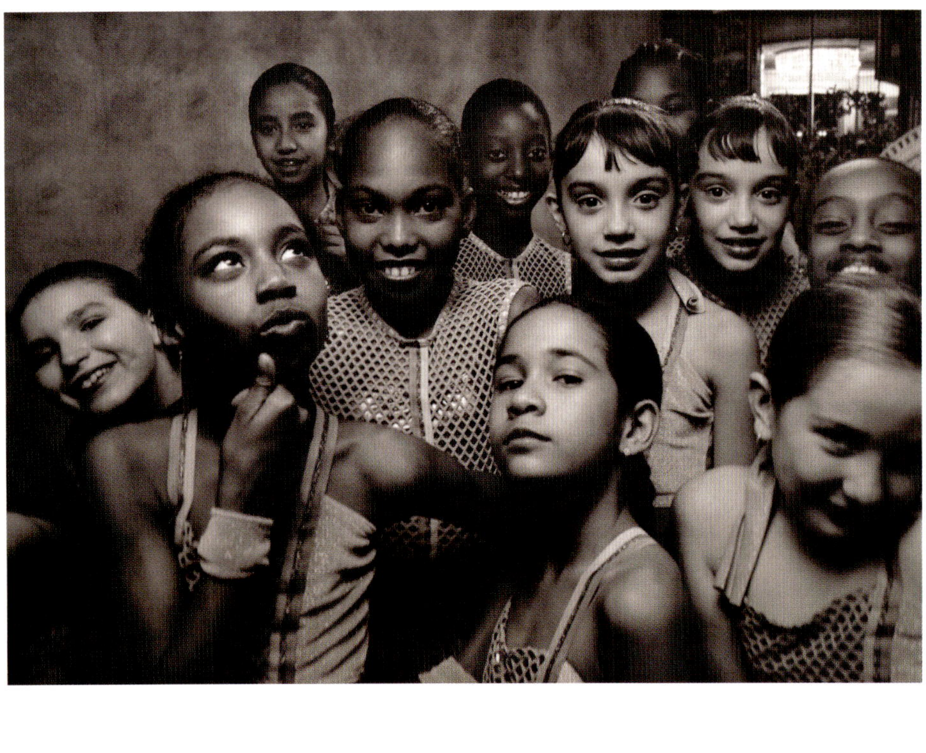

Ricky Flores, *Liz*, 1985. Black-and-white film.

Russell Frederick, *Dancers*, ca. 2000. Silver gelatin print.

Opposite: Terrence Jennings, *Cuba*, 2007. Digital c-print.

Opposite: Richard E. Green, *Celebrate Rites* (Mali, West Africa), 1993. Archival pigment print.

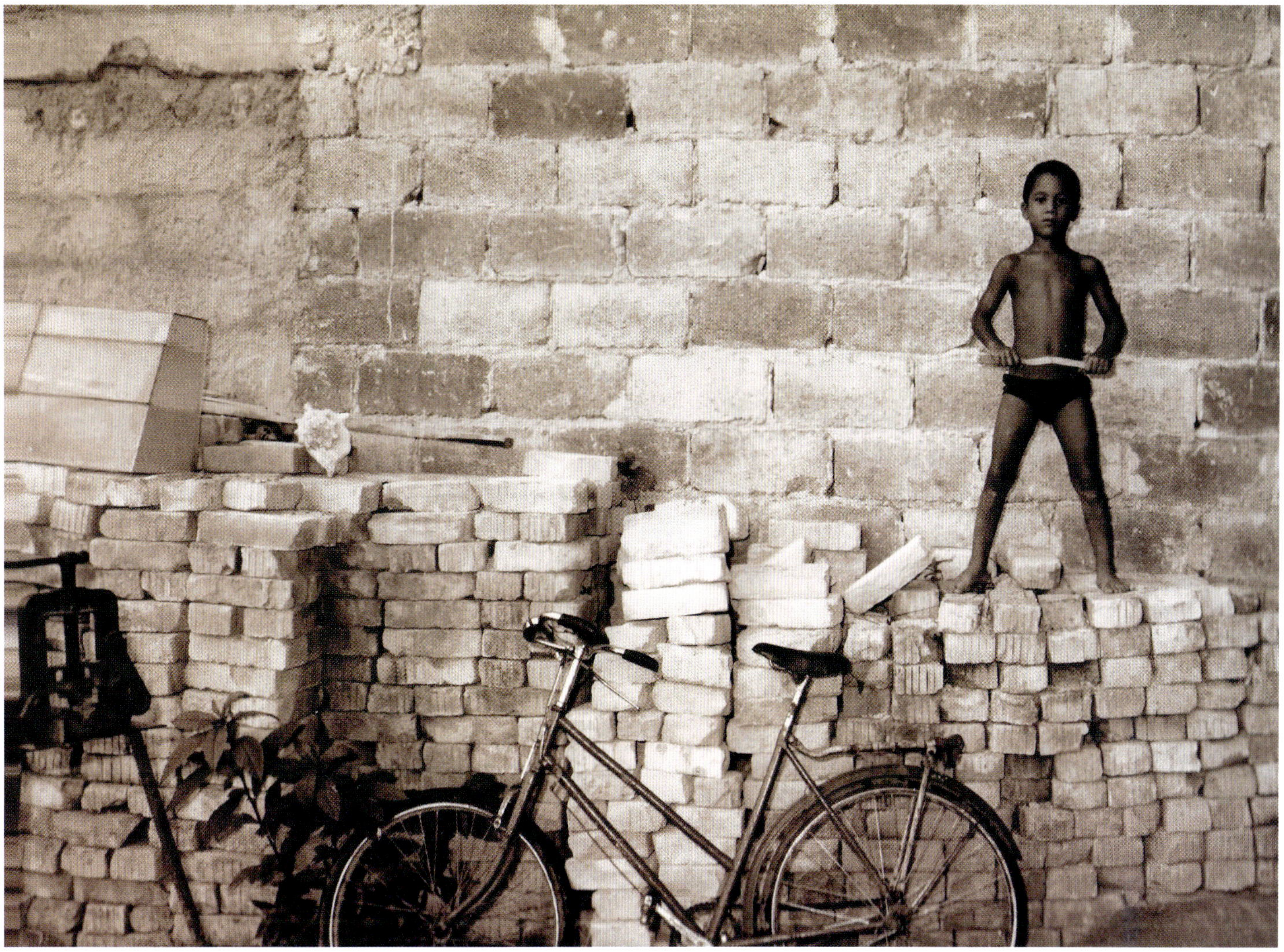

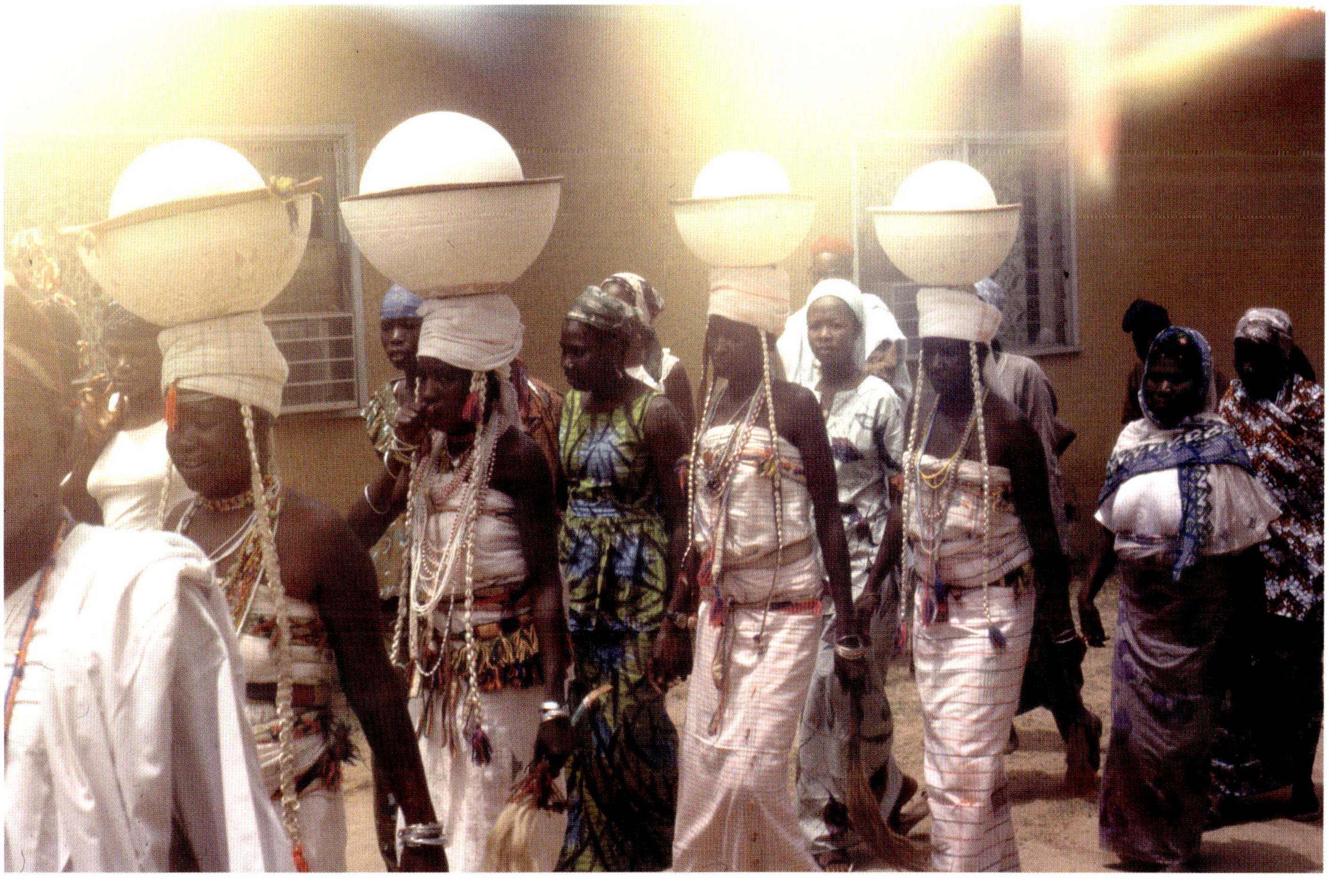

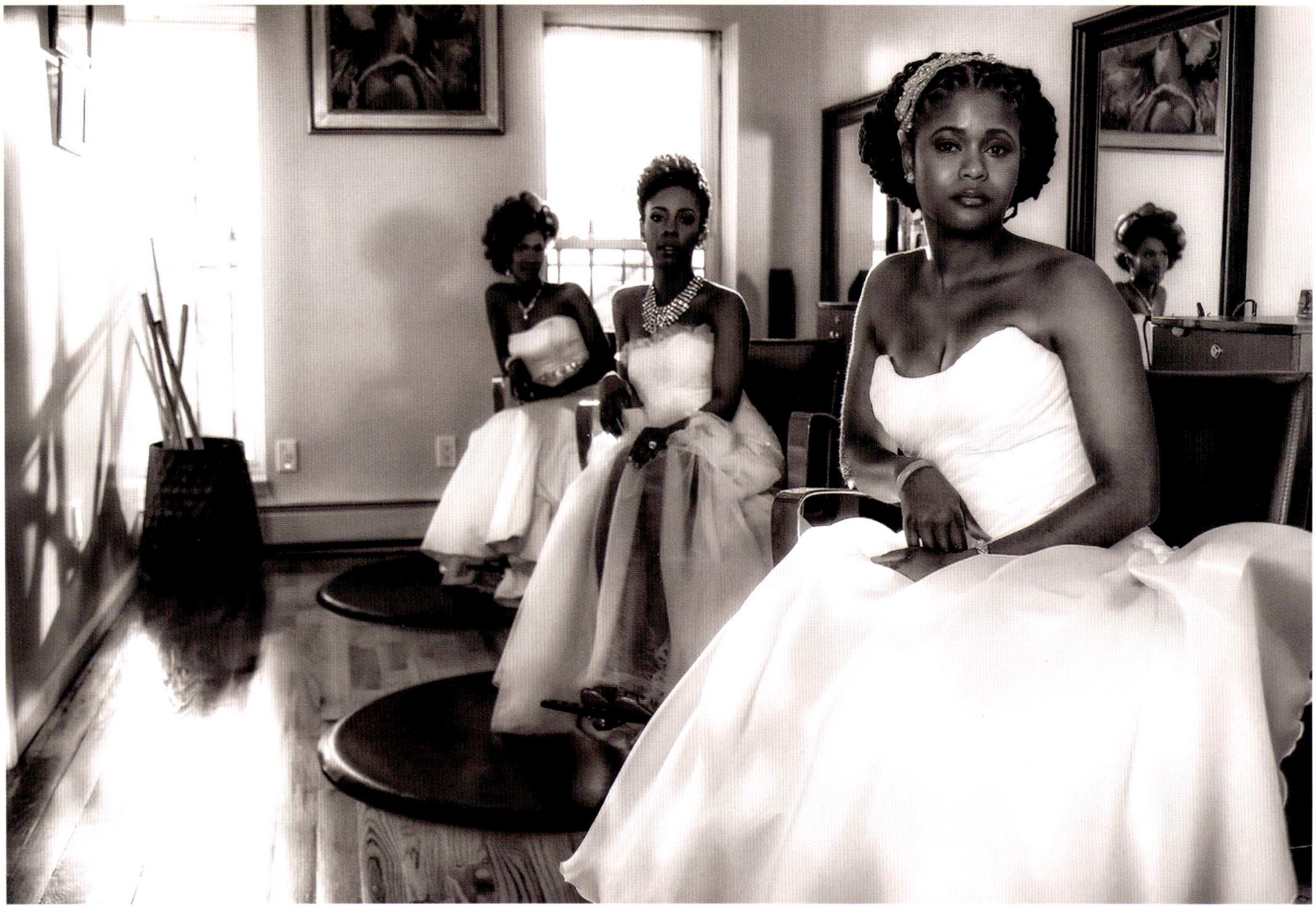

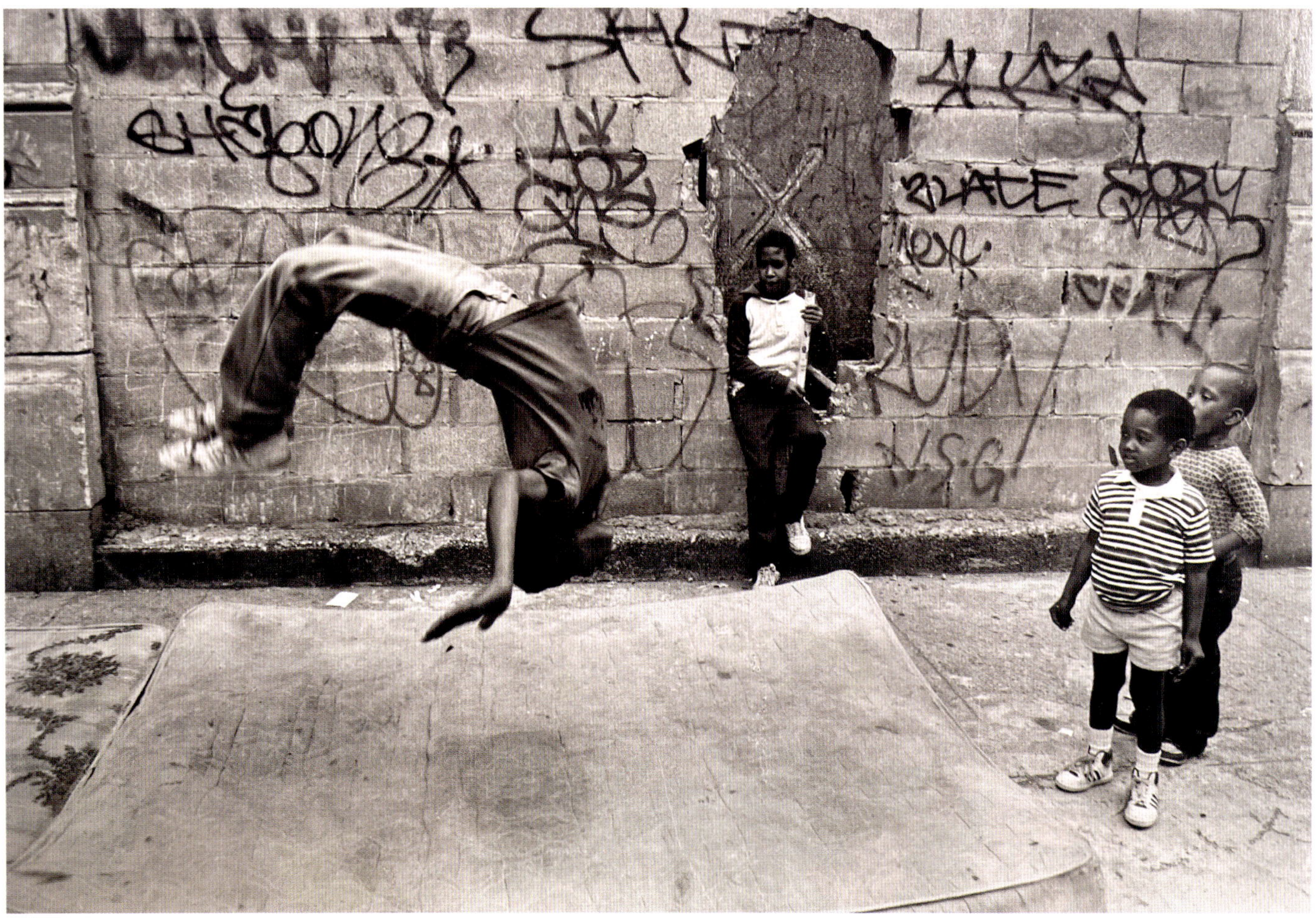

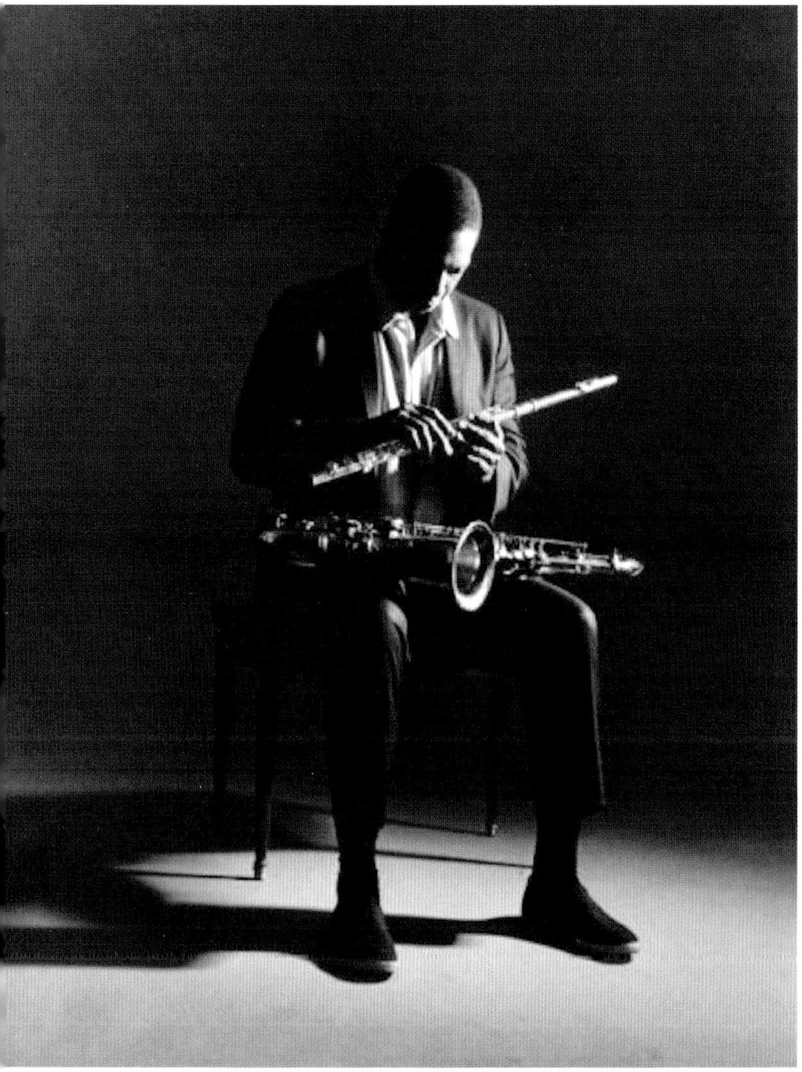

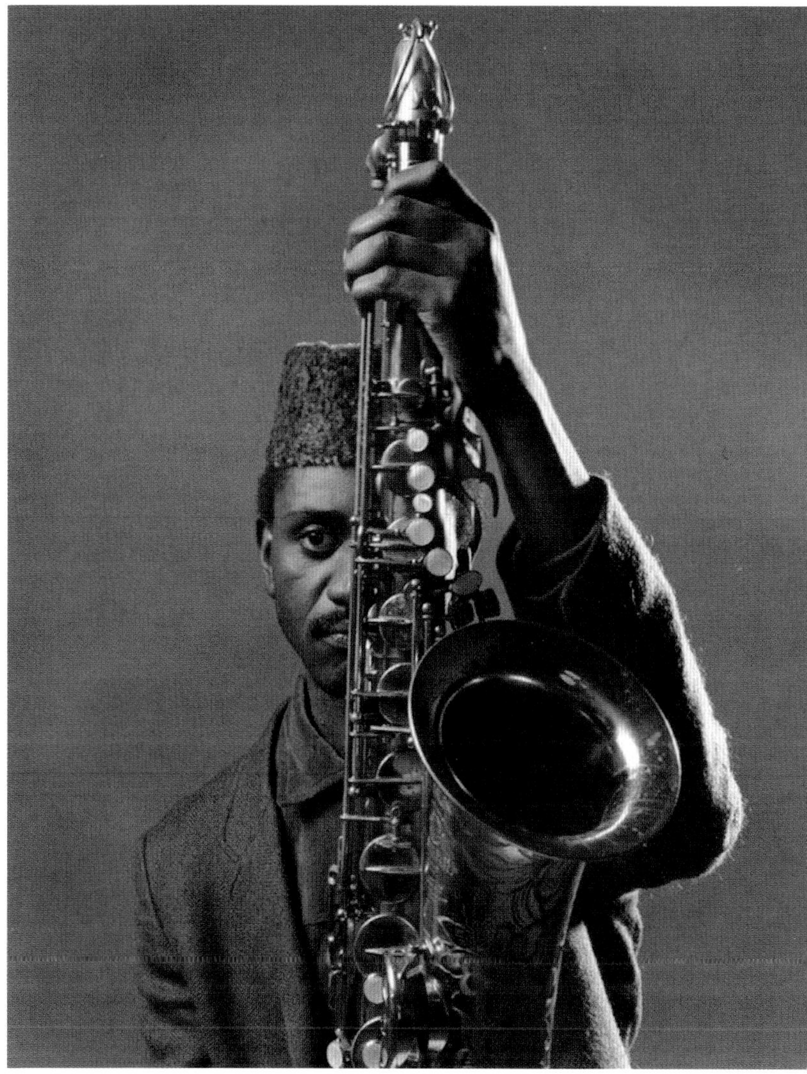

Opposite: Michael Young, *Brides*, 2016. Archival pigment print.

Opposite: Bud Williams, *Untitled* (Harlem), ca. 1989. Black-and-white film.

Chuck Stewart, *John Coltrane*, ca. 1965. Silver gelatin print.

Chuck Stewart, *Pharaoh Sanders*, ca. 1965. Silver gelatin print.

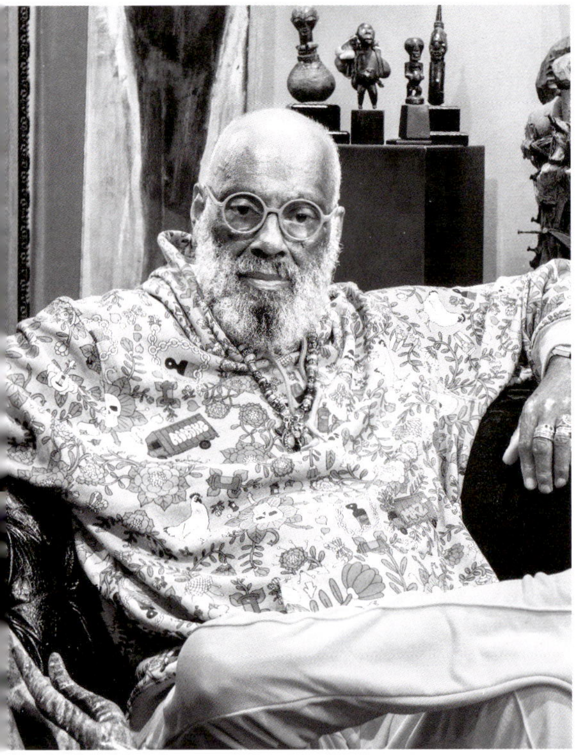

Photo: William Toney

DANNY SIMMONS
COMIC BOOKS AND FIGURINES

DR. MYRAH: What was the first piece of art you ever collected and when?

DANNY SIMMONS: A Dan mask from the Ivory Coast, collected in the late 1970s.

DR. MYRAH: Why are you a Keeper of comic books and paraphernalia?

DANNY SIMMONS: They give me joy. I've been collecting comic books since I was a kid and have continued to collect them. They make me feel good; the stories are usually uplifting, and I enjoy the art associated with comics—also some have increased in value over the years. The most expensive comic ever sold was *Superman* #1 for $5.3 million dollars in April 2022—of course this wasn't my comic. My favorite comic book artist is R. Crumb, who created Fritz the Cat and Mr. Natural, two of my favorite nonsuperhero characters.

When I was a kid, I started my art career by drawing comic book figures; the Hulk was my favorite character. I was reading comics before Marvel started, so at that time I had all of the Marvel first issues: *Spider-Man*, *The Hulk*, *Fantastic Four*, *Iron Man*, and the *X-Men*. I wish I had all of these comics now!

I enjoy going to the comic book store on Wednesdays, when new issues first come out; being there is so familiar to me, it feels like going home.

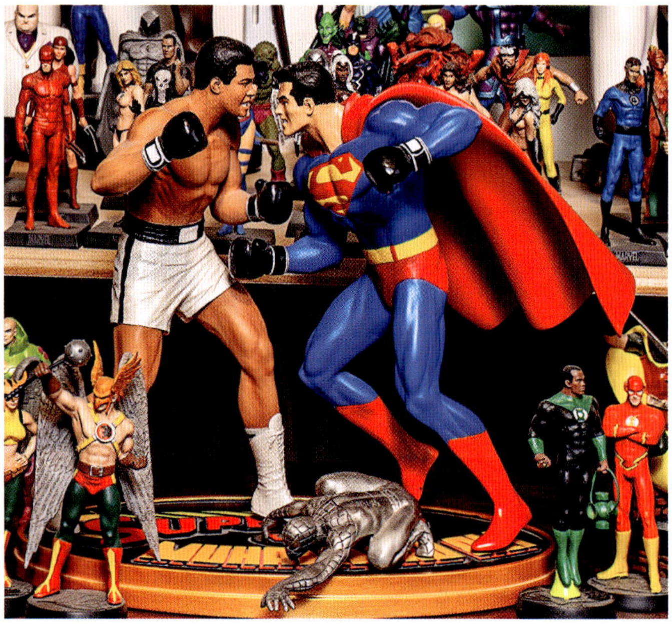

Muhammad Ali vs. Superman figurines, 2010.
Photo: William Toney

Opposite: All-Negro Comics, 1947 (published by Orrin Evans).
Photo: William Toney

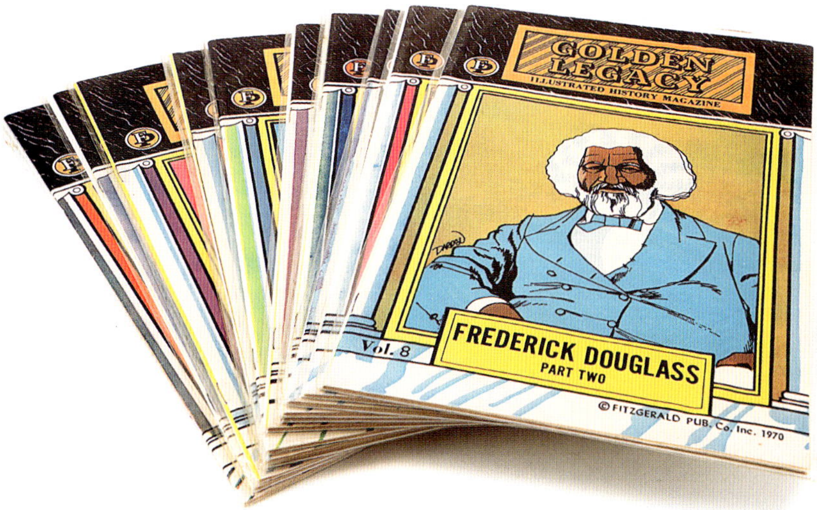

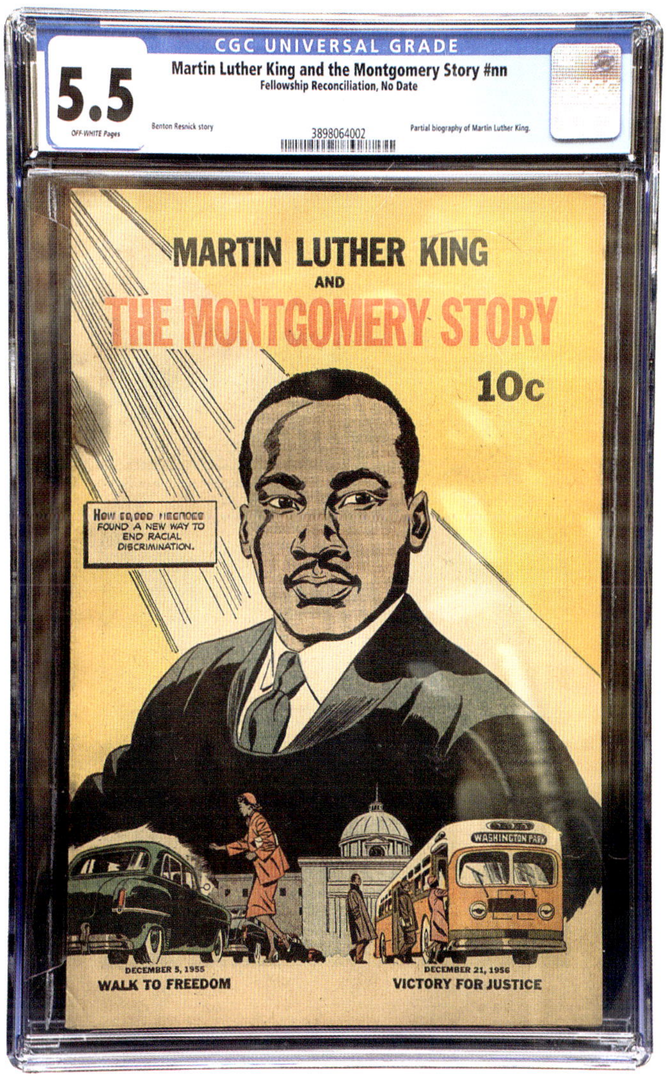

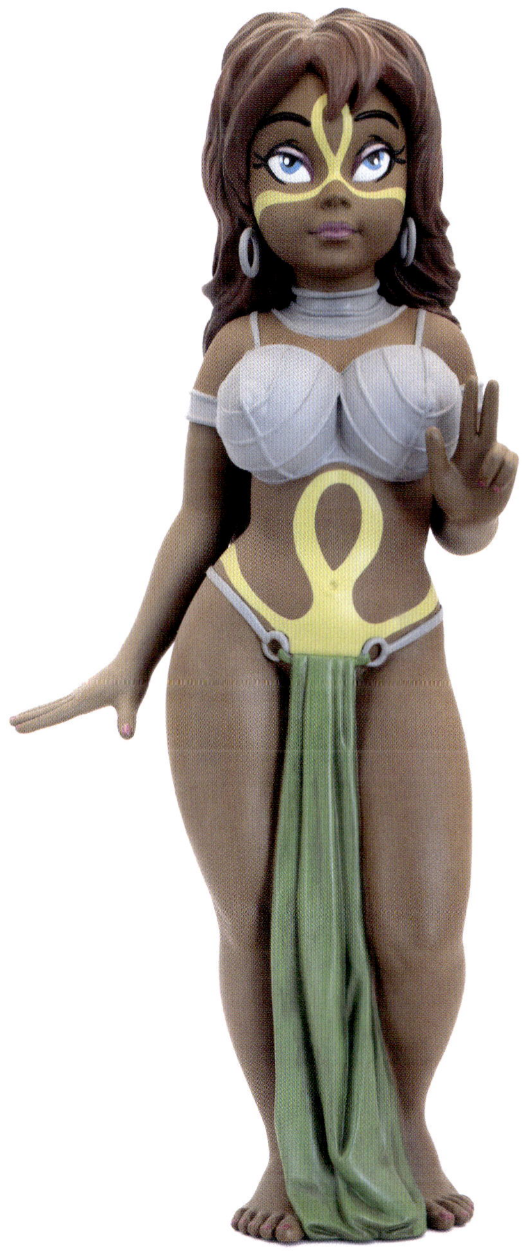

Top: Golden Legacy Comics, 1966–1970. *Photo: William Toney*

Martin Luther King Jr. and the Montgomery Story, Arthur Hassler, 1958 (published by Top Shelf). *Photo: William Toney*

Bode Broad by Vaughn Bode from *Cheech Wizard's Comics*, published in 1966. *Photo: William Toney*

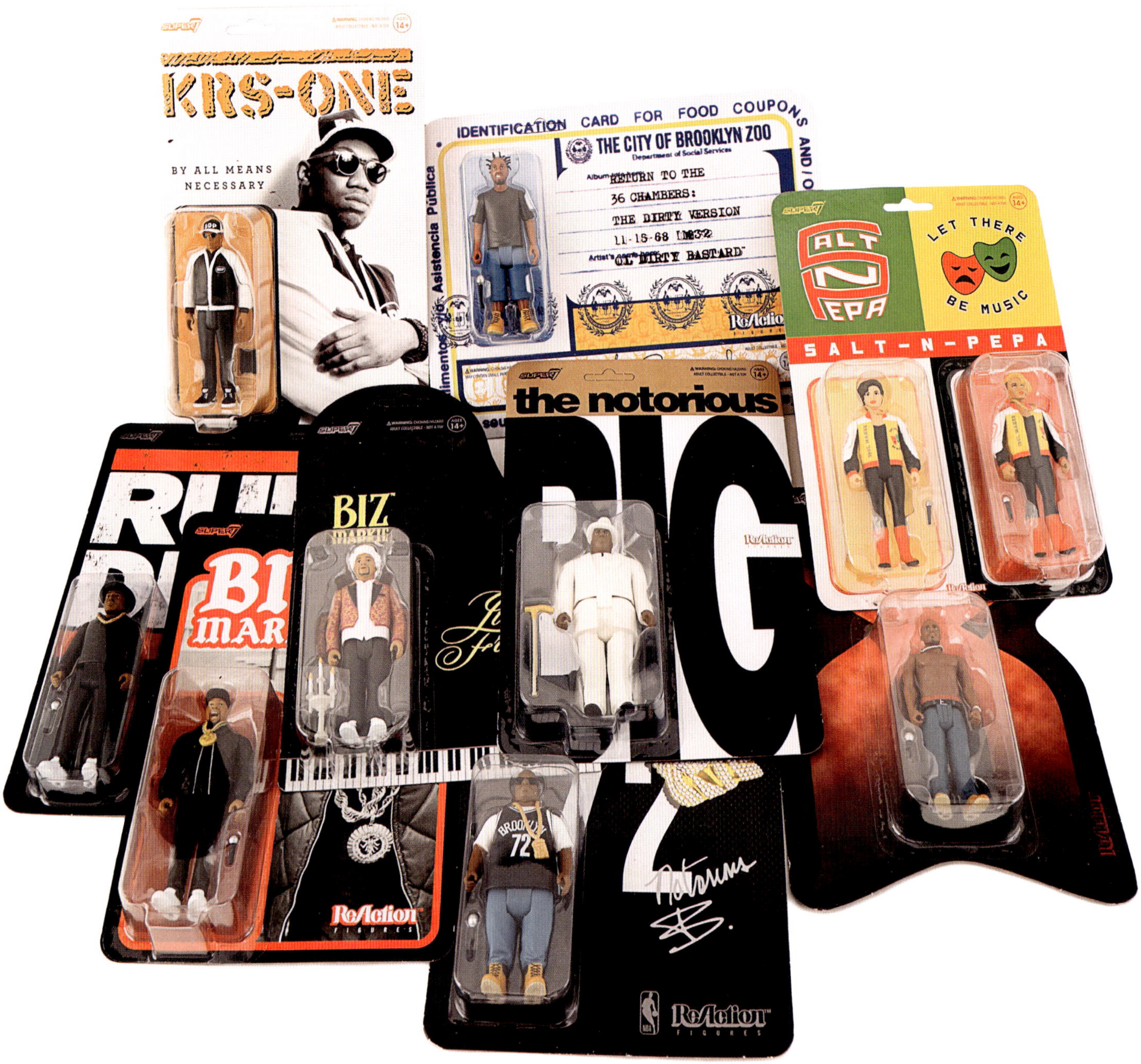

Hip-Hop Icon Legend figures by Re-Action, 2020–2024. *Photo: William Toney*

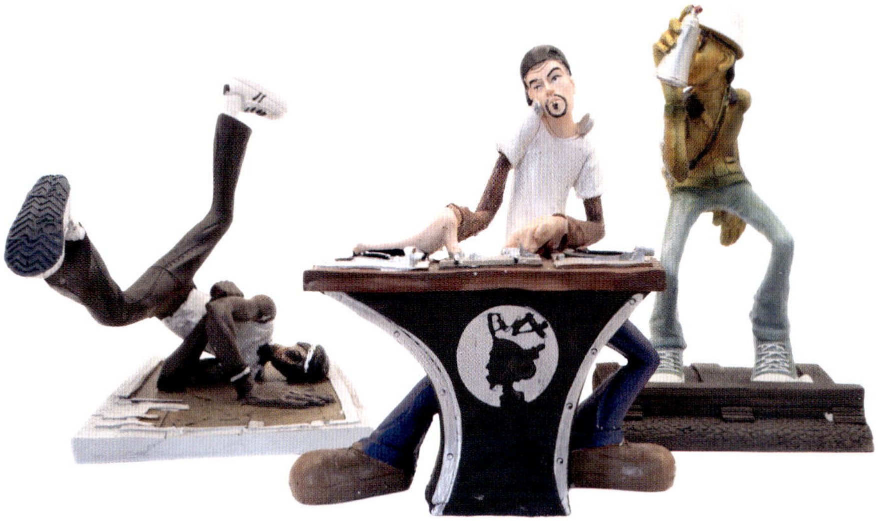

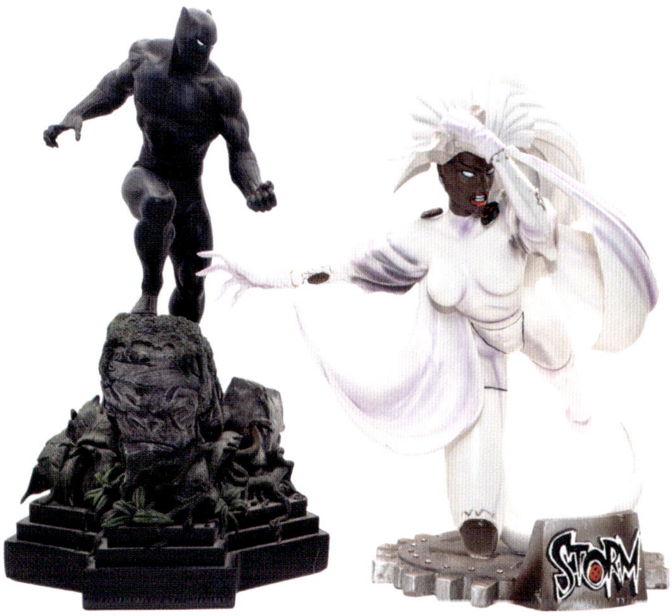

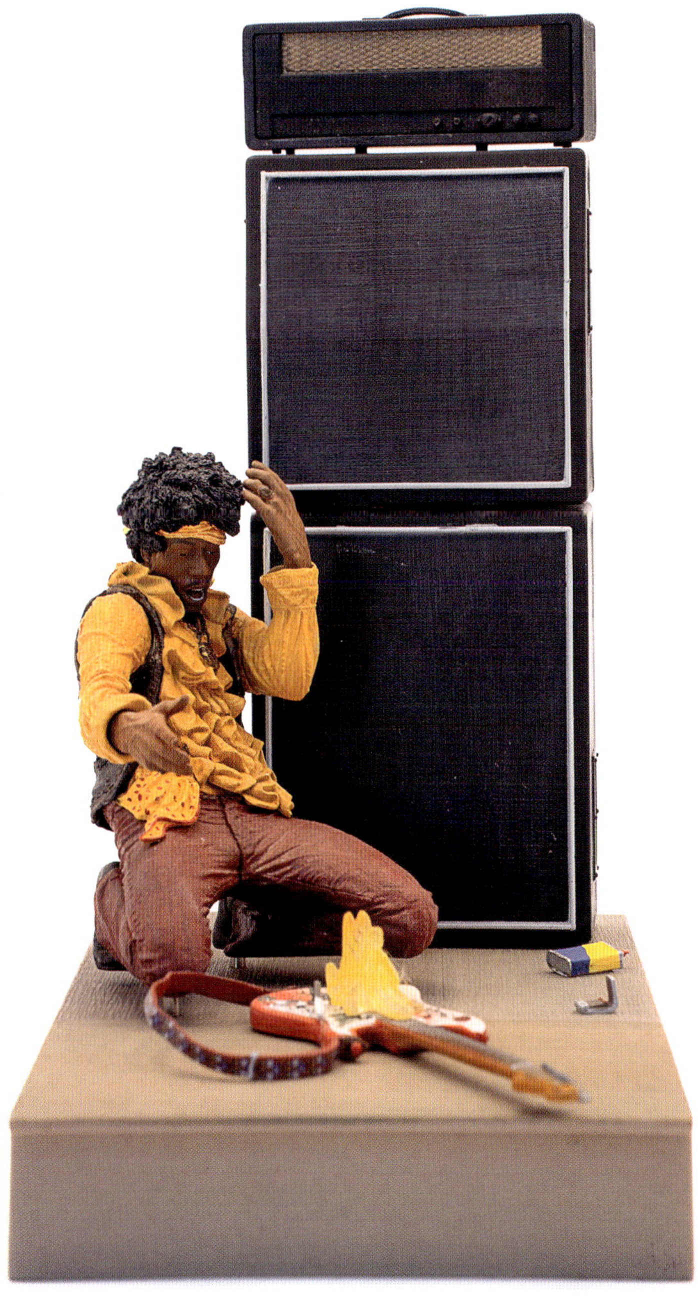

Top: Elements of Hip-Hop figures by Todd McFarlane, 2003. *Photo: William Toney*

Black Panther and *Storm*, Marvel Comics, ca. 1997. *Photo: William Toney*

Jimi Hendrix by Todd McFarlane, 2003. *Photo: William Toney*

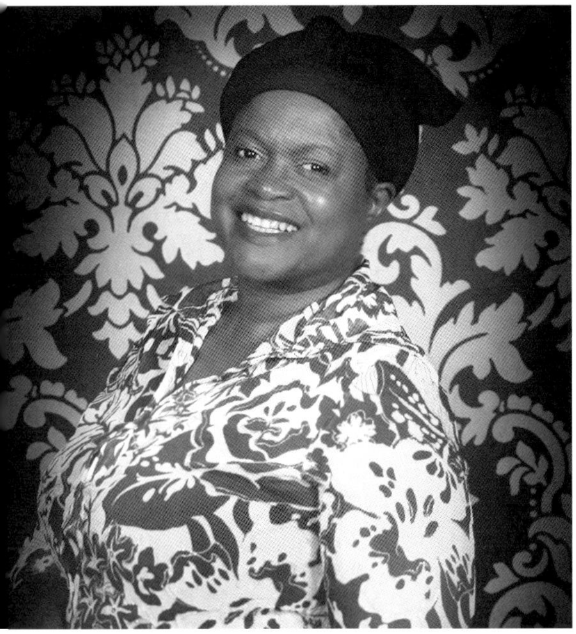

Photo: Kameron Hutchinson

THE STEWART-HUTCHINSON COLLECTION

HAITIAN MASTERS

DR. MYRAH: What is the first piece of art that you have collected and when?

JENNIFER STEWART-HUTCHINSON: The first piece of original art I ever purchased was Romare Bearden's *Sunburst at Moonbay*, and it holds a special place in my heart. I found it at the Essie Green Gallery in Park Slope, Brooklyn, in 1981. Bearden had painted it while visiting St. Maarten, his wife Nanette's family home in the West Indies. I wasn't an art collector at the time, but something about this piece spoke to me deeply.

I had learned that Bearden was passionate about seeing his work in the hands of young Black professionals, and that idea resonated with me. I felt inspired to own this piece, not only for its beauty, but for what it represented: the birth of a new beginning and optimism coming out of the dark. *Sunburst at Moonbay* has been hanging above my couch ever since, marking the beginning of my journey into collecting art by African American artists.

DR. MYRAH: Why are you the Keeper of Haitian Masters?

JENNIFER STEWART-HUTCHINSON: Becoming the Keeper of Haitian Masters was something we stumbled upon by accident, but it has brought us immense joy and fulfillment over the years.

It began with my dear friend the late James Brown, an African American artist who frequently traveled to Haiti for both pleasure and creative inspiration. James would sit on my couch, vividly recounting his experiences—staying at the legendary Hotel Oloffson, visiting Le Centre d'Art, and dancing at RA-RA in Port-au-Prince. His stories filled me with such intrigue that I convinced my friend Cynthia Barnes and my sister, Norva Hutchinson, to join me on a trip to Haiti—not once, but twice.

At the time, the media's portrayal of Haiti was overwhelmingly negative, which made us hesitate. But James had already planted a seed of curiosity in me. He recommended I read *Peintures Haïtiennes* and *Where Art is Joy* by Selden Rodman to better understand the richness of Haitian art. Through James, I was introduced to artists like Wilson Bigaud, Hector Hyppolite, Bernard Sejourne, and Jacques-Enguerrand Gourgue, and I began forming a list of artists whose work I wanted to collect during my visits.

Our first trip to Haiti, in 2001, was a revelation. I was struck by the raw beauty and rich cultural vibrancy of the Haitian people. Everything in Haiti—art, furniture, flags, dishes, even the homes—was a piece of art, and every person seemed to have the soul of an artist. We visited the studios of incredible artists such as Valcin II, Ludovic Booz, Ralph Allen, and Francois Sanon, and we, of course, spent time at Le Centre d'Art. I returned home with several remarkable pieces, and that's when the real journey began.

We visited again two years later, diving deeper into the museums, churches, and cultural landmarks. Each time I left Haiti, I felt like I was taking a piece of its extraordinary artistic legacy with me. The talent of Haitian artists is truly extraordinary, and their work deserves to be cherished and preserved for generations to come.

I'm a keeper of the masters because I feel an obligation to honor the stories, the history, and the extraordinary artistic vision of these artists. What began as a personal curiosity has grown into a profound responsibility to preserve and share their work with others. I see myself as a custodian of a vibrant and essential cultural legacy, one that deserves to be protected and celebrated for future generations.

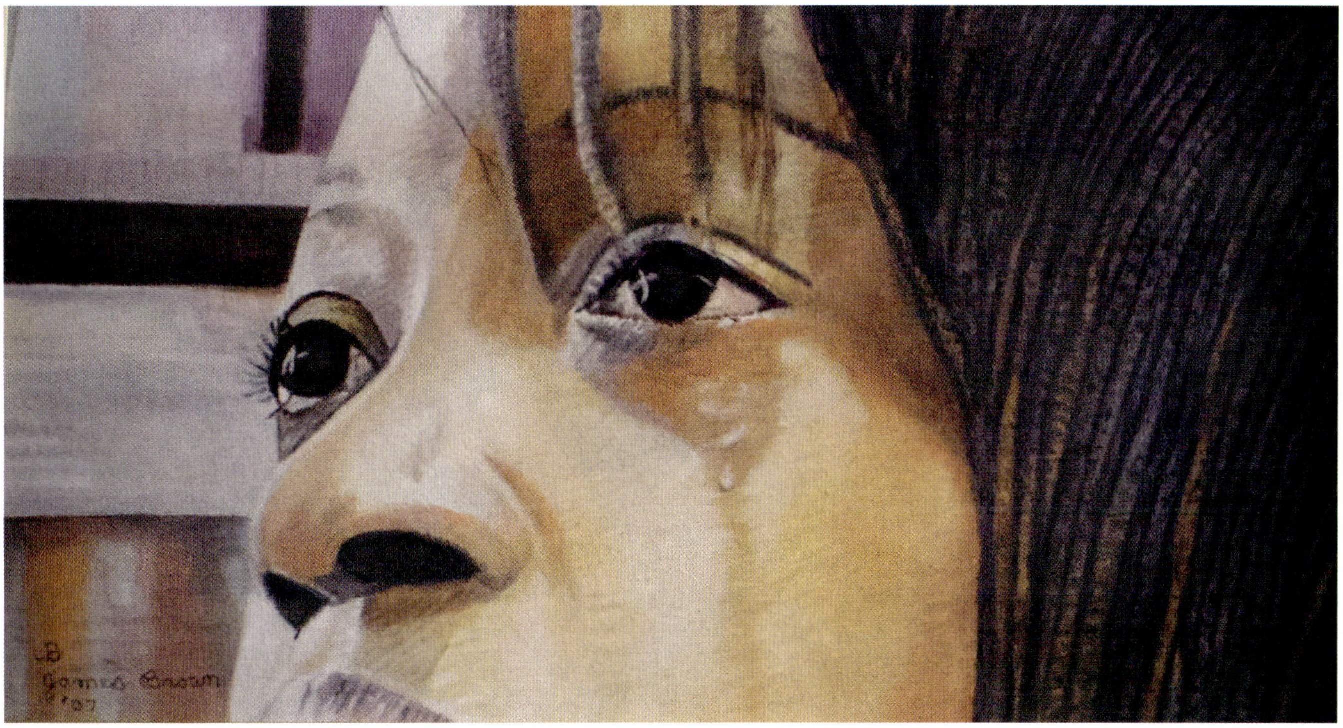

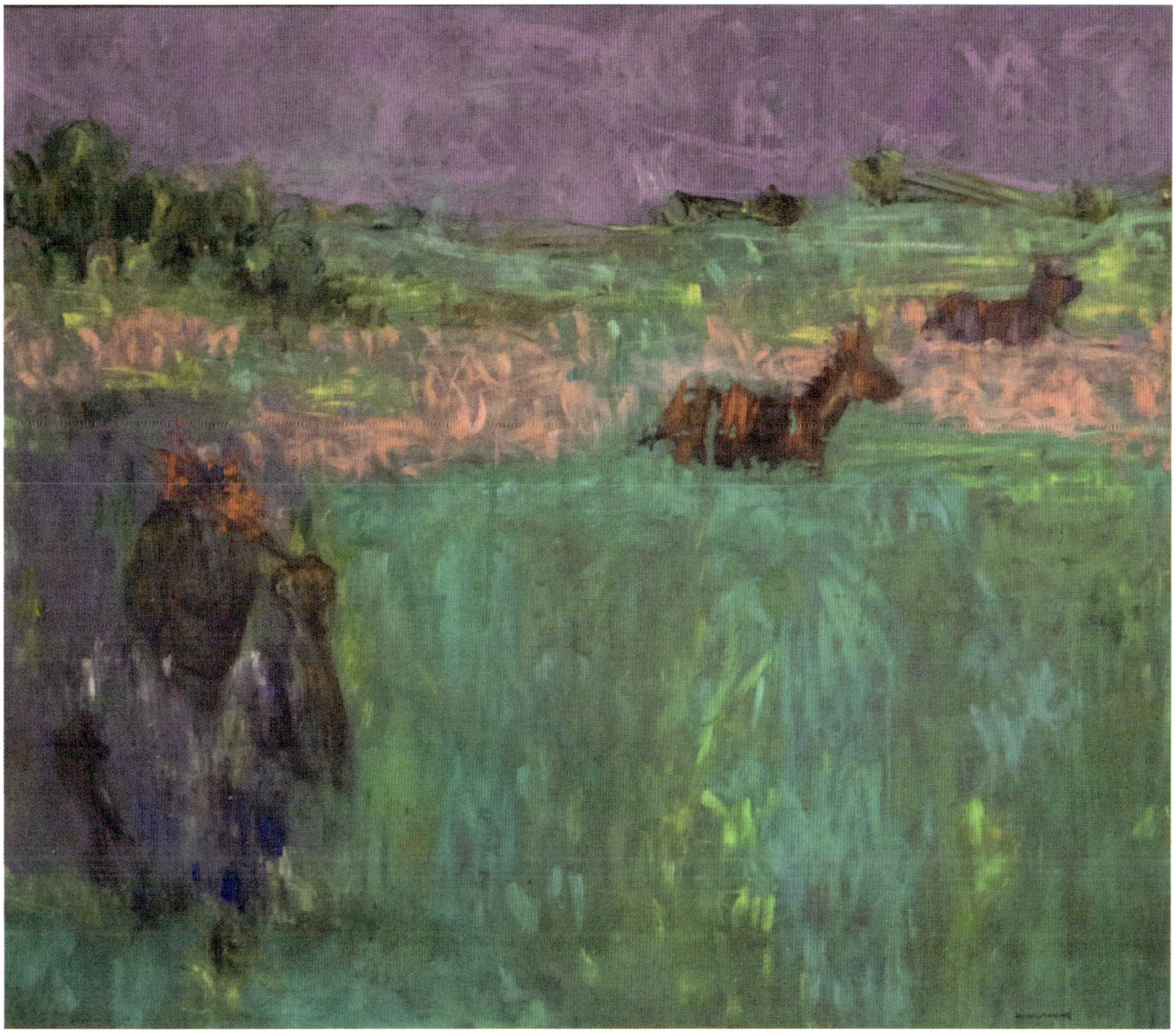

James Brown, *A Mother's Love* (year unknown). Acrylic on canvas, 9" × 17". *Photo: Myrah Brown Green*

Gesner Armand, *Untitled* (year unknown). Acrylic on canvas, 40" × 48". *Photo: Myrah Brown Green*

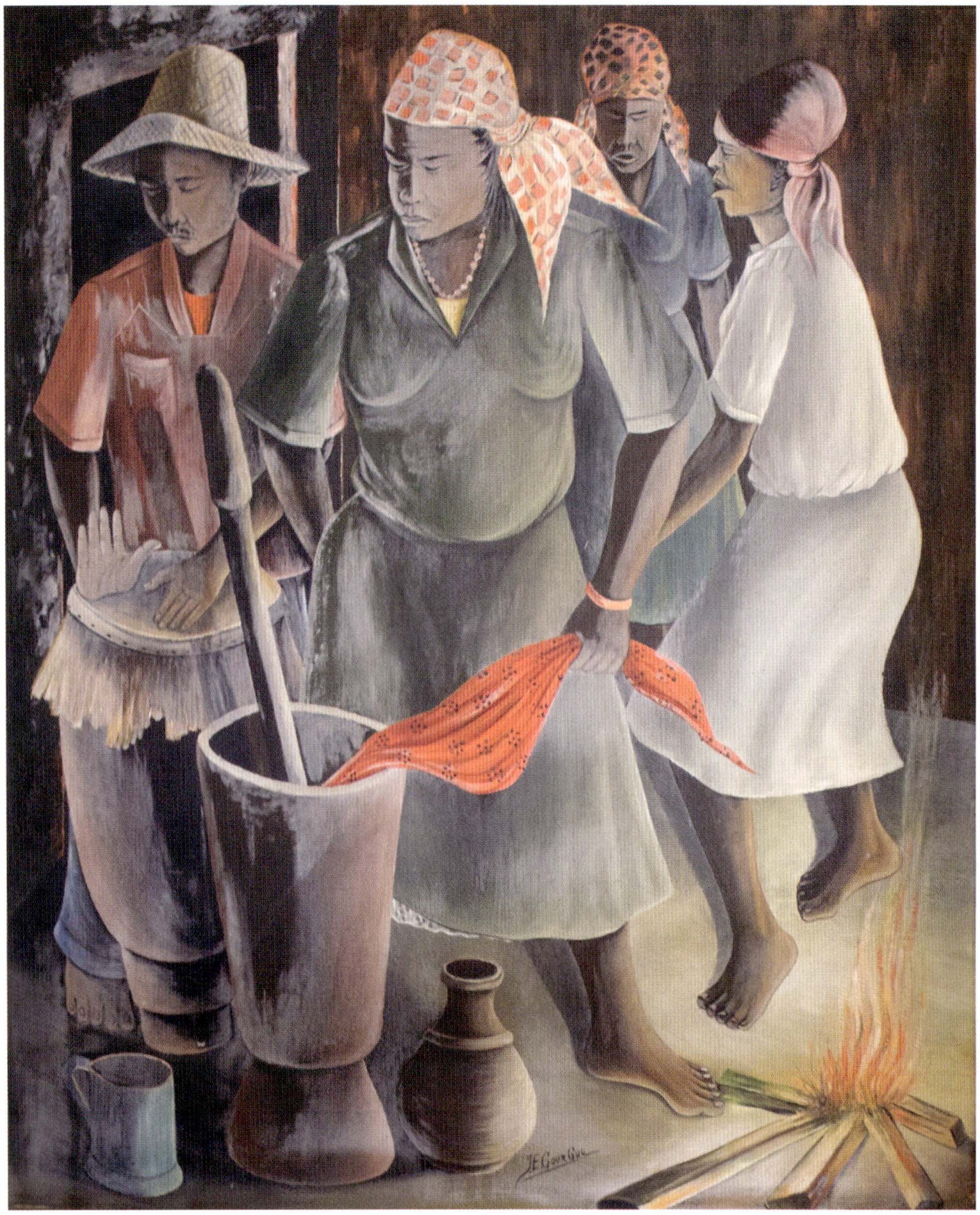

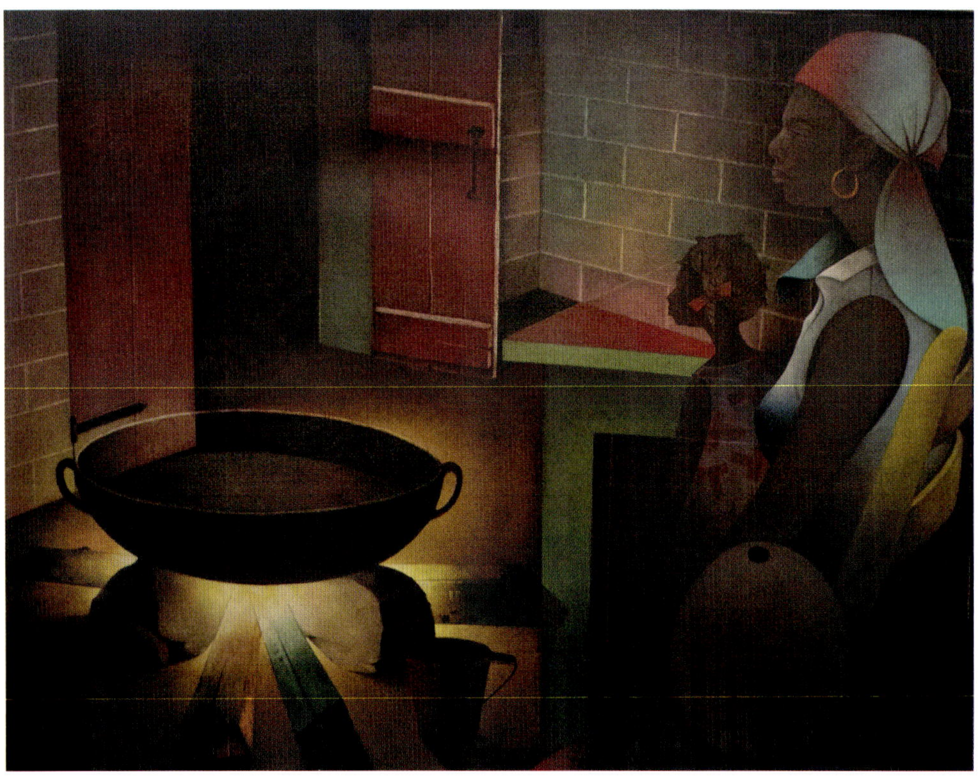

Jacques-Enguerrand Gourgue, *Untitled* (year unknown). Oil on board, 24" × 20". *Photo: Myrah Brown Green*

Jacques-Enguerrand Gourgue, *Untitled* (year unknown). Oil on board, 30" × 40". *Photo: Myrah Brown Green*

Opposite: Jean-Bernard Etienne, *Pretty Girl*, 1990. Acrylic on canvas, 20" × 24". *Photo: Myrah Brown Green*

Opposite: Henry-Robert Bresil, *Untitled*, 1990. Acrylic on Masonite, 20" × 24". *Photo: Myrah Brown Green*

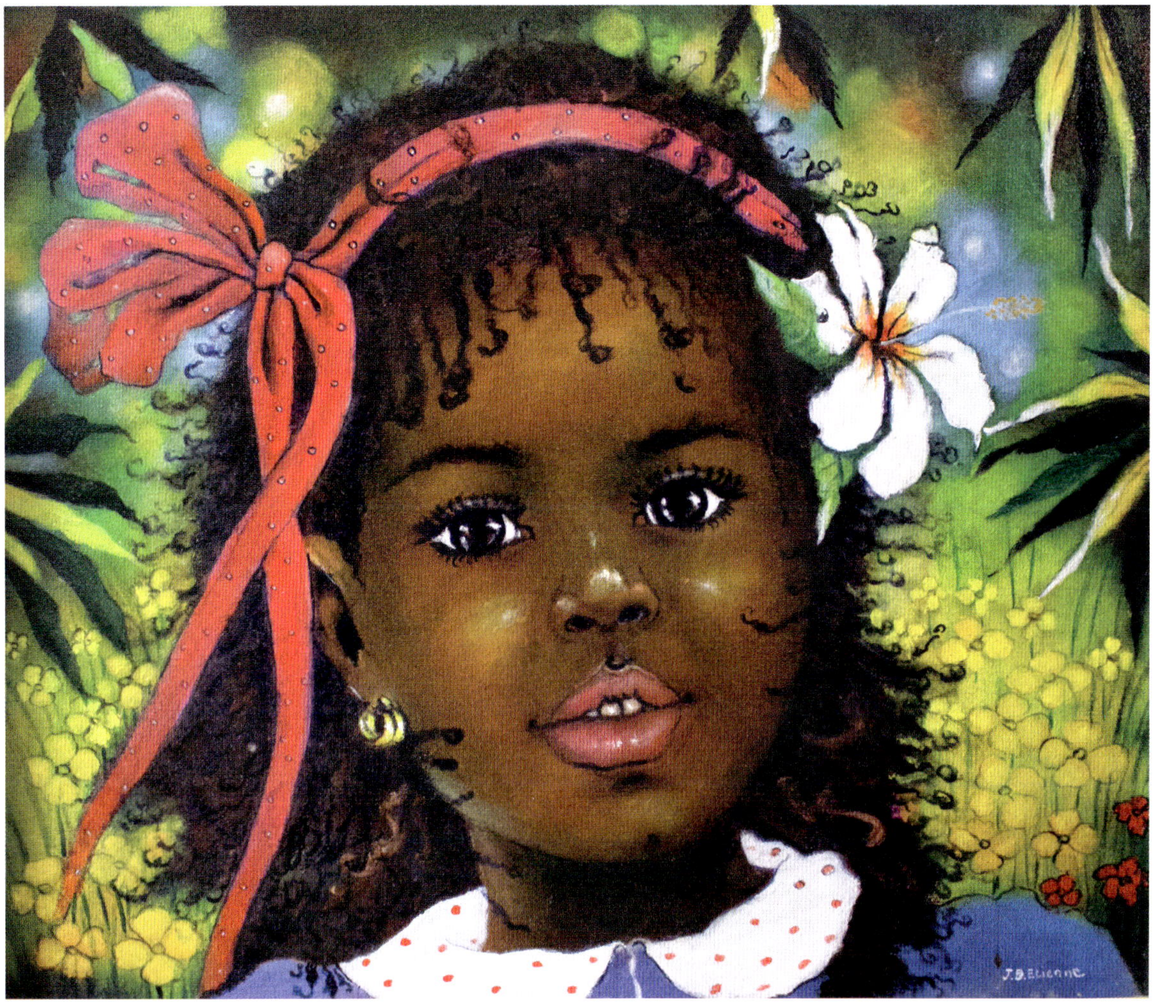
J.B.Etienne

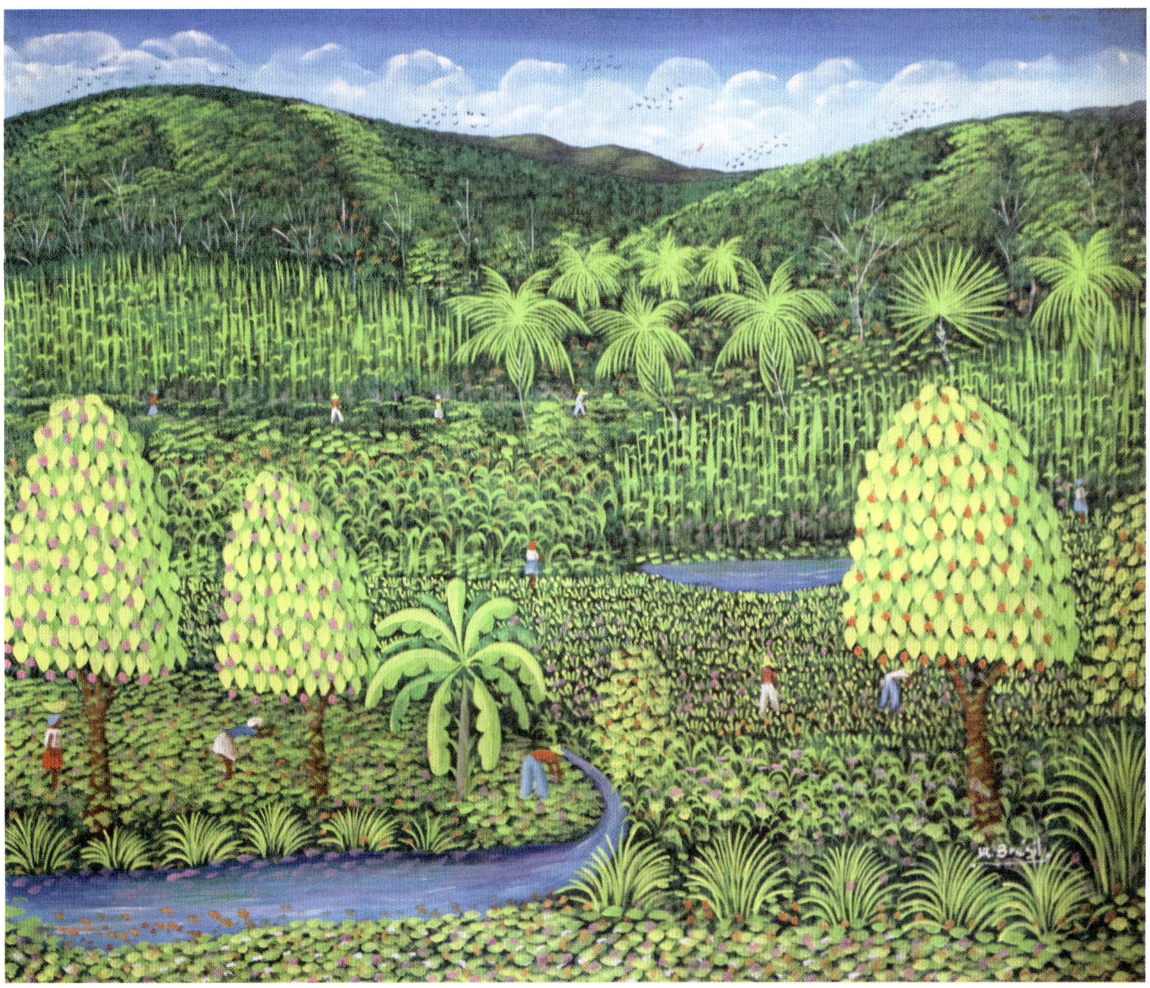

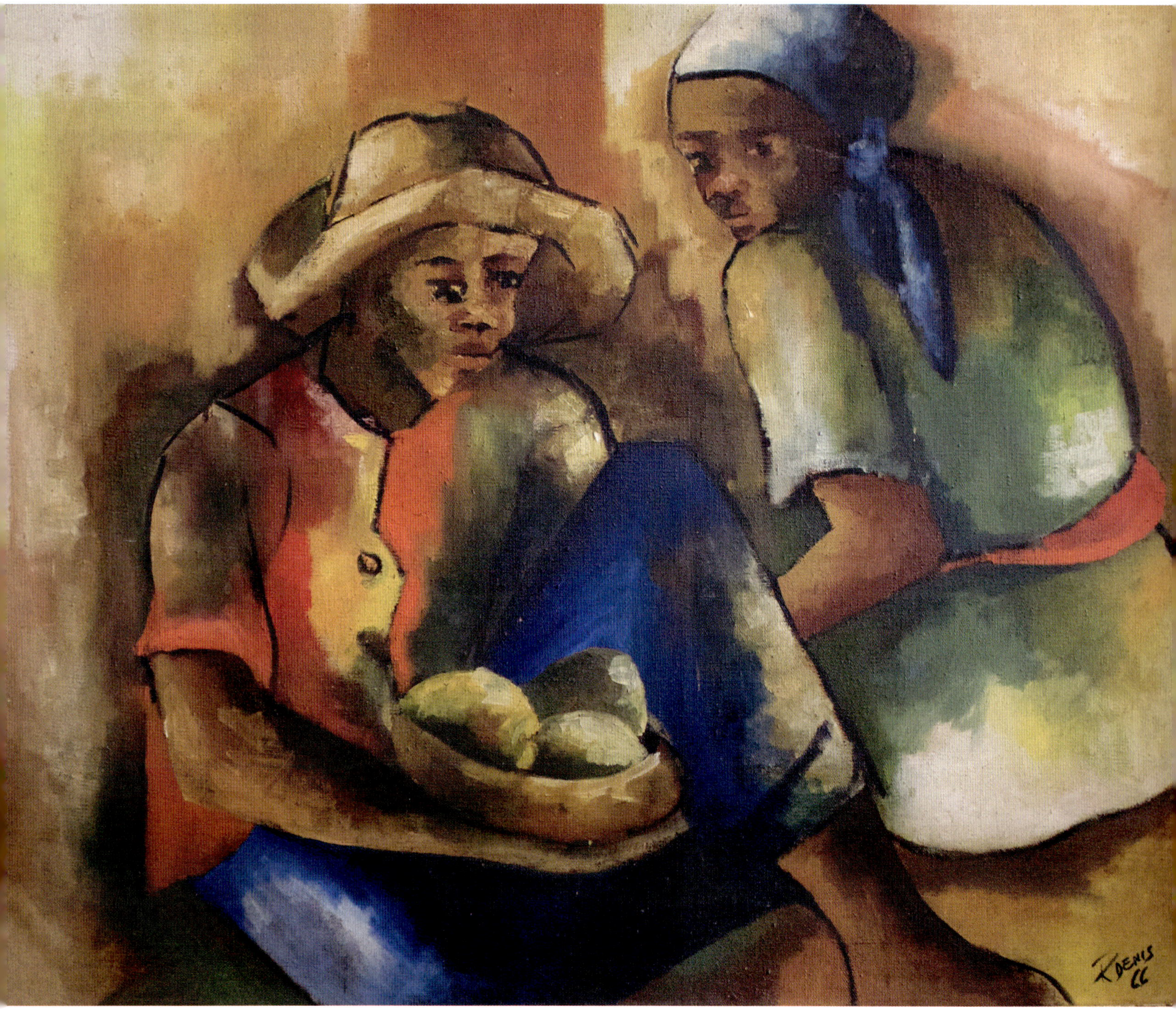

Raphael Denis, *Untitled*, 1966. Oil on canvas, 24" × 30". *Photo: Myrah Brown Green*

Paul Beauvoir, *Untitled*, 1956. Oil on canvas, 24" × 20". *Photo: Myrah Brown Green*

Ralph Allen, *Untitled*, 1999. Acrylic on canvas, 36" × 24". *Photo: Myrah Brown Green*

Albert Desmangles, *Untitled*, 1988. Acrylic on Masonite, 12" × 16". *Photo: Myrah Brown Green*

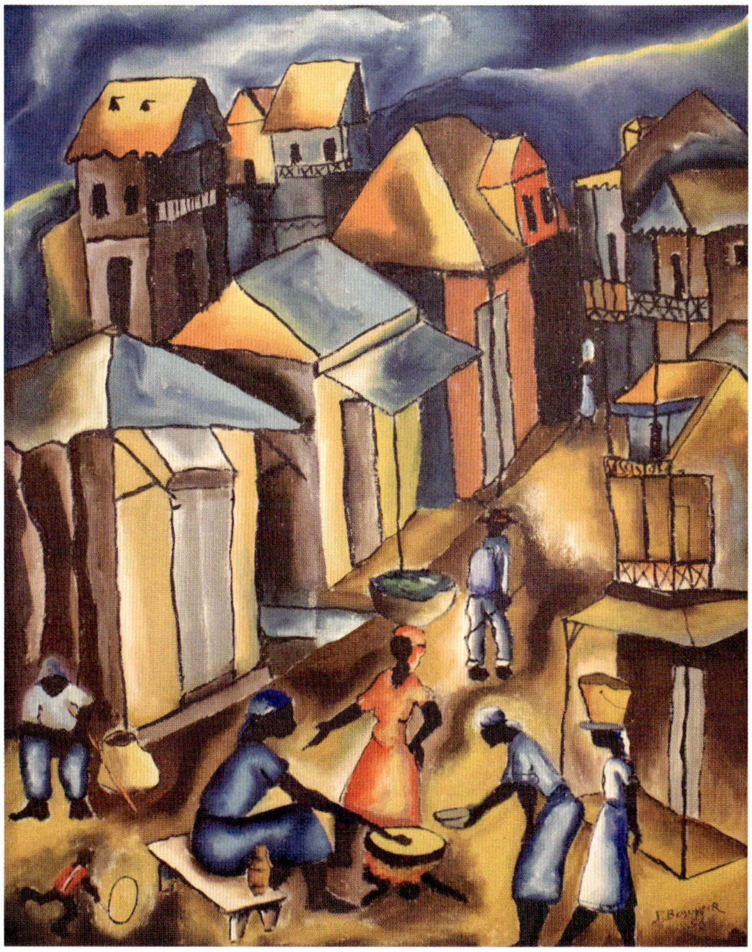

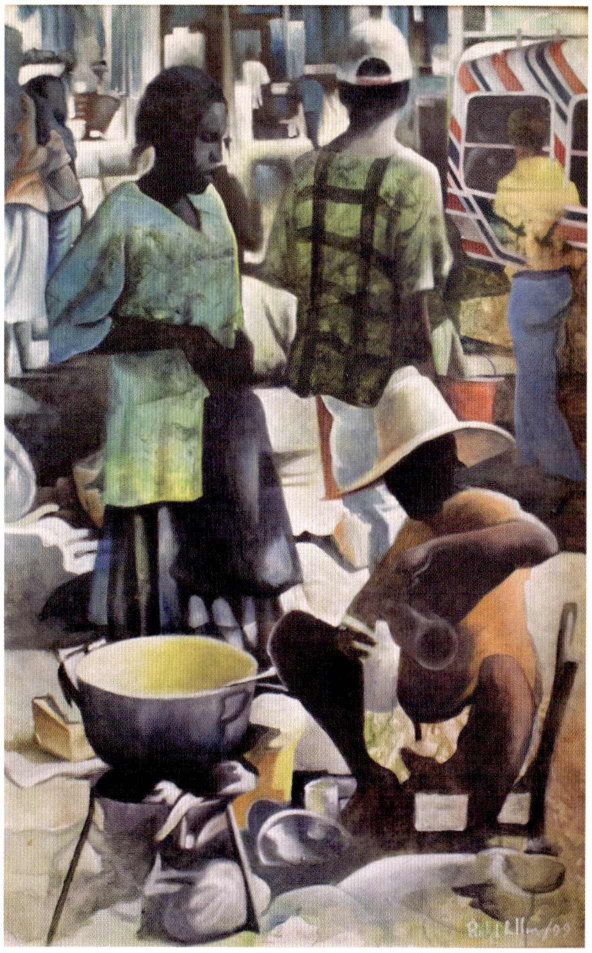

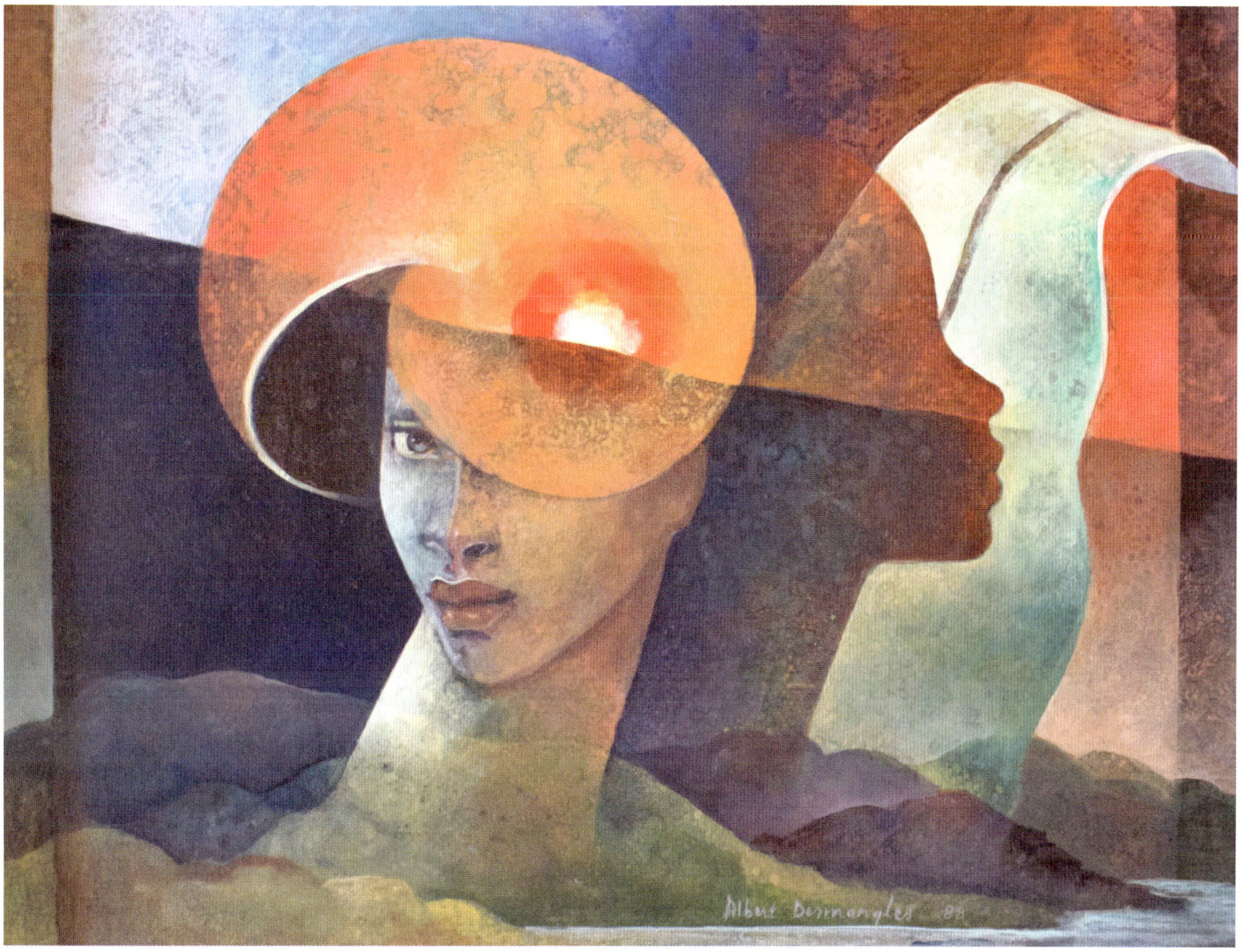

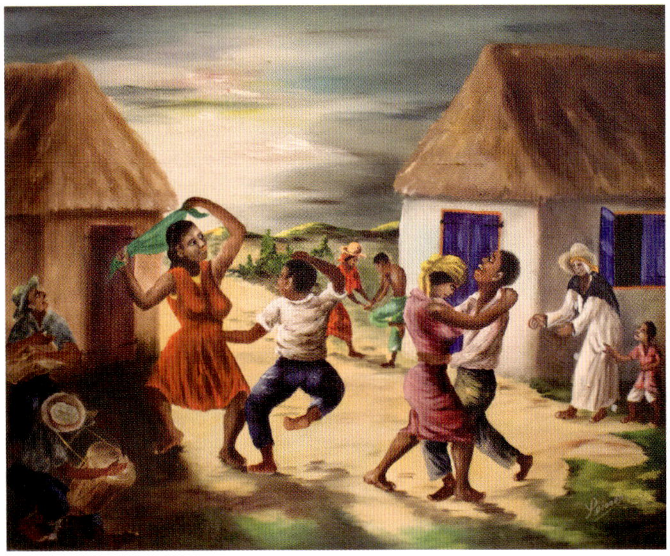

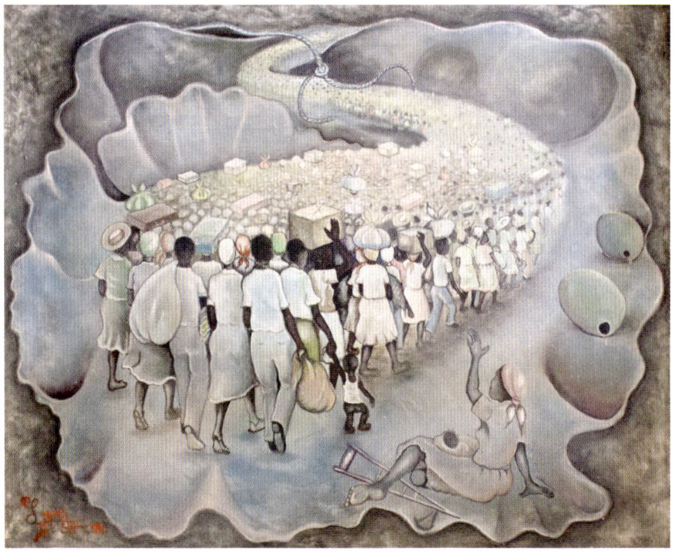

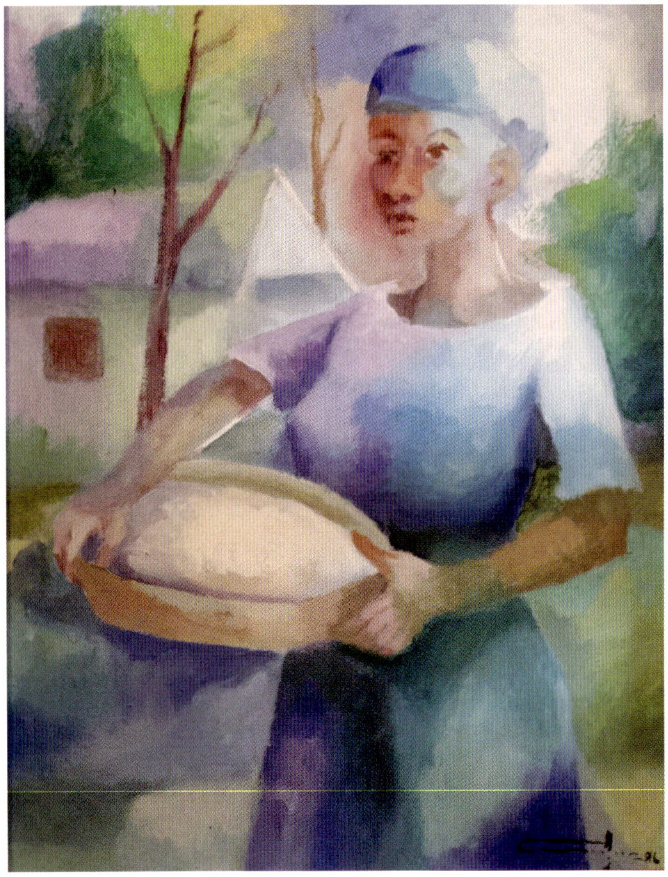

Top left: Louveture Poisson, *Untitled*, 1960. Oil on canvas, 17" × 22". *Photo: Myrah Brown Green*

Top right: Lionel St. Eloi, *Untitled*, 1976. Oil on canvas, 15.5" × 19.5". *Photo: Myrah Brown Green*

Dieudonné Cedor, *Untitled*, 1986. Acrylic on canvas, 20" × 16". *Photo: Myrah Brown Green*

Opposite: Bernard Sejourne, *Untitled*, 1987. Acrylic on Masonite, 30" × 24". *Photo: Myrah Brown Green*

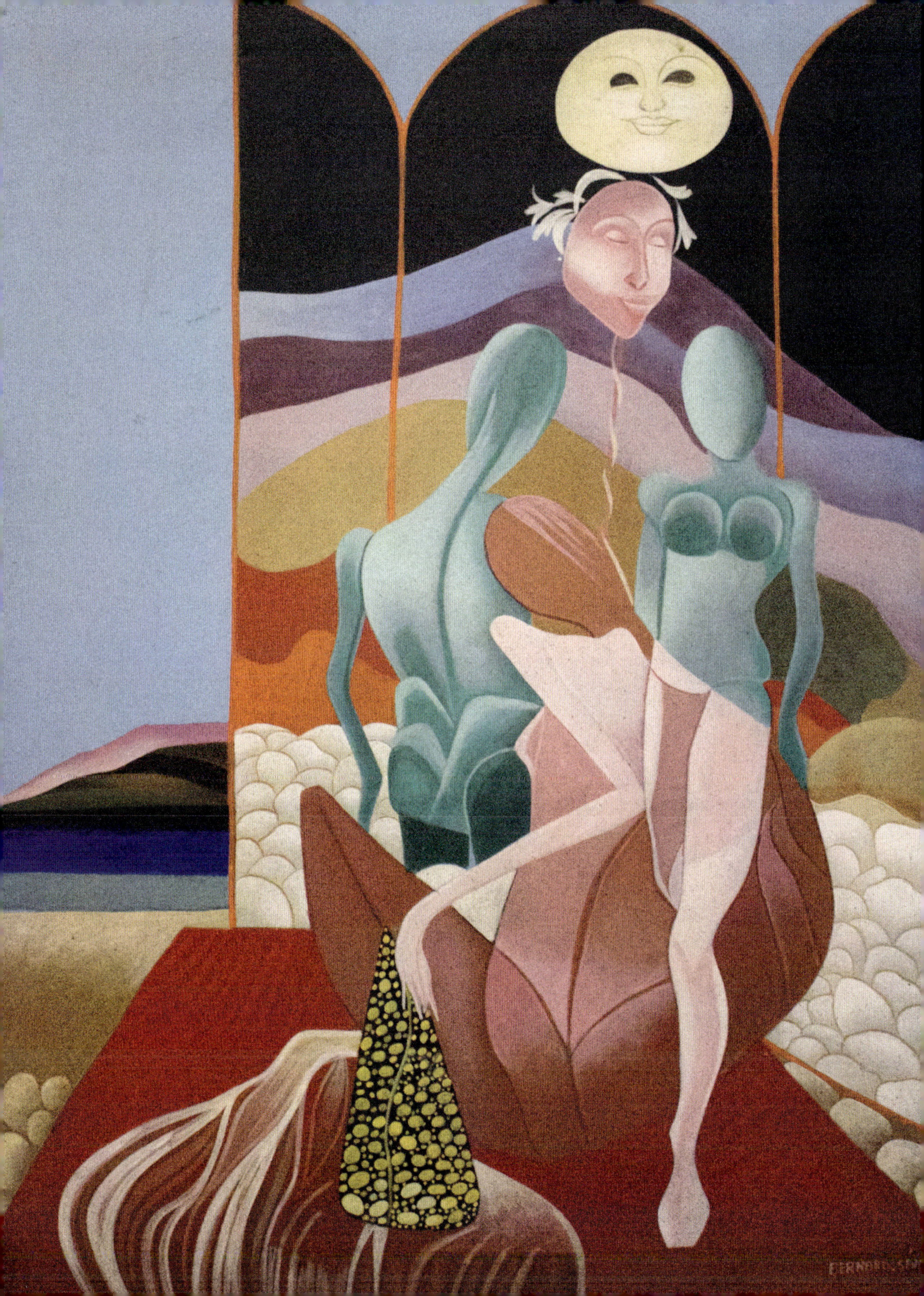

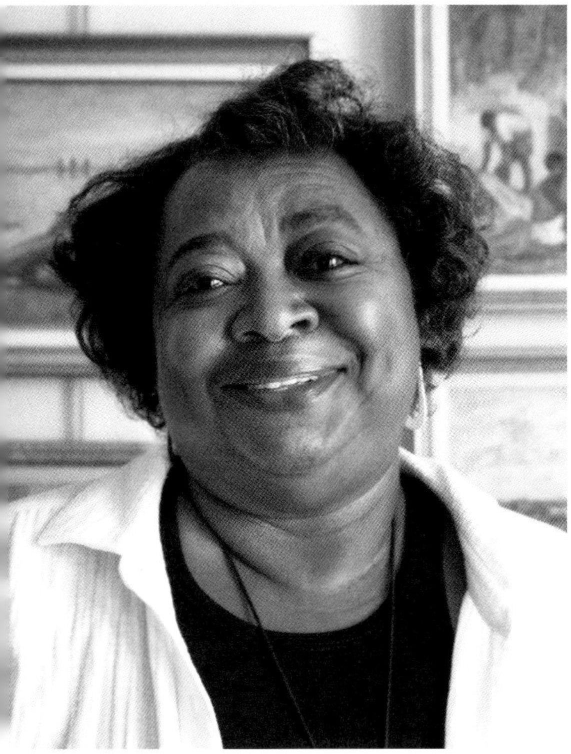

Photo: Myrah Brown Green

LINDA SUTTON
CARIBBEAN ART

DR. MYRAH: What was the first piece of art that you collected and when?

LINDA SUTTON: The first piece of art that I collected was an Otto Neals collage in 1982 from the Dorsey Art Gallery. Mr. Dorsey was very patient. It took me a year to pay for it. But my art education and my collection started right there at the Dorsey Art Gallery.

DR. MYRAH: Why are you a Keeper of Caribbean Art?

LINDA SUTTON: I've done many adventures in the arts with Caribbean artists. In 1982, right after I graduated from Adelphi, I became the director of the Afro-American Caribbean Cultural Center here in Brooklyn, and that's where it all started . . . and it followed me, and I followed the artists around the world and collected. I did a show in Aguila—the first International Arts Festival on the island of Anguilla. It was a mix of Caribbean artists and American artists. Verna Hart won the grand prize. The other artists in the show were Lester Gunter from Jamaica, Carlton Morell from Barbados, and then we had Arthur Coppedge from Brooklyn, New York. We came out victoriously. When Verna Hart won, her art became a postage stamp on the island of Anguilla.

My travels throughout the Caribbean and other parts of the world inspired me to collect and showcase art at my Gallerie St. Charles. We currently support young artists with academic scholarships and encourage them as they map out their career journeys while keeping the legacy of the late master artist Verna Hart alive.

Eric Gerault, *Market Place*, 1986. Oil on canvas, 10" × 10". *Photo: Myrah Brown Green*

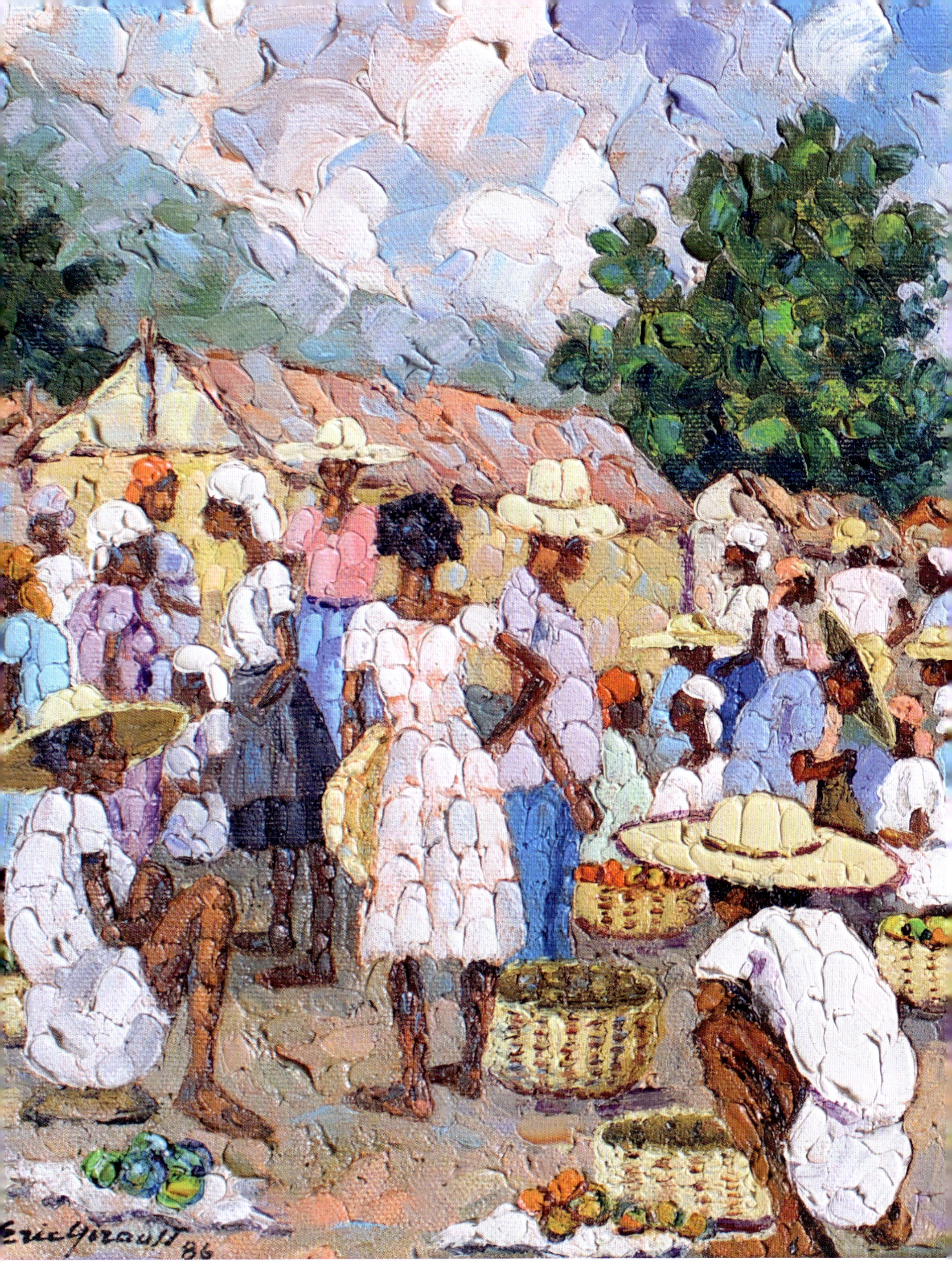
Eric Girault 86

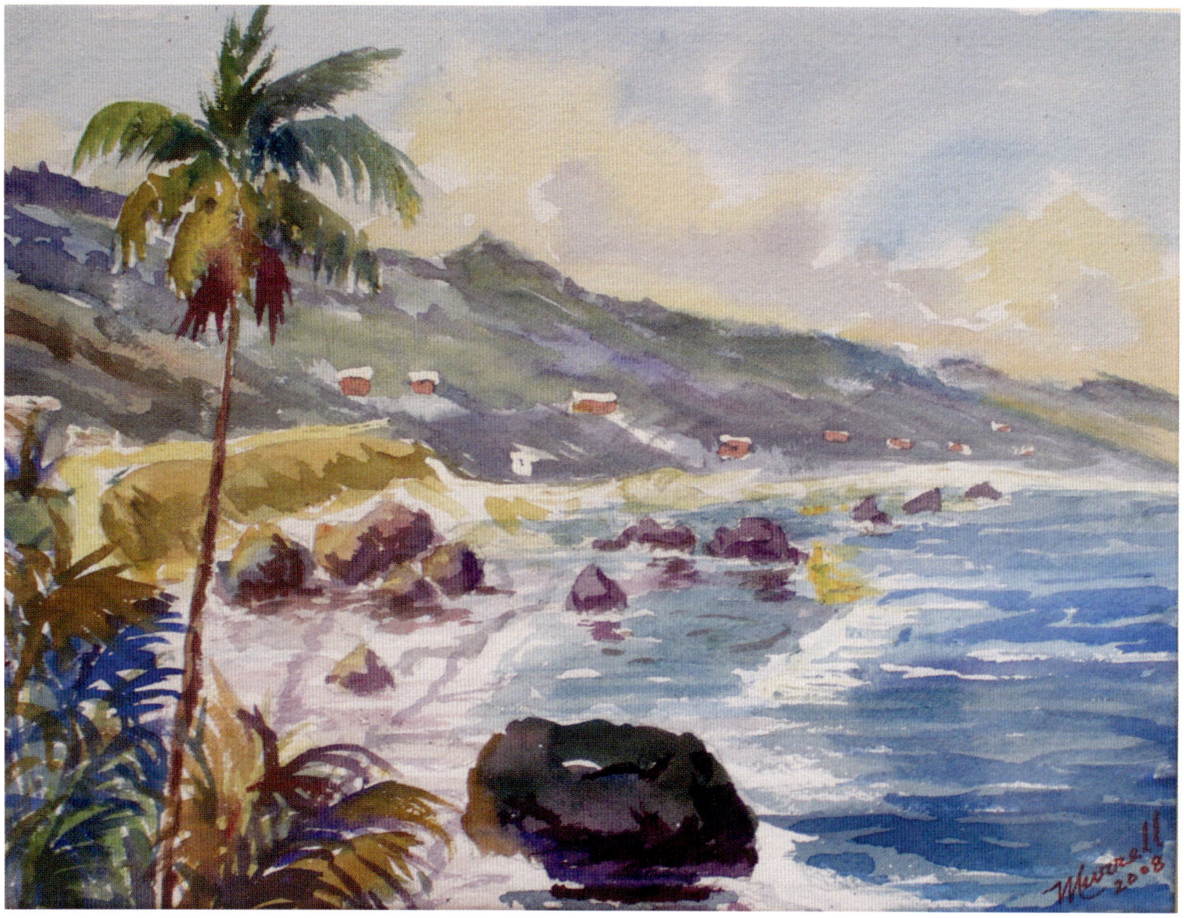
Murrell
2008

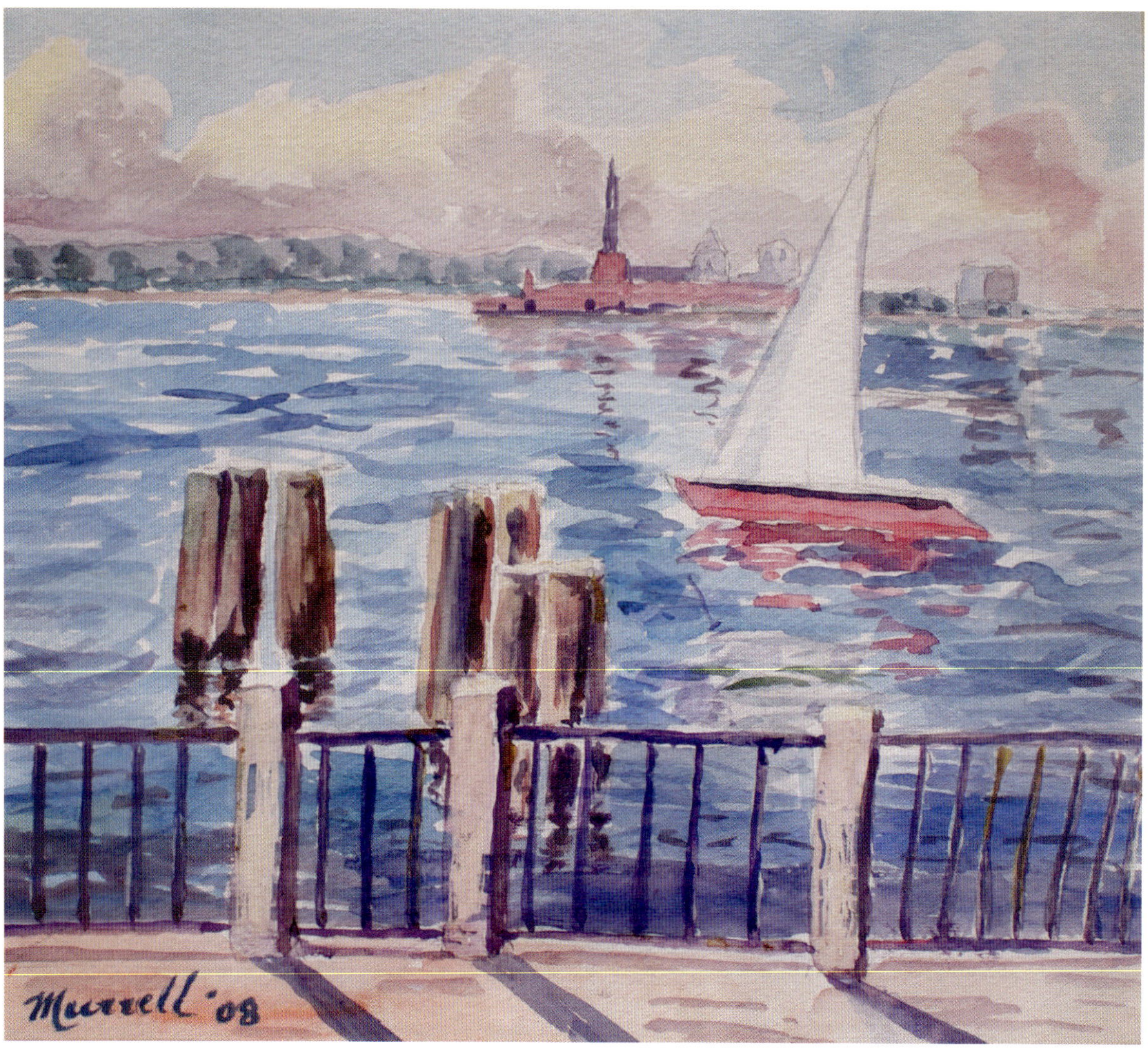
Murrell '08

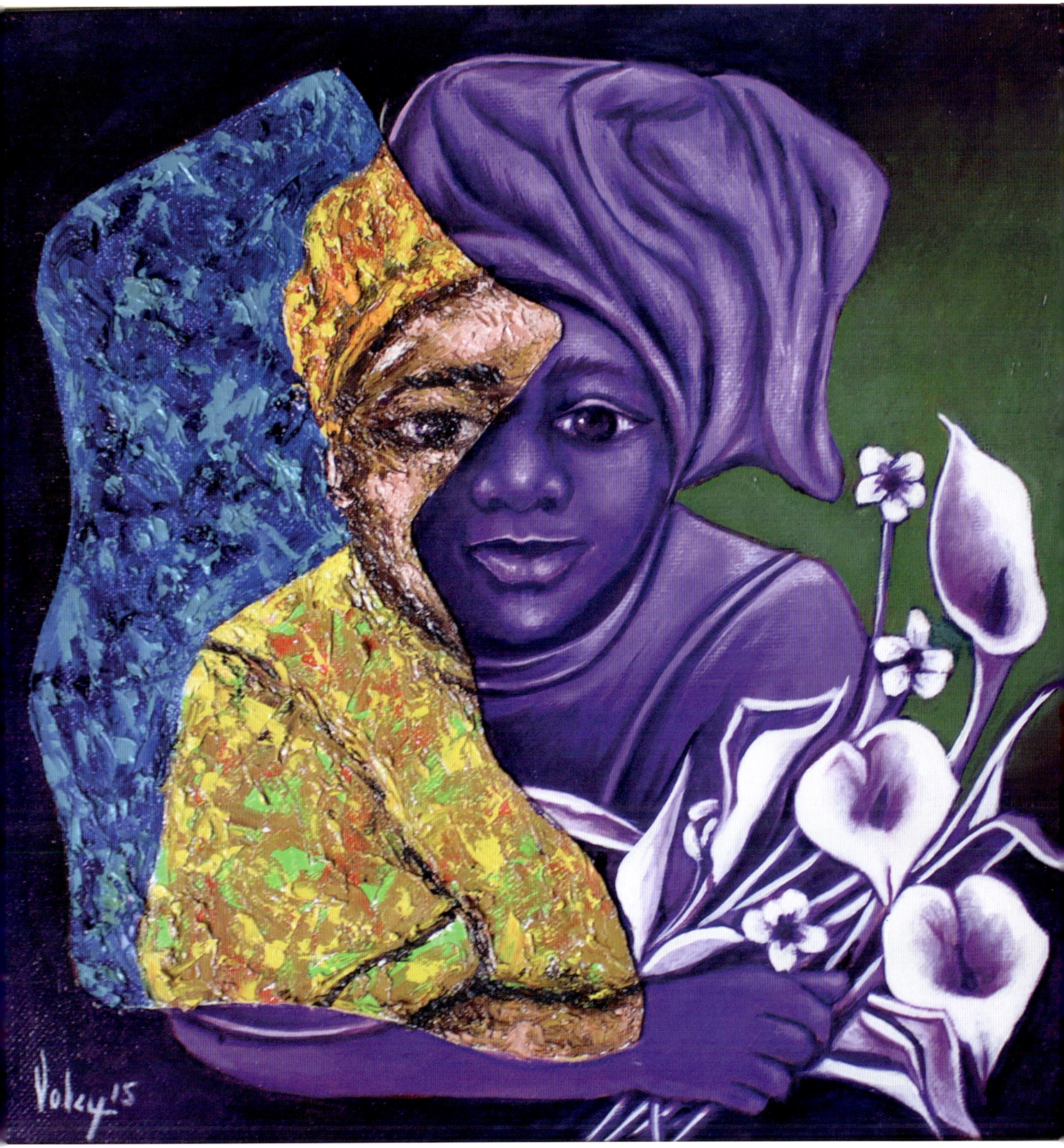

Carlton Murrell, *Bathsheba Beach, Barbados*, 2008. Watercolor, 11" × 14". *Photo: Myrah Brown Green*

Carlton Murrell, *Red Boat in Pier*, 2008. Watercolor, 11" × 14". *Photo: Myrah Brown Green*

Above: Jean Dominique Volcy, *Girl with Flowers*, 2015. Mixed media, 12" × 12". *Photo: Myrah Brown Green*

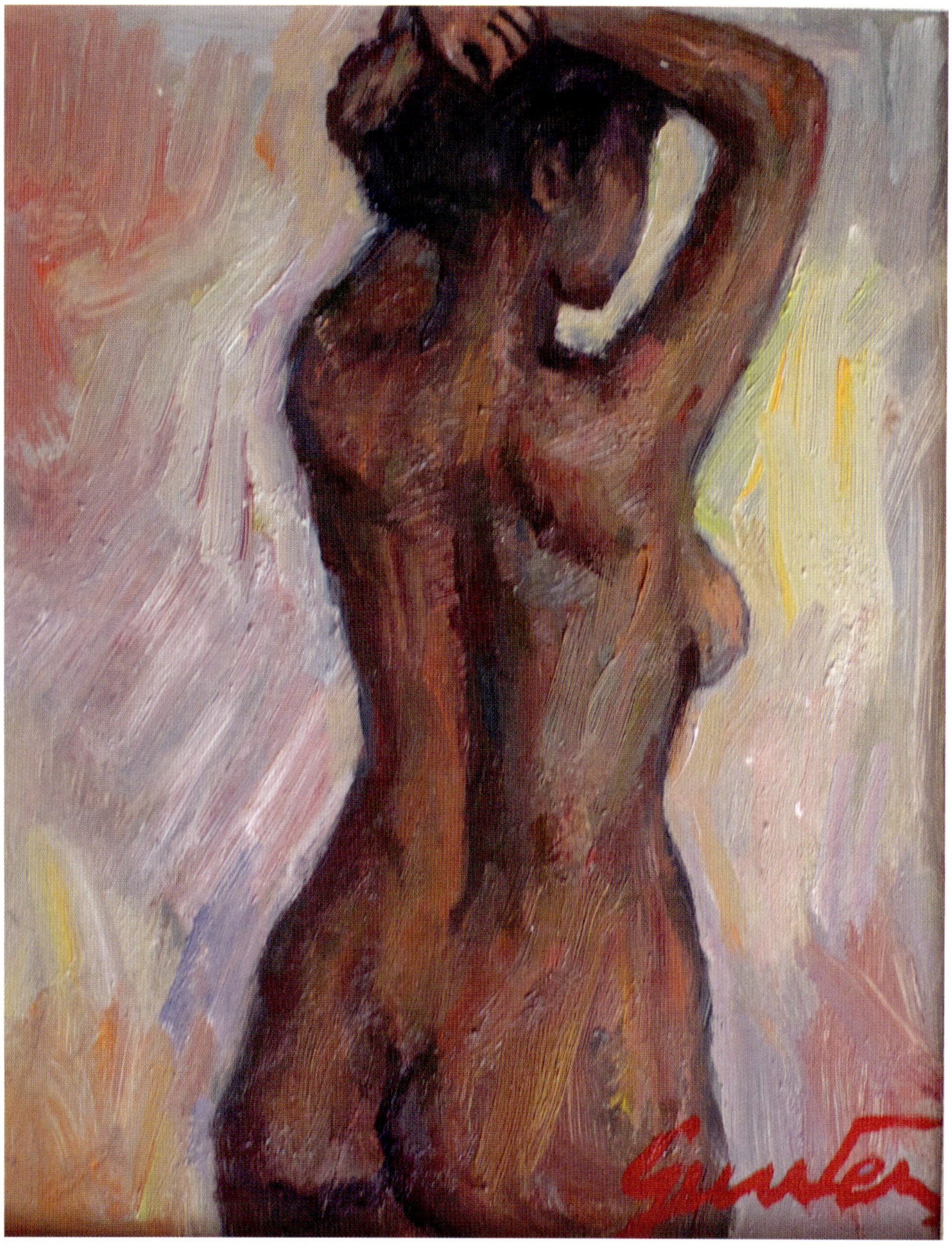

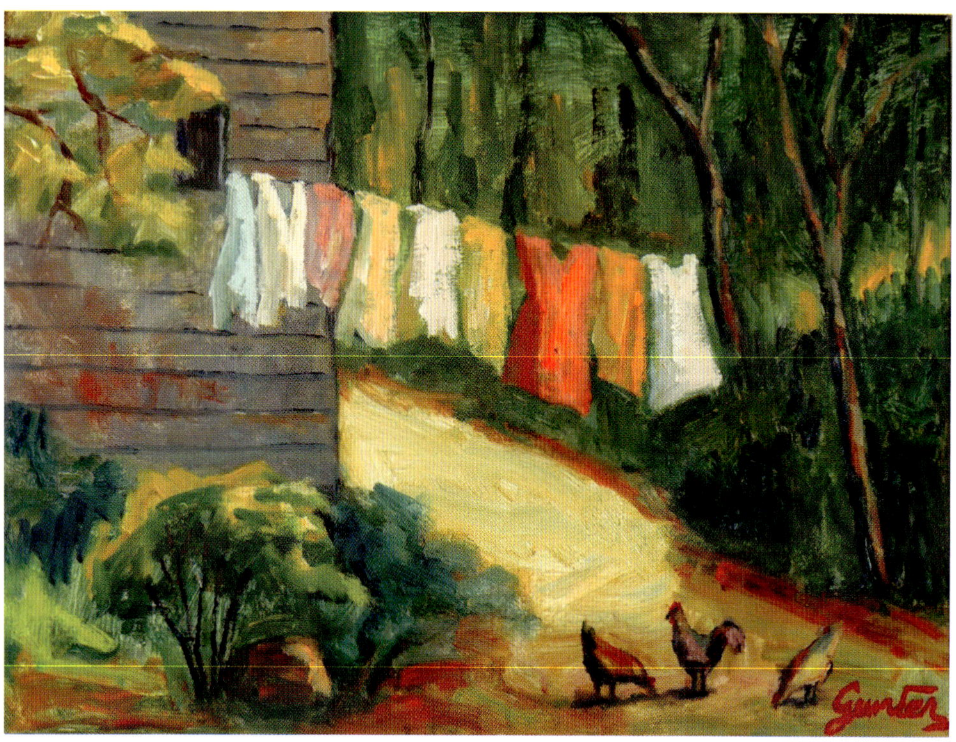

Lester Gunter, *Heads Up* (nude), 2010. Oil on masonite, 8" × 10". *Photo: Myrah Brown Green*

Lester Gunter, *Airing Laundry*, 2010. Oil on masonite, 10" × 12". *Photo: Myrah Brown Green*

Opposite: Lester Gunter, *The Fruit Vender*, 2010. Oil on masonite, 10" × 12". *Photo: Myrah Brown Green*

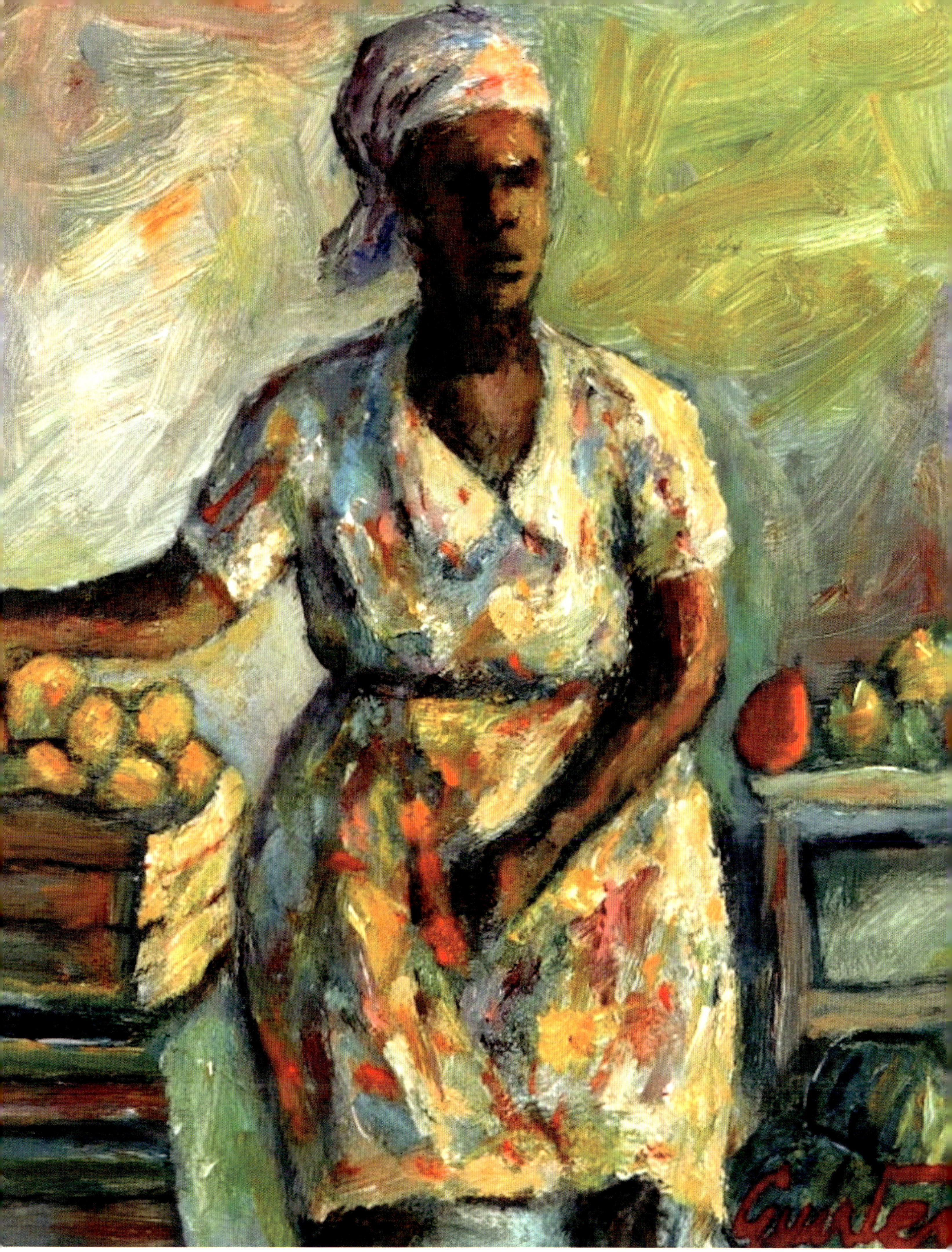

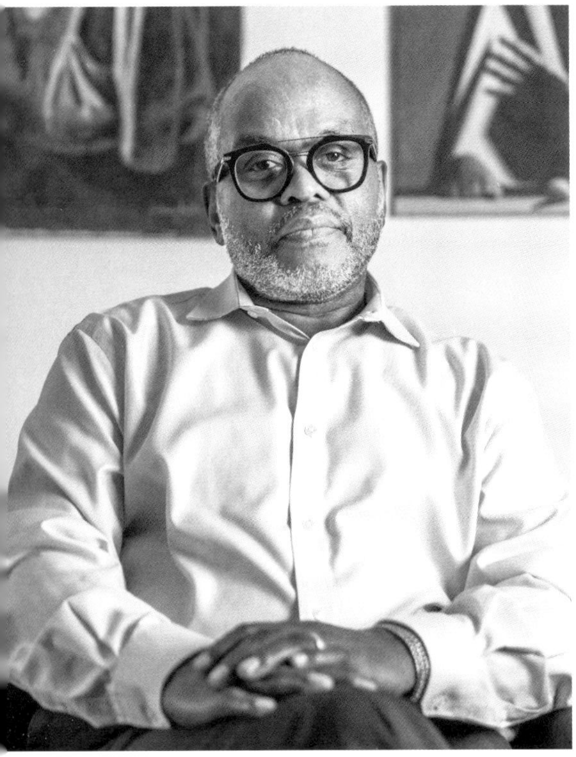

Photo: Ed Ryder

DONNELL WALKER
TEACHABLE MOMENTS

DR. MYRAH: What was the first piece of art that you collected and when?

DONNELL WALKER: The first piece of art that I collected was by an artist named Darrell Mackey. He and his mother moved from Harlem, and he also became a member of the church that I attended in south Philly. He created murals and taught art classes there. He was my first introduction to real art. He was older than I was, but we became friends. I saw this one painting in his studio that kind of reminded me of myself. It was a painting of a young boy. After a while, because he realized how much I liked it, he felt that I should have it. He gave it to me. That painting was the first piece of art that I collected.

DR. MYRAH: Why are you a Keeper of work that is created by or reflects Those Not Forgotten?

DONNELL WALKER: When I started really collecting, initially I couldn't afford to buy certain works that I saw. I started reading, researching, and realized that there were artists out there working all over the country. So I would track down their work. I would go to flea markets, thrift stores, house sales, and auctions. I was drawn to more of the artists who were kind of forgotten about, or who scholars were not really writing about. I guess that many of the curators or historians at the time didn't know about many of those artists. They were writing more about popular artists. I was more interested in the artists that worked alongside the known artists, like Jacob Lawrence, Bearden, and other well-known African American artists. Many of those artists were just as good as some of the artists that museums, galleries, and other art institutions were pushing out into the mainstream. Once doing more-intensive research, I realized that there were artists who were unknown, forgotten, and brilliant. While books were not being written about them, I decided to do my own research. I found that once the WPA ended, many of them had to find other jobs and careers while they made art. While most collectors were buying works by well-known artists, I was buying work by lesser-known artists who were great artists too. One of my goals in buying art is to help continue to keep the legacy of a forgotten artist alive.

Benjamin Britt, *Yield Not*, 1957. Oil on canvas, 34" × 20".
Photo: Courtesy of the Athenaeum of Philadelphia–Digital Imaging

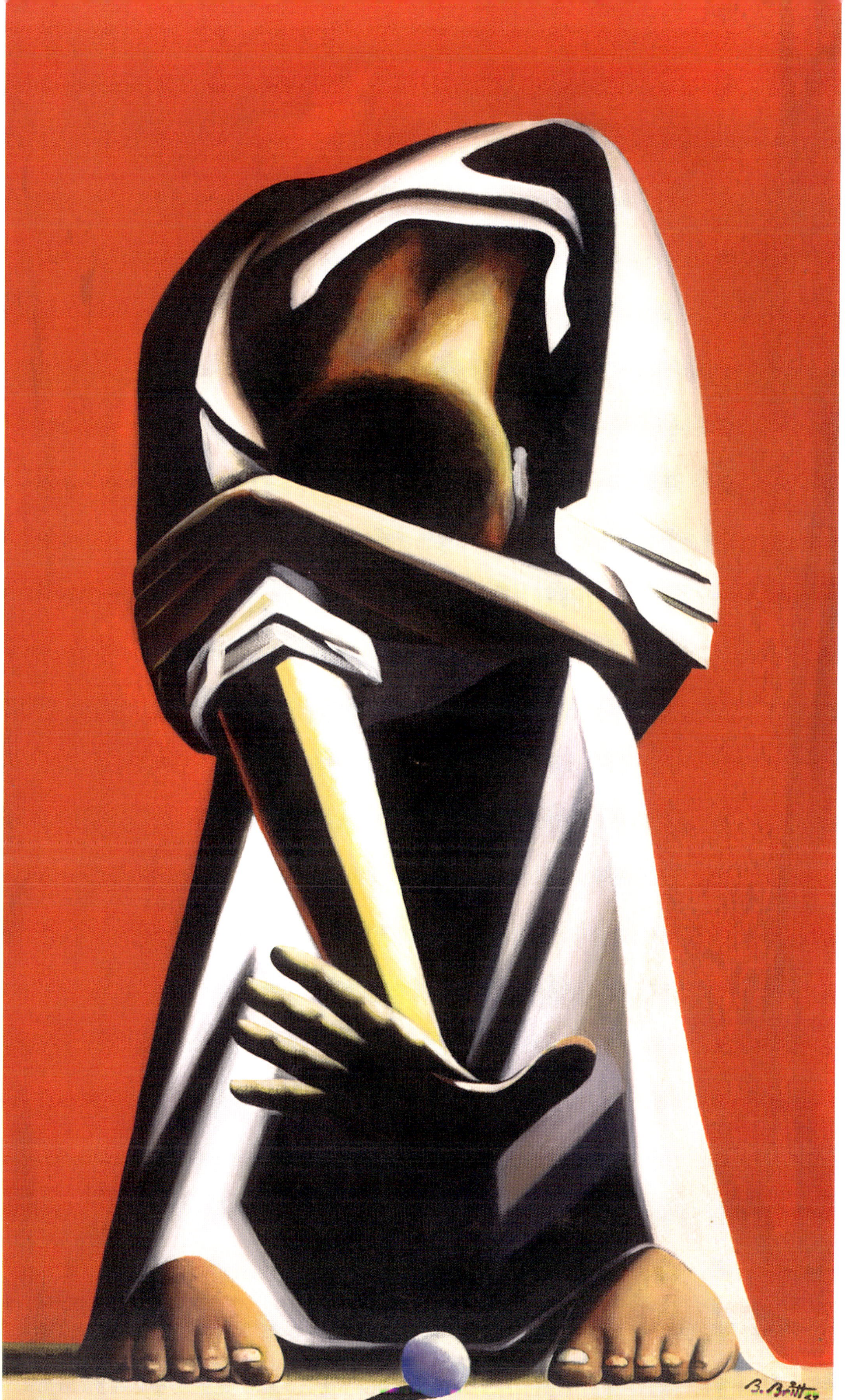
B. Britt 57

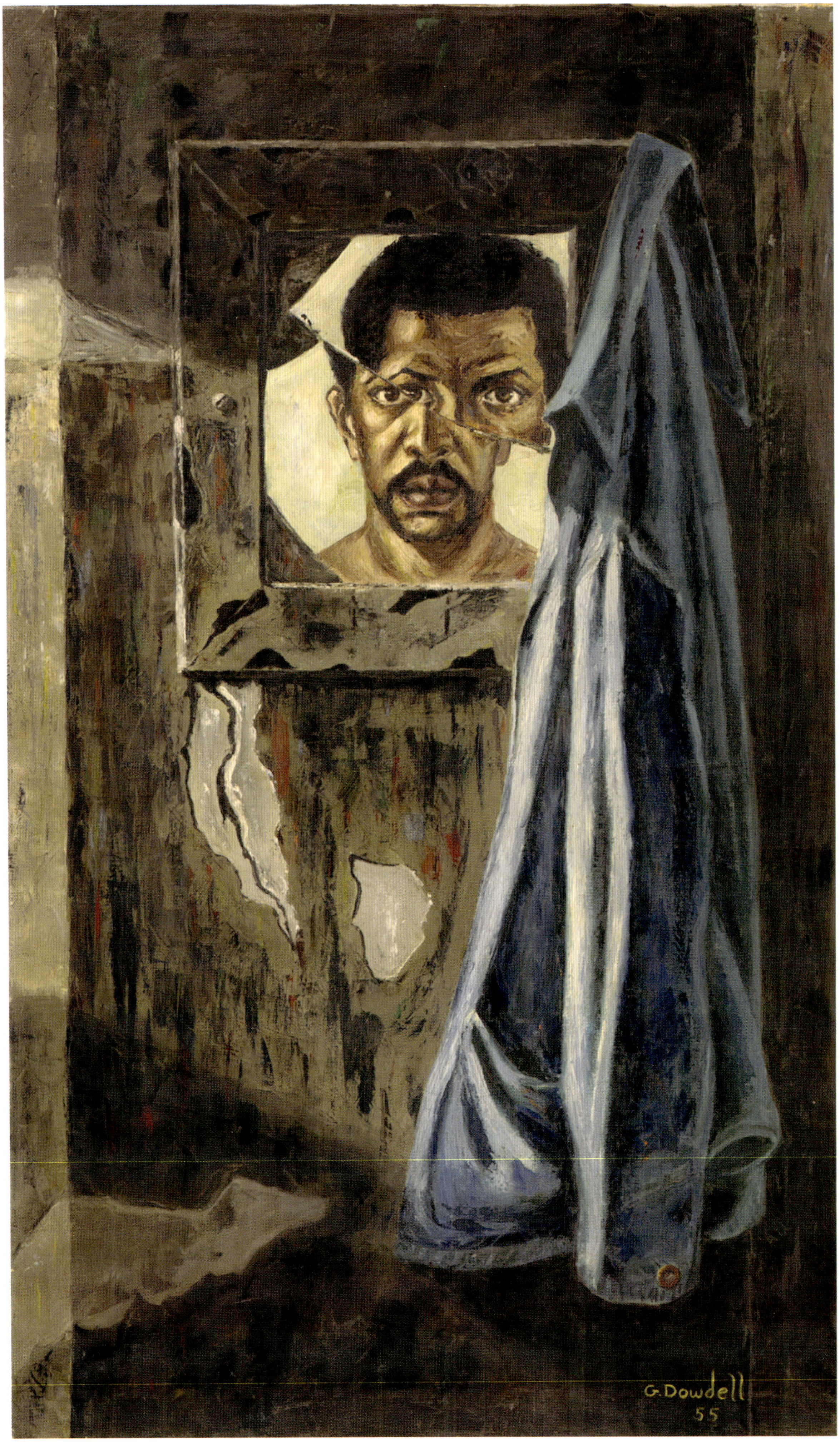
G. Dowdell
55

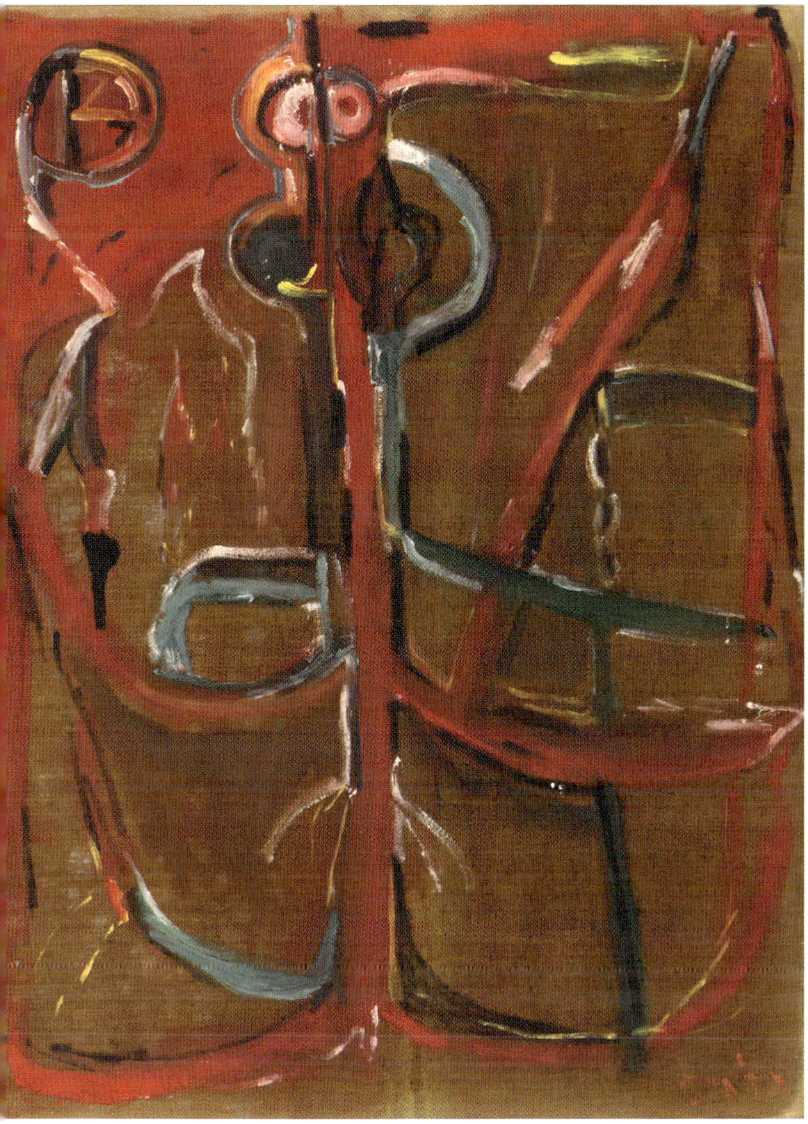

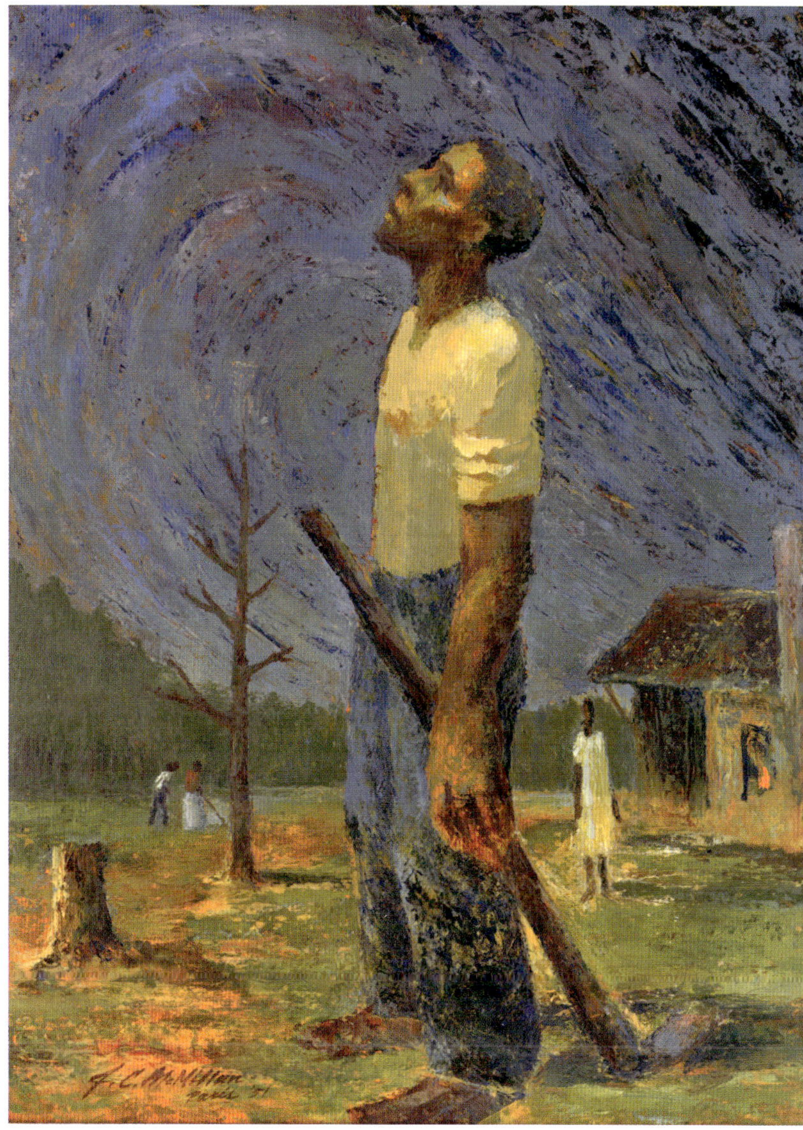

Opposite: Glanton Dowdell, *South East Corner of My Cell*, 1955. Oil on canvas, 40" × 24". *Photo: Courtesy of the Athenaeum of Philadelphia–Digital Imaging*

Herbert Gentry, *Untitled*, 1964. Oil on canvas, 36" × 28". *Photo: Courtesy of the Athenaeum of Philadelphia–Digital Imaging*

James C. McMillan, *Give Us This Day*, 1952. Oil on board, 28" × 22". *Photo: Courtesy of the Athenaeum of Philadelphia–Digital Imaging*

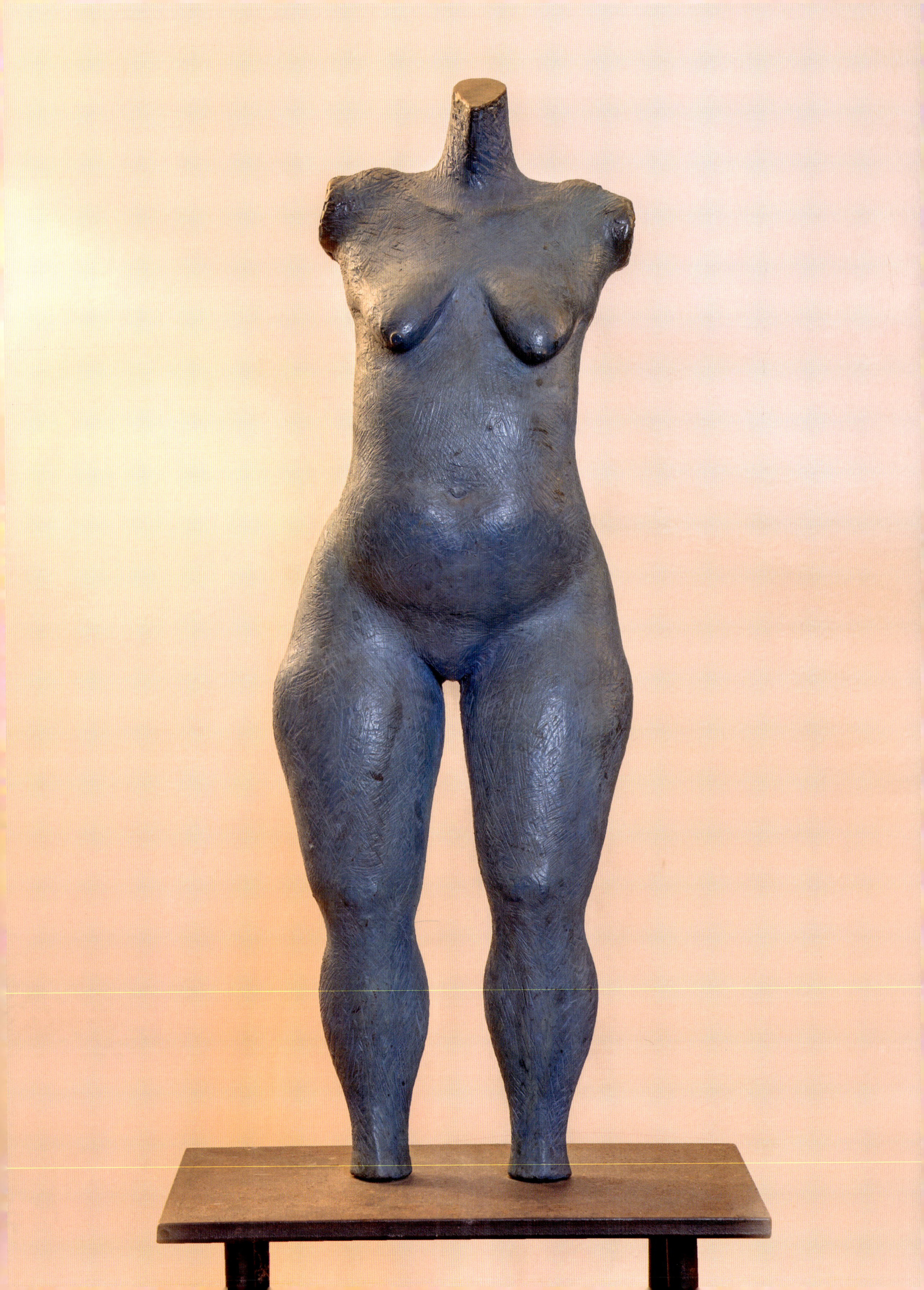

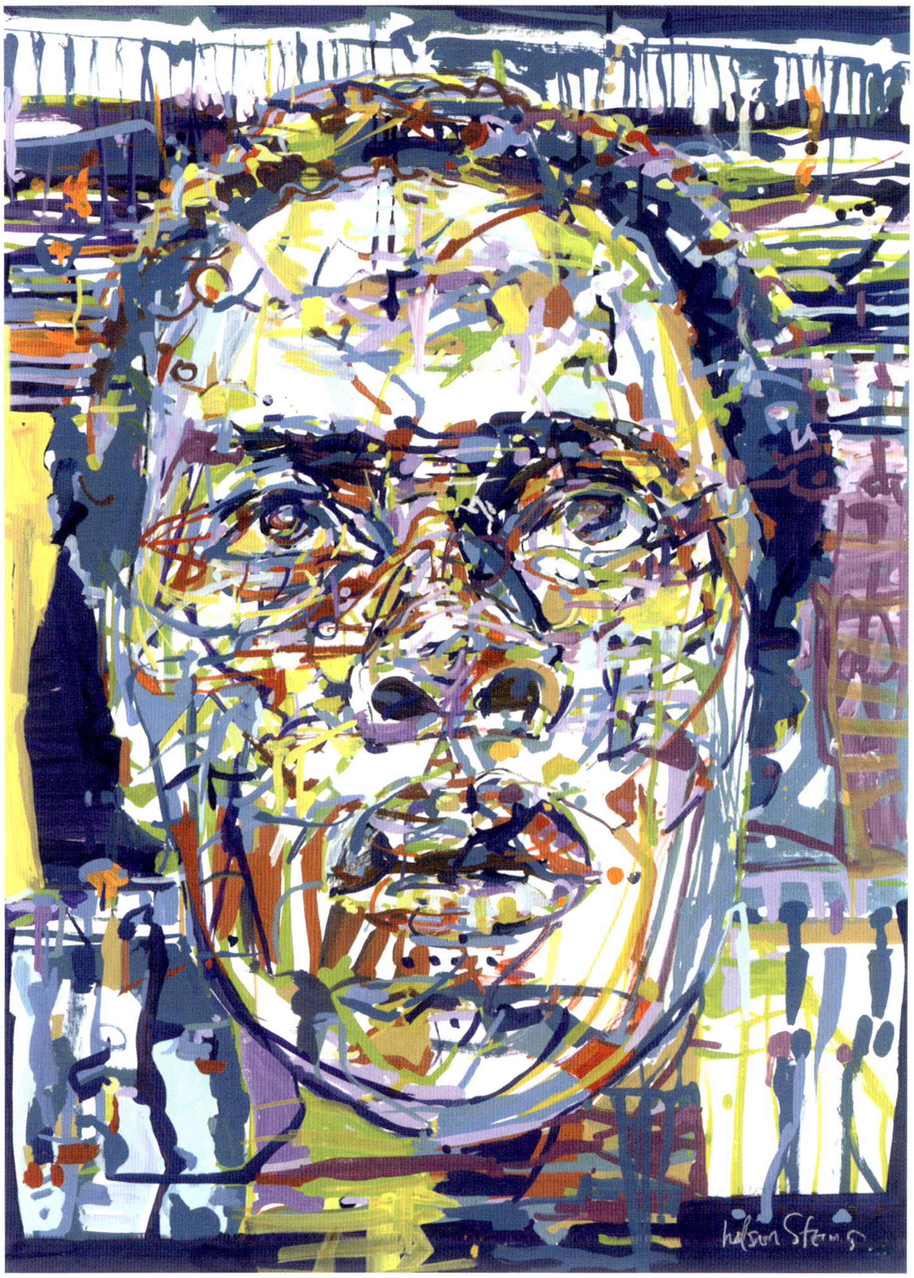

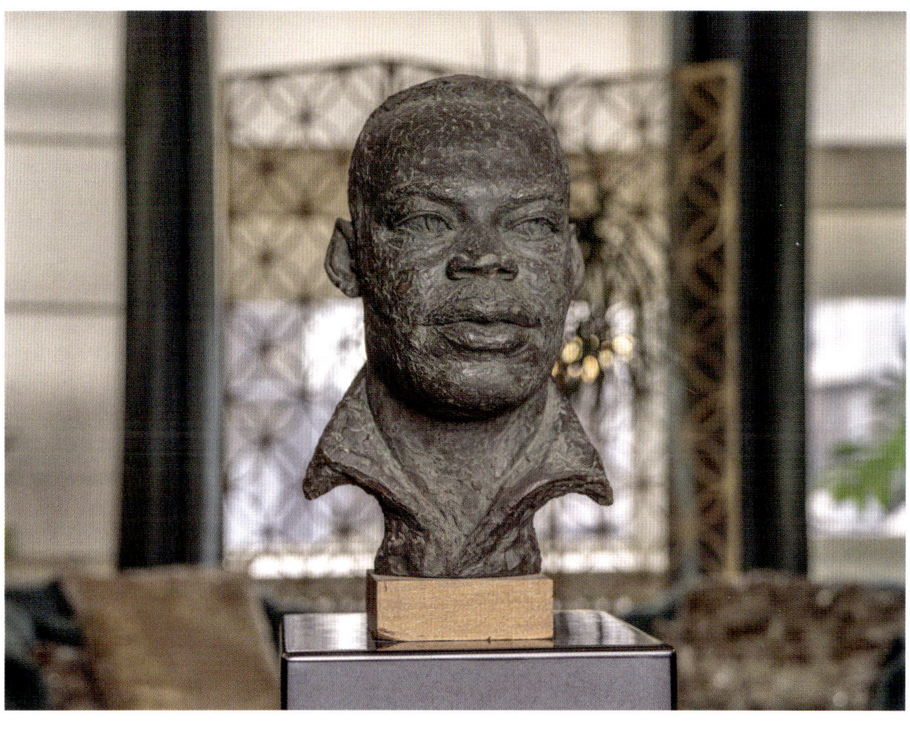

Opposite: Donald Locke, *Female Torso*, 1995. Bronze (#6 of 9), 28.5" × 10" × 10". *Photo: Ed Ryder*

Nelson Stevens, *Jessie*, 1979. Mixed media on illustration board, 40" × 30". *Photo: Courtesy of the Athenaeum of Philadelphia–Digital Imaging*

Inge Hardison, *Dr. Martin Luther King Jr.*, 1968. Clay, 17" × 10" × 10". *Photo: Ed Ryder*

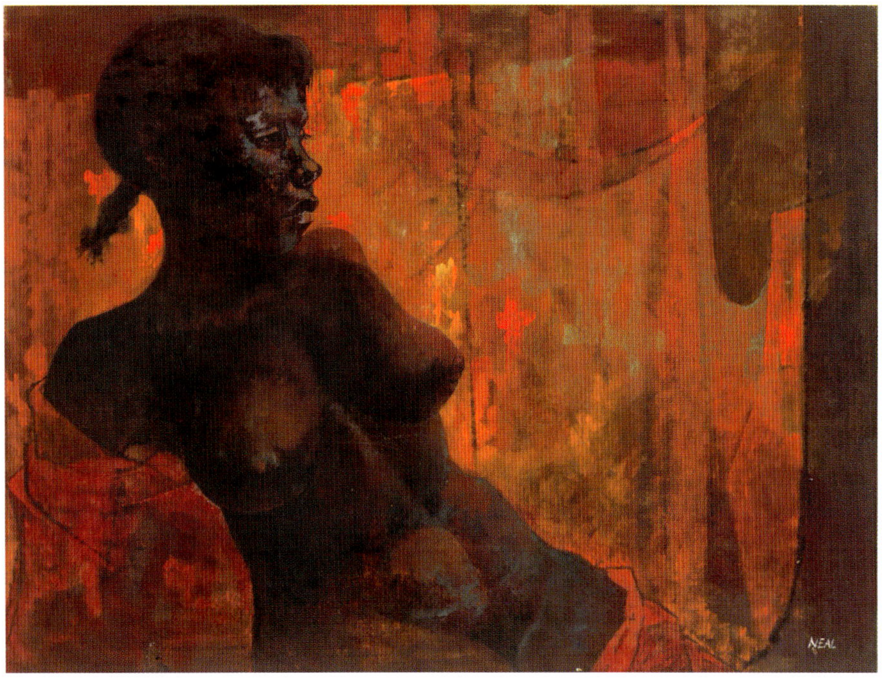

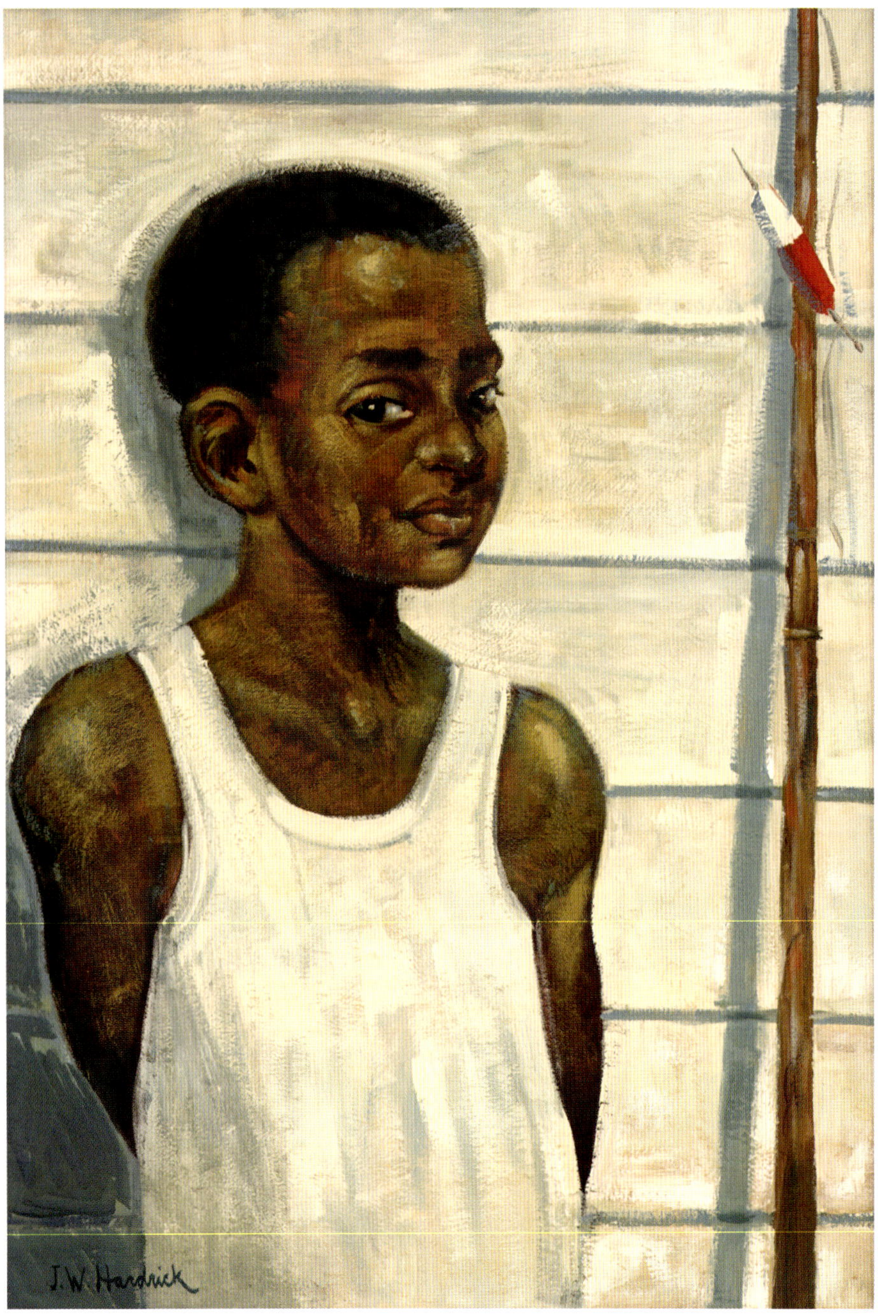

Harold Neal, *Beth Sheba*, 1961. Oil on masonite, 24" × 36". *Photo: Courtesy of the Athenaeum of Philadelphia–Digital Imaging*

John Wesley Hardrick, *A Seasoned Angler*, 1940. Oil on canvas, 30" × 20". *Photo: Courtesy of the Athenaeum of Philadelphia–Digital Imaging*

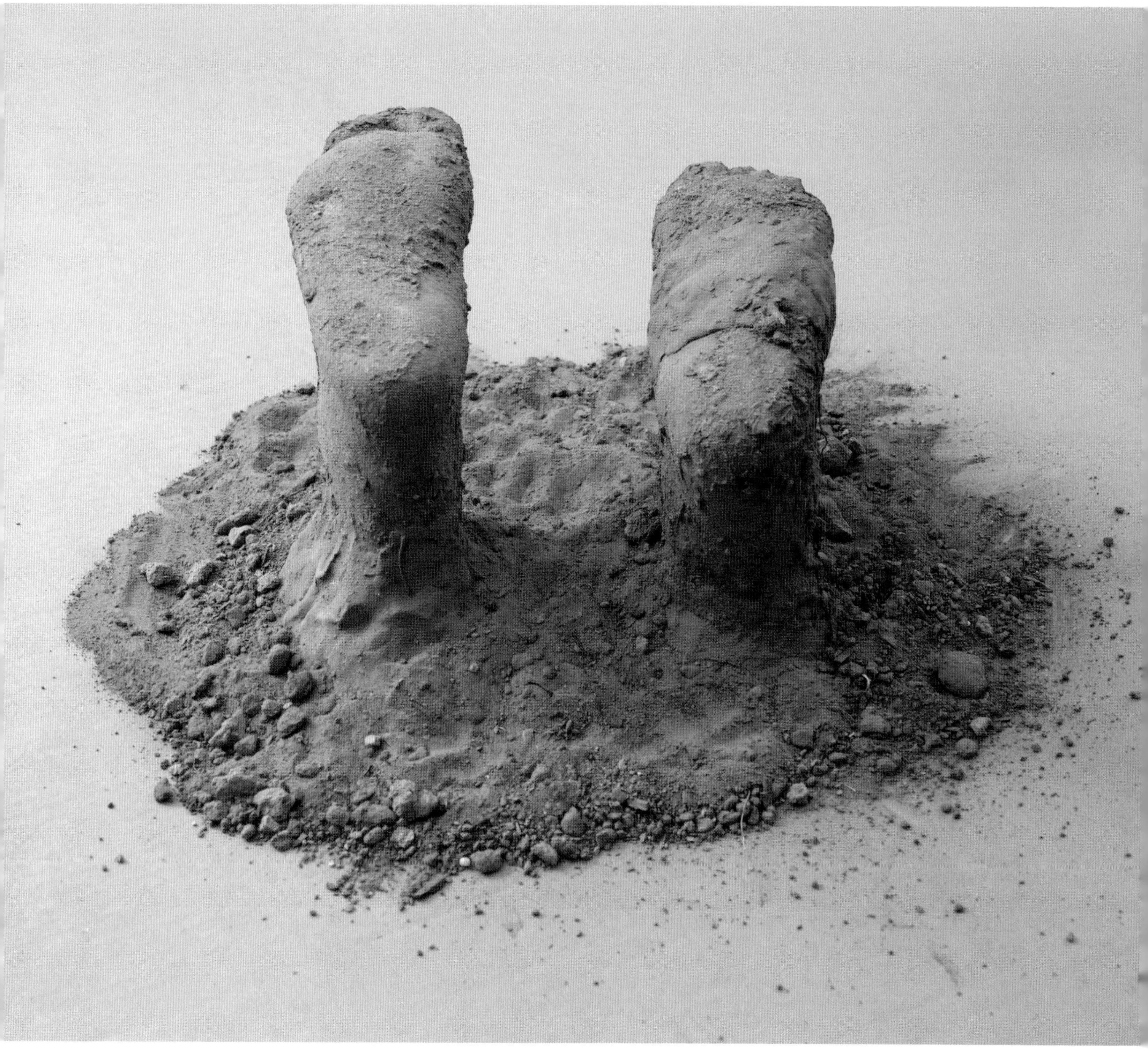

Jasmine Murrell, *The Beginning and the End*, 2011.
Mixed media; each piece is 15" × 5" × 7". *Photo: Ed Ryder*

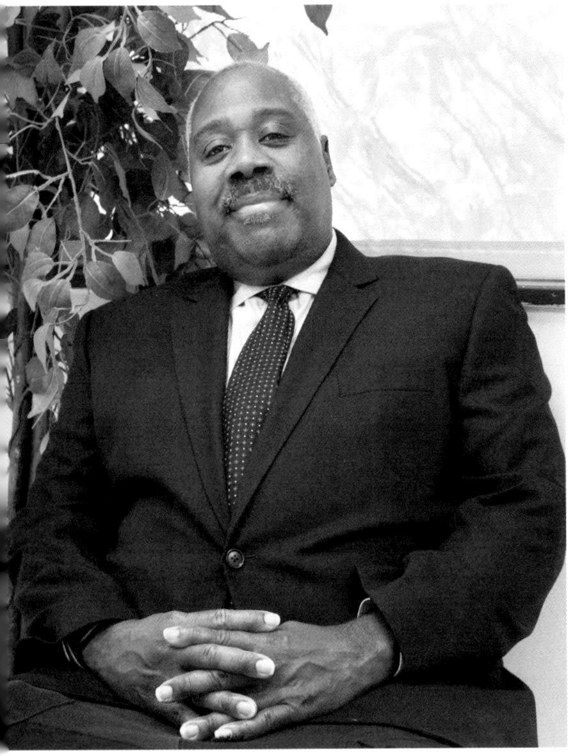

Photo: Myrah Brown Green

ANTHONY WALTERS
HAND-PULLED PRINTS

DR. MYRAH: What was the first piece of art that you collected and when?

ANTHONY WALTERS: My first serious print was a Joseph Holston etching called *Old Man* that I saw in a gallery, beautifully framed. I particularly loved the etching because, when I ran my finger around the indented paper, I loved the feel of something that was more than just a flat surface. I learned more about etchings in particular, then I gained an appreciation for other printmaking mediums, such as silkscreens, woodcuts, linoleum cuts, etc.

DR. MYRAH: Why are you a Keeper of Hand-Pulled Prints?

ANTHONY WALTERS: The support and advocacy of African American art is critically important not only to document the visual excellence of our culture, but is also a sound financial investment. As the contemporary African American art market has exploded in popularity and cost, prints are an excellent way to support the culture, support the artist, and surround oneself with the beauty of our visual griots. I say griots because in Africa, griots are local storytellers who verbalize local history, and I've always believed that our African American artists are indeed visual griots who have told our stories. Collecting original prints is not for the uninformed! To collect prints of great value, you must know the difference between silkscreens, woodcuts, linocuts, etchings, and other print mediums. These are by far the most-valuable print mediums, in my opinion. With rare exceptions, collectors should stay away from offset lithographs, most giclées, and other digitally reproduced mediums. I met the phenomenal artist Camille Billops midway through my art-collecting journey, and she really took my information level to greater heights. She told me to read as much as I could about African American artists and to also increase my knowledge about the various print mediums, as Camille herself was a very good printmaker. Several prints later, I am now honored to be included in this book, and I hope that others will begin their journey of collecting African American art at whatever financial levels they are comfortable with. Again, it is critically important that we support our culture, because if not us, no one else will.

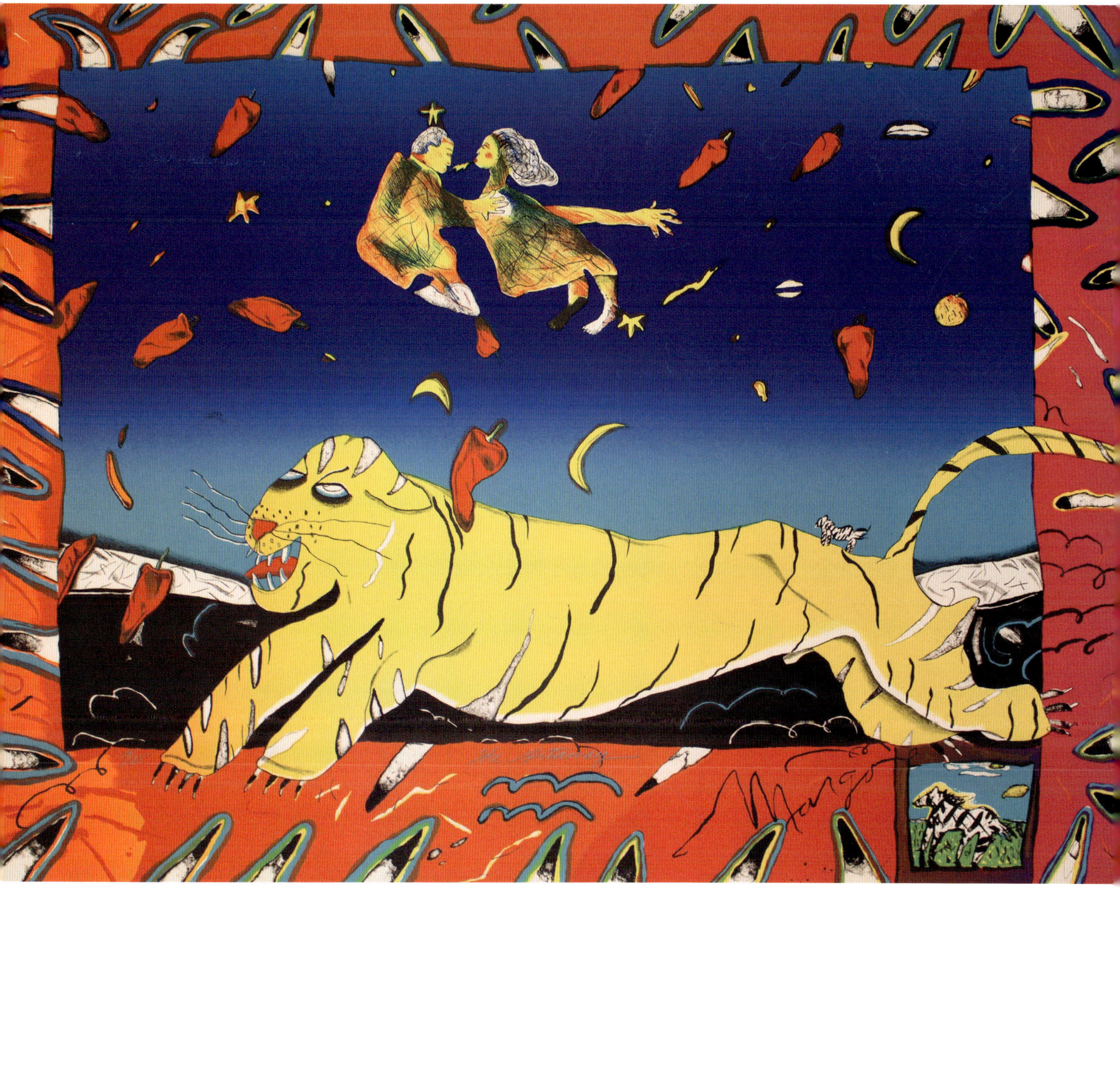

Margo Humphrey, *The Getaway*, 1977. Color lithograph, 25.5" × 30". *Photo: Myrah Brown Green*

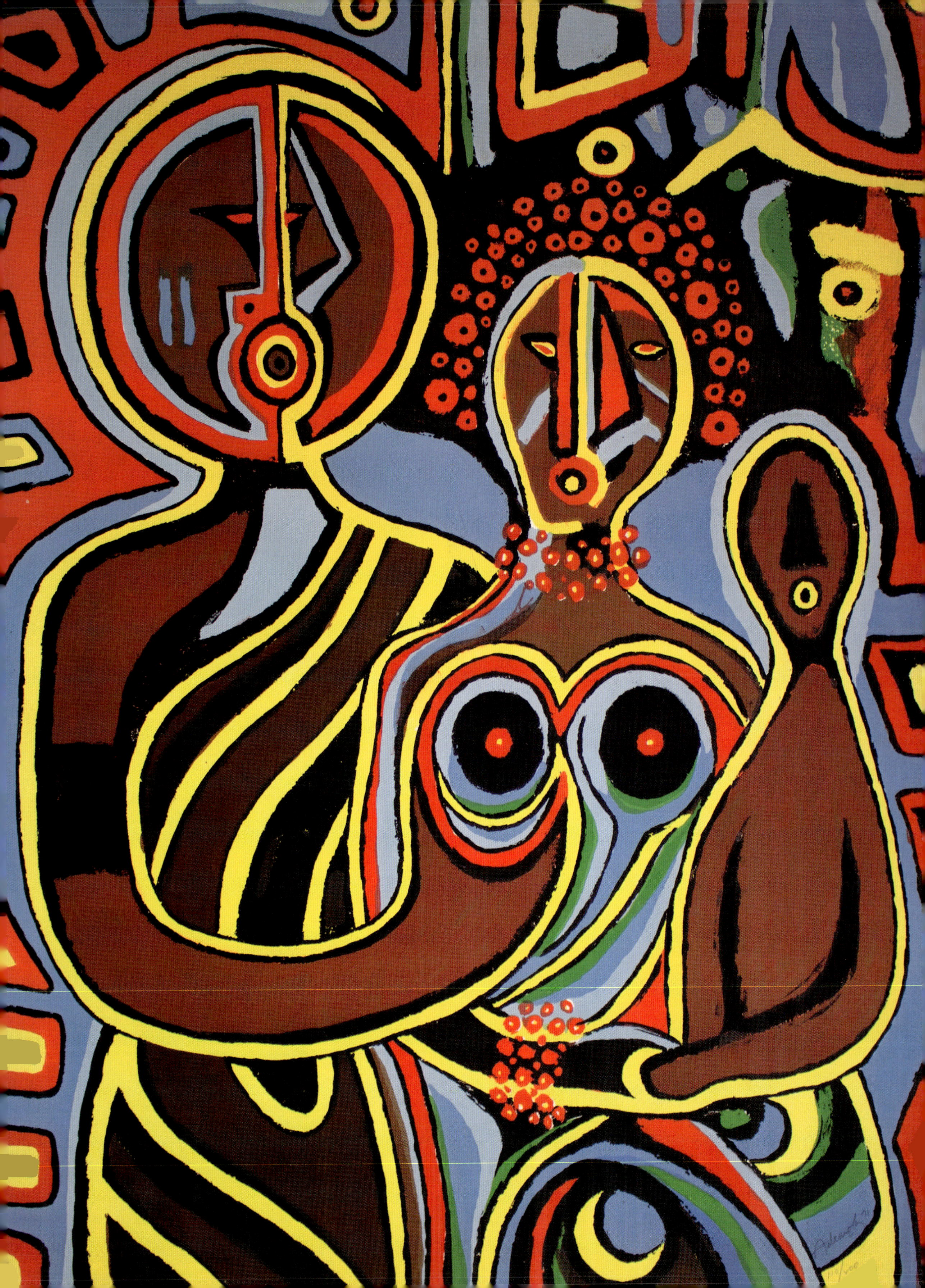

Opposite: Ademola Olugebefola, *The Family*, 1971. Silkscreen, 36" × 28". *Photo: Myrah Brown Green*

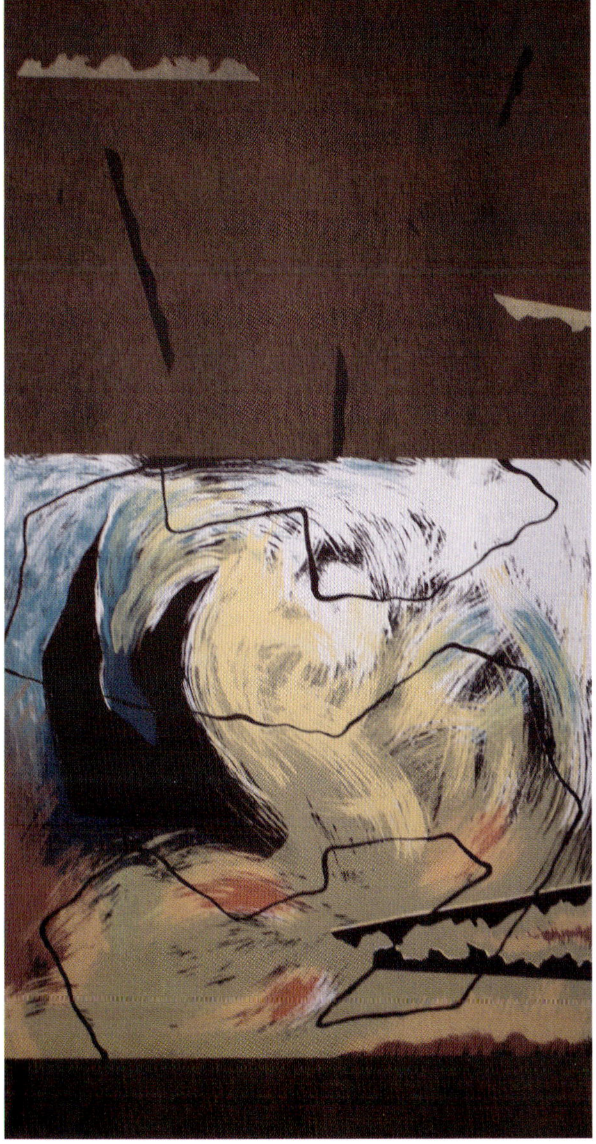

Nanette Carter, *Winter Wind*, 1992. Woodcut and lithograph, 42" × 22". *Photo: Myrah Brown Green*

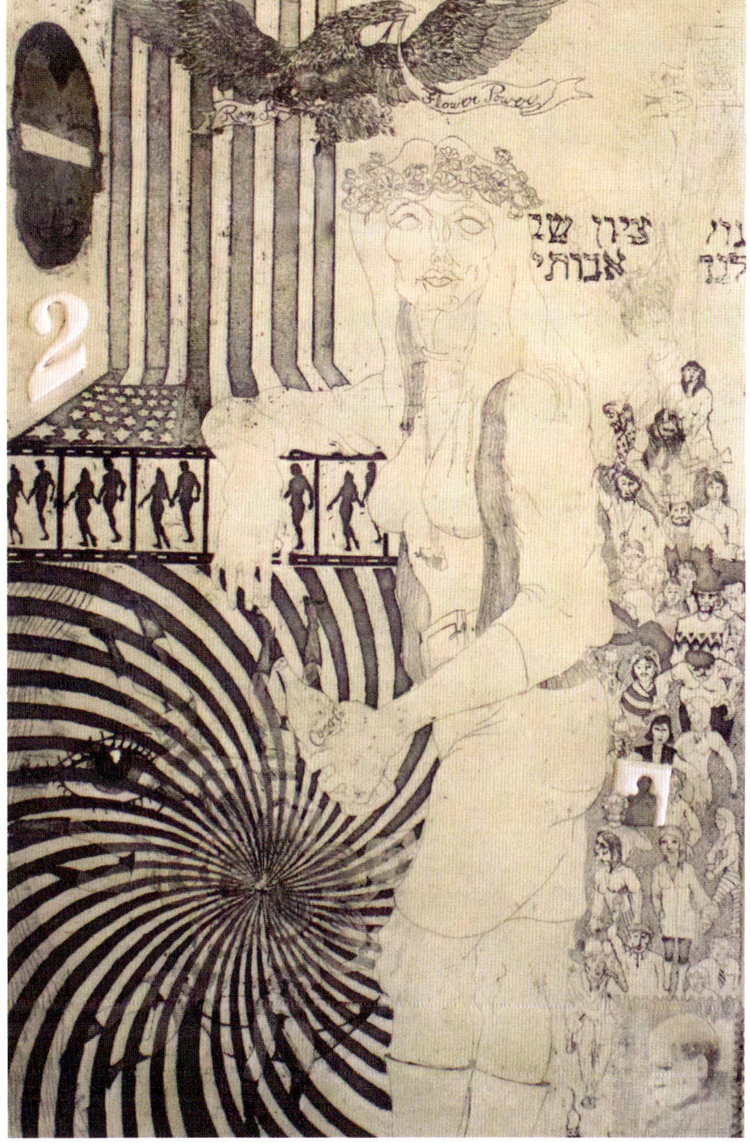

Ron Adams, *Flower Power*, 1967. Etching with intaglio, 19" × 12.5". *Photo: Myrah Brown Green*

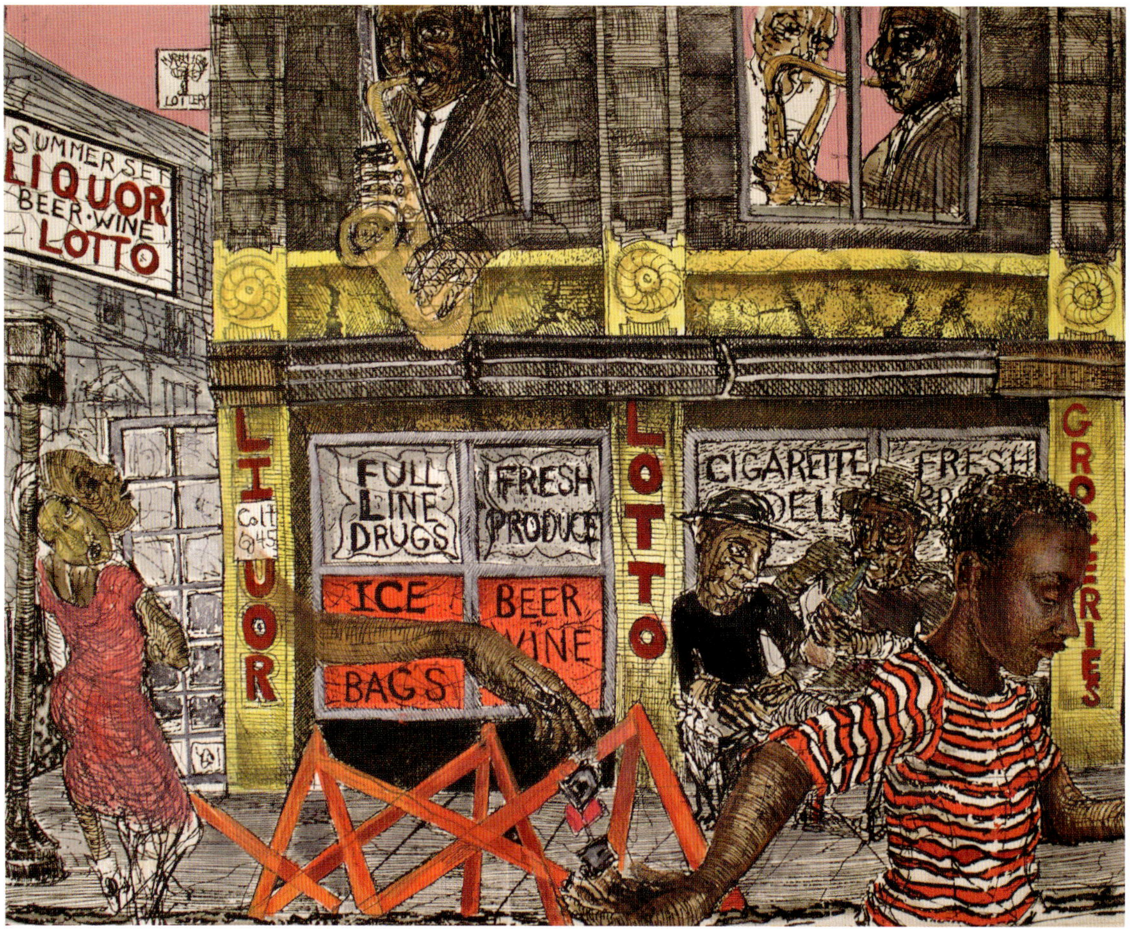

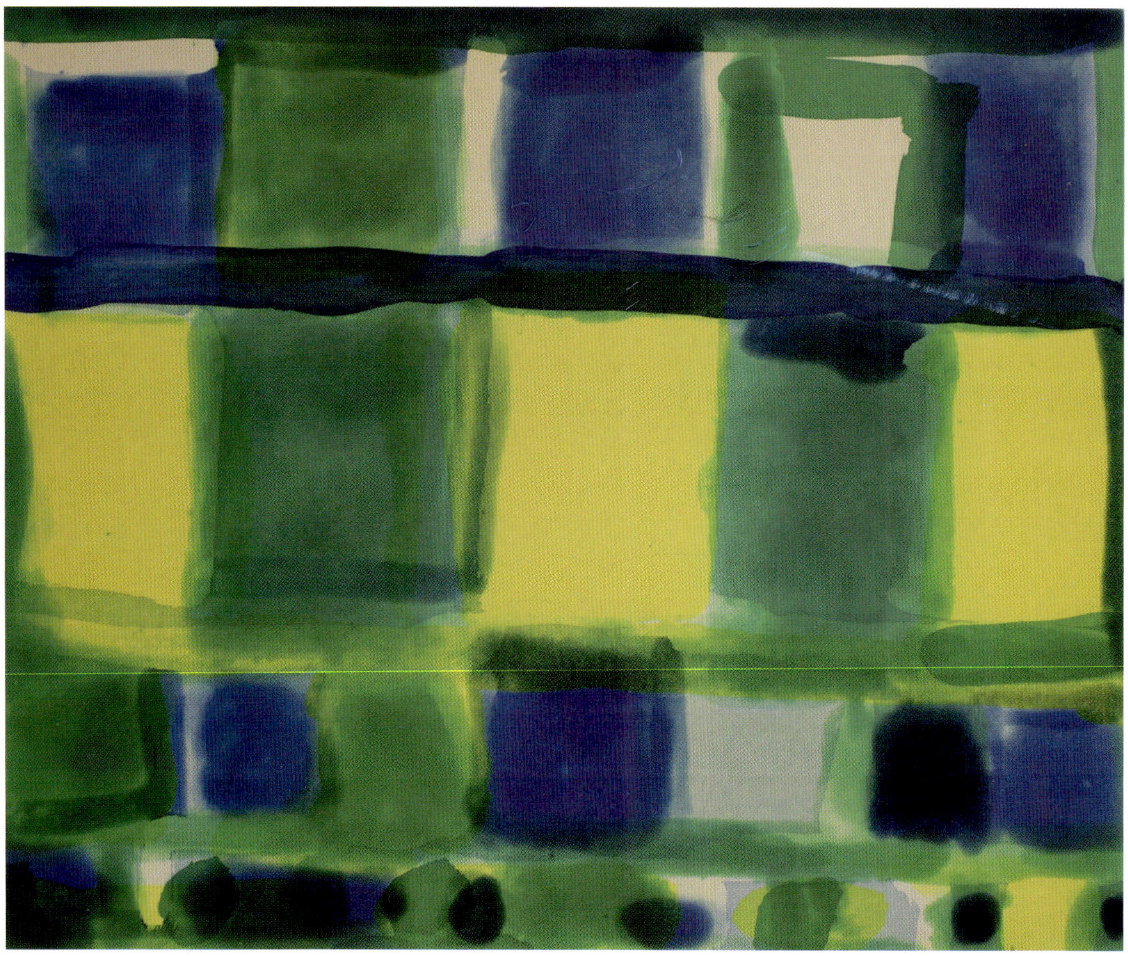

Stefanie Jackson, *A Dream Deferred*, 1994.
Color etching, 20" × 15.5". *Photo: Myrah Brown Green*

Stanley Whitney, *Yellow Changing*, 2011.
Aquatint etching, spit bit, and watercolor, 15" × 16".

Opposite: Varnette Honeywood, *Saint Sapphire* (date unknown).
Color lithograph, 26.75" × 40.5". *Photo: Myrah Brown Green*

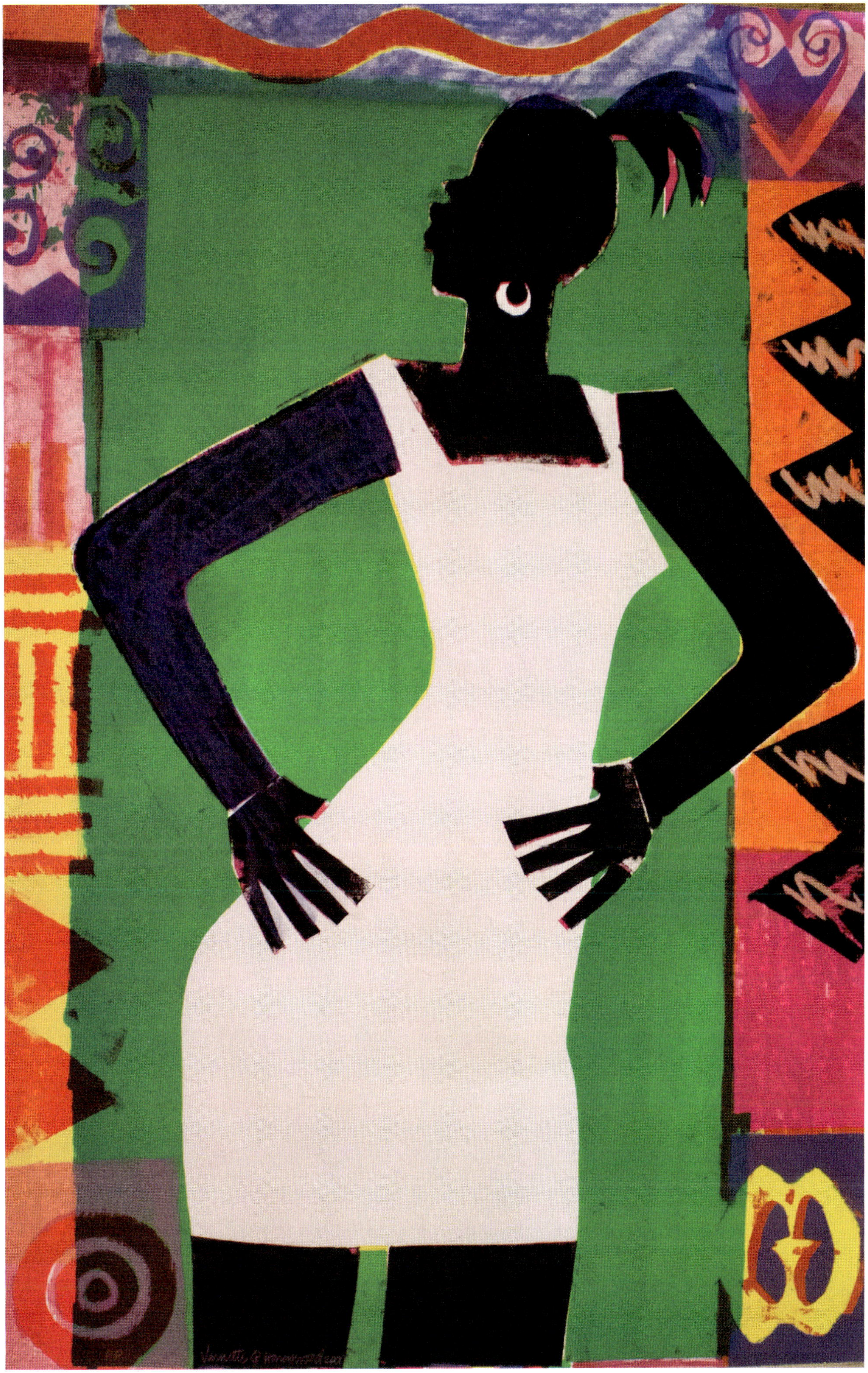

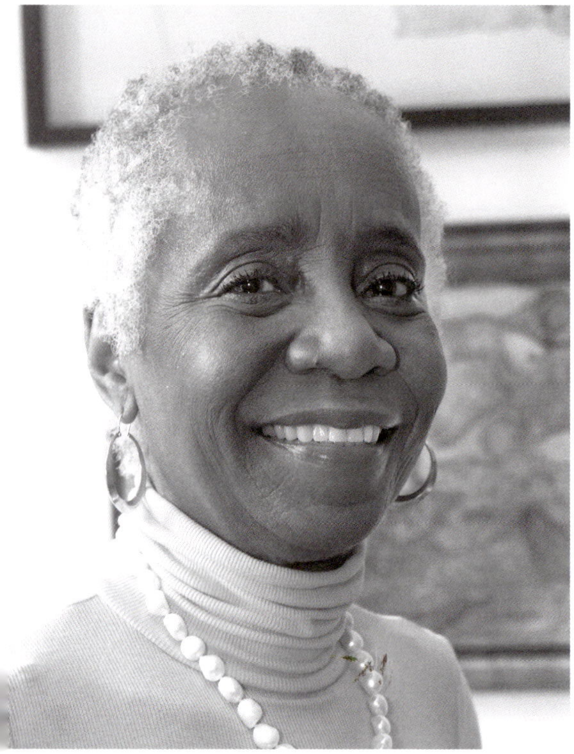

Photo: Rudolph Waterman

CHERYLE E. WILLIAMS
ABSTRACT

DR. MYRAH: What was the first piece of art that you collected and when?

CHERYLE E. WILLIAMS: The first piece of art that I collected was in Dorsey's Gallery in 1970. I was exposed to so many different artists. However, the first piece of art that I purchased was either created by Karl A. McIntosh or Otto Neals.

DR. MYRAH: Why are you a Keeper of Abstract Art?

CHERYLE E. WILLIAMS: To me, abstract art is powerful because it has no fixed definition. That's what I love about it. It allows for interpretation. It allows for emotion. A piece can make me feel happy, centered, moved—or even sad. It stirs something in me that awakens my imagination.

I remember the first abstract that truly spoke to a moment in my life: *In Total Darkness* by Ron Walton. I bought it before I was married, likely in 1978. At the time I was searching for meaning, direction, and was probably in a very dark place emotionally. That piece reflected exactly where I was, even before I had the words for it. The moment I saw it, I knew I had to have it.

One example that still stands out in my collection is a piece by James Denmark. He's known for his collage work, usually of people, places, and nature. But a very rare piece of his that I found fascinating was an abstract. When I asked what inspired it, he said, "I was just feeling good that day and wanted to do something different." That joy, that freedom, is embedded in the work. And that's what connected me to it.

Abstracts speak to my spirit. They remind me that art doesn't always need to explain itself; sometimes it just needs to be felt. And when it is, it becomes a kind of mirror. One that reflects not just the artist's journey, but my own.

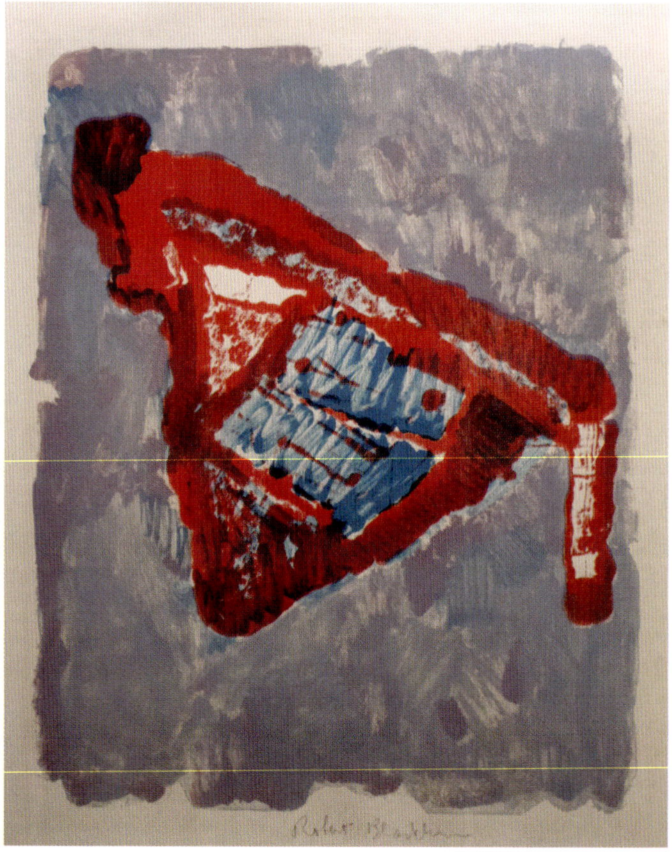

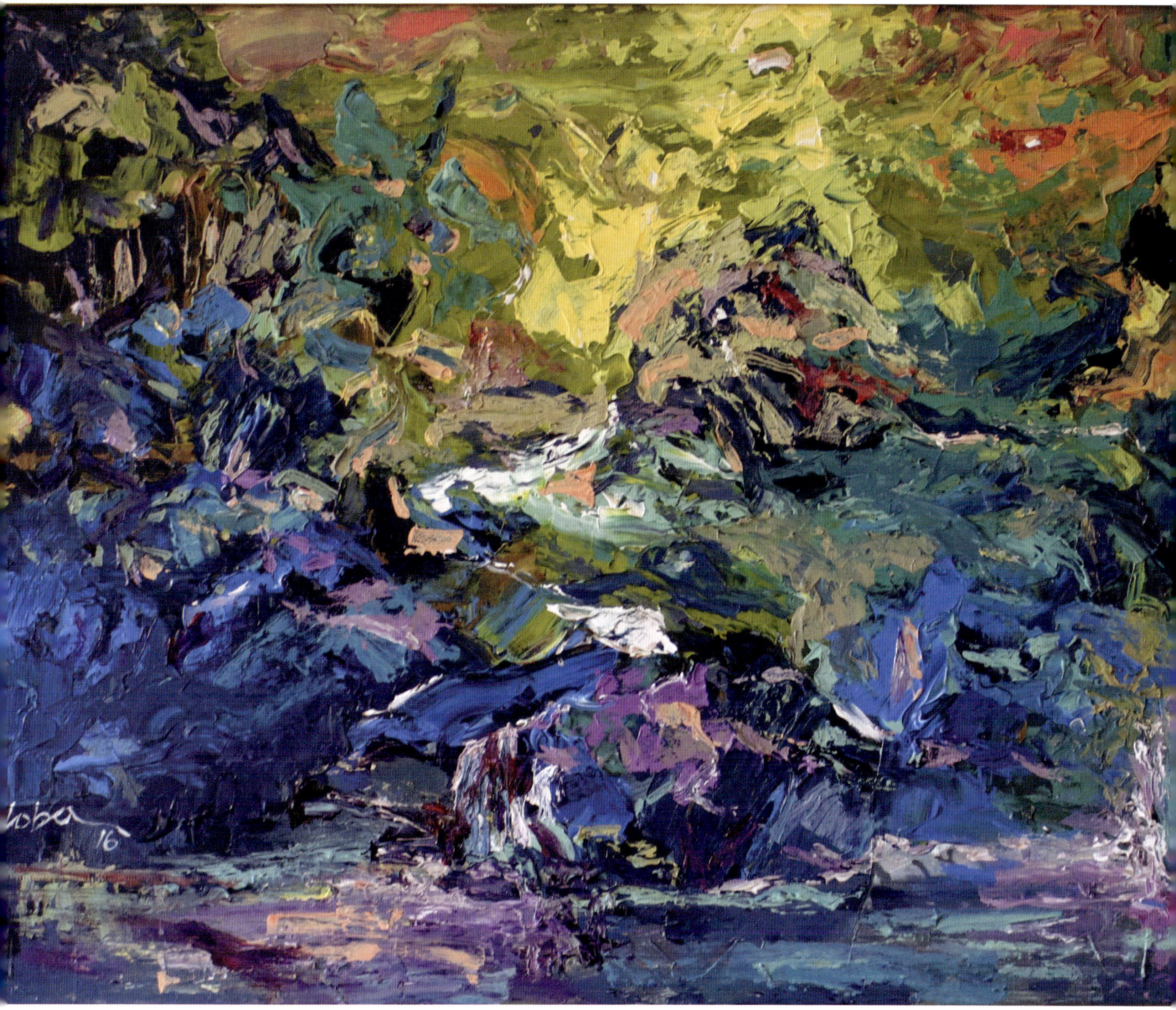

Robert Blackburn, *Untitled*, 1970. Monotype, 22.5" × 19.5". *Photo: Myrah Brown Green*

Opposite: Doba Afolabi, *Untitled*, 2016. Acrylic on canvas, 24" × 30". *Photo: Myrah Brown Green*

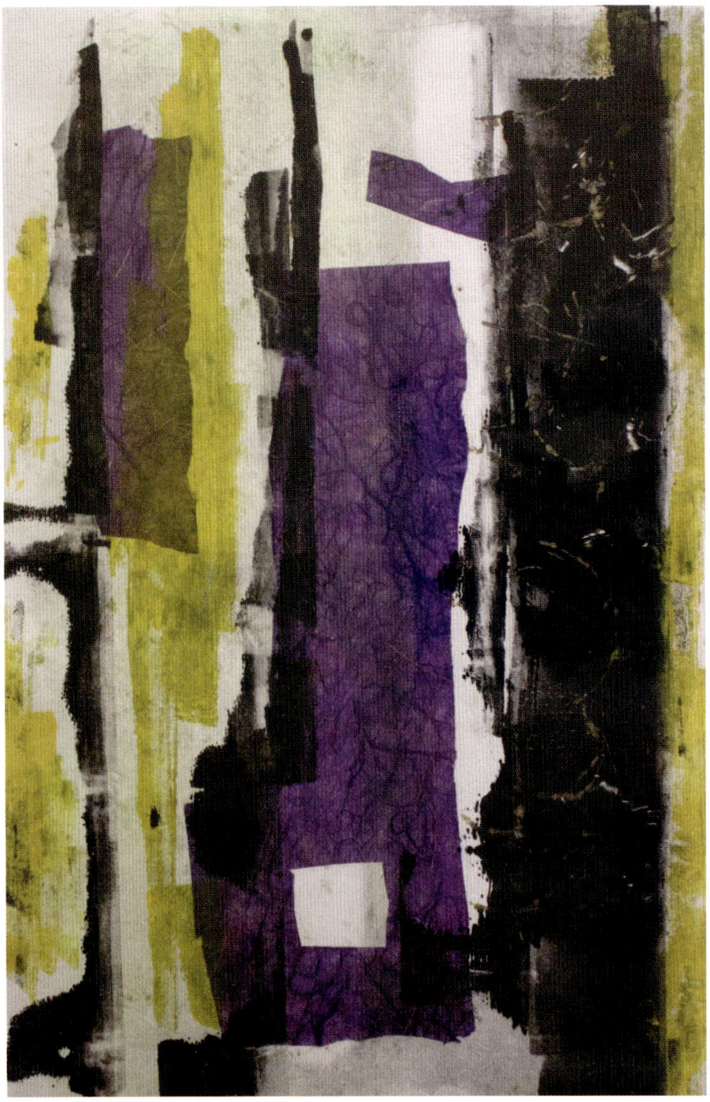

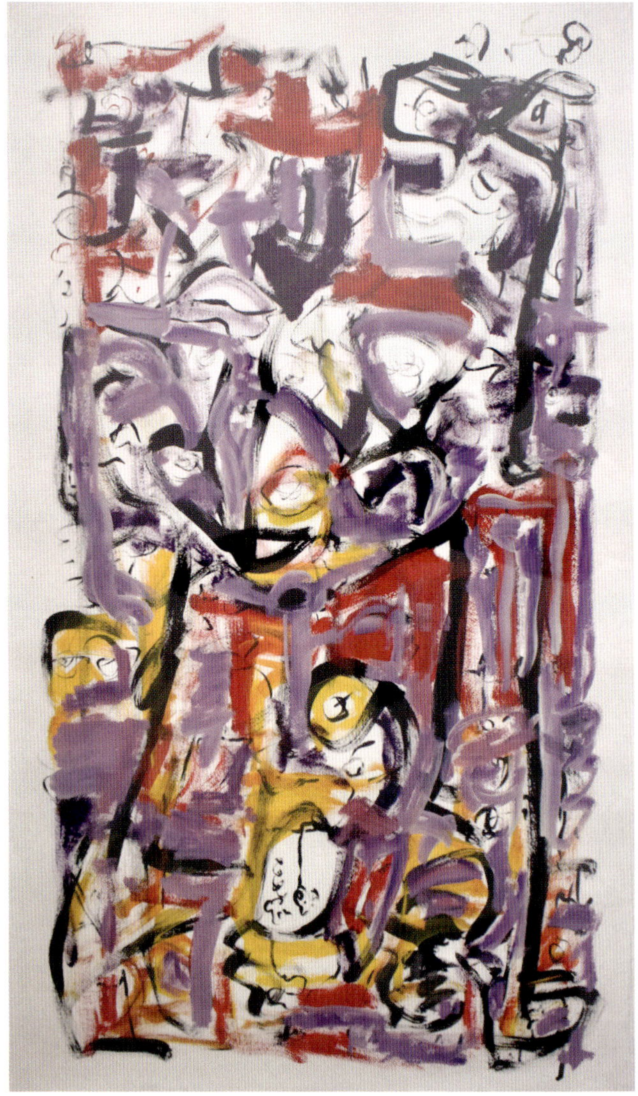

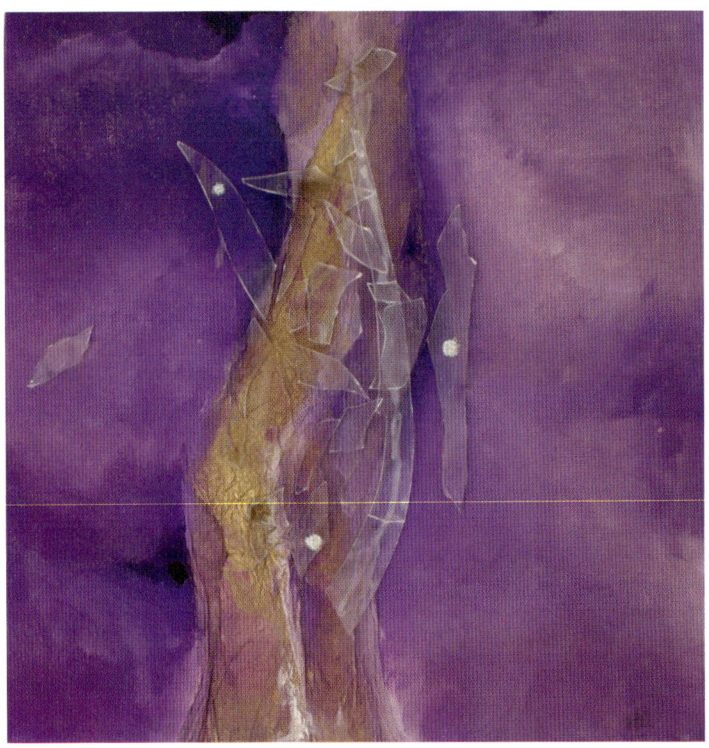

Top left: Ramona Candy, *Purple Promenade #9*, 2008. Monotype with chine collé, 16" × 11". *Photo: Myrah Brown Green*

Top right: Claude Lawrence, *Untitled*, 2014. Acrylic on paper, 47" × 27". *Photo: Myrah Brown Green*

Heather Williams, *Broken Glass II*, 2019. Mixed media, 12" × 12". *Photo: Myrah Brown Green*

Opposite: Ronald Walton, *In Total Darkness*, 1978. Oil on canvas, 38" × 24". *Photo: Myrah Brown Green*

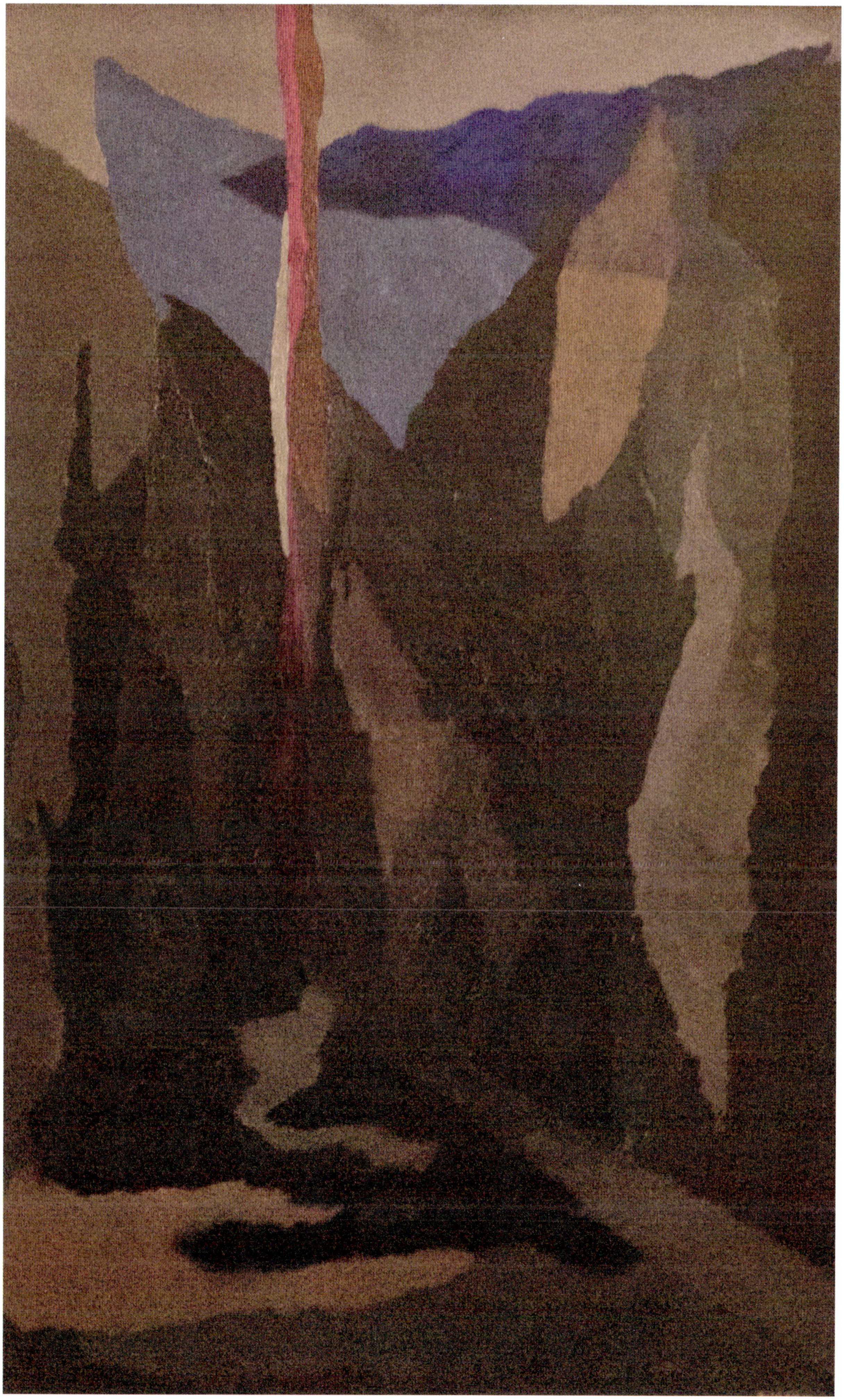

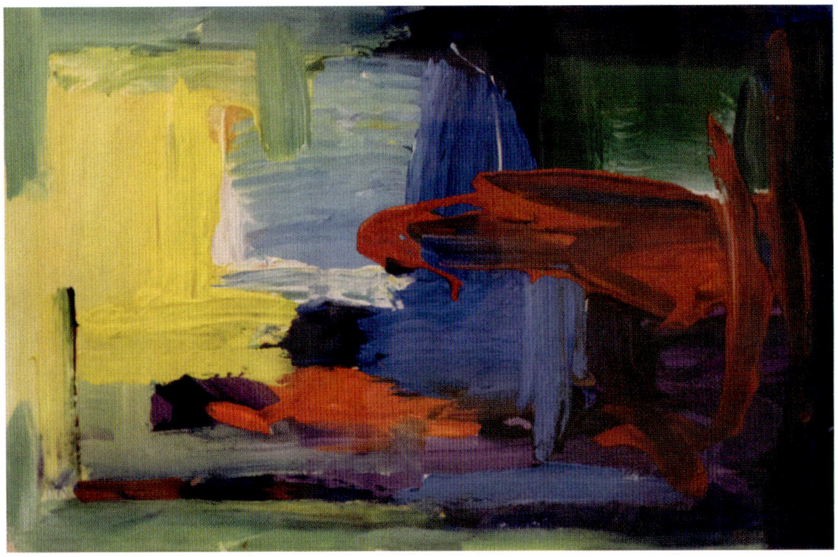

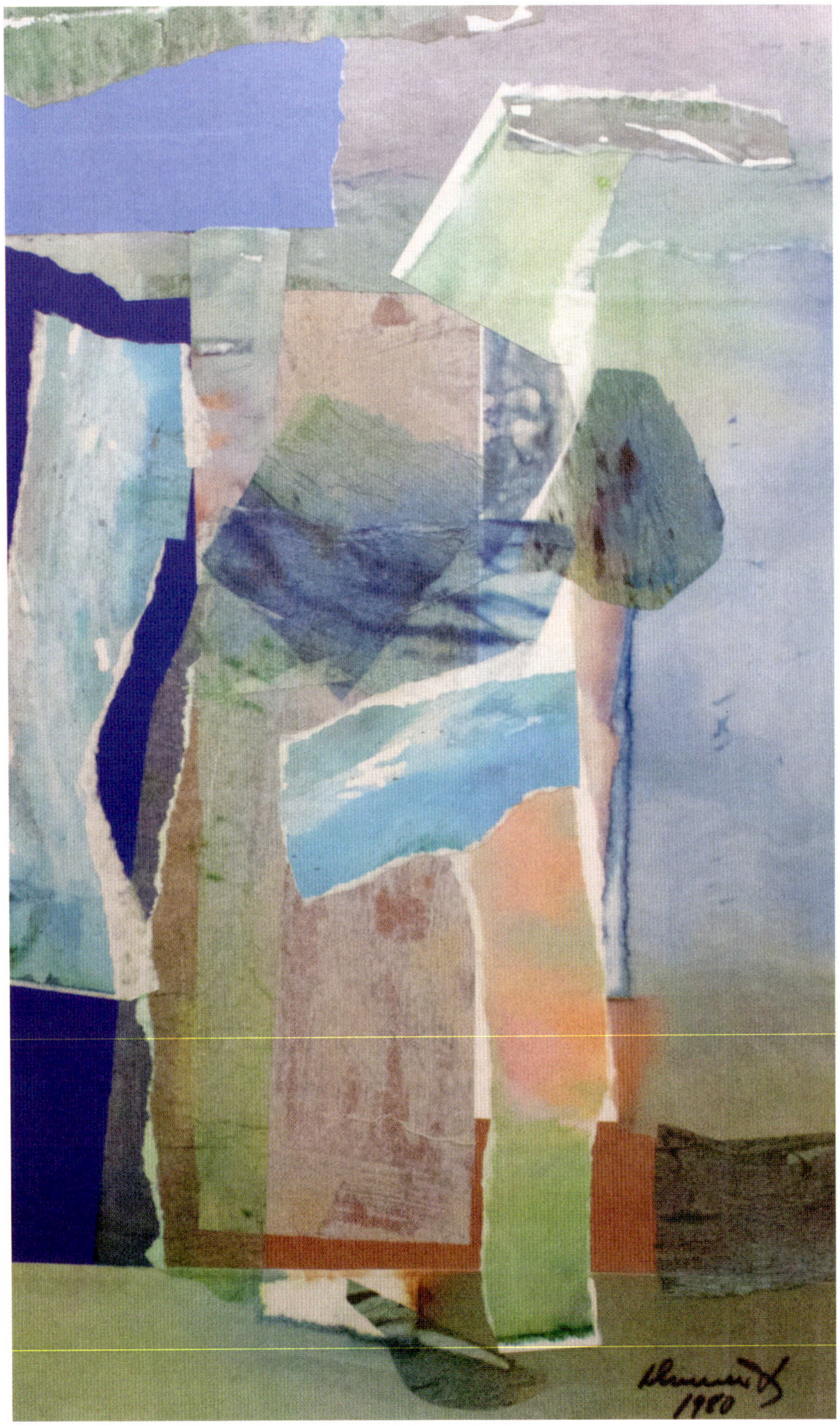

Donovan Nelson, *New Birth 21*, 2013. Acrylic on paper, 12" × 18". *Photo: Myrah Brown Green*

James Denmark, *Untitled*, 1980. Collage, 30.5" × 19". *Photo: Myrah Brown Green*

Opposite, top: Clive Tucker, *Untitled*, 1970. Oil on canvas. 32" × 28". *Photo: Myrah Brown Green*

Opposite, bottom: Gina Sampson, *Untitled*, 2016. Acrylic on canvas, 10" × 14". *Photo: Myrah Brown Green*

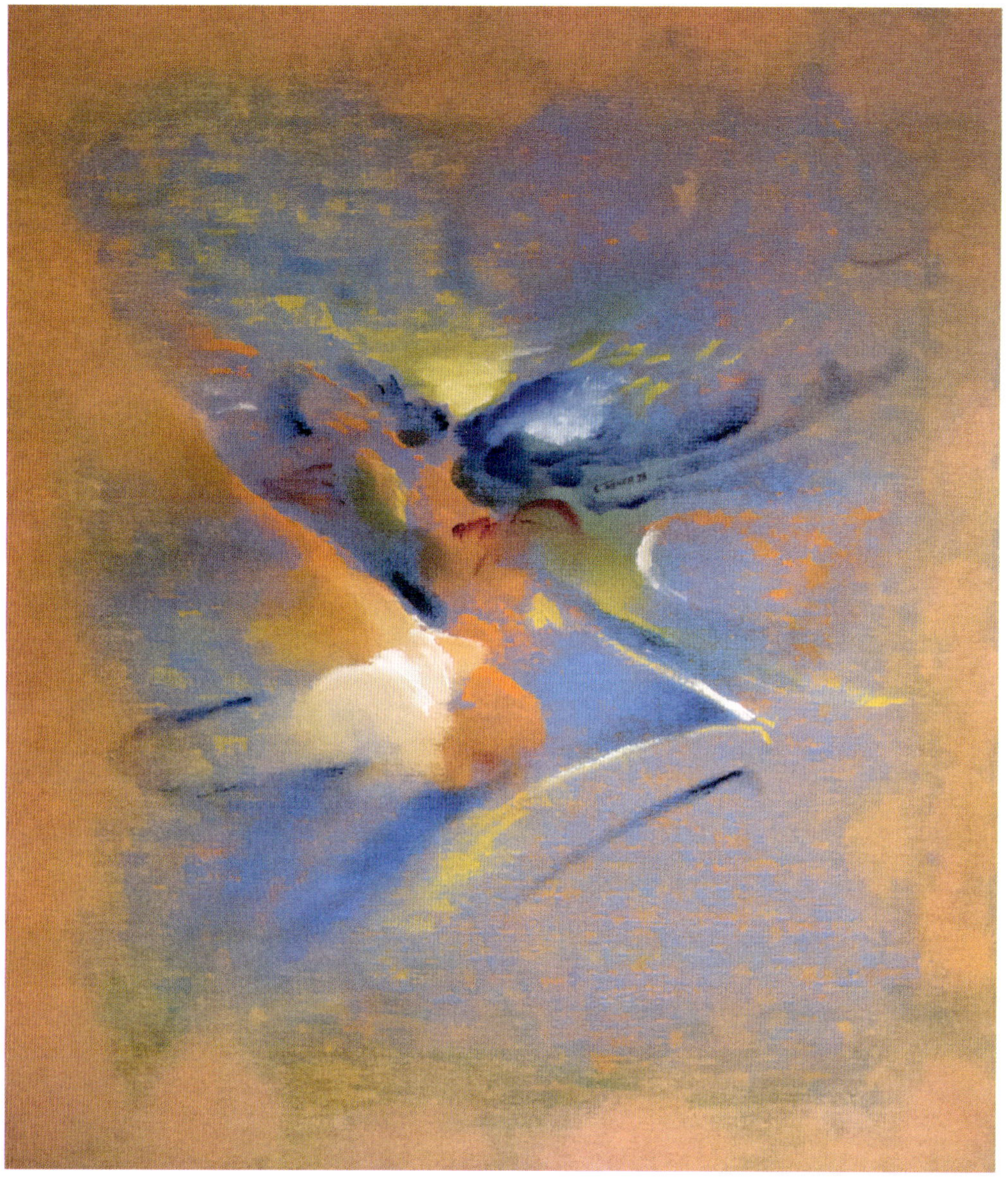

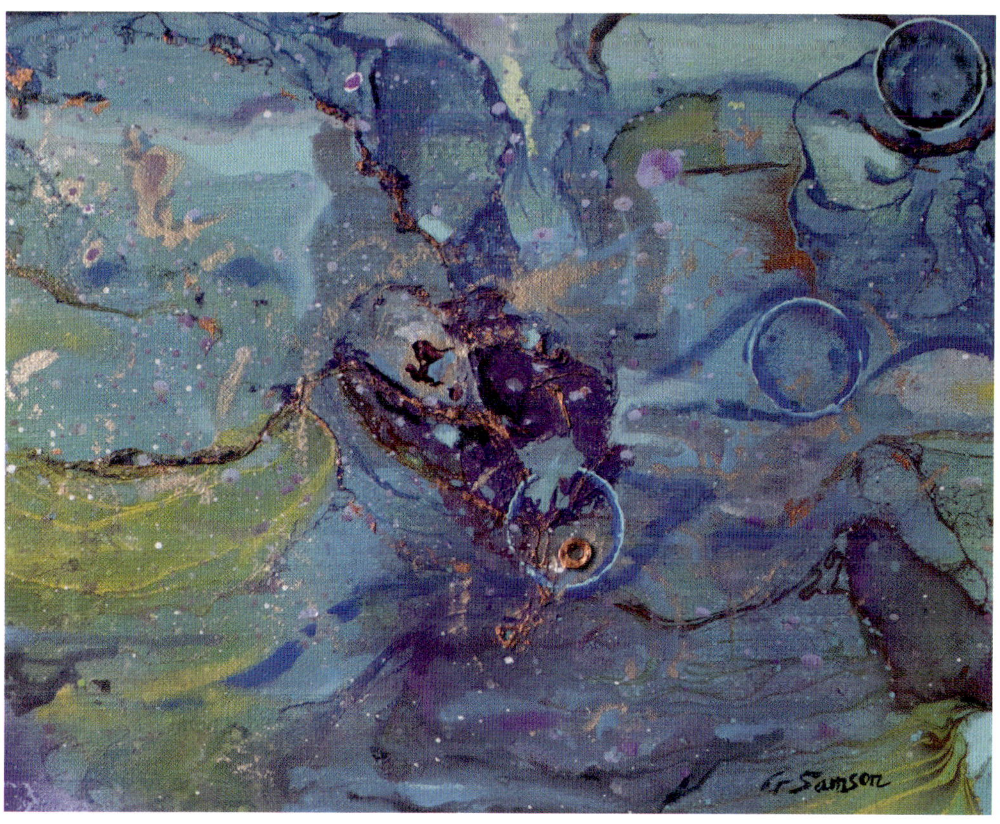

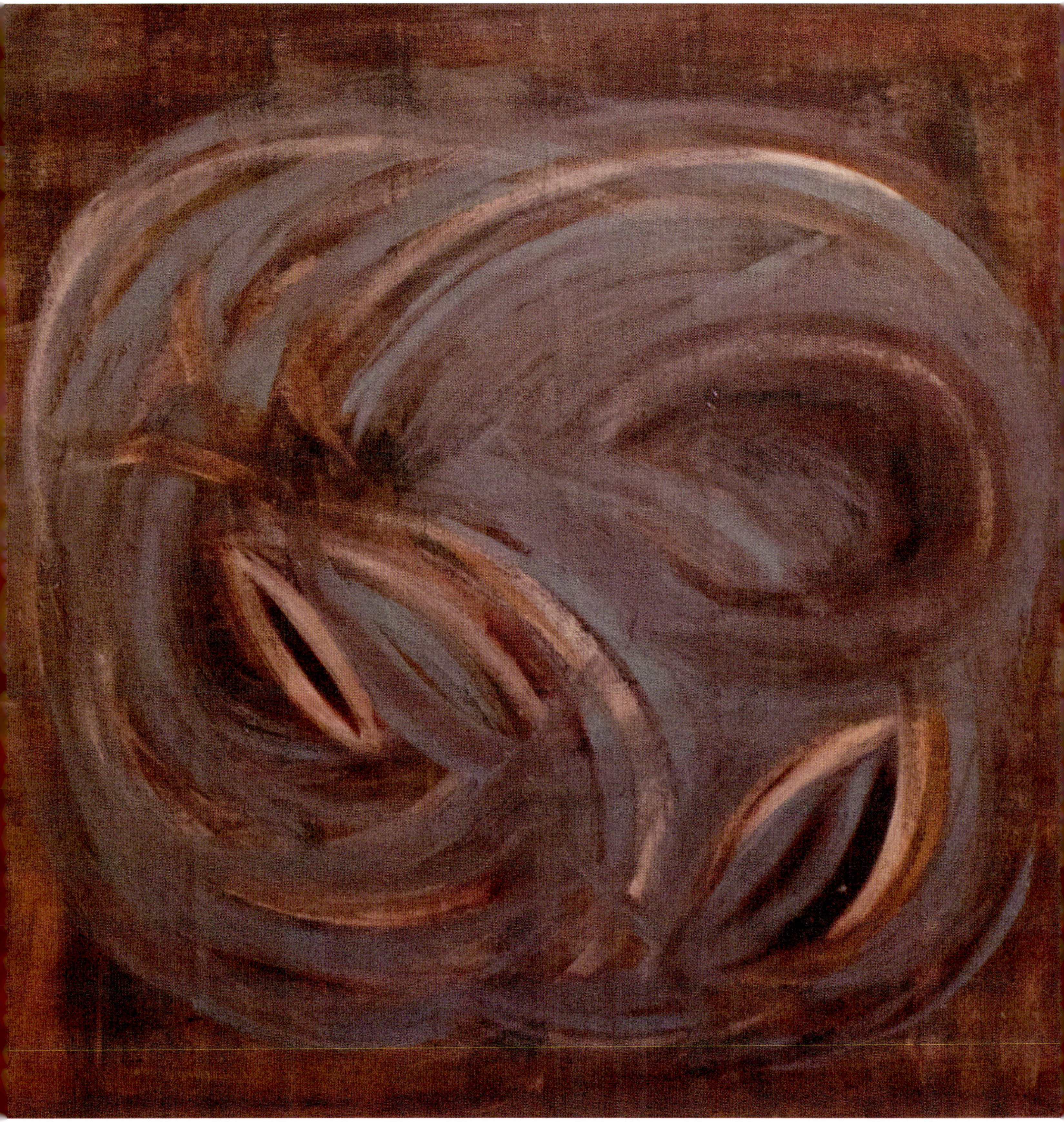

Above: Willie Mae Brown, *Dozing: If Your Mama Calls, Tell Her I am Sleep* (year unknown). Acrylic, 36" × 36". *Photo: Myrah Brown Green*

Karl A. McIntosh, *Untitled*, 1972. Oil on canvas, 16" × 22". *Photo: Myrah Brown Green*

Nia Mason, *Untitled*, 1978. Etching, 19.5" × 16". *Photo: Myrah Brown Green*

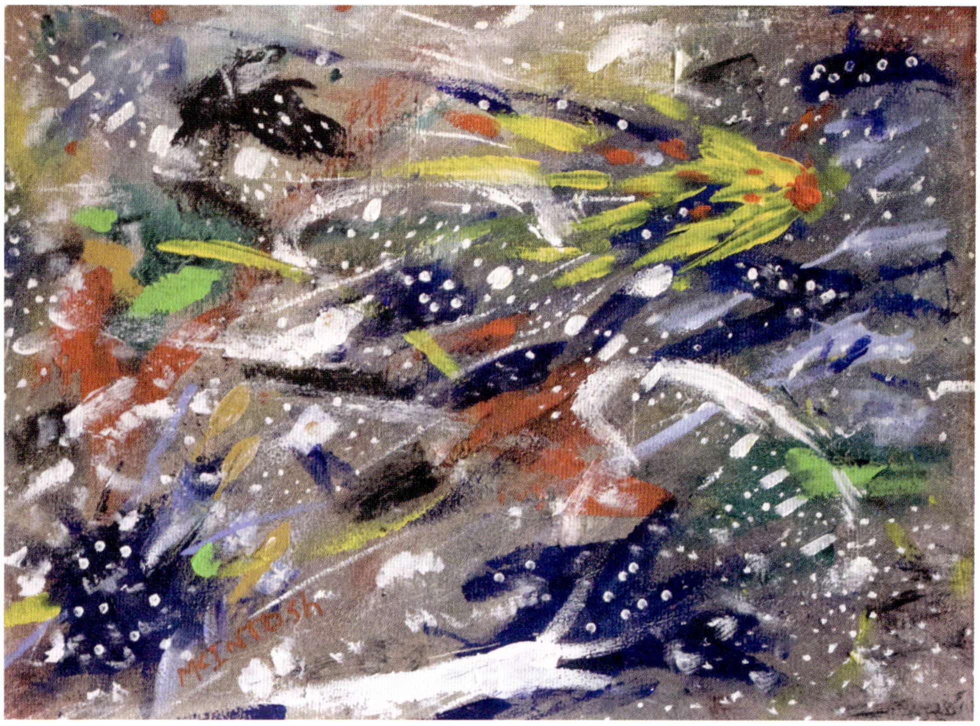

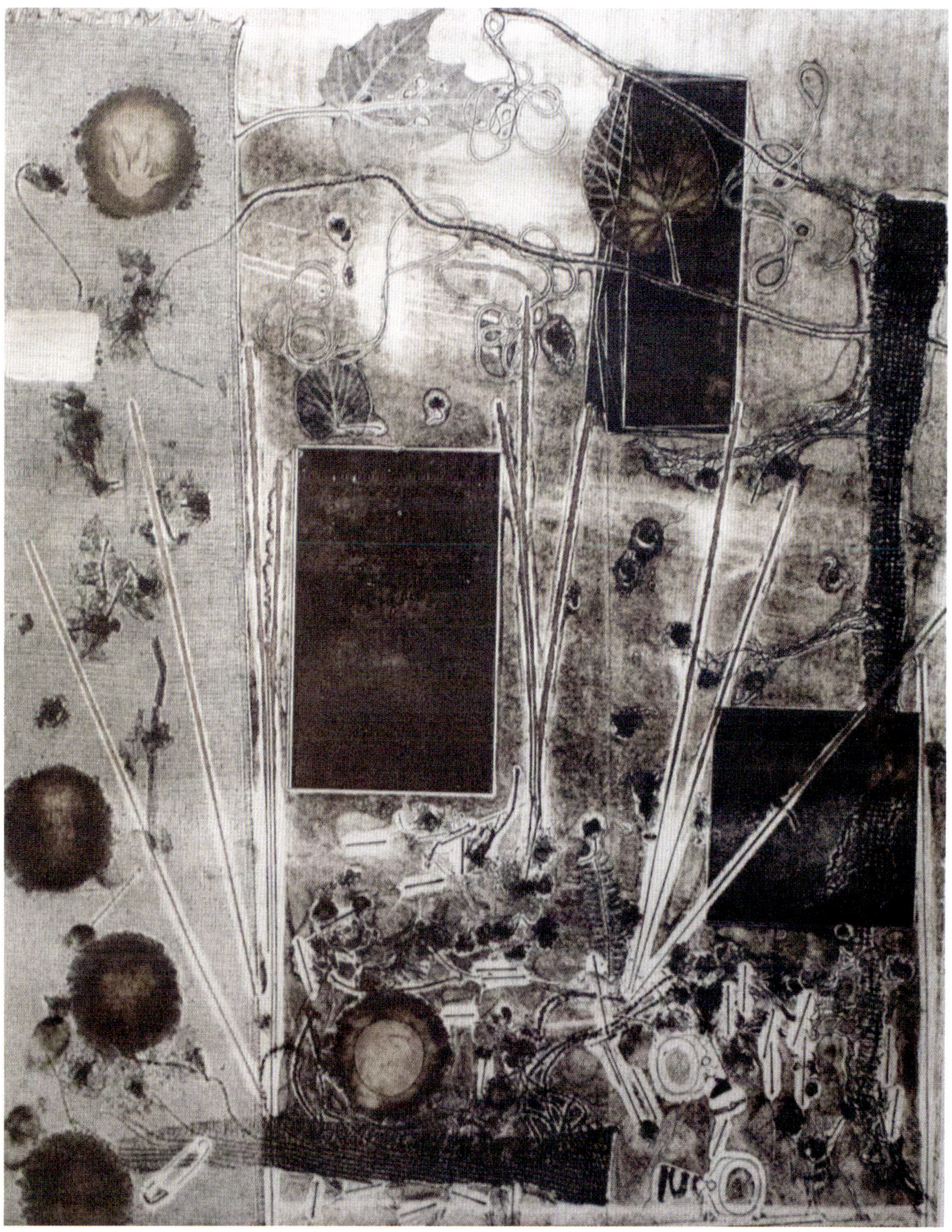

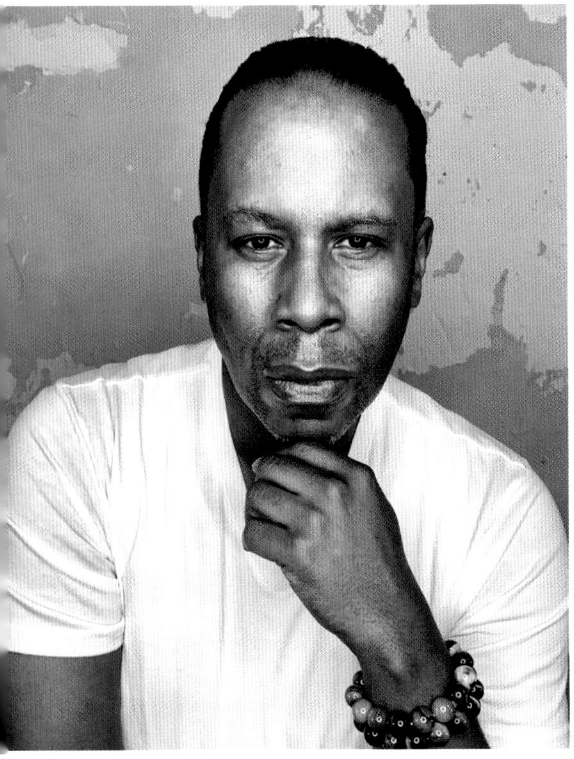

Photo: Deme Brown

ULYSSES WILLIAMS
STORIES IN PROCESS

DR. MYRAH: What was the first piece of art that you ever collected and when?

ULYSSES WILLIAMS: The first piece of art I ever collected was while in college. I went to a small fair with a group of friends. Small-business owners had rented tables and were selling their products. I came across this artist table and was captivated by their colorful African-inspired paintings. For some reason I just had to have one. I purchased this 8" × 10" flat canvas painting depicting three Black female figures dancing. The movement and vibrancy of the piece immediately resonated with me, giving me a joyous diaspora feeling. It wasn't just an artwork; it was a reflection of culture, celebration, and connection. Something about the movement, the energy, and the celebration of Black womanhood spoke to me. That piece marked the beginning of my journey as a collector, shaping how I appreciate and connect with art today.

Unknowingly, I guess that moment marked the beginning of my journey as a collector, shaping how I engage with art that tells stories, evokes deep emotions, and speaks to traditions of Black people.

I eventually gave that piece of art to a friend as a gift. I believe that art is a perfect gift no matter how big or small.

DR. MYRAH: Why are you a Keeper of art that is about Stories in Process?

ULYSSES WILLIAMS: As a Keeper of art that embodies Stories in Process, I see art as a living, evolving dialogue—never static, always unfolding. My mother was not necessarily a collector, but she liked nice things. She was a resident family photographer throughout many years. She loved having a camera in hand and taking snapshots. She chronicled the process of her family in physical growth, celebration, and so much more.

My role as a Keeper of art is an extension of my mother's interest in photography. I'm not just a collector, but a steward of artists' narratives that I relate to. Artists have this innate ability to put experience and expectations on canvas, collage, within sculpture, and photography in the written word that is legacy building. As a people, our stories are still being written, whether through artists' creative journeys or the conversations their work sparks. Art isn't just about the finished piece; it's about the histories, cultures, and personal experiences woven into it. By championing these works, I ensure that their stories are true and just, while supporting continued growth within their artistic process. I collect works that resonate and inspire new perspectives.

Michael Obele, *Fefekondoh* (Boundaries and Connections), 2021. Charcoal and graphite pencil on paper, 22" × 18". *Photo: Myrah Brown Green*

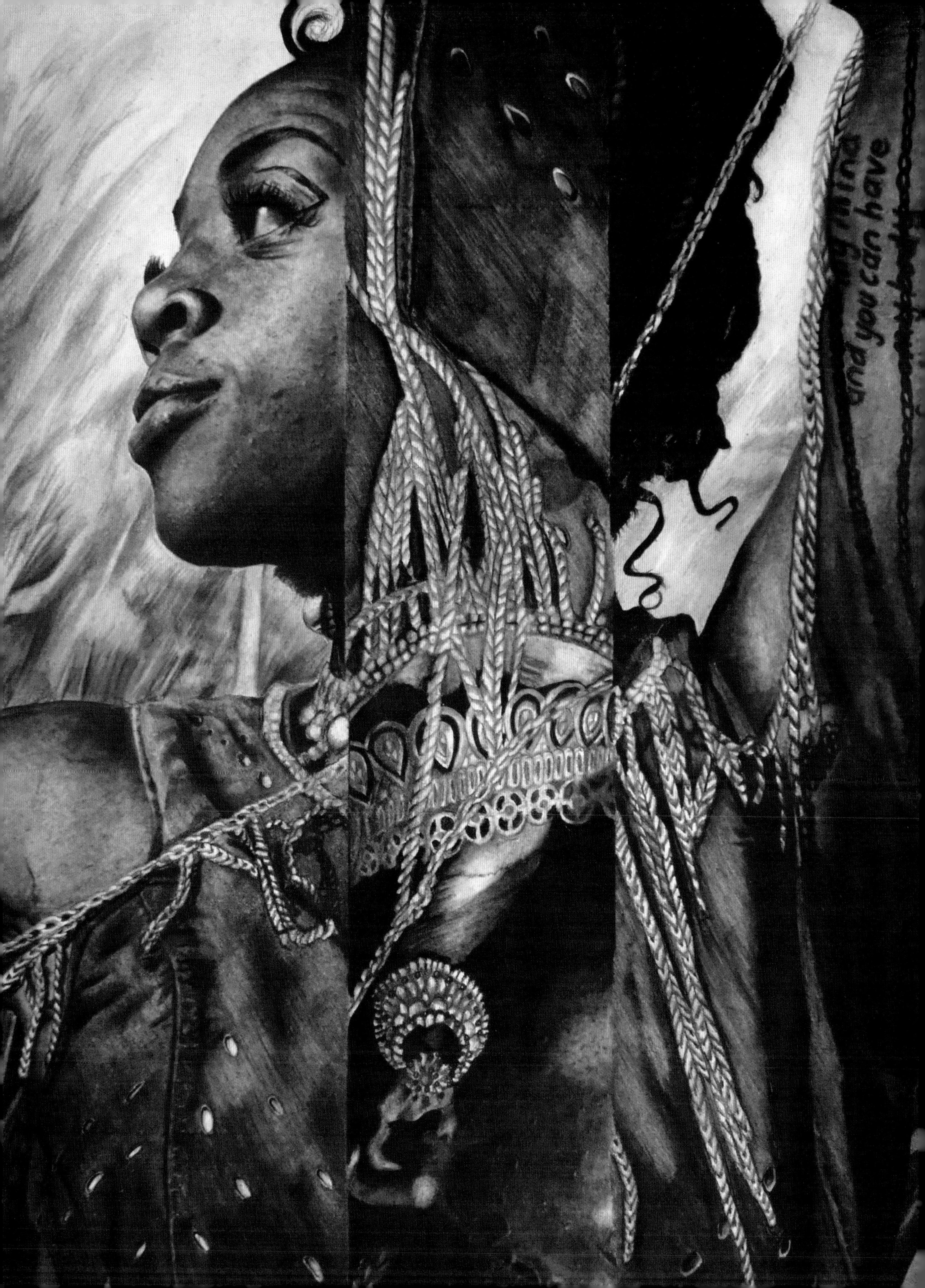

mind
and you can have

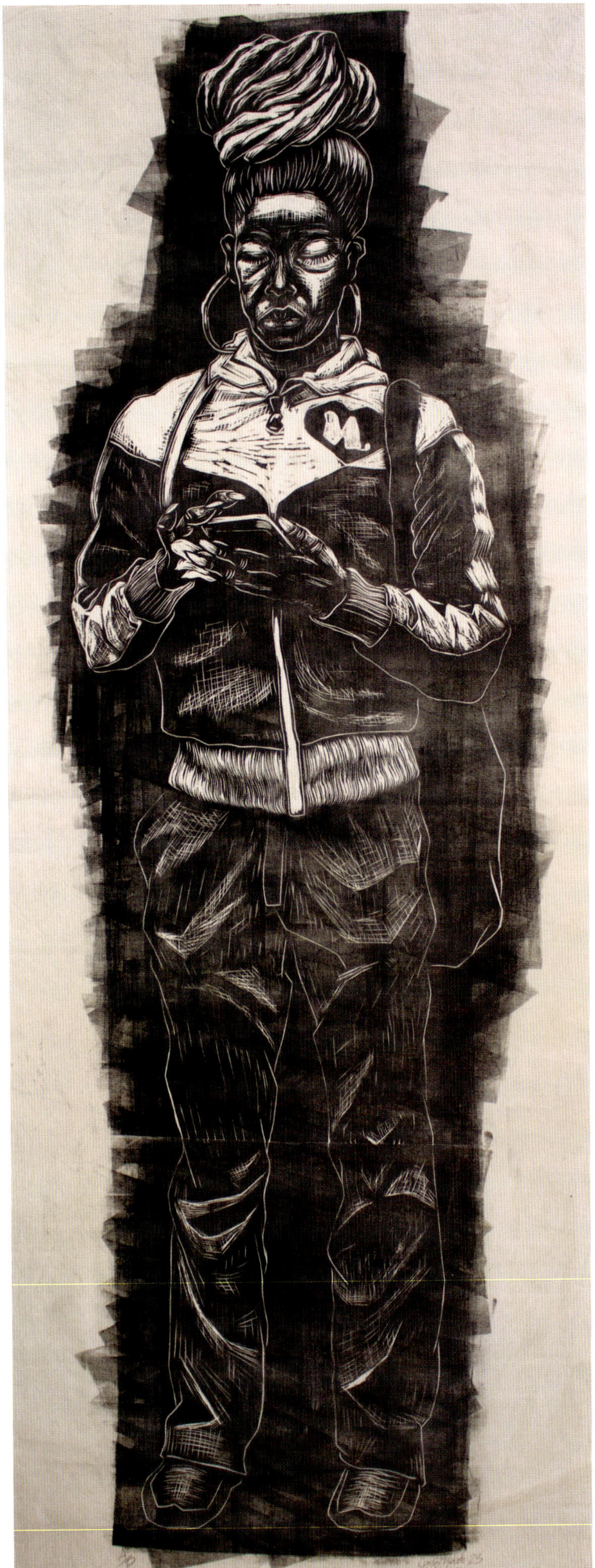

Left: Carlos Llobet Montealegre, *Untitled*, 2023. Relief print on textile, 70.5" × 29.5". *Photo: Myrah Brown Green*

Lakeem Wilson, *Listen, Learn and Observe* (year unknown). Ink on paper, 8.5" × 11" *Photo: Myrah Brown Green*

Jonte Drew, *Man and Lamb*, 2021. 3-D-printed sculpture in black, 12.5" × 7" (man) and 8" × 8.5" (lamb). *Photo: Myrah Brown Green*

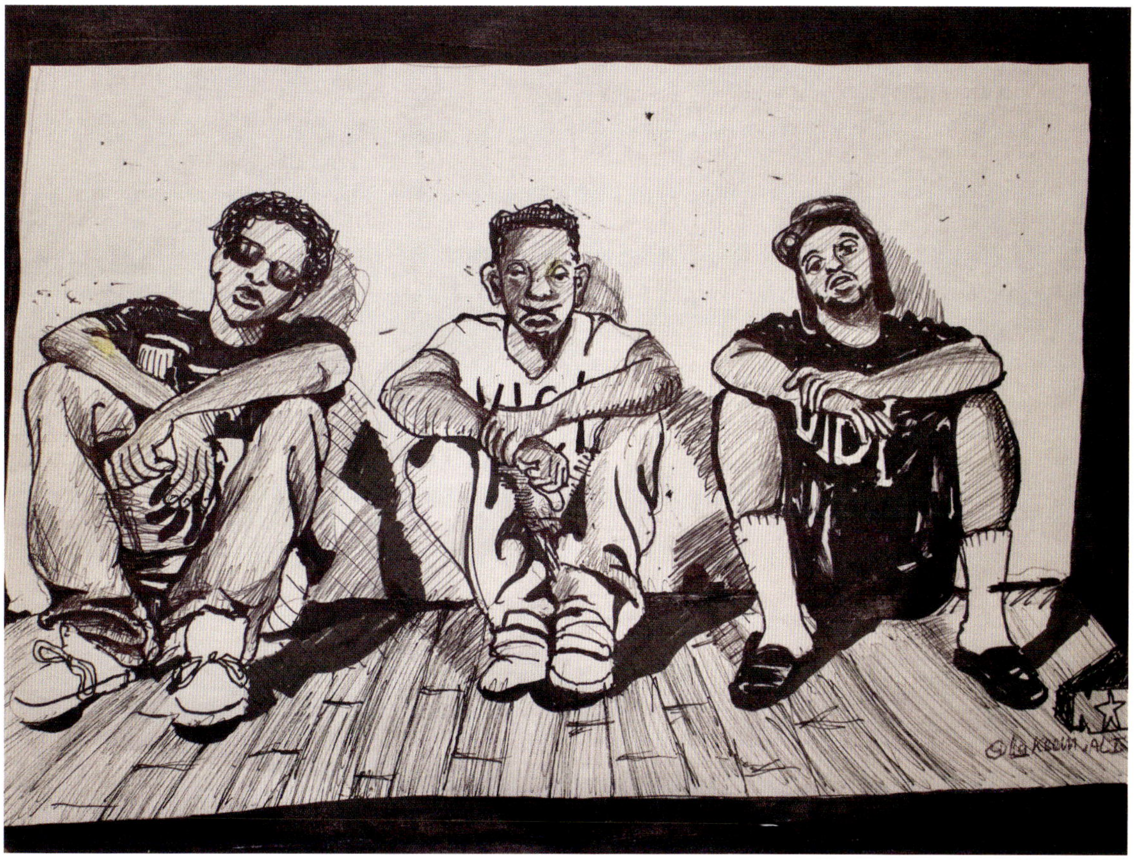

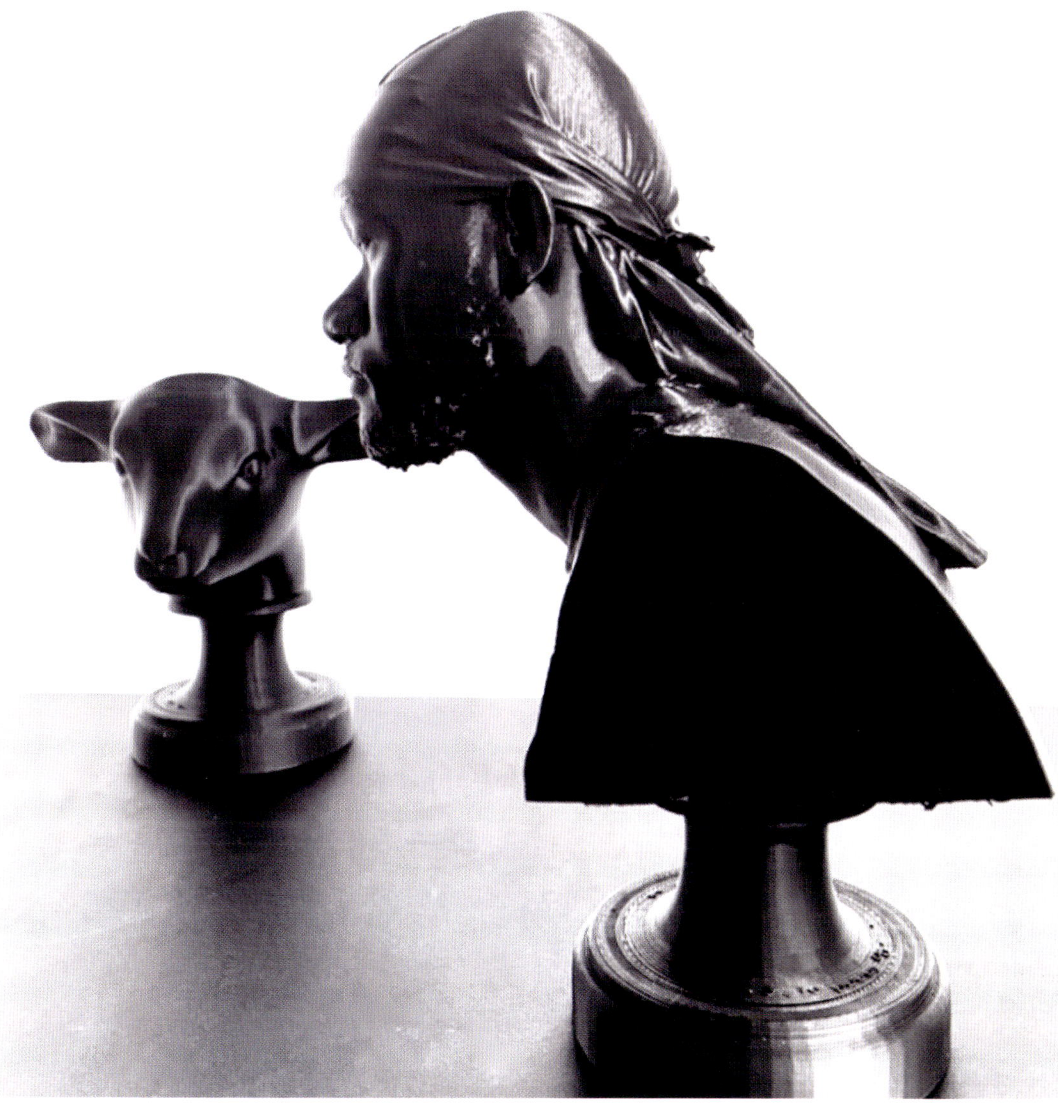

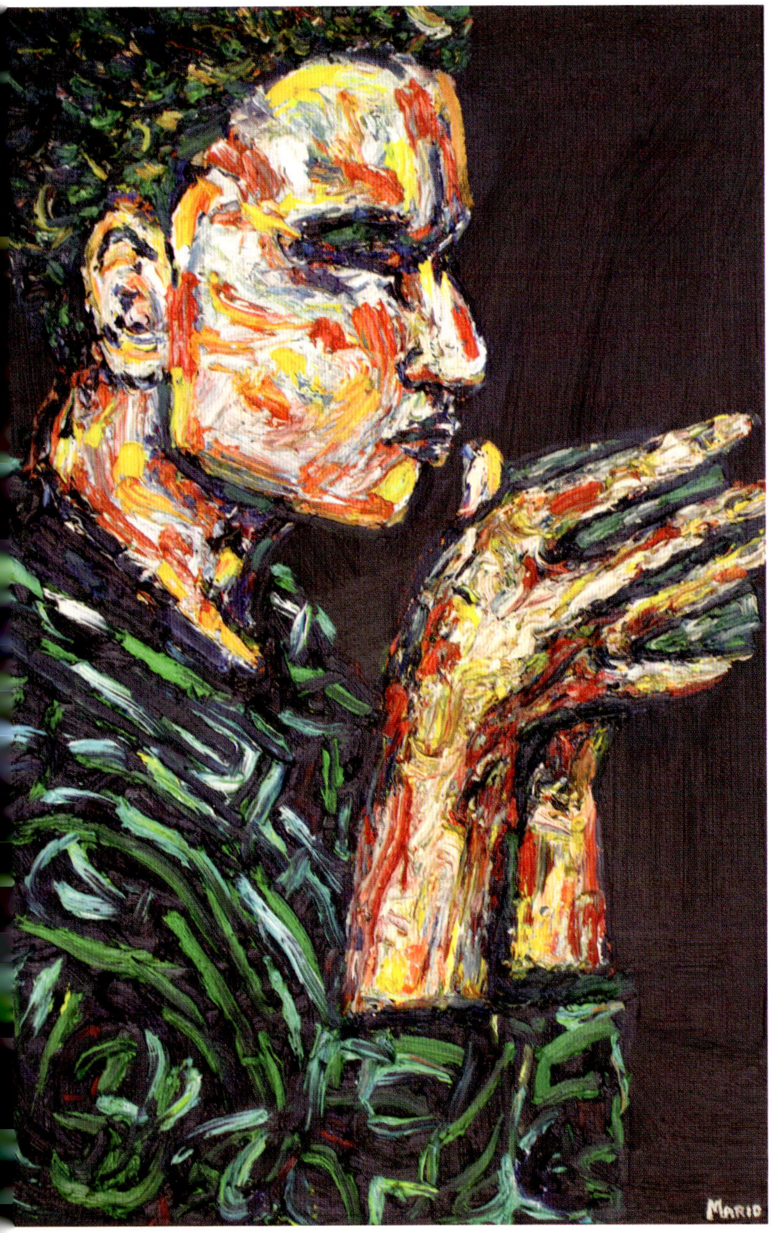

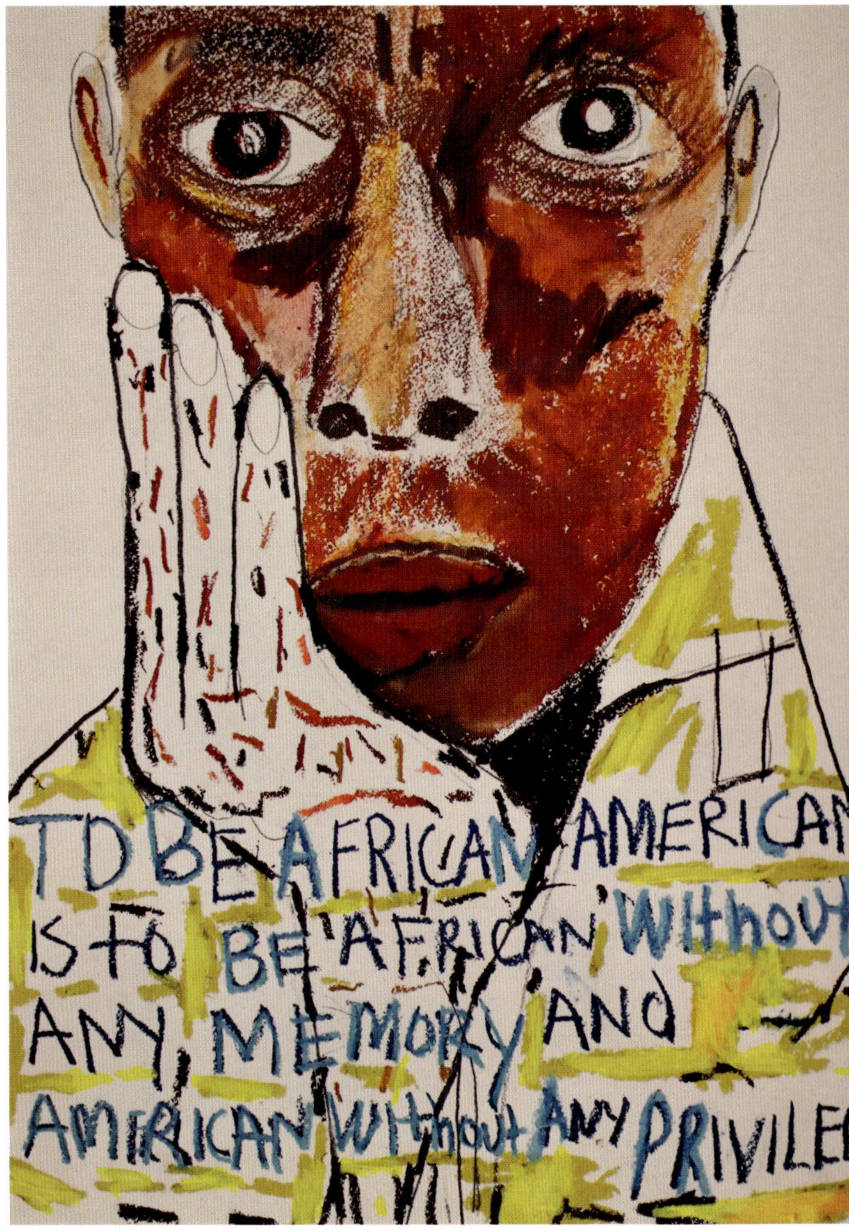

Mario Joyce, *Triggered*, 2017. Oil on canvas, 30" × 20". *Photo: Myrah Brown Green*

Daniel Robin Clurman, *Meditation Baldwin*, 2021. Limited-edition print, 24" × 18". *Photo: Myrah Brown Green*

Opposite: Fable Jones, *Portrait of a Man*, 2021. Watercolor on watercolor paper, 14$\frac{1}{16}$" × 10". *Photo: Myrah Brown Green*

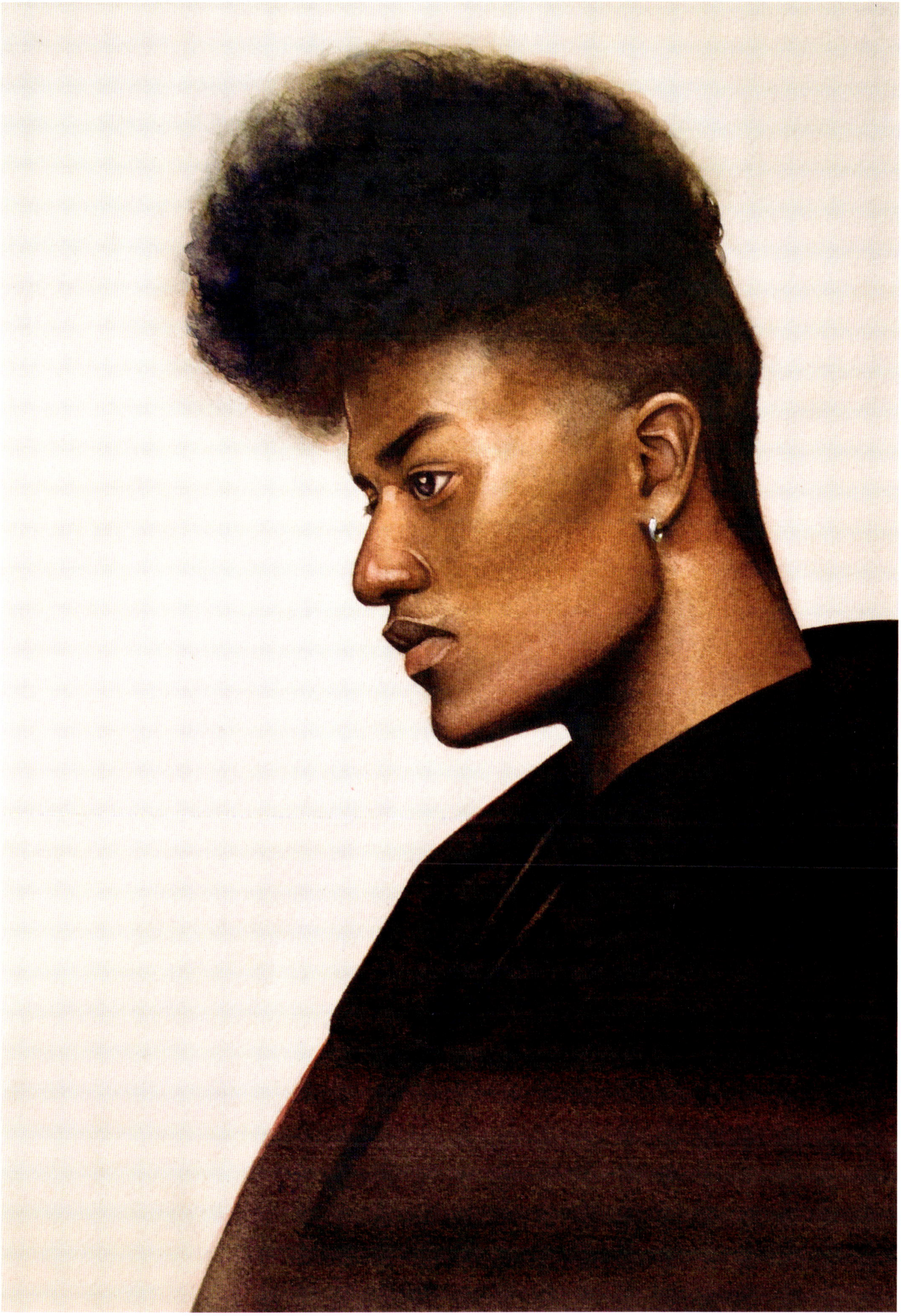

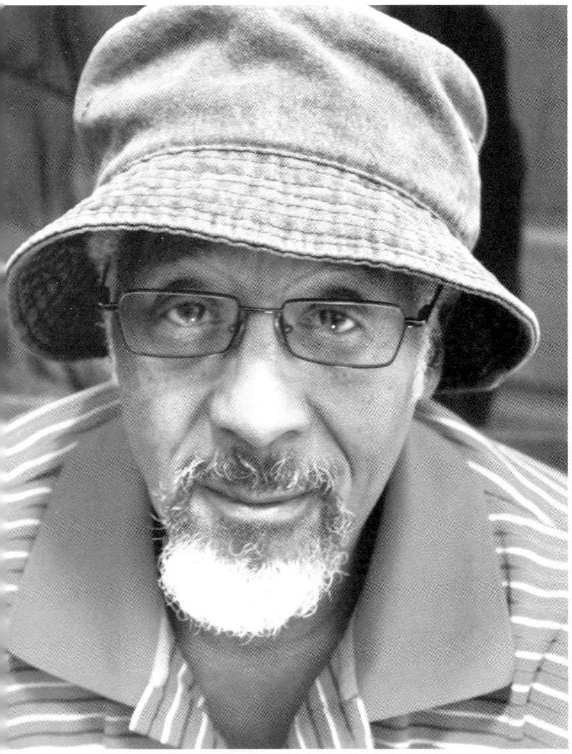

Photo: Myrah Brown Green

KEN WRIGHT
ROMANCE

DR. MYRAH: What was the first piece of art that you collected and when?

KEN WRIGHT: The first piece of art that I collected was a painting by my uncle Clarence Eastmond. It was done in black and white that looked like a wave in the water, and when you looked closely, it was a woman swimming in the water. You could only see part of her body. This I collected when I was about sixteen. He gave it to my mom, and my mom gave it to me. It was an original.

DR. MYRAH: Why are you a Keeper of Couples in Romance?

KEN WRIGHT: The foundation of romance in the art that I create and collect is about unity. I believe that unity in romance begins with a man and a woman, which is the basis of a family. That union is the combination that can create life. As far as unity in romance is concerned, for me, that's the foundation of these pieces of art. Over the years, I have watched couples in romance experience a unity between one another. I have seen those expressed feelings between the two extend to the family, the community, the city, and then extend to the nation. For me that's the core of it all. Romance is something that I aspire to because it can be positive and rewarding . . . and with its rewards, unlimited possibilities may be manifested. I am a keeper of couples in romance because each image may be different or have its own unique style. However, in life, that's what makes it original.

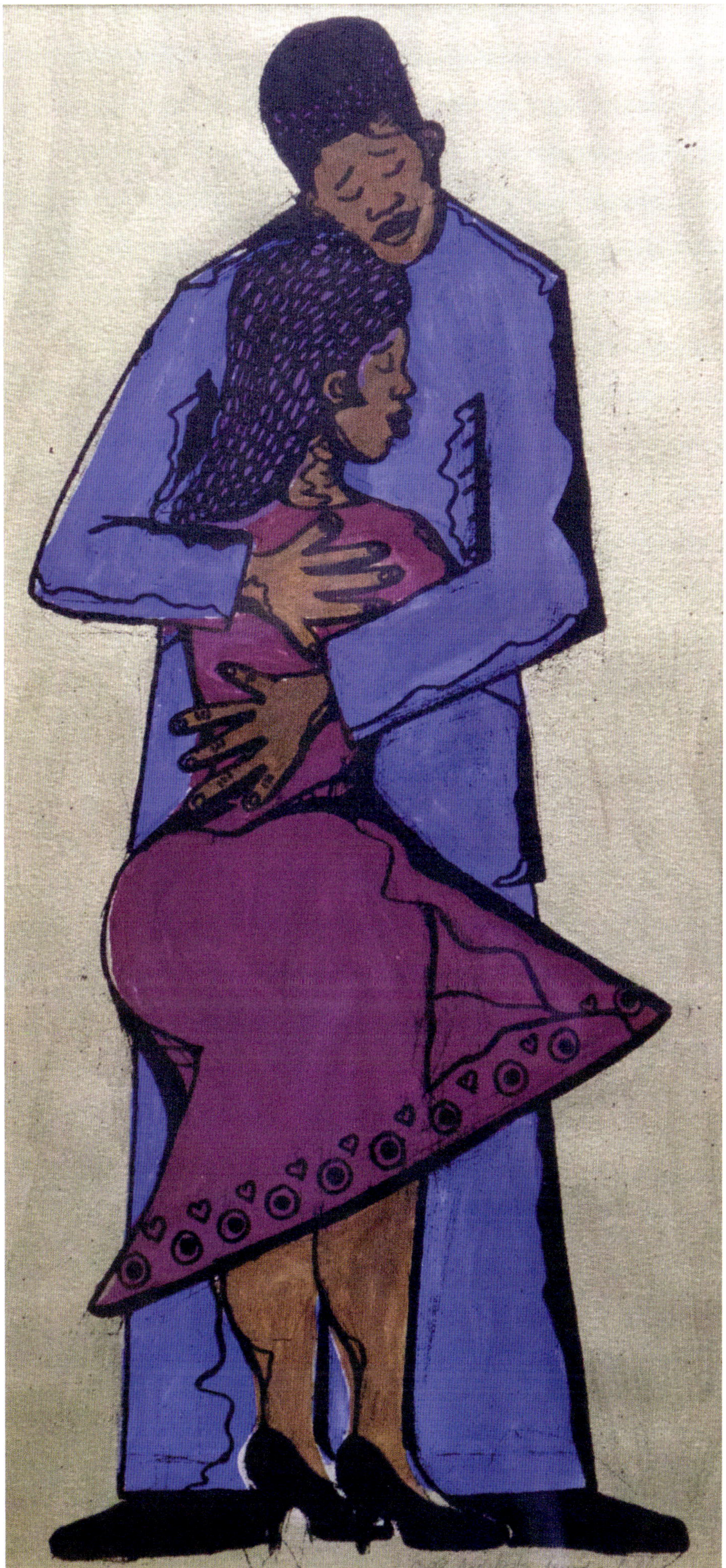

Sadikisha Saundra Collier, *The Lovers*, 1998. Monoprint, 18" × 9". *Photo: Ken Wright*

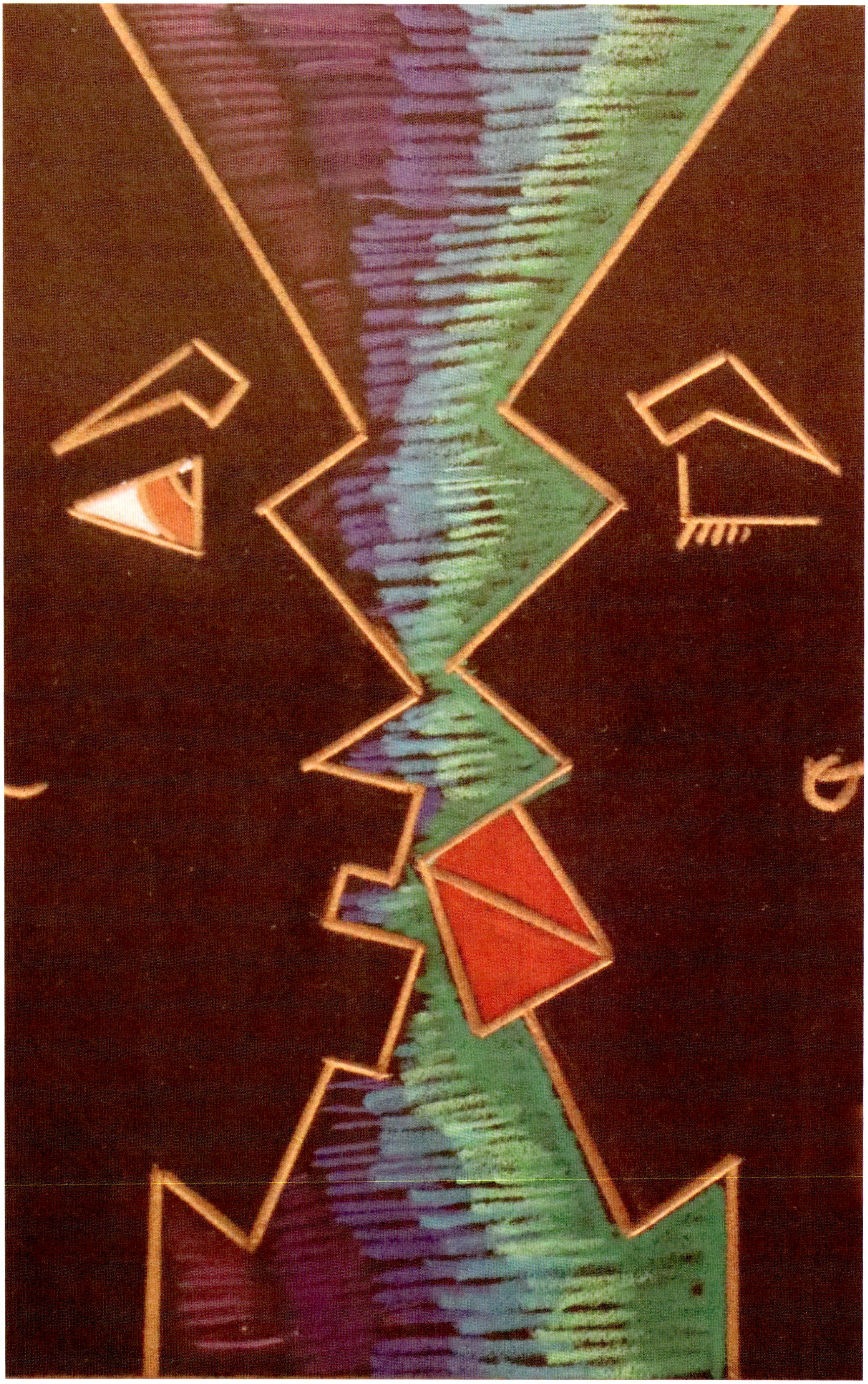

Above: Donovan McClean, *The Kiss*, 1994. Colored pencil, 6" × 8". *Photo: Ken Wright*

Leroy Campbell, *Untitled*, 1988. Acrylic, 7.5" × 7". *Photo: Ken Wright*

Deborah Singletary, *Hot House Rose and the Handyman*, 2004. Tableau in shadow box, 12" × 17". *Photo: Ken Wright*

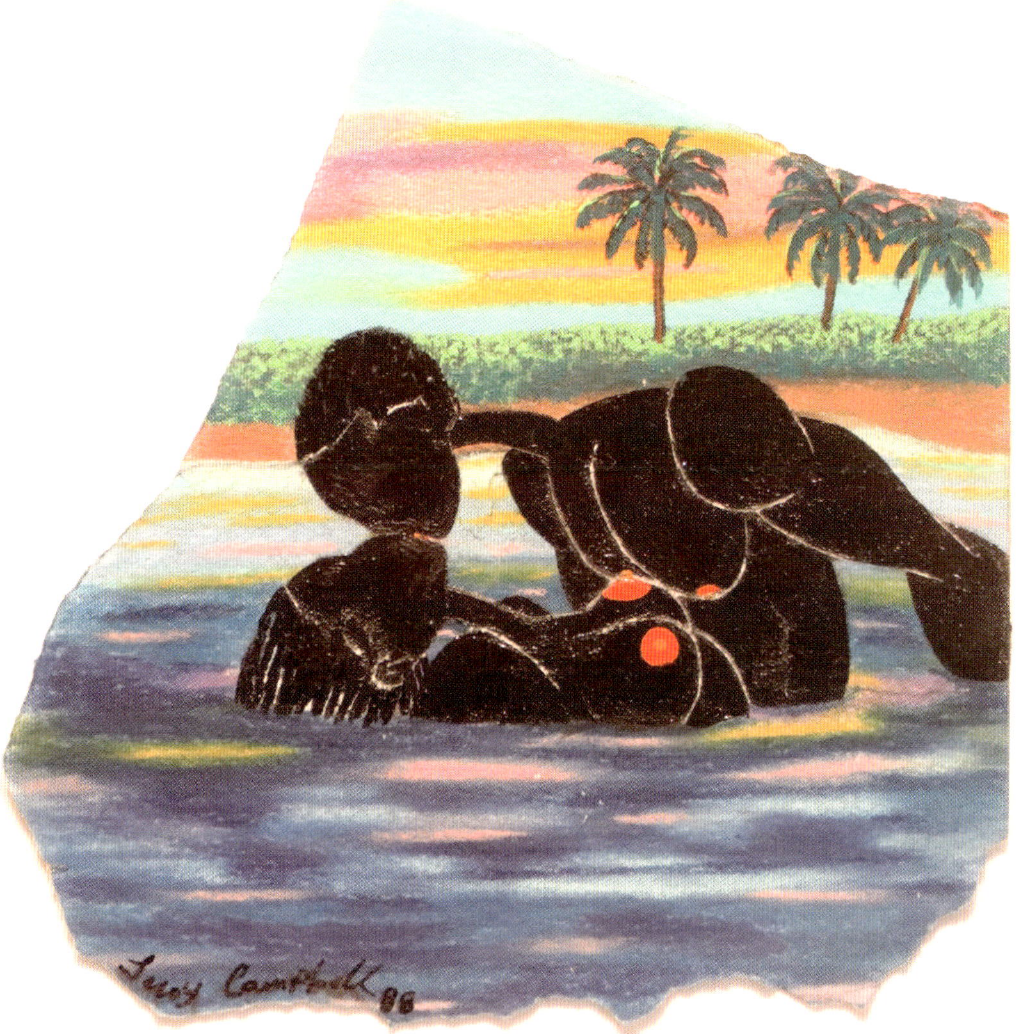

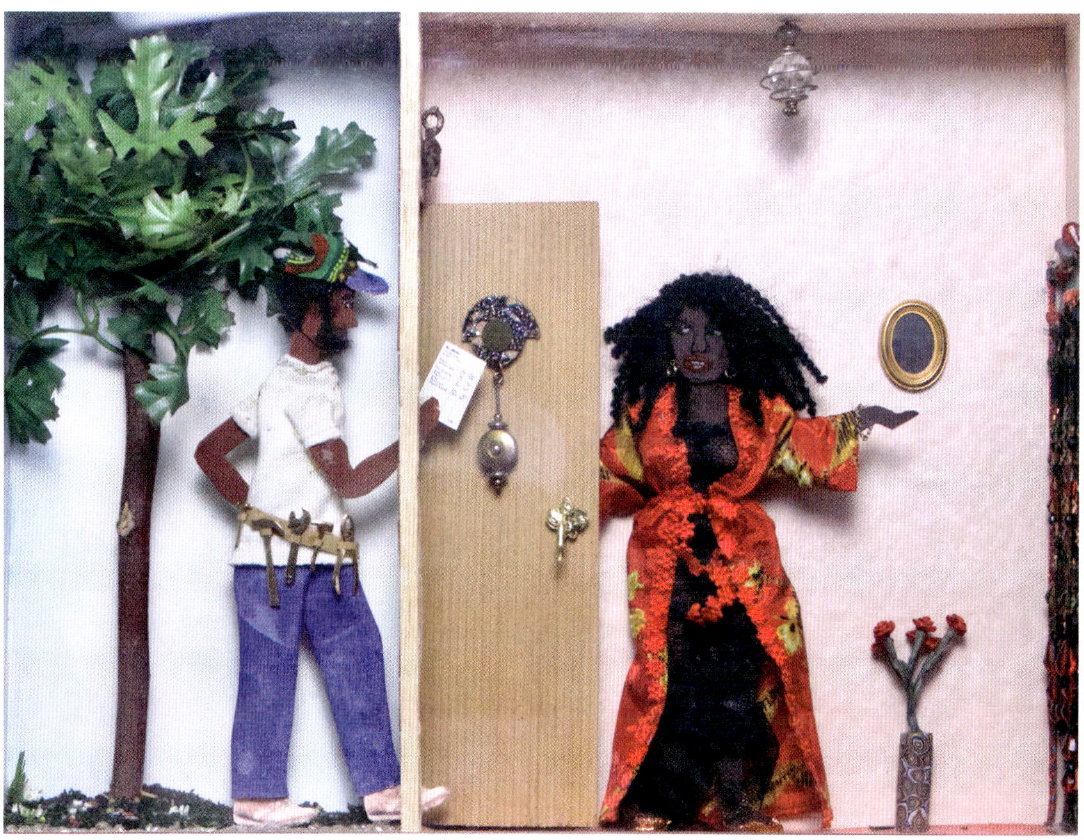

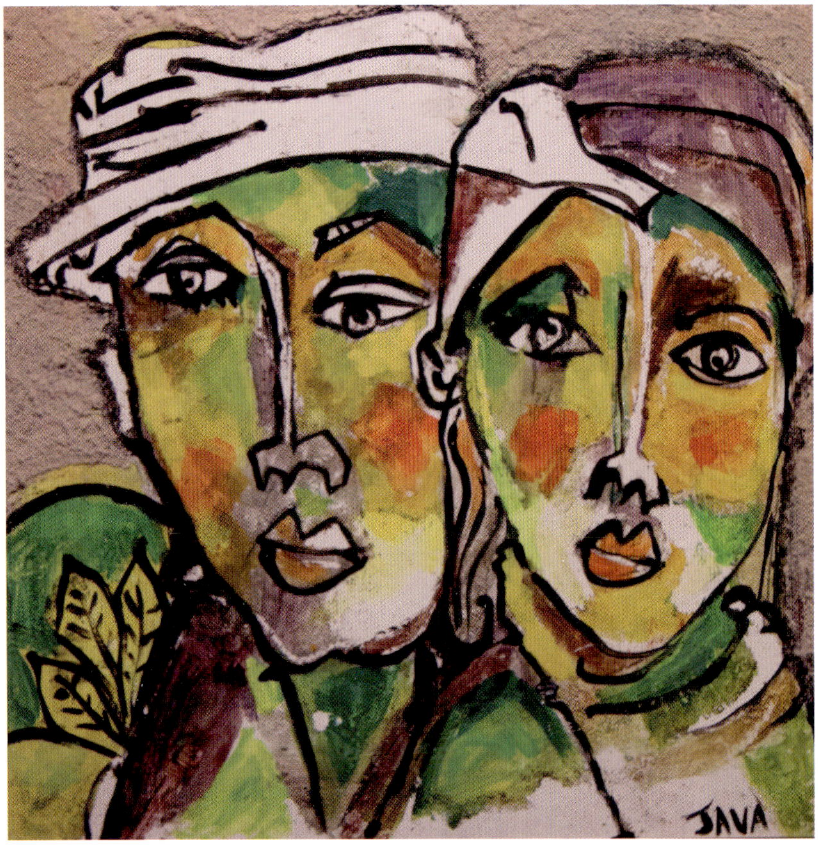

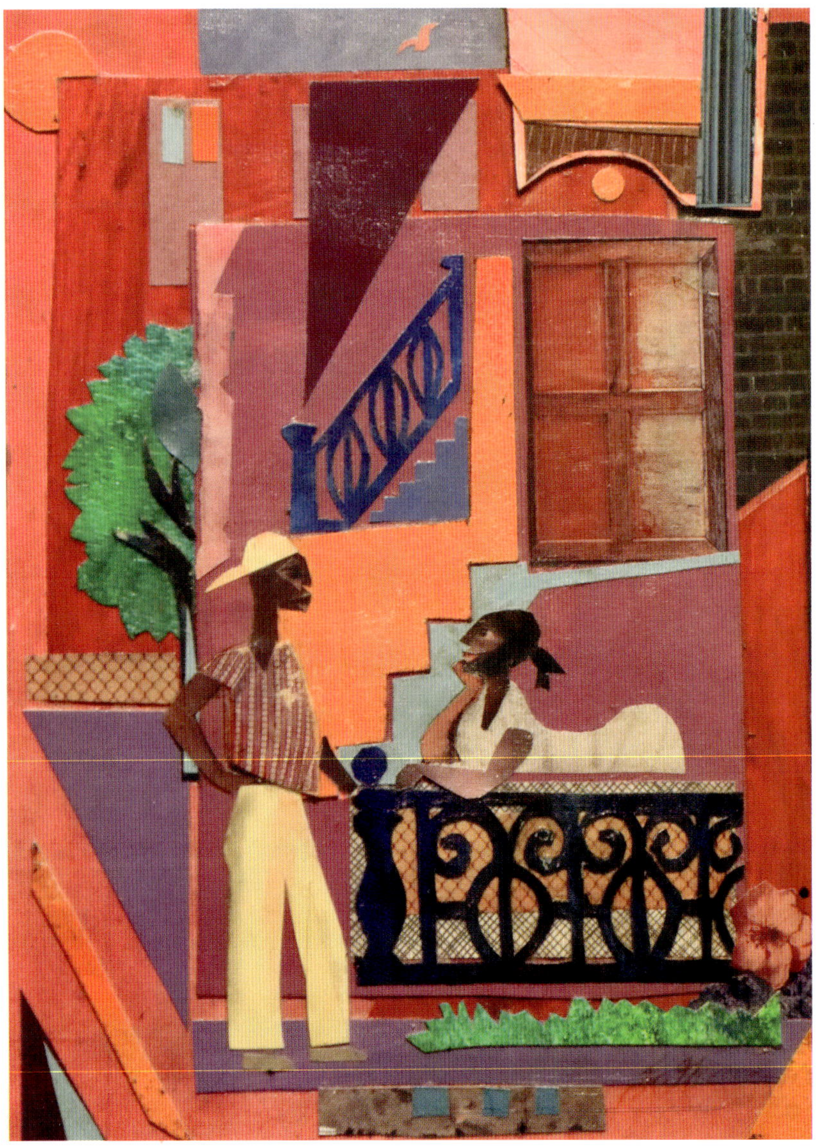

Java, *Untitled*, 2019. Acrylic on tile, 12" × 12". *Photo: Ken Wright*

Jimmy James Greene, *The Meeting*, 2019. Collage, 9" × 6.5". *Photo: Ken Wright*

Opposite: Otto Neals, *Untitled*, 2019. Collage and acrylic, 12" × 19". *Photo: Ken Wright*